Teaching Language and Literacy

Preschool through the Elementary Grades

James Christie

Arizona State University

Billie Enz

Arizona State University

Carol Vukelich

University of Delaware

Boston   New York   San Francisco
Mexico City   Montreal   Toronto   London   Madrid   Munich   Paris
Hong Kong   Singapore   Tokyo   Cape Town   Sydney

Series Editor: *Aurora Martínez Ramos*
Editorial Assistant: *Beth Slater*
Marketing Manager: *Liz Fogarty*
Production Editor: *Kathy Smith*
Editorial Production Service: *Chestnut Hill Enterprises*
Composition Buyer: *Linda Cox*
Manufacturing Buyer: *JoAnne Sweeney*
Cover Administrator: *Kristina Mose-Libon*
Electronic Composition: *Omegatype Typography, Inc.*

For related titles and support materials, visit our online catalog at www.ablongman.com.

Between the time Website information is gathered and then published, it is not unusual for some sites to have closed. Also, the transcription of URLs can result in unintended typographical errors. The publisher would appreciate notification where these occur so that they may be corrected in subsequent editions.

Library of Congress Cataloging-in-Publication Data

Christie, James F.
    Teaching language and literacy : preschool through the elementary grades / James Christie, Billie Enz, Carol Vukelich.—2nd ed.
      p. cm.
    Includes bibliographical references and index.
    ISBN 0-321-04905-5
    1. Language arts (Elementary)—Case studies. 2. Language arts (Preschool)—Case studies. 3. Curriculum planning. 4. Portfolios in education. 5. Education—Parent participation. I. Enz, Billie. II. Vukelich, Carol. III. Title.

  LB1576 .C5564 2003
  372.6—dc21

                                            2002026173

Printed in the United States of America

10 9 8 7 6   08 07 06 05

CONTENTS

6 Teaching Early Reading and Writing   160

PART THREE   **Language and Literacy Learning in the Elementary Grades   191**

7 **The Reading Workshop: A Balanced Approach to Reading Instruction   191**

8 **Embedded within Reading Workshop: Teaching Meaning and Skills   222**

PREFACE

Teaching Language and Literacy, Second Edition is about teaching the language arts: facilitating children's reading, writing, speaking, and listening development in prekindergarten through the upper elementary grades. The language arts are essential to everyday life and central to all learning; through reading, listening, writing, and talking children come to understand the world. To be a successful teacher of language and literacy, you need to understand how children's language and literacy develop and how to help children become fluent, flexible, effective users of oral and written language.

Themes

Children are at the center of all good language and literacy teaching. This principle underlies the three themes that run throughout this book: a **constructivist perspective on learning, respect for diversity,** and **instruction-based assessment.**

We believe that children construct their own knowledge about oral and written language by engaging in integrated, meaningful, and functional activities with other people. Children do not first "study" speaking, then listening, then reading, then writing. Children learn by engaging in activities in which language and literacy are embedded. We begin this book with a discussion of these basic assumptions about learning and then show how these principles translate into practice in teaching the language arts, starting at the early childhood level and continuing through the elementary grades. *Teaching Language and Literacy, Second Edition* describes how children acquire language and literacy knowledge in many different contexts and how teachers can design authentic classroom reasons for using oral and written language.

The constructivist view of learning maintains that children build knowledge by combining new information with what they already know. Thus, children's personal experiences, both at home and at school, are important factors in learning. In U.S. society, children come to school with vastly different backgrounds, both in terms of life experiences and language. This diversity needs to be taken into account when designing instructional activities for children and in evaluating their responses to these activities. Illustrations of how teachers can work effectively with diverse learners can be found throughout this book, and special emphasis is given to linguistic diversity. In a series of special features, Sarah Hudelson and Irene Serna describe how teachers can help second-language learners become bilingual and biliterate.

Every child comes to school with a wealth of information about how written and spoken language works in the real world. Teachers must discover what each student already knows in order to build on his or her knowledge through appropriate classroom activities. Because we recognize that assessment—understanding what children know and have learned—cannot be separated from good teaching, instructionally linked assessment is our third major theme. We introduce the principles of instruction-based assessment in

Chapter 1. Many subsequent chapters contain information on strategies that teachers can use to understand children's language and literacy knowledge in the context of specific learning and teaching events. In addition, Chapter 11 describes how to combine the chapter-by-chapter assessment strategies into a coherent assessment program centered around portfolios.

Organization

Part I deals with the foundation of language and literacy learning. Chapter 1 discusses three basic assumptions about language and literacy learning: constructivism, respect for diversity, and instruction-based assessment. These themes run throughout the book and underlie all the teaching strategies that we recommend in subsequent chapters. Chapter 2 describes the phenomenal development of oral language that occurs in a child's home between birth and age five.

Part II describes strategies for teaching language and literacy at the preschool and kindergarten level. Chapter 3 explains what parents and teachers can do to facilitate children's oral language learning by providing opportunities for reciprocal conversation and discussion, activity-centered language (e.g., dramatics play, cooperative learning), and language-centered activities (e.g., sharing, movie and book reviews). Chapter 4 details what young children learn about reading and writing at home and in preschool. We explain how both forms of language—oral and written—are acquired in much the same way. Children learn by using language in connection with meaningful activities. In Chapter 5, the focus shifts to building a foundation for literacy instruction. Key teaching strategies include provision of a print-rich classroom environment, read-aloud experiences, the Language-Experience Approach, and literacy-enriched dramatic play centers. Chapter 6 discusses practices for teaching reading and writing in the early grades.

Part III examines the teaching of reading and writing in the elementary grades. Chapter 7 discusses the best practices involved in a balanced reading program. This chapter features information about Reader's Workshop and highlights how to select books for elementary-grade students. Chapter 8 provides detailed examples of how the principles of Readers' Workshop are applied in both a primary and intermediate-grade classroom. Chapter 9 describes the writing workshop and explains why it is an ideal strategy for helping students become proficient writers. In Chapter 10, we explain how instruction in mechanical skills—handwriting, spelling, capitalization and punctuation, and grammar—can be embedded within the writing workshop.

Part IV deals with organizing the language arts curriculum. Chapter 11 describes how teachers can integrate the various language arts to study topics of interest to their students. Through these interdisciplinary studies, children use and enhance their language and literacy knowledge while at the same time learning content relevant to other areas of the school curriculum. Chapter 12 explains how to create portfolios and use them to assess children's language and literacy learning. Portfolios are an effective means for organizing, sharing, and evaluating the information gained using the various assessment procedures described in other chapters of this book. Finally, Chapter 13 discusses the importance of home–school collaboration and describes strategies for promoting parental involvement in language arts education.

Key Features

In order to give concrete illustrations of language and literacy learning, this book contains several detailed **case studies.** Chapter 2 contains the story of Dawn's oral language acquisition from birth to age five. Chapter 4 describes the early literacy development of Tiffany, a monolingual English speaker, and Alicia, a Spanish-speaking kindergartner who is just beginning to learn oral English. Tiffany's and Alicia's stories are continued in Chapter 8, where we follow their reading and writing development in the elementary grades. The instruction they receive also reflects many of the best practices described in the previous chapters.

   Special Feature boxes are interspersed throughout the book to provide in-depth information about topics relating to language and literacy learning and to teaching the language arts. Most notable are the series of features by Sarah Hudelson and Irene Serna, which provide information about how teachers can adjust instruction to meet the needs of second-language and bilingual learners.

   The book also contains a number of **Trade Secrets boxes** in which veteran teachers describe in their own words how they provide children with effective language arts instruction. These trade secrets illustrate how teaching strategies can be applied in specific situations and reveal how teachers deal with practical problems that arise in the course of daily life in the classroom.

   Another notable feature is the **broad scope** of this book, covering language arts instruction from preschool through the upper elementary grades. This coverage makes the book suitable both for elementary (K–8) and early childhood (preschool-grade 3 or preschool-grade 5) language arts methods courses.

Changes in the Second Edition

The most important change from the first edition involves a shift in emphasis away from competing conceptions of the reading instruction (transmission versus constructivist; skills-centered versus meaning-centered) toward a balanced approach to teaching reading. There is increased coverage of how to teach skills such as phonemic awareness, phonics, and comprehension strategies. We have also broadened the instructional scope of this text to include the upper elementary grades, and have included case studies, examples, and teaching strategies that deal with older students.

   We have also added a number of pedagogical features designed to make this textbook easier for students to read and comprehend. All chapters begin with an introductory vignette that illustrates a major concept to be presented in that chapter. Next the vignette is analyzed in a manner that helps the student begin to develop an interest in the topic. In addition, as part of the introduction, each chapter asks a series of "Think about" questions that enable students to connect new material in the book with past personal experiences and prior knowledge. The beginning of each chapter also includes definitions of key terms and a series of focus questions that alert the reader to key concepts presented in the chapter. The summary section at the end of each chapter contains answers to each of the focus questions at the beginning of the chapter, providing a review of the key concepts in each chapter and an opportunity for readers to self-check their comprehension. In addition, **Linking Knowledge to Practice activities** at the end of each chapter allow students to connect the theories and practices discussed in the book to practices they are observing in real classrooms.

ACKNOWLEDGMENTS

Many outstanding educators helped us write *Teaching Language and Literacy*. Our very special thanks to Sarah Hudelson and Irene Serna for their special features on second-language and bilingual learners. Like us, they sat before their computers for many days. From them, we learned how our ideas about teaching the language arts are appropriate for use with children whose primary language is a language other than English.

Many classroom teachers shared their secrets, showing how theory and research link with quality classroom practice. We are grateful to Mary Christie, John Falconer, Michelle Gary, and Carolyn Lara (Phoenix, AZ), Karen Eeds (Tempe, AZ), Kathy Eustace and Anne Foley (Gilbert, AZ), Marianne Bors, JoAnne Deshon, Dawn Downs, Ellen Fanjoy, Linda Hand, Marianne Kellner, Janice Medek, and Lisa Wrenn (Wilmington, DE), Jackie Shockley (Lewes, DE), Laurel Bok Swindle (Dover, DE), Nancy Edwards (Newark, DE) Bernadette Watson (St. Georges, DE), and Maryanne Lamont (Oxford, PA) for their descriptions of exemplary teaching practices. From these teachers, and others like them, we have seen how exciting language and literacy learning can be when teachers and children are engaged in purposeful language arts activities. From them, and their students, we have learned much.

Several of our colleagues played a role in the construction of this book through their willingness to engage us in many conversations about children's language and literacy learning. Never unwilling to hear our ideas and to share their own, colleagues like Kathy Roskos (John Carroll University), Susan B. Neuman (University of Michigan), Mary Roe (University of Delaware), Lesley Mandel Morrow (Rutgers University), Brenda Powers (University of Maine), Doreen Bardsley, Cory Hansen, Lyn Searfoss, Jill Stamm, Elaine Surbeck, and Chari Woodward (Arizona State University), Sandy Stone (Northern Arizona University), and Cookie Bolig and Mike Kelly (Delaware Department of Public Instruction) have greatly helped us frame our arguments.

Graduate students, including Myae Han, Kari Croce, Debbie Lubitz, and Maria Rascon (Arizona State University) and Deirdra Aikens, Deanne McCredie, JoAnne Deshon, Marlanne Kellner, Marcia Lawton, Linda Rogers, Sharon Saez, and Linda Zankowsky (University of Delaware) have been helpful in contributing features, locating references, cross-checking the reference list, and constructing the index.

The students we have nurtured and taught, both young children and college students, have also influenced the development of our ideas. Through their questions, their talk, their play, their responses, and their enthusiasm, each one of them has taught us about the importance of the language arts in our lives. Their positive responses to our ideas fueled our eagerness to share those ideas more broadly. What better honor than to learn that a "black market" of photocopies of the early drafts of the chapters of this book had developed on our campuses.

The final draft of this book is much better because of the feedback we received during our writing. Our students came to us with questions and suggestions. We revised. Alice Shepard (office specialist) and Monique Davis and Allison Mendoza (program coordinators) read drafts of chapters numerous times and offered valuable suggestions. The "official" reviewers of this manuscript—Diane Barone (University of Nevada, Reno), Kathryn Leo-Nyquist (Champlain College), Shelly Xu (Texas Tech University), Sara Ann Beach (University of Oklahoma), Harry Weisenberger (Tulsa Community College), and Carla B. Gable (Minnesota State University, Moorhead)—provided just the right amount of thoughtful praise, suggestions, and criticisms. We revised. Julia Penelope, copyeditor, read our final drafts with a critical eye and proposed numerous suggestions for clarity in wording and consistency in style. We revised and edited. Kathy Smith provided a well-chosen selection of photographs for our consideration. Casey Cook, our illustrator, helped to make our visions into realities.

Finally, our families have helped us write this book. Tiffany and Dawn Enz have provided wonderful examples of their use and enjoyment of oral and written language. The story of their journey to being competent language users brings life to the research and theory discussed in our book. Mary Christie, Don (Skip) Enz, and Ron Vukelich gave us time to write but also pulled us from our computers for antique shows, museums trips, and home repairs lest we forget we had lives. Then, of course, there are our extended families—our parents, David and Dorothy Palm, Art and Emma Larson, Bill and Jeannine Fullerton, John and Florence Christie—who provided our early reading, writing, speaking, and listening experiences and helped us know firsthand the joys of learning and teaching the language arts.

Jim Christie
Billie Enz
Carol Vukelich

1

Foundations of Language and Literacy

Tiffany and Dawn are shopping with their mother. Two-year-old Tiffany is sitting in the grocery cart as her five-year-old sister Dawn picks up a box of Cheerios.® "No, Dawn," says Tiffany as she vigorously shakes her head. Dawn replies, "Well then, what?" Tiffany points to a brightly colored box containing her favorite cereal, Trix.® "Dat." Dawn places the box in the cart as Tiffany nods in approval.

In the past two decades we have learned much about children's early literacy development. This new knowledge of how children learn language, reading, and writing has resulted in a major shift in our beliefs about how to teach and assess children's literacy development. While we once thought that learning to read began in first grade, we now know that the process of learning to read begins long before children come to school. Like learning to speak and to listen, learning about print begins in the home at birth, as soon as children's parents begin to read stories to them or when children begin to notice the print that surrounds them.

In the mid-1970s, cognitive psychologists, child psychologists, and anthropologists confirmed that children become aware of print at very early ages (Teale & Sulzby, 1989). The vignette of Dawn and Tiffany shopping for cereal provides an illustration of young children's early awareness of print. As this interaction demonstrates, children as young as two years old can identify signs, labels, and logos they see in their homes and communities (Goodman, 1986; Hiebert, 1981). Similarly, home-based case studies of children under the age of three reveal that children have extensive knowledge of the practical functions of print—of writing lists to aid memory, of writing signs to control other people's behavior, and of writing letters to communicate (Bissex, 1980; Heath, 1983; Taylor, 1983; Taylor & Strickland, 1986).

The term *emergent literacy* is often used to refer to children's early understanding of reading and writing. This somewhat new line of investigation has significantly changed educators' view about two aspects of literacy: (1) how and when children begin to construct knowledge about reading and writing, and (2) how parents and early childhood teachers can most effectively support young children's ongoing literacy development (Morrow, 2001).

The emergent literacy perspective provides a clear and powerful example of how the *constructivist theory of learning* works. Drawing on a synthesis of current research in cognitive psychology, anthropology, and philosophy, the theory defines learning as the result of many "self-motivated interactions, a process of resolving inner cognitive conflicts that often become apparent through concrete experience, collaborative discourse, and self-reflection"

(Fosnot, cited in Brooks & Brooks, 1993, p. vii). Although the constructivist theory is relatively new, it offers far-reaching implications for schools, for teachers, and for instruction. This theory reflects our beliefs about learning and provides the framework supporting the views about language and literacy presented in this book.

Before Reading This Chapter, Think About . . .

- your beliefs about how young children first learn to read and write. At what age do children begin to learn about literacy? Is knowledge about reading and writing transmitted from adults to young children, or do children construct this knowledge on their own?
- your beliefs about effective language and literacy instruction. How can teachers best help young children become skilled speakers, listeners, readers, and writers?
- your memories about how you learned to talk, read, and write. Do you recall, for example, reading cereal labels at an early age? Do you recall writing messages to loved ones?
- your memories about how you were taught to read and write in elementary school. Do you recall participating in a reading group or a book discussion group? Do you recall completing workbook pages or using the stories you read as models to write your own stories? Do you recall writing to teacher-created prompts, like writing about what you did during your summer vacation, or writing stories about topics of your choosing?

Focus Questions

- How do young children learn about language and literacy?
- Why is it crucial for teachers to respect children's diversity when teaching language and literacy?

BOX 1.1
Definition of Terms

constructivist theory of learning: the view that children actively construct meaning by making connections between new experiences and their prior knowledge, by making and testing their own hypotheses, and by interacting with peers and more knowledgeable others.

emergent literacy: children's early understandings about reading and writing.

scaffolding: temporary assistance and support that enable young children to do things that they could not do on their own.

schemas: the mental structures that store and organize knowledge.

zone of proximal development: a stage at which a child has partially mastered a skill but can use this skill only with the help of others.

- How should children's literacy learning be assessed?
- What are the best practices in teaching language and literacy to children?

Language and Literacy: Definitions and Interrelationships

The terms *language* and *literacy* can be defined in many ways. *Language* can be defined very broadly as any system of symbols that is used to transmit meaning (Bromley, 1988). These symbols can consist of sounds, finger movements, print, and so on. *Literacy* also has several different meanings. It can refer to the ability to create meaning through different media (e.g., *visual literacy*), knowledge of key concepts and ideas (e.g., *cultural literacy*), and the ability to deal effectively with different subject areas and technologies (e.g., *mathematical literacy, computer literacy*).

Because the topic of this book is the teaching of the language arts—the part of the school curriculum that deals with helping children learn to speak, listen, read, and write—we use school-based definitions of these terms. *Language* refers to oral language, (communicating via speaking and listening), and *literacy* refers to reading and writing (communicating through print). However, as we describe how children grow in both these areas, it will become obvious that language and literacy acquisition are closely tied to the total development of the child—learning to think, to make sense of the world, to get along with others, and so on.

While we have organized this book into separate chapters on oral language and literacy, it is important to note that the two types of language are integrally connected and related to each other. Oral language provides the base and foundation for literacy. Oral language involves first-order symbolism, with spoken words representing meaning. Written language, on the other hand, involves second-order symbolism that builds on the first-order symbolism of oral language. Printed symbols represent spoken words that, in turn, represent meaning. Do you see the connections between language and literacy?

One obvious connection between oral and written language is vocabulary. In order for a reader to recognize and get meaning from text, most of the words represented by the text must already be in the reader's oral vocabulary. If the reader can recognize most of the words in the text, context cues might be used to figure out the meaning of a few totally unfamiliar words. Similarly, a writer's choice of words is restricted by his or her oral vocabulary.

Catherine Snow and her colleagues (1991) point out a less obvious, but equally important, link between oral language and literacy. She points out that oral language is actually an array of skills related to different functions. One set of skills is relevant to the negotiation of interpersonal relationships and involves the child's ability to engage in face-to-face conversations (contextualized language). Another involves the ability to use language to convey information to audiences who are not physically present (decontextualized language). Decontextualized language has a vital role in literacy because it is the type of language that is typically used in written texts.

Children gain experience in these different aspects of language through different activities. They become skilled at contextualized language by engaging in conversations with others, whereas they gain skill at decontextualized language by listening to stories and by engaging in explanations and personal narratives and by creating fantasy worlds (Snow et al., 1991). It not surprising, therefore, that research has shown that children with rich oral language experiences at home tend to become early readers (Dickinson & Tabors, 2000) and have high levels of reading achievement during the elementary grades (Wells, 1986).

The relationship between literacy and oral language becomes reciprocal once children become proficient readers. Extensive reading begins to build children's oral language capabilities, particularly their vocabulary knowledge. Cunningham and Stanovich (1998) present evidence that people are much more likely to encounter "rare" unfamiliar words in printed texts than in adult speech, and Swanborn and de Glopper's (1999) meta-analysis of studies on incidental word learning revealed that, during normal reading, students learn about 15 percent of the unknown words they encounter. The more children read, the larger their vocabularies become.

Anything teachers can do to build children's oral language skills, particularly their vocabulary knowledge and ability to deal with decontextualized language, will also benefit children's literacy development. So even if a school's primary mission is to boost children's literacy skills, attention also needs to be given to building children's oral language abilities.

The Way Children Learn

> A restless Hannah is standing next to her mother in the dance studio, eating a piece of chocolate. As she begins to take another bite, she runs her finger over the raised letters imprinted on the candy. Hannah asks her mother, "What does this say?" Her mother replies, "HER-SHEY, it says HER-SHEY." In a very puzzled voice, with a perplexed look, Hannah repeats "Her-she" several times. Then she asks, "Mommy, is this a girl candy bar?"

Close observations of very young children can provide interesting and sometimes humorous insights about how they construct hypotheses about print through everyday interactions (Holdaway, 1979; Teale, 1986a). As young as she is, 32-month-old Hannah demonstrates a delightful understanding of language and literacy. She knows that the symbols on the candy bar have meaning. She is also aware that the pronouns *her* and *she* are equivalents to the word *girl*. However, Hannah's confusion indicates that this new information did not make sense; nothing in her prior experiences had led her to believe that candy bars had a particular gender.

Supporters of the constructivist perspective on learning would assert that learners like Hannah actively construct their own knowledge by connecting new experiences with what they have previously come to expect and understand (Brooks & Brooks, 1993). Children learn by (1) making a connection between new information and prior known information and then (2) organizing that information into structures called *schemas*. Lea McGee and Don Richgels (1996, p. 5) explain that a schema is a "mental structure in which we store all the information we know about people, places, objects, or activities."

To illustrate this point, please take a few moments to think about vanilla. Do you remember the first time you smelled vanilla extract? (If you have never smelled it, buy a bottle and try it.)

- How would you describe the aroma? (sweet)
- How did you expect it to taste? (good)
- What were your reactions when you finally tasted it? (surprise—because it tasted bitter)

In daily living, we frequently encounter materials (such as vanilla extract), ideas, or words that do not make sense or fit into the way we presently organize our knowledge. For example, how vanilla smells (appealing) does not fit with how it tastes (bitter). When initially confronted with such a contradiction, we either

- interpret what we experience by incorporating new information into our present rules for explaining our world (anything that smells as good as vanilla must also taste good, so this must be a pleasant taste, and the initial judgment of bitter must be wrong), or
- hypothesize a new rule or a new set of rules that better accounts for what we perceive to be occurring (perhaps some things, like vanilla, that smell appealing may have an unappealing taste).

In either case, we are learning through a continual process of perceiving, interpreting our perceptions, confirming our predictions, and adapting our prior knowledge to make sense of new information. Therefore, our schemas about our world are expanding and changing daily as we constantly engage in the learning process.

According to constructivist theory, learning is basically a social process that takes place through the interactions between and among children and others in their environment (Vygotsky, 1978). It is through social interactions that children learn new things. "Working with others and talking about what they are doing is the way in which children learn

*Teachers should teach in ways that allow children to work to their strengths—
and these strengths are going to be related to children's cultural backgrounds.*

because the roots of language and thought are social" (Galda, Cullinan, & Strickland, 1993, p. 10). This tenet is clearly illustrated by the following vignette:

> "I can do it, Mom," said three-year-old Zach as he watched his mother breast-feed his new-born sister. "Thank you, Zach, but only mommies make milk," replies his mother. Thinking for a minute, Zach ran to his bedroom and brought out his monkey doll. As he raised his shirt and brought the doll to his chest, Zach proudly announced "Zach makes apple juice!"

As Zach watches his mother feed and take care of his baby sister, he constructs a great deal of knowledge about his sister; about babies in general; and about the language, rituals, and complex routines that accompany child care. In fact, Zach is continually learning as he engages in activities and casual conversation with his parents. For instance, while shopping with his parents, he may learn about the functions and qualities of specific brands of diapers, baby cereal, and baby powder. As Zach reaches to retrieve these items in the store, his parents casually and immediately confirm the predictions he has made about the print on the baby-product labels. Zach is growing into literacy in much the same way as he learned to speak, by engaging in everyday activities with other people.

As the Zach vignette illustrates, it is the verbal interaction between the young child and someone more knowledgeable (parent, sibling) that helps children build new knowledge. Vygotsky referred to this as operating within the child's "zone of proximal development." A more knowledgeable other (parent, older sibling, other adult) supports a child's completion of a task, allowing the child to succeed and eventually to complete the task independently. Often the adult or older child completes a part of the task (the part of the task the child cannot do on his or her own), and the child completes another part of the task (the part the child can do independently). The adult or older child talks, as well as offers physical support, while the task is completed. In this way, the more knowledgeable other *scaffolds* the child's learning. Just as in constructing a building, this scaffold builds a support structure to help the child build a richer knowledge base, to create and extend held schema.

Auntie Carol's reading of one of her favorite books to two-and-a-half-year-old Lauren illustrates how an adult might scaffold a young child's learning. The book is *Caps for Sale* (Slobodkina, 1947).

> **CAROL (READS):**   Once there was a peddlar who sold [pauses] . . .
>
> **LAUREN:**   Caps.
>
> **CAROL (READS):**   He walked up the street and he walked down the street, holding himself very straight so as not to upset his caps, and as he walked along he called . . .
>
> **LAUREN:**   Caps! Caps!
>
> **CAROL:**   Ah! You're such a good reader, Lauren.

Lauren has heard this story numerous times. Her aunt "turns over" some of the reading to Lauren. Through her voice and her pausing, Carol signals Lauren that it is her turn to read. Carol scaffolds Lauren's reading of the book, supporting Lauren when Carol thinks

Lauren needs help and encouraging her to "read" those parts Carol thinks Lauren can "read."

In sum, then, there are two features central to the constructivist learning theory. First, learners make connections between new experiences and their prior knowledge, constructing and testing hypotheses to make meaning. They revise existing schema or create new schema daily. Secondly, learners learn through social interaction with more knowledgeable others in their environment, in which they assume the role of the apprentice. Children watch and mimic the more knowledgeable others as these experts talk and engage in behaviors. With the appropriate support from these experts, children's learning is scaffolded, creating a richer knowledge base.

Respect for Diversity

Zach, like most children, is growing up in a family or home setting. Further, his family exists within a community (maybe rural, maybe inner city, maybe suburban). Zach's social, cultural, and economic background will have a profound effect on his oral language and on his home reading and writing experiences. "We come to every situation with stories: patterns and sequences of events which are built into us. Our learning happens within the experience of what important others did" (Bateson, 1979, p. 13). In other words, the ways in which we make meaning and use words are dependent on the practices shared by the members of our community—the words chosen; the sentence structures used; the decision to talk after, or over, another's comment; and so on. As Allan Luke and Joan Kale (1997, p. 13) point out, "different cultures make meaning in different ways, with different patterns of exchange and interaction, text conventions and beliefs about reading and writing."

Given our increasingly diverse communities composed of many different cultures, teachers are more challenged than ever before to understand what this diversity means for their teaching and for their children's learning. Children cannot be asked to leave their family and cultural backgrounds at the classroom door and enter into a "hybrid culture" (Au & Kawakami, 1991). Teachers must teach in ways that allow their children to work to their strengths—and these strengths are going to be related to children's cultural backgrounds.

Some children will come to school having learned how to talk in ways that are consistent with their teachers' expectations; other children will not. Luke and Kale (1997, p. 11) provide an illustration of how disparate a child's language might be from school expectations. They share a story told by a young child, Elsey.

> *Tell you 'baut the crocodile first.*
> *Well, this crocodile 'e small tha/watnau? the chicken smell.*
> *It's a raw one.*
> *It's not a cook one*
> *but they eat raw one.*
> *So . . . This first big crocodile where they wanna send them away*
> *well, 'e smell/ 'e 's/ take the smell of it*
> *so 'e went down an' just' stop . . .*

Luke and Kale ask readers to pause and try to "hear" Elsey's contribution. They ask readers to consider the judgments they would make about the child. They ask readers to think about what Elsey *can* do, not what she cannot do.

Unfortunately, we know far less about children like Elsey's early language and literacy learning than we know about mainstream children's home experiences. In fact, it is only since the 1980s that researchers have investigated early literacy learning in nonmainstream homes and communities. In a pioneering study, Shirley Brice Heath (1983) described how children growing up in one working-class community learn that reading is sitting still and sounding out words, following the rules; whereas children in another working-class community learn that being able to tell a story well orally is more important than being able to read written texts. These conceptions of literacy were quite different from those found in children from middle-class families. The important question is: Should these types of cultural differences be viewed as deficits that must be "fixed" in order for children to succeed in school, or should these differences be viewed as positive characteristics that teachers can take advantage of when helping children learn language and literacy?

In the early 1960s, the "deficit" theory was in favor. For example, researchers and educators viewed use of a different language dialect as an explanation for why some children, particularly those from poverty environments, did not achieve in school. Programs like Head Start and Follow Through were funded to "fix" low-socioeconomic children's language. Specific language programs, like DISTAR, were designed to ameliorate the disadvantaged children's language deficiencies. DISTAR developers believed that if disadvantaged children repeated the structural patterns common to Standard English, the mainstream school dialect, these children would be ready to learn better and achieve more.

Today we know that this "deficit" view of some young children's language learning is based on incorrect language learning assumptions. Linguistically, dialects are just as rich and complex as Standard English. Children who use a dialect like Black English are equally as capable of encoding complex thoughts as those who use Standard English. These dialects need to be respected by teachers and viewed as a difference rather than a deficit.

When children who speak a dialect come to an educational institution outside the home, they are faced with the challenge of learning English as it is spoken by the mainstream culture. For example, Elsey, an English-dialect speaker, had to learn which auxiliaries (might, have) to select; the rules for posing a question; how to use English pronouns; the rules governing what can be said to an adult; how to get and hold the floor; a sense of the social purposes for literacy and the interaction patterns around text; the form and content of conventional children's literature stories; and how to use English appropriately in a variety of different settings.

Will children like Elsey meet teachers who have engaged in the study of the children's community's ways with words and texts? Will their teachers provide scaffolded language activities and instruction that will enable these children to be successful in their efforts to learn mainstream English? Will they meet teachers who have redesigned early reading lessons so the lessons better fit the speech events the children are accustomed to at home and in their community (Au & Jordan, 1981)? Will their teachers understand and value the patterns of teaching and learning evidenced in their homes, and build on these patterns so that these children are drawn into the school world (Tharp & Gallimore, 1988)? Will their teachers understand that these children might be quiet in school because their parents have taught them to show respect by being quiet and deferential (Volk, 1997)? Throughout this book, we give pointers on providing culturally sensitive language and literacy instruction.

Another significant and growing group of diverse learners are second language learners. The population of children who speak English as a second language was estimated at 3.5 million in the year 2000 and is projected to grow to 6 million by 2020 (Faltis, 2001). Of this group, those children who speak little or no English are referred to as limited English proficient (LEP). Other children are bilingual and can speak both English and their native language with varying degrees of proficiency. These children's native language might be Spanish, Portuguese, Japanese, or some other world language. When they come to school, young second-language learners are typically competent users of their native language. Their native language competence is a strength to be exploited by sensitive teachers.

We have included several Special Feature sections in subsequent chapters of this book that focus on second-language and bilingual learners' literacy development. From these features, readers will learn which strategies presented in this book are appropriate for use with children whose primary language is a language other than mainstream English and which strategies need to be adapted to meet the needs of these children.

Assessing Children's Literacy Learning

How do we know what children are learning? Changes in what we know about literacy learning have necessitated changes in our ways of measuring young children's knowledge about reading and writing. One of the central tenets of the new view on language and literacy teaching and learning is that assessment should be embedded in instruction. This is one of the underlying themes of this book. We provide illustrations of instructionally linked assessment in many subsequent chapters.

Because literacy learning is no longer viewed as a transmitted process of adding the discrete parts in order to form the whole, it makes more sense to base assessment on the constructive nature of reading and writing processes. From this new perspective, assessment is viewed as an ongoing process in which the teacher uses a variety of techniques to gather information about what children know and can do. This information is then used to form a portrait that reveals a child's literacy development. The success of the constructivist approach, then, rests with classroom teachers. In fact, Karen Wixson (1992) says that "the teacher is the most important assessment instrument."

Several elements have been identified by various experts as critical components of this new approach to literacy assessment. These elements are summarized in the following points.

1. **Assessment is embedded in instruction.** While children are engaged in learning, the teacher is simultaneously assessing the children's literacy learning. Hence, the teacher does not take time away from teaching, and the children do not take time away from learning for their teacher to assess them. A result is that curriculum, instruction, and assessment are all closely connected.

2. **Teachers use assessment to improve instruction.** Teachers gather information, analyze the information, and use what they learn to inform their instruction. In fact, this

should be the main purpose of assessment. Using this approach, teachers observe and listen to their students' responses, simultaneously assessing their students' knowledge and process. Based on these on-the-spot assessments, teachers might change their questions or change the activities they had planned. The link between assessment and instruction enables teachers to adapt instruction to meet the needs of specific children.

3. Multiple sources are used to gather evidence to support different perspectives of the child's literacy abilities. When multiple sources of data ("observations made in different situations, . . . by different people at different times, or [using] different assessment instruments") are used, then the likelihood of an accurate understanding of children's literacy knowledge and learning is increased (IRA/NCTE, 1994, p. 30).

4. Assessment should be a chronology of each child's development based on data collected over time. The goal is to compare each child's progress over time. A child's current performance should be compared against that child's previous performance rather than against the performance of others in the classroom.

5. The children's knowledge and learning are assessed while the children are engaged in authentic literacy events. Grant Wiggins (1993), a leading voice supporting authentic assessment, defines authenticity as the "faithful representation of the contexts encountered in a field of study or in the real-life 'tests' of adult life" (p. 206). In other words, authentic literacy tasks must be real ones that could and do occur in the world outside of school. The tasks must be functional, meaningful in a particular social context, and have all the characteristics of natural discourse.

6. Students should engage in self-reflection and self-evaluation. Students become more interested in and responsible for their own learning when they participate in assessing their own progress. "Self-evaluation leads to the establishment of goals. That is what evaluation is for. We evaluate in order to find out what we have learned so we will know what to study next" (Hansen, 1994, pp. 36–37). In this way, learning is advanced.

Many of the assessment techniques described above will be discussed at length in later chapters of this book. In addition, Chapter 11 features an in-depth discussion on how teachers can maintain and manage multiple sources of data and how these data can be organized into portfolios and used to analyze each child's literacy development over time.

Teaching Language and Literacy to Children

The authors of this book share several beliefs that form the foundation of our approach to teaching language and literacy. We believe that

- children learn by constructing and testing their hypotheses about language and literacy;
- children make sense of their world by integrating new experiences into what they understand, making connections between new information and previously known information and then organizing that information;
- learning is a social process that takes place through interactions between and among children and more knowledgeable others (e.g., parents, teachers, older siblings, other children);

- learning is a social act—children learn by watching, practicing, mimicking, and absorbing what those around them do;
- to support children's learning, teachers must "fit the child's needs at the moment" and operate within the child's zone of proximal development (the range of activities that children can do with help from others);
- teachers should study the cultures of the children in their classrooms in order to teach in ways that allow their young students to work to their strengths.

These beliefs are in direct contrast with those of the transmission approach to teaching language and literacy. The transmission model, with its part-to-whole orientation, emphasizes a highly sequential path toward literacy. As this approach also stresses a single correct answer to each question, it is likely to reflect only the values, ideas, and experiences of the dominant culture (Au, 1993). Furthermore, as instruction focuses on the end product, little recognition is given to the influence of the students' life experiences and cultural background. In Figure 1.1, we summarize the major differences between the transmission and the constructivist approaches to language and literacy learning and teaching.

	Transmission	Constructivist
How children learn	• When the teacher presents information directly • When children reach certain levels of maturity or skill readiness • Piece-by-piece	• Through observations, explorations and interaction with others • Continuously, actively, developmentally • Integrating prior knowledge with new experiences
Teacher's role in the learning process	• Disseminator of information, director of curriculum	• Facilitator, colearner
The language-art curriculum	• Part-to-whole • Reading, writing, listening, and speaking taught separately • Predetemined by district, teacher • Skills driven • Text/workbook dependent	• Whole-to-part • Reading, writing, listening, and speaking taught together • Evolving from student concerns • Centered around concepts • Real data/manipulatives
Student diversity	• All children follow same developmental pattern • All children will learn same information presented in sequential manner regardless of background	• Each child is unique • Background/prior experience significantly influences child's interests and learning
Asessment of children's learning	• Finished-product orientation • End-of-unit emphasis • Single measures (tests) used to make vital decisions • Teacher as sole evaluator	• Process-of-learning orientation • Ongoing and over time • Multiple sources (tests, observations, artifacts) • Teacher/child/parent as assessment partners

FIGURE 1.1 Learning Theories

Given our shared beliefs, we will emphasize constructivist teaching principles in this book. We believe the following principles should guide how children are taught spoken and written language in elementary classrooms.

Knowledgeable Teachers Provide Children with a Print-Rich Classroom Environment

High-quality literacy programs require a literacy-rich environment with many materials to support children's learning. As Susan Neuman and Kathy Roskos (1993, pp. 20–21) explain, a print-rich classroom can help children to learn about language and literacy:

> The quality of the physical environment is a powerful factor in language learning. The objects and opportunities it provides are the stuff out of which basic concepts are spun. What is available to label and to talk about, how accessible it is to touch and explore, and how it is organized influence both spoken and written language development.

Rich physical environments do not just happen; the creation of a classroom environment that supports children's learning, teacher's teaching, and the curriculum requires forethought. Some characteristics of this type of classroom environment include a well-stocked library corner and writing center, lots of functional print, theme-related literacy props in play areas, displays of children's writing, and so on. This type of environment offers children opportunities to talk, listen, read, and write to one another for real-life purposes.

Knowledgeable Teachers Demonstrate, Model, and Scaffold Instruction

Children will try to do what others do. Therefore, demonstrating and modeling literacy events will lead to children imitating these events. When a teacher reads books to young children, children independently pick up the books and say words in ways that would lead a listener to think they are reading. The children sound as though they are reading words, yet their eyes are focused on the illustrations. When children see parents and teachers using print for various purposes—writing shopping lists, looking up information in a book, and writing notes—they begin to learn about the practical uses of language and to understand why reading and writing are activities worth doing.

Deborah Rowe (1994) provides an example of a preschool teacher's demonstration of the use of exclamation points. The teacher is sitting in the writing center with a small group of children. She writes a get-well card to a sick colleague. She writes: "Dear Carol, We hope you get well SOON!!!" She explains, "exclamation mark, exclamation mark, exclamation mark. Because I want her to get well *soon*." Moments later, Kira and Hana talk about exclamation marks.

KIRA: And this is [pause] extamotion [sic] point. How come?

HANA: Put three cause it's big letters.

Still later, Hana and Christina include exclamation marks in their writing. Christina writes the letters COI over and over inside one band of a rainbow and exclamation marks inside another band, and Hana writes her name and fills the bottom of the page with upside-down exclamation marks (Rowe, 1994, pp. 168–169). This preschool teacher probably did not set out to teach her young students about exclamation points. In the act of writing and talking about her writing, she demonstrated to three curious, observant preschool apprentices the purpose of using an exclamation mark. Notice how she showed her student "observers" what is done during reading and writing. She acted as a writer; not as teacher of reading and writing. In this way, she shared with the children how a reader or a writer thinks as well as acts.

Yet, knowledgeable teachers do not hesitate to directly teach children those skills and strategies they likely would not learn through discovery on their own. Initially, the teacher might model and describe the skill or strategy. Then, the teacher might ask the children to practice the skill or strategy. While the children practice, the teacher will provide them with as much support and feedback as they need. Finally, the teacher will provide opportunities for the children to work independently to apply the newly learned skill or strategy. This "gradual release of responsibility and scaffolded instruction" provides children with appropriate support "when they are used within meaningful, authentic contexts" (Gambrell & Mazzoni, 1999, p. 16).

Knowledgeable Teachers Provide Opportunities for Children to Work and Play Together in Literacy-Enriched Environments

Of course, teachers are not the only people in the classroom environment who offer demonstrations of literacy. "Knowledgeable teachers understand that the social, collaborative nature of learning to read and respond to books goes beyond the relationship between adult and child, teacher and student, and includes peers" (Galda, Cullinan, & Strickland, 1993). This statement about learning to read is equally applicable to learning to write. Creating a "community of literacy learners" is often suggested in the professional literature. Children select books to "read" because their peers have selected the book. Children talk to each other about books they are reading or have had read to them. Children turn to each other for information and help in decoding or spelling words. "How do you spell *morning*?" "What's this word say?"

When teachers know that learning is a social act and that readers, writers, and speakers develop new understandings as a result of the rich exchange of ideas in collaborative learning contexts, teachers intentionally create new kinds of classroom participation opportunities for their students. For example, these teachers provide their students with opportunities to engage in discussion groups about books, to form literacy clubs, or to work in small groups to investigate specific topics within a content area.

Such collaborative learning opportunities will not "just happen." Teachers must create an environment where children can demonstrate for, or coach, each other. Several researchers have documented what happens when teachers create such opportunities. For example, researchers (e.g., Christie & Stone, 1999; Vukelich, 1993) have studied how play in literacy-enriched play settings provides children with opportunities to teach each other. Carol Vukelich (1993), for example, studied how children teach each other about the functions, features, and meaning of print in play. The following peer-to-peer interaction illustrates how one child coaches another child about how to spell his name.

> Jessie is the forest ranger. She is seated at the entrance to the camp site, directing potential campers to get a sticker from her before entering the campground, and *then* she'll tell them which tent they can use.
>
> **JESSIE:**   Ronald, how do you spell your name?
>
> **RONALD:**   *R.* [Jessie writes *r.*] No, it's the big kind.
>
> [Ronald forms the letter with his finger on the table. Jessie writes *R.*] Good!
>
> **JESSIE:**   What else?
>
> [Jessie writes as Ronald dictates each letter of his name, looking up at him after each one. When finished, she gives Ronald the sticker with his name on it.] (p. 390)

When teachers value children's contributions and celebrate what they know, children see the strengths in each other. Within such a supportive climate, children practice what they know and take the risks necessary for learning to occur. This kind of environment encourages children to learn from themselves, from each other, and from the teacher.

Knowledgeable Teachers Link Literacy and Play

The example above of children teaching each other how to spell occurred in literacy-enriched play settings in Karen Valentine's kindergarten classroom. The play setting was a park. Karen and the children generated ideas for the dramatic play setting. There needed to be a place to fish, so the water table became the fishing pond labeled "Lum's Pond" after the nearby pond. Fish and fishing poles were made in the art center. Paper clips were attached to the fish and magnets to the end of the string attached to the fishing pole. Soon children were reeling in fish. But to fish, you need a fishing license. A form was created and placed in the writing center. Park rangers ensured that no one fished who did not have a license. Soon the children needed clipboards with paper; tickets had to be issued to children caught fishing without a license.

A beach (blue water) with beach chairs (brought from homes) grew in another section of the play center. Soon, books found their way into beach bags, and sunglasses were needed to shade reading eyes. Samatha insisted that people on vacation write postcards. Karen, the teacher, provided models of several postcards in the writing center; the children used magic markers to draw postcard pictures on one side of 4 × 6-inch index cards. Pens found their way into the beach bags so the writing of postcards could occur while sitting at the beach.

And so the setting developed. By making the tools of literacy available to the children, the children began to incorporate print in very natural and real-world ways into the dramatic play theme. They wrote for many purposes (e.g., to control others' behavior, to share stories of vacation experiences, to reserve a tent). They read books and each other's writing. They talked "park" talk, negotiating their various "camping/park" schema to create a new shared schema. Within this play setting, they had the opportunity to practice the literacy events they had witnessed in the world outside the classroom and to add to their knowledge about literacy. Enriching play settings with appropriate literacy materials provides young children with important opportunities for literacy learning and for practicing literacy.

Knowledgeable Teachers Support Children's Experimentation in a 'Risk-Free' Environment Where Children Use What They Know to Make Sense of the New

Years ago, young children were not considered to be writing until they were writing conventionally, that is, correctly forming the letters and spelling the words. They were not considered to be reading until they could correctly recognize numerous printed words. In the 1970s, Marie Clay (1975) and Charles Read (1971) helped us understand emergent forms of writing and reading. We learned that children construct, test, and perfect hypotheses about written language. Their research lead to Elizabeth Sulzby's and her colleagues' (Sulzby, 1985a, 1985b; Sulzby, Barnhart, & Hieshima, 1989) creation of developmental sequences that children pass through on their way to becoming conventional readers and writers.

Today outstanding early childhood teachers do not expect young children's notions of writing and reading to conform to adult models of correctness. They expect children to experiment with print: to scribble, to make marks that look something like letters, to write strings of letters, and so forth. They expect children to look at pictures and "read" a story with an oral telling voice, to look at pictures and "read" a story with a written story voice, to attend to print and "read" in a written story voice, and so forth. As children experiment, these teachers compliment the children on their reading and writing expertise (e.g., "What good readers you are!" "What a wonderful story you have written!" "And you wrote all this?"). Through such explorations, children create meaning and communicate. Their teachers support their explorations with materials and with comments. Their teachers confirm when their hypotheses about print are correct.

Teachers' support for the construction of knowledge through experimentation and risk-taking does not end when children's print understandings more closely resemble adults'. When children reach this stage in their literacy development, teachers support their efforts to search for and construct new meanings in reading and through writing. They encourage them to test the word: Does it make sense in this sentence? They work to make children strategic readers, readers who dare to employ different strategies with different texts read for different purposes. These teachers and their children view reading and writing as meaning making or producing events.

Knowledgeable Teachers Provide Opportunities for Children to Use Language and Literacy for Real Purposes and Audiences

Most research on learning supports the proposition that knowing the reason for a learning situation and seeing a purpose in a task helps children learn. Through their lives outside the classroom, children have experienced a wide variety of purposes for writing to various audiences. If children are allowed to experiment with paper and pencils and to write on topics of their choice, these purposes will begin to show up in their early attempts at writing. They will jot down lists of things they need to do, make signs for their doors warning intruders to stay out, and write letters to the editor to complain about injustices.

Similarly, children have experienced many opportunities to read for real purposes. They have shopped in grocery and toy stores, and sometimes screamed when their mothers refused to purchase the cereal or toy whose label they read and wanted. They have told the car driver who slowed but didn't come to a full stop at the stop sign to STOP! They have read the address on an envelope collected at the mailbox and said, "You won't like this one. It's a bill!"

Notice how many of these reading and writing opportunities are literacy events woven into daily life. The event defines the purpose of the literacy activity. When children read and write for real people, for real purposes, and in ways that are linked with their lives outside of school, the students are more likely to be motivated, and motivation is believed to result in learning that is deep and internalized (Gambrell & Mazzino, 1999). Furthermore, through such meaningful literacy events, school and community are bridged. Just outside the walls of every school lie any number of real problems awaiting study. Reading and writing for real purposes abound.

Knowledgeable Teachers Read to Children Daily and Encourage Them to Read Books on Their Own

Living in a print-rich world provides children with many opportunities to read *contextualized* print. That is, children form hypotheses about what words say because of the context in which the words are embedded. As described in other sections of the chapter, children learn to read cereal boxes, stop signs, and the McDonald's sign early in life. While making such connections with print is important, young children also need multiple experiences with decontextualized print. Susan Neuman and Kathy Roskos (1993, p. 36) explain the meaning of decontextualized print:

> Essentially, this means that unlike contextualized print experiences, written language has meaning apart from the particular situation or context of its use. The meaning of decontextualized print is derived from the language itself and from the conventions of the literary genre. . . . Over time, [children] develop a frame, or sense of story, . . . a mental model of basic elements of a story.

Reading stories to children is one of the best ways to familiarize them with decontextualized print. Effective teachers plan numerous opportunities for storybook reading experiences. These teachers read aloud daily to individual children, small groups of children, and the whole class. Sometimes the books are regular-sized books, like the ones obtained from the public or school library. Other times, the books are big books, enlarged (about 24 × 26 inch) versions of regular-sized books.

But hearing stories read aloud is not enough for children of any age. Studies have shown the importance of talking about the books read (Heath, 1983; Yaden, Smolken, &

Conlon, 1989). Many teachers begin their read-alouds by engaging children in a discussion related to the story they are about to read. A teacher might read the title and ask the children what they think the story might be about or ask a question related to the book's content. While reading, the teacher might invite the children to make comments, to share reactions, or to ask questions. They might invite the children to turn to their reading partner to discuss a section of the book just read. After reading, the teacher will likely engage the children in a discussion aimed at extending their understanding of the story. This framework for read-alouds has been called a "grand conversation" (Clay, 1991). Such conversations help children understand how to process the decontextualized text found in books both in terms of the story's structure and by making connections between the text and their experiences.

It is also important to provide opportunities for children to read books to themselves and to one another. Through such occasions, children have the opportunity to practice what they have learned during the interactive storybook readings and to refine the strategies needed to construct meaning from texts. To learn to enjoy making meaning from written texts, each person must do the work, the thinking, independently. Children learn to read by reading.

Knowledgeable Teachers Use Authentic Forms of Assessment to Find Out What Children Know and Can Do

Is the child's development following the expected stages? Is the child learning? We know that standardized group paper-and-pencil tests do not reveal useful information about individual children's literacy development. Rather than testing children, teachers need to assess children's performance in a variety of contexts under many different conditions. Teachers assess to learn about children's strengths and weaknesses in order to plan the best instruction possible for every child in the classroom.

The 1998 joint International Reading Association and National Association for the Education of Young Children position statement on developmentally appropriate practices for young children suggests the following:

> **Accurate assessment** of children's knowledge, skills, and dispositions in reading and writing will help teachers better match instruction with how and what children are learning. However, early reading and writing cannot simply be measured as a set of narrowly-defined skills on standardized tests. These measures often are not reliable or valid indicators of what children can do in typical practice, nor are they sensitive to language variations, culture, or experiences of young children. Rather, a sound assessment should be anchored in real-life writing and reading tasks and continuously chronicle a wide range of children's literacy activities in different situations. Good assessment is essential to help teachers tailor appropriate instruction to young children and to know when and how much intensive instruction on any particular skill or strategy might be needed (p. 38).

The joint statement advises teachers of young children to use multiple indicators (observations of children engaged in reading, writing, and speaking events; evaluations of such children's products as writing samples; children's performance during reading and writing) to assess and monitor children's development and learning. While the IRA/NAEYC statement addresses the assessment practices of young children (ages 0–8), the suggestions echo those put forth by the International Reading Association and the National Council of Teachers of English in 1994 about the assessment of children of all ages.

Knowledgeable Teachers Respect and Make Accommodations for Children's Developmental, Cultural, and Linguistic Diversity

Children arrive in the classroom with different individual language and literacy needs. Our challenge is to offer good fits between each child's strengths and needs and what we try to give the child. The instruction we provide needs to dovetail with where children are developmentally and with their language and culture.

In the previous section about diversity, we wondered about the *how* of connecting children's classroom learning with their home cultural and linguistic experiences. We challenge readers to

- engage in the study of their children's community's ways with words and texts;
- carefully consider how to scaffold the classroom language activities and instruction so that all their children will experience success in their efforts to learn mainstream English;
- consider how to teach their young children about print in ways that better fit the speech events their children are accustomed to from their home and community;
- connect with their children's parents so that they can learn from each other how to best serve these children's needs; and
- look for ways to bring the community into the classroom and to connect children's outside learning experiences with their school and child care center learning experiences.

Knowledgeable Teachers Recognize the Importance of Reflecting on Their Instructional Decisions

The importance of "learning by doing," standing back from each teaching/learning event to learn from one's teaching, is not new. John Dewey (1938) is usually credited with proposing the importance of this activity, and Donald Schon (1983) with reintroducing the idea into the educational literature. To reflect is to take an active role in studying one's own instructional decisions in order to enhance one's knowledge and make informed decisions. Not all of such reflections will be on past actions (retrospective); some might be on the potential outcomes of future actions (anticipatory), while others will be "in action" while teaching (contemporaneous) (van Manen, 1995). To reflect is to problematize teaching: to consider and reconsider the procedures for technical accuracy (e.g., the procedural steps to follow while conducting a guided reading lesson), the reasons for instructional actions and outcomes, and the underlying assumptions of actions that impact social justice (e.g., curriculum mandates that affect teacher decision making or inequities that inhibit student learning).

Being a reflective practitioner assumes particular importance for literacy teachers who engage in constructivist literacy practices. In such literacy programs, the teacher builds the program in ways that are consistent with the students' needs. As the decision makers, these teachers determine which literacy skills or components to teach and when to move their community of learners toward the desired instructional goals, adjusting the when and how to meet each learner's needs. Reflection is central to making these critical decisions.

We have challenged ourselves to provide readers with information on what is known about ways to meet all children's needs.

Summary

One basic theory, called the constructivist theory of learning, underlies this book: Language and literacy learning is an active, constructive process. Children listen to and observe the oral and written language that surrounds them in everyday life, and they try to make sense of that language. In this chapter, we briefly explained this constructivist view of learning and discussed its implications for teaching language and literacy. How did the information match up with your own beliefs about literacy learning and instruction?

In subsequent chapters, we provide many explanations of how to implement constructivist teaching strategies aimed at promoting different aspects of language and literacy development. In addition, the themes of respect for student diversity and instructionally linked assessment appear throughout the book. When appropriate, Special Features about the special needs of second-language learners are included. Further, a section titled "Assessment: Discovering What Children Know and Can Do" is included in several of the chapters.

To summarize the key points about the foundations of language and literacy learning, we return to the focus questions at the beginning of this chapter:

■ *How do children learn about language and literacy?*

Children learn about language and literacy by observing, exploring, and interacting with others. Children assume the role of apprentice—mimicking, absorbing, and adapting the words and literacy activities used by more knowledgeable others. As they engage in these social interactions, children integrate new experiences with prior knowledge, constructing and testing hypotheses to make meaning. They store this newly constructed knowledge in mental structures called schemas.

■ *Why is it crucial for teachers to respect children's diversity when teaching language and literacy?*

Children's oral language, the way they make meaning, and their early literacy experiences all are dependent on the practices shared by the members of their cultural community. Language-minority children—children who speak nonmainstream English dialects or whose native language is not English—represent a significant and growing group of diverse learners. When these children come to school or the day care center, they will come as competent users of their home language. Teachers must teach in ways that allow their young children to work to their strengths and use their existing language competence as stepping-stones toward learning mainstream English and literacy skills that are so crucial for success in school and adult life.

■ *How should children's literacy learning be assessed?*

   Assessment—discovering what children know and can do with respect to reading and writing—should be ongoing and spread over time and should involve multiple sources of information. It should also be closely embedded with instruction, so that while children are engaged in learning, the teacher is simultaneously assessing the children's literacy learning. The main purpose of assessment should be to improve instruction. Teachers should use information gained from assessment to plan future learning activities that meet the needs of each child in the classroom.

■ *What are the best practices in teaching language and literacy to children?* Knowledgeable teachers
   ■ create print-rich classroom environments;
   ■ demonstrate, model, and scaffold instruction;
   ■ offer opportunities for children to work and play together;
   ■ link play and literacy;
   ■ support children's experimentation in a "risk-free" learning environment;
   ■ provide opportunities for children to read and write for real purposes and audiences;
   ■ establish daily read-alouds and opportunities for children to read books independently;
   ■ accept and take advantage of children's diversity; and
   ■ reflect on their instructional decisions.

L I N K I N G   K N O W L E D G E   T O   P R A C T I C E

1. Observe a young child interacting with print in a store, restaurant, or the like. Describe the setting in which the observation was made and the participants who were involved in the event. Describe the event exactly as it occurred. What does it indicate about the child's understanding of literacy?

2. Observe a teacher in a nearby classroom. How does this teacher's language and literacy instruction match up with the teaching principles described in this chapter?

3. Interview a parent or an older sibling about your early language and literacy development. What does this person recall about how you learned to talk, read, and write?

CHAPTER

2

Oral Language Development

Perched in the shopping cart, nine-month-old Dawn babbles away to her mother. As they approach the checkout register, the clerk greets her mother. Dawn smiles, loudly says "Hi!" and waves her hand. The startled clerk smiles at Dawn and begins to talk to her. Dawn, obviously pleased with this attention, now babbles back to the clerk.

As this scenario reveals, the power of language is evident to even its youngest users. Dawn demonstrates that she knows how to use language to express—and realize—her desire to become a significant, communicating member in her world. By age 18 months, Dawn will have a vocabulary of dozens of words, and she will begin speaking in rule-governed, two-word sentences. By age 36 months, her vocabulary will number in the hundreds of words, and she will be using fully formed, five- and six-word sentences.

Children's oral language development is remarkable. Lindfors (1987, p. 90) outlines the typical accomplishments of young language learners:

> Virtually every child, without special training, exposed to surface structures of language in many interaction contexts, builds for himself—in a short period of time and at an early stage in his cognitive development—a deep-level, abstract, and highly complex system of linguistic structure.

How does Dawn—and every other human child, for that matter—learn to communicate? How does this development occur so rapidly and without any seeming effort on the part of children or their parents? This question has fascinated scholars and parents for hundreds of years and is the subject of this chapter.

Before Reading This Chapter, Think About . . .

- What were your first words? Although you probably do not recall uttering those words, maybe your parents or older siblings recollect your having spoken to them.
- How do you think children acquire language? Is language development primarily a matter of genetics (an inborn ability to learn languages), the types of experiences and support children receive from their parents and other people, or a combination of these factors?

- When do children begin to express their thoughts orally? Why do some children develop language early while others experience language delays?
- Have you ever been in a situation where everyone around you used a language you don't know? How did you feel? How did you communicate with these speakers?

Focus Questions

- What are the major views on how children's language develops? Which aspects of language development does each view adequately explain?
- What are the major components of language?
- How does the structure of an infant's brain develop? How does this structural development affect language acquisition?
- What factors affect children's rate of language acquisition?
- How does children's acquisition of a second language compare with their first language acquisition? What should adults do to make it easier for children to learn English as a second language?

B O X   **2.1**

Definition of Terms

behaviorist perspective: the view that language acquisition is a result of imitation and reinforcement.

cerebral cortex: the largest part of the brain, composed of two hemispheres that are responsible for higher brain functions, including thought and language.

myelineation: a process in which the neurons of the brain become coated with a white substance known as myelin, which facilitates the transmission of sensory information and promotes learning.

morphemes: the smallest units of meaning in oral language. The word *cats* contains two morphemes: *cat* (name of a type of animal) and *s* (plural).

nativist perspective: the view that language development is a result of an inborn capacity to learn language.

neuro-biological perspective: the view that language acquisition can be explained by studying the structural development of the brain.

neurons: the impulse-conducting cells that make up the brain.

otitis media: an inflammation of the inner part of the ear that can retard language acquisition.

phoneme: the smallest unit of sound in a language. There are approximately 44 phonemes in English.

pragmatics: rules that affect how language is used in different social contexts.

semantics: the part of language that assigns meaning to words and sentences.

synapses: connections between the neurons of the brain.

syntax: rules for arranging words into sentences.

social–interactionist perspective: the view that language development is a result of both genetics and adult support.

Language Acquisition Theories

There are four views on how children learn language: behaviorism, linguistic nativism, social interactionism, and the neuro-biological perspective. We present a brief description of each perspective in this chapter. Our experiences as parents, teachers, and researchers lead us to believe that the social-interactionism perspective most realistically accounts for similarities and differences in young children's language development. Therefore, we present a more detailed description of what is presently known about children's language acquisition from this perspective. However, we also acknowledge the importance of the new neuro-biological information provided by neuroscientists to help us understand the biology of language acquisition. Together, the social-interactionist and the neuro-biological perspectives provide important insights for teachers and future teachers on how children acquire language. In Figure 2.1, we summarize these four views of language acquisition.

Behaviorist Perspective

The behaviorist view suggests that nurture—the way a child is taught or molded by parents and the environment—plays a dominant role in children's language development. Through

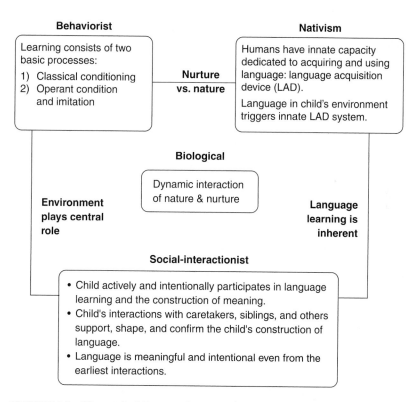

FIGURE 2.1   Theoretical Perspectives on Language Acquisition

the first half of the 20th century, this was the prevalent view. Researchers and teachers believed that all learning (language included) is the result of two basic processes—classical and operant conditioning (Skinner, 1957). Behaviorists attribute receptive language to associations that result from classical conditioning. For example, every time the baby is offered a bottle, the mother names the object, "Here's the bottle." After numerous repetitions with the adult presenting the action/object and phrase, the baby learns that the clear cylinder filled with food is called a bottle.

Behaviorists suggest that through operant conditioning, infants gradually learn expressive language by being rewarded for imitating the sounds and speech they hear. For instance, a baby spontaneously babbles and accidentally says or repeats the sound "mama." The mother responds joyfully, hugging and kissing the baby, saying "Yes, Mama!" The baby, given this reward, is reinforced and attempts to repeat the behavior. Once the behavior is repeated and rewarded often enough, the child connects the word sound to the object or event.

Nativist Perspective

The nativist view of learning and development, with its emphasis on nature, is at the opposite end of the continuum from the behaviorist perspective. According to the nativist view, a person's behavior and capabilities are largely predetermined. Nativists believe every child has an inborn capacity to learn language. If these theorists were using computer terminology, they would say that humans are hardwired for language. Noam Chomsky (1965) called this innate capacity a language acquisition device (LAD). Nativists posit that the LAD allows children to interpret phoneme patterns, word meanings, and the rules that govern language. For example, when children first begin to use past tenses, they often overgeneralize certain words, such as *goed* for *went,* or *thinked* for *thought.* Since *goed* and *thinked* are not words that children would hear adults say, these examples illustrate that children are using some type of internal rule system, not simple imitation, to govern their acquisition of language.

Nativists also believe that this innate language structure facilitates the child's own attempts to communicate, much the same way as the computer's wiring facilitates the use of a number of software programs. Nativists believe that language learning differs from all other human learning in that a child learns to communicate even without support from parents or caregivers. They view the environment's role in language acquisition as largely a function of activating the innate, physiologically based system. Environment, these theorists believe, is not the major force shaping a child's language development.

Social-Interactionist Perspective

Social interactionists do not come down on either side of the nature versus nurture debate; rather, they acknowledge the influence of genetics and parental teaching. They share with behaviorists the belief that environment plays a central role in children's language development. Likewise, along with nativists, they believe that children possess an innate predisposition to learn language. In addition, social interactionists stress the child's own intentional participation in language learning and the construction of meaning.

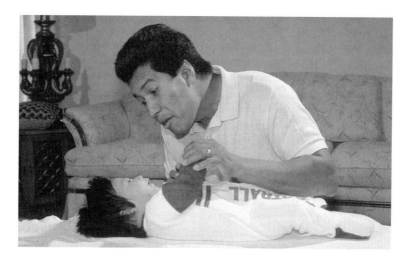

The social-interactionist perspective highlights the importance of infants'
verbal "bouts" with caregivers.

Lev Vygotsky's theory (1978) forms the foundation of the social-interactionist view of language development. Vygotsky believed that language develops in the context of social interaction and language use. As children experience the wide variety of functions and forms of language, they internalize the way that their society uses language to represent meaning. Social experiences shape the language the child internalizes. At the same time, the child is making an internal effort to assign meanings to experience and to communicate with the outside world. These efforts are simultaneous. Two forces, within and without the child, work together to propel language learning.

The social interactionist's point of view emphasizes the importance of the infant's verbal negotiations or "verbal bouts" (Golinkoff, 1983) with caregivers. These negotiations occur partly because mothers or other caretakers treat children's attempts at speech as meaningful and intentional (Piper, 1993). An example is shown by 11-month-old Dawn, standing by the garage door. Dawn is patting the door.

DAWN:	"Bice!"
MOM:	"Do you want ice?"
DAWN:	(shaking her head) "Biiisse."
MOM:	(opening the garage door) "Bise?"
DAWN:	(pointing at the bike) "Bise."
MOM:	"You want to go for a bike ride?"
DAWN:	(raising her arms, nodding her head vigorously) "Bice!"

As Dawn's mother (and most mothers) begins to make sense of her child's speech, she also begins to understand her child's meaning and/or intent. Lev Vygotsky (1962) described this type of adult support, or scaffolding, as facilitating the child's language growth within the zone of proximal development, the distance between a child's current level of development and the level at which the child can function with adult assistance. In the preceding example, the mother's questions enable Dawn to successfully communicate using a one-word sentence, something she could not have done on her own. Parents also support children's efforts to learn language by focusing the child's attention on objects in the immediate environment and labeling each object and its action. Special Feature 2.1 provides examples of how children use language for social purposes.

A Biological Perspective

The psychologists, linguists, and anthropologists who developed the three preceding perspectives of language acquisition had to infer the origins of language and brain activity from careful, long-term observations of external behavior. Over the past two decades, technological innovations have enabled neuroscientists to study the brain at a cellular level. Brain imaging techniques are noninvasive procedures that allow researchers to graphically record and simultaneously display three-dimensional, color-enhanced images of a living brain as it processes information (Sochurek, 1987). These data provide researchers with a better way to understand the organization and functional operations of the brain.

According to this new perspective, the capacity to learn language begins with brain cells called neurons. Neurons emerge during the early phases of fetal development, growing at the fantastic rate of 250,000 per minute (Edelman, 1995). As neurons multiply, they follow a complex genetic blueprint that causes the brain to develop distinct but interdepen-

---

Special Feature 2.1

Why Do Children Talk?

Why do children talk? Beyond being biologically designed to do so, children talk to share thoughts and feelings, to ask for things they need, to question new ideas, and just to enjoy speaking. There are as many reasons that children talk as there are children. It is for functional and social reasons that we all learned language.

Through observations of his young son, linguist Michael Halliday (1975) was able to distinguish seven different functions (uses) of language. These include language used to satisfy personal goals and needs; control others; share information about self; interact with someone else; learn; pretend and fantasize; and share information. After studying many preschool children, Joan Tough (1977) concluded that there

are four functional categories that account for language use: directing self and others; telling present and past experiences; predicting, imagining, and empathizing with others; and relating to others and maintaining self-control.

As you read Halliday's (1975) and Tough's (1977) descriptions of the different types of functional categories, you probably noticed a great deal of similarity among their classification systems. Without oversimplifying, and after much study and comparison, the authors believe that these many functional purposes can be organized into three broad domains. Children and adults, with varying degrees of sophistication, use language to express or assert their needs, connect with self and others, and create, comprehend, and expand their knowledge of their immediate environment and the world at large.

TABLE 2.1 Functional Uses of Language

Major Domains	Specific Functions	Halliday	Tough
Reveal or assert needs/wants	Satisfy personal needs	Instrumental	Directive
"My toy."	Accomplish goals		
"Mine!"	Direct self/others	Regulatory	Directive
"You do that."	Control self/others		
"I do it."			
Connect with self and others	Share information about self/others	Personal	Relational
"I like chips."	Interact with others	Interactional	
"Here I am."	Direct self/others		
"That's my baby sister."	Express feelings		
Create, comprehend, and expand knowledge	Learn—find out information	Heuristic	Projective
"Why?"	Communicate information to self/others	Imaginative	
"How come?"	Pretend and fantasize	Informative	
"Let's pretend that."			

dent systems—brain stem and limbic system, cerebellum and cerebral cortex (MacLean, 1978). New brain-imaging technology has allowed scientists to locate specific areas in the brain that are dedicated to hearing, speaking, and interpreting language. Thus, the nativist linguistic theory of language acquisition is, in part, correct—the human brain has dedicated structures for language, and infant brains are born capable of speaking any of the 3000-plus human languages (Kuhl, 1993). However, infants are not disposed to speak any particular language, nor are they born language proficient. The language that a child learns is dependent on the language that the child hears spoken in the home (Sylwester, 1995).

In fact, the recent discoveries in neuro-biology support elements of the nativist, behaviorist, and social-interactionist views of language development. These biological findings reveal that language learning is a reciprocal dialogue between genetics (nature) and environment (nurture). Clearly, infants are born with key brain areas genetically dedicated to language functions. Yet, for children to learn the language of their culture, it is necessary that they have consistent, frequent opportunities to interact with a persistent caregiver who models the language with the child. Likewise, neuroscientists agree that a child's language capacity is dependent on the quality of language input. Parents and caregivers who consistently engage in conversation with their infants actually help their children develop neural networks that lead to language fluency and proficiency (Healy, 1994; 1997; Kotulak, 1997; Sprenger, 1999). In Figure 2.1, we summarize the major concepts of these four perspectives of language acquisition.

Linguistic Vocabulary Lesson

Linguistics is the study of language. To better understand the complexities of linguistic acquisition, we provide a brief discussion of the components of linguistic structure, of phonology, morphology, syntax, semantics, and pragmatics.

Phonology

The sound system of a particular language is its phonology, and the distinctive units of sound in a language are its phonemes. Individual phonemes are described according to how speakers modify the airstream they exhale to produce the particular sounds.

Phonological development begins when sounds of speech activate neural networks in the infant's brain. This process begins during the last two months of prenatal development as babies are able to hear intonation patterns from their mother's voice (Shore, 1997).

Although the mechanical aspects of the auditory system are in place at birth, the neural network that supports language acquisition is just beginning to develop. Verbal interactions with caregivers allow babies to clearly hear sounds of their native language(s) and observe how the mouth and tongue work to create these unique sounds. Simultaneously, as babies babble, they gain motor control of their vocal and breathing apparatus. Interactions with caregivers allow babies an opportunity to listen, observe, and attempt to mimic sounds they hear and the mouth and tongue movements they see. Through this process, babies begin to specialize in the sounds of their native language(s). The developmental window of opportunity (sometimes called the critical period) for mastering sound discrimination occurs within the first six months of an infant's life. By this time, babies' brains are already pruning out sensitivity to sounds that are not heard in their environment (Kuhl, 1993). This pruning is so efficient that children actually lose the ability to hear phonemes that are not used in their mother-tongue. Children who consistently hear more than one language during this time may become native bi- or trilinguals, as they retain the ability to hear the subtle and discrete sounds.

Another important aspect of the English phonology is its prosody, or the stress and intonation patterns of the language. Stress refers to the force with which phonemes are articulated. Where the stress is placed may distinguish otherwise identical words (RECord [noun] versus reCORD [verb]). Intonation, on the other hand, refers to the pattern of stress and of rising and falling pitch that occurs within a sentence. These changes in intonation may shift the meaning of otherwise identical sentences:

IS she coming? (Is she or is she not coming?)
Is SHE coming? (Her, not anyone else)
Is she COMING? (Hurry up; it's about time)

Babies as young as four and five months begin to experiment with the pitch, tone, and volume of the sounds they make and often produce sounds that mimic the tonal and stress qualities of their parents' speech.

Morphology

As babies' phonological development progresses, they begin to make morphemes. Morphemes are the smallest units of meaning in oral language. While babies may begin to make word-like sounds (echolalia) around six to eight months, morphemes will not emerge until around the baby's first birthday. These real words are made up of one or more phonemes and fall into several categories:

> *Lexical*—individual meaning carrying words, such as *cat, baby.*
>
> *Bound*—units of sound that hold meaning (like *re, un*) but must be attached to other morphemes (*reorder, unbend*).
>
> *Derivational and inflectional*—usually suffixes that change the class of the word; for example: noun to adjective—*dust* to *dusty;* verb to noun—*teaches* to *teacher.*
>
> *Compound*—two lexical morphemes that together may form a unique meaning, such as *football* or *cowboy.*
>
> *Idiom*—an expression whose meaning cannot be derived from its individual parts; for example, *Put your foot in your mouth* carries a very different meaning from the visual image it conjures up.

Syntax

Syntax refers to how morphemes, or words, are combined to form sentences or units of thought. In English, there are basically two different types of order: linear and hierarchical structure. Linear structure refers to the object-verb arrangement. For example, *Building falls on man* means something very different than *Man falls on building.* Hierarchical structure refers to how words are grouped together within a sentence to reveal the speaker's intent. However, different languages have unique and inherent rules that govern syntax. A speaker of English might say: *The long, sleek, black cat chased the frightened tiny, gray mouse.* A language with syntactical rules that differ from English could state it this way: *Chasing the gray mouse, tiny and frightened, was the cat, long, sleek, and black.*

Shortly after their first birthdays, most children are able to convey their intentions with single words. Have you ever heard a young child use the powerful words *no* and *mine*? More complex, rule-driven communication usually emerges between the ages of two and three, when children are able to construct sentences of two or more words.

Though children have prewired capacity for language rules (such as past-tense), adult scaffolding or support plays a significant role in extending and expanding a child's language development. For instance, when Joe says *deenk,* his day care teacher can extend and clarify Joe's intentions: *Joe, do you want to drink milk or juice?* If Joe says *I drinked all the milk,* his teacher might tactfully expand his statement. *Yes, Joe, you drank all of your milk.* This type of subtle modeling is usually the most appropriate way to support children as they learn the conventional forms and complexities of their language. However, even when adults expand a child's speech, the child's own internal rule-governing system may resist modification until the child is developmentally ready to make the change. The following interaction between a four-year-old and an interested adult illustrates this phenomenon (Gleason, 1967):

CHILD: My teacher holded the baby rabbits and we patted them.

ADULT: Did you say your teacher held the baby rabbit?

CHILD: Yes.

ADULT: What did you say that she did?

CHILD: She holded the baby rabbits and we patted them.

ADULT: Did you say she held them tightly?

CHILD: No. She holded them loose.

Semantics

"How would you differentiate among the following words that a blender manufacturer has printed under the row of buttons: stir, beat, puree, cream, chop, whip, crumb, mix, mince, grate, crush, blend, shred, grind, frappe, liquify?" (Lindfors, 1987; p. 47). Semantics deals with the subtle shades of meaning that language can convey. Variations in language meanings generally reflect the values and concerns of the culture. For instance, dozens of Arabic words may be dedicated to describing the camel's range of moods and behaviors. The Polynesian language has many words that define variations in the wind; likewise, Eskimo languages include many words for snow.

Knowledge of word meaning is stored throughout the brain in a vast biological forest of interconnected neurons, dendrites, and synapses. Beyond culture, children's ongoing personal experience allows them to connect words and meaning. Since words are symbolic labels for objects, events, actions, and feelings, a child may initially call all four-legged animals *kittie*. However, after several firsthand encounters with kitties (with the support of adults who can help label and describe the event) a child will likely develop the concepts and vocabulary to discriminate kitties from doggies, kittens from cats, and eventually Persians from Siamese.

Pragmatics

Sitting in his bouncer, two-month-old Marcus studies his mother's face as she talks to him. In a high-pitched voice, she exaggerates her words in a singsong manner: *Lookeee at Mommeeee. I see baabee Marceee looking at Mommeee.* Baby Marcus appears to mimic her mouth movements and responds to her conversations with smiles, wiggles, and very loud coos. After Marcus quiets, his mother knowingly responds to her baby's comments, *Yes, you're right, Mommeee does love her Marceee-Boy.*

When parent and child engage in singsong conversation of "parentese" and baby vocalizations, the basic conventions of turn-taking are learned, but rarely does the teacher or student realize that a lesson was being taught. Pragmatics deals with the conventions of becoming a competent language user. These include rules on how to engage successfully in conversation with others, such as how to initiate and sustain conversation, how to take turns, when and how to interrupt, how to use cues for indicating subject interest, and how to tactfully change subjects.

Pragmatics also refers to the uses of language (spoken and body) to communicate one's intent in real life. The message of a speaker's actual words may be heightened or may even convey the opposite meaning depending on the manner in which the words are delivered. This delivery may include inflection, facial expressions, or body gestures. Take, for example, this statement: *I'm having such a great time.* Imagine that the person who is saying this phrase is smiling easily and widely, with eyes making direct contact with the person with whom she is sharing her time. Now, picture the person saying *I'm having such a great time* while sneering and rolling her eyes (see Figure 2.2). Though the words are identical, the intent of the two speakers is obviously completely different. Further, pragmatics deals with an increasing conscious awareness of being able to accomplish goals through the use of language.

As children mature, they are able to use social registers—or the ability to adapt their speech and mannerisms to accommodate different social situations. This level of communicative competence can be observed in children as young as five as they engage in pretend play. During dramatic play children may easily switch roles—baby to parent, student to teacher, customer to waiter—by using the vocabulary, mannerisms, and attitudes that convey the role they wish to play.

FIGURE 2.2   Language is more than words

In reviewing these linguistic structures—phonology, morphology, syntax, semantic, and pragmatics—it seems amazing that children acquire these components naturally. Parents rarely teach these intricate conventions directly. Instead, children acquire these intricate communication skills by listening, imitating, practicing, observing, and interacting with supportive caregivers and peers.

Observing the Development of Children's Language

"One of the most remarkable cognitive achievements of early childhood is the acquisition of language" (Black, Puckett, & Bell, 1992, p. 179). By the time they enter school, most children have mastered the basic structures of language and are fairly accomplished communicators. Though individual variations do occur, this rapid acquisition of language tends to follow a predictable sequence.

This progression will be illustrated by following Dawn from infancy through second grade. Dawn is the child of educational researchers. Her development is like that of almost every other normal child throughout the world, except that it was documented by her researcher-parents. Dawn's parents used a simple calendar-notation procedure to collect information about their children's language development. When Dawn's parents reviewed the date book/calendar each morning, new words were recorded. Thus, it became quite easy to document Dawn's growth over time. When these busy parents had a reflective moment, they recorded their recollections (vignettes) of an event and dated it. Often, at family celebrations, a video camera was used to record the events of Dawn's use of language in great detail. Occasionally, videotapes also documented story times. By using the calendar vignettes and the videotapes, Dawn's parents were able to marvel at her growth and development.

In Dawn's seven-year case study, we observe her language acquisition from a social-interactionist perspective and a *neuro-biological view*. By intertwining the two views we can easily see how Dawn's language development is a dynamic interaction of her intentions, the physical coordination of her mouth and tongue, her neural development, and the support of her family members. This complex dance of nurture and nature reveals that Dawn's skills do not automatically develop at a certain point in brain maturation but, by the same token, without a particular level of neural growth, Dawn would not be able to accomplish her goals.

Birth–1 month

During the first month of Dawn's life, most of her oral communication consisted of crying, crying, crying. The greatest challenge her parents faced was interpreting the subtle variations in her cries. It took about three weeks for them to understand that Dawn's intense, high-pitched cry meant she was hungry. Dawn's short, throaty, almost shouting cries indicated a change of diaper was necessary, while the whining, fussy cry, which occurred daily at about dinner time, meant she was tired.

At birth, the human brain is remarkably unfinished. Most of the 100 billions neurons, or brain cells, are not yet connected. In fact, there are only four regions of the brain that are fully functional at birth including the brain stem, which controls respiration, reflexes, and heartbeat, and the cerebellum, which controls the newborn's balance and muscle tone. Like-wise, infants' sensory skills are rudimentary; for instance, newborns can only see objects within 12–18 inches of their faces. Still, newborns are able to distinguish between faces and other objects and they recognize the sound of their parents' voices.

2 to 3 months

During the second to third months after Dawn's birth, she began to respond to her parents' voices. When spoken to, Dawn turned her head, focused her eyes on her mother or father, and appeared to listen and watch intensely. Her parents and grandparents also instinctively began using an exaggerated speech pattern called *parentese* (often called *baby talk*). Until recently, parents were cautioned against using baby talk or parentese with their infants because it was believed to foster immature forms of speech. However, recent studies have demonstrated that this slowed-down, high-pitched, exaggerated, repetitious speech actually seems to facilitate a child's language development because:

- The rate and pitch of parentese perfectly matches the infants' auditory processing speed. As babies mature their brain eventually reaches normal speech rates.
- Parentese also allows babies many opportunities to see and hear how sounds are made and, thus, to learn how to control their own vocal apparatus. As babies carefully observe parents, siblings, and other caregivers, they often mimic the tongue and mouth movements they see (Cowley, 1997; Field, Woodson, Greenberg, & Cohen, 1982; Healy, 1994; Shore, 1997).

During the first three months of life, the number of neural synapses, or connections, increases twenty times to more than 1,000 trillion. These neural connections are developed through daily verbal and physical interactions that the infant shares with parents, siblings, and other caregivers. Daily routines such as feeding and bathing reinforce and strengthen particular synapses, while neural networks that are not stimulated will eventually wither away in a process called neural pruning.

4 to 6 months

During conversations with her parents, Dawn would often move her mouth, lips, and eyes, mimicking the facial movements of her parents. At the beginning of the fourth month, Dawn discovered her own voice. She delighted in the range of sounds she could make and some-times chuckled at herself. At this point, Dawn (and most normally developing infants) could make almost all of the vowel and consonant sounds. She cooed and gurgled endlessly, joy-fully experimenting with phonemic variations, pitch, and volume. When spoken to, she often began her own stream of conversation, called "sound play," which would parallel the adult speaker. At six months, Dawn was becoming an expert at imitating tone and inflection. For example, when her mother yelled at the cat for scratching the furniture Dawn used her own vocal skills to yell at the poor animal, too.

The cerebral cortex, the part of the brain that is responsible for thinking and problem solv-ing, represents 70 percent of the brain and is divided into two hemispheres. Each hemi-sphere has four lobes—the parietal, occipital, temporal, and frontal. Each of these lobes has numerous folds, which mature at different rates as the chemicals that foster brain development are released in waves. This sequential development explains, in part, why there are optimum times for physical and cognitive development. For instance, when a baby is three or four months old, neural connections within the parietal lobe (object recognition and eye–hand coordination), the temporal lobe (hearing and language), and the visual cortex have begun to strengthen and fine-tune. This development allows babies' eyes to focus on objects that are more than two feet away from their faces. This new ability allows babies to recognize themselves in a mirror and begin to visually discern who's who. At this same time, babies begin to mimic the tongue and mouth movements they see. Babies also experiment with the range of new sounds they can make. These trills and coos are also bids for attention, as most babies have begun to make simple cause-and-effect associations, such as crying equals Momma's attention.

6 to 9 months

During her sixth month, Dawn's muscle strength, balance, and coordination allowed her to have greater independent control over her environment as she mastered the fine art of crawling and stumble-walking around furniture. These physical accomplishments stimulated further cognitive development, as she now had the ability to explore the world under her own power.

At seven months, Dawn's babbling increased dramatically. However, the sounds she produced now began to sound like words, which she would repeat over and over. This type of vocalizing is called "echolalia." Though "MmmaaaMmmaaa" and "Dddaaaddaaa" sounded like "Mama" and "DaDa," they were still not words with a cognitive connection or meaning.

In her eighth month, Dawn's babbling began to exhibit conversationlike tones and behaviors. This pattern of speech is called "vocables." While there were still no real words in her babble, Dawn's vocalizations were beginning to take on some of the conventions of adult conversation, such as turn-taking, eye contact, and recognizable gestures. These forms of prelanguage are playlike in nature, being done for their own sake rather than a deliberate use of language to communicate a need or accomplish a goal.

At approximately nine months, Dawn first used real, goal-oriented language. As her father came home from work, she crawled to him shouting in an excited voice, "Dada, Dada," and held her arms up to him. Dawn's accurate labeling of her father and her use of body language that expressed desire to be picked up were deliberate actions that revealed that Dawn was using language to accomplish her objectives.

As a child matures, the actual number of neurons remains relatively stable. However, the human brain triples its birth weight within the first three years of a child's life. This change is caused as neurons are stimulated and synapse connections increase, as the message-receiving dendrite branches grow larger and heavier. In addition, the long axons over which sensory messages travel gradually develop a protective coating of a white, fatty substance called myelin. *Myelin insulates the axons and makes the transmission of sensory information more efficient. Myelineation occurs at different times in different parts of the brain and this process seems to coincide with the emergence of various physical skills and cognitive abilities. For instance, the neuromuscular development during the first months of life is dramatic. Within the first six months, helpless infants develop the muscle tone and coordination that allows them to turn over at will. Babies develop a sense of balance and better eye–hand coordination as neural connections in the cerebellum and parietal lobe strengthen. This allows most six-month-old babies to sit upright, with adult support, and successfully grasp objects within their reach. The ability to hold and inspect interesting items gives babies a lot to "talk" about.*

Between six to seven months, the brain has already created permanent neural networks that recognize the sounds of a child's native language(s) or dialect. Next, babies begin to distinguish syllables, which soon enables them to detect word boundaries. Prior to this, "doyouwantyourbottle?" was a pleasant tune, but was not explicit communication. After auditory boundaries become apparent, babies will hear distinct words, "Do / you / want / your / BOTTLE?" As sounds become words that are frequently used in context to label a specific object, the acquisition of word meaning begins. At this stage of development, babies usually recognize and have cognitive meaning for words such as bottle, momma, *and* daddy. *Their receptive or listening vocabulary grows rapidly, though it will take a few more months before their expressive or oral language catches up.*

From about the eighth to the ninth month, the hippocampus becomes fully functional. Located in the center of the brain, the hippocampus is part of the limbic system. The hippocampus helps to index and file memories and, as it matures, babies are able to form memories. For instance, babies can now remember that when they push the button on the busy box it will squeak. At this point, babies' ability to determine cause-and-effect and remember words greatly increases.

9 to 12 months

Between age nine months and her first birthday, Dawn's expressive (speaking) and receptive (listening and comprehending) vocabulary grew rapidly. She could understand and comply with dozens of simple requests, such as "Bring Mommy your shoes" or the favorite label-the-body game, "Where is Daddy's nose?" In addition, Dawn's command of nonverbal gestures and facial expressions were expanding from waving "bye-bye" to scowling and saying "no-no" when taking her medicine. In addition, holophrastic words began to emerge, in which one word carried the semantic burden for a whole sentence or phrase. For example, "keeths," while holding her plastic keys, purse, and sunglasses meant "I want to go for a ride," or "iith" meant "I want some ice." Dawn also used overgeneralized speech in which each word embraced many meanings. For instance, *doll* referred not only to her favorite baby doll but to everything in her toy box, and *jooth* stood for any type of liquid she drank.

At the end of the first year, the prefrontal cortex, the seat of forethought and logic, forms synapses at a rapid rate. In fact, by age one, the full cortex consumes twice as much energy as an adult brain. This incredible pace continues during the child's first decade of life. The increased cognitive capacity and physical dexterity stimulates curiosity and exploration and a deep desire to understand how things work. Neural readiness, in combination with countless hours of sound play and verbal exchanges with loving caregivers, allows most children to begin speaking their first words.

12 to 18 months

At this time Dawn's vocabulary expanded quickly. Most of her words identified or labeled the people, pets, and objects that were familiar and meaningful to her. Clark's research (1983) suggests that young children between one and six will learn and remember approximately nine new words a day. This ability to relate new words to preexisting internalized concepts, then remember and use them after only one exposure, is called *fast mapping* (Carey, 1979).

Because chronological age is not a reliable indicator of language progression, linguists typically describe language development by noting the number of words used in a sentence, which is called "mean length of utterance" (MLU). At this point, Dawn was beginning to use two-word sentences such as "Kitty juuth." Linguists call these two- and three-word sentences "telegraphic speech" as they contain only the most necessary of words to convey meaning. However, these first sentences may have many interpretations; for instance, Dawn's sentence "Kitty, juuth" might mean "The kitty wants some milk," or "The kitty drank the milk," or even "The kitty stuck her head in my cup and drank my milk." Obviously the context in which the sentence was spoken helped her parents to better understand the intent or meaning of her communication.

By 18 months neural synapses have increased, strengthened, and are beginning to transmit information quite efficiently; hence, most toddlers begin to experience a language "explosion." Brain imaging technology clearly reveals that the full cortex is involved in processing language. During this time children are able to learn as many as twelve words a day. Linguists call this phonenomenon "fast mapping."

18 to 24 months

Around age 18 months to two years, as Dawn began using sentences more frequently, the use of syntax became apparent. "No shoes" with a shoulder shrug meant she couldn't find her shoes, but "Shoes, no!" said with a shaking head, meant Dawn did not want to put on her shoes

At two years of age, most children have fully wired brains, nimble fingers, are sturdy on their feet. Though they are generally aware of cause-and-effect, they are still unable to foresee potential problems. In other words, children's physical abilities may exceed their common sense. By this time, most children are able to use language to communicate their needs and accomplish their goals. Increased neural activity, plus verbal expression and physical skill, also give rise to greater independence. At this time parents may hear the word "No!" quite often.

Biologically, the brain is fully functional by this time. The remainder of a child's language development relies on the experiences and opportunities the child has to hear and use language with more experienced language users.

24 to 36 months

Though Dawn's vocabulary grew, her phonemic competence did not always reflect adult standards. Many of her words were clearly pronounced (*kitty, baby*), while others were interesting phonemic attempts or approximations (*bise* for *bike*, *Papa* for *Grandpa*, *bawble* for *bottle*); others were her own construction (*NaNe* for *Grandma*). At this age, most children are unable to articulate perfectly the sounds of adult speech. Rather, they simplify the adult sounds to ones they can produce. Sometimes this means they pronounce the initial sound or syllable of a word (*whee* for *wheel*), and at other times they pronounce only the final sound or syllable (*ees* for *cheese*). Another common feature is temporary regression, meaning that they may pronounce a word or phrase quite clearly, then later produce a shortened, less mature version. This, too, is a normal language developmental phase for all children. Thus,

FIGURE 2.3   Parental expansion of telegraphic speech

it is important that parents accept their child's language and not become overly concerned with correcting their pronunciation.

Likewise, children's early attempts to use sentences need thoughtful support, not critical correction. Parents can best support their child's attempts to communicate through extensions and expansions. Extensions include responses that incorporate the essence of a child's sentence but transform it into a well-formed sentence. For example, when Dawn said, "ree stor-ee," her father responded, "Do you want me to read the story book to you?" When parents and caregivers use extensions they model appropriate grammar and fluent speech and actually help to extend a child's vocabulary.

When parents use expansions, they gently reshape the child's efforts to reflect grammatical appropriate content. For example, when Dawn said, "We goed to Diseelan," instead of correcting her ("We don't say *goed* we say *went*") her mother expanded Dawn's language by initially confirming the intent of Dawn's statement while modeling the correct form, "Yes, we went to Disneyland."

The adaptations parents make when talking to young children such as slowing the rate of speech, using age-appropriate vocabulary, questioning and clarifying the child's statements, and extensions and expansions occurs in all cultures. These early interactions with children and the gradual and building support is called *parentese* or, more gender-specifically, *motherese* and *fatherese.* When parents use this form of support they are actually helping their children gain communicative competence and confidence (White, 1985). Between the ages of two and three years, Dawn's language had developed to the point where she could express her needs and describe her world to others quite well. In addition to using pronouns, she also began to produce grammatical inflections: *-ing,* plurals, the past tense, and the possessive.

Statements	Age
"I lub you, Mama."	2.0*
"Boot's crywing."	2.1
"Dawn's baby dawl."	2.2
"My books."	2.4
"Grover droppted the radio."	2.6
"Cookie monster shutted the door."	2.8
"She's not nice to me."	2.9
"Daddy's face got stickers, they scratch."	3.0

*Indicates age by years and months.

Dawn also loved finger plays such as the "Itsy, Bitsy Spider" and "Grandma's Glasses," poems such as "This Little Pig," and songs such as "Jingle Bells," "Yankee Doodle," and the "Alphabet Song." She was also beginning to count and echo-read with her parents when they read her favorite stories, like the "Three Little Pigs." Dawn would "huff and puff and blow your house down" as many times as her parents would read the story.

3 to 5 years

Dawn had become a proficient language user. She could make requests, "Please, may I have some more cake?" and demands, "I need this, now!" depending on her mood and motivation. She could seek assistance, "Can you tell me where the toys are?" and demonstrate concern, "What's the matter, Mama?" She sought information about her world, "Why is the moon round one time and just a grin sometimes?" She could carry on detailed conversations just as she did in the grocery store at 4.0 (4 years and 0 months):

MOM: Dawn, what juice did you want?

DAWN: Orange juice. But not the kind that has the little chewy stuff in it.

MOM: That is called pulp.

DAWN: Pulp—ick! I don't like it because it tasted badly.

MOM: Well, do you remember what kind has the pulp?

DAWN: You know, it comes in the orange can and has the picture of the bunny on it.

MOM: Well, there are several kinds in orange cans.

DAWN: Mom, I know that, cause orange juice is orange. But this one I don't like, at all, has a bunny on it.

MOM: Can you remember the name?

DAWN: Yeah, the writing words have A-B-C-O.

MOM: Oh, I know, the store's brand, ABCO.

DAWN: Yes, here it is. Now DON'T BUY IT!!

4 to 5

Dawn began to engage in dramatic play, using her knowledge of common events in familiar settings such as the grocery store and the doctor's office to act out life scripts with other children. These dramas allowed Dawn and her peers the opportunity to use their language in many functional and imaginative ways. Her favorite script was the restaurant, as she always enjoyed being the waitress, describing the daily special to her customers, then pretending to write their orders.

Jim Johnson, Jim Christie, and Thomas Yawkey (1999) suggest that during dramatic play, two types of communication can occur. First, *pretend communication* takes place when the child assumes a role and talks, in character, to other characters in the drama. The second type, *metacommunication,* occurs when the children stop the ongoing dramatic-play script and discuss the plot or character actions. The following is an example of metacommunication between Dawn and her friend Jennifer at age 5.6 years:

DAWN: Pretend you ordered pizza and I have to make it, okay?

JENNIFER: Okay, but it should be cheese pizza, 'cause I like it best.

DAWN: Okay, I can use yellow strings (yarn) for the cheese.

JENNIFER: Waitress, I want yellow cheese pizza, in a hurry. I'm hungry.

6 to 7

Almost all six- to eight-year-old children have extremely elaborate vocabularies, with estimates ranging between 2500 and 8000 words (Gleason, 1967). During these years, Dawn's expressive and receptive vocabulary continued to grow as she interacted with teachers, classmates, and family. There are, however, differences between home and school language. Classroom language may be more formalized, as children respond to specific, fact-oriented, teacher-directed questions. To illustrate this point, the following dramatic-play scenario took place in Dawn's bedroom, where she had established a pretend school, consisting of a teacher's desk, student's table, chalkboard, reading books, paper, pencils, and markers. Dawn (age 6.6 years), wearing high heels, a long dark dress and jacket, and an old pair of glasses, had assumed the role of teacher, while two classmates, Amy and Jennifer, took the roles of students.

DAWN: (standing very straight and holding the chalk) What is the first thing we write on the page? Class, together, one, two, three.

CLASS: (in unison) Our name.

DAWN: What goes on the paper next? Class, together, one, two, three.

CLASS: (in unison) The date.

DAWN: Good thinking, students. You may begin your assignment.

During this play episode, it became clear that Dawn had carefully observed her teacher's dress, mannerisms, voice inflection, and tone. Dawn's portrayal of her teacher also demonstrated how easily children may adapt their speech pattern to effectively role-play adult characters or to interact with adults or other children in many different contexts. Children appear to intuitively modify their communication style by assessing multiple social factors such as the age, gender, and status of the person with whom they are interacting, and the context in which the conversation is taking place. The combination of these variables will significantly influence what children say and how they say it. In other words, Dawn might behave and communicate quite freely with peers her own age, yet she might act much more formally and maturely around the teenage babysitter. This ability is sometimes called "**language register.**"

While classroom conversation may be more structured, playground conversations with peers are generally more colorful and imaginative, as children integrate information from television, movies, books, and comics. The following scenario with Dawn at age 7.0 years provides an illustration.

DAWN: Jason, Jason, *Jason!!!!*

JASON: What?

DAWN: I'm going to be Princess Leia from Star Wars for Halloween.

JASON: Well, you maybe can be her, but you can't have the "force" with you.

DAWN: I can too.

JASON: Nu-uh.

DAWN: Yes, sir.

JASON: You can't 'cause only boys can have the force, like Luke Skywalker and Yoda.

DAWN: Well, Princess Leia can shoot zappers and boss Han Solo.

JASON: Maybe so, but she'll never be a boy!

Dawn's language development, though completely normal, is also a human miracle. Language plays a central role in learning, and the success of children in school depends to a very large degree on their ability to speak and listen. Dawn's case study also confirms the critical role of social interaction in language development. In recognition of this importance, the following section provides more information about how parents and caregivers can support a child's language acquisition.

What Is Normal Language Development?

While the process of learning to talk follows a predictable sequence, the age at which children say their first word may vary widely from one child to another. Developmental guidelines provide descriptions of specific behaviors and delineate the age at which most children demonstrate this physical or cognitive skill. This type of information helps parents and physicians anticipate normal physical and cognitive growth. While physical maturation is easy to observe, cognitive development is less obvious. Fortunately, children's language development provides one indication that their cognitive abilities are developing normally. In Table 2.2, we present the average ages for language acquisition and review Dawn's development from birth to age two. In comparing their progress, it is clear that both children followed the same sequence of language acquisition, but at different rates. Though the age they displayed specific skills differed, their language abilities matured within the age range offered for normal language development. While most children demonstrate language skills well within the normal age range, some do not. If a child's language is delayed more than two months past the upper age limits, caregivers should seek medical guidance, as delays may indicate problems (Copeland & Gleason, 1993; Weiss, Lilly-White, & Gordon, 1980). Early identification of problems leads to appropriate intervention.

While helpful, developmental guidelines are not perfect. To determine norms, data must be collected on specific populations. In most cases these data were collected on middle-income Caucasian children born in modern industrial-technological societies. Since this sample does not represent the world's population, the upper and lower age limits of these "universal" norms must be interpreted carefully.

Factors Contributing to Variation in Rate of Language Acquisition

Since the critical period for language development occurs within the first 36 months of a child's life, significant language delay may indicate specific medical or cognitive problems. Beyond medical problems, there are several factors that could modify the rate of normal language production. We review these factors in the following discussion.

TABLE 2.2   **Normal Language Development**

About 90 percent of children will develop the following language skills by the ages indicated. If a child does not demonstrate these behaviors by these ages, it is important for parents to seek medical guidance.

Age	Language Skill
2 months	Make sounds in response to stimulus
3 months	Make cooing sounds
7 months	Make sounds such as "giving a raspberry"
10 months	Single-syllable babbling ("ma," "pa," "ba," "da")
11 months	Multiple-syllable babbling ("mama," "dada," "baba")
14 months	Uses *mama* and *dada* (or similar sounds) to call parents
16 months	Uses some words besides *mama* and *dada*
22 months	Has a vocabulary of four to six words Can express some wants Can be understood by strangers about half the time
23 months	Can form two-word sentences
26 months	Has a 50-word vocabulary
29 months	Uses *me, you,* and *my*
34 months	Uses prepositions Can carry on a conversation Can identify and use *cup, spoon*
37 months	Can be understood by strangers about three quarters of the time
47 months	Can be understood by strangers most of the time

Source: Copeland & Gleason (1993).

Gender Differences

Are there differences in the rate and ways that boys and girls develop language fluency and proficiency? This question reflects another facet of the ongoing nature versus nurture debate. Observational research consistently reveals that a majority of girls talk earlier and talk more than the majority of boys. It is also true that the majority of late talkers are young boys (Healy, 1997; Kalb & Namuth, 1997). However, it is difficult to determine whether differences in the rate of language acquisition are biological or if biological differences are exaggerated by social influences. There is evidence for both views. For example, neural-biological research offers graphic images that illustrate how men's and women's brains process language somewhat differently (Corballis, 1991; Moir & Jessel, 1991). Though this research appears to support nature as the dominant factor in language differences, it is also important to consider how powerful a role nurture plays. Experimental research consistently documents differential treatment of infants based on gender. In other words, men and women tend to cuddle, coo at, and engage in lengthy face-to-face conversations with baby girls. Yet, with baby boys, adults are likely to exhibit "jiggling and bouncing" behaviors but are not as likely to engage in sustained face-to-face verbal interactions. Perhaps girls talk earlier and talk more because they receive more language stimulation (Huttenlocher, 1991).

Socioeconomic Level

Numerous studies have long documented the differences in the rate of language acquisition and the level of language proficiency between low and middle socioeconomic families (Hart & Risley, 1995; Morisset, 1995; Walker, Greenwood, Hart, & Carta, 1994). These studies found that children, especially males, from low-income homes were usually somewhat slower to use expressive language than children from middle-income homes. These findings likely reflect social-class differences both in language use in general and in parent–child interaction patterns. For example, Betty Hart and Todd Risley (1995) estimate that, by age four, children from professional families have had a cumulative total of 50 million words addressed to them, whereas as children from welfare families have been exposed to only 13 million words. The children from professional families have had more than three times the linguistic input than welfare families' children; this gives them a tremendous advantage in language acquisition.

Results of long-term observations of middle-income and lower-income families concluded that all mothers spent a great deal of time nurturing their infants (e.g., touching, hugging, kissing, and holding), but that there were differences in the way mothers verbally interacted with their children. Middle-income mothers spent a great deal more time initiating verbal interactions and usually responded to and praised their infants' vocal efforts. Middle-income mothers were also more likely to imitate their infants' vocalizations. These verbal interactions stimulate neural-synapse networks that foster expressive and receptive language. It is still unclear why lower-income mothers do not engage their children in verbal interactions at the same level as middle-income mothers. The authors of these studies speculate that this may be a reflection of social-class differences in language use in general.

Cultural Influences

The rate of language acquisition may be somewhat different for children of different cultures. Since spoken language is a reflection of the culture from which it emerges, it is necessary to consider the needs verbal language serves in the culture. Communication may be accomplished in other meaningful ways (Bhavnagri & Gonzalez-Mena, 1997). Janet Gonzalez-Mena (1997, p. 70) offers this example:

> The emphasizing or de-emphasizing of the verbal starts from the beginning with the way babies are treated. Babies carried around much of the time get good at sending messages nonverbally—through changing body positions or tensing up or relaxing muscles. They

are encouraged to communicate this way when their caregivers pick up the messages they send. They don't need to depend on words at an early age. Babies who are physically apart from their caregivers learn the benefits of verbal communication. If the babies are on the floor in the infant playpen or in the other room at home, they need to learn to use their voices to get attention. Changing position or tensing muscles goes unperceived by the distant adult.

Likewise, some cultures do not view babies' vocal attempts as meaningful communication. Shirley Brice Heath (1983) describes a community in which infants' early vocalizations are virtually ignored and adults do not generally address much of their talk directly to infants. Many cultures emphasize receptive language, and children listen as adults speak.

Medical Concerns

Beyond gender, socioeconomic, and culture differences, other reasons that children's language may be delayed include temporary medical problems and congenital complications. In Special Feature 2.2, "She Just Stopped Talking," we provide an example of one the most common childhood problems—otitis media—that, left unattended, could cause significant language delays and speech distortion and ultimately difficulty in learning to read and write.

Congenital Language Disorders

For most children, learning to communicate is a natural, predictable developmental progression. Unfortunately, some children have congenital language disorders that impair their ability to learn language or use it effectively. The origin of these disorders may be physical or neurological. Examples of physical problems include malformation of the structures in the inner ear or a poorly formed palate. Neurological problems could include dysfunction in the brain's ability to perceive or interpret the sounds of language.

Though the symptoms of various language disorders may appear similar, effective treatment may differ significantly, depending on the cause of the problem. For example, articulation problems caused by a physical malformation of the palate might require reconstructive surgery, while articulation problems caused by hearing impairment might require a combination of auditory amplification and speech therapy. Two of the most common symptoms of congenital language disorders are disfluency and pronunciation.

Disfluency. Children with fluency disorders have difficulty speaking rapidly and continuously. They may speak with an abnormal rate—too fast or too slow; in either case, their speech is often incomprehensible and unclearly articulated. The rhythm of their speech may also be severely affected. Stuttering is the most common form of this disorder. Many children may have temporary fluency disruptions or stuttering problems as they are learning to express themselves in sentences. Children who are making a transition to a second language may also experience brief stuttering episodes. It is important for parents or teachers to be patient and supportive, as it may take time to distinguish normal developmental or temporary lapses in fluency from a true pathology. Stuttering may have

Special Feature 2.2

She Just Stopped Talking

On her first birthday, Tiffany mimic-sang "Hap Birffaay meee" over and over. She said "Sank oo" when she received her birthday gifts and "Bye, seeoo" when her guests left. Later that summer, after a bad bout with an ear infection, Tiffany's mother noticed she was turning up the volume on the television when she watched *Sesame Street.* A few days later, after several restless nights, Tiffany became very fussy and irritable and began tugging on her ear. Her parents again took her to the doctor, who diagnosed another ear infection. After a ten-day treatment of antibiotics, Tiffany appeared to be fine, except that she seemed to talk less and less.

About a month later, the situation worsened. Tiffany would not respond to her mother's speech unless she was looking directly at her mother. At that point Tiffany had, for the most part, stopped talking.

Tiffany's story is all too common. She was suffering from otitis media, an inflammation of the middle part of the ear. The symptoms of otitis media usually appear during or after a cold or respiratory infection. Because fluid can collect in the middle ear (behind the eardrum) without causing pain, children with otitis media may not complain. The following is a list of possible symptoms; any one of these symptoms could indicate that a child has otitis media:

- earaches or draining of the ears
- fever
- changes in sleeping or eating habits
- irritability
- rubbing or pulling at the ears
- cessation of babbling and singing
- turning up the television or radio volume much louder than usual
- frequently need to have directions and information repeated
- unclear speech
- use of gestures rather than speech

- delayed speech and language development.

From 12 months through four years of age, language development is at its peak. Even a temporary hearing loss during this time interferes with speech articulation and language learning. Otitis media causes temporary loss of hearing when the fluid pushes against the eardrum. The pressure prevents the eardrum from vibrating, so sound waves cannot move to the inner ear and the child's hearing is greatly distorted or muffled. Consequently, final consonant sounds and word endings are often unheard, and words blend into one another. Because one of the main reasons people talk is to communicate, a child who cannot understand what is said becomes frustrated and easily distracted. This type of hearing loss may continue for up to six weeks after the ear infection has healed.

Though hearing loss caused by otitis media is described as "mild and fluctuating," it is a major cause of speech distortion and language delay in the preschool years. If left untreated, young children with recurrent and persistent otitis media may develop permanent hearing loss, speech distortions, language delays, and problems with focusing attention.

When Tiffany's parents realized that she had stopped speaking, their pediatrician referred them to an otolaryngologist (ear, nose, and throat specialist). The doctor was pleased that Tiffany's parents had written down new words she used on the family calendar. As the doctor reviewed the calendar, it became apparent that Tiffany's normal language development had virtually stopped. He did not seem surprised when her parents mentioned that she had also stopped babbling and singing and that she no longer danced when music was played. Because Tiffany's pediatrician had already tried three months of antibiotics to control the infection with no success, the specialist suggested surgically placing bilateral vent tubes in the eardrum to drain the fluid from the middle ear. When the

(continued on next page)

multiple origins and may vary from child to child. Regardless of cause, recently developed treatment protocols have been effective in helping stutterers.

Pronunciation. Articulation disorders comprise a wide range of problems and may have an equally broad array of causes. Minor misarticulations in the preschool years are usually developmental and will generally improve as the child matures. Occasionally, as children lose their baby teeth, they may experience temporary challenges in articulation. However, articulation problems that seriously impede a child's ability to communicate needs and intentions must be diagnosed. Causes of such problems may include malformation of the mouth, tongue, or palate; partial loss of hearing due to a disorder in the inner ear; serious brain trauma; or a temporary hearing loss due to an ear infection (Copeland & Gleason, 1993).

It is important to remember that some children may simply show delayed language development; this may mean that a child is gaining control over speaking mechanisms at a slower rate than same-age peers or has had limited opportunity to hear speech or interact with others. Children who are learning a second language may also appear to have articulation difficulties when they attempt to use their second language. As we explain in Special Feature 2.3, anyone learning a new phonemic system will experience some difficulty in expressing new sound combinations. "Bilingual children should be assessed in their native language and referred for therapy only if an articulation disorder is present in that language" (Piper, 1993, p. 193). Caregivers and teachers need to be careful not to confuse the normal course of second-language acquisition with speech disorders.

Summary

Children's acquisition of oral language is truly remarkable. By the time they enter kindergarten, most children have mastered the basic structures and components of their native language, all without much stress or effort. How did the information contained in this chapter compare with what you were able to discover about your own first words and early language learning? Which of the four perspectives described above comes closest to your view about children's language development?

Special Feature 2.3

Young Children's Second-Language Development
Sarah Hudelson and Irene Serna

Have you ever been in a situation where everyone around you is using a language that you don't know? How did you feel when the language around you sounded like gibberish? How did you respond? Were there some strategies that you used to cope? Think about yourself in this kind of situation as you read about young children learning a second language.

In Chapter 2 you have learned about how children acquire their native language. Dawn's language acquisition is typical for a child brought up in a monolingual home—that is, a home where one language is spoken. However, a growing number of children in the United States are raised in homes where two languages are used regularly, and where two languages are addressed to young children. Children raised in such bilingual environments have not one but two native languages, what Swain (1972) refers to as bilingualism as a native language.

Years ago there was concern that young children would be cognitively damaged by such early exposure to two languages, that there would be considerable confusion on the child's part and that normal language development would be delayed (Hakuta, 1986). Recent investigations, however, have made it clear that this is not the case. There is now ample evidence that young children raised from birth with two languages develop language at rates comparable to monolingual children. They begin to use single words and multilingual word combinations at the same time as monolingual children. Young bilingual children develop separate language systems and use them appropriately (Hakuta, 1986). Depending on the frequency of use, one language may develop more fully than the other. It is also common for young bilinguals to borrow words from one language and use them in speaking the other language in order to communicate

their intentions. But fluency in two languages is a common occurrence among young children (see Goodz, 1994, for a recent review of research on preschool bilingualism). It is certainly possible that some of the young children in your prekindergarten or primary grade classrooms will be bilingual in English and another language.

It is even more probable, however, that your classroom will contain some children whose native language is other than English—Spanish, French, Russian, Polish, Croatian, Arabic, Vietnamese, Chinese, Khmer, Japanese, Urdu, Navajo, Hopi, Apache, to name a few. There are currently millions of young children in this country who are being raised in households where a language other than English is spoken (Waggoner, 1992). Cultural and linguistic diversity is increasing in our schools. Like monolingual English speakers, non-English speaking children have learned their native languages by living in and being socialized into particular speech communities. Non-English speaking children come to school having acquired the structural systems (phonological, syntactic, morphological, semantic) of one language as well as the pragmatics of what is appropriate language use—in terms of social and cultural norms—of their native language speech community. Thus, these learners bring to school understandings of what language is, what language can do, what language is for, and how to use language appropriately in their own communities (Lindfors, 1987).

Often, appropriate ways of using language in these diverse communities are significantly different from the ways of mainstream English-speaking children. For example, Delgado-Gaitan and Trueba (1991), studying the language socialization of Mexican immigrant children in a California town, discovered that young children were socialized to talk with their siblings and other children, yet to be quiet around adults.

When young speakers of languages other than English enter school, they may be fortunate enough to be placed in bilingual classrooms, where children and adults make use of the native

(continued on next page)

language for learning and where the English language and academic instruction through English are introduced gradually. Or they may find themselves in settings where English is the basic language of the class and of instruction. In either case, children find themselves in the position of acquiring English as a second or additional language (ESL). What this means is that children must develop new ways of expressing themselves, new ways of talking about their experiences, new ways of asking questions, new ways of using language to help them learn. They must also learn to behave appropriately in settings, including school, where the new language is used. This is hard work that involves them in striving both to understand the language around them and to use that language for themselves and with others (Lindfors, 1987; Tabors & Snow, 1994).

The perspective on child second-language acquisition that most researchers and educators take is similar to the social-interactionist perspective articulated in Chapter 2. That is, in learning a new language children engage in the creative construction of the rules of the new language, and this creative construction occurs within the context of multiple social interactions as children use the new language with others (Allen, 1991). The discussion that follows summarizes some essential points about children's ESL acquisition. Most of the understandings presented have been formulated through careful observation of children and teachers in prekindergarten and primary grade settings.

As discussed in Chapter 1, creative construction means that the ESL learner is not simply an empty jar into which the new language is poured. Rather, the learner is an active participant in the development of abilities in the new language. Learners use language from the environment and from specific others to make predictions about how English works and then to try out these predictions in the form of English utterances. Sometimes learners predict that the second language works like the first one, and

sounds, lexical items and morpho-syntactic patterns from the native language may influence English. Always, creative construction involves making mistakes, but mistakes need to be seen as the learner's attempt to make sense of the new language, to figure out how that language is put together (Allen, 1991).

Nora, a first-grade, Spanish-speaking child whose acquisition of English was studied by respected researcher Lily Wong Fillmore (1976), provides a good demonstration of the child as creative constructor. Early in first grade, Nora memorized such phrases as "Do you wanna play?" and used them to initiate contact with English-speaking children. Soon she began to use the phrase "How do you do dese?" as a general formula to ask for information and help. After a while she added elements to the formula so that she could ask such questions as: "How do you do dese little tortillas? How do you do dese in English?" Gradually she was able to vary the sentence after the word you to produce: "How do you like to be cookie cutter? How do you make the flower? How do you gonna make these?" She was also able to use *did* as in "How did you lost it?" Later still she was able to use *how* in sentences very different from the original formula; for example, "Because when I call him, how I put the number?" (pp. 246–247) These efforts illustrate how Nora, over time, constructed and reconstructed her English to convey her meanings and accomplish her purposes.

Tabors and Snow (1994) have documented a general sequence in young children's ESL acquisition that appears to be fairly common. When they first encounter the new language, many young learners will continue to use their native language when speaking to English speakers. This behavior is often followed by a period when they do not talk at all but instead attempt to communicate nonverbally through gestures, mimes, and cries or whimpers to attract attention. Young ESL learners also have been observed to engage in spectating—paying close attention to the actions and utterances of English

(continued on next page)

Special Feature 2.3 *(continued)*

speakers (so that they can connect words to activities)—and rehearsing—practicing the new language to, by, and for themselves, repeating words, phrases, and sounds in English at a very low volume. Following the nonverbal period, children begin to use formulaic expressions in English (e.g.: "What's that?" "Wanna play?" "I want that." "I don't know." "Gimme!"), which may get them into the action with other children. From formulas, as Nora demonstrated, children gradually begin productive language use, moving beyond memorized utterances and formulaic expressions to creative construction. Although this sequence has been described as if it were discrete and unidirectional, this is not necessarily so for all learners.

There are tremendous individual differences in children's second-language learning. Learners differ in the rate at which they learn the second language. They differ in their willingness to learn English and in their avoidance or non-avoidance of the new language. They differ in the language-learning strategies they use. They differ in whether their stance is more participator or observer. The least successful English learners seem to be those who avoid contact with English speakers and who do not engage with what is going on around them in English (Fillmore, 1976; Saville-Troike, 1988). Some research has suggested that the best ESL learners are those children who are most eager to interact with English speakers, who are most willing to participate and use whatever English they have at a particular point in time, who are risk takers and are not afraid to make mistakes, and who identify with English speakers (Fillmore, 1976; Strong, 1983). However, researchers also have discovered that quiet children who pay close attention to what is going on around them (the careful observer stance) may also be quite effective language learners (Fillmore, 1983; Flanigan, 1988). So not all young children learn a second language in exactly the same way.

What is crucial to children's successful second-language acquisition is the learner's choosing to work at communicating with people who speak the new language. Young ESL learners find themselves in environments where English is used. But they must choose to work at learning the new language; they must want to interact with others in English if acquisition is to occur. Interaction is critical in two ways: (1) it gives learners opportunities to try out the new language to see if they can make themselves understood; and (2) fluent English speakers respond to the learner's efforts, providing both additional language input and a gauge on how well the learner is communicating. This language give and take is critical to continued learning (Ellis, 1985; Tabors & Snow, 1994).

In the ESL setting both adults and other children may act as language teachers for children. Adults tend to modify or adapt their ways of speaking to what they think the ESL learner will understand and respond to. Studies of primary teachers working with ESL learners have reached the following conclusions: As with "baby talk" in native language settings, effective teachers tend to speak more slowly, using clear enunciation, somewhat simplified sentences, and exaggerated intonation. They often use repetitions or restatements of sentences. They also contextualize their speech by using objects and physical gestures so that learners may use non-linguistic cues to figure out what has been said. Finally, adults make concerted efforts both to encourage the ESL child to talk and to understand what the learner is saying. In their efforts to understand children, adults frequently expand children's incomplete sentences or extend what they have said (Enright, 1986; Fillmore, 1982, 1983). Through all of these provisions of "comprehensible input" (Krashen, 1982), adults are responsive persons with whom to try out the new language.

Fluent English-speaking children are also important language models and teachers for

(continued on next page)

their ESL counterparts. During interactions, English-speaking children may assist their non-English speaking peers by gesturing, correcting, giving feedback, engaging in language play, and encouraging the second-language learner to talk (Ventriglia, 1982). But children do not make the consistently concerted efforts that adults do to be understood by and to understand ESL learners unless they have been coached to do so (see Tabors & Snow, 1994). They may tire of the teacher role and move away from it more quickly than an adult would. And children do not tend to focus as exclusively on understanding the ESL child as adults do; what is often most important is carrying out whatever activity they happen to be engaged in (Fillmore, 1976; Peck, 1978). But given that children often (but not always) are more interested in interacting with other children than they are with adults, other children provide strong incentives for ESL children to use their developing English and to make themselves understood. The desire to communicate is at the heart of young children's second-language learning.

Earlier we distinguished bilingual from ESL classrooms. In spite of research evidence that speaks to the efficacy of teaching children through their native language, a major issue with regard to non-English-speaking learners has been the role that languages other than English play in children's learning. The common-sense belief that the most efficient way to encourage English language proficiency is to use only English is still adhered to by numbers of early childhood educators (see Fillmore, 1991). This has meant that numbers of Head Start and kindergarten programs have embraced the idea of an early school introduction of, and sometimes school immersion in, English—with the understanding that parents will continue to use their native languages at home so that young children continue to develop linguistic abilities and communicative competence in their home tongues while acquiring English (Tabors & Snow, 1994). Theoretically,

this situation should result in young children becoming bilingual, but using their two languages in different settings.

Unfortunately, the reality is that early introduction to English in school has often meant that non-English-speaking children refuse to communicate in their native languages and try to use English exclusively. In a study of the home language practices of more than 300 immigrant preschoolers, Fillmore (1991) discovered that these young learners, whether they were enrolled in bilingual or English-only classrooms, were particularly vulnerable to language loss. The longer they stayed in school, the more they relied on English for communication, even at home. This jeopardized non-English-speaking parents' abilities to interact verbally with their children and socialize them.

Fillmore raises the issue of whether English-language acquisition has to come at the expense of other languages. Her data point out the potentially devastating consequences of children's refusal to speak their native languages. Parents anguish over how to communicate with their children, how to pass on family and community histories, how to transmit cultural expectations, how to discipline them, and so on if they are unable to communicate with them. We believe that not only early childhood educators but all educators, whether bilingual or not, must wrestle with the reality of how to respect and value children's home languages and cultures.

In many important ways, second-language acquisition in young children is quite similar to first-language acquisition. This general statement means that adults working with second-language learners need to focus both on making themselves understood by children and on understanding children and encouraging them to use their new language. Adults need to focus on the learners' communicative intentions, not on the conventionality of their utterances. Adults also need to be sensitive to individual differences in children's rates of second-language

(continued on next page)

Special Feature 2.3 *(continued)*

learning and accepting of these differences. Children should be encouraged but not forced to use the new language, and children should not be belittled for hesitancy in trying out English. Adults need to recognize that children are learning English even if they are not responding verbally. Adults need to encourage other children who are native speakers of English to have patience with ESL learners and to assist them in their learning. Finally, adults should value the native languages that children bring to school with them and encourage them to continue to use their native languages.

To summarize the key points about oral language development, we return to the guiding questions at the beginning of this chapter:

■ *What are the major views on how children's language develops? Which aspects of language development does each view adequately explain?*

Four competing perspectives have been used to explain how children acquire language. The behaviorist perspective emphasizes the important role of reinforcement in helping children learn the sounds, words, and rules of language. This view handily explains the imitative aspects of initial language learning. Nativists stress the importance of children's inborn capacity to learn language and suggest that a portion of the brain is dedicated to language learning. Nativist theory explains how children "invent" their own two- and three-word grammars and overgeneralize rules for past tense ("He goed to the store") and plural ("I saw two mouses today!"). The social-interactionist perspective emphasizes the importance of both environmental factors and children's innate predisposition to make sense out of language and use it for practical purposes. According to this view, children learn about language by using it in social situations. The social-interactionist view highlights the role of parental support in language acquisition. Finally, new technology has allowed scientists to observe how the brain perceives, interprets, and expresses language. These developments have lead to a new perspective of children's language learning, the neuro-biological view, which complements the three earlier views on language development. This perspective explains how the structural development of the brain is related to language acquisition. It helps explain why children's experiences during infancy have such a crucial effect on later language learning.

■ *What are the major components of language?*

The major components of language are (1) phonology—the sounds that make up a language; (2) morphology—the meaning bearing units of language, including words and affixes; (3) syntax—the rules for ordering words into sentences; (4) semantics—the shades of meaning that words convey; and (5) pragmatics—the social rules that enable language to accomplish real-life purposes.

■ *How does the structure of an infant's brain develop? How does this structural development affect language acquisition?*

At birth, the human brain is remarkably unfinished. Most of the 100 billion neurons or brain cells are not yet connected. During the first month of life, the number of neural synapses or connections increases 20 times to more than 1000 trillion. As a child matures, the actual number of neurons remains stable; however, the number of synapse connections increases, and the message-receiving dendrite branches grow larger and heavier. At age one, the full cortex consumes twice as much energy as an adult brain. This neural readiness, in combination with countless hours of sound play and verbal exchanges with loving caregivers, allows most children to begin speaking their first words at this age.

By 18 months, neural synapses have increased and strengthened and are beginning to transmit information efficiently. Hence most toddlers begin to experience a language explosion, particularly in the areas of vocabulary and syntax. During this time, children are able to learn as many as 12 words a day. Thus, the neuro-biological perspective reveals how the rapid development of the brain during the first few years of life makes it possible for children to acquire language so quickly and efficiently. This perspective also explains why the first 36 months are a critical period for language development.

■ *What factors affect children's rate of language acquisition?*

While language development follows a predictable sequence, the rate at which children acquire language varies tremendously. Gender, socioeconomic level, and cultural influences all can affect the rate of language acquisition. A child's language learning can also be impeded by illnesses, such as otitis media, and by a variety of congenital problems of a physical and/or neurological nature. Parents and caregivers are cautioned to seek a medical diagnosis if language development is significantly delayed, as early identification and treatment can often avoid irreparable disruption of the language acquisition process.

■ *How does children's acquisition of a second language compare with their first language acquisition? What should adults do to make it easier for children to learn English as a second language?*

In many ways, second-language acquisition in young children is similar to their acquisition of their first language. In learning a new language, children engage in the creative construction of the rules of the new language, and this creative construction occurs within the context of multiple social interactions as children use the new language with others.

Adults working with second-language learners need to focus both on making themselves understood by children and encouraging these children to use their new language. Adults need to focus on the learners' communicative intentions, not on the conventionality of their utterances. Children should be encouraged but not forced to use the new language, and children should not be belittled for hesitancy in trying it. Adults need to recognize that children are learning English even if they are not responding verbally. Adults need to encourage other children who are native speakers of English to have patience with ESL learners and to assist them in their learning. Finally, adults should value the native languages that children bring to school with them and encourage them to continue to use their native languages.

LINKING KNOWLEDGE TO PRACTICE

1. Interview two parents and two early childhood teachers regarding how they believe children learn language. Consider which theory of language acquisition best matches each interviewee's beliefs.

2. Interview a school nurse or health care aide about the numbers of children she or he sees who are affected by illnesses and congenital problems. From the health care worker's perspective, what effect do these medical problems have on children? How often should children be screened for auditory acuity? If a family has limited financial recourses, what agencies can provide medical services?

3. Observe a second-language learner in a preschool or day care setting. Does the second-language learner comprehend some of the talk that is going on in the classroom? How does the child communicate with other children? How does the teacher support the child's second-language acquisition? Are other children helping? Does the second-language learner have any opportunities to use his or her native language?

3 Facilitating Early Language Learning

Four-year old Evan, from Arizona, was visiting his grandmother in Vermont during the Christmas holiday. Upon opening the drapes one morning, he viewed snow-covered trees and fields. Evan gasped, "Grammie, who spilled all the sugar?" His grandmother responded, "Evan, that's very clever. It sure looks like sugar. Actually, it's snow."

Clearly, Evan's unfamiliarity with snow didn't prevent him from drawing a clever comparison. His grandmother responded by first showing appreciation for Evan's deduction and then providing the correct word, *snow*. Evan had a great opportunity to learn about the qualities of snow through conversations with his parents, grandparents, and older sister as they played together in the snow. During these adventures, they offered appropriate words for and information about all the new sights, sounds, tastes, smells, and feelings. By the end of the week, Evan knew the difference between wet and powder snow. He made snow angels, helped build a snowman and snow fort, engaged in a snowball war, and had an exhilarating ride on a sled. The new experiences he shared with older and more snow-experienced language users allowed Evan to build new vocabulary and cognitive understandings.

Chapter 2 discussed how infants and toddlers learn their native language through complex social interactions with parents, siblings, and other caregivers. These individuals are essentially a child's first and most important teachers. Throughout the preschool years, the family plays a significant role in helping children become accomplished language users. In this chapter, we examine the talk that goes on in homes and describe ways parents can support and enrich language development. Next, we discuss the many ways teachers can create learning environments that invite the types of rich oral interactions that promote language acquisition and enhance learning in all areas of the curriculum.

Before Reading This Chapter, Think About . . .

- Your home language environment when you were a child. Did you engage in lengthy conversations with your parents and siblings? Did you have an appreciative audience when you told stories about your own experiences? Did your family discuss the TV shows that you watched?
- The conversations that took place in your classroom when you were in school. Were these mainly teacher-centered exchanges in which you and your classmates responded

to questions asked by the teacher, or did you have the opportunity to engage in two-way conversations with the teacher and other students?

■ Sharing or show-and-tell. What did you like about this activity? Was there anything that you did not like about it?

■ The make-believe play you engaged in when you were a child. What were some of the favorite roles and themes that you acted out during this play?

■ How did you feel when you gave an oral presentation in class? Did you fell embarrassed or confident?

Focus Questions

■ How can parents best facilitate their children's oral language development?

■ What is the initiation, response, evaluation (IRE) pattern of class talk? What problems are associated with this type of discourse? How can teachers provide children with more stimulating conversations in the classroom?

■ How do group activities, learning centers, and dramatic play promote oral language acquisition?

BOX **3.1**

Definition of Terms

active listening: the listener combines the information provided by the speaker with his or her own prior knowledge to construct personal meaning.

anecdotal record: a brief note describing a child's behavior.

checklist: a observation tool that specifies which behaviors to look for and provides a convenient system of checking off when these behaviors are observed.

dramatic play: an advanced form of play in which children take on roles and act out make-believe stories and situations.

initiation, response, evaluation (IRE): a pattern of classroom talk in which the teacher asks a question, a student answers, and the teacher either accepts or rejects that answer and then goes on to ask another question.

metalinguistic awareness: the ability to attend to language forms in and of themselves. For example, a child may notice that two words rhyme with each other.

metaplay language: comments about play itself ("I'll be the mommy, and you be the baby.").

personal narrative: a story told in the first person about a personal experience.

pretend language: comments that are appropriate for the roles that children have taken in dramatic play. For example, a child pretending to be a baby might say "Waah! Waah!"

rubric: a scoring tool with a list of criteria that describe the characteristics of children's performance at various proficiency levels.

scaffolding: temporary assistance that parents and teachers give to children to enable them to do things that they cannot do on their own.

- What can teachers do to promote language-rich dramatic play?
- How can sharing or show-and-tell be turned into a valuable oral language activity?
- How can teachers effectively assess children's oral language development?
- What can teachers do to optimize oral language experiences for bilingual and second-language learners?

Home Talk: A Natural Context for Learning and Using Language

Evan's family helped him understand and label his new experience with snow. Their language support was natural and was guided by Evan's constant questions "Why doesn't this snow make a snowball? Why can't I make an angel on this snow?" Evan's learning while he played was nothing new or extraordinary; he has received language support from his parents and sibling from the moment he was born. His parents and older sister intuitively supported his attempts to communicate. When Evan was an infant his parents, like most parents, naturally used parentese. That is, they talked to him in higher pitched tones, at slower rate of speech, and with exaggerated pronunciation and lots of repetition of phrases. Parentese helped Evan hear the sounds and words of his native language. Between the age of 18 months and three years, as Evan's communicative competence grew, his family intuitively adjusted their verbal responses so that he could easily learn new vocabulary and grammatical structures.

In Special Feature 3.1, we describe the types of verbal scaffolding Evan's family and most adults automatically use to support children's language development. This type of scaffolding is a prime example of Vygotsky's (1978) zone of proximal development in which adults help children engage in activities that they could not do on their own. Through ongoing interactions with his parents, sister, and other caregivers, Evan (and most children) quickly learn basic conversation skills (Danst, Lowe, & Bartholomew, 1990; Manning-Kratcoski & Bobkoff-Katz, 1998; Norris & Hoffman, 1990). By age three, Evan, like most children, had learned to take turns, back-channel (use fillers like "uh-huh" to keep conversations going), be polite, and make appropriate responses (Menyuk, 1988). He knew how to engage in conversations with adults and his peers.

Encouraging Personal Narratives

Evan's family played a vital role in helping him interpret, label, and recall his new experiences with snow. Back in Arizona, Evan had many stories to tell his teacher and playmates at preschool. For the next several months, each time he spoke with his grandparents, he relived his snow-day tales. The stories, or personal narratives, that Evan told helped him make sense of this new experience, broadened his vocabulary, and reinforced his expressive language skills. Likewise, each time Evan told the story about how the snow ball he threw at his sister knocked off the snowman's nose and made his dad laugh, he deepened his memory of the event.

Children's personal narratives are a window into their thinking. Their language also reveals how they use current knowledge to interpret new experiences. Evan's first interpretation of a snowy field was to relate it to a recent incident with a broken sugar bowl. These

Special Feature 3.1

Caregivers' Strategies for Supporting Children's Language Development

In almost all cases, caregivers intuitively scaffold children's language development. These communication strategies have been observed across all cultures.

Expansions—Adult recasts the child's efforts to reflect appropriate grammar. When adults use expansions they help introduce and build new vocabulary.

Child: Kitty eat.
Adult: Yes, the kitty is eating.

Extensions—Adult restates the child's telegraphic speech into a complete thought and may add new information in response to the child's comments.

Child: Kitty eat.
Adult: Kitty is eating his food.
Child: Kitty eat.
Adult: The kitty is hungry.

Repetitions—Adult facilitates the development of new sentence structure by repeating all or part of the child's comment.

Child: Kitty eat.
Adult: Time for kitty to eat. Time for kitty to eat.

Parallel talk—Adult describes the child's actions. Parallel talk is an effective way to model new vocabulary and grammatical structure.

Child: Kitty eat.
Adult: Jimmy is watching the kitty eat.

Self-talk—Adult describes their actions. Like parallel talk, self-talk effectively models new vocabulary and grammatical structures.

Adult: I'm feeding the kitty.

Vertical structuring—Adult uses questions to encourage the child to produce longer or more complex sentences.

Child: Kitty eat.
Adult: What is the kitty eating?
Child: Kitty eat cat food.

Fill-ins—Adult structures the conversation so that the child must provide a word or phrase to complete the statement.

Adult: The kitty is eating because she is—
Child: Hungry!

Adapted from Manning-Kratcoski, A., & Bobkoff-Katz, M. (1998). Conversing with young language learners in the classroom. *Young Children,* 53(3): 30–33.

verbal expressions of new mental constructions can be both fascinating and humorous. Likewise children's personal narratives offer insight into their language development and overall intellectual, social, and emotional growth.

Though children instinctively know how to put experiences, feelings, and ideas into story form, parents and caregivers can encourage their children's language development by offering many storytelling opportunities and attentively listening while children share their accounts of events (Canizares, 1997). Though nothing can replace quiet and private time to listen to children, many working parents report that they use the time in the car, bus, or subway going to and from day care and/or errands to listen carefully to their children.

Children often share what they know or have learned in story form. This is because the human brain functions narratively—for most of us it is much easier to understand and remember concepts when we are given information in story form rather than as a collection of facts. Since the human brain retains information more efficiently in story form, parents can explain new information using stories. For example, when five-year-old Tiffany wanted to know how to tie her shoelaces, her daddy told her the following story:

> Once upon a time, there were two silly snakes [the shoelaces] who decided to wrestle. They twisted around each other and tied themselves together very tightly [first tie]. The snakes became scared and tried to curl away from each other [the loops]. But the snakes tripped and fell over each other and tied themselves in a knot.

Reading Storybooks

Research reveals a connection between the amount of time adults spend reading storybooks to children and the level of children's oral language development. The stories, pictures, and accompanying adult-to-child interactions facilitate language use and increase expressive and receptive vocabulary. Further, children who have been read to frequently are better able to retell stories than children who have had few opportunities to engage in storytime (Barrentine, 1996; Durkin, 1966). Caregivers may also encourage discussion and comprehension by asking open-ended questions about the story. Children often relate to the characters and story lines, and, when encouraged, they reveal interesting views. The following conversation occurred when Dominique was four-years-old, after a reading of *Goldilocks and the Three Bears.*

MOM: What part of the story did you like the best?

DOMINIQUE: When Goldilocks kept messing up baby bear's stuff.

MOM: Who did you like best in the story?

DOMINIQUE: Baby bear.

MOM: Why?

DOMINIQUE: 'Cause baby bear is like me. All of his stuff is wrecked up by Goldilocks, like Sheritta [her 18-month-old sister] messes up mine.

Notice that Dominique's mother asked open-ended opinion questions and accepted her child's responses. This type of question encourages oral responses and children's personal interpretation of the story. Adults should refrain from asking interrogation or detail questions, such as "What did Goldilocks say when she tasted the second bowl of porridge?" Detail questions tend to make storytime avoidable, not enjoyable.

As children snuggle in a parent's lap or beside their parent in a chair or bed, storytime creates a comforting, private time to talk together. In addition to providing wonderful language opportunities, storytime also establishes a foundation for children to become successful readers (See Chapter 4).

In today's culturally, linguistically, and socioeconomically diverse society, teachers may find that some of their students' parents may not have the ability to read to their children or the financial means to purchase storybooks. Even more parents are unsure how to successfully engage their children in storytime. Special Feature 3.2 offers several suggestions for parents. In addition, teachers may need to help parents by acting as a resource. In Chapter 13, readers will discover a number of concrete suggestions for ways in which teachers can help parents support their children's language and literacy growth.

Television as a Language Tool

Television has been a major influence in family life in almost all U.S. households since the 1950s. In the 1980s the availability of video rentals and inexpensive video players, video movies, and video storybooks, cartoons, and games have added yet another dimension to television watching. During the 1990s, it was estimated that 99 percent of U.S. homes had at least one television set. In addition, the TV is usually in the part of the home where most family interactions occur (Miller, 1997). Sadly, the average child between two and five years of age will spend 27 hours a week viewing television programming. Anything that occupies children for so many hours a week deserves careful consideration.

Time.   Research regarding the amount of time young children watch TV and the effect of viewing on later academic success is inconclusive, though the data clearly suggest that watching for many hours per day or week has a negative effect on children's academic performance. Susan Neuman (1988) suggests that more than four hours of TV viewing a day has a negative effect on children's reading achievement. Likewise, Angela Clarke's and Beth Kurtz-Costes' (1997) study of low-socioeconomic African American preschool children shows that children who watched the most television (between 30 and 55 hours per week) exhibited poorer academic skills than their peers who watched fewer than 25 hours per week. On the other hand, moderate amounts of TV viewing may be beneficial. The Center for the Study of Reading landmark report, "Becoming a Nation of Readers," suggests that there is actually a positive link between watching up to 10 hours of television a week and reading achievement (Rice, Huston, Truglio, & Wright, 1990). Clarke and Kurtz-Costes (1997) suggest that the variation in researchers' findings may be due in part to the home climate. They suggest that **who** watches TV with young children and **how** TV is watched may have a greater effect on children's learning than simply the **amount** of TV viewing.

Choosing Programming for Children.   Selecting appropriate children's programming has become more challenging in recent years. In addition to regular public access, cable service may offer as many as 100 options to choose from each hour of the day. And while there are a number of proven classics—such as *Sesame Street, Reading Rainbow,* and *Mister Rogers*—children's programs change from year to year. One way parents can determine the quality of children's programming is through considering children's needs. Diane Levin and Nancy Carlsson-Paige (1994) created a list of children's developmental needs and suggested program criteria to accommodate these concerns.

Language Development via Storybook Reading

In recent years, studies have revealed that home literacy experiences, or the lack of them, profoundly influence children's later literacy development and language development. However, storybook reading is not an instinct. Knowing how to interact with children and storybooks takes time and practice. One simple approach that significantly increases a child's involvement in the story time experience is called "Dialogic Reading." It involves parents asking questions about the stories as they read, such as asking children

FIGURE 3.1   Closed- and Open-Ended Questions

Closed-ended questions usually only require a single word answer—"yes" or "no" or require the "right answer." Open-ended questions, on the other hand, have no right or wrong answers and encourage students to talk more and to use richer language.

This set of example questions for early primary-grade children refers to Maurice Sendak's *Where the Wild Things Are.*

Closed-Ended Questions	Open-Ended Questions
Did you like Max?	What did you think about Max?
Why did Max get in trouble?	How did you feel when Max's mother sent him to bed?
Were the wild things monsters?	Tell me about the wild things. What did they look like?
What did Max do to the wild things?	Why did Max stare at the wild things? How would you tame wild things?
Did you like the story?	What part of the story did you like best?

This set of questions for middle-school children refers to J. K. Rowling's *Harry Potter and the Sorcerer's Stone.*

Closed-Ended Questions	Open-Ended Questions
Do you like the Dursleys?	How would you describe the Dursleys?
Is Hagrid a giant?	How do you think the Dursleys felt when Hagrid arrived?
Did Mr. Dursley let Harry read the letter from Hogwarts?	Why didn't Mr. Dursley want Harry to read the letter from Hogwarts?
How many wands did Harry try?	What do you think it means when the wand seller said "The wand chooses the wizard?"
What did Harry get at Gringotts?	Hagrid got something secret at Gringotts. What do you think it was?

Remember to ask questions before, during, and after the story as this helps to maintain child involvement.

(continued on next page)

Special Feature 3.2 (continued)

to describe what they are seeing on the page. In addition, parents are also encouraged to add information.

The following scene illustrates the Dialogic Reading approach. Dad is reading Jane Manning's *Who Stole the Cookies from the Cookie Jar?* (Harper Festival, 2001) to three-year-old Jasper. Before Dad even reads begins the story, he asks Jasper about the cover illustration.

Dad: Jasper, who is on the cover?
Jasper: Doggie, kitty, piggy, rabbit, and mouse..
Dad: Look, Jasper. Do you see that the book is shaped like our cookie jar?
Jasper: Daddy, see the cookies, they are chocolate chip!
Dad: Your favorite. Jasper, the title of this book is *Who Stole the Cookies from the Cookie Jar?* Who do you think stole the cookies?
Jasper: I think Piggy or Cookie Monster.

The reading and conversation about this twelve-page storybook lasted more than a half hour with Jasper deeply engaged with describing the richly detailed illustrations and guessing who had stolen the cookies.

In addition to dialogic reading, there are other simple and enjoyable strategies parents can use to help their children get the most from storytime:

- Read the same books again and again. Children learn new things each time they hear story and look at the pictures.
- Ask children to find and label objects. This helps to keep them involved in the story.
- Ask open-ended questions. Asking questions like "What do you think will happen next?" or "What was your favorite part of the story?" encourages children to share their feelings and opinions. Figure 3.1 provides several examples of open-ended questions.
- Expand your child's answers. Adding to your child's responses encourages him or her to interact with you and keeps him or her involved.
- Read with enthusiasm. Taking on the voices of the three little pigs and the wolf is fun and exciting and brings the story to life.

Active Viewing.   Children are extremely impressionable, and television's visual imagery is a powerful force in their lives. Therefore, it is important for parents to help guide and mediate the viewing process. Susan Miller (1997) suggests a number of ways parents and caregivers may interact with children as they view television.

- *Watch television together*—Help children interpret what is seen on the screen.
- *Talk about the programs*—Conversations initiated by television programming offer opportunities to discuss a wide variety of issues.
- *Observe children's reactions*—Ask children to label or describe their feelings.
- *Foster critical thinking*—Ask children what they think about a program. Would they have handled the problem differently? Did they agree with the character's actions?
- *Extend viewing activities*—Children are often motivated to learn more about a topic or activity once television has sparked their interests.

In short, while the television can be a powerful tool in children's learning, careful consideration of how much, what, and how children view TV programs is needed.

School Talk: A Structured Context for Learning and Using Language

By the time most children enter preschool, they are capable of conversing with both adults and their peers. Language learning, however, is far from complete. Research has revealed that the semantic, syntactic, and pragmatic aspects of oral language continue to develop throughout the elementary school years (Chomsky, 1969; Karmiloff-Smith, 1979; Menyuk, 1988). Teachers, therefore, have the responsibility to promote language learning by engaging in conversations with students and by encouraging children to converse with each other (Roser, 1998). In fact, national teaching standards require elementary educators to be able to apply their knowledge of linguistics (morphemes, syntax, grammar, etc.) and theories of language learning. More specifically, elementary-grade teachers are expected to use teaching strategies that:

- build on students' experiences and current oral language skill,
- enhance students' listening skills,
- support students who are learning English as a second language and those who speak with dialects.

In addition, teachers are expected to be able to assess students' ability to accomplish their goals using language and use language assessment information to plan and modify future instruction.

Teacher Discourse

Over every school day, there are dozens of possibilities for verbal interactions (Smith & Dickinson, 1994). Unfortunately, research indicates that this opportunity is often overlooked in traditional transmission-oriented classrooms. Studies have shown that in many classrooms the teacher dominates the language environment; this does little to promote the children's oral language growth (Cazden, 1988; Howard, Shaughnessy, Sanger, & Hux, 1998; Wells, 1986). For example, these studies suggests that in some classrooms:

- teachers spend most of the time talking **to** rather than talking **with** children.
- teachers dominate discussions by controlling how a topic is developed and who gets to talk.
- children spend most of their time listening to teachers.
- when children do talk, it is usually to give a response to a question posed by the teacher.
- teachers tend to ask test-like, closed-ended questions that have one right answer (that the teacher already knows).

The typical pattern of classroom discourse is characterized by teacher initiation, student response, and teacher evaluation. In the IRE pattern, the teacher asks a question, a student answers, and the teacher either accepts or rejects that answer and goes on to ask another question (Galda, Cullinan, & Strickland, 1993). For example, before the following discussion, the kindergarten children had listened to *The Three Little Pigs.*

TEACHER: What material did the pigs use to build their first house?

BOBBIE: They used sticks.

TEACHER: Yes. That is correct, the pigs used sticks for the first house. What did the pigs use to build the third house?

MANUEL: They used cement.

TEACHER: No. Who remembers what the book says? Jon?

JON: Bricks.

TEACHER: Yes. The pigs used bricks.

Notice how the teacher's questions are not real questions; rather they test whether these young students recalled specific details of the story. Note also that children have no opportunity construct their own meaning of the story by combining text information with their prior knowledge. For example, Manuel's answer, *cement,* suggests that Manuel was making inferences based on prior experience. The teacher's negative response to Manuel's comment probably communicates to him that it is incorrect to make inferences when reading. This sends a message to students that one should recall exactly what is said in the text. Finally, notice that there is absolutely no interaction from student to student. The turn-taking pattern is teacher–student–teacher–student.

These types of IRE interactions are sometimes appropriate because teachers do need to get specific points across to students (Dyson & Genishi, 1983). However, problems ensue if this is the only type of talk that is taking place in the classroom. IRE discussions do not provide the type of language input and feedback that "advance children's knowledge of language structure and use" (Menyuk, 1988, p. 105). In addition, these teacher-dominated exchanges do not allow students to negotiate and build meaning through dialogue (Hansen, 1998).

What can early childhood teachers do to provide children with more stimulating experiences with language? We offer three recommendations:

1. Engage students in reciprocal discussions and conversations.
2. Provide ample opportunities for activity-centered language that invite (and, at times, require) students to use language to get things done.
3. Provide language-centered activities that focus students' attention on specific aspects of language.

In the sections that follow, we present guidelines for implementing each of these recommendations.

Reciprocal Discussions and Conversations

Teachers' verbal interaction styles set the general tone for classroom language environments. The worst-case scenario occurs when a teacher insists on absolute silence except during teacher-led initiation, response, evaluation discussions. Such environments definitely limit continued oral language development. Other teachers provide ideal language environments by engaging students in genuine conversations, conducting stimulating reciprocal discussions, and allowing children to converse with each other at a moderate volume during classroom learning activities, using "inside voices" (soft voices that do not disrupt classroom learning).

Teachers have many opportunities to talk with students throughout the school day, ranging from one-to-one conversations to whole-group discussions. Following is an example of an effective conversation between Ms. E., a preschool teacher, and Roberto, age four:

ROBERTO: See my new backpack, Teacher?

MS. E: What a neat backpack, Roberto. Show it to me.

ROBERTO: It has six zippers. See? The pouches hold different stuff. Isn't it neat?

MS. E: I like the different size pouches. Look, this one is just right for a water bottle.

ROBERTO: Yeah. The arm straps are great too. See, I can make 'em longer.

MS. E: Yes [nods and smiles]. It fits your arms perfectly. Where did you get this nifty backpack?

ROBERTO: We got it at the mall.

MS. E: What store in the mall?

ROBERTO: The one that has all the camping stuff.

MS. E: The Camping Plus store?

ROBERTO: Yeah. That's the one.

Notice how Ms. E. allowed Roberto to take the lead by listening carefully to what Roberto said and by responding to his previous statements. She let him do most of talking, using back-channeling (nodding and smiling) to keep the conversation going. Ms. E. asked only three questions, and they were genuine—she wanted to know where Roberto purchased the backpack.

Reciprocal conversations are not restricted to one-to-one situations. Teachers can also engage children in genuine discussions pertaining to ongoing instructional activities. Cory Hansen (1998) gives an example of group discussion of George MacDonald's 1872 classic, *The Princess and the Goblin* (Puffin Books). The chapter book is being discussed by a group of kindergarten students in Chris Boyd's classroom.

Previously in the story, the grandmother had given the princess a gift of a glowing ring from which a thread would lead her to comfort if she were frightened. The princess assumed it would lead her to her grandmother, but one night it led her deep into a cave and stopped at a heap of stones. The chapter ("Irene's Clue") ends with the princess bursting into tears at the foot of the rocks. Curdie, the fearless miner's son, was missing.

JOSEPH: I think that Curdie's on the other side of the rocks.

MRS. B.: Where'd you get the clue for that?

ANNA: Because the strings led her to the mountain. That means it was close to Curdie because Curdie lived by the mountain.

KIM: Maybe Curdie's on the other side of the stones!

JAMAL: I think her grandmother was a goblin since she could have went through the rocks.

JORDAN: I know. Maybe—when she was falling asleep on the other side—but how could the goblins be that fast?

ANNA: Because they're magic.

RICHARD: I know how Curdie got to the other side. . . .

CHORUS: Children begin to talk in small groups simultaneously.

JOSEPH: Maybe Curdie's in the heap of stones.

MRS. B.:   What makes you say that?

JOSEPH: Because in the last chapter—Curdie's Clue—it said they piled the rock—a big stone in the mouth of the cave.

KIM: The grandmother said the ring always led to the grandmother's bedroom so she . . .

ANNA: No it didn't. It said, "This will take me to you—wherever it takes you, you go." And the grandmother said, "Wherever it takes you, you will go."

MRS. B.:   Can you think of any reason why the princess should go to the cave?

JOSEPH: Because it said, "You must not doubt the string."

ADAM: The grandmother said the thread would lead to her but it ended up leading her to Curdie.

ALONDRA: I think the grandmother knows about Curdie.

KIM: It's because her grandmother wanted her to save Curdie!

ANNA: That was the clue.

JAMAL: To get Curdie out cuz she know about him.

JOSEPH: Yeah. (Hansen, 1998, pp. 172–173)

Here, Mrs. B. let the students take the lead by listening closely to what they said and responding to their comments. Her questions were genuine (she did not know what the children's responses would be) and were open-ended in nature ("What makes you say that?"). By welcoming the children's viewpoints, she encouraged them to bring their personal interpretations to the story. Also note that the children talked to each other; they engaged in real conversations. The teacher facilitated this child—child turn-taking pattern by encouraging the students to respond to each other's ideas.

Ms. E.'s and Mrs. B.'s effective use of reciprocal questions allowed students to engage in authentic discussion with the teacher and each other. Obviously, the way a teacher interacts with children influences the way children communicate. Therefore, it is important for teachers to reflect on the quality of their conversations and discussions with students of all ages.

As teachers work with the students in their classrooms it is important to remember that many children do not speak academic or "standard" English. Teachers must be sensitive and respectful to the wide range of dialects they hear, always remembering that the language of the child's home must be valued even as teachers help children learn a more academic vocabulary. Special Feature 3.3 offers some guidance for teachers in understanding and supporting language variation.

Contexts for Encouraging Language for Children

We know that what students say and do is greatly influenced by where they are and what is around them. For example as Evan played in the snow, he learned snow-related vocabulary with his family. Teachers must create dynamic learning environments that are contexts for language development. In other words the curriculum must give children something to talk about. In the following section, we describe how teachers might use group activities, learning centers, and dramatic play to expand students' learning and opportunities to use language.

Group Activities. Teachers can support language by involving children with group activities that encourage, and at times necessitate, verbal interaction. What sort of activities would require children to talk? As Celia Genishi (1987) points out, "almost every object or activity presents an opportunity for talk when teachers allow it to" (p. 99). In the following vignette, we provide an illustration of a whole-group activity that required a rather large group of multilingual, four-year-old children to reveal and assert needs and wants and connect with themselves and others.

The young students have been learning about manners and balanced meals. As part of a culminating activity, the entire room has been transformed into a restaurant. Twelve little tables are draped with tablecloths, and each table has a vase of flowers. Today, the teachers are waitresses, and a few parents have volunteered to cook real food. The children must choose between the Panda Café (spaghetti, meatballs, garlic toast, juice or milk) or the Café Mexico (burrito, chips, salsa, juice or milk). Each café has a menu with words and pictures. The children must select the specific items they wish to eat and give their orders to the waitress. The waitress takes the children's orders on an order form and gives the order form to the cooks. The cooks fill the orders exactly as the children request. Then, the waitress returns with the food and the order form and asks the children to review the order.

TEACHER: What café would you like, sir?

ROBERTO: [Points to menu.]

TEACHER: Which café? You must tell me.

ROBERTO: The Café Mexico.

TEACHER: Right this way, sir. Here is your menu. Take a moment to decide what you want to eat. I'll be right back to take your order.

ROBERTO: [Looks over the menu and shares his choices with his friend by pointing to the items he wants.]

Special Feature 3.3

Understanding and Supporting Language Variation

Welcome to my home. Please, do come in.

Hey yaw'l. Jes come rite-on in ta mah plaaace.

Dude, catch the pad. Wanna crash?

As you read the sentences above, did you begin to form mental images about the speakers? Did you make predictions about their ages, places of origins, and social status? If you did you are not alone, the study of dialects offers a fascinating look at how the language we use is linked to our social identity. Likewise, the study of dialects often provides the most vivid illustration of how language changes over time (Hazen, 2001).

Many people believe there is only one correct form of English, what is often called Standard English. According to this view, the phrase, *My sister is not home* will always be preferred to the phrase, *My sister ain't home.* However, linguists suggest that what is appropriate language depends on the situation. In many contexts, *My sister ain't home.* is more acceptable. This is called Rhetorically Correct English, which suggests that what is "correct" varies and is governed by the speaker's intention, the audience, and the context (Crystal, 1995; Demo, 2000).

Unfortunately, dialect discrimination is widely tolerated in the United States. Many people believe that there is only one kind of appropriate English that all children should learn and that all teachers should be required to teach. However, even this long-held view is being challenged. In the mid-1990s the Oakland, California, school board, proposed that Ebonics be accepted as a school language. The outcry against this idea was national! Only Standard English should be taught in schools, was frequently heard. When educator-linguist Lisa Delpit (1997) was asked if she was for or against Ebonics her answer was complex:

My answer must be neither. I can be neither for Ebonics nor against Ebonics any more than I can be for or against air. It exists. It is the language spoken by many of our African-American children. It is the language they heard as their mothers nursed them and changed their diapers and played peek-a-boo with them. It is the language through which they first encountered love, nurturance and joy. On the other hand, most teachers of those African-American children who have been least well-served by the educational system believe that their students' chances will be further hampered if they do not learn Standard English. In the stratified society in which we live, they are absolutely correct (p. 6).

As Delpit suggests, no matter how accepting teachers may be of a child's home language in the classroom, a child's dialect may serve as a source of discrimination as they mature. So what is the role of the teacher? According to Lily Wong Fillmore and Catherine Snow (2000, p. 20), "Teachers must provide children the support needed to master the English required for academic development and for jobs when they have completed school. However, this process does not work when the language spoken by the children—the language of their families and primary communities—is disrespected in school."

In summary, teachers need to teach children the dialect of school and work. To accomplish this goal, teachers need to provide the same type of scaffolding parents used when children were first learning to talk (Manning-Kratcoski & Bobkoff-Katz, 1998). Teachers must extend and expand children's language in a respectful manner, for example, as a simple expansion:

Child: That ain't right.
Teacher: I agree, this isn't right.

(continued on next page)

Special Feature 3.3 *(continued)*

Notice how the teacher recasts the child's effort in Standard English. Note also that the teacher doesn't emphasize the correct form, but uses it naturally. When adults use expansions they help to introduce and build new vocabulary.

TEACHER: OK, sir. What would you like?

ROBERTO: [Points to the items on the menu.]

TEACHER: Please, sir. You will have to tell me.

ROBERTO: [Hesitates for a few seconds.] I want the burrito and chips and juice.

TEACHER: Do you want salsa? [She leans over so he can see her mark the items on the order form.]

ROBERTO: No. [Firmly.]

Notice how the teachers organized this activity so that the children had to verbally express their needs multiple times throughout the restaurant adventure. In addition, the children had many opportunities to see how print is used in real life. However, teachers are not the only valuable source of language input. Children can also gain valuable oral language practice from talking with peers who are not as skilled as adults in initiating and maintaining conversations. To encourage peer-to-peer interactions, these teachers also created a miniature version of the restaurant in a dramatic play learning center. In this center, Roberto and his classmates will be able to play restaurant together for a few weeks.

As teachers of children observe their students in a variety of learning situations that require the children to use their language skills, they will often notice some who are having difficulty with the production of speech. Good teachers know that children with speech challenges and language delays should receive specialized support. Trade Secret 3.1 provides a brief overview of the most common speech challenges children display.

Learning Centers.   Since children's learning and language is greatly influenced by their environment, good teachers guide children's language development through the deliberate structuring of the classroom environment. For example, the teachers in the previous vignette created a restaurant to encourage talk about food, ordering meals, taking orders, cooking meals, and the like. Later, as the children interacted together in the restaurant dramatic play center, they continued to help each other build and reinforce their knowledge of restaurants. In learning center classrooms, the teacher's role is to set up the environment, observe as children interact with the materials, supply help and guidance when needed, and engage in conversations with the children around the materials and the children's use in their learning. A good deal of the teacher's effort is expended on the setting-up or preparation phase. Centers are created when the teacher carves the classroom space into defined areas. (See Chapter 9 for ideas on how to carve the classroom space into learning centers.)

Trade Secret 3.1

Supporting Children Who Experience Language Delay or Speech Challenges
By Kathy Eustace

I teach in an inclusion preschool of four-year-olds. Each year nearly half my students exhibit some type of speech production challenge. As their teacher I see one of my roles as being a language facilitator for **all** my students. Whether the child is classified as typically developing or exhibits a speech production disorder or presents evidence of language delay, each is merely at a specific stage of development. My job is the same for all students: to assess their current level of ability, support mastery at this stage, and then help them learn the skills necessary to move on to the next stage. The most common challenges I see when I work with children include articulation disorders, fluency disorders, and language delay.

Articulation disorders account for the majority of all speech production difficulties in young children. These generally involve the mispronunciations of the *s, r, l, th,* and *sh* sounds. The child either:

- omits the sound completely (e.g., *alt* for *salt*),
- substitutes one sound for another consistently (e.g., *wabbit* for *rabbit*), or
- distorts or does not produce the sounds precisely (e.g., *Eidabeth* for *Elizabeth*).

Nearly all children experience some level of misarticulation while they are learning to speak and most children correct through normal development. Speech therapy is usually only necessary if the misarticulations prohibit others from understanding the child's verbal communication or if the problem persists and becomes embarrassing for the child.

Fluency disorders occur when the normal rate of speech "flow" is atypical. Stuttering is one form of fluency disorder. Stuttering occurs when repetitions of sounds interrupt the child's flow of speech, for example, *ppppp please.* Cluttering is another form of disfluency. Cluttering involves excessively fast speech in which word boundaries are often obscured or garbled, for example, *Idonwnnagotoleep for I don't want to go to sleep.* Once again, nearly all children occasionally stutter and/or clutter when they are excited or tired. Disfluency disorders are not considered problematic unless they are constant and prevent a child from communicating his or her intentions.

Language delay is diagnosed when children have difficulty understanding a communicated message or expressing their thoughts verbally as contrasted to a developmental standard. For example, a two-year-old who responds in one- or two-word sentences is developmentally normal, but a four-year-old who only responds in one- or two-word sentences would be classified as language delayed.

Language delays may be exhibited as a primary condition caused by temporary health concerns such as colds or ear infections. Other more serious causes of language delay also include language-impoverished home environments or damage to the areas of the brain that process language. Language delays also occur as secondary symptoms to other physical conditions such as mental retardation, autism, cleft plate, or cerebral palsy.

While there are many reasons children many not acquire the typical language skills expected for their age, the cause is less important than the treatment. For example, a child may exhibit language delays due to mental retardation or a child with normal intelligence may not have acquired normal language due to temporary hearing loss or an environment that was not verbally interactive. Regardless of the circumstance, the instructional goal is to increase the production of verbal communication, and therefore the treatment is nearly identical.

When I plan activities for my inclusive class, I plan language opportunities that would be appro-

(continued on next page)

Trade Secret 3.1 *(continued)*

priate for a range of abilities, from the typically developing child to the children who exhibit speech production challenges to language delays. I also facilitate student participation based on the ability level of each child, always keeping the child's individual goals in mind. The activities are open-ended and designed to elicit responses at all four levels. The following examples are based on a discussion I had with my class after we had read *Little Cloud* by Eric Carlile (Scholastic, 1996).

Level 1—involves an indication that the child has a receptive understanding of a new concept, in this case, clouds. At this level I merely ask the child to demonstrate his or her understanding of the new concept by pointing to a visual representation of the concept. *Where are the clouds in this picture, Jamie?*

Level 2—asks a child to use a one-word response to communicate. This one word may help me gauge a child's receptive understanding or a linguistic concept, or it may include a targeted speech sound that is typically mispronounced by this child. For example, *On this page what did little cloud turn into? Gustavo? Yes, that is right RRRRabbit.*

Level 3—involves a multiword response from a child whose goal it is to increase his or her mean length of utterance or who is working on syntax. *Can you tell me three or four things that Little Cloud changes into? Sarafina?*

Level 4—involves helping children make inferences or comparisons. This level of response gives children an opportunity to elaborate their thoughts and to work on the aspect of their language that is in question. *How are sheep and clouds alike? Who helped Little Cloud make the rain?*

Readers seeking more information on establishing centers will find *The Creative Curriculum for Early Childhood Education* (Dodge & Colker, 1992) to be a useful resource. This book presents detailed, easy-to-follow instructions for setting up popular interest areas (centers). It also contains practical tips on schedules, routines, and other aspects of classroom management, plus good suggestions for encouraging parental involvement.

Dramatic Play. Another context for activity-centered language is dramatic play. Dramatic play occurs when children take on roles and use make-believe transformations to act out situations and play episodes. For example, several children might adopt the roles of family members and pretend to prepare dinner, or they may become superheroes who are engaged in fantastic adventures. This type of play—also called sociodramatic, make-believe, pretend, or imaginative play—reaches its peak between the ages of four and seven.

Although to some dramatic play appears simple and frivolous at first glance, close inspection reveals that it is quite complex and places heavy linguistic demands on children (Fessler, 1998). In fact, Jerome Bruner (1983, p. 65) reported that "the most complicated grammatical and pragmatic forms of language appear first in play activity." When children work together to act out stories, they face formidable language challenges. They not only need to use language to act out their dramas, they must also use language to organize the play and keep it going. Before starting, they must recruit other players, assign roles, decide on the make-believe identities of objects (e.g., that a block of wood will be used as if it were a telephone), and plan the story line. Once started, language must be used to act out the story, keep the dramatization heading in the right direction (e.g., be sure that everyone is doing things appropriate to their role), and re-energize the play if it is becoming repetitious and boring.

To accomplish these tasks, children must use two different types of language: (1) pretend language that is appropriate for their roles, and (2) metaplay language about the play itself. Children switch between their pretend roles and their real identities when making these two types of comments. This linguistic complexity is illustrated in the following example.

Three preschoolers are enacting a domestic scene in their classroom's housekeeping corner. John has taken the role of the father; Wendy is the mother; and George, the youngest of the three, has reluctantly agreed to be the baby.

WENDY: Baby looks hungry. Let's cook him some food. [Pretend.]

JOHN: Okay. [Pretend.]

WENDY: [Addressing George.] Cry and say that you're hungry. [Metalanguage.]

GEORGE: But I'm not hungry. [Metalanguage.]

WENDY: Pretend that you are! [Metalanguage.]

GEORGE: [Using a babyish voice.] I'm hungry. [Pretend.]

WENDY: [Addressing John.] Father, what should we have for dinner? [Pretend.]

JOHN: How about eggs. [Pretend.]

WENDY: I'll go get some eggs from the 'frigerator. [She goes to a wall shelf and takes several cube-shaped blocks.] [Pretend.]

GEORGE: Aah! I'm hungry! [Pretend.]

WENDY: [Pretending to scold George.] Be quiet! [She puts the blocks in a toy pan and places the pan on the toy stove.] The eggs are cooking. Father, you'd better set the table.

JOHN: Okay. [Pretend.]

GEORGE: Let me help, Daddy. [Pretend.]

JOHN: No! Babies don't set tables! You're just supposed to sit there and cry. [Metalanguage.] (Johnson, Christie, & Yawkey, 1999, p. 1)

In this example, Wendy is in her role as mother when she makes her initial comment about the baby. She reverts to real-life identity when she tells George what to say next and to pretend to be hungry. Then she shifts back to the role of mother when she asks father what he wants for dinner.

In order to take full advantage of dramatic play's potential as a medium for language development, attention needs to be given to three factors: (1) the settings in which play occurs, (2) the amount of time allocated for play activities, and (3) the type of teacher involvement in play episodes.

*Dramatic play is an ideal medium for
promoting oral language development.*

Play settings.   It is important to remember that children play best at what they already know. Therefore, dramatic play settings need to be familiar to children and consistent with their culture (Neuman, 1995). For example, the domestic play themes, such as parents caring for a baby or a family eating a meal, are very popular with young children because these are the roles and activities with which they are most familiar. For this reason, we recommend that preschool and kindergarten classrooms contain a housekeeping dramatic play center equipped with props that remind children of their own homes. Not only do such centers encourage dramatic play, but they also provide a context in which children can display the types of literacy activities they have observed at home.

The range of children's play themes and related literacy activities can be greatly expanded by the addition of a theme center to the classroom. These centers have props and furniture that suggest specific settings that are familiar to children, such as a veterinarian's office, restaurant, bank, post office, ice cream parlor, fast-food restaurant, and grocery store (Table 5.1 contains lists of literacy materials that can be used in a variety of theme centers). For example, a veterinarian's office might be divided into two areas: (1) a waiting room with a table for a receptionist and chairs for patients, and (2) an examination room with another table, chairs, and a variety of medical props (doctor's kit, scales, etc.). Stuffed animals can be provided as patients. Theme-related literacy materials—appointment book, patient folders, prescription forms, wall signs, and so on—should also be included to encourage children to re-enact the literacy activities that they have observed in these settings. Children will use their knowledge of visits to the doctor to engage in play with their peers. The following scenario illustrates how three preschoolers verbalize their knowledge of what occurs at the animal hospital.

SERGIO: [The vet is looking at the clipboard.] It says here that Ruffy is sick with worms.

MARIE: [Owner of a toy kitty named Ruffy.] Yep, uh huh. I think she ate bad worms.

SERGIO: That means we gotta operate and give Ruffy big horse pills for those worms.

JOY: [The nurse.] OK, sign here. [Hands Marie a big stack of papers.] Sign 'em all. Then we'll operate. But you gotta stay out in the people room. You could faint if you stay in here.

Chari Woodard (1984), a teacher who has had considerable success with theme centers in her university's laboratory preschool, recommends that one theme center be introduced at a time and left for several weeks. Then the center can be transformed into another theme. She also advises locating these centers near the permanent housekeeping center so that children can integrate the theme center activities with their domestic play. Children acting as parents for dolls, pets, or peers in the housekeeping area might, for example, take a sick baby to the doctor theme center for an examination. Or, children might weld or examine cars in the classroom garage (Hall & Robinson, 1995). Woodard found that children, particularly boys, began engaging in more dramatic play when the theme corners were introduced.

Time.   Dramatic play requires providing a considerable amount of time for children to plan and initiate. If play periods are short, children have to stop their dramatizations right after they have started. When this happens frequently, children tend to switch to less advanced forms of play, such as functional (motor) play or simple construction activity, which can be completed in brief sessions.

Research has shown that preschoolers are much more likely to engage in rich, sustained dramatic play during 30-minute play periods than during shorter 15-minute sessions (Christie, Johnsen, & Peckover, 1988). Our experience indicates that even longer periods are needed. For example, Billie Enz and Jim Christie (1997) spent a semester observing a preschool classroom that had 40-minute play periods. Very often, the four-year-olds had just finished preparing for a dramatization when it was time to clean up. Fortunately, the teachers were flexible and often let the children have an extra 10 to 15 minutes to act out their dramas. We recommend that, whenever possible, center time last for at least 60 minutes.

Teacher Involvement.   For many years, it was believed that teachers should just set the stage and not get directly involved in children's play activities. This hands-off stance toward play has been seriously challenged by a growing body of research that suggests that classroom play can be enriched through teacher participation. Teacher involvement has been found to assist nonplayers to begin to engage in dramatic play, to help more proficient players enrich and extend their dramatizations, and to encourage children to incorporate literacy into their play episodes (Enz & Christie, 1997; Roskos & Neuman, 1993). However, teachers need to use caution because overzealous or inappropriate forms of involvement can interfere with ongoing play and sometimes cause children to quit playing altogether (Enz & Christie, 1997).

The simplest and least intrusive type of teacher involvement in play is observation. By watching children as they play, teachers demonstrate that they are interested in the children's play and that play is a valuable, worthwhile activity. Observation alone can lead to more sustained play. Bruner (1980) reported that preschoolers' play episodes lasted roughly twice as long when a teacher was nearby and observing than when children played completely on their own. In addition, the children were more likely to move toward more elaborate forms of play when an adult was looking on.

Observation can also provide clues about when more direct forms of teacher involvement in play are appropriate. A teacher may find that, in spite of conducive play settings, some children rarely engage in dramatic play. Or the teacher may notice that there is an opportunity to extend or enrich an ongoing play episode, perhaps by introducing some new element or problem for children to solve (Hall, 1999). Both situations call for active teacher involvement.

Chapter 5 describes three roles that are ideal for initiating and extending dramatic play: the stage manager role, in which the teacher supplies props and offers ideas to enrich play; the co-player role, in which the teacher actually takes on a role and joins in the children's play; and the play leader who stimulates play by introducing, in a role, some type of problem to be resolved. For more information about these roles and other roles that teachers can adopt during play, see Jones and Reynolds (1992).

In addition to promoting language acquisition, dramatic play encourages children to help each other learn academic skills and content (Hansen, 1998; Christie & Stone, 1999), make friends, and develop important social skills (Garvey, 1977). Peer-to-peer interaction is particularly important for the growing numbers of students who are learning English as a second language and need help with more basic aspects of oral language (Fessler, 1998). For these reasons, dramatic play centers need to be a prominent feature in early childhood classrooms.

Language-Centered Activities for Children

Beyond creating contexts that encourage language and facilitate verbal interactions, teachers can also provide activities that focus specifically on language. Read-alouds, sharing, storytelling, and language play all fall into this category. The first of these, teacher read-alouds, is the subject of an entire section in Chapter 5. Storybook reading can be an ideal context for promoting attentive listening and oral discussion skills. We discuss the remaining four language-centered activities below.

Sharing. Sharing, or show-and-tell, is a strategy designed to promote students' speaking and listening abilities. Traditionally, sharing has been a whole-class activity in which one child after another gets up, takes center stage, and talks about something of her or his own choosing—often some object brought from home (Gallas, 1992). Children in the audience are expected to quietly listen and not participate.

In this traditional format, sharing is not a very productive language experience for the child who is speaking or for those who are listening. The large group size can intimidate the speaker and reduce participation—only a small percentage of students get to share on a given day. Or if many students share, it becomes a very drawn-out, boring affair. The lack of participation on the part of the audience leads to poor listening behavior. Listening is an active, constructive process in which listeners combine information provided by a speaker with their own prior knowledge to build personal meaning. Mary Jalongo (1995) relates a teacher's definition of listening that captures the essences of active listening: "it is hearing and making and shaping what you heard—along with your own ideas—into usable pieces of knowledge" (p. 14). The passive role of the audience in traditional sharing works against this process.

With two modifications, sharing can be transformed into a very worthwhile language activity. First, group size should be "small enough to reduce shyness, encourage interaction, permit listeners to examine the object, and afford everyone a long enough turn without tiring the group" (Moffett & Wagner, 1983, p. 84). Groups of three to six students are ideal for this purpose. Second, listeners should be encouraged to participate by asking questions of the child who is sharing. "Let the sharer/teller begin as she will. When she has said all that initially occurs to her, encourage the audience by solicitation and example to ask natural questions" (Moffett and Wagner, 1983, p. 84). The teacher's role is to model questioning that encourages elaboration and clarification ("When did you get . . . ?" "What happened next?" "What's that for?"). After asking one or two questions, teachers should pause and encourage the audience to participate. Prompts, such as "Does anyone have questions for Suzy?" may sometimes be needed to get the process started. Once children realize that it is acceptable for them to participate, prompting will no longer be necessary.

This peer questioning stimulates active listening by giving the audience a reason to listen to the child who is sharing. Children know that, in order to ask relevant questions, they are going to have to listen very carefully to what the sharer has to say. The child who is sharing benefits as well. Children can be encouraged to elaborate their brief utterances or to organize their content more effectively and to state it more clearly (Moffett & Wagner, 1983).

Teachers can add variety to sharing by occasionally giving it a special focus, such as by asking children to bring something that

1. has a good story behind it, which encourages narrative discourse,
2. they made or grew, which facilitates explanation or description, or
3. works in a funny or interesting way, which fosters expositive communication.

Storytelling.   Chapter 5 discusses many of the values of reading stories to children. Telling stories to children is also very worthwhile. The direct connection between the teller and audience promotes enjoyment and active listening. Marie Clay (1989) describes some of the values of storytelling:

> Storytelling is more direct than story reading. Facial expressions, gestures, intonations, the length of pauses, and the interactions with the children's responses create a more direct contact with the audience, dramatic in effect. The meaning can be closer to the children's own experiences because the teller can change the words, add a little explanation, or translate loosely into a local experience (p. 24).

The first stories that children tell usually involve real-life experiences—they relate something that has happened to them. Sharing, discussed in the previous section, can be an ideal context to allow children to tell these types of stories in the classroom. Small-group, interactive sharing provides feedback that enables children to tell clearer, better-organized stories about personal experiences (Canizares, 1997).

Some children need assistance in broadening the range of their storytelling to imaginative, fictional stories. The following suggestions can help with this task:

- Open up the sharing period to include fantasy stories. Once teachers begin permitting their children to tell "fictitional" stories, the children may begin sharing imaginative, creative stories that feature language that is much richer than that used in their show-and-tell sharing (Gallas, 1992).
- Encourage children to retell the stories contained in their favorite storybooks. Books remove the burden of creating an original story to tell. Story retelling has other benefits for children, including enhanced oral fluency and expression and improved story comprehension (Morrow, 1985).
- Have children make up words for the stories in wordless picture books, such as *Pancakes for Breakfast* by Tomie dePaola (Harcourt, Brace, Jovanovich, 1978). Here again, the book is providing the content for the child's story. See Appendix A, Quality Literature for Young Children (page 249) for a list of other exemplary wordless picture books.
- Link storytelling with play and writing. Vivian Paley (1990) has developed a strategy in which children come to a story table and dictate a story that the teacher writes down. During this dictation, the teacher asks the children to clarify any parts of the story that are unclear or difficult to understand. The teacher reads the story plays to the class. Finally, children serve as directors and invite classmates to join in acting out their stories. Children enjoy watching their stories dramatized, motivating them to create additional imaginative stories.

Language Play.   In addition to using language in their dramatic play, children also play with language. This intentional "messing around" with language begins as soon as children have passed through the babbling stage and have begun to make words (Garvey, 1977). This play involves the phonological, syntactic, and semantic aspects of language. By age two, language play becomes quite sophisticated. Ruth Weir (1962) placed a tape recorder in her two-and-a-half-year-old son Anthony's crib and turned it on after he had been placed in his crib for the evening. During this presleep time, Anthony engaged in an extensive amount of systematic language play. He experimented with speech sounds ("Babette . . . Back here . . . Wet"), substituted words of the same grammatical category ("What color. What color blanket. What color mop. What color glass"), and replaced nouns with appropriate pronouns ("Take the monkey. Take it." and "Stop it. Stop the ball. Stop it"). These monologues constituted play because language was being manipulated for its own sake rather than being used to communicate.

Young children also make attempts at humor, playing with semantic aspects of language. Kornei Chukovsky (1976) explains that "Hardly has the child comprehended with certainty which objects go together and which do not, when he begins to listen happily to verses of absurdity" (p. 601). This, in turn, leads children to make up their own nonsense. Chukovsky uses his two-year-old daughter as an example. Shortly after she had learned that dogs say "bow wow" and cats say "miaow," she approached him and said, "Daddy, 'oggie—miaow!' and laughed. It was his daughter's first joke!

Children gain valuable practice while engaging in these types of language play. They also begin to acquire metalinguistic awareness, the ability to attend to language forms as objects in and of themselves. Courtney Cazden (1976) explains that when language is used for its normal function—to communicate meaning—language forms become transparent. We "hear through them" to get the intended message (p. 603). When children play with language, the situation is reversed. The focus is on the language—the grammatical rules and semantic relationships they are manipulating.

The type of language play children engage in is also age related (Geller, 1982). At age three, children like to repeat traditional rhymes ("Mary Had a Little Lamb"). They eventually begin to make up their own nonsense rhymes, playing with sound patterns ("Shama sheema / Mash day n' pash day . . ."). By ages five and six, children delight in verbal nonsense ("I saw Superman flying out there!") and chanting games ("Cinderella, dressed in yellow / Went upstairs to kiss her fellow / How many kisses did she get? / 1, 2, 3, 4, 5, . . .")—forms themselves rather than meaning. Children become aware of the sounds (Cinderella dressed in yellow, went upstairs to kiss her fellow./ How many kisses did she get?/ 1, 2, 3, 4, 5 . . .").

The obvious educational implication is that language play should be encouraged and supported at school (Cazden, 1976). Judith Schwartz (1983) recommends that teachers try three things to stimulate their students to play with language.

1. Create a climate that allows play to flourish—a classroom atmosphere in which "children and teacher laugh easily and often."
2. Serve as a model by sharing humorous anecdotes, word play, folk literature, jokes, and stories with children and by using gentle humor in interpersonal relationships with children.
3. Value each child's contributions by allowing many opportunities for sharing oral and written language play.

Songs and Finger Plays.   Sitting on the floor with a small group of preschoolers, Ms. K. begins:

> *Where is Thumbkin?*
> *Where is Thumbkin?*
> *Here I am! Here I am!*
> *How are you today, sir?*
> *Very well, I thank you.*
> *Run away, Run away.*

The three- and four-year-old children quickly join in and immediately start the finger movements that accompany this familiar song. Very young children love to sing. The human fondness for a catchy tune and a snappy, clever rhyme begins early. Beginning in infancy and continuing on throughout their childhood, they are experimenting with their voices and the sounds that they can make. In Special Feature 3.4, we describe children's

Special Feature 3.4

Musical Development from Infancy through Kindergarten

Age 0 to 9 months

- Begins to listen attentively to musical sounds; is calmed by human voices. Starts vocalization, appearing to imitate what he or she hears.

Age 9 months to 2 years

- Begins to respond to music with clear repetitive movements. Interested in every kind of sound; begins to discriminate among sounds and may begin to approximate pitches. Most attracted to music that is strongly rhythmic.

Age 2 to 3 years

- Creates spontaneous songs, sings parts of familiar songs; recognizes instruments and responds more enthusiastically to certain songs. Strong physical response to music.

Age 3 to 4 years

- Continues to gain voice control; likes songs that play with language; and enjoys making music with a group as well as alone. Concepts such as high and low, loud and soft are beginning to be formed. Likes physical activity with music.

Age 4 to 6 years

- Sings complete songs from memory, is gaining pitch control and rhythmic accuracy. Loves language play and rhyming words. Attention span increases for listening to tapes and compact discs.

Adapted from Collins, M. (1997). Children and music. In B. Farber (Ed.), *The parents' and teachers' guide to helping young children learn.* Cutchogue, NY: Preschool Publication.

musical development from infancy through kindergarten. Singing encourages risk-free language play, especially for children who are learning a second language (Freeman & Freeman, 1994b; Jackman, 1997). Singing songs in a new language allows children to make safe mistakes as they experiment with the new phonemic system—similar to the way toddlers may begin to sing jingles they hear on the television long before they can actually speak in full sentences. As noted in a recent report by Catherine Snow and her colleagues (1998), singing songs is an important literacy activity.

Therefore, teachers of young children would be wise to build in singing as part of their language arts curriculum (Collins, 1997). In particular, children enjoy songs that

- offer repetition and chorus, such as "Polly Put the Kettle On," "Mary Had A Little Lamb," or "Here We Go Round the Mulberry Bush";
- provide repeated words or phrases that can be treated like an echo, such as "Miss Mary Mack" or "She'll Be Comin' Round the Mountain";
- require sound effects or animal noises, such as "If You're Happy and You Know It" or "Old MacDonald Had a Farm";

- tell a story, such as "Hush, Little Baby," "Humpty Dumpty," or "Little Bo Peep"; and
- ask questions, such as "Where Is Thumbkin?" or "Do You Know the Muffin Man?"

In addition to singing, many songs or poems include finger plays. Do you recall the "Itsy-Bitsy Spider" and how your fingers became the spider who climbed up the water-spout? Children's minds are fully engaged when they act out the words of a song or poem with their fingers (Collins, 1997).

Many preschool and kindergarten teachers write the songs the children love to sing on chart paper or purchase the big book format of these beloved songs. As the children sing, the teacher uses a pointer to underline each word. The follow-the-bouncing-ball approach to teaching reading is quite effective with some children (Segal & Adcock, 1986). Singing is a wonderful way for children to play with and enjoy language.

Children who are learning a second language need many opportunities to practice their new language in a safe classroom environment. Special Feature 3.5 offers classroom teachers suggestions on how to encourage language learning in their classrooms.

Contexts for Encouraging Language for Older Children

Just like teachers of younger children, the teachers of older students also need to provide specific contexts for helping their students to interact verbally. Older students need opportunities to learn how to share their views in an organized manner, listen thoughtfully to others, and use language for the sheer enjoyment of communicating. One context for facilitating language is Reading Workshop, discussed in Chapter 8. Here, we present three language-centered activities for older students.

Cooperative Learning Groups

Cooperative groups are an instructional context that provides the social structure for students to work together in small groups to accomplish a common goal (Calderon & Slavin, 1999). These cooperative learning groups are an ideal context for language development. Students in a cooperative group are more motivated to speak because they: (1) need to communicate to accomplish the common goal; (2) students are taught to praise and encourage each other; and (3) students are made interdependent so they need to know what the others know. Because of these factors, cooperative learning provides a supportive, motivating context for speech to emerge. Cooperative learning groups allow for multiple opportunities for listening and speaking. The talk between students is:

- Frequent: The single greatest advantage of cooperative learning over traditional classroom organization for the acquisition of language is the amount of talking students do within the group.
- Redundant: Students become fluent if they have the opportunity to speak repeatedly on the same topic. Many cooperative learning structures, such as Three Pair Share, are

Special Feature 3.5

Optimizing Oral-Language Learning Experiences for Bilingual and Second-Language Learners

Sarah Hudelson and
Irene Alicia Serna

In Chapter 2, several general points were made about young children's second-language acquisition. Second-language development was discussed from the perspective of creative construction, suggesting that learners, at their individual rates and using their individual styles, engage in figuring out how their new language works, much as they had to figure out how their native language works. The focus was on the social-interactionist perspective on language acquisition, noting that children learn a second language as they interact with others (adults and other children) in that language. This means that teachers and English-speaking children in classrooms are all language teachers. Also, as noted earlier, there is evidence that teachers of second-language learners use language in ways that are similar to the talk parents use with their young children. This observation suggests that the attributes of parental talk discussed at the beginning of Chapter 3 also would apply to adults working with second-language learners.

With this general perspective in mind, the specific recommendations for promoting oral language articulated in this chapter are discussed as they relate to educators who work in bilingual and second-language settings.

The Use of Reciprocal Discussions and Conversations with Bilingual and Second-Language Learners

Environments that promote genuine conversations and discussions—both among children themselves and between children and adults—are critical to the language growth of bilingual and second-language learners. Teachers' understandings and attitudes are central to the establishment of these linguistic contexts. In bilingual education settings, where the philosophy is to use both the children's native language and English as vehicles for learning, teachers provide non-native-English-speaking children with opportunities to extend both native and English language ability by using both languages in academic settings. As they provide these opportunities, bilingual teachers must decide how to allocate the use of the two languages in the classroom. Such allocation often depends on program design and goals, and on the language abilities of specific teachers and children (Lessow-Hurley, 1990).

Bilingual teachers may use one language for certain content or activities (such as language arts and mathematics) and the other language for other content and activities (such as science and art). Instead, one language may be used for part of the day and the other language for the rest of the time. Alternatively, the teacher and the children may use both languages freely, alternating between them in the ways that bilingual people often do (Jacobson & Faltis, 1990). In some settings, more of the native language is used in conversations and discussions when children are less comfortable in English. As the children gradually become more fluent in English, more time is spent in English. In other settings, teaming occurs, with one teacher using only a language other than English for instruction and the other educator using only English. Across these settings, the message that teachers send to children is that of valuing and using both languages and that it is possible to learn English without sacrificing their home language. In many classrooms, teachers also encourage English speakers to try to learn some of the non-English language, just as they encourage non-English speakers to use English (Reyes, Laliberty, & Orbansky, 1993; Turner, 1994).

Many elementary school teachers, however, are not bilingual and will therefore use only English

(continued on next page)

Special Feature 3.5 *(continued)*

in their teaching, even though several of their students may use languages other than English. In these settings, it is necessary for teachers to make adjustments in their ways of talking and presenting content, in order for children who are still learning English to participate more fully. These adjustments are also the case for bilingual teachers when they are working in the learners' second language. Teachers need to make adjustments in the following ways:

- Teachers need to provide contextual, extralinguistic support for their spoken language in the form of gestures, acting out, facial expressions, and use of visual aids (e.g., objects, pictures, diagrams, or films), so that visual information makes clear what is being said. Early in their language acquisition, second-language learners need more than the spoken language to understand what is going on in the classroom (Enright, 1986; Freeman & Freeman, 1994b). Their reliance on extralinguistic cues and modified input diminishes over time as they learn more English (Willett, 1995).

- Teachers need to organize class environments that are rich with materials and that provide opportunities for collaborative, hands-on experiences (Enright, 1986; Enright & McCloskey, 1988).

- Teachers need to adjust their own speech when speaking with and responding to second-language learners—focusing on the here and now, slowing down their delivery, simplifying their syntax and repeating and rephrasing, attending carefully to children's understandings or confusion, focusing on the child's meaning over correctness, and extending and expanding the second-language learner's language (Enright, 1986; Freeman & Freeman, 1994b; Lindfors, 1987).

- Teachers need to structure opportunities for second-language learners to experi-

ment with English and need to encourage learners to do so (Ernst, 1994). Early on, second-language learners may do better in situations where teachers are involved directly. As these children become more fluent, they need to interact with their peers in English and to use the new language for academic content (Willett, 1995).

- Teachers need to acknowledge that mistakes are a natural and necessary part of language learning and to set up environments that encourage risk taking and allow mistakes (Freeman & Freeman, 1994b).

- Teachers need to provide learners with feedback on their efforts within the context of their engagement with content. The focus needs to be on the learners' ability to communicate, not simply on the accuracy of grammatical forms (Freeman & Freeman, 1994b).

- Teachers need to allow children to use languages other than English as a way to negotiate content before expressing their understandings in English (Freeman & Freeman, 1994b; TESOL, 1996).

- Teachers may need to sensitize native or fluent English-speaking children to the struggles of children who are working both to learn English and to use English to learn. This may be done, for example, through using a language other than English to teach a lesson or to read a story to English-speaking children and then discussing how the children felt, what problems they had in understanding, and how they could help others in similar situations (Rudnick, 1995).

Keeping the factors just mentioned in mind should mean that children who are learning English as a second language have more opportunities to participate in classroom activities, conversations, and discussions.

(continued on next page)

The Use of Contexts for Activity-Centered Language with Bilingual and Second-Language Learners

Children, including English-language learners, learn a lot of language from each other and often prefer to interact with peers instead of with adults. English learners will learn the new language most naturally when they need to use it to engage with others, at least with some others who are more proficient in English than they are (TESOL, 1997). In a school setting, such engagement logically springs from interesting and meaningful content that children examine in collaboration with others in thematic units, in centers, and in paired and group projects. One challenge many teachers may face is how to structure activities to promote collaboration, including verbal interactions. An added challenge is how to structure groups to maximize the participation of children who are learning English.

Teachers whose classes include second-language learners need to give serious consideration to the linguistic abilities of children as they form groups. There are times when children organize their own groups. There is evidence that ESL learners who choose to work with others still learning the language can be successful at negotiating content and using English to learn, especially if the learners come from different native language backgrounds and are in the numerical minority in a classroom (Willett, 1995). At other times, however, teachers may assign children to work or play with others. At these times, particularly if the teachers have an agenda of language development along with academic learning, teachers may group heterogeneously in terms of language ability, making sure that groups contain more- and less-able users of English. In this way, the less proficient speakers learn from those with more proficiency. However, factors other than language proficiency may also need to be taken into account when organizing groups. Jerri Willett, for example, has reported that a teacher grouped

two English speakers with a Spanish speaker, thinking that the English speakers would work with the other child and thus facilitate his English development (1995). However, the two English speakers were girls, and they resisted collaborating with the Spanish-speaking boy, refusing to interact with him. Collaboration became a reality only when this young child worked (and played) with other boys.

In settings where many of the learners come from one home language (e.g., Spanish), groups may be formed that include at least one native English speaker, one child who is bilingual, and one child who speaks Spanish fluently but is not yet fluent in English. In these groupings, the bilingual learner often acts as a language broker, assisting the other children in communicating with each other (Fournier, Lansdowne, Pastenes, Steen, & Hudelson, 1992). This assumes that children are free to use languages other than English in the classroom, even if children ultimately share their work in English.

The Use of Language-Centered Activities with Bilingual and Second-Language Learners

In bilingual and second-language classrooms, many activities that teachers organize focus specifically on language. This chapter discusses the language-centered practices of read-aloud experiences, sharing, storytelling, and language play, all of which need to be considered for bilingual and ESL learners. Each language-centered practice is discussed in turn.

Read-Aloud Experiences

Reading aloud is a central component of instruction, not a frill. It is central to both first- and second-language development. Reading aloud should be done in children's home languages, as well as in English, even if there is not a formal bilingual program in place. In some Spanish-English bilingual classrooms, teachers group children by

(continued on next page)

Special Feature 3.5 *(continued)*

language for one read-aloud experience daily, so that the Spanish-dominant children listen and respond to Spanish-language literature and the English-dominant children do the same in English. At other times, the children are mixed, and both languages are used to negotiate story content.

Read-aloud experiences need to be chosen carefully. Ms. Espinosa and Ms. Moore chose some books, particularly those read early in the children's second-language development, on the basis of predictability, to ensure that the children would understand the stories. Other books should be chosen for the quality of the story, the potential for discussion by children and teacher, and cultural relevance and authenticity (Espinosa & Fournier, 1995; Hudelson, Fournier, Espinosa, & Bachman, 1994). It is important to choose some books that reflect the experiences of the children (Barrera, Ligouri & Salas, 1992).

Sharing

Sharing is a practice employed by many teachers because it gives children an opportunity to talk about aspects of their own lives and encourages them to listen to each other. There is evidence that successful participation in such classroom activities is important for ESL learners' linguistic development and for their ability to negotiate in mainstream classrooms (Ernst, 1994). However, children who are just learning English may be much less confident in using the new language than their English-speaking peers. They may speak more slowly, with more hesitations. They may not articulate as native speakers do. Their verbalizations may be incomplete or unconventional syntactically. This may make it more difficult for them to share their experiences and to get and maintain the attention of their peers. Given these realities, teachers may need to take an active role in facilitating the participation of ESL children. This role may include negotiating with others opportunities for ESL learners to talk, assisting children in articulating what they want to contribute, and sensitizing other children to their

struggles to express themselves (Ernst, 1994; Rudnick, 1995).

Storytelling

It has been our experience working with bilingual and second-language learners from many different backgrounds that many of them come from cultures where oral stories abound and storytelling traditions are strong (Au, 1993). Therefore, storytelling should occupy a prominent place in classrooms that are populated by numbers of culturally and linguistically diverse students. When teachers are telling stories, they need to incorporate stories that reflect the heritages of the children with whom they work (see, for example, Bishop, 1994; Bosma, 1994; Harris, 1992; and Miller-Lachman, 1995, for animal stories, fables, folktales, legends, and myths that might be used). Children need to be encouraged to tell stories from their cultural backgrounds. Parents may also be invited to classrooms to participate in storytelling. Storytelling opens up multiple possibilities for understanding diverse world views.

Language Play

Across cultures, children engage in language play (Lindfors, 1987). One of the oral traditions of many cultures is the sharing of rhymes, songs, riddles, games, tongue-twisters, jokes, and so on across generations and among children. Teachers should make deliberate plans to use these forms, both to foster appreciation for other languages and cultures and to provide children with opportunities to manipulate the sounds of familiar and new languages. For example, teachers can make written records of these rhymes, songs, and finger plays in Spanish and English and can use them repeatedly in daily routines such as opening exercises, transitions between activities, introduction to read-aloud time, and school closing. Because children usually chant these forms in chorus, practice with the sounds of the new language takes place in a risk-free environment.

(continued on next page)

There are many collections of such traditional lore in Spanish readily available in the United States (e.g., Bravo-Villasante, 1980; Delacre, 1989; Jaramillo, 1994; Schon, 1994). Shen's Books and Supplies (8221 South First Avenue, Arcadia, CA 91006) has collections of traditional poetry available in Japanese, Chinese, Korean, and Vietnamese, as well as in English translations. In languages where material is not available commercially, teachers might invite parents to share traditional forms. The use of material from the oral tradition is strongly recommended.

explicitly designed to provide redundancy of talking opportunities. Even informal, cooperative learning discussion provides redundancy as students discuss a topic with each of their teammates. There is not enough time in the traditional classroom to call on each student to talk more than once on a topic.

■ Developmentally appropriate: Speech to a whole class is often formal and less contextualized than speech within a cooperative group. It is easy to share an idea with a friendly peer; it is hard to answer a question or speak on an assigned topic before the whole class. Students within a small group have more opportunities to enter conversation at the level appropriate to their own development.

■ Feedback rich: Students talk to each other, providing immediate feedback and correction opportunities. Feedback and correction in the process of communication ("Give me that," "Sure, you take the ruler," etc.) lead to easy acquisition of vocabulary and language forms, whereas formal correction opportunities ("What is this?" "This is a ruler," etc.) lead to self-consciousness and anxiety, which inhibit, rather than facilitate, language acquisition.

The nature of cooperative learning activities also facilitates second-language learning because students speak in real time, about real events and objects, to accomplish real goals. They talk over things they are making and therefore negotiate meaning (Ovando & Collier, 1998).

Dramatic Simulations

Another language-centered activity ideally suited for older children is dramatic simulation or role-play. Like dramatic play for younger children, simulations allow students to try on different personas, create scripts, engage in meta-play language, and enjoy oral presentation (Brice-Heath, 1993). The following Trade Secret 3.2 by multi-age teacher Carolyn Lara shows how she uses dramatic simulations to encourage language.

Movie, Videos, Book, and Music Reviews

Another interesting way teachers can provide time for older students to share their thoughts and opinions orally is through the use of movie, book and music reviews. The following scenario provides an example of how fifth- and sixth-grade students in Mr. Falconer's

Trade Secret 3.2

How My Fourth- to Fifth-Grade Multi-Age Class Becomes Television Journalists: Using Dramatic Simulations to Encourage Language, Reading, and Cooperating

By Carolyn Lara

As a teacher of a combined fourth- and fifth-grade multi-age class, I have a number of objectives that include oral presentation and language skills. Some of the academic goals for my elementary students include being able to:

- retell stories,
- express themselves in small group settings,
- express themselves in large group settings, and
- use their language skills work cooperatively in small groups.

One way I help my students learn presentation skills is through dramatic simulations. I use this approach because I have found that older children often express themselves more freely and are less self-conscious when they role-play. I have also observed that my students use more mature vocabulary when they play adult roles.

To begin this process I schedule the first field trip of the year to a local television station. The students observe the mid-day news being televised and they have an opportunity to talk to the anchors, field reporters, and the news producer. For the next few days the class watches videos of the mid-day news show.* As a class, we analyze the news, talk about story length (typically one to two minutes), and discuss how the newscasters summarize the "who, what, when, where, and why" of each story. We also talk about how newscasters use graphics to illustrate their stories.

During our reading time we also study the characteristics of print media: the newspaper,

news magazines, our weekly readers, and so on. We examine stories for the main ideas, for supporting details, and also look at how news reporters can tell a story from multiple points of view. We practice this by reading two versions of the "Three Little Pigs": the traditional story, told from the pig's view, and *The True Story of the Three Little Pigs* (by Jon Scieszka), told from the wolf's perspective.

After the basics of newscasting have been explored, we begin to do our own weekly news show. We usually do newscasts on Friday mornings. I begin by randomly assigning students to five news beats (I pull their name cards from a bowl). One group takes world and national news, another group takes state and local news, a third group handles entertainment and the arts, a fourth takes sports, and the fifth handles the weather. After the students receive their group assignment, they individually review their section of the newspaper (each student receives a copy of the local newspaper). After ten minutes I ask the groups to convene and to decide which stories they want to report about "on air." I serve as the news producer and each group must receive story approval from me (this prevents stories that could be considered too controversial for fourth- and fifth-graders from being "aired"). Each news-beat group may only report three two-minute stories. After the news-beat groups decide which stories they want to report, they have another fifteen to twenty minutes to figure out how to summarize and present the information. During this process they have to determine the facts, write their script, and figure out the type of reporting style they wish to use: the news anchor reader approach, the "in-the-field" reporter, live on-camera eye-witness interviews, or a combination of approaches. They also must decide on graphics or props. The students are free to use any art materials they need. Among their favorite graphics are transparencies and overhead pens as they find it enjoyable to project the graphic on the screen.

Next the broadcast begins. I am the video camera operator but I also draw two student's

(continued on next page)

Trade Secret 3.2 *(continued)*

names to be coproducers. The coproducers watch the time and cue the group and the camera when to start and stop. The following is an example of a weather script the students wrote.

Celina: Today it is cold in Phoenix, just 45 degrees. (She is wearing five or six coats.) Let's ask the average person on the street what they think of our record-breaking temperatures. What do you think average person? Is it cold?

Marcus: Hey lady, I'm from Michigan, this feels like summer to me (he has put on sunglasses to make his point and he is pretending to put on sun block). I'm just afraid I'm going to get a burn.

Celina: Well, let's find an Arizona native and see what he or she thinks. You over there, yes, you. What do you think?

Regina: (wearing an sign that says AZ native) It is so cold! Did you

know that this is the coldest it has been on this day since 1943? The cold weather is being caused by a low front coming from the Gulf of Mexico.

George: (wearing a sign that says farmer) Yes, and the farmers in the area are worried about their citrus crops. If it gets too much colder we could lose a lot of grapefruits and oranges.

During this process the students have a wonderful time figuring out how to share their stories and keep the "viewing audience" watching. Many students who are too shy to raise their hands during classroom discussion often blossom in during news cast days. In addition to being a wonderful opportunity for oral expression, this project helps students with reading comprehension and learning how to work together in small groups.

Due to the oftentimes sensitive and violent nature of the news, many districts now require the news broadcast to be videotaped and prescreened by the teacher prior to the students' viewing it. Prescreening gives the teacher an opportunity to edit out any material that might cause concern to the local community. The prescreening also gives the teacher an opportunity to observe and highlight specific newscasting techniques that might be of interest to the students.

multi-age classroom have arts in review time. For a half hour after lunch on Mondays Mr. Falconer asks his students to break into small groups of three to four students to share their views of recent movies, videos, books, and music. The students are reminded to discuss only G or PG-13 movies (school-board policies restrict students and teachers from discussing R-rated movies in class).

MALCOLM: I watched *Shrek* this weekend. I saw it when it first came out but I missed some of the funny stuff the first time, like when the Gingerbread Man said "Eat Me" to the bad guy. The video also added a special feature where the characters sang and danced. That was excellent!

BRITTANY: I saw the movie but not the video. Did you know they (the filmmakers) are making fun of the guy that runs Disney. I wonder what he felt like when he saw how short they made that Lord Farquaad guy? Is he really that short?

> **JESSIE:**   I don't think he is that short, but I liked the fact that when the spell was broken that Pincess Fiona was still an ogre. It was a surprise 'cause I thought it was going to end like *Beauty and the Beast.*
>
> **BRITTANY:**   I know what you mean. It was surprising, but I thought, if she turned into a beautiful princess, how could they have a happy ending?
>
> **JESSIE:**   I think that they don't have to be the same physically to be happy—you know, both beautiful like *Beauty and the Beast* or both ogres, like Shrek. I would have liked it if they are different. How would it have been if she were an ogre and Shrek became a handsome prince?

In other parts of the room, students were talking about *Harry Potter, Lord of the Rings,* and a television special, *Walking with Prehistoric Beasts.*

During these sessions Mr. Falconer drops into the groups to listen and to share his views as a member of the discussion. He gives the small groups about fifteen minutes to talk. At the end, he asks if any group would like to share opinions with the whole group. Several of the groups talk about their discussions, and other individuals in the class offer additional comments. Mr. Falconer has noticed that since he began using this strategy to encourage oral discussion with older students, they are more willing to discuss their views during Readers' Workshop and Writing Workshop.

Assessment: Finding Out What Children Know and Can Do

By the time most children are preschoolers, their oral language is quite rich and complex. This complexity makes assessment difficult. The only way to truly capture the full richness of children's language is to tape record their conversations and then make a verbatim transcription of what is said, along with a detailed description of the context in which the language occurred. The transcript can then be analyzed to determine the mean length of sentences used, which forms of language the child used, the pragmatic rules followed, and so forth (see Genishi & Dyson, 1984). Unfortunately, such endeavors are very time-consuming and not practical in most teaching situations.

A number of more practical options are available for assessing children's oral language abilities. To illustrate these options, we use an incident recently observed by two of the authors in a university preschool. Julie is a four-year-old Korean girl who has been in the United States for about eight months. She participates in classroom activities, especially dramatic play, but rarely speaks either in Korean (she is the only child from Korea in the class) or in English. Chari, Julia's teacher, is playing with several other children at the time of the incident. Chari takes on the role of a customer and asks to use the toy phone in a post office theme center. She picks up the phone and makes a pretend phone call to Buddy, whose behavior is becoming very raucous. Chari says, "Ring, ring, ring . . . Buddy, there's a package waiting here for you in the post office." This is successful in redirecting Buddy away from the rough-and-tumble play that he had been engaging in.

Julia is playing by herself in the housekeeping center, pretending to be a parent taking care of a baby (a doll). Julia overhears Chari's pretend phone call to Buddy, but she continues with her solitary play. A few minutes later, Julia picks up a toy phone in the housekeeping center, and says: "Ring, ring ... Miss Chari, will you come over to my house?" This is Julia's first complete sentence used in the classroom!

Chari has several options for recalling Julia's language breakthrough. She might use a checklist. Figure 3.2 is a checklist used in a multilingual classroom. This checklist focuses on Michael Halliday's (1975) functional uses of language (see Table 2.1, page 27). Such checklists are easy to use and require little time. This checklist can be easily modified to fit other situations (for example, for a monolingual classroom, the language columns could be eliminated) or to focus on other aspects of language (grammatical forms could replace Halliday's functional uses of language). Such instruments provide a broad view of the language that children use in the classroom. However, much of the richness of the children's actual language is lost.

Chari might use an anecdotal record. Anecdotal records are even less structured than an observation recording form (Figure 3.3). Here, the teacher writes a brief description of the language incident on a piece of paper, index card, or Post-it-Note™. Later, Chari can

Child's Name	Language			Partner(s)			Location								Function						
	English	Spanish	Other	Child	Several Children	Adult	Library	Writing	Listening	Housekeeping	Theme (play)	Blocks	Math/Sci	Art	Instrumental	Regulatory	Interaction	Personal	Heuristic	Imaginative	Informative
Julia	✓									✓										✓	

FIGURE 3.2   Oral language checklist

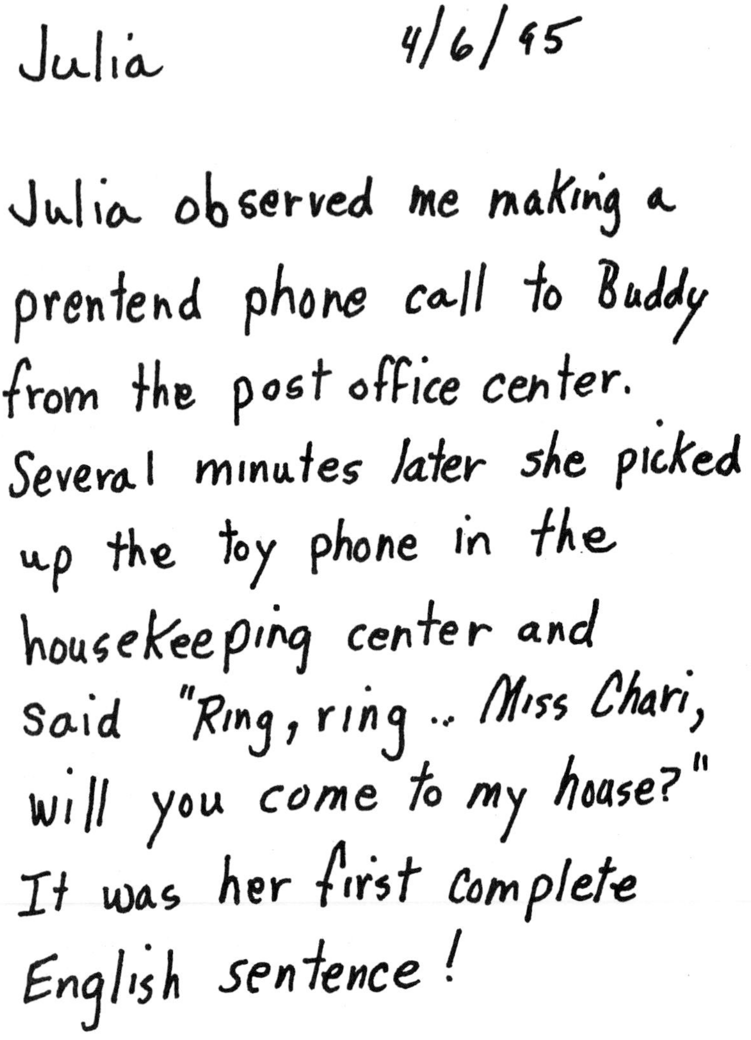

Julia   4/6/95

Julia observed me making a prentend phone call to Buddy from the post office center. Several minutes later she picked up the toy phone in the housekeeping center and said "Ring, ring ... Miss Chari, will you come to my house?" It was her first complete English sentence!

FIGURE 3.3   Anecdotal record

file these anecdotes in individual folders for each of her children. This unstructured format allows Chari to make a detailed description of Julia's language exchange with her. Of course, anecdotal records require more time and effort on the part of the teacher than do the two previous methods.

As suggested earlier, teachers may elect to make audio or video recordings of children's language activity. Genishi and Dyson (1984) have developed guidelines for making audio recordings. These are adapted to include video recordings:

- Select an activity setting that encourages language interaction. (Dramatic play areas are a good place to start.)

- If you are using a tape recorder, place it in the target setting and turn it on, checking first to make sure that the equipment is working. If using a video camcorder, place the camera on a tripod and adjust the zoom lens so that it covers the main area where children will be interacting. Turn the camera on, and check it occasionally to make sure that the camera angle is capturing the significant action.
- Do a trial recording to make sure that the equipment is working correctly and that the children's language is being clearly recorded. This trial will also help desensitize the children to the equipment.
- Listen to or view the recordings as soon as possible so that your memory can help fill in the gaps in unintelligible parts of the recordings.

An effective way to analyze the data contained in audio and video recordings is to use a rubric to judge the quality of individual's oral language behavior. A rubric is a set of criteria that describe student performance in terms of proficiency levels (O'Neil 1994). Figure 3.4 offers an example of a rubric that can be used to assess older children's oral presentations and guide their efforts to develop more effective presentations.

Summary

This chapter began with a review of the many ways parents can support their child's language development within the home. The remainder of the chapter described ways that teachers can provide young children with stimulating oral language experiences that promote active listening and more precise, sophisticated speech. How did your own experiences at home and at school compare with those described in this chapter? Did you recall other types of beneficial oral language activities that were not covered?

To summarize the key points about facilitating oral language learning, we return to the guiding questions at the beginning of this chapter:

- *How can parents best facilitate their children's oral language development?*

Parents can promote their children's oral language by scaffolding their language, encouraging them to tell personal narratives about their experiences, reading stories to them on a regular basis, and monitoring their children's TV viewing and encouraging active viewing.

- *What is the initiation, response, evaluation (IRE) pattern of class talk? What problems are associated with this type of discourse? How can teachers provide children with more stimulating conversations in the classroom?*

The IRE pattern of discourse occurs when the teacher asks a question, a student answers, and the teacher either accepts or rejects that answer and goes on to ask another question. These types of question-and-answer exchanges do not provide the type of language input and feedback needed to advance children's language skills. Teachers can provide richer oral language experiences for children by engaging them in reciprocal conversations and discussions—listening closely and responding to their comments; asking genuine, open-ended questions; welcoming the interjection of personal experiences; and encouraging child–child turn-taking.

FIGURE 3.4 A Rubric to Assess Oral Presentations

Evaluating Student Presentations

	1	2	3	4	Total
Organization	Audience cannot understand presentation because there is no sequence of information.	Audience has difficulty following presentation because student jumps around.	Student presents information in logical sequence that audience can follow.	Student presents information in logical, interesting sequence that audience can follow.	
Subject Knowledge	Student does not have grasp of information; student cannot answer questions about subject.	Student is uncomfortable with information and is able to answer only rudimentary questions.	Student is at ease with expected answers to all questions, but fails to elaborate.	Student demonstrates full knowledge by answering all class questions with explanations and elaboration.	
Graphics	Student uses superfluous graphics or no graphics.	Student occasionally uses graphics that don't support text and presentation.	Student's graphics relate to text and presentation.	Student's graphics explain and reinforce screen text and presentation.	
Mechanics	Student's presentation has four or more grammatical errors.	Presentation has three misspellings and/or grammatical errors.	Presentation has no more than two misspellings and/or grammatical errors.	Presentation has no misspellings or grammatical errors.	
Eye Contact	Student reads all of report with no eye contact.	Student occasionally uses eye contact, but still reads most of the report.	Student maintains eye contact most of the time but frequently returns to notes.	Student maintains eye contact with audience, seldom returning to notes.	
Elocution	Student mumbles, incorrectly pronounces terms, and speaks too quietly for students in the back of class to hear.	Student's voice is low. Student incorrectly pronounces terms. Audience members have difficulty hearing presentation.	Student's voice is clear. Student pronounces most words correctly. Most audience members can hear presentation.	Student uses a clear voice and correct, precise pronunciation of terms so that all audience members can hear presentation.	

Adapted from a rubric developed by Information Technology Evaluation Services, NC Department of Public Instruction

■ *How do group activities, learning centers, and dramatic play promote oral language acquisition?*

These types of activities create language content (i.e., give children something to talk about). In addition, children must use language to participate successfully in these types of activity.

■ *What can teachers do to promote language-rich dramatic play?*

Teachers can promote language-rich play by providing (1) settings equipped with theme-related, culturally-relevant props; (2) scheduling lengthy play periods; and (3) being actively involved in children's play activities.

■ *How can sharing or show-and-tell be turned into a valuable oral language activity?*

Traditional sharing involves having one child speak to the entire class. This activity can be transformed into a valuable oral language activity by limiting group size and encouraging children in the audience to actively participate by ask questions and making comments.

■ *How can teachers effectively assess children's oral language development?*

Teachers should observe children interacting during regular classroom activities and use checklists, observation sheets, and/or anecdotal records to document significant milestones in their oral language acquisition.

■ *What can teachers do to optimize oral language experiences for bilingual and second-language learners?*

The same strategies recommended for native English speakers are also appropriate for use with bilingual and second-language learners. The major adaptations that are needed are (1) exposing children to books and other print in child's native language, and (2) allowing children lots of opportunity to speak, listen, read, and write in their native language.

LINKING KNOWLEDGE TO PRACTICE

1. Visit an early childhood classroom and observe children interacting in a dramatic play center. Note the theme that the children are acting out and the roles that they are playing. Record examples of both metaplay language and pretend language.

2. Observe children engaging in a sharing (show-and-tell) activity. Describe the teacher's role and the children's behavior (both the speaker and the audience). Did this sharing time involve most of the students in active listening?

3. Make an observation recording form similar to the one in Figure 3.3. Visit an early childhood classroom and observe a small group of children interacting at a learning center. Use the observation recording form to record several significant utterances from each child. What do these behaviors indicate about each child's language development?

4 The Beginnings of Reading and Writing

Snuggled next to her mother, one-year-old Tiffany is listening to one of her best-loved bedtime stories, Goodnight Moon, *by Margaret Wise Brown (1947, Scholastic). Her mother reads:*

> And two little kittens
> And a pair of mittens
> And a little toy house
> And a young mouse.

Pointing to the picture, Tiffany says, "Mamma, da mousey."
"That's right, Tiffany," says her mother, who resumes reading:

> And a comb and a brush and a bowl full of mush
> And a quiet old lady who was whispering Hush.

Tiffany, touching the pictures of the bunny mother sitting in the rocking chair, says, "Dat's like Nane Gammaw."
Her mother replies, "Yes, Tiffany, she looks like Grandma."
Throughout the story, Tiffany comments on the illustrations. As her mother finishes the last line,

> Goodnight stars, goodnight air, goodnight noises everywhere.

a very sleepy Tiffany yawns, "Ganight, Mamma."

As children sit in their parents' or other caregivers' laps, surrounded with love and attention, the storybook is a wonderful introduction to the world of print. Are you surprised to learn that *Goodnight Moon* was the first book Tiffany read to her teacher in first grade?

For children living in a culture that values literacy, the process of learning to read and write begins very early, often before their first birthdays. In recent years, researchers have made great progress in expanding our understanding of early literacy development. We now know that children acquire written language in much the same way that they learn oral language. Both are social, constructive processes. With oral language, children listen to the language that surrounds them, detect patterns and regularities, and make up their own rules for speech. Children then try out and refine these rules as they engage in everyday activities with others. With written language, children observe the print that surrounds them and watch their parents and others use reading and writing to get things done in daily life. They then construct their own concepts and rules about literacy, and they try out those ideas in social situations. With experience, these child-constructed versions of reading and writing become increasingly similar to conventional adult forms. Yet, as noted in Chapter 1, children need more instruction from adults to become readers and writers than they do to become speakers.

Social interaction plays a key role in early literacy learning. Susan Neuman (1998, p. 68) explains:

> Especially in these early years, literacy is a profoundly social process that enters children's lives through their interactions in a variety of activities and relationships with other people. Close observations suggest that children often become interested in writing and reading because it can be useful for them in their social relationships; it can give them power, help them to better understand the world around them, and enable them to express their feelings of friendship or frustration. As they learn about written language and how to use it in contexts and activities that are personally meaningful, children will even seek help from others who are more competent and who can serve as spontaneous apprentices.

To place this current view of early literacy development in historical perspective, we begin by describing its predecessors. These traditional ways of looking at beginning reading and writing are commonly known as the readiness and earlier-is-better views. Next, we discuss the new view of early literacy learning and the research on which this perspective is based. Finally, two case studies are used to illustrate two children's early literacy development: Tiffany, a native English speaker, and Alicia, a Spanish-speaking kindergartner.

Before Reading This Chapter, Think About . . .

- your early experiences with storybooks. Do you recall snuggling into an adult's lap and sharing a storybook? Did this happen regularly, at bedtime? In line at the supermarket? On the bus? What were your favorite books as a young child?
- how you learned to read and write. Do you remember reading and writing at home before going to school? Do you remember having lots of books in your home? Do you remember having access to paper and pencils? Were you an early reader—that is, did you learn to read without any formal instruction from an adult?

Focus Questions

- How does the early literacy view of young children's literacy development compare with the readiness and earlier-is-better views?
- What knowledge about written language do young children exhibit when adults watch them closely?
- What is the relationship among oral language, phonemic awareness, and phonics?
- What are emergent writing and emergent reading?
- What home factors affect young children's literacy development?
- What does early literacy look like in a language other than English?

BOX **4.1**

Definitions of Terms

alphabetic principle: knowing that there is a systematic relationship between the letters of written language and the sounds of oral language.

conventions of print: social rules (left-to-right and top-to-bottom sequence, spaces between words) and terminology (letter, word, page) of written language.

early literacy: the new view of literacy development suggesting that children learn literacy by constructing, testing, and refining their own hypotheses about print.

emergent reading: forms of reading young children use as they move toward conventional reading.

emergent writing: forms of writing young children use as they move toward conventional writing.

graphic awareness: visually recognizing environmental print, letters, and words.

logographic reading: using environmental print's entire context to give meaning to the print, to read the word.

phonemes: smallest units of speech that make a difference in meaning. For example, toad has three phonemes: /t/, /o/, /d/.

phonemic awareness: understanding that words consist of a sequence of phonemes.

phonics: making connections between letters in written words and sounds (phonemes) in speech.

Traditional Views of Literacy Development

Some years ago, it was assumed that written language is acquired in a totally different manner than is speech. According to this view, literacy development starts much later than oral-language acquisition, and it involves totally different learning processes. Children were not considered to be ready to begin learning to read and write until about age six, and this learning was not believed to occur naturally (Durkin, 1987). Children needed to be taught, using basal readers, worksheets, handwriting practice, spelling workbooks, and grammar exercises. Literacy instruction was serious business, best left in the hands of specially trained teachers. Parents were cautioned not to try to encourage early reading or writing for fear that children might learn incorrect concepts and skills, which would later have to be untaught by teachers.

This traditional view of literacy development can be traced to the maturational theories of the mid-1920s (Gesell, 1928). It was believed that children had to reach a certain level of intelligence and physical maturity before they could learn to read and write. During this same period, the concept of readiness skills took hold. According to this view, children needed to master a number of visual, auditory, and motor skills before they could learn to read. Reading readiness tests were developed to measure children's mastery of these skills, and readiness workbooks designed to promote perceptual-motor growth soon became a standard component of the beginning levels of basal reading programs (Stallman & Pearson, 1990).

The merger of the maturation and readiness orientations led to the persistent belief that early childhood was a time during which readiness skills should be taught as a prelude

FIGURE 4.1   Visual discrimination worksheet

to real reading and writing (Teale & Sulzby, 1986). As a result, kindergarten and beginning first-grade students did lots of readiness activities that had little to do with actual reading. Figure 4.1 illustrates a typical reading readiness worksheet item. This visual discrimination exercise requires students to find the house that matches the one on the far left. Children usually did not have access to books until the middle part of first grade. Writing instruction was postponed even later, after handwriting, spelling, and phonics skills had been mastered.

Sparked by the launching of the Soviet satellite *Sputnik* in 1957 and the resulting uproar that American education needed to catch up with Soviet education, attitudes about delaying reading instruction finally started to change. This event, combined with a growing awareness of the importance of early learning and a concern about the education of children from low-income families, led to a movement to begin academic instruction at a much younger age (Elkind, 1990). The result of this earlier-is-better orientation was to shift the timing of traditional practices downward. Reading readiness workbooks and worksheets, which had been used in kindergarten and first grade, now began appearing in preschools. Basal preprimers and worksheets providing isolated drill on letter recognition and phonics became common in kindergartens.

This earlier-is-better phenomenon was hardly an improvement over the traditional readiness approach. Both had serious shortcomings. The traditional approach withheld reading and writing activities from many faster-developing children who were ready and eager to begin mastering written language. In contrast, the earlier-is-better movement required slower-developing children to engage in structured instructional activities (phonics worksheets, lengthy teacher-led lessons, basal preprimers) for which they were not developmentally ready. The resulting mismatch between the instructional demands and children's capabilities often caused slower-developing children to fail in their initial school-literacy experiences. This failure, in turn, fostered negative attitudes about reading and writing that were very difficult to reverse later on.

Current Perspectives on Early Literacy

Fortunately, at the same time that the earlier-is-better movement was taking hold, several new areas of research emerged, which were eventually to lead to a radically different conception of early literacy development. According to this new perspective, which has come to be commonly known as emergent literacy (Yaden, Rowe, & MacGillivray, 2000), written language acquisition has much in common with oral language development. Children begin learning about reading and writing at a very early age by observing and interacting with readers and writers and through their attempts to read and write (Sulzby & Teale, 1991). Each reading and writing attempt teaches children, as they test out what they believe about how written language works. Based on others' responses, their beliefs are modified. The next time they read or write, they test out their new knowledge. The term *emergent* conveys the evolving nature of children's concepts as they move from personalized, idiosyncratic notions about the function, structure, and conventions of print toward conventional reading and writing. As Catherine Snow and her colleagues (1998, p. 45) note, "growing up to be a reader [and writer] is a lengthy process. . . ."

Susan Neuman and Kathy Roskos (1998) point out several problems associated with the terms *emergent* and *conventional*. *Emergent* implies that there is a distinct point at which literacy acquisition begins, and *conventional* implies that there is a point at which acquisition suddenly ends with the appearance of fully mature reading and writing. Neuman and Roskos (1998, p. 2) argue, to the contrary:

> It is now recognized that there is no beginning point. Even at a young age, children are legitimate writers and readers. Similarly, there can be no end point, no single boundary denoting conventionalized practices. Rather, literacy development begins early, is ongoing, and is continuous throughout a lifetime.

We are going to follow Neuman and Roskos' lead and use the term *early literacy* throughout this book to refer to the new perspective on literacy acquisition.

Interest in early literacy began with studies of early readers, children who learned to read before they entered kindergarten. This research led to investigations of what preschool-age children typically learn about print. At the same time, researchers began to investigate children's home literacy experiences, seeking to discover the factors that promote early literacy acquisition.

The following sections review major findings of four strands of research on early literacy: early readers, children's concepts about print, early forms of reading and writing, and home literacy experiences. Many of these research studies link acquisition of knowledge or skills with specific ages. It is important to note that there are large individual differences in literacy development and that the ages at which particular knowledge or skills appear will vary widely for specific children. In fact, it is not unusual to find up to a five-year range in children's literacy development within a kindergarten classroom (IRA/NAEYC, 1998).

Part of this variation in the rate of literacy acquisition is due to differences in children's innate intelligence and aptitude. Considerable diversity also exists in children's experiences with oral and written language during the early years (IRA/NAEYC, 1998). That is, some children live in homes with adults who provide the kind of resources and support that optimize literacy acquisition, and others do not. In addition, variations exist in how essential written language is for communicating in different cultures (Neuman & Roskos, 1993). In cultures with a strong oral tradition, the motivation for acquiring literacy may not be as strong as in cultures emphasizing the importance of written language.

Early Readers

Early readers are children who learn to read during the preschool years without receiving formal instruction from their parents or teachers. Teachers who subscribed to the traditional readiness view were well aware that such children existed. These children created problems because their needs did not match with the reading readiness curriculum (Hall, 1987). The general consensus was that these early readers were intellectually gifted and that their high IQ was responsible for their early acquisition of literacy.

In the mid-1960s and early 1970s, researchers in the United States and Great Britain began to study these children (Clark, 1976; Durkin, 1966). Results showed that many early readers were of normal intelligence, contradicting the commonly assumed link between early reading and giftedness. Parental interviews revealed that these children shared several characteristics:

1. They were curious about written language at a very young age, asking many questions about letters, words, and print.
2. They showed an early interest in writing and liked to scribble, write their names, send notes, and so forth.
3. They loved to have favorite stories read to them over and over again.
4. They had a parent, older sibling, or other adult who answered their questions about written language and who read to them on a regular basis.

These findings suggested that home experiences had an important role in promoting early reading.

Concepts about Print

Research on early readers in turn stimulated interest in what typical children were learning about literacy during the preschool years. The earliest studies on this topic were conducted in laboratory settings and had rather negative results, reporting that preschool-age children had only vague conceptions about reading and writing (Downing & Oliver, 1973–1974). In these studies, children were typically taken out of their classrooms and interviewed by a researcher; the adult, the setting, and the situation were not familiar to the children.

More recent studies have shifted the focus to the knowledge about literacy that young children exhibit in everyday situations at home or in school classrooms. This shift in perspective has resulted in an entirely different picture of preschool-age children's print awareness.

One of the first concepts about literacy that children learn is the distinction between print and pictures. Most children discover the print—picture distinction quite early, often by age three. Ask three-year-olds to draw a picture and to write their names. Their markings when asked to draw a picture likely will be quite different from those made when asked to write their names. This distinction is important because it establishes a separate identity for print and allows children to begin learning about its functions and structure.

Research indicates that children's knowledge about print follows a loose developmental sequence (Lomax & McGee, 1987):

1. general concepts about the purpose and functions of print;
2. graphic awareness—the ability to visually recognize environmental print, letters, and words;
3. phonemic awareness—the concept that words consist of a sequence of spoken sounds (phonemes); and
4. letter–sound relationships (phonics).

In the following sections, we provide brief reviews of the research on each of these topics.

Purpose and Functions of Print.   One of the earliest discoveries that children make about written language is that print has meaning. Jerry Harste, Virginia Woodward, and Carolyn Burke (1984) found that many three-year-olds expect print to be meaningful. This understanding becomes evident when children point to words on signs, cereal boxes, or menus and ask, "What does that say?" Alternatively, after making marks on a piece of paper, children make comments such as, "What did I write?" or "This says . . . "

A related discovery is that print is functional; it can be used to get things done in daily life. Children's knowledge of the practical uses of print grows substantially during the preschool years. Elfrieda Hiebert (1981) found that three-year-olds demonstrated limited knowledge of the purposes of several types of print, such as labels on Christmas presents, street signs, and store signs, but five-year-olds showed much greater knowledge of these functions.

Children's knowledge of the functional uses of literacy frequently shows up in their make-believe play. For example, Marcia Baghban (1984) recounts how she took her 28-month-old daughter Giti out to eat at a restaurant. On returning home, Giti promptly acted out the role of a waitress, making marks on a pad of paper while recording her mother's food orders. Other researchers have reported numerous incidents of preschoolers' engaging in a variety of functional literacy activities while engaging in dramatic play, including jotting down phone messages, writing checks to pay for purchases, looking up recipes in cookbooks, and making shopping lists (Neuman & Roskos, 1991b, 1997; Vukelich, 1992).

Graphic Awareness.   Children begin to recognize environmental print—print that occurs in real-life contexts—at a very early age. Several researchers (e.g., Goodman, 1986; Lomax & McGee, 1987; Mason, 1980) have shown that many three- and four-year-olds can recognize and know the meanings of product labels (Colgate, Cheerios, Pepsi), restaurant signs (McDonald's, Pizza Hut), and street signs (Stop). Even if children do not say the correct word when attempting to read such print, they usually will come up with a related term. For example, when presented with a Coke can, the child might say "Pepsi."

In recognizing environmental print, children attend to the entire context rather than just the print (Masonheimer, Drum, & Ehri, 1984). This *logographic reading* begins quite early. Yetta Goodman (1986) found that 80 percent of the four-year-olds in her study could recognize environmental print in full context—they knew that a can of Pepsi Cola said

Grocery stores are many children's first libraries.

Pepsi. Typically, by mid-kindergarten, many children learn to recognize a limited set of whole words without environmental context clues, using incidental cues such as shape, length, and pictures (Ehri, 1991).

Children often begin to recognize the letters of the alphabet at about the same time as they "read" environmental print. This ability varies considerably among children, with some children recognizing one third of the alphabet by age three (Hiebert, 1981), and others not learning any letters until they enter kindergarten (Morgan, 1987). As is explained later in this chapter, variations in children's home literacy experiences appear to be responsible for some of these differences.

Interest appears to be a key factor in determining the specific letters that children learn first (McGee & Richgels, 1989). Children's own names and highly salient environmental print are often the source of initial letter learning. Marcia Baghban (1984), for example, describes how K (K-Mart), M (McDonald's), and G (Giti) were among the first letters recognized by her two-year-old daughter Giti.

The ability to recognize letters is an important step in early literacy development. Children must realize that words are made up of individual letters in order to grasp the *alphabetic principle* that underlies written English. As explained in the next section, this principle is an important prerequisite to invented spelling, decoding, and independent reading. Children's letter recognition ability has been repeatedly shown to be a powerful predictor of later reading achievement (Adams, 1990). We present strategies for helping children learn the alphabet in Chapter 7.

Phonemic Awareness.   In order to become fluent readers and writers, children need to move beyond *logographic* reading (recognition of environmental print and whole words) and understand that sentences are composed of individual words, that words are composed of combinations of individual letters, and that these letters have a relationship to the phonemes (smallest units of sound) of speech. Understanding this *alphabetic principle—* that there is a systematic relationship between the letters of written language and the sounds of oral language—requires more than letter recognition. Children must also become aware that the words in speech are composed of sequences of individual sounds or phonemes. This conscious awareness of phonemes sets the stage for children to discover the relationship between letters and sounds that will, in turn, facilitate the recognition of words that are in their oral vocabulary but are not familiar in print (Stanovich, 1986). In addition, children need to be able to isolate sounds in words in order to use invented spellings in their writing (Richgels, Poremba, & McGee, 1996).

Most children come to understand the phonological structure of speech gradually during their preschool years. Adults report observing children as young as two or three years of age playing with sounds. For example, young children rhyme words, (e.g., bunny, sunny, funny), or they mix words (e.g., pancake, canpake). These children are exhibiting phonological awareness. According to Catherine Snow and her colleagues (1998), for most children phonemic awareness begins when they appreciate alliteration. That is, they under-stand that two words begin with the same sound (e.g., baby and boy begin with /b/). This is a challenging task for young children. It is not until children are five or six that the major-ity of them can identify words that begin with particular phonemes. Those children whose oral language is the most proficient are the children whose phonemic awareness is the most developed.

On entering school, children's level of phonemic awareness is one of the strongest predictors of success in learning to read (Adams, 1990). In fact, phonemic awareness has been shown to account for 50 percent of the variance in children's reading proficiency at the end of first grade (Adams, Foorman, Lundberg, & Beeler, 1998).

Unfortunately, phonemic awareness is difficult for many young children to acquire. Marilyn Adams and her colleagues (1998, p. 19) report that

> Phonemic awareness eludes roughly 25 percent of middle-class first graders and substan-tially more of those who come from less literacy-rich backgrounds. Furthermore, these chil-dren evidence serious difficulty in learning to read and write.

One reason that phonemic awareness is difficult to learn is that there are few clues in speech to signal the separate phonemes that make up words (Ehri, 1997). Instead, phonemes over-lap with each other and fuse together into syllabic units. Adams and her colleagues (1998) give the example of *bark*. They point out that this word is not pronounced /b/, /a/, /r/, /k/. Instead, the pronunciation of the medial vowel *a* is influenced by the consonants that pre-cede and follow it. Because phonemes are not discrete units of sound, they are very abstract and are difficult for children to recognize and manipulate (Yopp, 1992).

Ample evidence exists that phonemic awareness can be developed through instruction (Adams et al., 1998). However, there is considerable controversy over how this important skill should be taught. A variety of strategies are available, ranging from direct instruction using isolated words to activities involving rhymes and games. As will become apparent in Chapter 7, we favor approaches that make this difficult concept enjoyable and interesting for young children to learn.

Letter–Sound Relationships (Phonics).   Once children have acquired phonemic awareness, they can begin to make connections between letters in written words and the phonemes in speech. Young children's knowledge of letter–sound relationships becomes evident when they begin using invented spellings in their early writing. Figure 4.2 illustrates young Sareena's invented spelling. Note how she used letter–sound relationships in choosing the one or two letters used to represent each word: *g* for going, *pz* for pizza, *ht* for hut, and so on. In Chapter 7, we present developmentally appropriate strategies for promoting children's phonics learning.

Conventions of Print.   Conventions of print refer to the social rules (left-to-right and top-to-bottom sequence, spaces between words, capitalizing the first letter of each sentence) and terminology (letter, word, page) that surround written language. Knowledge of these conventions tends to grow slowly. For example, knowledge of the left-to-right and top-to-bottom sequence of print is often not acquired until age five or six, and metalinguistic terms such as *letter* and *word* continue to confuse many children during the primary grades (Clay, 1972).

Early Forms of Reading and Writing

Traditionally, strict criteria have been used to define the onset of reading and writing. Children were not considered to be reading until they could correctly recognize numerous printed words, and they were not considered to be writing until they had mastered correct letter formation and could spell words conventionally. Children's early attempts at reading (labeling illustrations or making up a story to go along with the pictures in a book) and their early tries at writing (scribbles or random groups of letters) were dismissed as insignificant and inconsequential.

As interest in early literacy increased during the 1970s, some researchers began focusing attention on these initial attempts at reading and writing (Clay, 1975; Read, 1971). It soon became clear that these early forms appeared to be purposeful and rule governed. Children appeared to construct, test, and perfect hypotheses about written language. Research began to reveal general developmental sequences, with the early forms of reading

FIGURE 4.2   Sareena's invented spelling: "I am going to Pizza Hut today"

and writing gradually becoming more conventional with age and experience (Ferreiro & Teberosky, 1982; Sulzby, Barnhart, & Hieshima, 1989). In Table 4.1, we describe the stages that most children progress through in their early reading and writing.

Emergent Writing.   Building on the earlier work of Marie Clay (1975) and of Emilia Ferreiro and Ana Teberosky (1982), Elizabeth Sulzby asked preschool children to write stories and to read what they had written (Sulzby, 1985b, 1990). Based on this research, Sulzby (1990) has identified seven broad categories of early writing: drawing as writing, scribble writing, letter-like units, nonphonetic letter strings, copying from environmental print, invented spelling, and conventional writing (see Figure 4.3).

Sulzby believes that these categories do not form a strict developmental hierarchy. While there is a general movement from less mature forms toward conventional forms, children move back and forth across these forms when composing texts, and they often combine several different types in the same composition. Several of the examples in Figure 4.3 show this type of form mixing. Angela's shopping list contains drawings to represent cookies and a hamburger, while a scribble stands for the word *and*. Pierce used both invented spelling and copying from environmental print to write his prescription for the sick teddy bear. Children also appear to adjust their form of writing to the task at hand. Kindergartners tend to use invented or conventional spellings when writing single words. When writing longer pieces of text, they often shift to less mature forms, such as nonphonetic letter strings or scribbles, which require less time and effort (Sulzby & Teale, 1991).

TABLE 4.1   The Stages of Emergent Reading and Writing

Emergent Reading	Emergent Writing
1. **Attending to pictures, not forming stories**—The child looks at the pictures in the book and labels or makes comments about them.	1. **Drawing as writing**—The child draws a picture or set of pictures to represent writing.
2. **Attending to pictures, forming oral stories**—The child looks at the book's pictures and creates a story, using intonation that sounds like he or she is telling an oral story.	2. **Scribble writing**—The child writes using continuous wavy lines.
3. **Attending to pictures, forming written stories**—The child looks at the book's pictures and creates a story, using intonation that sounds like reading.	3. **Letter-like units**—The child writes using a series of separate marks that have some letterlike characteristics.
4. **Attending to print**—The child attends to the print rather than to the pictures when attempting to read the story. The child may refuse to read because of print awareness, may use only selected aspects of print (e.g., letter–sound relationships), or may read conventionally.	4. **Nonphonetic letter strings**—The child writes using strings of real letters that show no evidence of letter–sound relationships.
	5. **Copying from environmental print**—The child copies conventional print found in the environment.
	6. **Invented spelling**—The child spells words using letter names and letter–sound relationships.
	7. **Conventional spelling**—The child uses correct spelling for most words.

Based on Sulzby (1990) and Sulzby and Barnhart (1990).

Drawing as writing—Pictures represent writing.

Context: Angela (age 4), who is playing in the housekeeping center, makes a shopping list for a trip to the supermarket.

Text: "Hamburgers [the two bottom circles] and chocolate chip cookies [the two top circles]"

Scribble writing—Continuous lines represent writing.

Context: Rimmert Jr. (age 6) writes a thank-you letter to a family friend.

Text: "Thank you for your letter from America."

Letter-like units—The child makes a series of separate marks that have some letter-like characteristics

Context: Lauren (age 4) writes a story about a recent experience.

Text: "I buy the food at the store. I baked it, and I washed it and ate it."

Nonphonetic letter strings—The child writes strings of letters that show no evidence of letter–sound relationships. These can be random groups of letters or repeated clusters of letters.

FIGURE 4.3   Sulzby's Categories of Emergent Writing

(continued)

Context: Debbie (age 4) writes in her journal about a recent school experience.
Text: "We play together, and Bobby fought with us. We fight with him, then we play again."

Copying from environmental print—The child copies print found in the environment.

Context: Pierce (age 4), in the role of a veterinarian, writes a prescription for a sick teddy bear. He
               copies the words *apple juice* from a can he has retrieved from a nearby garbage can.
Text: "Penicillin" [invented spelling]
               "Apple juice" [copying]

Invented spelling—The child creates his or her own spelling using letter–sound relationships. This
can range from using one letter per word to using a letter for every sound in each word (as in the
example below).

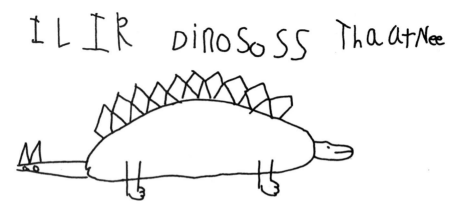

FIGURE 4.3   Continued

Context: Chris (age 5) writes in his journal.
Text: "I like dinosaurs. They are neat."

Conventional—The child uses correct spelling for most of the words.

Context: Johnny (age 5) writes in his journal.
Text: "This is a dog jumping over a box."

FIGURE 4.3   Continued

Sulzby cautions teachers against having unrealistic expectations of children's emergent writing capabilities. Case studies of early readers (Baghban, 1984; Bissex, 1980) might lead teachers to expect that invented spelling is a common occurrence among four- and five-year-olds. However, Sulzby's longitudinal research has revealed that children's writing development is typically much slower, with invented spelling not arriving until late kindergarten for some and not until the end of first grade for others (Sulzby & Teale, 1991). Both groups of children (the early and the late spellers) are normal.

Emergent Reading.   Sulzby has also investigated the patterns in children's early attempts at reading familiar storybooks (Sulzby, 1985a). She found that children's storybook-reading behaviors appeared to follow a developmental pattern, with their attention gradually shifting from the pictures to the text and their vocalizations changing from sounding like oral storytelling to sounding like reading. The following is a condensed list of Sulzby's storybook-reading categories (Sulzby & Barnhart, 1990):

1. *Attending to pictures, not forming stories*—The child looks at the pictures in the book, labeling or making comments about them.

2. *Attending to pictures, forming oral stories*—The child looks at the book's pictures and weaves a story across the pages. However, the child's intonation sounds like she or he is telling an oral story. The listener must be able to see the pictures to follow the story.

3. *Attending to pictures, forming written stories*—The child reads by looking at the book's pictures, and the child's wording and intonation sound like reading. The listener does not usually have to see the pictures to follow the story.

4. *Attending to print*—The child attends to the print rather than to the pictures when attempting to read the story. The child may refuse to read because of print awareness, may use only selected aspects of print (e.g., letter–sound relationships), or may read conventionally.

Allison's (age five) emergent reading of "The Hare and the Tortoise" is illustrated in Special Feature 4.1. Her reading is representative of Sulzby's category, "attending to pictures, forming written stories." Notice how Allison has memorized parts of the story and paraphrases the rest of the text, using her own words to reconstruct its meaning.

Other studies by Sulzby revealed that children's reading of their own emergent writing follows roughly the same pattern (Sulzby, Barnhart, & Hieshima, 1989). First, children refuse to read or claim that they did not write. Next, they label or describe what they have written. This is followed by making up stories to go along with their writing, with their voice shifting gradually from sounding like oral language to sounding like reading. Finally, children begin to actually attend to the print that they have written, reading "aspectually" (just attending to letter–sound relationships or to selected whole words that can be recognized by sight) at first and then conventionally.

Research has shown that young children's emergent readings can be influenced by the number of times a child has heard a book read (Pappas & Brown, 1987) and how many times the child has read the book independently (Pappas, 1993). Repeated readings of a book, either by the child or adult, increases the degree to which children's subsequent emergent reading approximates the actual text of the book. In addition, text features, such as pictures and grammatical subordination, and narrative structure have been found to affect children's emergent reading, as measured by the Sulzby scale (Elster, 1998). Thus, children's emergent reading levels should be expected to vary, depending on the features and familiarity of the texts being read.

Interestingly, children's level of early reading does not always correspond to their early writing (Sulzby, Barnhart, & Hieshima, 1989). For example, a child might be able to write with invented spelling, using letter–sound relationships to encode words. However, the same child might not use letter–sound relationships when decoding words during reading. So children who begin to use invented spelling are not automatically able to read their

Allison's Emergent Reading of "The Hare and the Tortoise"

Text	Re-enactment
Once upon a time, a hare and a tortoise lived near a large. . . . They lived in a large open field.	Once upon a time there lived a hare and a tortoise.
Every day, the hare went zigzagging across the field, with a *hippity-hop, hoppity-hop*. His long hind legs made it easy for him to move quickly. If danger was near, off he would scamper, quick as a flash.	Every day the hare goes zigzagging across the field, with a *hippity-hop, hoppity hop*. When danger was near, he would scamper off in the quick of the night.
The tortoise, on the other hand, was not very fast. He plodded along slowly, without a care in the world.	The tortoise and the hare were slow. He didn't care if the tortoise—the hare made fun of him. He plodded along slowly, without a care in the world.
It so happened that the hare loved to make fun of how slowly the tortoise moved. The tortoise tried not to let it bother him, but he did not like it. One day the hare began teasing the tortoise in front of other animals.	One day the hare decided to tease the tortoise. When the tortoise passed by the hare started teasing the tortoise. You are so slow, I'll bet I could even beat you in a race.
"You are so slow." said the hare, "that I get tired just watching you! Why, if you were any slower, you would be standing still."	You are so slow, so slow. You are like a statue.

own writing. The pattern of relationships between the emergent forms of literacy are far from simple!

Home Literacy Experiences

The fourth and final strand of research has focused on young children's home environments in an attempt to discover factors that promote early literacy development. Whereas the first three groups of studies are concerned with what children learn about written language, home literacy research is concerned with how this learning takes place.

Early studies in this area focused on umbrella characteristics such as family income and parents' levels of education (Sulzby & Teale, 1991). Results revealed positive relationships between these variables and reading achievement in the early grades. For example, children from middle-income families tend to be better readers than those from low-income families. Unfortunately, such findings do little to explain how these variables directly affect children's literacy growth.

More recent studies have narrowed their focus and have attempted to describe the actual literacy-related experiences that children have at home. These home literacy studies have identified several factors that appear to have important roles in early literacy acquisition. These factors are described in the sections that follow.

Access to Print and Books

In order to learn about literacy, young children must have opportunities to see lots of print and must have easy access to books. Plentiful home supplies of children's books have been found to be associated with early reading (Durkin, 1966), interest in literature (Morrow, 1983), and positive orientation toward schooling (Feitelson & Goldstein, 1986).

Because of the literate nature of our society, all children are surrounded by large amounts of environmental print. For example, they see print on product containers (Cheerios, Pepsi), street signs (Stop), and store signs (McDonald's, Pizza Hut). Differences do occur, however, in children's exposure to books and other forms of reading materials. Bill Teale's (1986b) descriptive study of the home environments of 24 low-income preschoolers revealed that, while some of the homes had ample supplies of children's books, other homes contained none. This is not to suggest that all children from low-income families lack exposure to reading materials at home (see Special Feature 4.2). However, those children who do not have access to books at home are at a great disadvantage in acquiring literacy.

Adult Demonstrations of Literacy Behavior.   Children also need to observe their parents, other adults, or older siblings using literacy in everyday situations (Smith, 1988). When children see their family members use print for various purposes—writing shopping lists, paying bills, looking up programs in the television listings, and writing notes to each other—they begin to learn about the practical uses of written language and to understand why reading and writing are activities worth doing. If their parents happen to model reading for pleasure, so much the better. These children see literature as a source of entertainment. Children's exposure to these types of functional and recreational literacy demonstrations has been found to vary greatly.

Supportive Adults.   Early readers tend to have parents who are very supportive of their early attempts at literacy (Morrow, 1983). While these parents rarely attempt to directly teach their children how to read and write, they do support literacy growth by doing such things as (1) answering their children's questions about print; (2) pointing out letters and words in the environment; (3) reading storybooks frequently; (4) making regular visits to the local library; (5) providing children with a wide variety of experiences such as trips to stores, parks, and museums; and (6) initiating functional literacy activities (such as suggesting that a child write a letter to grandmother or help make a shopping list).

Special Feature 4.2

The Home Literacy Experiences of Nonmainstream Children

The majority of the research on the home literacy experiences of young children has been conducted in white, middle-class homes. In recent years, however, increasing attention is being given to the home literacy experiences of nonmainstream children—children from low-income and ethnically diverse families. The findings are mixed and show a complex picture of these children's early experiences with language and literacy.

On the one hand, some studies have shown that many poor families have had difficulty providing their children with the rich types of language and literacy experiences that middle-income families typically provide (Vernon-Feagons, Hammer, Miccio, & Manlove, 2001). The Hart and Risley (1995) study, described in detail in Chapter 2, reported that low-income mothers used fewer words and a more restricted vocabulary in conversations with their children. Other studies suggest that many low-income children may have less experience with rhyming activity (Fernandez-Fein & Baker, 1997) and are less likely to visit public libraries (Baker, Serpell, & Sonnenschein, 1995).

Other studies have documented a wide range of home literacy environments and practices within nonmainstream families (Purcell-Gates, 1996; Taylor & Dorsey-Gaines, 1988; Teale, 1986b). For example, Purcell-Gates's study of twenty low-income families of differing ethnic backgrounds revealed great variability in the literacy experiences of children. The total number of literacy events in the low-income

homes ranged from .17 to 5.07 per hour, meaning that some children had opportunities to experience more than 25 times the amount of literacy than other children! Similarly, Teale's study of low-income children in San Diego, California, revealed that the average number of minutes per hour that children engaged in literacy activities ranged from 3.6 to 34.72, almost a tenfold difference. While on average the home literacy experiences of low-income children may not be as rich as those of the average middle-class children, some nonmainstream children do have frequent interactions with print.

Vernon-Feagons, Hammer, Miccio, and Manlove (2001, p. 194) point out a shortcoming of research on nonmainstream children's home literacy environments: "most studies of poverty have generally measured environmental factors in the home at the exclusion of measuring health and the larger discrimination in the larger society." For example, they cite Vernon-Faegans's (1996) study of rural African American children in the Piedmont area of North Carolina. This study found that, within this group of children, those with early nutritional deficits were at much greater risk of having problems acquiring literacy. Larger societal factors also enter the picture. Neuman and Celano (2001), for example, found that low-income families had much more restricted access to public libraries and places to buy books. In addition, the school libraries in low-income neighborhoods had fewer books per child, lower quality books, less qualified librarians, and fewer computers. So limited access to literacy materials and good places to read, caused by societal inequities, may be contributing factors to many low-income children's "at-risk" status.

The amount of such support that children receive during the preschool years varies greatly from family to family, and these differences have been found to have a considerable effect on children's literacy learning during kindergarten and the elementary grades (Christian, Morrison, & Bryant, 1998).

Independent Engagements with Literacy

Young children need to get their hands on literacy materials and to have opportunities to engage in early forms of reading and writing. This exploration and experimentation allows children to try out and perfect their growing concepts about the functions, forms, and conventions of written language.

Independent engagements with literacy often take place in connection with play. Don Holdaway (1979) has described how, as soon as young children become familiar with a storybook through repetitive read-aloud experiences, they will begin to play with the books and pretend to read them. He believes that this type of reading-like play is one of the most important factors promoting early literacy acquisition.

Young children also incorporate writing into their play. Sometimes this play writing is exploratory in nature, with children experimenting with different letter forms and shapes. At other times, emergent writing occurs in the context of make-believe play. Figure 4.4 is an example of this type of play-related writing. Four-year-old Ben was engaging in dramatic play in the housekeeping center. He wrote a Post-it™ Note message to another child, who was acting out the role of his mother, informing her that he was at soccer practice.

Sulzby (1985b) has described how children's early writing follows a loose developmental sequence, becoming more conventional over time (see Figure 4.3). Play provides

FIGURE 4.4   Ben's Post-it™ **Note message: "My sister and dad took me to soccer practice. Be back at 4"**

children with highly pleasurable and meaningful opportunities to experiment with these early forms of writing. In addition, social interaction during play (such as when other players cannot read a shopping list written in scribble writing) may provide motivation for children to develop more conventional forms of script.

Young children also use literacy in functional, nonplay situations. An excellent example is Glenda Bissex's (1980) account of how her four-year-old son Paul, after failing to get her attention by verbal means, used a stamp set to write "RUDF" (Are you deaf?). He also attempted to secure his privacy by putting the sign "DO NOT DSTRB GNYS AT WRK" (Do not disturb . . . Genius at work) on his door.

Opportunities to engage in these types of independent engagements with literacy depend on access to books and writing materials. As mentioned previously, research on children's home environments indicates that there are wide discrepancies in the availability of children's books and other reading materials. Similar differences also exist in the availability of writing materials. Teale's (1986b) descriptive study of the home environments of low-income preschoolers revealed that only 4 of 24 children had easy access to paper and writing instruments. He noted that these particular children engaged in far more emergent writing than did the other subjects in the study.

Storybook Reading

Storybook reading is undoubtedly the most studied aspect of home literacy. Quantitative studies have attempted to establish the importance and value of parents' reading to their children. A recent meta-analysis of 29 studies spanning more than three decades indicated that parent–preschooler storybook reading was positively related to outcomes such as language growth, early literacy, and reading achievement (Bus, van Ijzendoorn, & Pellegrini, 1995).

Other studies have attempted to describe and analyze what actually takes place during storybook-reading episodes and to identify the mechanisms through which storybook reading facilitates literacy growth (e.g., Altwerger, Diehl-Faxon, & Dockstader-Anderson, 1985; Heath, 1982; Holdaway, 1979; Snow & Ninio, 1986; Taylor, 1986; Yaden, Smolkin, & Conlon, 1989). These studies have shown that parent–child storybook reading is an ideal context for children to receive all of the previously mentioned factors that promote literacy acquisition:

1. Storybook reading provides children with access to enjoyable children's books, building positive attitudes about books and reading.

2. During storybook reading, parents present children with a model of skilled reading. Children see how books are handled, and they hear the distinctive intonation patterns that are used in oral reading.

3. Parents provide support that enables young children to take an active part in storybook reading. Early storybook-reading sessions tend to be routinized, with the parent first focusing the child's attention on a picture and then asking the child to label the picture. If the child does so, the parent gives positive or negative feedback about the accuracy of the label. If the child does not volunteer a label, the parent provides the correct label (Snow &

Ninio, 1986). As children's abilities grow, parents up the ante, shifting more of the responsibility to the children and expecting them to participate in more advanced ways.

4. Storybook reading encourages independent engagements with literacy by familiarizing children with stories and encouraging them to attempt to read the stories on their own (Holdaway, 1979; Sulzby, 1985a).

Other researchers have studied how cultural factors affect the manner in which parents mediate storybook reading for their children. Shirley Brice Heath (1982) found that middle-class parents tended to help their children link book information with other experiences. For example, John Langstaff's popular predictable book *Oh, A-Hunting We Will Go* (1974, Macmillan) contains the following lines:

> *Oh, a-hunting we will go.*
> *A-hunting we will go.*
> *We'll catch a lamb*
> *And put him in a pram*
> *And then we'll let him go.*

To help the child understand the term *pram,* a middle-class parent might say, "The pram looks just like your sister's baby carriage." Working-class parents, on the other hand, had a tendency to not extend book information beyond its original context and would simply define the word *pram* for the child. Sulzby and Teale (1991) speculate that these differences in story-reading style may have a considerable effect on children's early literacy acquisition.

Case Studies

The following sections present two case studies of early literacy development. Tiffany, a native English-speaking child, is the subject of the first case study. The second study describes Alicia's literacy acquisition. Alicia is a native speaker of Spanish, and English is her second language. There are many interesting similarities and differences in the early literacy acquisition of these two girls.

Tiffany

Tiffany's parents began reading to her soon after birth, and by age one, she was actively participating in storybook-reading sessions. Now, nearly two years later, 30-month-old Tiffany has begun to attempt to read on her own. The story begins in her bedroom, where she was looking at Richard Scarry's *Best Word Book Ever* (1980, Western Publishing Company) with her sister Dawn. Though her house has many children's books, this book was one of her favorites. Tiffany delighted in labeling the pictures and describing the actions of the Bunny family as they engage in familiar, everyday situations. As Tiffany pointed to the pictures of Nicki Bunny going to the doctor for a checkup, both she and Dawn laughed at the animals who are all dressed up in clothing: "Nicki Bunny wears shoes!" While attempting to read this text, Tiffany displayed many aspects of her concepts about print, including book handling and turning pages (starting at the front of the book and progressing to the back), as well as an appreciation of storybook reading.

On the way to the grocery story several months later, Tiffany's family passed a McDonald's sign. Thirty-three-month-old Tiffany shouted with gleeful recognition, "Donald's—ummm, eat burgers." Tiffany, like most children brought up in a literate culture, had already begun to recognize that her world is full of environmental print. Though Tiffany's reading of the McDonald's sign came more from interpreting the color and shape of the logo than from differentiating letters, it demonstrated her understanding that print carries meaning—another important developmental milestone.

Tiffany was also beginning to demonstrate an understanding that writing, as well as oral language, communicates meaning. Waiting with her mother in the bank, 36-month-old Tiffany took a handful of bank forms. While her mother talked to the bank manager, Tiffany occupied herself by using a pen to fill out the many forms. Her writing contained many squiggly lines and some picture-like forms (Figure 4.5). When Tiffany's mother asked her what she had written, Tiffany replied, "I write, 'Tiffy can buy money.'" At this stage, it is typical for children's writing to include both pictographs (pictures that represent writing) and scribble writing. Notice that her scribbling has the appearance of an adult's English cursive writing.

Sitting on her father's lap, 42-month-old Tiffany was reading him Maurice Sendak's *Where the Wild Things Are* (1963, Scholastic):

> *This bad boy in the wolf pajamas is mean to his mommy.*
> *He runs away 'cause he is mad.*
> *He gets in a boat, like "rubba a dub" [Tiffany's bathtub toy boat].*
> *Then he meets some big bad chicken monsters and yells at them.*
> *They make him the King, 'cause he yelled so loud!!!*
> *Then he goed home 'cause he wanted to eat.*

FIGURE 4.5   Tiffany (age 36 months) writes a note using a drawing and scribbles: "Tiffany can buy money"

The story she told consisted of her interpretations of the text's illustrations, and she used a storytelling tone as she held the book and turned the pages. As explained earlier, this behavior is indicative of Elizabeth Sulzby's category of emergent reading, "attending to pictures, forming oral stories" (Sulzby & Barnhart, 1990). Though Tiffany's oral retelling of the story was fairly accurate, her father noted that she did not include the monster refrain—"and they rolled their terrible eyes, gnashed their terrible teeth, and showed their terrible claws!" Her omission of this salient part of the story was probably caused by the fact that, during this stage of emergent reading, story retelling is guided by the illustrations rather than by the words in the text. As the pictures did not explicitly detail this refrain, Tiffany lacked the visual cues that would have triggered the recitation of this phrase.

At age four years, Tiffany continued to refine her understanding of the many functions of print. Sitting at her child-sized table in her playhouse with her best friend Becca, Tiffany pondered a piece of paper with her pencil in her mouth.

TIFFANY: What do you think the babies will eat?

BECCA: Baby food, Tiff.

TIFFANY: I know that! What kind of baby food?

BECCA: Oh, I think the orange stuff, but not the green.

TIFFANY: [Now writing this information down.] Okay. What else?

BECCA: You need to write down cat food and take the coupons.

TIFFANY: [Pulling out a bunch of coupons from her drawer, she sorts through them until she finds the Purina Cat Chow coupon.] Yeah, that coupon says "free cat food."

Figure 4.6 demonstrates that Tiffany had begun to produce letter-like forms. Though she continued to use pictographs, Tiffany could distinguish print from pictures. Pointing to the drawing she said, "This is a picture of baby food." She went on to describe her letter-like forms with the comment, "This says buy peaches and diapers."

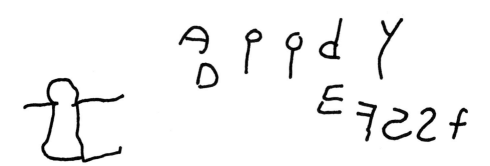

FIGURE 4.6   Tiffany (age 48 months) makes a shopping list using a picture of baby food plus "Buy peaches and diapers"

This episode also reveals that Tiffany was continuing to expand her environmental print vocabulary. In fact, she was becoming quite adept at recognizing dozens of product names. This ability was fostered by parental praise and encouragement each time Tiffany joined her parents as a member of the grocery-shopping expedition.

At age four years, Tiffany started preschool. One of the first academic activities her preschool teachers undertook was helping the children recognize and print their own names. As is often the case, Tiffany's first attempts to print her name were somewhat frustrating. Though she was quite accomplished at making letter-like forms, trying to reproduce specific letters in a specified sequence was definitely a challenge. At that time, Tiffany received a chalkboard from her grandparents. The new writing implement seemed to inspire her to practice more frequently, and soon Tiffany had mastered the fine art of printing her name (Figure 4.7).

Along with printing her name, Tiffany, like most of her preschool classmates, was becoming interested in naming and printing the alphabet. This interest was sparked by her teachers through direct, developmentally appropriate instruction. Prior to her preschool experience, Tiffany only casually watched the *Sesame Street* letter segments, paying attention instead to the social drama of the *Sesame Street* characters. However, between the ages of four and five years, Tiffany became an astute alphabet hunter—shouting with great authority the names of the letters as they flashed across the television screen. Tiffany sang the alphabet song, read alphabet books, did alphabet puzzles and alphabet dot-to-dot worksheets, and molded clay letters. She diligently wrote alphabet symbols with every type of writing tool imaginable—markers, pens, pencils, and water paints and paint brushes. She wrote her letters on every surface conceivable, including her bedroom walls! Her all-time favorite alphabet activity was writing her letters with soap crayons on the bathtub wall.

Tiffany's new proficiency with letter formation resulted in the production of many strings of random capital and lowercase letters, or using Sulzby's (1990) terminology, strings of nonphonetic letter strings (see Figure 4.8). Notice that though Tiffany knew many upper- and lowercase letters, she was not yet forming words or clustering her letters in word-like units.

Soon after Tiffany entered preschool, she became interested in joining her sister Dawn (age seven) in playing school. During these dramatic play sessions, Tiffany would

FIGURE 4.7 **Tiffany (age 52 months) writes her own name**

FIGURE 4.8   Tiffany (age 54 months) writes a stream of random letters

listen to Dawn as she read basal texts and their favorite literature. In the role of teacher, Dawn would ask factual questions during and after reading storybooks to Tiffany. For example, after reading Maurice Sendak's *Where the Wild Things Are* (Harper & Row, 1963), Dawn asked, "What did the monsters say to Max? What did Max say to the monsters?" Dawn would model writing letters on the chalkboard and then ask Tiffany to copy what she had written. Tiffany did her best to reproduce the words that Dawn wrote. Every so often, Tiffany would run out to her mother and proclaim, "Look it! What it say?"

Later in the year, when Dawn was at school, Tiffany would play school by herself, only this time she was the teacher. Dressed in a long white pleated skirt, heels, and jacket, she looked like Ms. O'Bannon, her sister's second grade teacher. She would "read" stories to her teddy bear and to rows of doll students, and she would use her ruler to point to alphabet cards posted on the wall. She would ask Teddy to pay attention and ask Annie (a doll) to tell her what the letters said. It is interesting to note that, when Tiffany pretended to be the teacher, her writing became more conventional. She carefully wrote her letters as she practiced saying the phrases that Dawn had used earlier: "Start at the top, draw a flat-hat top, then find the middle and draw a straight line. Now you see, you have a *T*."

Sitting in her miniature rocker holding her beloved baby doll Ramalda, four-and-a-half-year-old Tiffany began reading another favorite story, *Old Hat, New Hat* by Stan and Jan Berenstain (1970, Random House). Pointing to the pictures, Tiffany recited the story line, "new hat, new hat, new hat" and "too feathery, too scratchy," then the rousing finale, "just right, just right, just right!" Tiffany's recitation involved following the pictures and recalling the phrases she had heard and repeated with her parents virtually dozens of times. At this point in her development, her storybook reading was beginning to sound like reading as she imitated the expression and phrasing her parents used when they read this story to her.

When Tiffany began kindergarten at age five, she could recognize most alphabet letters. During her kindergarten year, Tiffany learned that each alphabet letter made a specific sound, but some alphabet letters made two or three sounds. For Tiffany, this phonics knowledge was an exciting step toward literacy. She reveled in baking Big Bird's brown banana bread with butter and studying the scientific qualities of bubbles and bouncing balls billions of times.

Her teacher, Ms. C., also modeled the writing process at the end of each day. She began by asking the children to summarize what they had learned that day, and as the children volunteered ideas, she would write their statements. While Ms. C. wrote, she would ask, "Who knows what letter Baby Bear starts with? What other sounds do you hear?" This type of informal modeling provided the spark that ignited Tiffany's reading—writing connection. This very sensitive teacher also had the kindergarten children write in their journals at their own developmental level. Figure 4.9 illustrates one of Tiffany's first invented-spelling journal entries. At this point, she was beginning to separate her words.

During the latter part of the kindergarten year, Tiffany used sophisticated invented spelling to express her thoughts and feelings. Simultaneously, Tiffany's interest in interpreting written materials of all types was increasing. In addition to reading product labels, she attempted to decode greeting cards, print she saw on television, and billboards. She also insisted that her parents use manuscript printing as opposed to cursive writing. Tiffany was spending a great deal of time reading texts that contained predictable patterned rhythm and rhyme. After these predictable books were read with Tiffany several times, she could begin to read them to herself. Her read-by-myself books included *Oh, A-Hunting We Will Go* by J. Langstaff (1974, Houghton Mifflin) and *Chicken Soup with Rice* by M. Sendak (Harper & Row, 1962).

As is the case with most children, Tiffany's writing did not correspond directly to her early reading development. Though her use of invented spelling seemed to suggest that she would be able to decode a great number of words, she refused to attempt to decode the text in literature books that had not been read to her previously. Tiffany needed to have a sense of context, or an understanding of what the print was about, before she felt comfortable attempting to read the material. Notice that the items she was decoding earlier—grocery products, greeting cards, and the print used in TV or magazine advertisements—provided strong contextual clues that indicated what the script might be saying.

When six-year-old Tiffany entered first grade, she had made tremendous progress in acquiring literacy. She was able to write and instantly recognize all the upper- and lowercase

FIGURE 4.9   Tiffany (age 60 months) uses invented spelling in her journal: "I love papa and Nannie"

alphabet symbols. She was also able to distinguish and label all single consonant and vowel sounds. She was able to express her thoughts in written form by using invented spelling, and she could read some familiar predictable books. Tiffany had a strong foundation for more formal reading instruction that would follow in first grade.

Alicia

In Special Feature 4.3, Irene Serna and Sarah Hudelson present a second case study of early literacy. This case study features, Alicia, who came from a home in which Spanish was the primary language. When she entered kindergarten, Alicia was speaking perfect Spanish but was only partially proficient in oral English. She was fortunate to attend a bilingual kindergarten in which she was allowed to learn to read and write in Spanish and then transfer what she had learned to English literacy. It is interesting to compare Alicia's acquisition of reading and writing in Spanish with Tiffany's literacy development in English. As you will see, there are many interesting parallels.

Summary

The four research strands reviewed in this chapter have joined to provide a picture of the new early literacy perspective. How does what you read in this chapter compare with how you learned to read and write? Were the supportive factors described in the section "Home Literacy Experiences" present in your home?

Here, we return to the questions posed at the beginning of the chapter, and briefly summarize the information presented.

■ *How does the early literacy view of young children's literacy development compare with the readiness and earlier-is-better views?*

According to the early literacy view, the literacy learning process shares much in common with the oral language development process. Literacy acquisition, like oral language development, begins early. For many children, literacy development begins in infancy when caregivers read storybooks to children and children begin to notice print in the environment. Literacy learning is an active, constructive process. By observing print and having stories read to them, young children discover patterns and create their own early versions of reading and writing that initially have little resemblance to conventional forms; the story they read may be quite different from the one in the book, and their writing may look like drawing or scribbles. As children have opportunities to use these early forms of literacy in meaningful social situations and as they interact with adults who draw their attention to the features and functions of print, their constructions become increasingly similar to conventional reading and writing.

According to the readiness view, literacy development begins much later (at about age six). The process through which children acquire literacy is unlike the oral language acquisition process. Rather than constructing knowledge about literacy by experimenting with forms of literacy in supportive environments, supporters of this view believed that children must be directly taught by specially trained teachers who guided children's acquisition of literacy concepts and skills, known as reading readiness skills, which had little to

Alicia's Early Literacy Development in Spanish
Irene Serna and Sarah Hudelson

As Tiffany's case study illustrates, young children begin to read and write English by engaging in daily literacy activities with family members and teachers. These adults support early literacy by creating opportunities for reading and writing and by responding to children's requests for assistance. What does early literacy look like in a language other than English? Alicia, a Spanish-speaking kindergartner we came to know through our research, provides a good example of how children construct their literacy in Spanish (Serna & Hudelson, 1993).

Alicia's Home Language and Literacy

Spanish was the dominant language in Alicia's home. Her mother reported that Alicia had requested that books be read to her since she was four years old. In addition, Alicia had been eager to engage in writing within family activities. At home, Alicia helped produce shopping lists, notes, and cards sent to family members. Of course, these were written in Spanish. Clearly, Alicia came from a very literate home environment that featured frequent storybook reading, many opportunities to write in connection with daily activities, and adults who supported her early attempts at reading and writing. In this regard, Alicia's early literacy development was quite similar to Tiffany's and that of other English-speaking children who come from supportive home environments. There was one significant difference—Alicia reported that her mother and grandmother frequently told her *cuentos* (folk tales) and family stories. Thus, storytelling (oral literacy) was also a strong part of Alicia's home literacy experiences.

Alicia's Literacy Development in Kindergarten

Though Alicia participated in a bilingual Head Start program as a four-year-old, when she entered kindergarten, her score on an oral language proficiency test identified her as limited-English proficient. Two-thirds of the children in her bilingual kindergarten program spoke English, and one-third spoke Spanish. Alicia used both languages to socialize with her peers. However, she primarily used Spanish to explain her thinking, to narrate stories, and to express herself personally. At the beginning of kindergarten, Alicia only discussed books that were read aloud in Spanish. By the latter half of the year, she was discussing books read in both languages. This was particularly helpful to the monolingual children because Alicia could interpret books and communications in English or Spanish. Alicia's role in the classroom became that of translator. Thus, while her one year of Head Start was not sufficient time for Alicia to develop oral proficiency in English, the second year of bilingual programming in kindergarten did allow her to develop bilingual abilities.

Writing

Beginning in October of her kindergarten year, Alicia was asked to write in a journal for 45 minutes daily. Throughout the year, she also drew and wrote in learning logs to record information from study in thematic units. She contributed to group language experience charts, which summarized findings from the children's thematic studies. In her earliest journal entries, Alicia wrote a patterned and familiar phrase in English, "I love my mom." A November entry demonstrated that Alicia had moved from producing a patterned phrase to creating a label for her picture: *"Mi papalote"* (my kite). In November, Alicia also wrote her first sentence describing a picture, *"Yo ciro mi babe Martinsito"* (I love my baby Martincito), using both invented (*ciro* for *quiero*) and conventional spelling. She also wrote additional patterned sentences, *"Mi Nana bonita come sopa Mi mami bonita come sopa"* (My pretty grandmother eats soup. My pretty mother eats soup). In December, Alicia repeated phrases to write two lines of text describing her picture, *"Los colores del arco iris son bonitos Colores del arco ids"*

(continued on next page)

(The colors of the rainbow are pretty. The colors of the rainbow). Her writing did not become more expressive until February when she wrote about playing in the pile of snow that had been trucked to the school (see Figure 4.10).

This February sample demonstrates that Alicia's invented spellings included most sounds in each syllable, that the vowels were standardized, and that she confused some of the consonants. Though she put spaces between most words, conventional word separation was not used consistently.

In April, Alicia wrote a personal narrative about her little cousin Martincito, primarily describing how she cared for and played with him. Figure 4.11 contains two of the ten sen-

tences she wrote in this personal narrative. Written over a three-week period, Alicia's personal narrative illustrates that her invented spellings were very close approximations of standard Spanish spellings. Alicia also separated words more consistently. Syntactically, all of her sentences were complete, and all grammatical inflections were correct. By the end of kindergarten, Alicia was the classroom's most fluent writer in Spanish. As a result, other children often asked her to write their personal narratives.

Reading

From September through February, Alicia retold stories from familiar, predictable picture books using some of the story language in Spanish and

FIGURE 4.10   Alicia's February writing sample

(continued on next page)

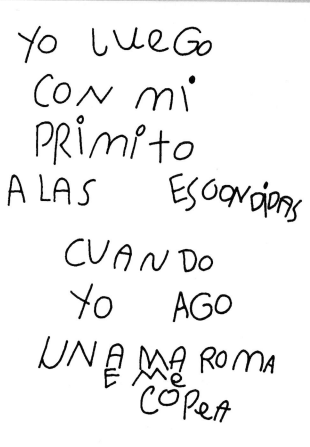

Alicia's Spelling	Conventional Spanish Spelling	English Translation
Yo juego	Yo juego	I play
con mi	con mi	with my
primito	primita	little cousin
alas escondidas	a las escondidas	hide-and-seek
Cuando	Cuando	When
Yo ago	yo hago	I make
una ma roma	una moroma	a somersault
e me copea	el me copea	he copies me

FIGURE 4.11   Alicia's April writing sample

(continued on next page)

some in English. In March, her first story was typed for publication (in Spanish). Alicia read this text for the first time using letter–sound cues and a phonetic decoding strategy (i.e., she tried to sound out the words). While this initial reading was not very smooth, Alicia practiced reading the words until she could reread her own story fluently. From March to the end of the year, Alicia used this same strategy with familiar, predictable books in Spanish. Initially, each book was read utilizing the phonetic decoding strategy, focusing on sounding out unfamiliar words. Subsequently, she reread the text until she could read it fluently. Alicia chose to read books that had plain print, with only one or two lines of text per page. She rejected books with too many words or italic print. By the end of May, Alicia read the Spanish versions of Maurice Sendak's *Where the Wild Things Are* (1963, Harper & Row) and Robert Kraus's *Herman the Helper* (1974, Windmill), familiar and unfamiliar texts, respectively. She

made a few mistakes, primarily grammatical. She did not correct these mistakes, but they were rather minor and did not change the meaning of the story. Alicia read more effectively, using multiple cues (letter–sound, meaning, and grammatical) as well as illustrations to decode unfamiliar words. Alicia also demonstrated that she was reading to construct the meaning of each text because she was able to retell each story accurately. By the end of kindergarten, Alicia had become a fluent writer and reader in Spanish. She was able to use sophisticated invented spellings that were very close approximations of standard Spanish spellings, and she could compose coherent narrative stories. Alicia learned to read in Spanish through reading both her own writing and familiar, predictable books. By April, Alicia was reading picture books fluently and independently. She was able to use multiple cueing systems and reading strategies in Spanish.

do with actual reading. Children did not meet real reading materials, like books, until the middle of first grade. Children did not write to communicate until much later, after they knew how to form letters and spell words.

The earlier-is-better view borrowed the practices of the readiness view and moved them to earlier grades. What children had been guided to do in first grade now was moved to the kindergarten and preschool years.

■ *What knowledge about written language do young children exhibit when adults watch them closely?*
Watch children and you will see the following:

Children as young as three years of age know the difference between drawing and writing, expect print to be meaningful (to say something), and know something about the purposes of print.

Two- and three-year-olds play with sounds, thus exhibiting their phonological awareness knowledge.

Three- and four-year-olds read product labels, restaurant signs, and street signs.

Three-year-olds can name about one-third of the letters of the alphabet.

Five- and six-year-olds identify words that begin with the same phoneme, thus exhibiting their phonemic awareness knowledge.

Young children write /m/ for man, thus exhibiting their knowledge of phonics.

Young children show that they know such concepts as print moves from left-to-right and top-to-bottom across the page and that words have spaces between them.

Young children use early forms of writing and of reading, becoming more conventional with age and experience.

■ *What is the relationship among oral language, phonemic awareness, and phonics?*

Research data suggest that those children whose oral language is the most proficient typically are the same children whose phonemic awareness is the most developed. That is, these tend to be the children who best understand that words in speech are composed of sequences of individual sounds or phonemes. Once children have acquired this critically important concept, they are then able to make connections between letters in written words and the phonemes in speech.

■ *What are emergent writing and emergent reading?*

On their way toward reading and writing conventionally, young children construct, test, and perfect hypotheses about written language. Research has shown general developmental sequences, with children's early forms of reading and writing gradually becoming more conventional with age and experience. These early reading and writing forms are known as emergent. Children using all forms of reading and writing are legitimate writers and readers.

■ *What home factors affect young children's literacy development?*

Several factors have been identified as having important roles in early literacy acquisition. These include

opportunities to see lots of print and have easy access to books;

opportunities to observe adults using literacy in everyday situations;

adults who support children's literacy development by answering children's questions, pointing to letters, taking the children to the library, providing children with a wide variety of experiences, and initiating functional literacy activities;

literacy materials that support children's engagement in early forms of reading and writing; and

experiences with adults who share books with children.

■ *What does early literacy look like in a language other than English?*

Children learn the dominant language of their home. When these homes—be they English-speaking, Spanish-speaking, or Arabic-speaking—provide a literate model, typically the young children who live in them are eager to engage in talking, writing, and reading in the home's dominant language. So early literacy across languages looks quite similar. Some cultures and families place emphasis on oral storytelling in addition to reading and writing. Adults in these homes share stories with their young literacy learners and with each other. Of course, children from families whose dominant language is a language other than English will enter school using the language that works for them in their home environment. A quality program that supports these children's emergence as readers and writers is important.

LINKING KNOWLEDGE TO PRACTICE

1. With a group of colleagues, talk about an early childhood classroom you have seen. Which view of literacy was evidenced in this classroom? Provide specific descriptions of what you observed (like the vignette at the beginning of this chapter) to support your decision of the view evidenced.

2. Read a storybook with a child three years or older. Ask the child to point to where you should begin reading. Does the child know that you will read the print, not the pictures? After you have read the story to the child, ask the child to read the story to you. What form does the child use to read the story (e.g., attending to pictures, forming oral stories; attending to pictures, forming written stories; attending to print)? When you have finished reading the book, select an important word from the story. Can the child tell you the name of the letters in this word? Say a word that rhymes with this word. Now, it's the child's turn. Can the child say another word that rhymes with this word? Say a word that begins with the same sound. Can the child say a word that begins with the same sound? Point to each letter. Can the child say the sound of each letter? Can the child blend the letter sounds to form the word? Compare your findings with those gathered by your colleagues.

3. Observe young children at play in a literacy-enriched dramatic play setting (for example, a home center equipped with paper, pencils, telephone books, television guides, cookbooks, junk mail, cereal boxes, etc.) Watch two or three children while they play in this setting. What do they talk about? What do they write? For example, do they make grocery lists? What does their writing tell you about what they know about the kinds of written language (lists, letter writing, check writing) and forms of written language (scribbles, nonphonetic letter strings, invented spellings)? Do they expect their writing to say something? How do they use the reading materials in the setting? Can they read the cereal boxes? What form of reading do they use to construct meaning from the print? What does your observation tell you about these children's development as readers and writers? If possible, complete this activity with a colleague who watches other children in the play setting. Compare the children's literacy behaviors in the same play setting.

CHAPTER

5 Building a Foundation for Literacy Learning

As Isaac enters his kindergarten classroom, he and his classmates collect laminated helper necklaces from their name pockets on the attendance chart. Each necklace has a tag listing a classroom task. Isaac "reads" his tag—Errand Runner. He checks the nearby Helper Board where all the duties for each task have been described in both words and pictures. Today he will run any errands his teacher may have, such as taking the attendance count to the center's office. Yesterday, Isaac was Pencil Sharpener, which involved gathering and sharpening pencils. He hopes to be Pet Feeder tomorrow.

In Chapter 4, we described how most children begin to learn about reading and writing at an early age by engaging in everyday activities with their family and peers. Research has revealed that several types of home experiences stimulate early literacy learning: (1) easy access to print and books; (2) supportive parents or other caregivers who read stories aloud, demonstrate different types of literacy behaviors, answer children's questions about print, and scaffold children's literacy efforts; and (3) opportunities for children to engage in emergent forms of reading and writing. But just as children have varying degrees of verbal interactions with their families (Chapter 2), research also has revealed that children may have vastly different opportunities to interact with print in their homes.

Home literacy experiences help children develop an awareness of the forms and functions of print. Therefore, developmentally appropriate early childhood programs feature literacy activities that mirror the types of literacy experiences found in enriched home environments, such as print-rich settings, storybook reading, demonstrations of various forms of literacy, and lots of opportunities for children to engage in meaningful reading and writing activities. These types of experiences build on what children have already learned about written language, provide a smooth transition between home and school, and help ensure initial success with language arts instruction.

In the sections that follow, we discuss four strategies that form the foundation of developmentally appropriate preschool and kindergarten language arts programs: functional literacy activities, sharing literature, literacy play, and the language experience approach (also known as shared writing). These strategies are particularly valuable because they provide a broad spectrum of learning opportunities that are appropriate for children at different ages and with different prior experience with print. When used with large groups of children, opportunities exist for *all* children to gain valuable knowledge about literacy.

Before Reading This Chapter, Think About . . .

- how you used print as a child. Did you write notes to your family? Did you pretend to write checks? Send a letter to Santa? Write a thank-you card to Grandma?
- advertisement logos you remember from your childhood. Could you spot a McDonald's a mile away? Did your favorite toy or snack food have a special logo or trademark?
- the favorite books from your childhood. Did you have one or two favorite books that you liked to have your parents, siblings, or other adults read to you? Or did you have a favorite book that you liked to read on your own?
- how you played house as a child. Did you have real cereal boxes and egg cartons for your pretend kitchen? Did an interested adult join in your pretend play?

Focus Questions

- What are functional literacy activities, and how can teachers use these activities in a preschool or kindergarten classroom?
- How can teachers set up a well-designed library center?
- What are the characteristics of effective adult storybook reading?
- How can dramatic play centers be used to encourage young children's literacy development?
- How does the language experience approach (or shared writing) increase a child's understanding of print and facilitate reading development?

BOX **5.1**

Definition of Terms

broad-spectrum instructional strategy: Strategies that are effective and appropriate for a wide-range of learner abilities.

environmental print (EP): Includes the real-life print children see in the home or community, including print on food containers and other kinds of product boxes, store signs, road signs, advertisements, and the like. Because the situation gives clues to the print's meaning, EP is often the first type of print young children can recognize and understand.

functional literacy activities: Reading and writing activities that accomplish real-life purposes, such as writing lists and reading directions.

functional print: Print that guides everyday classroom activity (e.g., labels, lists, directions, sign-up sheets).

language-experience approach/shared writing: The teacher works with whole groups, small groups, or individual children to write down the children's oral language stories. These highly contextualized stories are easy for children to read.

literacy-enriched dramatic play centers: Sociodramatic play centers that are enhanced with appropriate theme-related literacy materials, such as recipe cards, cookbooks, and food containers for the kitchen center.

shared book experience: The teacher reads a big book with enlarged print and encourages children to read along on parts that they can remember or predict.

Functional Literacy Activities

As we explained earlier in Chapter 4, children's home reading experiences are usually functional in nature. Children watch their parents and older siblings use reading and writing to accomplish real-life purposes. They often join in these activities (e.g., reading food labels and signs in the environment). It is important for teachers to provide opportunities for children to continue to learn about functional qualities of reading and writing.

In the vignette at the opening of this chapter, note how the helper necklaces in Isaac's classroom provide the same type of functional literacy experiences that children have at home. The print on the helper necklaces serves a real purpose and assists with everyday activities (classroom chores). The surrounding context—the chores that are done on a daily basis in the classroom—makes the print on the necklaces easy to recognize and understand.

Functional literacy activity is a broad-spectrum strategy that provides opportunities for children who are at different stages in their literacy development to learn new skills and concepts. For example, if Isaac is just beginning to learn about the meaning and functions of print, the helper necklaces provide an opportunity to learn that print can inform him about his assigned chores and help him remember these chores. If he has already acquired this basic concept, the necklaces provide opportunities to learn about the structure of print. For example, he may eventually learn to recognize some of the printed words on the necklaces (*runner, pencil, pet*), or to figure out some related letter-sound relationships (the letter *p* represents the sound that *pencil* and *pet* begin with).

In the sections that follow, we describe two types of print that can provide children with functional literacy activities: (1) environmental print that exists in everyday life outside of school, and (2) functional print that is connected with classroom activities.

Bringing Environmental Print into the Classroom

At home and in their neighborhoods, children are surrounded by print that serves real-life functions: labels on cereal boxes and soft-drink cans, road signs, billboards, and restaurant menus. This type of functional print is referred to as environmental print (EP). Because the situation gives clues to the print's meaning, EP is often the first type of print that young children can recognize and understand. Because EP is so meaningful and easy to read, it should be available in all preschool and kindergarten classrooms.

Unfortunately, EP tends to be rather scarce in school settings (Morrow, 2001). Therefore, teachers must make an extra effort to make this type of print available to their children. Following are several strategies that can be used to bring real-world EP into the classroom:

■ *EP alphabet chart*—The teacher places pieces of chart paper around the room for every letter of the alphabet. Each day, children bring to class product labels they can "read." During circle time, these labels are read and attached to the correct chart. For example, the Kix (cereal) label would go on the *K k* page. Then the group reads the labels on all the charts, starting with the *A a* page. After several months, when most of the chart pages are full, the teacher can use the product labels from the charts to make books such as "I Can Read Cereals."

■ *EP folders*—Selected pieces of EP can be attached to file folders to make EP books (Anderson & Markle, 1985). For example, a pizza book could be made by pasting or laminating the product logos from pizza advertisements, coupons, and delivery containers onto the inside surfaces of a file folder (see Figure 5.1). Children can decorate the front cover with pizza-related illustrations. Other book possibilities include toothpaste, cookies, milk, cereal, and soft drinks. These EP folders should be placed in the classroom library so that children can show off to their friends how well they can read this type of contextualized print.

FIGURE 5.1   EP folder

■ *EP walks*—This strategy involves taking a class for a walk in the neighborhood surrounding the school (Orellana & Hernández, 1999). Before leaving, the children are told to be on the lookout for EP. As examples of EP are encountered during the walk, they are pointed out by the teacher or by the children. After the children return to the classroom, they draw pictures of the print they could read on the walk. The pictures are put into a group book, which the teacher reads aloud to the class. The children can then take turns reading EP items in the book.

■ *Individual EP booklets*—This approach involves using magazine coupons or advertisements that feature products children are familiar with to make personalized "I Can Read" books. Children sort through the ads or coupons, select the products they recognize, and then use glue sticks to secure the coupons to pre-made construction paper booklets. The children can share their booklets with each other and take them home to read to family members.

■ *Sociodramatic play*—As will be explained later in this chapter, environmental print can be used as props in children's dramatic play. For example, empty product boxes such as cereal containers and milk cartons can be used in the kitchen area of housekeeping or home centers. As children act out home-related themes such as making dinner, they will have opportunities to attempt to read the print on the containers.

Functional Print Connected with Classroom Activities

Unlike environmental print that is found in the world outside of school, functional classroom print is connected with everyday school activities. This print is practical as well as educational. The helper necklace in the opening vignette helps children remember their assigned chores, making the classroom run more smoothly. Simultaneously, the necklaces offer opportunities for children to learn about the functions and structure of print. As with all functional print, the context helps children discover the meaning of the print.

Nancy Taylor and her colleagues (1986) observed the print in a number of preschool classrooms and used qualitative procedures to develop categories of written language displays, many of which involved functional uses. The following are the major types of functional print that they discovered in classrooms: labels, lists, directions, schedules, calendars, and messages.

Labels.   As illustrated by the helper necklaces in the vignette at the beginning of this chapter, labels may be used to delineate tasks that students are assigned to complete, such as line leader, pencil sharpener, pet feeder, or paper passer. Labels can also be used to help organize the classroom. For example, cubbies can be labeled with children's names so that students know where their belongings are stored. Containers can be labeled to designate their contents, and labels can be used on shelves to indicate where materials are to be stored. Labels can also be used for designating different areas of the classroom (library, home center, blocks, games, art), informing children about the types of activities that are supposed to take place in each location. Finally, labels can be used to convey information. For example, teachers often use labels to identify objects in displays (e.g., types of sea shells) and pictures ("This is a . . . ").

Lists.   Lists have a variety of practical classroom uses. Attendance charts can be constructed by placing each child's picture and name above a pocket. The children sign in by finding their name card in a box and by matching it with their name on the chart. After the children become familiar with their printed names, the pictures can be removed. In Trade Secrets 5.1, a preschool teacher offers another way of using this approach to take attendance and to document ongoing literacy development.

The teacher can use a second set of name tags to post jobs on a helper chart. This chart, which is an alternative to the helper necklaces described at the beginning of this chapter, contains a description of jobs needing to be done and display pockets that hold the children's name cards (see Figure 5.2). When attendance and helper charts are used on a daily basis, children quickly learn to recognize their own names and the names of their classmates.

Directions.   Instructions can be posted for using equipment such as tape recorders and computers. Classroom rules (e.g., "We walk in our classroom") can be displayed to remind children of appropriate behavior. In addition, children can create their own personal directives. For example, a child may place a "Look, don't touch!" sign on a newly completed art project or block structure. At first, children will need help from the teacher or from peers in reading these types of directions. Soon, however, they will learn to use the surrounding context to help them remember what the directions say. Teachers can help this process by constantly referring children to these posted directions. For example, if a child is running in the classroom, the teacher could direct the child's attention to the "We walk in our classroom" sign and ask, "What does that sign say?"

Trade Secrets 5.1

Connecting Names and Faces

Ms. Martinez uses a visual approach to help her three- and four-year old preschool students recognize their names and document their literacy growth over time. During the first day of school, Ms. Martinez takes an individual picture of each of her students using an instant camera. As the child's image emerges on the photo, she asks each child to write his or her name on a piece of construction paper. (If the child's writing is completely illegible, she writes the child's name conventionally next to the child's personal script and then explains, "This is how I write your name.") She places the child's picture above the name and places the page in a clear plastic page protector. She places the pictures on a child's eye-level bulletin board. She uses the bulletin board to help the children take attendance (as the children enter the room in the morning they attach a brightly painted clothespin to their pictures).

In five or six weeks, Ms. Martinez repeats this process. She takes new pictures of the children and again asks them to print their names on a new piece of construction paper. In addition, she asks them to write anything else they would like to share. She is always amazed at how much the children's ability to print their names and their understanding about print has developed during the first few weeks. Instead of sending the first set of pictures home, she organizes the pages in a book-like fashion and places the "Our Class" book in the library. It is one of the children's favorite library books.

Ms. Martinez repeats this process four to five times during the year. By the end of the year, Ms. Martinez has a visual record of her students' writing development throughout the school year.

FIGURE 5.2   Helper chart

Directions can also include recipes for cooking or directions for art activities. The directions can be put on wall charts. Even very young children can follow simple directions that use both words and pictures.

Schedules.   A daily schedule can be presented at the beginning of class to prepare children for upcoming activities. Pictures can be used to help children remember the different segments of the day (see Figure 5.3). If children ask what is going to happen next, the teacher can help them use the chart to figure it out.

Calendars.   A monthly calendar can be set up at the beginning of each month and used for marking children's birthdays, parties, and other special events (field trips, classroom visitors, when a student's dog had puppies, etc.). The teacher can encourage the children to use the calendar to determine how many more days until a special event takes place and to record events of importance to them.

FIGURE 5.3   **Daily schedule**

Messages.   Often, unforeseen events change the day's plans. It's raining, so there can be no outdoor playtime. Instead of just telling children, some teachers write a message. For example,

> Circle time will be first thing this morning.
> We have a special visitor!
> She will share her cookies with us.

Because these messages inform children about activities that directly affect their day, even the youngest children quickly learn to pay close attention to these notices.

Sign-In and Sign-Up Lists.   Children can write their names on lists for a variety of functional purposes. For example, kindergarten teacher Bobbi Fisher (1995) writes the date and day at the top of large 9 × 18-inch piece of drawing paper and has her children write their names on the paper each morning when they first arrive in the classroom. Bobbi and her assistant teacher sign the list also. During circle time, the list is read to the class as a means of taking attendance and to build a sense of community. As the children become familiar with each other's printed names, they take over the activity. She periodically uses this sign-in procedure to assess the children's emerging writing abilities.

Lists can also be used to sign-up for popular classroom centers and playground equipment. Judith Schickedanz (1986) describes how teachers at the Boston University laboratory preschool have children sign up on lists to use popular centers such as the block and dramatic play areas. If children do not get a chance to use the area on a given day, they are first in line to use it the next day. Sign-up sheets are also used to get turns using tricycles on the playground.

Children should be encouraged to use emergent forms of writing. If a child's writing is completely illegible, the teacher may need to write the child's name conventionally next to the child's personal script. The teacher can explain, "This is how I write your name." Once the child's name is recognizable, this scaffold can be discontinued.

Inventory Lists. Lists can also be used to create inventories of the supplies in different classroom areas. Susan Neuman and Kathy Roskos (1993) give an example of a chart that contains an inventory of the supplies in the art area. The list contains a picture and the name of each item, as well as the quantity of each item available. The sign informs children that there are 8 paintbrushes, 12 pairs of scissors, lots of paper, and so on. During cleanup, children can use this information to make sure the center is ready for future use.

Sharing Literature with Children

As early as 1908, Edmond Huey wrote about children's acquisition of reading and noted that "the key to it all lies in the parent's reading aloud to and with the child" (p. 332). Today, after decades of research on the teaching of reading, we continue to agree with Huey. More recently Marilyn Adams (1990) summarized what many educators believe and research supports: "The single most important activity for building the knowledge and skills eventually required for reading appears to be reading aloud to children" (p. 46). This single act—parents and teachers reading aloud to children—has received more research attention than any other aspect of children's literacy development. The findings of this vast body of research support the claims of Huey and Adams. The National Education Goals Panel (1997, p. 20) summarizes:

> Early, regular reading to children is one of the most important activities parents can do with their children to improve their readiness for school, serve as their child's first teacher, and instill a love of books and reading. Reading to children familiarizes them with story comprehension such as characters, plot, action, and sequence ("Once upon a time . . . ," " . . . and they lived happily ever after"), and helps them associate oral language with printed text. Most important, reading to children builds their vocabularies and background knowledge about the world.

Unfortunately, not all children have equal access to this wonderful literacy-building experience. Data suggest that only about 45 percent of children below the age of three and

56 percent of three- to five-year-olds are read to daily by their parents (National Education Goals Panel, 1997).

This section is about how to share books with young children. We begin by explaining how teachers can set up inviting library centers in their classrooms and how they can effectively read stories to young children. Finally, we discuss how story-reading sessions can be an ideal context for assessing children's literacy growth.

Selecting Good Books for Children

The careful selection of quality picture storybooks can play an important role in young children's development. According to Charlotte Huck, Susan Hepler, Janet Hickman, and Barbara Kiefer (1997), quality picture storybooks can

> enlarge children's lives, stretch their imaginations, and enhance their living. The phenomenal growth of beautiful picture books for children of all ages is an outstanding accomplishment of the past fifty years of publishing. Children do not always recognize the beauty of these books, but early impressions do exert an influence on the development of permanent tastes for children growing up (p. 250).

To help teachers with the task of making appropriate selections of quality books, we suggest two resources. First, we suggest readers consider obtaining a copy of Charlotte Huck, Susan Hepler, Janet Hickman, and Barbara Kiefer's (2000) book, *Children's Literature in the Elementary School.* Though the title says "elementary school," the book is a rich resource for teachers of children of all ages. It alerts readers to titles, and titles, and titles of outstanding literature, noting the likely age of children who would enjoy each book most. At the end of each chapter, readers will find pages and pages of recommended titles. The latest edition, the seventh edition, of this book, reproduces many pages from quality picture books and picture storybooks for teachers' examination. This book is a *must* for every teachers' professional library.

Jim Christie recommends "Children's Choices," a yearly feature that appears in each October's issue of *The Reading Teacher.* It consists of an annotated list of new children's books that have been field-tested with thousands of children across the United States. The books on the list are the ones that are most popular with children. The books are grouped in broad age ranges, from those intended for beginning readers to those written for advanced intermediate-grade readers.

Teachers should be sure to share tales representative of various cultures. Many resources are available to locate high quality multicultural literature. For example, the National Association for the Education of Young Children (1509 16th Street, N.W., Washington, D.C. 20036-1426) publishes a brochure, *African American Literature for Young Children,* developed by the National Black Child Development Institute. The most up-to-date information on multicultural books can be found on the World Wide Web. A variety of sites can be found using the descriptors "multicultural children's literature" with any of the major search engines (Yahoo, MSN, Google, etc.). For example, a recent search located the site, POWERFUL ASIAN AMERICAN IMAGES REVEALED IN PICTURE BOOKS compiled by Kay Vandergrift (http://www.scils.rutgers.edu/special/kay/asian.html) and a number of similar sites with lists of books about children from different cultures.

Once appropriate selections have been made, the teacher's challenge is to organize the books to make them accessible to their students—to encourage them to voluntarily read, read, read.

Classroom Library Centers

A key feature of a classroom for young children is a well-stocked, well-designed library center. Classroom libraries promote independent reading by providing children with easy access to books and a comfortable place for browsing and reading. Children have been found to read more books in classrooms with libraries than in ones without libraries (Morrow & Weinstein, 1982). As Stephen Krashen (1987, p. 2) has pointed out, this finding supports "the commonsense view that children read more when there are more books around."

However, the mere presence of a classroom library is not enough to ensure heavy use by young children. The library must contain an ample supply of appropriate and interesting books for children to read. Design features are also important. Lesley Morrow and Carol Weinstein (1982) found that children did not choose to use "barren and uninviting" library corners during free-play time. However, when the design features of centers were improved, children's library usage increased dramatically.

Unfortunately, classroom libraries are not a universal feature of early childhood classrooms, and many of the libraries that do exist are not well-designed. Jann Fractor, Marjorie Woodruff, Miriam Martinez, and Bill Teale (1993) collected data on the libraries in 89 kindergarten through second-grade classrooms and found that only 58 percent of classes had a library center. Only 8 percent of these classroom libraries were rated as being good or excellent (having large numbers of books, partitions, ample space, comfortable furnishings, book covers rather than book spines facing out on book shelves, and book-related displays and props). The vast majority of libraries were rated as basic, containing small numbers of books and few desirable design characteristics.

Books.   In order to attract and hold children's interest, a classroom library must be stocked with lots of good books to read. Experts recommend that classroom libraries contain 5 to 8 books per child (Fractor et al., 1993). According to these guidelines, a class of 20 children would require 100 to 160 books. These books should be divided into a core collection and one or more revolving collections. The core collection should be made up of high-quality literature that remains constant and available all year. These should be books that appeal to most of the children in class and that most children will enjoy reading on more than one occasion. Lesley Morrow (2001) also recommends that the books be color-coded according to type. For example, all animal books could be identified with blue dots on their spines so they can be clustered together on a shelf marked *Animals.* Each category would be distinguished by a different color. Morrow also suggests a simpler alternative—storing books in plastic tubs or cardboard boxes, with labels on the front describing the type of book in the container.

Revolving collections change every few weeks to match children's current interests and topics being studied in class. For example, if several children become hooked on an author, such as Tomie de Paola or Maurice Sendak, collections of the author's books could be brought into the library to capitalize on this interest. If the class were studying seeds and plants, then picture storybooks and informational books relating to these topics could be

A well-designed library center invites children to read books.

added. When student interest shifts to a new author or when a new topic is under investigation, the old sets of revolving books are replaced with new ones.

Quality and variety are also of utmost importance in selecting books for the classroom library (Fractor et al., 1993). In order to motivate voluntary reading and to instill positive attitudes toward written texts, books must catch children's attention, hold their interest, and captivate their imaginations. Only high-quality literature will achieve these goals.

Physical Characteristics.   A number of physical features have been identified that make libraries attractive to children and that promote book reading (Morrow, 1983, 2001):

- *Partitions*—Bookshelves, screens, large plants, or other barriers set the library center apart from the rest of the classroom. This gives children a sense of privacy and provides a cozy, quiet setting for reading.
- *Ample space*—There should be room enough for at least five or six children to use the library at one time.
- *Comfortable furnishings*—The more comfortable the library area, the more likely it is that children will use it. Soft carpeting, chairs, old sofas, bean bags, and a rocking chair all help create a comfortable atmosphere for reading.
- *Open-faced and traditional shelves*—Traditional shelves display books with their spine out, whereas open-faced shelves display the covers of books. Open-faced shelves are very effective in attracting children's attention to specific books. Researchers have found that, when both types of shelves are used, kindergartners chose more than 90 percent of their books from the open-faced displays (Fractor et al., 1993). Traditional shelves are also useful because they can hold many more books

than open-faced shelves. Many teachers rotate books between traditional and open-faced shelves, advertising different books each week.

■ *Book-related displays and props*—Posters (available from such sources as the Children's Book Council, 67 Irving Place, New York, NY 1003; the American Library Association, 50 East Huron Street, Chicago, Illinois 60611; and the International Reading Association, 800 Barksdale Road, Newark, Delaware 19711), puppets, flannel boards with cutout figures of story characters, and stuffed animals encourage children to engage in emergent reading and to act out favorite stories. Stuffed animals also are useful as listeners or babies for children to read to.

■ *Label the center*—Like cordoning off the area from the classroom space, symbolic cues help define the space and identify appropriate activities for young children. Using both print, "Library Corner," and symbols associated with the library—book jackets, a photograph of a child looking at a book—helps even the youngest child read the label for the corner.

■ *Writing center*—Some teachers like to place a writing center near the library corner. This accessibility seems to prompt young children to make illustrations and write in their personal script or dictate a sentence to an adult about the stories they are reading.

Remember, the better designed the library corner, the more use children will make of it—that is, more children will choose to participate in book reading and literature-related activities during free-choice periods. Therefore, a classroom library corner that is voluntarily used by few children is suspected to be a poorly designed center. What might an enticing library corner look like? We provide a drawing of a possible library corner for an early childhood classroom in Figure 5.4.

Effective Story-Reading Techniques

The verbal interaction between adult and child that occurs during story readings has a major influence on children's literacy development (Cochran-Smith, 1984). Much of the research on effective story-reading techniques reports on the interactions between a parent and his or her child during story reading. We have extrapolated the findings of this research to teacher–children story-reading interactions.

Some of this research discusses the affective benefits of story reading. For example, researchers like David Yaden, Laura Smolkin, and Laurie MacGillivray (1993, p. 60) describe story reading as a pleasurable activity. "Children learn very quickly that bringing a book to a parent or caregiver will begin a certain predictable and, for the most part, pleasurable activity." Bill Teale (1986b) describes the exchange as a dance, a choreographed interaction between adult and child reader (sometimes the adult and sometimes the child) and listener (sometimes the adult and sometimes the child).

Adult Behaviors While Reading.   The majority of researchers have concentrated on the human interactions during story reading. From this research, we learn about turn-taking in story reading. Through story reading, very young children are guided into the turn-taking pattern inherent in all conversation: the adult (in this research the adult is usually a parent) talks, then the child talks, then the adult talks, and so forth.

FIGURE 5.4   Library Center

It is within this verbal exchange that the dyad (parent and child) engages in its most significant negotiations: negotiating the meaning of the story. Obviously the adults' understanding exceeds the child's understanding of the text. Through scaffolding, the adult gently moves the child toward the adult's understanding of the text. That is, the adult questions the child about the text's meaning. The child replies, and this reply gives the adult a cue. Based on the child's response, the adult adjusts the kind of support (the scaffold) provided. To aid the child's construction of the meaning, the adult behaves in three ways: (1) as a co-respondent who shares experiences and relates the reading to personal experiences, (2) as an informer who provides information, and (3) as a monitor who questions and sets expectations for the reading session (Roser & Martinez, 1985). Adults play these roles differently depending on the child's response and age. (See Figure 5.5 for a summary of how adults read to children of different ages.)

Child Behaviors During Reading.   What do children do when they are being read to by a caring adult? Several researchers (e.g., Baghban, 1984; Morrow, 1988) have studied young children's behavior, often their own children, during adult–child readings. These

FIGURE 5.5 Typical adult behaviors when reading aloud to children of different ages

12 Months or Younger	12 to 15 Months	15 to 36 Months	36 Months and Older
Adult does most of the talking. Adult labels the pictures ("Look, a train!") and answers ("Yup, it's a train.") Adult points to object.	Adult asks rhetorical questions ("Is that a bus, Kareen?") Adults answer question ("Yup! It's a bus allright!")	Adult asks child to label the object ("What's that?") If the child does not answer, the adult provides the answer ("It's a peach.") If the child provides the correct answer, the adult repeats and reinforces the child's correct answer ("Peach! Yeah! This is a peach.") As the child's competence increases, the adult asks for more ("What color is that peach?" "When do you eat a peach?")	Adult expects child to attend and listen to larger chunks of the text. Adult questions child about characters and story meaning ("Who brought the goodies to her grandmother?" "What did the wolf first say when he saw Little Red Riding Hood?") Most questions are literal (the answers are in the text). Adult points to object. Adult encourages child to read a section of book with support ("What did the Gingerbread Man say to the Little Old Woman?" "Run, run, as fast as you can. . . .")

researchers tell us that even infants focus on the book. They make sounds even before they are speaking, as if they are imitating the reader's voice. They slap at the picture in the book. A little older child with some language facility begins to ask questions about the pictures. They play the "What's that?" game, pointing and asking "What's dat? What's dat? What's dat?" almost without pausing for an answer.

David Yaden, Laura Smolkin, and Mark Conlon's (1989) longitudinal case studies of preschoolers, age three to five, revealed an interesting trend in the questions children ask during reading aloud at home. Initially, most of the children's questions were about the pictures in books. Over time, there was an increase in the number of questions about word meanings and the story being read, and a decrease in picture-related questions. The investigators concluded that "it is possible that after 4 years of age, children begin to pay more attention to the story itself and to the written displays than they do at age 3" (p. 208).

Cultural Variations in Story-Reading. Do children from nonmainstream families have similar early childhood home reading experiences? Shirley Brice Heath's answer to this question is no. In her book *Way with Words* (1983), Heath provides a rich description of the literacy experiences of working-class African American, working-class Caucasian, and mainstream families in the Piedmont area of the Carolinas. From her research, Heath learned that the parents from mainstream families read to their children well into elementary school; use a wide variety of complex questioning strategies to develop their children's understanding of story, plot event sequence, and characterization; and look for ways to connect the text information to their children's experiences. Parents from the working-class

Caucasian families also read to their children, but what they do while they read is different. They stress the sequence of the stories and ask children literal meaning questions ("What did the little boy do then?" "What's the hen's name?"). Further, they make few attempts to connect the events described in the books to their children's experiences. Finally, Heath learned that the African American families tell lots of stories, but reading is strictly for functional purposes. These families read forms, recipes, and the newspaper. They tend not to read books to their children. Of course, Heath's work can not be generalized to all mainstream, Caucasian working class, or African American families. As Teale (1987) notes, there is a great deal of variation among and within social and cultural groups. Teachers need to learn from their students' parents about the experiences their young children have had with books.

We believe that children who have had experiences with books and have experienced dialogic interactions with adults with books are advantaged over children who have no experiences with books and whose parents or early teachers have not shared books with them. Therefore, we strongly encourage teachers and parents of young children to read, read, read to their children.

Classroom Read-Alouds

When a parent and a child read together, the child typically sits in the parent's lap or snuggles under the parent's arm. Many parents establish a bedtime reading ritual, cuddling with the child for a quiet reading time before the child goes to bed. Teachers of the very youngest children, infants, and toddlers should follow parents' lead and apply what is known about how parents read to infants and toddlers to their reading to their young students. The low teacher–child ratio recommended by the National Association for the Education of Young Children for infant (one adult to one infant) and toddler (one adult to four toddlers) programs helps permit this kind of adult–child interaction—though with toddlers, such one-on-one reading together requires some careful arranging (Bredekamp, 1989). We recommend that teachers create a daily reading ritual, perhaps just before naptime. Some day care centers connect with church groups or nearby residential facilities for elderly citizens for the explicit purpose of adults coming to the center just before naptime to read to the children. Now, like at home, every child can have a lap, a cuddle, and a "grandparent" all alone.

The older the child, the larger the permitted-by-law number of children in the group. The typical kindergarten class, for example, is often one teacher and 20 (unfortunately, sometimes even more) children. Teachers of these children are challenged to keep read-alouds enjoyable, pleasurable experiences. Of course, selecting age- and interest-appropriate books is important. Read-aloud experiences are one means to ensure that high-quality literature is accessible to all students, something that is especially important for children who have had few storybook experiences outside school.

The *how* of reading is also important. Now there are too many children for everyone to cuddle next to the adult reader. Yet physical comfort is important. Having a special carpeted area for reading to the group is important. Often this area is next to the library center. Nancy asks her young learners to sit in a semicircle. Patty asks her young learners to sit on the X marks she has made using masking tape on the carpet. Lolita asks her three-year-olds to sit or lie wherever they like in the small carpeted area—as long as they can see the pictures. Each day a different child gets to snuggle with her. In each of these classrooms, the teacher sits at the edge of the circle or the carpet on a low chair, holding the picture book about at the children's eye level. The chair the teacher sits in to read from is a special chair, used both for teacher read-alouds and for the children to read their own writing to the class. Each teacher calls this chair *the author's chair.* Nancy, Patty, and Lolita have mastered reading from the side. Thus the children can see the illustrations while the teacher reads. These teachers know the story they are about to read. They have carefully selected it and read it through, practicing how it will sound when read aloud, in advance. They know how to read it with excitement in their voices. They are careful not to overdramatize, yet they use pitch and stress to make the printed dialogue sound like conversation. They show that they enjoy the story.

The following sequence describes the typical read-aloud strategies recommended by several groups of of researchers based on their survey of research studies, reading methods textbooks, and books and articles about reading to children (Teale & Martinez, 1988).

- *Select high-quality literature*—A key element to a successful read-aloud experience is the book that is being read. Try to find books that will appeal to the children's interest, evoke humor, stimulate critical thinking, stretch the imagination, and so on. While a good story is always effective, also try to include informational books and poetry written for young audiences. A great source for locating good read-aloud books is Jim Trelease's (1989) *The New Read-Aloud Handbook.*

- *Show the children the cover of the book*—Draw the children's attention to the illustration on the cover ("Look at the illustration on this book!"). Tell the children the title of the book, the author's name, and the illustrator's name. ("The title of this book is . . . The author is . . . The illustrator is . . . ") Draw your finger under the title, the author's name, and the illustrator's name as you read each. Remind the children that the title, author's name, and illustrator's name are always on the front of the book. Remember that these are new concepts for young children.

- *Ask the children for their predictions about the story*—("What do you think this story might be about?") Take a few of the children's predictions about the story's content. ("Let's read to see what this story is about.")

- *Or provide a brief introduction to the story*—This can be accomplished in a number of ways. You might provide background information about the story ("This story is going to be about . . . "), connect the topic or theme of the story to the children's own experiences, draw the children's attention to familiar books written by the same author, draw the children's attention to the book's central characters, clarify vocabulary that might be outside the children's realm of experiences, and so on. Keep the introduction brief so there is ample reading time.

- *Identify where and what you will read*—Two important concepts about print for young children to learn is that readers read the print on the pages, not the pictures, and where readers begin reading. Begin read-alouds by identifying where you will start reading and what you will read. Repeating this information often ("Now, I'll begin reading the words right here") weaves this important information into the read-aloud. Be sure to point to the first word on the page as you say where you will begin. Eventually the children will be able to tell you where to begin reading. After many exposures to this important concept, you might playfully ask, "Am I going to read the words or the pictures in this book?" "Where should I begin reading?"

■ *Read with expression and at a moderate rate*—When teachers read with enthusiasm and vary their voices to fit different characters and the ongoing dialogue, the story comes alive for children. It is also important to avoid reading too quickly. Jim Trelease (1989), a leading authority, claims that this is the most common mistake that adults make when reading aloud. He recommends reading slowly enough that children can enjoy the pictures and can make mental images of the story.

■ *Consider reading some stories interactively; that is, encourage children to interact verbally with the text, peers, and the teacher during the book reading*—Some teachers pose questions throughout their book reading to enhance the children's meaning construction and to show how one makes sense of text (Barrentine, 1996). They encourage their students to offer spontaneous comments, to ask questions, and to respond to others' questions, to notice the forms and functions of print features (words, punctuation, letters) as the story unfolds. They use the during-reading book discussions to help children understand what to think about as a story unfolds. According to Brian Cambourne (1988), children learn through active engagement with literacy events, not through passive absorption. Interactive storybook reading provides an opportunity for such needed engagement. However, all this talk while reading might interfere with children's ability to appreciate the literature. Perhaps some books lend themselves better to interactive storybook reading experiences while others should be enjoyed and discussed after the reading.

■ *Read favorite books repeatedly*—Not every book you read has to be a book the children have never heard before. In fact, repeated readings of books can lead to enhanced comprehension and better postreading discussions (Martinez & Roser, 1985; Morrow, 1988). In addition, reading a book three or more times increases the likelihood that young children will attempt to select that book during free-choice time and will try to re-enact or read it on their own (Martinez & Teale, 1988). Of course, the benefits of repeated reading need to be balanced against the need to expose children to a wide variety of literature.

■ *Allow time for discussion after reading*—Good books arouse a variety of thoughts and emotions in children. Be sure to follow each read-aloud session with a good conversation, with questions and comments ("What part of the story did you like best?" "How did you feel when . . . ?" "Has anything like that ever happened to you?" "Who has something to say about the story?"). This type of open-ended questioning invites children to share their responses to the book that was read. After listening to a book read aloud, children want to talk about the events, characters, parts they liked best, and so forth. As children and teacher talk about the book together, they construct a richer, deeper understanding of the book.

When teachers follow the preceding guidelines, they can help ensure that their story reading has the maximum impact on children's literacy learning.

Shared Reading

Teachers usually read picture books to their classes by holding the books so that the children can see the illustrations, pausing occasionally to elicit students' reactions to the stories or to ask story-related questions. This traditional whole-class read-aloud experience differs from parent–child storybook reading interactions in a very important way: Most children can see only the pictures, not the print. To remedy this situation, Holdaway (1979) devised the shared book experience, a strategy that uses enlarged print, repeated readings, and increased pupil participation to make whole-class storybook reading sessions similar to parent–child reading experiences. Today, the shared book experience has become an important component of a quality early literacy program.

To use this strategy, the teacher first needs to select an appropriate book. Andrea Butler and Jan Turbill (1984) recommend stories that have (1) an absorbing, predictable story line; (2) a predictable structure, containing elements of rhyme, rhythm, and repetition; and (3) illustrations that enhance and support the text. These features make it easy for children to predict what is upcoming in the story and to read along with the teacher.

Once a book has been selected, an enlarged copy needs to be obtained. This can be done in several ways. The teacher can (1) rewrite the story on chart paper, using 1-inch or 2-inch tall letters and hand-drawn illustrations; (2) make color transparencies of the pages from the original picture book and use an overhead projector; or (3) acquire a commercially published big book (about 24 × 26 inches) version of the story. Commercial big books are becoming increasingly available. Scholastic and Wright Group/McGraw-Hill, for example, publish enlarged versions of a number of high-quality picture books. Initially, only picture storybooks were available in the big book size. Today informational books also can be located in big book size. These ready-made big books have the advantage of saving teachers time by eliminating the need to make enlarged texts. Understandably, they are expensive since they include large versions of the original illustrations.

Unlike when regular-sized books are shared with children, big books permit all children to see the print. Teachers may take advantage of the enlarged print by drawing young children's attention to the print in the same ways that an adult draws a child's attention to the print in a regular-sized book during a read-aloud. Typically, teachers use a pointer to point to the words as they read big books and invite the children to read along, particularly to the words in a familiar text or to the refrain in a book. As children "read" along with the teacher, they internalize the language of the story. They also learn about directionality (reading from left to right with return sweeps), one important convention of print.

Through the use of big books, teachers can introduce children to other conventions of print—to letter–sound relationships (phonics); to the sequence of letter sounds in words (phonemic awareness); to the difference between letters, words, and sentences; to the spaces between words; to where to start reading on the page; to reading left to right; to return sweeps; to punctuation. In addition, through the use of big books, teachers are able to further children's development of important concepts about books (e.g., the front and back of a book, the difference between print and pictures, that pictures on a page are related to what the print says, that readers read the print, where to begin reading, where the title is and what it is, what an author is, what an illustrator is). In essence, using big books teaches skills in context.

Linking Literacy and Play

In Chapter 3, dramatic play is described as an ideal context for developing young children's oral language. Dramatic play can also offer a context in which children can have meaningful, authentic interactions with reading and writing in early childhood classrooms (Christie, 1991; Roskos & Christie, 2000; Yaden, Rowe, & MacGillivary, 2000). The following vignette, which involves four-year-old preschoolers, illustrates some of the advantages of integrating play and literacy:

> With some teacher assistance, Noah and several friends are getting ready to take a make-believe plane trip to France. The elevated loft in the classroom has been equipped with chairs and has become the plane, and a nearby theme center has been turned into a ticket office. Noah goes into the ticket office, picks up a marker, and begins making scribbles on several small pieces of paper. The teacher passes by with some luggage for the trip. Noah says, "Here Kurt . . . Here are some tickets." The teacher responds, "Oh great. Frequent flyer plan!" Noah then makes one more ticket for himself, using the same scribble-like script. The teacher distributes the tickets to several children, explaining that they will need these tickets to get on board the plane. As Noah leaves the center, he scribbles on a wall sign. When asked what he has written, Noah explains that he wanted to let people know that he would be gone for a while.

The most obvious benefit of linking literacy and play is that play is fun. When children incorporate literacy into their play, they begin to view reading and writing as enjoyable skills that are desirable to master. This is in marked contrast to the negative attitudes that can be perpetuated by dull skill-and-drill lessons and worksheets found in some classrooms.

The airplane trip vignette illustrates how the nonliteral nature of play makes literacy activities significant to children. The pieces of paper that Noah produced would be meaningless in most situations. However, within the context of a make-believe plane trip, Noah's scribbles represent writing, and the pieces of paper signify tickets—not just to Noah, but also to the teacher and the other children. This make-believe orientation enabled Noah to demonstrate his growing awareness of the practical functions of print. He showed that he knew that printed tickets can grant access to experiences such as trips and that signs can be used to leave messages for other people.

The low-risk atmosphere of play encourages children to experiment with emergent forms of reading and writing. When children play, their attention is focused on the activity itself rather than on the goals or outcome of the activity. This means-over-ends orientation promotes risk taking. If outcomes are not critical, mistakes are inconsequential. There is little to lose by taking a chance and trying something new or difficult. Noah felt safe using scribble writing to construct tickets and signs. In nonplay situations, the tickets and signs themselves would assume more importance, decreasing the likelihood that Noah would risk using a personal form of script to construct them.

Like functional literacy, linking literacy and play is a broad-spectrum instructional strategy that offers children many opportunities to learn a variety of different skills and concepts. In addition, children can learn these skills in a variety of ways, including observation, experimentation, collaboration, and instruction. As a result, there are greater opportunities for children at different levels of development to learn new skills and to consolidate newly acquired skills that are only partially mastered. Unlike narrowly focused skill-and-drill activities, opportunities exist for every child in the classroom to advance his or her literacy development.

Literacy-Enriched Play Centers

Nigel Hall (1991) recommends that classroom play areas be subjected to a print flood, an abundance of reading and writing materials that go along with each area's play theme. The goal is to make these play centers resemble the literacy environments that children encounter at home and in their communities. For example, a restaurant center might be equipped with menus, wall signs, pencils, and note pads (for taking food orders). These props would invite children to incorporate familiar restaurant-based literacy routines into their play. Research has shown that this print-prop strategy results in significant increases in the amount of literacy activity during play (Morrow & Rand, 1991; Neuman & Roskos, 1992, 1997).

Different types of literacy materials have been found to stimulate different kinds of literacy play. Lesley Morrow and Muriel Rand (1991) reported that unthematic literacy materials such as pens, pencils, felt-tip markers, and books encouraged children to practice and to experiment with the form and structure of print. For example, children practiced writing letter characters and/or jotted down all the words they knew how to spell. These literacy activities tended to be unconnected with other play activities. In Figure 5.6, we present an example of four-year-old Ryan's unthematic writing. He picked up a piece of paper at the writing center and proceeded to write his name and several random strings of letters and black dots. When asked what he was writing, he responded, "Letters and periods." He had just noticed this punctuation convention (in books or environmental print) and decided to include it in his writing.

In contrast, the thematic literacy props in a veterinarian play center tended to elicit reading and writing activities that were related to the play theme. The thematic literacy play activities appeared to focus on the functional uses of print rather than on its form and structure. For example, children acting in the doctor role wrote make-believe prescriptions, jotted down notes on patients' charts, and filled out appointment cards for future checkups. Other children, in the role of pet owners, pretended to read the pamphlets in the waiting room while their pets were examined. Both thematic and unthematic literacy materials should be included so that children will be encouraged to explore the structural features and practical functions of print.

Beyond writing implements such as pencils, markers, crayons, and pens, we provide examples of thematic and unthematic literacy materials that can be used with a variety of dramatic-play themes in Table 5.1 (Christie & Enz, 1992).

Preparatory Experiences

Matching the classroom settings to children's experiences outside the classroom is important. Children can play only what they know. Nigel Hall and Anne Robinson (1995), for example, used a mechanic's garage as a classroom play setting and as a stimulus for multiple kinds of reading and writing. Prior to initiating the garage play theme, the children were

FIGURE 5.6   Unthematic play writing—Ryan writes "letters and periods"

taken on a field trip to visit a neighborhood mechanic's garage. This firsthand, direct experience greatly increased the children's understanding of what goes on in a mechanic's garage, helped them plan and construct a realistic garage play center, and enhanced their subsequent play.

Using Hall and Robinson's book as their guide, a group of undergraduate students at the University of Delaware designed a bakery play setting in their kindergarten field placement classroom. First, they took the kindergartners on a walk to the neighborhood bakery. There the children saw how bread, cookies, cakes, and so forth were made. They watched cakes and cookies being decorated. The children also recorded the kinds of environmental print they saw in the bakery on the clipboards they had carried with them. They watched the bakery's owner serve a customer. They heard about the importance of cleanliness in preparing food and of being certain to get the correct spelling of names for writing on cakes.

On return to the classroom, the undergraduate students talked with the children about setting up a bakery play setting. How could they create a display case? "Put some of that um, um paper you can look through on one side of those shelves [shelves open on both sides]." What should we call our bakery? "McVey Bakery." What do we need in the bakery? "Cakes, cookies, a cash register," and the list grew.

The next day, the undergraduate students had created a bakery. They brought cooking pans from home, posters borrowed from a bakery, Styrofoam™ circles of various sizes with

TABLE 5.1   Literacy Materials Added to Play Settings in the Christie and Enz Study

Home Center	Business Office
Pencils, pens, markers	Pencils, pens, markers
Note pads	Note pads
Post-It ® notes	Telephone message forms
Baby-sitter instruction forms	Calendar
Telephone book	Typewriter
Telephone message pads	Order forms
Message board	Stationery, envelopes, stamps
Children's books	File folders
Magazines, newspapers	Wall signs
Cookbooks, recipe box	
Product containers from children's homes	
Junk mail	

Restaurant	Post Office
Pencils	Pencils, pens, markers
Note pads	Stationery and envelopes
Menus	Stamps
Wall signs ("Pay Here")	Mailboxes
Bank checks	Address labels
Cookbooks	Wall signs ("Line Starts Here")
Product containers	

Grocery Store	Veterinarian's Office
Pencils, pens, markers	Pencils, pens, markers
Note pads	Appointment book
Bank checks	Wall signs ("Receptionist")
Wall signs ("Supermarket")	Labels with pets' names
Shelf labels for store areas ("Meat")	Patient charts
Product containers	Prescription forms
	Magazines (in waiting room)

Airport/Airplane	Library
Pencils, pens, markers	Pencils
Tickets	Books
Bank checks	Shelf labels for books
Luggage tags	("ABCs," "Animals")
Magazines (on-board plane)	Wall signs ("Quiet!")
Air sickness bags with printed instructions	Library cards
Maps	Checkout cards for books
Signs ("Baggage Claim Area")	

paper disks of the same size that could be decorated with magic markers to look like cakes, a cash register, play money, checkbooks with blank checks, an order pad, cookbooks, wall signs, brown foam pieces that looked like doughnuts, and two chef hats. Together, the college students and the children set the limit on the number of children who could play at any one time—five. This necessitated a sign-up sheet. The children played and wrote orders, decorated cakes with messages ("Happy Birthday"), made signs advertising specials, wrote checks to pay for ordered cakes, wrote receipts, and so forth. The trip to the bakery clearly provided the children with lots of literacy-rich ideas for play.

Notice how easy it was for the undergraduate students to provide the needed preparatory experience (the field trip) and to gather the materials needed to create the bakery. Most were inexpensive, or free. To convert traditional play areas into literacy-enhancing play centers requires a minimum of resources and effort. In return, children's play options are expanded, and the children are presented with opportunities to have meaningful engagements with reading and writing.

Teacher Involvement in Play

Lev Vygotsky (1978) has described how adult interaction can facilitate children's development within the children's zone of proximal development. That is, adults can help children engage in activities that go beyond their current level of mastery, which the children could not do on their own without adult mediation. Many opportunities for this type of adult scaffolding occur when children are engaged in dramatic play in literacy-enriched settings (Roskos & Neuman, 1993). Teachers can encourage children to incorporate literacy activities into ongoing play episodes and can help children with reading and writing activities that the children cannot do independently. This, in turn, can promote literacy growth. Carol Vukelich (1994) found that when adults assumed the role of a more knowledgeable play partner with kindergartners in print-rich play settings, the children's ability to read environmental print was enhanced.

The following vignette illustrates how one teacher used literacy scaffolding to enrich her four-year-olds' pizza parlor dramatization.

> Channing and several friends ask their teacher whether they may play pizza parlor. The teacher says "Yes" and brings out a prop box containing felt pizza pieces, pizza boxes, menus, tablecloths, and so on. The children spend about ten minutes separating the pizza ingredients (olives, pepperoni slices, onions, and cheese shavings made out of felt) into bins. When they have finished, the teacher asks which pizza shop they would like to be today. They respond, "Pizza Hut." While the children watch, the teacher makes a sign with the Pizza Hut name and logo. Channing requests, "Make a 'closed for business' sign on the back." The teacher turns over the paper and writes "CLOSED FOR BUSINESS." She then hangs the "CLOSED" sign on the front of the play center. The children spend another ten minutes rearranging furniture and setting up the eating and kitchen areas in their pretend restaurant. When the children have finished their preparations, the teacher asks, "Is it time to open?" Channing responds, "Yeah. Switch the sign now." The teacher turns the "CLOSED" sign over so that the Pizza Hut logo is showing. The teacher then pretends to be a customer, reads a menu, and orders a pizza with pepperoni, green peppers, onions, and lots of cheese. Once the cooks have piled the appropriate ingredients onto the pizza, the teacher carries it

over to a table and pretends to eat it. When she finishes eating, she writes a make-believe check to pay for her meal.

The teacher played several important roles in this episode. First, she served as stage manager, supplying the props that made the pizza play possible. She also provided scaffolding, making signs that the children could not make on their own. The "Pizza Hut" and "CLOSED" signs provided environmental print for the children to read and also created an opportunity for the children to demonstrate their growing awareness of the regulatory power of print. The pizza shop could not be open for business until the "CLOSED" sign was taken down.

The teacher also served as a co-player, taking on a role and becoming a play partner with the children. Note that she took the minor role of customer, leaving the more important roles (pizza cooks) to the children. While in the role of customer, the teacher modeled several literacy activities—menu reading and check writing. Several children noticed these behaviors and imitated them in future play episodes.

Research has revealed that teachers assume a variety of roles when interacting with children during play (Enz & Christie, 1997; Roskos & Neuman, 1993). As we illustrate in Figure 5.7, these roles form a continuum from no involvement to complete domination of play. The roles in the center of this continuum have been found to be the most effective for enriching the quality of children's play and encouraging play-related literacy activities:

■ *Stage manager*—In the stage manager role, the teacher stays on the sidelines and does not enter into children's play. From this position outside the play frame, the teacher helps children prepare for play and offers assistance once play is underway. Stage managers respond to children's requests for materials, help the children construct costumes and props, and assist in organizing the play set. Stage managers also may make appropriate theme-related script suggestions to extend the children's ongoing play.

FIGURE 5.7   Teacher's roles in play

Uninvolved	Interviewer/ Narrator	Stage Manager	Co-Player	Play-Leader	Director
Out of room Engaged in other activities	Asks literal nonplay-related questions Engages in informal conversation, "chatting" Narrates activities	Gathers materials Makes props Constructs costumes Organizes set Script suggestions	Assumes role and within the role: Supports dialogue Guides plot Makes plot suggestions Defines roles and responsibilities of different characters	Introduces conflicts Facilitates dialogue Problem solving	Delegates props Dictates actions Directs dialogue

■ *Co-player*—In the co-player role, the teacher joins in and becomes an active participant in children's play. Co-players function as an equal play partners with children. The teacher usually takes a minor role in the drama, such as a customer in a store or a passenger on a plane, leaving the prime roles (store clerk, pilot) to the children. While enacting this role, the teacher follows the flow of the dramatic action, letting the children take the lead most of time. During the course of play, many opportunities arise for the adult to model sociodramatic play skills (e.g., role-playing and make-believe transformations) and play-related literacy activities (e.g., writing a shopping list, ordering food from a menu).

■ *Play leader*—As in the co-player role, play leaders join in and actively participate in the children's play. However, play leaders exert more influence and take deliberate steps to enrich and extend play episodes. They do this by suggesting new play themes and by introducing new props or plot elements to extend existing themes. For example, if the teacher has taken on the role of a family member preparing a meal, she might exclaim, "Oh my goodness, we don't have any meat or vegetables for our soup! What should we do?" This creates a problem for the children to solve and may result in the writing of a shopping list and a trip to a nearby store center. Teachers often adopt this role when children have difficulty getting play started on their own or when an ongoing play episode is beginning to falter.

Other roles tend to be less effective—uninvolved, interviewer (the teacher quizzes children about their play activities), and director, in which the teacher takes over control of the play and tells children what to do. These latter two roles tend to disrupt children's play rather than to enhance it. When adults take over control of children's play and intervene too heavy-handedly, children lose interest and often stop playing.

The key to successful play involvement is for teachers to observe carefully and to choose an interaction style that fits with children's ongoing play interests and activities. Kathy Roskos and Susan Neuman (1993) observed six experienced preschool teachers and found that they used a repertoire of interaction styles to encourage literacy-related play. These veteran teachers switched styles frequently, depending on the children who were playing and the nature of the play. The teachers' ability to switch styles to fit the children's play agenda appeared to be as important as the specific interaction styles the teachers used.

When teachers set up literacy-enriched play settings and become involved in play in appropriate ways, they provide children with opportunities to have meaningful engagements with emergent reading and writing. These playful literacy activities go hand-in-hand with the functional, real-world writing activities such as signing up to use a popular center, making an invitation to class parties or performances, writing a message to custodians ("Plz du nt tch"), and so on. Both types of literacy engagements give children opportunities to form, try out, and perfect their own hypotheses about the function and structure of print.

Shared Enactments

In sociodramatic play, children make up their own stories as the play progresses. In shared enactments, on the other hand, the players enact a written story. This story can be composed by the children in the classroom or by an adult author.

Written Story to Dramatization.   Vivian Paley (1981) has developed a strategy that combines storytelling and play. Children first dictate stories that are tape recorded and later written down by the teacher. The teacher reads the stories aloud to the class, and then the children work together as a group to act out the stories. This strategy promotes children's narrative skills—over time, their stories become better organized and increasingly more complex—and makes contributions to many aspects of their social, oral language, and cognitive development.

In her book, *Boys and Girls: Superheros in the Doll Corner,* Paley (1984, pp. 50–51) gives an example of a story written by one of her kindergarten boys:

> Superman, Batman, Spiderman, and Wonderwoman went into the woods and they saw a wicked witch. She gave them poisoned food. Then they died. Then Wonderwoman had magic and they woke up. Everybody didn't wake up. Then they woke up from Wonderwoman's magic. They saw a chimney and the wolf opened his mouth. Superman exploded him.

Note how this story has a rudimentary narrative plot: the main characters encounter a problem (dying as a result of eating poison); an attempt is made to solve the problem (magic); and there is a resolution (waking up). Then a new problem comes along (the wolf), and the narrative cycle continues. Also, notice that this child has incorporated superheroes from popular media with elements from classic fairy tales to build his story: finding a cottage in the woods (*Hansel and Gretel*), a witch who gives poison food (*Snow White*), and a wolf and a chimney (*The Three Pigs*).

Greta Fein, Alicia Ardila-Rey, and Lois Groth (2000) have developed a version of Paley's strategy that they call *shared enactment.* During free-choice activity time, the teacher sits in the classroom writing center (see Chapter 7), and children are encouraged to tell the teacher stories. The teacher writes down the children's words verbatim. When a child finishes with his or her story, the teacher asks if there is anything else he or she wishes to add. Then the teacher reads the story back to the child to make sure that it matches the child's intentions. The child decides whether to share the story with the group. If the child does, it is put in a special container called the story box.

Later, during shared enactment time, the teacher reads the story to the class, and the story is dramatized. Fein, Ardila-Rey, and Groth (2000, p. 31) describe a typical shared enactment session:

> The children gathered along two sides of a large space used for circle time and the teacher sits among them. The empty space before them became the stage. The teacher summoned the author to sit by her side and read the story out loud to the group. The teacher then asked the author what characters were needed for the enactment. The author identified the characters (often with the eager help of other children) and chose a peer to portray each one. When the actors had been assembled, the teacher read the story slowly as a narrator would, stopping to allow for action and omitting dialogue so that the actors could improvise. The players dramatized the story, following the lead of the author who acts as director. At the completion of the enactment and the applause, another story was selected for dramatization.

Fein and her colleagues used the shared enactment procedure with a class of kindergartners twice a week for 12 weeks and found that it resulted in a substantial increase in narrative activity (story enactment and storytelling) during free play. The investigators noted that this brief intervention appeared to penetrate the daily life of the classroom and promised to make important contributions to the children's narrative development.

Dramatization to Written Story.   Another version of combining play and storytelling for preschool children involves an observant teacher who witnesses an interesting drama emerging from the children's pretend play. At the conclusion of the dramatic play, the teacher privately asks these children if they would like to retell their drama with the class. If the children wish to share their pretend adventure, the teacher quickly writes it down as the entire group listens. This strategy helps the children realize how spoken words and actions can be written down and shared with others. The following is an example of dramatic play-to-written story told by three four-year-old girls.

> There were two mommies who were going to take their babies to the doctor 'cause their babies were sick from a sleeping spell. On the way to the doctor they got lost in the forest. Just then Xena came by on her big white horse. They all got on the horse together and they found Dr. Mary, Medicine Woman. The doctor gave the babies shots and medicine and the babies got better.

Notice how the children's story reflected a traditional plot line—a problem that needed to be solved, a crisis, and two heroines who saved the day. Once again the children had interwoven story elements from classic fairy tales (*Sleeping Beauty*) with current TV heroes.

Language Experience Approach or Shared Writing

The language-experience approach (LEA), which became popular in the 1970s (Allen, 1976; Veatch et al., 1979), has children read texts composed of their own oral language. Children first dictate a story about a personal experience, and the teacher writes it down. The teacher reads the story back to the children and then gives them the opportunity to read it themselves. Sometimes the children illustrate their dictated sentences. This strategy is also referred to as shared writing.

The LEA or shared writing strategy is an excellent means for teachers to demonstrate the relationship between speaking, writing, and reading. It can help children realize that (1) what is said can be written down in print, and (2) print can be read back as oral language.

Like functional print and play-based literacy, the language experience or shared writing strategy presents children with a broad array of learning opportunities. At the most basic level, LEA/shared writing helps children learn that the purpose of written language is the same as that of oral language: to communicate meaning. For other children, the strategy enables teachers to demonstrate explicitly the structure and conventions of written language. The children watch as the teacher spells words conventionally, leaves spaces between words, uses left-to-right and top-to-bottom sequences, starts sentences and names with capital letters, ends sentences with periods or other terminal punctuation marks, and so on. This is an ideal means to show children how the mechanical aspects of writing work.

LEA/shared writing has the additional advantage of making conventional writing and reading easier for children. By acting as scribe, the teacher removes mechanical barriers to written composition. The children's compositions are limited only by their experiential backgrounds and oral language. Reading is also made easier because the stories are composed of the children's own oral language and are based on their personal experiences. This close personal connection with the story makes it easy for children to predict the identity of unknown words in the text.

A number of variations of LEA/shared writing have been developed. In the sections that follow, three that are particularly appropriate for use with young children are described: group experience stories, individual experience stories and classroom newspapers.

Group Experience or Shared Writing Stories

This strategy begins with the class having some type of shared experience: The class takes a field trip to a farm, to a zoo, across the street to the supermarket, to see a play; the class guinea pig has babies; the class completes a special cooking activity or other project. Whatever the event, the experience should be shared by all members of the group so that everyone can contribute to the story.

The following is a description of how early childhood teachers might engage their children in a group shared story-writing experience. The "make-a-word" and "make-a-sentence" ideas described below are Pat Cunningham's (1995b). Many early childhood teachers have begun to weave activities like these into their children's LEA/shared writing experiences. Many believe their children are much more knowledgeable about print because of their use of Cunningham's ideas.

Teachers need to be selective about which of these activities to use in a single LEA/shared writing. To use all of these activities in one LEA/shared writing might take too much time. It is important to keep the group's attention and to ensure that this reading and writing activity remains enjoyable.

1. The teacher begins by gathering the children on the rug in the whole-group area to record their thoughts about the experiences—to preserve what they recall in print. Teachers often begin with a request to "tell me what you remember about . . . ?"

2. As children share their memories, the teacher records exactly what they say. The teacher does not rephrase or correct what a child says. The teacher records the children's language, just as they use it. The sentence structure, or syntax, is the child's. The spellings, however, are correct. As the teacher writes the child's comments on a large sheet of chart paper with a magic marker in print large enough for all the children to see, the teacher verbalizes the process used to construct the text. (The teacher might choose to write on the chalkboard, overhead transparency, or chart paper.) The following dialogue (sometimes a bit of a monologue) illustrates what the teacher might say as the child's language is recorded:

> ### Our Trip to the Farm
> LOLLIE: We went on a hayride.
>
> TEACHER: *We*—because that word is the first word in Lollie's sentence, it needs to be capitalized.

> **TEACHER:**   Lollie's next word is *went*. I need to make a space between *We* and *went*. [Teacher reads: "We went."] How many letters are in *went*? Let's count them.
>
> **CHILDREN:**   1–2—3–4
>
> **TEACHER:**   *On*. Does anyone know how to spell *on*? No? *O—n*. *On* is spelled *o—n*. Another space before I write the *o*. Watch while I write a *n*. First I draw a straight line down, from top to bottom. Then I come to the top of the straight line, and I make a curved line like that. That's a *n*. Another space. *A*. Watch while I make an *a*. First make a circle, and then I make a line on the right-hand side of the circle, from top to bottom. *Hayride*. That sounds like two words, doesn't it? What two words, Marcus?
>
> **MARCUS:**   Hayride. [He says them together.]
>
> **TEACHER:**   That's right. *Hay* and *ride*. That's the end of Lollie's sentence. What do I need to put at the end of this sentence?
>
> **KRISTOL:**   A period.
>
> **TEACHER:**   Right. A period. [She makes a large dot and rereads Lollie's sentence.] [Teacher points and reads the whole sentence.]

Many concepts about the structure and conventions of print are taught during the creation of this single sentence—capitalize the first word of a sentence; put a space between words; form an *n* like this; an *h* and an *n* are formed the same way; letters make up words, and so forth. Every sentence in LEA/shared writing lends itself to exploring how our language conventions work, to introducing and reinforcing young children's knowledge of the mechanics of writing. In addition, by reading each word as it is written, the teacher promotes word recognition and one-to-one matching of speech and print.

Because of the amount of time spent on each sentence, the teacher takes sentences from only a small number of students. Taking sentences from all the children would make the sitting time too long for the young learners.

If a student's contribution is vague or unclear, the teacher might have to ask the child to clarify the point or may have to do some *minor* editing to make the sentence comprehensible to the rest of the class. The teacher must exercise caution when a student's contribution is in a divergent dialect (e.g., "He be funny."). Changing this utterance to so-called standard English may be interpreted as a rejection of the child's language. This, in turn, might cause the child to cease to participate in future experience stories. In such cases it is usually better to accept the child's language and not change it. As Nigel Hall (1987) points out, this dialect sensitivity does not need to extend to differences in pronunciation. If a child pronounces a word in a divergent manner (e.g., *bes* for *best*), the conventional spelling of the word can still be used. The child is still able to pronounce the word as *bes* when reading it.

3. When the whole story is created, the teacher rereads it from beginning to end, carefully pointing to each word and emphasizing the left-to-right and return-sweep progression. Then the class reads the story as a group (a practice called choral reading). Often a child points to the words with a pointer as the class reads.

4. The teacher hangs the story in the writing center, low enough so interested children can copy the story. Because the teacher wrote the story on chart paper (teachers' preferred medium for group stories), the story can be stored on the chart stand and reviewed periodically by the class. Sometimes the teacher rewrites each child's sentence on a piece of paper and asks the originator to illustrate his or her sentence. The pages are then collected into a book, complete with a title page listing a title and the authors' names, and placed in the library corner. These books are very popular with the children. Other times, the teacher makes individual copies of the story—via photocopying or word processing—for each child.

Individual Language Experience Stories

In an individual language experience story, each student meets individually with the teacher and dictates her or his own story. As the child dictates, the teacher writes the story. Because the story is not intended for use with a group audience, editing can be kept to a minimum, and the child's language can be left largely intact. Once the dictation is completed, the teacher reads the story back to the child. This rereading provides a model of fluent oral reading and gives the child an opportunity to revise the story ("Is there anything you would like to change in your story?"). Finally, the child reads the story.

A variety of media can be used to record individual experience stories, each with its own advantages. Lined writing paper makes it easier for teachers to model neat handwriting and proper letter formation. Story paper and unlined drawing paper provide opportunities for children to draw illustrations to go with their stories. Teachers can also use the classroom computer to make individual experience stories. Children enjoy watching the text appear on the monitor as the teacher keys in their story. Word-processing programs make it easy for the teacher to make any changes the children want in their stories. Stories can then be printed to produce a professional-looking text.

Individual experience stories can be used to make child-generated books. One approach is to write children's stories directly into blank books. Blank books are made of sheets of paper stapled between heavy construction paper or bound in hard covers. An alternative approach is to staple completed experience stories between pieces of heavy construction paper. For example, books can be made up of one student's stories ("Joey's Book") or of a compilation of different children's stories ("Our Favorite Stories" or "Our Trip to the Fire Station"). Child-authored texts can be placed in the classroom library for others to read. These books tend to be very popular because children like to read what their friends have written.

Individual experience stories have several important advantages over group stories. The direct personal involvement produces high interest and motivation to read the story. There is a perfect match between the child's experiences and the text, making the story very easy to read. Children also feel a sense of ownership of their stories and begin to think of themselves as authors.

The one drawback to this strategy is that the one-to-one dictation requires a considerable amount of teacher time. Many teachers make use of parent volunteers or older students (buddy writers) to overcome this obstacle. Another strategy is to have a tape recorder available for children to dictate their stories. Teachers can then transcribe the children's compositions when time allows. Of course, children miss out on valuable teacher modeling when tape recordings are used.

Classroom Newspaper

The classroom newspaper strategy (Veatch, 1986) begins with oral sharing in which individual children discuss recent events that have happened to them. For example, Bobby might say, "We went to the lake, and I saw a big fish swimming in the water. I tried to catch it, but I fell in and got all wet." After five or six children have shared their personal experiences, the teacher picks several of the most interesting to put in the classroom newspaper. The teacher then writes these experiences on a piece of chart paper with the date on the top. The teacher rephrases the children's contributions, polishing them up a bit and converting them to the third person. For example, Bobby's contribution might be edited into the following: "Bobby and his family went to the lake. He tried to catch a large fish and fell into the water. He got all wet!" Note that Bobby's thoughts are preserved, but the text is transformed into third-person, newspaper-style writing.

Children then take turns reading the day's news. The charts can be saved and reviewed at the end of the week. Classroom news does not require a shared experience, making it easier to use this technique on a regular basis than to use the group experience story. This technique also can give quite an ego boost to the children whose experiences are reported. For this reason, an effort should be made to ensure that all children get a turn at having their stories included in the news.

The classroom newspaper is an excellent way to help shift children from first-person narrative style used in individual and group stories to the third-person narrative styles used in many magazines and adult-authored children's books. We describe two variations of this strategy—daily time capsules and headline news—in Trade Secrets 5.2 and 5.3.

Trade Secrets 5.2

Daily Time Capsules

Just before class is dismissed each day, Cyndy Schmidt asks her kindergartners what they have learned. As students tell their "significant learnings," she lists them on the chalkboard. Next, Cyndy asks the children to pick the one that they are most likely to remember next year. The item picked by the most children becomes the Time Capsule for that day. The Capsule item can be written, along with the day's date, on a large piece of construction paper and illustrated by student volunteers. These Capsules are permanently displayed on the classroom wall. By the end of the year, several rings of Capsules encircle the entire classrooms! Other teachers prefer to put Capsules into a book that is displayed in the library center. Daily Time Capsules can be reviewed occasionally with children to reinforce learning and to give them additional reading practice. Cyndy has found that these Capsules also make a very favorable impression on parents and others who visit the classroom.

Trade Secrets 5.3

Headline News

Kindergarten teacher Nancy Edwards begins each Monday's class with a group session called Headline News. The children are divided into pairs. They talk to each other about what they did over the weekend. Then each child shares her partner's news. Emma, for example, tells about Jordan's adventure getting new tennis shoes at the mall. When Emma finishes, Nancy says, "What was the most important thing about Jordan's weekend?" The children agree: getting the new shoes. On a strip of paper Nancy writes: "Jordan gets new shoes!" This strip, along with a strip for every other child, is posted on the Headline News bulletin board.

Summary

When most children enter preschool or kindergarten, they already possess considerable knowledge about reading and writing. Teachers can capitalize on this prior learning by using a number of effective yet remarkably simple instructional strategies that link home and school literacy learning. In this chapter, we discussed four strategies that form a solid foundation for an effective, developmentally appropriate early childhood language arts program: functional literacy activities, storybook reading, play-based literacy, and language experience or shared writing approach.

- *What are functional literacy activities, and how can teachers use these activities in a preschool or kindergarten classroom?*

   Functional print (labels, lists, directions, and schedules) is ideal for beginning readers because the surrounding context helps explain its meaning. This contextualized print is easy for young children to read and helps them view themselves as real readers. In addition, functional literacy activities help develop the concept that reading and writing have practical significance and can be used to get things done in everyday life. This realization makes print more salient to children and provides important motivation for learning to read and write. Functional print also presents opportunities for children to learn to recognize letters and words in a highly meaningful context.

- *How can dramatic play centers be used to encourage young children's literacy development?*

   Dramatic play provides an ideal context for children to have meaningful, authentic interactions with print. Dramatic play offers children of all ages and abilities multiple low-risk opportunities to explore and experiment with reading and writing.

- *How can teachers set up a well-designed library center?*

   A well-stocked and managed classroom library should be a key feature of every early childhood classroom. To encourage young children to engage in book reading in this area, the classroom library must be well-designed with partitions, ample space, comfortable furnishings, open-face and traditional bookshelves, and book-related props and displays. Teachers will know quickly if their classroom library meets the well-designed criteria; inviting classroom libraries are heavily used by the children.

■ *What are the characteristics of effective adult storybook reading?*

What adults say—the verbal interaction between adult (parent or teacher) and child—during story readings has a major influence on children's literacy development. During storybook readings, children learn about the turn-taking inherent in all conversation. The adult helps the child negotiate the meaning of the text, assisting by relating the content to personal experiences, providing information, asking questions, and setting expectations. Who talks the most and the content of the talk varies with the age of the child.

Specific read-aloud strategies have been recommended for use in early childhood classrooms. These include: read aloud every day, select high-quality literature, show and discuss the cover of the book before reading, ask children to make predictions about the story, provide a brief introduction, identify where and what you will read, read with expression at a moderate rate, read some stories interactively, read favorite stories repeatedly, and allow time for discussion after reading.

Shared reading, the reading of big books, is also recognized as a critically important practice in quality early childhood literacy programs because big books permit all children to see the print, something not possible when teachers read aloud a regular-sized book. By using big books, teachers can introduce children to the conventions of print and the concepts about books.

■ *How does the language experience approach (or shared writing) increase a child's understanding of print and facilitate reading development?*

The language experience approach/shared writing strategy involves having the teacher write stories that children dictate. The resulting experience stories are a dynamic means to demonstrate the connections among talking, reading, and writing. As the teacher writes the children's speech, the children immediately see the one-to-one correspondence between spoken and written words. Because the children are the authors of these highly contextualized stories, they can easily read the stories. Experience stories can be composed by either a single child or a group of children. Group stories are more time-efficient, but individual stories are more personalized and ensure a perfect match between reader and text. Classroom newspapers and daily time capsules are current-event variations of the LEA strategy, and provide children the same opportunities to read print in highly contextualized, authentic situations.

LINKING KNOWLEDGE TO PRACTICE

1. Visit a preschool or kindergarten classroom and record the different types and ways functional literacy activities are used in the classroom. How did the children respond to or use functional print within classroom? Did the teacher refer to the functional print?

2. Observe a library center in an early childhood classroom and evaluate its book holdings and design features. Are there a large number and wide variety of books available for the chil-

dren to read? Are any basic types of books missing? Does the library center contain partitions, ample space, comfortable furnishings, open-face and traditional bookshelves, and book-related props and displays? Is there a writing center nearby?

3. Tape yourself during a read-aloud with a small group of children. Analyze your read-aloud for the strategies suggested in this chapter. What goals would you set for yourself?

4. With a partner, design plans for a literacy-enriched play center. Select a setting appropriate for a group of children. Describe how this center might be created in a classroom. What literacy props could be placed in the play center? What functional uses of print might be used to convey information? What literacy routines might children use in this center? What roles might children and teacher play? How might you scaffold children's play and literacy knowledge in this play center?

5. Observe a LEA/shared writing activity. Describe how the teacher used this opportunity to teach children about the forms and functions of print.

6 Teaching Early Reading and Writing

When Carol was three and four, she lived in California, and her beloved Grammy lived in Minnesota. Whenever her mother wrote home, Carol wrote to her grandmother. When she had completed her letter, her mother always asked, "And what did you tell Grammy?" Carol pointed to the scribbles on the page, every scribble, and eagerly told her mother exactly what the letter said. Her mother listened intently, always ending with, "And you wrote all that?" Later, her clever mother inserted a slip of paper into the envelope telling Grammy the gist of Carol's message. Grammy's response to Carol's letter always arrived within a week or two. Carol and her mother snuggled together on the overstuffed green sofa to read Grammy's letter, over and over. When her daddy came home from work, Carol met him with "It's a Grammy letter day!" Then, she'd "read" Grammy's letter to her Daddy.

Some contend that children learn written language just like oral language. That is, children learn to read and write simply by having opportunities to see print in use and by engaging in activities where literacy is embedded in the task, just like Carol did in the vignette above. These people believe that children learn without ever knowing they are learning. This view supports the implicit teaching of literacy. Others believe that children need to engage in activities that help them focus on the abstract features of our written language, like on letter names and sounds. This perspective supports the explicit teaching of literacy. We believe the truth lies somewhere in the middle: Children do need opportunities to see reading and writing in use and to experience the purposes of literacy. Children also need to be directly taught about the functions and features of print. The key is that the activities and experiences that early childhood teachers offer young children must be appropriate for the children's age and stage.

Chapter 5 presents the core components of a balanced early childhood language arts program:

- daily storybook reading by the teacher,
- opportunities for children to attempt to read books on their own in the library center,
- functional reading and writing activities,
- literacy activities linked to play, and
- language experience or shared writing activities.

This chapter is about three other key components of a balanced early literacy program: writing instruction, reading instruction, and assessment. The chapter begins with a discussion of several effective means for teaching children about writing: the writing center, writing workshop, interactive writing, and publication. Then, developmentally appropriate forms of reading/decoding instruction are explored. Skill areas include phonological awareness, of which phonemic awareness is a component, letter recognition, letter–sound correspondences (phonics), and sight word recognition. Finally, we describe how teachers can assess children's early literacy skills and knowledge.

Before You Read This Chapter, Think About . . .

- how you learned to write. Not handwrite, but write. Do you remember writing messages to special people, maybe messages that were lines and lines of scribble? Do you remember writing on walls, much to someone's dismay?
- how you learned the names of the letters of the alphabet. Did you learn by singing the alphabet song?
- how you learned the sounds letters make. Do you remember phonics workbooks or learning phonics rules (e.g., when two vowels go walking, the first one does the talking)?

Focus Questions

- Why is a writing center an important area in the preschool classroom? How might an adult teach in the writing center?
- How does a teacher teach during a writing workshop?
- Why is it important to publish children's writing?
- What does it mean to offer young children a balanced approach to reading instruction?
- What is the difference between phonological awareness, phonemic awareness, and phonics? In what sequence do young children typically acquire these skills? What does this sequence suggest about classroom instructional strategies?
- How might early childhood teachers introduce young children to the letters of the alphabet?
- What types of assessment methods are used to collect data about children's early literacy learning?

Writing Instruction

Even the youngest of children like to write—not only on paper, but also on walls and floors. As Pam Oken-Wright notes, "The urge to make one's mark is such a strong one that it is manifest on many a bedroom wall, executed with whatever implement was handy or seemed exciting" (1998, p. 76). Early childhood teachers, then, must take advantage of this natural urge by providing a variety of writing materials to their young writers, learning to ask the right question at the right time, and providing the right instruction at the right time to nudge their young writers' development. In this section, we explore the what and the how of writing instruction in an early childhood classroom.

BOX **6.1**

Definition of Terms

alphabetic principle: the idea that letters, or groups of letters, represent phonemes.

ongoing assessment: a form of assessment that relies on the regular collection of children's work to illustrate children's knowledge and learning. The children's products are created as they engage in daily classroom activities. Thus, children are learning while they are being assessed.

onsets: the beginning parts of words.

phonemes: the individual sounds that make up spoken words.

phonemic awareness: the awareness that spoken words are composed of individual sounds or phonemes.

phonics: the relationship between sounds and letters in written language.

phonological awareness: awareness of the sound structure of oral language.

rimes: the endings parts of words.

writing center: an area in the classroom that is stocked with materials (lots of kinds of paper, different writing tools) to invite children to write.

writing workshop: a time in the schedule when all children meet to study the art and craft of writing.

The Context for Writing: The Writing Center

A writing center is a special area in the classroom that is stocked with materials that invite children to write. When setting up such a center, teachers need to remember that writing is a social act. Children want to share their writing with peers, to know what their peers are writing, to ask for assistance with the construction of their text. "Morning. How do you spell 'mororornnn-nnninggg'?" Knowing children's need for talk while writing, teachers typically provide a table and chairs in the writing center.

Gather the Needed Materials.   In addition to a table and chairs, teachers stock the writing center with materials that invite children to write, to play with writing materials. Such materials include but are not limited to the following:

- many different kinds of paper (e.g., lined theme paper, typical story paper, discarded computer or office letterhead paper with one side clean, lots of unlined paper, paper cut into different shapes to suggest writing about particular topics, paper folded and made into blank books, stationery and envelopes, cards);
- various writing tools (e.g., pencils, markers—be certain to purchase the kind that can withstand the kind of pressure young children exert as they write—crayons, felt-tip pens, a computer or computers with a word-processing program);
- writing folders for storage of each child's writing efforts; and
- a box or file drawer in which to store the file folders.

Notice that oversized (fat) pencils and special primary-lined paper were not recommended as the only paper and pencils to be provided. For young children, Miriam Martinez and Bill Teale (1987) recommend unlined paper because it does not signal how writing is supposed to be done. Children are freer to use the emergent forms of writing—pictures used as writing, scribble writing, letter-like units, and so on—that do not fit on the lines of traditional lined writing paper or story paper (e.g., top half blank, bottom half lined).

In addition to these required items, many teachers include the following items in their classroom writing center:

- a bulletin board for displaying such items as samples of the children's writing, examples of different forms of writing (e.g., thank you notes, letters, postcards, stories), writing-related messages (e.g., "Here's our grocery list"), messages about writing (e.g., "Look at this! Shawn's sister published a story in the newspaper"), and the children's writing;
- posters showing people engaged in writing;
- clipboards for children who want to write someplace other than at the table;
- mailboxes (one for each child, the teacher, the principal or center director, and other appropriate persons, as determined by the children) to encourage note and letter writing;
- alphabet strips on the writing table so that the children have a model readily available when they begin to attempt to link their knowledge of letter sounds with their knowledge of letter formations.

Most teachers introduce the materials to the children gradually, that is, they do not place all these materials in the writing center on the first day of school, which young children would find overwhelming. They make the writing center new and exciting over the year by regularly adding new materials and tools. Pam Oken-Wright (1998) suggests that when new materials are added to the writing center, it is important not to substitute the new materials for the old materials; young children like the familiar along with the new.

Arrange the Materials.   With so many different materials in the writing center, keeping the supplies orderly and replenishing them can be time-consuming. Some teachers label the places where the various tools and paper belong in the writing center; this helps all the children know where to return used materials, and it helps a child "clerk" know how to straighten the center at cleanup time. Further, labeling the places where the items belong permits a quick inventory of missing and needed items. Figure 6.1 provides an illustration of a well-equipped, well-arranged writing center.

Computers and Word Processing.   A growing number of early childhood classrooms have computers in the writing center. Teachers in these classrooms are indeed fortunate! Early childhood computer expert Dan Shade highly recommends the following relatively new software packages for their user-friendly qualities; that is, young children can easily use them to write: *Orly's Draw-a-Story* (Dan's personal favorite), *Claris for Kids,* and *The Writing Center* (the new and improved version). Some older favorites include *Kid Works 2*

FIGURE 6.1   A well-equipped writing center

(Davidson), *Storybook Weaver* (MECC), *Wiggins in Storybook Land,* and *The Incredible Writing Machine* (The Learning Company).

Marilyn Cochran-Smith, Jessica Kahn, and Cynthia Paris (1986) point out that all writers, regardless of age, require time at the computer when their attention is focused on learning word-processing skills. For example, Bev Winston, a kindergarten teacher, introduced her young students to word processing during the school's orientation days, those days that precede the first full day of school. Then she watched her children as they played with word processing during their free-play time and provided instruction as each child needed it. Word processing is a tool to preserve children's important first writings. It is important for teachers to keep this in mind. Young children need time to experiment with this tool just as children need time to experiment with pencils, pens, markers, and so forth.

The Writing Workshop

By the time children reach kindergarten, many teachers add a writing workshop, with some direct teaching of writing, to the daily schedule at least once a week.

The writing workshop was first described by Donald Graves (1983) in his book *Writing: Teachers and Children at Work.* All members of the writing workshop meet to intensively study the art and craft of writing. The workshop typically has the following components:

- *Focus lesson*—A five-minute lesson to teach children about the writing process ("I want to make a change in my writing. I'm going to *revise*. Here's how I'll do it."); a procedural aspect of the writing program ("We help our friends while they write. We say things like, 'Tell me more about your dog. What color is he?' "); a quality of good writing ("I can tell more about my dog by adding his color, black. So I'll write 'I hv a blk dg.' "); a mechanical feature of writing ("Always make *I* a capital, a big letter."); or about why people write ("We need to make a list.").
- *Writing*—A 10 to 15 minute period during which children write and meet with peers and the teacher.
- *Group share*—A ten-minute period during which one or two children read their writing pieces to the group and receive positive feedback and content-related questions.

While the writing workshop was originally designed for use in the elementary grades (see Chapter 9), it can be easily adapted for use with younger children. Here are examples of how one kindergarten teacher has used variations of the workshop approach to help her students develop as writers.

Focus Lessons. Focus lessons, (also called mini-lessons) are short lessons that focus on an aspect of writing. Kindergarten teacher Bernadette Watson uses focus lessons to teach her students how to match letter sounds with the correct letter symbols. In one lesson, she helped the children sound out the spellings of the words in the sentence "I went to New York." She

---

Trade Secrets 6.1

Teaching about Sound–Symbol Relationships: An Invented-Spelling Mini-Lesson

Bernadette Watson

Teacher: I didn't tell you this before. I went on a trip to New York this weekend. The New York Marathon (the running race) was on this weekend, so there was a lot of traffic! It took us a long time to get to New York. That's what I'm going to write about today. I'm going to start by drawing a picture. I'll just draw a road. That will help me remember what I'm going to write about. [Teacher draws a road]. I'm going to write "I went

to New York City." Will you help me write the words? "I" Oh, that's an easy one. [Writes "I"] W-e-n-t [stretches word]. "w"-"w"-"w."

Child: "Y."

Teacher: It does sound like a "Y." We'll use "Y" for that sound. E-N-T.

Children: "N!" "N!" [Teacher writes "N."]

Teacher: W-E-N-*T*-T-T

Children: "T!" [Teacher writes "T."]

Teacher: to

Child: I know how to spell to—"t" "o."

Teacher: How do you know that?

Child: I don't know. I just do. [Teacher writes *to*.]

Teacher: [Reads, I went "to."] New. "N"-"N"-"N."

Child: It's like my name. "N"

. . . and so on.

stretched the words out (e.g. w-e-n-t) and focused the children's attention on sound of each letter ("What letter makes the /w/ sound?) or letter cluster ("How about /ent/?). Because she knows that her students will not fully understand the relationship between sounds and symbols as a result of one lesson, Ms. Watson weaves the content of this lesson into many lessons and reinforces this understanding when she talks with her young writers about their writing.

Writing Time.   The focus lesson is followed by a time for the children to write. Ms. Watson teaches in a public school and has to make do with an occasional parent as a teacher assistant. She presents a writing lesson on Monday. Five children begin their free-play time in the writing center, writing with Ms. Watson's support and reading their text to Ms. Watson before they leave the writing center. The other children proceed to centers of their choice. Tomorrow another five children will begin their free-play time in the writing center. Each child begins free-play in the writing center once each week. Certainly the children can choose to write on more than their writing day, but all children must write at least one day each week. Requiring the children to begin their play time in the writing center one day each week allows Ms. Watson to support and observe each child's writing development at least once each week.

While the children write, Ms. Watson and other adults who might be in the classroom, meet with the young writers about their writing. The opportunity to talk while writing is a critically important component of writing workshop. The talk is about the content and the mechanics (usually the letter–sound relationships) of the piece. Through conferences, teachers can provide one-on-one instruction, providing the child with just the right help needed at that minute.

Group Share Time.   The workshop is culminated by group share time. During the group share session, two or three children sit, one at a time, in the author's chair and share their pieces with the other writers in the class. (See Trade Secret 6.2 for a description of how one teacher uses the "author's chair" strategy.) Typically, the other children are gathered at the sharing writer's feet, listening attentively while the writer reads the piece, preparing to make comments or ask questions. The following describes one group share in Ms. Bernadette Watson's kindergarten classroom.

> **DEMETRI:**   "I like your story."
>
> **MS. WATSON:**   "Remember, Demetri, when we talked about how we tell the writer what we really liked about his or her story? Can you tell Aaron what you liked about his story?"
>
> **DEMETRI:**   "I really liked the part where you thought you would get a dog, because I want a dog, too."
>
> **AARON:**   "Thanks."

The classroom rule is that the writer calls on three children for a question or a comment. The first response is a comment. The other two must be questions. Ms. Watson uses this time to help her children begin to understand the difference between a comment (statement or sentence) and a question. Learning the difference takes lots of practice.

Through group shares, young children learn that writing is meant to be shared with others. Writers write to communicate their thoughts and ideas with their readers. Young

Trade Secret 6.2

The Author's Chair

Ms. Garcia has taken a regular classroom chair and taped the label "Author's Chair" on its backrest. The chair is placed in front of the carpeted area where her kindergartners sit during circle time. She uses this chair on a daily basis to read good literature to her class. Ms. Garcia also uses the Author's Chair to read stories that her students have written, treating them in the same manner as the adult-authored books. Her students use the chair too, taking turns reading their own writing from the Author's Chair.

Regardless of who is doing the reading (Ms. Garcia or her students) or what type of book is being read (adult-authored or child-authored), the children in the audience respond in the same way. First, they *receive* the story, making positive comments about their favorite part, what they liked best about the story (e.g., "It was funny!"), or their views of what the story was about. Then the students may ask questions, requesting additional information or inquiring about specific events in the story. If the book was written by a professional author, Ms. Garcia and the children speculate on how the author might answer these questions.

The Author's Chair strategy, developed by Donald Graves and Jane Hansen (1983), provides a powerful incentive for young children to write. They know that selected pieces of their writing will be published by being read from the Author's Chair. Another advantage of this strategy is that the chair serves as a link between child and adult authors. When children sit in the chair and read their published books, their books are treated just like those of professional writers. They are received and questioned in the same manner. This adds status to their writing, helps children perceive themselves as being real authors, motivates young children to write, and helps them to develop a sense of authorship.

children also learn how to share their writing with others (reading in a loud voice so others can hear, holding their writing so others can see) and about the difference between a question and a comment. Teachers use children's texts and questions and comments as a context to teach about writing.

We return to the writing workshop in Chapter 9, where we describe how the workshop is used in the elementary grades.

Journals and Interactive Forms of Writing

Teachers want to provide young children with opportunities to write for many different purposes and to use different forms (or modes) of writing. Ms. Murphy modeled writing a letter (a form or mode) to stay in contact with people (a purpose) in the writing center. Ms. Edwards demonstrated writing a list (a form or mode) to help her remember (a purpose) in a writing workshop mini-lesson. In this section, we describe three kinds of writing that are particularly beneficial for beginning writers: journals, dialogue writing, and pen pals.

Journals.   Journals focus on personal expression and learning. Children write to themselves about what is happening in their lives in and out of school, the stories they are reading, and what they are learning in different subject areas. The writer is his or her own audience. The text might be pictures and writing, just pictures, or just print.

Many teachers ask their children to keep learning logs while engaging in the study of different topics. Learning logs are little books in which children record their thinking and their discoveries. Children in Nancy Edwards' classroom keep a science learning log when they study the pond, a project that extends over several months. Each week the children record at least one new learning about the pond. Figure 6.2 shows an example of a page from one child's journal. Notice the range of ways this young child responds to the writing task—by drawing and writing letter strings relationships.

Dialogue Writing.   By the time children are four or five years old, most have become quite proficient at oral dialogue. Teachers can capitalize on this strength by engaging children in written conversations (Watson, 1983). In written conversations, the teacher and child use shared writing paper or dialogue journals to take turns writing to each other and reading each other's comments. This strategy makes children's writing more spontaneous and natural by helping them see the link between written and oral language. In addition, the teacher serves as an authentic audience of children's writing, providing motivation for engaging in the writing process.

The teacher initiates these written conversations by writing brief messages to each student, who in turn reads what the teacher has written and writes a response back to the teacher. The teacher then reads these responses and writes additional comments, and this continues in a chain-like fashion.

Teachers usually begin by making declarative statements about personal experiences rather than by asking children questions. Questions have a tendency to result in brief, stilted

FIGURE 6.2   **Learning log entries (This is a cattail.)**

replies from children (similar to their oral responses to verbal interrogation by a teacher). For example,

> **TEACHER:**   Did you do anything nice over the weekend?
> **CHILD:**   No.

On the other hand, when teachers write personal statements to the children, they respond more spontaneously. Nigel Hall and Rose Duffy (1987, p. 527) give the following example:

> **TEACHER:**   I am upset today.
> **CHILD:**   What is the matr with you?
> **TEACHER:**   My dog is sick. I took her to the vet, and he gave her some medicine.
> **CHILD:**   I hop she get betr sun did the medsn wok?

Obviously, it is helpful if children are able to use legible forms of invented spelling to write their messages. However, this strategy can be used even with children who are at the scribble or nonphonetic letter string stage of early literacy. With these children, a brief teacher–child conference is needed so that children can read their personal script messages to the teacher.

Pen Pals.   Once children get used to engaging in written conversations with their teachers, they will naturally want to engage in written exchanges with their peers. Miriam Martinez and Bill Teale (1987) describe how a "postal system/pen pal" program was successfully implemented in several Texas early childhood classrooms. Children in the morning half-day classes wrote weekly letters to pen pals in the afternoon classes; children in full-day programs were assigned pen pals in other full-day program classrooms. Children were purposely paired with partners who used different writing strategies. For example, a scribble writer was matched with an invented speller. Letters were exchanged once a week and placed in mailboxes located in the writing center. A teacher or aide was at the center to assist in cases where children received letters they could not read. Teachers reported that student response was overwhelmingly positive. Here, real audiences and real purposes for writing were provided.

Publishing Children's Writing

"Helping children make and publish their own books taps into [their] love of creating and owning written words" (Power, 1998, pp. 31–32). Brenda Power suggests several reasons why teachers should help young children publish their writing in books. Making their own books helps children learn:

- to hold the book right side up and to turn the pages correctly;
- that books have covers, titles, and authors;
- letter and sounds through their writing of the book and how to decode words by reading their own words;
- about the importance of an author and an illustrator to a book.

To publish with young children is to take their written texts and do something special with them. To publish is to make the writing public, to present it for others to read. There are many different ways to publish young children's writing. For example:

- Ask each child to bring a clear, plastic 8½ × 11-inch frame to school. (Of course, frames must be purchased for those children whose parents can not provide them.) Have the children publish their work by mounting their selected pieces, one at a time, in their frames. Hang the frames on the back wall of the classroom on a Wall of Fame.
- String a clothesline across the classroom. Using clothespins, clip the children's writings to the clothesline.
- Punch a hole in the upper left corner of several pages. All pages may be construction paper pages. If not, include a piece of colored construction paper or poster board on the top and bottom of the pile of pages for the book's cover. Thread string, yarn, or a silver ring through the hole to hold the book together.
- Purchase a low-cost photo album with large, stick-on plastic sleeves. (These can be found at discount stores and occasionally at flea markets or rummage and garage sales.) Place one page of each child's writing in one of the plastic sleeves. The same photo album can be used over and over as one piece of writing can be substituted for another piece of writing.
- While engaging in a special experience, take photographs of the children. Glue the picture to a piece of colored construction paper. Ask each child to select a photo. Ask the child to write about the chosen picture on a piece of white paper. Cut the white paper into an interesting shape, and mount it on the construction paper below the photo. Laminate each page and put the pages together with spiral binding.
- Cover a large bulletin board with bright paper or fabric. In large cut-out letters, label the bulletin board something like "Young Authors" or "Room 101 Authors." Divide the bulletin board evenly into rectangular-shaped sections, one section for each child in the class, using yarn or magic marker. Label each section with a child's name. Encourage the children to mount one of their pieces of writing in their special section each week. A staple or pushpin might be used to mount the writing.

These are but a few of the many ways that children's writing might be published. We repeat: Publishing with young children means making their writing public—available for others to read. It is important to note that it is developmentally inappropriate to require young children to revise or recopy their writing, though sometimes they are willing to add to their text. Most young children do not have the attention span or interest to make revisions or to recopy the text.

If the child's writing is a personal script—that is, if it is a form of emergent writing that needs the child's reading for meaning to be constructed—the teacher might elect to include a conventionally spelled version of the message with the child's personal script version. It is important to include the child's personal script version on the page with the conventionally spelled version to avoid taking ownership from the child.

Handwriting

So far, we have focused on providing young children with opportunities to write. What about handwriting? Drilling young children on how to form the letters of the alphabet correctly also is a developmentally inappropriate practice. Forming letters correctly requires a good bit of manual dexterity, something most young children are developing. Teachers should provide young children with numerous opportunities to engage in activities that help develop their dexterity, like puzzles, sewing cards, table games, cutting, and drawing. Models of appropriately formed letters should be available for the children's reference. This means that teachers should correctly form the uppercase and lowercase letters when writing for and with the children, and an alphabet chart of uppercase and lowercase letters should be available at eye-level for the children's use in the writing center. When children have achieved some control, the teacher might work one-on-one with the children. Since the letters in a child's name are the most important, the teacher might choose to begin instruction by helping the child correctly form these letters. Do not expect perfection, and be sure to keep the instruction playful.

Reading Instruction

As explained in Chapter 4, the early literacy perspective has successfully replaced the readiness view as the dominant theory of early literacy development. According to this view, the best way to help preschoolers and kindergartners learn to read is to provide them with the types of experiences described in Chapter 5. However, when it comes to decoding instruction—helping young children learn the alphabetic principle and use this knowledge to recognize unfamiliar printed words—some controversy exists. While there is general agreement that most children need to be taught decoding skills, there are divergent views about when and how these skills should be taught. Morrow and Tracey (1997, p. 645) explain:

> Advocates of whole language suggest that phonics should be taught in the context of reading and writing activities and not be isolated. Materials such as worksheets and flashcards are considered inappropriate. Instead the teaching of skills emerges naturally from activities in which the class is engaged. . . . Others, however, contest that teaching phonics only through naturally occurring activities in context is not systematic enough and leaves a lot to chance. These writers argue that children need some systematic sound–symbol instruction to learn to read.

We prefer teachers to use an activity-based, in-context approach to skills instruction with young children. The sections that follow describe a number of strategies for teaching the major decoding skills: phonological and phonemic awareness, alphabet letter recognition, word recognition, and phonics. Readers will find examples of activity-based, in-context strategies for introducing and teaching these skills to young children.

Phonological and Phonemic Awareness

Phonological and phonemic awareness are two important, closely related skills that play an important role in early literacy development. Phonological awareness is a broader term, referring to awareness of the sound structure of speech. Phonemic awareness is a subset of phonological awareness that involves awareness that spoken words are composed of individual sounds or phonemes (Yopp & Yopp, 2000). Both are important for all young children to possess if they are to become successful readers (Stahl, Duffy-Hester, & Stahl, 1998).

Marilyn Adams (1990) suggests that if children are to succeed at reading, especially if the reading program they meet in the primary grades relies heavily on phonics, phonemic awareness is the most crucial component of an early literacy program. This is a new challenge for early childhood teachers. In the past, the teaching of letter–sound associations (phonics) has dominated early childhood programs; for the most part, children have been denied phonological and phonemic awareness experiences. Now we know that before phonics instruction can be fully useful to young children, they need phonological and phonemic awareness experiences. Even after children begin to read, they need continued instruction in phonological awareness, phonemic awareness, and phonics.

Growth in phonological awareness begins in infancy, so even the teacher of the youngest child is a phonological awareness instructor. Initially, babies hear language "as one big piece of 'BLAH BLAH BLAH'." However, as discussed in Chapter 2, babies quickly learn to hear the unique phonemes that comprise their native language. These early speech lessons occur naturally as most adults use parentese to communicate with infants (parentese is an exaggerated, slowed, and highly articulated form of speech that allows infants to see and hear their native language). Phonological awareness begins when young children are able to hear the boundaries of words (for example, *Seethekitty* becomes *See the kitty*). As sounds become words that are frequently used in context to label specific objects, the acquisition of word meaning begins.

The ability to hear distinct words and make meaningful associations usually emerges between 9 and 18 months (Cowley, 1997), and children quickly become specialists in their native tongue. However, as children begin to hear and consistently produce the discreet sounds that comprise their language, the ability to hear and accurately produce the phonemes of other languages rapidly diminishes. Robert Sylwester (1995) calls this process "neural selectivity." The networks for phonemes that aren't in the local language may atrophy over time due to lack of use. This creates a challenge for children who do not speak the language of instruction when they enter school, as they often experience difficulty with hearing the phonemes and word boundaries of a second language. Therefore, oral language in the early childhood classroom is central and is a prerequisite to children's phonological and phonemic awareness development.

Marilyn Jager Adams (1990) suggests that before young children can become aware of phonemes—the individual sounds that make up spoken words—they first must become aware of larger units of oral language. Thus, children must first realize that spoken language is composed of words, syllables, and sounds. As mentioned earlier, this broader understanding is referred to as phonological awareness.

So, what can a child who is phonologically aware do? According to Catherine Snow, Susan Burns, and Peg Griffin (1998, p. 52), a child who is phonologically aware can enjoy and produce rhymes, count the number of syllables in a word, and notice when words begin or end with the same sound.

What kinds of preschool activities help children develop an appreciation of the sounds of spoken words? Marilyn Adams and several colleagues recommend a sequence of instructional activities that starts by building the most basic concepts of phonological awareness and then moves toward awareness of smaller and smaller units of sound (Adams, Foorman, Lundberg, & Beeler, 1998):

- *Rhyming activities*—Plan activities that focus the children's attention on the sounds inside words. For example, invite the children to recite or sing well-known nursery rhymes such as "Jack and Jill," "Humpty Dumpty," or "Hickory Dickory Dock." Once children are familiar with the rhymes, repeat a rhyme leaving out the rhyming word. Ask the children to guess the missing rhyming words ("Humpty Dumpty sat on a wall. Humpty Dumpty had a big _____.") (Ericson & Juliebö, 1998).
- *Words and sentences*—Plan activities that develop children's awareness that language is made up of strings of words. For example, recite a familiar nursery rhyme and invite the children to join in. Explain that rhymes are made up of individual words. Recite the rhyme again, clapping as each word is spoken. Then construct the rhyme by inviting each child to say one word of the rhyme in sequence (The Wright Group, 1998). Activities in which children track print, such as the shared reading strategy described in Chapter 5, are also effective ways to help children discover the concept of words.
- *Awareness of syllables*—Plan activities that develop the ability to analyze words into separate syllables and to combine syllables into words. For example, clap and count the syllables in the children's first and last names. Start with several names with one syllable, then with multiple syllables. Say the names slowly, and clap for each syllable. Then ask the children to say the names and clap along. After each name has been "clapped," ask children how many syllables they heard.

Note that these phonological awareness activities are sequenced to provide progressively closer analysis of the units of sounds. Young children will need many of these kinds of activities. Teachers will need to be alert when their children are ready for a new challenge.

Phonological awareness exercises build a base for phonemic awareness activities in which children manipulate phonemes, the individual sounds that make up syllables and words. Phonemic awareness is a more advanced form of phonological awareness. Knowledge that speech can be broken down into phonemes is very important for learning to read. Here are some activities that can be used to develop awareness of phonemes:

- *Sound matching*—Plan activities that ask children to decide which of several words begins with a specific sound (Yopp & Yopp, 2000). For example, show children pictures of familiar objects (cat, bird, monkey), and ask which begins with the /b/ sound.
- *Sound isolation*—Plan activities in which children are given words and asked to tell what sound occurs at the beginning, middle, or ending (Yopp, 1992). For example, ask "What's the sound that starts these words: *time, turtle, top*?" Or ask children to "Say the first little bit of *snap*" (Snow et al., 1998).
- *Blending*—Plan activities that invite children to combine individual sounds to form words. For example, play "What am I thinking of?" (Yopp, 1992). Tell the class that you are thinking of an animal. Then say the name of the animal in separate phonemes: "/c/-/a/-/t/." Ask the children to blend the sounds to come up with the name of the animal.
- *Segmentation*—This is the flip side of blending. Here, teachers ask children to break words up into individual sounds (Stahl et al., 1998). Lucy Calkins (1994) calls the ability to segment words "rubber-banding," stretching words out to hear the individual phonemes. For example, provide each child with counters and Elkonin boxes (a diagram of three blank squares representing the beginning, middle, and ending

sounds in a word). Ask the children to place counters in the boxes to represent each sound in a word. For the word *cat,* a marker would be placed in the left-hand square for /c/, another in the center square for /a/, and a third in the right-hand square for /t/. The concrete props often make this difficult task easier for children.

- *Phonemic manipulation*—Ask the children to mentally add, delete, substitute, or reverse phonemes in words. For example, ask them to say a word and then say it again without the initial sound (farm > arm), to substitute initial sounds in lyrics of familiar songs (Fe-Fi-Fiddly-i-o > De-Di-Diddly-i-o) (Yopp, 1992), or to build words by substituting onsets or rimes (c-ake, b-ake, sh-ake, m-ake).

Other ways to increase phonemic awareness include reading children's books that play with sounds of language (see Opitz, 1998, for a list); reading alphabet books (Murray, Stahl, & Ivey, 1996); inviting children to use computer software like *Reader Rabbit's Ready for Letters, Kid Pix, A to Zp, Bailey's Book House,* and *The Playroom* (Snow, et al., 1998); and encouraging children to use invented spelling (Stahl, et al., 1998). A recent meta-analysis of the results of fifty-two research studies revealed that phonemic awareness instruction is more effective when it is taught along with the letters of the alphabet (Ehri, Nunes, Willows, Schuster, Yaghoub-Zadeh, & Shanahan, 2001). Once children begin to recognize letters, they can use them to manipulate and reflect on the sounds in oral language (Yopp & Yopp, 2000). The activities in the "Alphabet Letter Recognition" section below will also indirectly help them develop phonemic awareness.

Some words of caution: Such activities can become developmentally inappropriate if the teacher does not keep them playful, weaving them intentionally and regularly into the day's activities in ways that do not dominate the early childhood program. Also, some of these activities will be inappropriate for some children. Children who are ready for such experiences will have had many experiences with books.

Letter Recognition

What do children seem to be learning when they begin to name and write alphabet letters? By the time young children say the alphabet letter names, they have begun to make discoveries about the alphabet. Children who have had experiences with print come to understand that the squiggles on the paper are special; they can be named. Toddler Jed, for example, called all letters in his alphabet books or in environmental print signs either *B* or *D* (Lass, 1982). At this very young age, he had already learned that letters were a special form of graphics with names. Three-year-old Frank associated letters with things that were meaningful to him. He argued with his mother to buy him the *Firetruck* (not just the car) because "It's like me!" He pointed to the *F.* (Incidentally, his argument was successful.) Giti pointed to the *z* on her blocks and said, "Look, like in the zoo!" (Baghban, 1984, p. 30). These three young children have learned to associate letters with things important to them.

Should early childhood teachers expect all children to say and write all letters of the alphabet by the time the children are five? Certainly not! By the age of three, some children can name as many as ten alphabet letters (Hiebert, 1981). Even children who read and write before entering kindergarten might not know the names of all the letters of the alphabet (Lass, 1982). As with other literacy learning areas, there is wide variation in what each child in a group of children will know and be able to do. Classroom strategies selected to teach young children alphabet letter names must be sensitive to these individual differences.

Knowing that some young children who are accomplished readers cannot name all the letters of the alphabet is a significant discovery. It is clear that learning to say the alphabet names need not be the first literacy skill children learn. Maybe it makes more sense to help children learn some whole words first, words that are important to them (e.g., their names, stores). Then, the letters within the words, like Cara's *C,* might hold more meaning.

Two methods are widely used to teach children the alphabet: the alphabet song and letter-of-the-week activities. Both methods have been criticized.

The alphabet song is the way children are most often introduced to letters at home (Adams, 1990). While there are some advantages to learning the names of letters in this fashion (e.g., the names give children a peg on which to attach perceptual information about letters), the song can also lead to misconceptions (e.g., that *lmnop* is one letter). In addition, Schickedanz (1998) argues that learning to recite the alphabet from memory is a trivial accomplishment that contributes little to children's learning to read. Yet, the recent report by the National Research Council (Snow et al., 1998) suggests singing the alphabet song as one of many activities early childhood teachers should use to support children's literacy learning.

The letter-of-the-week strategy involves introducing children to a different letter each week. During that week, children engage in a variety of activities related to the target letter. For example, during *A* week, children might establish an ant farm, eat apples, read a book about antelope, and the like. This strategy has been criticized for focusing on letters in isolation from meaningful reading and writing, for being too slow (it takes 26 weeks to introduce all the letters), and for not capitalizing on children's interests and prior knowledge (Schickedanz, 1998; Wagstaff, 1997–1998).

Some children learn to write simply by engaging in meaningful writing activities. Others need direct instruction.

Rather than introducing letters in a fixed, arbitrary sequence, Lea McGee and Don Richgels (1989) believe that it is preferable to teach letters that match children's current interests and activities. In order to deliver this type of individualized alphabet instruction, teachers need to observe closely to learn about the types of contexts in which children notice letters (e.g., environmental print, computer keyboards, books, friends' T-shirts). These contexts provide wonderful opportunities for informal talk and instruction about the alphabet.

It is these other kinds of alphabet learning activities that are more typical of quality early childhood activities. They include:

- *Environmental print*—Bring environmental print items to class (empty cereal boxes, cookie bags, etc.) and encourage children to read the print's message and discuss prominent letters (e.g., the letter *C* on a box of corn flakes).
- *Reading and writing children's names*—As discussed in Chapter 5, printed versions of children's names can be used for a variety of functional purposes, including attendance charts, helper charts, sign-up lists, and so on. Names of classmates have inherent high interest. Take advantage of every opportunity to read these names and to call attention to letters in the names ("Look, Jenny's and Jerry's names both start with the same letter. What letter is it?").
- *Writing*—Whenever children engage in writing, on their own or with a teacher (e.g., shared writing), their attention can be drawn to the letters of the alphabet. Remember that even if children are using scribbles or another personalized form of script, they are attempting to represent the letters of alphabet and thus are learning about letters.
- *Alphabet books*—There are many types of alphabet books available. For young children who are just learning the alphabet, books with simple letter–object associations (e.g., illustrations that show a letter and objects that begin with the sound associated with the letter) are most appropriate (Raines & Isbell, 1994). Alphabet books offer an enjoyable way to introduce children to letters and the sounds they represent. Research has shown that repeated reading of ABC books can promote young children's letter recognition (Greenewald & Kulig, 1995). It is also beneficial for children to make their own alphabet books. These child-made ABC books typically have a letter at the top of each page. Children then draw pictures and/or cut and paste illustrations of objects that begin with the sound of each letter. They can also write any words they know that contain the target letter. An adult can label the pictures.
- *Alphabet games*—Schickedanz (1998) recommends two alphabet games in particular:
  - alphabet-matching puzzles, in which the children must match loose letter tiles with letters printed on a background board;
  - an alphabet clue game, in which the teacher draws part of a letter and then asks children to guess which letter he or she is thinking of. After children make their guesses, the teacher adds another piece to the letter and has the children guess again.
- *Special alphabet activities*—Young children enjoy finger painting letters; painting letters on the easel or on the sidewalk on a hot day with a brush dipped in water; rolling and folding clay or playdough to make letters; and making and eating alphabet soup or pretzels. All of these activities provide meaningful, playful contexts within which young children can learn alphabet names.

- *Traditional manipulatives*—There are many traditional early childhood manipulatives that can be used to support children's alphabet letter name learning. These manipulatives include alphabet puzzles, magnetic uppercase and lowercase letters, felt letters, letter stencils, and chalk and chalkboards.

Incidentally, Adams (1990) recommends that teachers help children identify uppercase letters first, followed by lowercase letters. She thinks uppercase letters are more familiar to children and are easier for children to visually discriminate between than their lowercase counterparts.

Word Recognition

According to the old readiness view of reading, children needed to learn to recognize the letters of the alphabet before they were ready to learn to recognize and read whole words. Research on early literacy has shown this to be incorrect (see Chapter 4). We now know that many children learn to recognize personally significant words, such as their names and environmental print (*Pepsi*), before they learn to recognize the more abstract letters that make up these words. We recommend that teachers work on the two skills in a simultaneous and connected fashion: provide experiences that draw children's attention to highly meaningful words and, at the same time, point out key letters in those words.

We have already described several basic strategies that parents and teachers can use to help young children learn to recognize whole words:

- *Storybook reading*—When adults read favorite books to children over and over again, repeated exposure to a small number of words can lead to the beginning of word recognition.
- *Environmental print*—Words connected with environmental print (e.g., cereal boxes, soft drink cans, road signs, billboards, and restaurant menus) are often among the first words that children recognize. As explained in Chapter 4, this type of print is easy to learn to recognize because the context gives clues to the print's meaning. Adults can assist this process by drawing children's attention to environmental print and by using the environmental print and functional print strategies described at the beginning of Chapter 5.

In the following sections, we discuss two other strategies that are ideally suited for building young children's recognition of words: key words and word walls.

Key Words.   The key word strategy, developed by Sylvia Ashton-Warner (1963), is an excellent way to build young children's ability to recognize words. It is a very simple and elegant strategy: children choose words that are personally meaningful and that they would like to learn to read. Real-life experiences, favorite children's books, writing workshop, and language experience stories are primary sources for these key words. Children learn to recognize these words quickly because of their high meaning and personal significance.

Here is how the key word strategy works: The teacher asks each child in the class to pick a favorite word that he or she would like to learn to read. This word is written on a large card while the child watches. (This is sometimes done in circle time so that the whole class learns about each child's key word.) The children then write their key words plus any other words that they remember. Finally, they engage in various games and practice activities with their key words.

The following are some of the key word games and practice activities recommended by Jeanette Veatch and her associates (Veatch, Sawicki, Elliot, Flake, & Blakey, 1979, pp. 30–32):

- *Retrieving words from the floor*—The children's words (with young children this will be the words of a partner or a small group) are placed face down on the floor. On the signal, each child is to find one of her or his own words, hold it up, and read it aloud.
- *Claiming the cards*—The teacher selects many words from the class, holds them up, and the child who "owns" each word claims it.
- *Classifying words*—The teacher selects categories that encompass all of the words selected by the children. The categories are introduced, and labels are placed on the floor for each category. The children must then decide in which category their words belong. For example, the children who have animal words would stand next to the sheet of paper that says *animals.*
- *Making alphabet books*—Children record their words in the correct section of an alphabet book that is divided by initial letters. This is a good example of how children can learn about words and letters simultaneously.
- *Illustrating*—The child can draw a picture about the key word, dictate the word to a teacher to write on a card, and then copy the word into a picture dictionary word book.
- *Finding words*—Children might find their key words in books, magazines, and newspapers.

Veatch and her colleagues recommend that children collect key words and keep them in a box or on a ring file known as a "word bank." Another possibility is to have children keep their key words in a word book, as is illustrated in Trade Secret 6.3. In this variation, the teacher writes a word on a card for the child, then the child copies the word into his or her word book. Notice how the teacher, Bernadette Watson, prompts Amanda to use letter–sound relationships when she writes Amanda's key word, *elephant,* on the card.

Periodically, the teacher can have children review the words in their word banks or word books. Besides providing opportunities for children to practice recognizing key words, word banks and word books serve other valuable functions. They provide children with a concrete record of their reading vocabulary growth. It is very motivating for children to see their collections of words grow larger and larger. In addition, the words can be used to help children learn about letters and the sounds they are associated with. For example, if children are learning the sound associated with *b,* the teacher can have children find all the words in their collections that begin with that letter.

Word Walls.   A word wall is a word bank for an entire classroom. Category labels are posted at the top of one or more bulletin boards, and then words are selected by the teacher and/or children and placed on the board under the appropriate label. Wagstaff (1998) sug-

Trade Secret 6.3

My Word Book

Bernadette Watson

As the children entered the classroom, Ms. Watson greeted them, gave them a 3   5-inch card, and asked them, "What is your word for today?" Children answered. Amanda said, "Elephant." Ms. Watson positioned her hand to write *elephant* on the card. Before she wrote the word, she asked Amanda how she decided on this word as her word for the day. Amanda had seen a program on television about elephants the night before and had decided, right then and there, that *elephant* would be her word today.

"So," asked Ms. Watson, "what letter do you think *elephant* begins with?"

"I don't know," responded Amanda.

"It's an *e*," said Ms. Watson. "What letter is next?" She stretched the sound, "l-l-l-l-l."

Amanda responded, "L!"

"You're right," exclaimed Ms. Watson, "and then it's another *e*, and a *p-h-a-n*. And what do you think the last letter is? T-t-t-t-t."

Amanda said, "T!"

"Absolutely," said Ms. Watson.

Amanda took her card with *elephant* written on it with her and set off to locate her word book. Having found it, she sat at a table to copy her word into her book. First, she drew a picture of an elephant. Above it, she copied the word *elephant*. At the beginning of the year, that is all she would have done. Now, she also wrote a sentence under the picture: "isnt.v" (I saw on TV).

When she was done, Amanda took her book to the library center. Here, she might read her words to herself or to a friend. The pictures she had drawn greatly help her remember her word for the day.

---

gests a strategy that is appropriate for kindergartners: the ABC word wall. The category labels are the letters of the alphabet. Each week, the class focuses on a different poem or nursery rhyme. After the rhyme or poem is read for the first time, several words are selected that begin with different letters. For example, if the rhyme was "Jack and Jill," *Jack, hill,* and *pail* might be selected as the focus words. The following sequence is used to familiarize children with these words and their initial sounds:

- The teacher emphasizes the beginning sound of each word, helping children hear and say the sounds.
- The words are written on colored pieces of construction paper and added to the word wall under the appropriate letter labels.
- The children engage in word play—putting thumbs up if words begin with the same sound as *Jack, hill,* or *pail,* and thumbs down if they start with a different sound; finding other words that start with the *j, h,* or *p* sounds; substituting words that rhyme with words in the nursery rhyme: "Back and Jill went up the pill to fetch a tail of water."
- The rhyme is reread, placing the words back into a meaningful context.

During the rest of the week, the rhyme can be revisited with shared reading, and the children can engage in different types of word play with the words on the word wall to build phonemic awareness and knowledge of letter–sound relationships.

Trade Secrets 6.4 describes another variation of the ABC word wall that might be used at the kindergarten level.

Trade Secret 6.4

Word Walls

At the beginning of the kindergarten year, Mrs. Burl begins each school day by asking her class to share any print items they brought from home. These items are usually packages or wrappers of products the children's family use at home. She asks each child who brought an item to read the name of the item to the rest of the class. After the children have read their environmental print, Mrs. Burl selects one of the products, Aim toothpaste, and asks the children where they think the Aim toothpaste container should go on their ABC word wall? The children think for just a moment when Anissa suggests cutting the wrapper into two parts—one part for *Aim* to go under the letter *Aa* on the word wall and the second for *toothpaste* to go under the letter *Tt*. Mrs. Burl asks the class for a thumbs-up (for yes) or thumbs-down (for no) vote. The children give her a unanimous thumbs up. Mrs. Burl quickly cuts the package, circles the appropriate words, and asks the child

who brought the wrapper to pin each word under the correct letter on the word wall.

The word wall concept allows teachers to stimulate children's awareness of words and knowledge of letters and sounds (Hedrick & Pearish, 1999; Morrow, Tracey, Gee-Woo, & Pressley, 1999; Wagstaff, 1998). Teachers may use a range of word wall activities to reinforce and support young children's growing phonemic awareness and reading skills. Mrs. Burl begins the kindergarten year with an ABC word wall that focuses on the initial letter sounds. Later, when the children's awareness of the sound—symbol relationship grows, she will add blends and consonant digraphs to the ABC word wall (see Figure 6.3).

Mrs. Burl found the word wall concept to be useful for teaching a variety of focus lessons and stimulating the children's interest in words and reading. She also found that parents are interested in the word walls because they provide an ongoing visual record of the many lessons Mrs. Burl uses to teach phonemic awareness to her students.

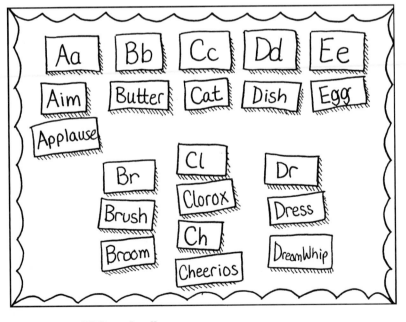

FIGURE 6.3   ABC word wall

Phonics

Phonics involves using the alphabetic principle (letters have a relationship with the sounds of oral language) to decode printed words. Young children differ greatly in their need for instruction in this important decoding skill. Stahl (1992, p. 620) explains: "Some will learn to decode on their own, without any instruction. Others will need some degree of instruction, ranging from the pointing out of common spelling patterns to intense and systematic instruction." Thus, as in all other aspects of literacy instruction, it is important for phonics teaching to match the needs of individual students.

The children who learn phonics more or less on their own simply need to be provided with the types of meaningful reading and writing activities described in Chapter 5—shared reading and writing, literacy-enriched play, and functional literacy activities. As these children engage in these purposeful literacy activities, they gradually discover the relationship between letters and sounds.

Those who need a moderate amount of assistance profit from what Morrow and Tracey (1997) term "contextual instruction." This type of instruction occurs in conjunction with the same types of activities described in the preceding paragraph—shared reading and writing, literacy-enriched play, and functional literacy activities. The only difference is that while children are engaging in these activities, the teacher draws children's attention to letter–sound relationships that are present.

Morrow and Tracey (1997, p. 647) give an example of how one teacher, Mrs. M., drew her students' attention to the letter *m* and its sound during an activity that involved both shared writing and functional writing:

> Because her class had finished putting on a show for their grandparents, Mrs. M. thought it would be a good idea if they wrote a thank-you note to the music teacher who assisted them with the performance. The note was composed by the students with the teacher's help. She wrote the note on the board and sounded out each word to help the students with spelling. After they finished writing, Mrs. M. read the entire note and had the students read the note aloud:
>
> **MRS. M.:** How should we start this letter?
>
> **STUDENT:** Dear Mr. Miller.
>
> **MRS. M.:** Very good [as she writes] "Dear Mr. Miller" has three words. *Dear* is the first word, *Mr.* is the second word, and *Miller* is the third word. I just realized that my name and Mr. Miller's name both begin with the same letter, *M.* Let's say these words together, "Mr. Miller, Mrs. Martinez."

This type of spontaneous teaching can occur in connection with all the literacy learning activities described in Chapter 5. Of course, such teaching requires a teacher who is on the lookout for teachable moments involving letter–sound relationships. Because most, if not all, preschool and kindergarten classes contain some children who need moderate assistance, we recommend that teachers make an effort to take advantage of these types of teaching opportunities when they arise.

Another way to help children acquire knowledge about phonics is through writing (IRA/NAEYC, 1998; Stahl, 1992). Once children have reached the invented spelling stage in their writing development, they begin to use their knowledge of letter names and letter–sound relationships to spell words. During this stage, children spell words the way that they sound rather than how they are conventionally spelled. For example a child may spell the word *leave* with the letters *lev* because this is how the word sounds. When children use invented spelling, their attention is naturally focused on letter–sound relationships.

Research indicates that temporary use of invented spelling can promote children's reading development (IRA/NAEYC, 1998). For example, a study by Clarke (1988) found that young children who were encouraged to write with invented spelling scored higher on decoding and reading comprehension tests than children who were encouraged to use conventional spelling.

Finally, teachers can provide preplanned phonics activities to children who have developed some awareness of the sounds that make up spoken words and who can recognize some of the letters of the alphabet. This can be done by adapting the phonemic awareness, letter recognition, and word recognition activities discussed earlier in this chapter so that they focus on letter–sound relationships. We recommend that letter–sound relationships be selected that fit in with ongoing class activities or that fit the needs of specific children, rather than using an arbitrary sequence (consonants first, short vowels second, long vowels third, etc.).

Several of the phonemic awareness activities described earlier in this chapter can easily be modified to teach phonics by having children identify which letters represents the various sounds and then writing words so that children can see the letter–sound relationships:

- *Letter–sound matching*—Show pictures of familiar objects (cat, bird, and monkey) and ask children which begins with the /m/ sound. Then ask which letter *monkey* starts with. Write the word on chalkboard. Ask children for other words that start with the /m/ sound, and write these words on the board.
- *Letter–sound isolation*—Pronounce words and asks children what sounds are heard at the beginning, middle, or end. For example, ask the children, "What sound is in the middle of *man, cat,* and *Sam*?" Once the sound is identified, ask the children what letter represents the sound. The words can then be written on the chalkboard, along with other short-*a* words.

In a similar fashion, letter recognition activities can be modified to teach phonics by shifting the focus from letters to their sounds.

- *Environmental print*—Discuss letter–sound relationships that occur in environmental print. For example, if children have brought in cereal boxes from home, the teacher could ask questions such as "What letters make the /ch/ sound in Cheerios?" Children could then be asked to identify other words that start with the /ch/ sound, and these words could be written on the chalkboard or added to an ABC word wall.
- *Reading and writing children's names*—When referring to children's names in attendance charts, helper charts, and other places, call children's attention to letter–sound correspondences in their names. For example, the teacher might say, "Jenny's and Jerry's names start with the same sound. What letter does both their names start with?"
- *Games*—Create games that enable children to reinforce their growing knowledge of letter–sound relationships in an enjoyable manner. A popular type of phonics game

requires children to match letters with pictures that begin with letter sounds. For example, the letter *b* might be matched with a picture of a bird. If you use this type of phonics matching game, be sure to tell the children the word that each picture represents in order to avoid confusion with other words that the picture could represent. In the example of the *b/bird* item, a child might justifiably believe that the picture of a bird represented the word *robin* or *sparrow* rather than *bird*.

Word banks and word walls, discussed in the section on word recognition, can also be invaluable aids in helping children learn phonics. The words in these collections are familiar to children and often have strong personal significance and meaning. These high-meaning words can serve as pegs on which children can attach letter–sound relationships. Teachers should routinely take advantage of these words by linking them with phonics activities and lessons. For example, if a teacher were trying to help children learn the *ch* sound–symbol correspondence, children could be asked to find all the letters in their word banks or on the word wall that contain this letter combination.

Some children will need more direct instruction on letter–sound relationships, but not during the preschool years. Preschool and kindergarten children who need extensive help learning phonics really need more experience with phonemic awareness, letter recognition, and informal types of phonic instruction described in this chapter. These activities will build a foundation that will help these children benefit from more systematic approaches to learning phonics later.

Assessment: Discovering What Children Know and Can Do

Remember from Chapter 1 that one of the main tenets of this book is that assessment and instruction should be linked. Assessment should provide teachers with information that they can use to enhance children's literacy learning. It should also be based on our current knowledge of early literacy learning—that is, the early-literacy perspective. Assessment should yield information about children's storybook-reading strategies, knowledge of the practical functions of reading and writing, concepts about book print, and emergent reading and writing behaviors (Teale, 1990).

Traditional standardized tests, such as the *Metropolitan Readiness Tests* (Nurss & McGauvran, 1976), do not measure up well against these criteria. These standardized tests use multiple-choice items to measure so-called prereading skills such as auditory memory, visual discrimination, rhyming, and letter recognition. For example, the children might be presented with a page containing rows of letters. The teacher is directed to read the following instructions from the test manual: "Put your finger on the first row of letters. Find the letter that is exactly the same as the first letter in this row. Draw a circle around it." Young children often respond inappropriately to such items because they do not understand the demands of the test situation or have trouble maintaining attention to abstract, uninteresting test items (Teale, 1989). More importantly, standardized readiness tests do not yield information that can help teachers to promote children's literacy development.

In Chapter 12, we describe how "ongoing assessment" provides teachers with much more useful types of data that can guide literacy instruction. Ongoing assessment strategies include anecdotal notes, vignettes, conferencing, audio and video recording, and the collection of artifacts and work samples. These types of performance-based assessment are conducted while children are engaging in everyday types of classroom activities, and the resulting data is often organized and reported in portfolios that show their progress over time.

Checklists are one of the most commonly used types of ongoing assessment tools. These lists are observational tools that specify what to look for and provide a convenient system for keeping records. A variety of checklists have been published that can help teachers keep track of children's early literacy learning. For example, Figure 6.4 presents an adapted version of Elizabeth Sulzby, June Barnhart, and Joyce Hieshima's (1989) Forms of Writing checklist, which can help identify the forms of emergent writing that children use during play and other classroom activities.

Teachers can also construct their own checklists to keep track of their data gathering. Some years ago the teachers at the St. Michael's Early Childhood Center worked together to construct a literacy checklist. They knew that children's book-reading behaviors were important for them to understand, but they were not certain just which book-reading behaviors were important to track as their young learners moved through their center. They agreed to form a study group to read and discuss professional literature on children's literacy development in order to understand better how they should conduct their read-aloud and shared reading sessions and what they should focus on during their observations of their students. One outcome of their study was a checklist. Following the publication of the National Research Council's report, *Preventing Reading Difficulties in Young Children* (Snow, Burns, & Griffin, 1998), the teachers worked together to reconsider their checklist to ensure that they were appropriately following the children's literacy accomplishments. We reproduce a version of their checklist in Figure 6.5 to guide our readers' consideration of their own students' literacy accomplishments.

Certainly, observing a behavior once is insufficient to justify drawing the conclusion that the behavior is a part of the child's permanent repertoire. Teachers will want to look for

---

FIGURE 6.4   Emergent Writing Checklist

Child's Name _____

Forms of Writing	Date(s) Observed	Situation
■ uses drawing (might be circular scribbles)	_____	_____
■ uses drawing and writing	_____	_____
■ uses linear scribble	_____	_____
■ uses letter-like shapes	_____	_____
■ uses random letters	_____	_____
■ uses invented spellings	_____	_____
■ uses conventional spellings	_____	_____

FIGURE 6.5   Checklist for Assessing Young Children's Book-Related Understandings

_____ can
     (Child's name)

Concepts about Books	Date	Comments
look at the picture of an object in a book and realize it is a symbol for the real object		
handle a book without attempting to eat or chew it		
identify the front, back, top, and bottom of a book		
turn the pages of a book correctly		
point to the print when asked, "What do people look at when they read?"		
show how picture and print connect		
point to where a reader begins reading		
point to a book's title		
point to a book's author		
recognize specific books by their covers		

Conventions of Print

	Date	Comments
show that a reader reads left to right with return sweeps		
find a requested letter or provide the letter's name		
ask questions or make comments about letters		
ask questions or make comments about words		
read words or phrases		
read sentences		
read along while adult reads familiar stories		

Comprehension of Stories

	Date	Comments
answer and ask literal questions about story (provide example)		
answer and ask interpretive questions about story (provide example)		
answer and ask critical questions about story (provide example)		
ask questions about story		
retell stories by relying on pictures and with help to recall details without book and with knowledge of the details without book and with knowledge of key story elements		
setting		

(continued)

FIGURE 6.5   Continued

characters	_____	_____
theme (what main character wanted or needed)	_____	_____
episodes (___/___)	_____	_____
ending	_____	_____
sequence	_____	_____
from beginning to middle	_____	_____
from middle to end	_____	_____
connect information in stories to events in his or her life	_____	_____

Attitude toward Books

participate in book-sharing routine with caregiver	_____	_____
listen to story	_____	_____
voluntarily look at books	_____	_____
show excitement about books and reading	_____	_____
ask adults to read to him or her	_____	_____
use books as resource for answers to questions	_____	_____

repeated evidence that the child is habitually exhibiting these accomplishments. We recommend that teachers indicate the dates of their observations on the checklist and make quick notes of the specific behaviors the child exhibited. At St. Michael's, the checklist follows the child from year to year as a part of the child's portfolio. Knowing when each child demonstrated each literacy accomplishment helps teachers and parents understand individual children's patterns of development. Reading each child's checklist informs the teacher of the child's strengths and the instructional program for that child. Collectively reading all children's checklists informs the teacher of the instructional needs of all the children in the class.

One problem with ongoing assessment is that teachers have to wait for literacy events to occur naturally and spontaneously. Teachers sometimes need to hurry things along a bit in order to gain the information they need to plan effective literacy instruction. They can do this by using performance sampling—setting up situations that enable the teachers to gather data about children's literacy abilities (Teale, 1990).

Performance samples of one-to-one storybook reading can provide insights into children's concepts about print. This involves reading a familiar storybook to a single child. The teacher can ask the child to point to words that are being read, providing information about print-to-speech matching and about directionality. Questions can also be asked to probe the child's understanding of concepts such as letters, words, capitalization, and punctuation (e.g., "Show me a question mark"). This type of informal performance sample is preferable to the more standardized *Concepts About Print* test (Clay, 2000) because it uses books that are familiar and highly meaningful to children (Goodman, 1981; Teale, 1990;).

Trade Secret 6.5 describes how Dawn Foley used performance sampling to assess four-year-old Serafina's ability to recognize environmental print. The procedure that Dawn

Trade Secret 6.5

Using Developmentally Appropriate Performance Sampling: What Does Sarafina Know about EP?

By Dawn Foley

Sarafina is a curious, loving, and talkative four-year-old who lives with her mother and father. She is an only child who is excited about "goin to preeeeschool" this fall. As a toddler, Sarafina developed a cataract on her left eye. This condition obscured her vision and also affected her depth perception. She recently received a cornea transplant and is now wearing prescription glasses. Her parents expressed concern about her ability to become a successful reader. Her mother commented that her interest in reading had greatly increased after her surgery. I have been asked to assess Sarafina's early literacy knowledge.

To determine Sarafina's awareness of print, I decide to use a performance sampling of her ability to recognize environmental print (EP). As discussed in Chapter 4, EP includes logos, labels, road signs, and billboards that are found in the child's immediate surroundings. Children's awareness of EP occurs at an early age and they often engage in reading EP long before reading print in books. EP recognition during the early years is known to be a good predictor of future reading ability (Adams, 1990).

The Environmental Print Assessment kit (Han, Chen, Christie, & Enz, 2000) consists of ten items that were identified as universal in U.S. culture, being recognized by 60 to 80 percent of the children in the Phoenix pilot study. The pilot group consisted of children ages three to five from diverse ethnic, linguistic, and socioeconomic backgrounds.

The kit has 4 different levels of print, ranging from highly contextualized to highly decontextualized:

- Level 1 consists of actual EP objects (M&M bag, STOP sign, Oreo cookie wrapper, Band-Aid box, Pokémon plate, Burger King Sack, Pepsi can, McDonalds fries container, Teletubbies plate, and a Blockbuster video container.
- Level 2 consists of ten cards with the color logo of each of the items.
- Level 3 consist of ten cards with a black-and-white logo without the color or background clues.
- Level 4 consists of ten cards with each of the words printed in a generic font.

The activity is presented as a game, with prompt questions such as *"Can you tell me what this is?"* Or *"What is in this container?"* Children are given:

2 points if they recognize the correct word (Pepsi, McDonalds, Blockbuster),
1 point for meaningful answers such as correctly identifying the categories (soda for Pepsi, burger for McDonalds, movie or video for Blockbuster), and
0 points for no response or a wrong answer.

On Level 1 (real objects), Sarafina correctly identified 90 percent of the items. She was able to automatically identify the product logo by name when shown the real product. On Level 2 (cards with colored logos), Sarafina was able to correctly identify the labels 80 percent of the time. Level 3 (logo names in black-and-white) was more challenging, but she was able to identify or read 50 percent of the logos correctly. Level 4 (reading decontextualized, generic print) proved to be too difficult. Sarafina was able to automatically identify only the words STOP and M&Ms, and she scored 15 percent on this test.

The results of this test demonstrate that Sarafina, like most emergent readers, is a logographic reader. She relies on pictures and the colors and shapes of the text art to decode the words in and out of context. She understands that these symbols have specific meanings and she distinguishes differences. She also is using letters to recognize the differences between familiar logo names that have similar contexts such as differentiating Burger King from McDonald's.

used was like a game. This game like format made the assessment enjoyable for Serafina and held her attention. All performance sampling procedures used with young children should have similar characteristics.

Summary

Whereas Chapter 5 describes activities that can implicitly teach children how to write and read, this chapter deals with explicit literacy instruction. It describes a variety of developmentally appropriate strategies that teachers can use to directly teach children how to write and read. Each skill has been found to be important to children's success as readers and writers. What have you learned?

■ *Why is a writing center an important area in the preschool classroom? How might an adult teach in the writing center?*

A writing center is that area of the classroom in which the teacher has stocked materials (different kinds of papers, various writing tools, alphabet strips, computers) that invite children to write. The teacher is an important other in the writing center. As a cowriter, the teacher writes alongside the children and models the writing process, informally teaching children about the forms (letters, thank-you notes) and features (spelling, letter formation) of print. As a skilled writer, the teacher can teach children as he or she writes by casually talking about letter–sound relationships, how to begin a letter, or what might be said in a letter.

■ *How does a teacher teach during a writing workshop?*

Each writing workshop begins with a mini-lesson. The goal of these lessons is to teach children about some aspect of writing (e.g., how to make revisions; how to add describing words; how to spell words). The mini-lesson is followed by writing time. During writing time, the teacher talks with individual children about their writing. Here, the teacher might help a child stretch words to hear sounds, add details to the child's drawing, or talk with the child about the topic of the piece. Through conferences, the teacher provides one-on-one instruction. After the writing time, two or three children will share their work with their peers and the teacher. Now, the teacher and the other children can ask questions about the writing.

■ *Why is it important to publish children's writing?*

Publishing helps young children understand that they write so others can read their thoughts. Making young children's writing efforts public is important. The publishing process need not be complicated.

■ *What does it mean to offer young children a balanced approach to reading instruction?*

Balanced reading instruction combines elements of meaning-centered and skill-centered reading instruction. Children do large amounts of reading and have opportunities to discuss and respond to what has been read. In addition, they receive direct instruction on basic reading skills. This instruction is linked to the texts they are reading.

■ *What is the difference between phonological awareness, phonemic awareness, and phonics? In what sequence do young children typically acquire these skills? What does this sequence suggest about classroom instructional strategies?*

Phonological awareness (realization that spoken language is composed of words, syllables, and sounds) is broader than phonemic awareness (realization that words are composed of phonemes). Both are important for all young children to possess if they are to become successful readers. Whereas phonological and phonemic awareness just involve sound, phonics involves learning the relationship between letters and the sounds they represent. The instructional sequence now recommended by research is to begin by helping children build the basic concepts of phonological awareness, then to move toward helping children develop awareness that words are composed of phonemes, and finally to help children develop awareness of letter–sound associations. Therefore, the instructional sequence is from broad concepts to smaller and smaller ones.

■ *How might early childhood teachers introduce young children to the letters of the alphabet?*

Some readers probably learned the names of the letters of the alphabet by singing the alphabet song. Today, the value of this activity gets mixed reviews. Some readers probably learned the names of the letters of the alphabet by studying a different letter each week. This approach receives strong criticism today. Early childhood teachers should teach their young learners the names of the letters that match their children's current interests and activities through informal talk and playful activities. Teachers should remember that most children will not know the names of all the letters of the alphabet before they recognize and read whole words. Skillful teachers can link children's attention to highly meaningful words and key letters simultaneously.

■ *What types of assessment methods are used to collect information about children's progress?*

Changes in what we know about literacy learning have necessitated major changes in our ways of measuring young children's literacy accomplishments and progress. Instead of sporadic tests and quizzes that yield isolated samples of student literacy behavior, teachers now rely on ongoing assessment procedures that are connected with the daily literacy activities that take place in the classroom. This ongoing assessment makes heavy use of systematic observation and the collection of samples of children's work. The classroom library, writing center, and dramatic play areas are ideal settings for this type of assessment, and anecdotal notes, vignettes, and checklists provide effective ways to record data.

LINKING KNOWLEDGE TO PRACTICE

1. Visit a classroom set up for three-year-olds and a classroom set up for five-year-olds in an early childhood center. Draw a diagram of each classroom's writing center, and make a list of the writing materials the teacher has provided. Describe the differences between the writing center set up for three-year-olds with that set up for five-year-olds. Observe the classrooms' teachers as they interact with the children in the writing center. Describe what they talk about with the children.

2. Create descriptions of several developmentally appropriate phonological or phonemic awareness activities, from the most basic concepts to the more advanced, that might be used with young children. Make copies of your activities for others in your class.

3. Create a description of several developmentally appropriate alphabet recognition activities for use with young children. Make copies of your activities for others in your class.

4. Interview a pre-K or kindergarten teacher about the information-gathering tools that he or she typically uses to collect information about children's literacy development. How does the teacher organize this information to share with parents?

7

The Reading Workshop: A Balanced Approach to Reading Instruction

Mrs. Smith's Classroom

If you were to enter Mrs. Smith's classroom, you would immediately notice how quiet it is. The desks are arranged in straight rows, all facing the front of the room. Mrs. Smith is sitting at the "reading" table with a group of eight students who are in the high-ability group. The children are taking turns reading a story out of their basal reader. Every few pages, Mrs. Smith intervenes and asks a series of questions about the story, using the basal's teacher manual as her guide. The rest of the students are at their desks doing blackline masters and workbook pages that provide practice on numerous word recognition skills (phonics, contextual analysis, etc.) that are taught in the basal program. After thirty minutes, the "high" group returns to their desks to do seatwork, and ten students in the "middle" group join Mrs. Smith at the reading table. Seatwork is checked, vocabulary is introduced, and then the children begin reading a new story. During this "reading" period, the focus is totally on reading. Writing and the academic subjects are taught at other times during the school day.

Mrs. Brown's Classroom

The reading period begins with Mrs. Brown pulling seven students together for a brief mini-lesson on three vowel digraphs (ea, oa, ai) that have been causing these students difficulty. The other students begin working on projects, sharing, and reading. Soon, a steady buzz of conversation can be heard as the students talk with others and engage in various activities. Some are reading tradebooks that they have chosen from the classroom library. A group of six children are sitting at a table with Mrs. Brown, discussing their reactions to folktales they have read. Each child has read a different book; they are comparing the structures of their tales. Others are working on projects for an integrated unit on transportation that has been ongoing for several months. After the literature study session has ended, Mrs. Brown checks on the progress of the different groups of students, offering assistance and guidance when needed. She then returns to her desk where she holds brief conferences with individual students about the tradebooks they have been reading.

How to teach children to read has been the subject of a series of highly charged controversies stretching back more than a century (Mathews, 1966). Initially, there was disagreement over whether letter names or sounds should be taught first. The argument then shifted to whether children should learn whole words or be taught phonics (Chall, 1967). These debates have been accompanied by dramatic shifts in instructional methods, giving the unfortunate appearance of "pendulum swings" (Holdaway, 1979).

Over the past several decades, the debate has been carried on between proponents of skill-centered and meaning-centered methods of instruction, as illustrated in the two vignettes of the two second-grade classrooms above. Mrs. Smith's teaching represents a skills-centered approach to teaching reading that places heavy emphasis on teaching a carefully sequenced set of skills. Mrs. Brown's teaching, on the other hand, embodies a meaning-centered approach to reading instruction in which children are taught skills as the need arises in the course of engaging in purposeful reading and writing activities. While these classroom scenarios are fictitious, they are representative of the extreme contrasts seen in many schools across the United States. Readers may even find two teachers like Mrs. Smith and Mrs. Brown teaching next door to each other in the same school.

When we wrote the first edition of this book in the mid-1990s, the "Reading Wars" between these two radically different approaches to reading instruction were in full swing. During the past five years, we have witnessed some encouraging developments. While the "wars" are by no means over (e.g., Allington & Woodside-Jaron, 1999; Stahl, 1999), there have been increasing calls for a cease-fire (e.g., Joyce, 1999) and a very encouraging trend toward what is termed "balanced" literacy instruction (e.g., Au, Carroll, & Scheu, 1997; International Reading Association, 1999; Pearson & Raphael, 1999). A balanced approach merges elements of the two opposing approaches in an attempt to take advantage of each approach's inherent strengths:

- Skills emphasis—direct, systematic instruction on skills needed for proficient reading, such as phonemic awareness, letter recognition, phonics, fluency, and comprehension strategies
- Meaning emphasis—lots of opportunities to engage in authentic reading and writing activities; contextualized, needs-based skills instruction; curricular integration

Of course, balance alone will not result in effective reading instruction. Experts such as David Pearson and Taffy Raphael (1999, p. 24) have warned about the dangers of "balance gone astray." Simply taking a little of this from one approach and combining it with a little bit of that from another approach can result in a contradictory, ineffective instructional program. We believe that an approach that relies primarily on the components of a meaning-centered approach to reading instruction, but that also includes direct, systematic instruction on key reading skills, is the best way to teach children to read.

We begin this chapter with a discussion of theories of the reading process that underlie different approaches to teaching reading. Next, we summarize the findings of the National Reading Panel, which conducted a massive synthesis of decades of reading research in an attempt to identify research-based principles of effective reading instruction. We then briefly discuss the key elements of effective reading instruction. We conclude with a description of the Reading Workshop, which we believe embodies the elements of a balanced, effective approach to teaching reading.

Before You Read This Chapter, Think About . . .

- the materials that were used to teach you to read. Did you spend most of your time reading stories from a basal reader and doing workbook pages and blackline masters? Or did you primarily read children's literature and other tradebooks?

- how you were grouped for reading instruction. Was reading taught to the whole class? If small groups were used, were you assigned to a permanent "ability" group or did you participate in a variety of different types of groups?
- what aspect of reading instruction helped you the most in learning to read? Skill lessons? Practice exercises? Literature discussions? Opportunities to read self-selected books?

Focus Questions

- What are the key differences between the subskill and constructivist views of the reading process? How does the inside-out/outside-in theory bridge the gap between these two opposing views of the reading process?
- Why are research syntheses so important in the field of reading?
- What are the key principles of "best practice" in teaching reading?
- What are the main components of a reading workshop?

Theories of the Reading Process

Two very different theories underlie the instruction described in the two vignettes at the beginning of this chapter. Ms. Smith subscribes to a *subskill theory of the reading process*.

BOX **7.1**

Definition of Terms

ability grouping: Students are grouped for instruction according to their reading ability, often into a low, a middle, and a high reading group.

comprehension: The ability to construct meaning from text, using both print information and prior knowledge.

decoding: The ability to translate text into oral language, using phonological, graphic, and con-textual cues.

engaged reading: Engagement occurs when students are motivated to read and understand a text.

flexible grouping: Students are placed into a variety of different, temporary groups for reading instruction.

independent reading: Reading that allows children an opportunity to read self-selected books on their own or with a partner.

inside-out factors: Aspects of the reading process that are involved in decoding written texts into meaningful language.

outside-in factors: Aspects of the reading process that support understanding of the meaning of text.

reading workshop: An approach to teaching reading that allows students choice in the books they read. Students are taught to record their responses to their reading and to work together in literature study groups to discuss their views about the stories they are reading.

This theory maintains that reading consists of a linear succession of subskills that can be learned one after another: letter recognition, letter—sound relationships (phonics), sight words, other decoding skills (context, word structure), and finally comprehension (Paris, Wasik, & Turner, 1991). The assumption is made that once students have mastered all these skills, they will be good readers. It is also assumed that reading is simply a matter of breaking the code—translating written text into oral language. Once a reader recognizes all the printed words in a text, comprehension occurs more or less automatically. Beginning reading instruction, therefore, should focus mainly on word-recognition and decoding skills.

Ms. Brown's instruction adheres to a *constructivist theory of the reading process.* Reading is viewed as an interactive, strategic process in which readers combine text cues with their own prior knowledge to construct meaning (Goodman, 1970; Rosenblatt, 1985; Rumelhart, 1977). Comprehension is not merely the passive, automatic absorption of meaning that has been decoded in text. Instead, comprehension is an active, constructive process in which readers build meaning by combining text information with what they already know (Anderson & Pearson, 1984). This is accomplished by the use of a variety of strategies that enable the reader to decode words, make inferences, read for different purposes, and self-monitor their comprehension (Paris et al., 1991).

Constructivist theories of the reading process highlight the importance of interest and of social interaction. These theories maintain that interest, a factor almost totally ignored in the past, has a profound effect on comprehension and learning from text (Hidi, 1990). The more interested the reader is in a text, the greater the comprehension and subsequent learning. Constructivist theories also emphasize the social aspects of learning and comprehension. For example, when children and adults share their insights into what stories mean, meaning can be expanded for all of the participants (Eeds & Wells, 1989).

Constructivist theories focus attention on the importance of engaging with text (Guthrie & Wigfield, 2000). According to Anne Sweet (1993, p. 4) an engaged reader

1. uses prior knowledge to gain information from new material;
2. uses a variety of skills in a strategic way to gain information independently;
3. is internally motivated to read for information and for pleasure; and
4. interacts socially to make gains in literacy development.

By implication, a major goal of reading instruction should be to provide children with the skills, strategies, and attitudes that will enable them to be engaged readers.

The subskill theory of the reading process aligns naturally with a skills-centered approach to reading instruction, and the constructivist theory has obvious connections with a meaning-centered approach. Is there a theory that supports a balanced approach to literacy instruction? Whitehurst and Lonigan (2001) have proposed an interactive model of the reading process that is ideally suited for this purpose (see Figure 7.1). This model proposes that reading requires people to utilize two interdependent types of information:

- Outside-in sources of information—such as knowledge of how texts are structured and knowledge of concepts—that support understanding of the meaning of text
- Inside-out sources of information—such as phonemic awareness, letter recognition, and knowledge of letter–sound relationships—that enable the reader to translate print into oral language

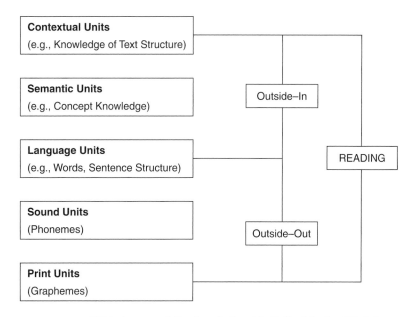

FIGURE 7.1   Whitehurst and Lonigan's Outside-In/Inside-Out Model of the Reading Process

Adapted from Whitehurst and Lonigan (2001).

Both sources of information are essential for successful reading. Children cannot read a text unless they can use inside-out information to recognize most of the words in it. At the same time, even if all the words in a text are recognized, successful reading is not possible unless children have the outside-in information that enables them to link information in text with their prior knowledge about text structure and their knowledge about the world in general.

This outside-in/inside-out model of the reading process provides a balanced approach to literacy instruction. It highlights the need for direct instruction in decoding skills (the smooth, effortless processing of inside-out information), while at the same time emphasizing the need for linking this instruction with authentic, interesting reading and writing activities that promote comprehension by maximizing the availability of outside-in information.

Research Synthesis: Guide to Effective Practice

Reading has been undoubtedly the most heavily researched area in the field of education. It has been estimated that approximately 100,000 research studies on reading have been published since 1966 (National Reading Panel, 2000). The sheer number of these research studies has made research synthesis a practical necessity. Research synthesis methodology allows one to derive generalizations from the findings of a group of existing studies on the same topic. Shanahan (2000, p. 209) points out some of the advantages of research synthesis:

> No single investigation is sufficient for creating a full understanding of any complex phenomena, and we thus need a systematic way for constructing insights and understandings from the findings from a multiplicity of studies. . . . By pooling the results of a collection of investigations, we can draw more reliable conclusions, resolve discrepancies and contradictions, and become more fully cognizant of the contexts that influence the phenomenon of interest.

Shanahan has identified twenty-five influential research syntheses that have been published since the mid-1960s. These reviews had a substantial impact on prevailing conceptions of best practice in literacy instruction.

In this chapter, we will summarize three recent major syntheses of research on reading that focus on different aspects of the reading process:

- *Becoming a Nation of Readers* by the Commission on Reading (Anderson, Heibert, Scott, and Wilkinson, 1985). This report was sponsored by the National Academy of Education and the National Institute of Education.
- *State of the Art: Transforming Ideas for Teaching and Learning to Read* by Anne Sweet (1993). This report was sponsored by the Office of Research of the U.S. Department of Education.
- *Teaching Children to Read: An Evidence-Based Assessment of the Scientific Literature and Its Implications for Reading Instruction* by the National Reading Panel (2000). This report was sponsored by the National Institute of Child Health and Human Development.

The two research syntheses by the Commission on Reading (Anderson et al., 1985) and Anne Sweet (1993) tap into a large body of research conducted in the 1980s and early 1990s that focused on factors that promote reading comprehension. In terms of Whitehurst and Lonigan's (2001) model of the reading process, the focus is on "outside-in" factors. It is not surprising, then, that the results align closely with "meaning-centered" approaches to teaching. Here is an abridged list of comprehension-related findings from these two influential research syntheses:

The Commission on Reading

1. Effective teachers create literate environments for their children (p. 92).

2. Both oral and silent reading are important for the beginner. Children should read selections silently before they are asked to read them orally (p. 58).

3. Priority should be given to independent reading. Two hours a week of independent reading should be expected by the time children are in the third or fourth grade (p. 82).

4. Workbook and skill sheet tasks take too much of the time allocated for reading. These should be pared to the minimum that will actually contribute to growth in reading (p. 81).

5. Students should do more extended writing. Writing is most beneficial when students have a reason to communicate to a genuine audience (p. 81).

6. Teachers need to teach comprehension skills directly. Teachers should devote more time to teaching strategies for understanding not only stories but also social studies and science texts (p. 81).

7. Grouping by ability may slow the progress of low-ability students. . . . Some of the problems with ability grouping can be alleviated by switching group assignments periodically, using criteria other than ability for group assignment, and, maybe, increasing the time devoted to whole class instruction (p. 92).

8. More comprehensive assessments of reading and writing are needed. Standardized tests do not provide a deep assessment of reading comprehension and should be supplemented with observations of reading fluency, critical analysis of lengthy reading selections, and measures of the amount of independent reading and writing done by children (p. 101).

State of the Art *report by Anne Sweet*

1. Storybook reading, done in the context of sharing experiences, ideas, and opinions, is a highly demanding mental activity for children. . . . Teachers who read aloud to children foster their ability to deal with narrative text (p. 7).

2. Effective reading instruction can develop engaged readers who are knowledgeable, strategic, motivated, and socially interactive. . . . Choosing to read is an important ingredient of engaged reading. It has been found that allowing students to choose reading material of interest to them is a powerful motivator that fosters independent reading habits (p. 4).

3. Children who engage in daily discussions about what they read are more likely to become critical readers and learners. . . . Research shows that students' verbal exchanges about content improve learning and increase their level of thinking (p. 9).

4. Responding to literature helps students construct their own meaning, which may not always be the same for all readers. . . . When students read a piece of literature they respond to it by using their prior knowledge to construct meaning. That is, their transaction with the text results in the construction of their own meaning (p. 8).

5. Expert readers have strategies that they use to construct meaning before, during, and after reading. . . . As students become proficient readers, they develop a set of plans or strategies for solving problems they encounter in their reading experiences. . . . Effective teachers incorporate these strategies into their ongoing literacy instruction (p. 10).

6. Children's reading and writing abilities develop together. . . . Teachers can be most effective in helping children to become better readers, writers, and thinkers when they weave integrated reading and writing activities into their literacy instruction (p. 11).

7. The most valuable form of reading assessment reflects our current understanding about the reading process and simulates authentic reading tasks. . . . Literacy assessments done in the classroom that involve performance tasks . . . provide valuable information needed to direct instructional decision making (p. 12).

National Reading Panel report

The report of the National Reading Panel (2000) reflects the recent rise in interest in phonics, word recognition, and fluent reading, "inside-out" factors in the Whitehurst and Lonigan model of the reading process. However, some of the recommendations also deal with facilitating comprehension. This research synthesis makes use of meta-analysis to statistically analyze the findings of multiple studies on the same topic (Glass, McGaw, & Smith, 1981). The findings support a skills-centered approach to teaching reading. Some of the key findings are paraphrased below:

1. **Phonemic awareness training improves students' phonemic awareness, reading, and spelling.** The effects on reading last well beyond the end of training.

2. **Systematic phonics instruction enhances children's success in learning to decode, spell, and comprehend text.**

3. **"One size fits all" does *not* apply to phonic instruction.** Teachers need to tailor instruction to meet the needs of specific children.

4. **Guided reading has a positive impact on word recognition, fluency (ability to read orally with accuracy, speed, and good expression), and comprehension.**

5. **Vocabulary instruction leads to gains in reading comprehension.** Learning in rich contexts and multiple exposures facilitate vocabulary knowledge.

6. **Comprehension is enhanced when readers actively relate the ideas contained in print to their prior knowledge.**

7. **Teaching a combination of strategies—such as self-monitoring, question generation, story structure, and summarization—is the most effective way to promote reading comprehension.**

Taken together, the findings of these three research syntheses lay the foundation for an effective, balanced approach to reading instruction. In the next section, we present a series of research-based "best practices" for teaching reading.

Best Practice in Reading Instruction

Given the widely discrepant views of the reading process discussed earlier in this chapter and the increasing "politicalization" of reading instruction (see Allington & Woodside-Jiron, 1999), it is hardly surprising that there is not universal agreement about what constitutes best practice in reading instruction. However, given the current movement toward balanced instruction and the overlapping findings of major research syntheses on reading, we agree with Linda Gambrell and Susan Mazzoni's (1999) contention that there is "common ground" for research-based best practices for teaching reading.

Drawing from the three research syntheses in the preceding section, we have assembled a list of practices that reflect a balanced approach to reading instruction. The reader should be aware of Gambrell and Mazzoni's (1999, p. 12) caveat about any list of best practices:

> We believe that there is no simple, narrow solution to the "best practices" debate. . . . For example, employing a method that research has shown to be effective for improving a particular aspect of literacy learning will not be a 'best practice' if instruction is not adapted to meet the strengths and needs of a particular group of learners, or if classroom management is an issue, or if a 'risk-taking' environment has not been fostered, or if other aspects of literacy instruction have not been included in the total program. Also, it is important to remember that teachers work with children who come to school with unique personalities and understandings; therefore different children will often respond differently to the same instruction. This means that best practices involve a 'custom fit'—not a simple 'one size fits all'—approach.

With this important caveat in mind, here is our list of best practices for teaching reading in the elementary grades (see Table 7.1) As you examine our list, please note the emphasis on balance. Direct instruction in decoding and comprehension skills is balanced with opportunities to listen to interesting stories and to engage in enjoyable, self-selected reading and writing activities.

- ■ **Read aloud to children on a daily basis** Earlier in this book, we discussed many of the benefits of reading aloud to children (see Chapters 4 and 5). Teacher read-alouds should *not* be phased out after kindergarten; rather, storybook reading should continue to be an integral part of the reading program. Even adults enjoy being read to!

TABLE 7.1   Best Practice in Reading Instruction

Read aloud to children on a daily basis

Create a literate classroom environment

Provide direct instruction on phonemic awareness, phonics, and word recognition

Provide opportunities for ample independent reading of self-selected books

Use guided reading to develop word recognition, fluency, and comprehension

Activate and build prior knowledge connected with texts

Teach vocabulary, both directly and indirectly

Provide opportunities for children to discuss the books they are reading

Provide a variety of reading response activities

Directly teach comprehension strategies

Keep seatwork to a minimum

Use a range of oral reading strategies

Integrate reading and writing activities

Use flexible grouping

Use authentic assessments to inform instruction

The benefits described earlier—promotion of positive attitudes about books and reading, exposure to new vocabulary and knowledge, increased familiarity with book language and story structure, accessibility to high quality literature, community building, "advertising" books for independent reading, opportunities for informal teaching—all apply from kindergarten on up through the grades. In addition, group storybook sessions allow students to begin sharing their developing insights about the deeper meanings of literature, setting the stage for literature study groups (Peterson & Eeds, 1990).

We recommend that all teachers follow the same general guidelines for read-alouds that were recommended in Chapter 5 for use at the preschool and kindergarten level. However, several adaptations are required because of older children's advanced development and changes in curriculum. Teachers of older children can assume a less directive role in post-reading discussions, allowing children more opportunity to share their personal reactions to the stories that they hear. This sharing of interpretations will help children build their own personal meaning for stories and presents opportunities for them to learn from their peers' insights. Teachers can encourage these story "conversations" by asking open-ended questions ("How did you feel when . . . "), by sharing their own personal reactions to the story ("I really liked the part where . . . "), and by accepting and respecting children's diverse responses to literature.

We also recommend that teachers balance the reading of narrative stories with the reading of expository texts (Doiron, 1994; Pearson & Raphael, 1999). Informational books, which become increasingly important as children progress through the grades, use very different organizational patterns than narrative stories: listing, time order or sequencing, description, cause/effect, problem/solution, and comparison/contrast. Read-alouds are a good way to begin to familiarize children with these expository text structures. In addition, some children prefer informational texts to stories. Reading nonfiction books aloud is an effective way to interest these reality-oriented children in reading.

- **Create a literate classroom environment** In Chapter 5, we discussed the importance of a literate classroom environment at the preschool and kindergarten levels. It is every bit as important to provide the same type of classroom environment in the elementary grades. In order for children to learn about literacy, they have to see lots of examples of meaningful print and have easy access to reading and writing materials. The same types of centers and materials that we recommended in Chapter 5 are also appropriate in the elementary grades:

- a well-designed,well-stocked classroom library
- a writing center
- lots of functional print
- lots of student work on display

Of course, adjustments need to made to the "level" of the print. For example, the books in the classroom library should represent a wide range of difficulty levels to match students' varying abilities. The higher the grade level, the larger the span of abilities. For example, when Mary Christie taught third grade, her classroom library contained books ranging from Dr. Seuss's Beginner Books (e.g., *The Cat in the Hat*

[Houghton Mifflin, 1957]) to books intended for sixth- and seventh-graders (e.g., *The Great Gilly Hopkins* by Katherine Paterson [HarperCollins, 1978]). This assures that children can choose books that match their reading abilities. This range also allows better readers to choose easy books for an enjoyable change of pace. Mary recalls that some of her best readers like to read the Dr. Seuss books on occasion.

Ideally, the classroom library should have a balance of easy-to-read materials and high quality literature (Pearson & Raphael, 1999). When students engage in self-selected independent reading, they often choose "page turners," easy books that are fun to read but not necessarily of high literary quality (Searfoss & Readence, 1994). Magazines also offer this type of easy reading practice.

At the same time, teachers also need to ensure that children also have opportunities to read high quality fiction and poetry. Good literature captures children's imaginations, which in turn fosters "engaged" reading. Rosenblatt (1985) has described the process of literary evocation "in which the reader selects out ideas, sensations, feelings, and images drawn from his past linguistic, literary, and life experience, and synthesizes them into a new experience" (p. 40). Only quality literature is likely to evoke this type of aesthetic experience.

Two particularly useful resources for locating good books for the classroom library are found in *The Reading Teacher,* the elementary-grade journal of the International Reading Association. Each October issue contains the "Children's Choices," a list of kid-tested books that are both above average in literary quality and popular with children. Each November issue contains "Teachers' Choices," a list of children's books that are especially popular with teachers. These are books that reflect exceptionally high literary value or have potential for use in other areas of the curriculum such as social studies and science. The books on the Teachers' Choices list are books that might not be discovered or appreciated by children without the help of an adult.

■ **Provide direct instruction on phonemic awareness, phonics, and word recognition**   Decoding is an essential part of the reading process. Text information cannot be accessed unless most of the words are recognized by sight recognition, phonics, context clues, or other means of decoding. Quick, automatic word identification is needed in order for the reading process to work properly and for comprehension to occur. Adams (1991) explains:

In fact, the automaticity with which skillful readers recognize words is the key to the whole system. It allows them to devote their conscious attention and effort to the meaning and significance of the text. . . . The reader's attention can be focused on the meaning of text to the extent that it's free from fussing with the words and letters (p. 207).

For some fortunate children who have had rich home literacy experiences, meaningful engagements with reading and writing will be sufficient for learning phonics and other word recognition skills. However, as the National Reading Panel's (2000) research synthesis revealed, most children profit from direct instruction in decoding skills. Here are some guidelines for delivering effective decoding instruction:

1. Just teach skills that children need to learn. If most students have not mastered a skill, then whole-class instruction is appropriate. On the other hand, if many children

Teachers should use direct instruction to teach phonics, letter recognition, and other decoding skills.

have already mastered a skill, use small-group instruction to teach it to just those children who need to learn the skills.

2. Provide direct instruction. Don't "beat around the bush" when teaching phonics, letter-recognition, and decoding skills. Tell the students which skill is being taught and why it is useful, then directly teach the skill.

3. Model how the skill is used. For example, if you are teaching the "sh" digraph, show how knowledge of this letter–sound relationship can help the children sound out unfamiliar words.

4. Tie the skill to students' prior knowledge and experience. For example, have the children think of other words that contain the "sh" sound.

5. Link the skill with the texts that children are reading. For example, have them be on the lookout for words that contain the *sh* digraph. Connecting decoding instruction with texts that students are reading is an ideal way to make instruction meaningful to students. They see immediately why skills are important and how these skills can help them become better readers. Because the decoding skills are learned in context, rather than in isolation, transfer to "real" reading is facilitated.

■ **Provide opportunities for ample independent reading of self-selected books**
Current theories of the reading process (and common sense) suggest that the best way to become a good reader is to do lots of reading. Ideally, readers themselves should select much of the material they read. Self-selection insures that books appeal to children's current interests, making reading an engaging and enjoyable activity.

Research has shown that the amount of independent reading children do—both in and out of school—is related to gains in reading achievement (Anderson, Wilson,

& Fielding, 1988). Unfortunately, the amount of time that children spend reading in traditional classrooms is quite small, averaging seven to eight minutes a day in the primary grades (Anderson et al., 1985). Children do not do very much reading outside of school either. One study found that fifth graders spent an average of about ten minutes per day at home reading books (Anderson et al., 1988).

An obvious implication of this research is that teachers need to encourage independent reading of self-selected books, both at school and at home. Time needs to set aside so that all children have opportunity to do recreational reading in the classroom. Pleasure reading should always be an option when children finish assignments early. But this type of "spare time" reading is rarely available to less able students, the ones that need it most. So teachers need to schedule a special time for pleasure reading, and this period needs to be long enough so that children can become fully engaged with the books that they are reading. The reading workshop, introduced in the next section and described in detail in Chapter 8, is an ideal way to provide students with ample amounts of free reading. Sustained Silent Reading (SSR) is another effective means for providing time for every child to engage in recreational reading (see Special Feature 7.1).

- **Use guided reading to develop word recognition, fluency, and comprehension**
  Guided reading is an instructional method teachers use to support individual readers' development of effective strategies for reading texts at increasingly challenging levels of difficulty (Fountas & Pinnell, 1996; Opitz & Ford, 2001). The goal is for students to be successful independent readers. Irene Fountas and Gay Su Pinnell (1996) outline the core components of a guided reading lesson:

  - The teacher works with a small group of children who are at about the same level of reading development.
  - The teacher chooses a book that is relatively easy for this group of children to read, but poses a few problems for them to solve. The books are often from a "leveled" set of books, classified by difficulty. Calkins (2001) presents an effective system for establishing and using a leveled classroom library.
  - The teacher briefly introduces the story. The goal is to interest the students in the story, relate the story to their experience, and give them clues that will help them process the text.
  - The students then each read the whole text, either softly out loud or silently to themselves. During reading, the teacher "listens in" to learn about the children's use of reading strategies. The teacher provides temporary assistance when needed.
  - The teacher invites children to share their personal responses to the story. Then the teacher selects one or two teaching points to present to the group following the reading.
  - If the book is liked by the children, it is made available for free-choice reading. Occasionally, the teacher engages children in extending the story through art, drama, writing, or additional reading.

  Over time the level of difficulty of the books increases, and the amount of scaffolding and support from the teacher decreases.

Special Feature 7.1

Sustained Silent Reading

Sustained silent reading (SSR) is a teaching strategy developed by Lyman Hunt (1971) and by Robert McCracken and Marlene McCracken (1978) that gives students fixed time periods to engage in the independent reading of self-selected books. SSR fits well with all major approaches to reading instruction. It is tailor-made for providing the extensive reading component of whole-language and literature-based programs. SSR is also an ideal supplement to basal reading series, helping to compensate for the lack of self-selected, independent reading in many programs.

The basic SSR strategy is to set aside a specific time each day for silent reading—first thing in the morning, at the end of the reading period, after lunch, recess, or right before school lets out. While there are many variations to this strategy, three basic rules always apply to SSR:

- *Everyone reads*—Both the students and the teacher read something of their own choosing.
- *No interruptions*—Students must hold their comments and questions until the period has ended.
- *No reports, postreading questions, or record keeping*—The focus is totally on reading for pleasure (Tierney, Readence, & Dishner, 1995).

Initially, SSR periods should be quite brief so that most of the students can sustain their silent reading for the entire time—five minutes or less in the lower grades. This time should gradually be extended as children get in the habit of reading silently. Many teachers use a kitchen timer to signal the end of the period. This enables the teachers to enjoy their own reading without having to be constantly monitoring the time.

First-grade teachers may wish to make some slight modifications to make SSR more developmentally appropriate for beginning readers. Laraine Hong (1981) recommends that young children be allowed to read in pairs and talk to each other quietly. This adds a social dimension to pleasure reading and opens up opportunities for collaborative literacy learning. It also permits beginning readers, who have not yet reached the silent-reading stage, to read orally to each other. Another variation of SSR for young children is called "DEAR," for "drop everything and read." It is described at the beginning of Chapter 7.

Some children are reluctant to participate in SSR at first, particularly those with limited home literacy experiences and those who are experiencing difficulty in learning to read. Modeling and peer pressure can help these reluctant readers to start reading. Students observe a respected adult—their teacher—reading for pleasure on a regular basis, something they may not have seen at home. This communicates to children that recreational reading is an enjoyable, worthwhile activity. Peers are another important factor. Reluctant readers look around and see that many of their friends are reading books and enjoying it. These students will often begin to read to fit in with what their friends are doing and often discover that reading a good book is better than just sitting around doing nothing (the only alternative to reading during an SSR period).

Michael Opitz and Michael Ford (2001) provide several scenarios to illustrate how guided reading is played out in different classrooms, from first grade to sixth grade. Through each scenario, these authors illustrate how teachers integrate numerous strategies into their reading instruction.

■ **Activate and build prior knowledge connected with texts** Current interactive theories of the reading process, such as the Whitehurst and Lonigan model (see Figure 7.1), maintain that comprehension is an active, constructive process. Simply identifying all the words in a text does not insure that comprehension will occur. Readers must build meaning by linking text information with what they already know (Anderson & Pearson, 1984). The obvious instructional implication is that teachers should help children **activate** or **build** text-relevant background knowledge prior to reading.

If students have already had some experience with the topic, then teachers should make them aware of this fact and bring this prior knowledge to their attention. If students know very little about the topic, then teachers should help them build the prerequisite background knowledge. A number of strategies are available for activating prior knowledge:

■ **Questioning**—Teachers can ask what children already know about a topic ("What happens at an airport?") or ask questions about students' personal experience with the topic ("Who has been to an airport? What did you see there?").

■ **Brainstorming**—Children are asked to call up all the words they can think of that are related to a topic. These words can be listed on a chart or the chalkboard.

■ **Predicting**—The teacher provides clues as to what a story is about by focusing on the title, key illustrations, or the introduction. Children are then asked what they think will happen in the story. In order to make these predictions, children must call up what they already know about the topic. In addition, they are motivated to read the story to find out if their predictions are confirmed.

■ **Webbing**—A chart is constructed that illustrates how different ideas connected to a topic are related to one another. Webbing is often used to organize the concepts activated with brainstorming. Figure 7.2 illustrates how a web could be constructed from words connected with the topic, *airport.*

If, while engaging in these types of knowledge activation activities, it becomes obvious that children know little about the topic, then the teacher should take steps to build the prerequisite background knowledge prior to reading. Read-alouds, films and videos, guest speakers, and direct experiences are ideal for this purpose. For example, if children know little about airports, the teacher could read aloud Byron Barton's *Airport* (Harper & Row, 1982) and then take the class on a field trip to a nearby airport.

The Commission on Reading cautions that not all background knowledge is beneficial (Anderson et al., 1985). Some activities recommended in teacher's manuals are too broad or unfocused to be useful, whereas others may actually divert students' attention from the central theme or plot of a story (Beck, McCaslin, & McKeown, 1981). One example that comes to mind involves a basal reader story about a South American boy who had recently immigrated to the United States. The main problem that this boy faced was understanding the nonliteral nature of figurative speech. For example, if someone said, "That's really cool," the boy assumed that the comment referred to temperature rather than how desirable something was. The teacher's manual recommended asking students what they knew about South America, a topic that had very little to do with the plot of the story! At best, this activity

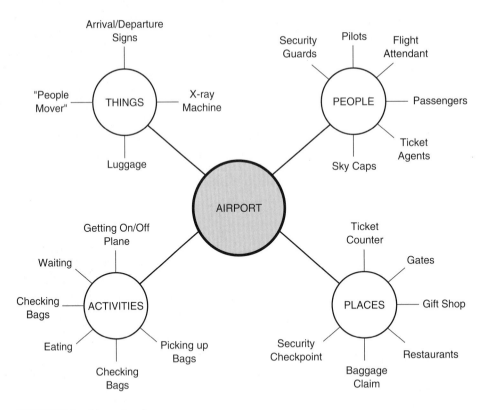

FIGURE 7.2   Airport web.

would be a waste of time. At worst, it may actually interfere with comprehension by directing children's attention away from the central plot. The Commission recommends that, when planning background knowledge activities, teachers should "focus on the concepts that will be central to the understanding of the upcoming story, concepts that children either do not possess or may not think of without prompting" (Anderson et al., 1985, p. 50).

■ **Teach vocabulary, both directly and indirectly** Vocabulary knowledge—knowing the meanings of words—has a crucial role in learning to read. It affects both decoding and comprehension. For example, in order to use phonics to decode and identify an unknown word, the word must be in the reader's oral vocabulary. Otherwise, the reader will not recognize the word, even if it is pronounced correctly. The relationship between vocabulary and reading comprehension is even stronger. It is impossible to understand the meaning of a text unless the reader knows the meaning of most of the words in the text.

The National Reading Panel (2000) reported that vocabulary instruction does lead to gains in reading comprehension. The panel recommends that vocabulary be taught both indirectly, in the context of storybook reading and other classroom activities, and directly through focused vocabulary lessons. Indirect or incidental teaching of vocabulary requires that teachers be alert for "teachable moments" involving words that are connected with ongoing activities. For example, the predictable book *A-Hunting We Will Go* by John Langstaff (D.C. Heath, 1989) contains the lines:

Oh, a-hunting we will go,
A-hunting we will go;
We'll catch a lamb
And put him in a pram,
And then we'll let him go!

Teachers can use this opportunity to teach the meaning of the word *pram,* a British term for a baby carriage, that will likely be unfamiliar to most U.S. children. This type of contextualized vocabulary instruction tends to be very effective because the context—in this case the storybook—helps solidify children's understanding of the new word.

Teachers should also use preplanned lessons to teach the meaning of passage-critical words, "words the teacher deems essential for understanding a text when the text provides insufficient clues to enable the reader to infer the meaning of the words" (Johnson, 2001, p. 42). Students' comprehension of the text is likely to suffer if they are not taught the meaning of such words prior to reading.

Direct vocabulary instruction should begin with a clear (and, if possible, concrete) explanation of the word. This should be followed by opportunities for students to "relate new words to their own prior knowledge, as well as to other related words" (Johnson, 2001, p. 48). For example, if the target word is *pram,* the teacher could have students generate other words they already know that have a similar meaning: *baby carriage, stroller,* and so on. Finally, children need active involvement with and multiple exposures to the new word (Blanchowicz & Fisher, 2000). Examples include using the word in oral and/ or written sentences, constructing a web of related terms (see Figure 7.2) and games and activities involving synonyms, antonyms, or other aspects of word meaning (see Trade Secret 7.1 for a collection of effective vocabulary teaching activities).

■ **Provide opportunities for children to discuss the books they are reading** To gain the maximum benefits from high quality literature, students need to have opportunities to discuss stories and share their interpretations (Sweet, 1993). This holds true whether the book is read aloud to the class by the teacher, students read the book in a small group with guidance from the teacher, or students read the book on their own.

We believe that literature study groups are the ideal context for book discussions. This strategy, which we will describe in Chapter 8, involves having a small group of students read the same story at the same time (on their own or with buddies). This group meets periodically to discuss the story. The teacher's role should be that of a guide and co-participant in the discussion, allowing children to construct their own meaning and interpretations for the story. Ralph Peterson and Maryann Eeds' (1990) classic book, *Grand Conversations: Literature Groups in Action,* contains

Trade Secret 7.1

Wonderful Words
Dawn Downes

"A definition is the enclosing of a wilderness of ideas within a wall of words."
Samuel Butler

Words are the building blocks of our language. Innocently masquerading as a simple string of letters, words carry with them an undeniable power. As students learn new words, they are gaining keys to the English language; keys that can do amazing work for them. Through learning words, students gain keys that will help them to comprehend text, speak and write with greater precision, and develop their thinking with greater depth.

The very best way to increase a student's vocabulary, or mental lexicon, is to engage the student with meaningful texts that are both self- and teacher-selected. When a student is engaged with a text that she finds interesting, meaning becomes paramount and vocabulary acquisition is a by-product of reading. However, sometimes curricula mandate topics and texts that students would not normally read if all reading was only based on their interest. In these cases, explicit strategies for teaching vocabulary are required to help students learn words outside of their natural word-learning processes. In the classroom, these explicit vocabulary-building strategies must reinforce the work that the students' mental lexicons are doing to learn new words. Additionally, vocabulary strategies should adhere to the three principles for effective vocabulary instruction as identified by Nagy (1988): integration, repetition, and meaningful use.

Word Collection Activities

When students are permitted to be involved in selecting their own vocabulary words for study, both their immediate interest in the words and their long-term retention of those words and word meanings increases (Blanchowicz & Fisher,

2000). There are several ways to structure self-selected vocabulary learning in the classroom:

- **Vocabulary Notebooks:** A vocabulary notebook can be an individual notebook, a section in a larger language arts notebook, or several papers stapled together in the reading/writing workshop folder. The vocabulary notebook is a place to collect lots of wonderful words. The notebook could be divided into sections where students write down words from various subject areas or from the classroom literature. As students are working in a particular unit of study or in a writing workshop, the vocabulary notebook serves as both a resource and a place to collect words.
- **Selecting Vocabulary Words from Whole-Class Literature Selections:** As students are reading, ask them to use post-it notes to mark words in the text that interfere with their being able to understand the reading. With older children, you may ask them to mark words that they think would confuse another student. If needed, create minimal requirements, such as mark three words in the whole book (for younger students) or two words in the chapter (for older students). If the whole class is reading a selected piece, everyone's confusing words could be compiled and the words that appear most frequently on everyone's list could be the vocabulary words to be learned from that reading selection. In a community of learners, the teacher is a reader too and is encouraged to contribute one or two words to the class list. This makes the final vocabulary list a negotiated list that involves all learners, not just the teacher.
- **Selecting Vocabulary Words from Literature Circles:** In literature circles students take ownership of the reading and learning process. In small groups, students select parts of the text to discuss, debate,

(continued on next page)

and learn. Included in Harvey Daniels' (1994) model of literature circles is a "Word Finder." As this student is reading, she looks for words that are new, different, strange, or interesting. When the group reconvenes to discuss the book, the Word Finder shares her words and the group decides which words to add to their group's vocabulary list.

Word Generation Activities

When a teacher wants to challenge her students to stretch their mental lexicons, word generation activities can offer some possibilities. Many literature anthologies come with art collections on transparencies. Place one of the transparencies on the overhead and ask students to brainstorm what words they are thinking of when they look at the artwork. Instead of art, the class can also generate words during a read-aloud. Find a place in the story that will generate interest for the students. When you reach this place in the read-aloud, interrupt your reading and ask students to make a list of words that describe how each of them feels about the character or the plot.

After brainstorming as individuals with either the picture or the literature, have the students share their words with a partner, and then collect all of the students' words on an easel at the front of the room. After examining the generated list, ask students to group words on the list together, or have them all choose a word and use the thesaurus to look up a new word that is a synonym or antonym.

Word Sort Activities

Word sorts are engaging activities in which students make comparisons between words and use those comparisons to arrange words into categories and lists (Bear, Invernizzi, Templeton, & Johnston, 2000). On each card is a word or a picture (for very young readers). To increase the repetition of words (Nagy, 1988), the words on the cards may be the words that were gathered dur-

ing the word collection or generation activities. Alternatively, the words may be drawn out of the content of science, social studies, mathematics, or other content areas. Through the school year, students could keep all of their vocabulary words on small cards (index cards cut in half). One side of the card has the vocabulary word and the other side of the card has the definition and, if possible, the sentence in which the word occurs in the reading. Words from various content areas could be kept separate in individual zipper bags, organized and ready to go for sorting activities.

When words and concepts are new to students, the teacher should engage the students in closed, or teacher-directed, sorts (Bear et al., 2000). In these sorts the teacher defines the categories or groupings into which the students sort and place their words. Children may sort words by beginning sounds, spelling patterns, parts of speech, thematic or semantic connections, or words known and unknown. After students have become skilled at sorting activities, the teacher may ask students to work independently or with a group to develop their own categories and groupings of words in an open-sort activity. After sorting, students should have the opportunity to share their open sort with another student or group and to articulate the words and how they are organized in the sort.

In the classroom, teachers have the wonderful opportunity to give children the words they need to send their thoughts and ideas out into the world. Words are packed with power, and as children increase their vocabulary, or mental lexicons, they become articulate and wise users of language. In the classroom, play with words. Roll them around in your reading, writing, speaking, and listening activities. Collect words in notebooks and on posters. Integrate words into all areas of your curriculum. Repeat words in meaningful contexts. Above all, engage students in creative word-learning activities that ask them to think about words, connect words to the concepts of the classroom, to the world, and to themselves. Teach students that words are wonderful, indeed!

wonderful examples of the deep discussions that elementary students can have about good literature.

As children share their thoughts about stories in literature study groups, they are often able to construct deeper levels of meaning. For example, one of us observed a group of six first-grade students discussing Maurice Sendak's *Where the Wild Things Are* (Harper & Row, 1963). At first, most of the children believed that Max actually sailed to the monster-filled island. But Tony pointed out that, at the end of the story, Max's supper was waiting for him "and it was still hot." So Tony reasoned that Max couldn't have been gone very long and that Max must have dreamed or imagined the whole thing. Several of the other children said, "Oh!" and it was obvious that they had accepted Tony's interpretation.

■ **Provide a variety of reading response activities** Rosenblatt's (1985) transactional theory maintains that the primary purpose for reading fiction and poetry is aesthetic: to evoke images and emotions. These aesthetic responses to literature are highly individualistic, as DeGroff and Galda (1992, p. 123) explain:

> Readers infuse intellectual and emotional meaning into what they read; the meaning they create is shaped by their experiences. Because no two people have had exactly the same experiences, no two readings are exactly the same. . . . We can, however, reach some measure of consensus about the meaning of a text. This consensus is possible because our experiences overlap to some extent.

Teachers can encourage aesthetic responses to fiction and poetry by offering a variety of options:

■ **Response journals**—As students read books, they jot down their ideas and reactions in a notebook. They can make comments about key events and favorite characters, or they may discuss their own thoughts and emotions as they read the story. Journal entries are treated as "first draft" expressive writing. When responding to student entries, teachers should focus on content (what is written) rather than on mechanics (how it is written).

■ **Drama**—Pretend play is a natural way for children to express their thoughts and feelings about real-life events, television shows, movies, and stories in books. By the time children enter the primary grades, most have become quite skilled at taking on roles and acting out stories (Johnson, Christie, & Yawkey, 1999). Teachers can capitalize on children's dramatic play abilities by encouraging them to act out stories that they have read and enjoyed. Drama allows children to express and explore their aesthetic responses to literature. In addition, dramatic reenactments can facilitate comprehension by building children's knowledge of story structure (Christie, 1987).

Students can respond to stories through drama in a number of different ways. Galda, Cullinan, and Strickland (1993) recommend the following basic strategies:

1. **Spontaneous reenactment**—Children act out the events of a story without a script or many props, often without an audience;
2. **Informal performance**—Children plan their enactment and make some basic props before acting out the story in front of an audience;

3. **Readers Theatre**—Children read aloud from scripts that are based on litera-ture selections.

Other options include pantomime, puppet shows, character study, and improvi-sation (see McCaslin, 1987). Whatever form of dramatization is used, emphasis should be placed on the experience itself rather than on a polished performance.

In Trade Secret 7.2, multi-age teacher Linda Hand describes the various types of literature-response activities that she uses with her first- and second-grade students.

■ **Directly teach comprehension strategies** A key goal of reading instruction is to help students become strategic readers who can develop a set of plans to overcome problems they encounter while reading and who can adjust their reading behavior to the task at hand (Sweet, 1993). Winograd (1989, p. 7) explains:

> Strategic readers approach the tasks of reading in a flexible manner that depends upon their purpose and the nature of the text. Strategic readers are skilled, of course; but, more important, they are capable of using those skills appropriately and willing to use them to achieve purposes they consider important (p. 7).

A number of strategies have been identified that can help readers construct mean-ing before, during, and after reading (National Reading Panel, 2000; Pressley, 2000):

■ **Question generating**—Readers ask themselves questions that they want to have answered, thus setting their own purposes for reading;

■ **Monitoring**—Readers learn to be aware of their understanding of text. They can detect when a problem occurs in decoding or comprehension, enabling them to take corrective action;

■ **Mental imagery**—Readers construct mental images that represent meanings expressed in a text;

■ **Text structure**—Readers analyze stories into story grammar elements;

■ **Summarizing**—Readers pull together and condense the information in a text passage.

To this list, we add one that we borrowed from Lucy Calkins (2001) that we find works well with children. What we and Lucy do is retype a story the children are reading, leaving boxes for the children's responses. The children read to the first box, and we ask, "What are you thinking right now?" The children discuss their ideas. Then they return to the text to underline that evidence in the text that supports their thinking. Finally, they read that portion of the text that supports their thinking. In this way, we are teaching children to think about the text as they read.

Research indicates that these types of strategies can best be taught through direct explanation and transactional types of strategy instruction, both involving direct explanation and teacher modeling of a strategy, followed by guided practice (National Reading Panel, 2000; Pressley, 2000). Because strategies are processes rather than sets of facts, modeling plays a key role in this instruction. Teachers have to show students how to use these processes. The teacher presents situations in which strategies are needed, models how to select an appropriate strategy to use, and then

Trade Secret 7.2

Responding to Literature
Linda Hand

Response plays an important role in my multigrade (first and second grade) language-arts program. As children participate in reading and writing workshops, they respond orally to their reading and writing and to that of others—conferring with the teacher, talking with each other in peer conferences, or sharing in small or large groups. Responding may also take the form of writing, art, or drama.

In my classroom, I read aloud many books to my students every day. Before reading a book, we discuss what we think the story will be about or what we will learn by reading it. During and after reading, we talk to make sense about what was read. We talk to connect reading to our lives and to connect with other books. Reading aloud gives me the opportunity to model ways to discuss books so that students are then able to discuss books in small literature circles with their peers.

Literature circles are an important part of our day. At the end of each reading workshop, the students discuss their books in small groups of three to five children. The books discussed may have the same title or author, or may be about the same theme. One child begins by telling the title, the author, and then something about the book that he or she would like to share. In each child's reading folder is a list of possible topics to discuss during literature circle:

- What did you notice that was special about the story?
- How did the story make you feel?
- What was your favorite part?
- Did the story remind you of your own life? How?
- Does the book remind you of any other books you have read?
- What did you learn from this story?

The students run their own discussion circles while I move from group to group, facilitating and modeling self-reflection and critical thinking. I find this difficult at times to manage, but when it goes well, it is extremely rewarding to hear the lively discussions.

Students also work independently to respond to favorite books. Inside each of their reading folders is a list of response options, including the following:

- Share your book with a friend.
- Make a story map of events—on bulletin-board paper.
- Construct a story web.
- Create a story frame.
- Put on a puppet show—retelling the story.
- Describe a character—brainstorm adjectives.
- Compare two characters in the story.
- Write a letter to a character, author, teacher, or peer.
- Write a new ending.
- Fill out an S.O.S. sheet—summary, opinion, support you opinion.
- Fill out a T.A.P.P.S. form—title, author, pizzazz words, picture, sentence.
- Draw a picture of a favorite part or character.
- Make a travel brochure for the story setting.
- Create a poster or a mural about the story.

These response activities help children construct their own personal meanings for the books they have read. The products of these activities serve other purposes as well. Children select favorite response products to include in their language-arts portfolios, aiding my assessment of their literacy growth. Selected pieces are also put on display in the library area, serving as effective advertisements for the books contained in the center.

"thinks aloud," sharing with the students the thinking process that one goes through when using the strategy (Spiegel, 1992, 1995).

■ **Keep seatwork to a minimum** Traditionally, decoding skills such as phonics and sight recognition of words have been taught using workbooks and skill sheets. Research conducted during the 1980s revealed that students often spent as much as 70 percent of the time set aside for reading instruction doing this type of independent practice. It was not uncommon for primary-grade children to do 1000 workbook pages and skill sheets a year (Anderson et al., 1985)!

Becoming a Nation of Readers by the Commission on Reading (Anderson et al., 1985) took a strong stand against this proliferation of seatwork. The Commission pointed out that the sheer quantity of seatwork was a serious problem, taking time away from meaningful reading activities. The Commission catalogued a number of other problems associated with skill sheets and workbook activities: (1) most seatwork exercises require perfunctory, passive reading instead of constructive, higher-level comprehension; (2) exercises usually involve filling in the blanks, circling, or underlining items rather than authentic writing; (3) exercises are often difficult to understand; (4) children often find repetitive seatwork to be boring and meaningless; and (5) skill practice is not integrated with the rest of the reading lesson. Given all these problems, it is not surprising that research has shown that seatwork tends to be associated with low levels of student engagement and lower achievement in reading (Adams, 1990).

We concur with the Commission's recommendations that teachers should only use seatwork exercises that: (1) focus on skills that children have begun to learn but have not fully mastered; (2) have clear directions; (3) involve "real" reading and writing; and (4) are related to other parts of the reading lesson. Teachers should also avoid using seatwork as a management technique to keep students busy.

■ **Use a range of oral reading strategies** "Round robin" oral reading occurs when children take turns reading a passage aloud, while the rest of the class reads along silently. Typically, the students have not read the selection silently prior to this oral reading. Round robin reading consumes a considerable amount of instructional time both in the primary grades, where it is used to read basal reader stories, and in the intermediate and upper grades, where it is used to cover content in social studies textbooks (Durkin, 1984, 1993).

While used extensively by some teachers, round robin reading has a number of serious shortcomings. Lower ability students often read very haltingly and make many errors, modeling poor oral reading for other students. This poor performance, coupled with corrections from the teacher or other students, can make oral reading a stressful and sometimes humiliating experience. In addition, other students must slow down their silent reading rate in order to keep pace with the sluggish rate of the oral reading. This can lead to excessive subvocalization and inefficient eye movements during silent reading (Durkin, 1993). A final problem concerns comprehension. Many students, especially higher ability readers, find round robin reading very boring, causing them to lose interest in stories and become disengaged. This lack of engagement can cause comprehension to suffer.

The Commission on Reading suggests that round robin oral reading can be used sparingly with beginning readers to provide these children an opportunity to share their newly acquired oral reading skills with others (Anderson et al., 1985). When used for this purpose, the group size should be kept small (three or four students is ideal) so that each child has ample opportunity to participate. Corrections should be kept to a minimum. Teachers should only correct mistakes that significantly change meaning, and children should never be allowed to correct each other. Further, the children should be reading books well within their instructional level.

Once children progress beyond the beginning reading stage, teachers can use other, more effective, strategies to provide them with oral reading practice:

- **Choral reading**—Children read the same text aloud simultaneously, providing practice without putting individual children in the "spotlight."
- **Buddy reading**—Pairs of children take turns reading a story aloud to each other. Compared with round robin reading, this strategy provides increased participation (each child reads 50 percent of the time) and lower stress (small audience).
- **Repeated reading**—Students practice reading a passage until they can read it fluently with no errors, and then read the story to the class. This strategy provides low-ability readers with much-needed success in oral reading.

- **Integrate reading and writing activities** Traditional basal reading programs were designed for use in "compartmentalized" language arts programs with separate periods for reading, English, handwriting, and spelling. Different aspects of written language were rarely linked together in meaningful ways (Noyce & Christie, 1989). The stories children read in their basal readers were not used as stimuli for writing assignments during English period, nor was writing used to help children better comprehend their basal reader selections. There was no connection between the words taught in the reading texts and those taught in the spelling program, and little attempt was made to link spelling instruction with the words children actually use in their writing. Handwriting, punctuation, and grammar were taught as separate English skills, disconnected from actual writing assignments. Reading and writing instruction were rarely connected with content area subjects such as social studies or science. This compartmentalization of the language arts came under attack in the 1980s and 1990s from a number of sources:

- Emergent literacy research revealed that reading and writing developed simultaneously in young children (see Chapter 4).
- Tierney and Pearson's (1983) "composing" model of the reading process suggested that reading and writing share the same basic processes.
- The Commission on Reading's influential report, *Becoming a Nation of Readers* (Anderson et al., 1985) emphasized the need for instructional integration, claiming that children learn more when reading and writing are taught together than when they are taught as separate subjects.
- A growing body of research revealed that reading and writing were closely related and that teaching them together can have positive results on literacy learning (Gavelek, Raphael, Biondo, & Wang, 2000; Shanahan, 1988).

Strategies for integrating the language arts are found throughout this book. Most of the strategies recommended for promoting emergent literacy in Chapters 5 and 6 involve both reading and writing. In Chapter 8, many of the reading workshops described in Martha Linn's first-grade and Anne Foley's fourth-grade classrooms involve writing and links with other areas of the curriculum. Finally, Chapter 11 describes how to use interdisciplinary/integrated units to connect the language arts with each other and with content areas such as social studies, science, and mathematics.

■ **Use flexible grouping** Traditional basal reading instruction has been organized around ability groups. Classes were usually divided into three reading groups (low, middle, and high) based on the students' performance on standardized or informal reading tests, or students were regrouped across classes to form homogeneous classes for whole-class instruction in reading (Reutzel, 1999). The goal was to reduce the range of reading ability in each group, making it easier for teachers to provide optimal instruction for each group of students. Teachers could select materials, goals, and instructional strategies that were ideally suited for students at each ability level.

While based on good intentions, ability grouping has a number of disadvantages, particularly for the students in the "low" group:

■ **Self-esteem**—Students tend to evaluate their abilities in terms of their group's status. If their group is labelled as "low," students begin to view themselves as poor readers (Anderson et al., 1985).
■ **Modeling**—Low-group students are surrounded by models of poor reading and rarely get to interact with high ability readers.
■ **Different instruction**—Children in the low group read more words out loud, do more skill drill, are asked lower-level comprehension questions, do less silent reading, and have less exposure to high quality literature than students in high groups (Flood, Lapp, Flood, & Nagel, 1992).
■ **Teacher expectations**—Teachers have far lower expectations for the progress of low-group students (Flood et al., 1992).

To make matters worse, once a child is placed in the low group, it may be very difficult to move to a higher group. Low-group students are taught lower-level materials and at a slower pace than other students, making it likely that they will fall further and further behind. Even when a low-group student begins to close the gap, labeling and low teacher expectations may block opportunities to change groups (see Special Feature 7.2).

Most of the problems associated with ability grouping occur when it is the *only* way that students are grouped for reading instruction and when these groups are static and semipermanent. Grouping students by ability on occasion can be beneficial, particularly when done on the basis of children's achievement in specific aspects of reading (rather than general achievement). But this needs to be balanced by other methods of grouping so that students' can interact with children of differing abilities, more skilled peers they can learn from and less skilled peers they can assist.

Flexible grouping offers an attractive alternative to static ability groups (Reutzel, 1999). The teacher varies the size of groups and the way that students are

Special Feature 7.2

Rae's Early Experience with Ability Grouping

My earliest literacy events were recorded by my mom. As a very attentive and loving mom, she did a lot to encourage my early literacy development. By the time I was 8 months old, I could label pictures in National Geographic, a magazine my mother read to me regularly. By age 20 months, I spoke in sentences. At age 3 years, 11 months, and 11 days, a monumental event occurred: I became a big sister! Until I began kindergarten, I was teacher and second mom to my little brother. I read to him, and he never criticized (maybe because he couldn't talk yet). I taught him how to write. You see, I was a reader and a writer. He was the focus of my life.

In school, my opinion of my reading and writing abilities quickly changed. I entered kindergarten young; I wouldn't turn five until December. Because I was behind in my motor skills, my teacher did not think highly of me. My penmanship, although quite legible, was not what she expected. She yelled at me because of my sloppy handwriting. She told my parents that I was a slow learner, a "C" student at best. When they requested ideas on ways they might help me, my teacher ignored their cries for assistance. By the end of the year, my parents had decided that was it: I would go to a different school the next year.

Unfortunately, my kindergarten teacher's opinion of my ability followed me to first grade. Based on comments by my kindergarten teacher that were in my cumulative record, my first-grade teacher decided I would need special help. Her decision was based on her sincere desire to help me. Unfortunately, I saw the additional instruction as punishment. While my peers had fun, I worked at the back of the room. I was different from the other children. I labeled myself "dumb." My self-esteem and confidence plummeted.

Despite negative feelings about myself, by March of my first-grade year, my teacher told my mother that I was really beginning to catch on, especially to reading. By September of my second-grade year, my reading and writing skills had caught up to my peers. My parents were delighted! To their surprise, however, they were told that I would need to continue to receive extra help. It seems that the school received some federal money because of my poor reading ability. The school received the money, so I had to receive the instruction—at the back of the room.

Third through sixth grades seemed to flow together. I do recall reading lots; I thought it would make me smart. By fourth grade, I began to earn A's and B's. Because of my performance, my parents requested that I be moved to a higher reading group. The work of the low reading group had become too easy for me. I was bored and unchallenged. The school's response was that reading groups were formed based on ability. Because I had a low ability, I needed to stay in the low reading group. My grades, the school said, were reflective of my overachieving performance, not my ability. Labeled as "slow" at four years of age, I was still labeled as slow through sixth grade—seven years later.

Early labels are hard to overcome!

grouped according to task demands and student characteristics. Whole-class grouping can be used for activities like teacher read-alouds, planning, brainstorming, sharing, performances, and focus lessons on skills that are unknown and necessary for all the students. Small groups, ranging in size from three to ten members, and pairs can be formed based on a number of factors:

- Skill development—Students who need instruction in a specific skill can be grouped together;

- Interests—Students sharing a common interest in a topic can form a group;
- Knowledge—Students possessing knowledge of specific content or strategies can be grouped together or spread among groups to act as experts;
- Work habits and social skills—Students with good work habits (e.g., persistence) or particular social skills (e.g., leadership) can be mixed with others to serve as models;
- Task characteristics—Students may be grouped together because they succeed best when doing certain types of activities;
- Random—Students are grouped by random means such as drawing numbers from a hat and putting all the "ones" in one group and "twos" in another; and
- Student choice—Children pick their own group members.

These small groups are temporary in nature. Once the activity is completed, the group ceases to exist and students move on to other activities. Children should also have opportunities to work *individually* on projects of personal interest and during free reading of self-selected books.

- **Use authentic assessments to inform instruction** As discussed in Chapter 1, one of the main tenets of this book is that assessment should be embedded in instruction. Teachers should assess children's reading skills and knowledge while the children are engaging in classroom learning activities. When done systematically over time, this type of instructionally embedded assessment provides valuable information about each child's reading development and, at the same time, enables teachers to fine-tune their literacy instruction to meet the needs of the students in their classroom.

In this book, we present a variety of assessment strategies that are ongoing, embedded in instruction, and involve authentic literacy tasks. These strategies include systematic observation and performance samples (Chapter 6), running records (Chapter 8), and portfolio assessment (Chapter 12). These procedures provide teachers with rich data about students' development as readers and writers and supply information that can be used to improve instruction.

The Reading Workshop

There are numerous approaches to teaching reading, ranging from systematic phonics programs to basal reading series to literature-based programs. *Approaches to Beginning Reading* (Aukerman, 1984) lists no fewer than 163 different programs for teaching reading. Out of this myriad of approaches, we believe that one approach has the best alignment with the "best practice" strategies discussed in the previous section, the reading workshop. The reading workshop was introduced in Nancy Atwell's (1987) classic book, *In the Middle*. While originally intended for the middle grades, over the past decade and a half, the reading workshop has been successfully adapted for use at all grade levels (e.g., Calkins, 2001; Serafini, 2001a).

The reading workshop is an approach to teaching reading that has an ideal balance between connected reading and skill instruction. Children spend a good portion of the time engaged in self-selected reading and responding to their reading through discussions, journals, and other types of book-related activities. Students are taught to record their responses to their reading in journals and to work together in literature study groups to discuss their views about the stories they are reading. Skill instruction takes place in whole-class focus lessons, small-group strategy lessons, and in teacher–student conferences.

While there are several variations in the reading workshop, the workshop typically has four main components:

- Focus lesson—This is a brief ten- to fifteen-minute lesson delivered to the whole class. The focus is on teaching skills that will help students become independent readers, including decoding skills and comprehension strategies. Lucy Calkins (2001) recommends that these lessons contain the following elements:

  - a *connection* that helps students realize how the lesson topic fits with earlier lessons and ongoing classroom activities;
  - a *teaching phase* in which students are taught a skill or strategy that can be used during independent reading. Modeling, in which the teacher actually shows children how to use the skill or strategy, is extremely important in this phase of the lesson.
  - an *active involvement phase* in which children have an opportunity to use the skill or strategy.

  Many teachers also include a brief follow-up period at the end of the workshop to ask children to discuss how they used the skill or strategy during the reading period.

- Reading Time—This is the longest (thirty to forty minutes) and most important part of the workshop. Students spend a big portion of this time engaged in self-selected reading, either by themselves or with a partner. Partner reading is especially important with first and second graders, who often lack the stamina to read on their own for long periods of time.

  During this time, the teacher engages in instruction during individual and small-group conferences with students. The teacher also occasionally teaches strategy lessons to small groups of children with similar instructional needs. These strategy lessons are actually a small-group variation of the whole-class mini-lesson that target skills and strategies that just a few students need. Literature study groups also meet during this part of the workshop, sometimes with guidance from the teacher and sometimes on their own.

- Response Time—After Reading Time, there is a brief period during which students write responses to the books they have been reading in logs or journals. The reading logs provide children with meaningful writing practice and keep the teacher informed about the books that students are reading during Reading Time. In addition, the journal entries can contain valuable assessment information about each student's reading progress.

- Sharing—At the end of workshop, the whole class gets back together, and students have an opportunity to discuss the books that they are reading. This sharing provides valuable oral language experience and helps students form a community that values and celebrates each member's reading accomplishments (Tompkins, 2001). In addition, when a student talks about the book that he or she has enjoyed reading, this creates a powerful "advertisement" for the book and will encourage classmates to read it.

Frank Serafini's (2001a) excellent book, *The Reading Workshop: Creating Space for Readers,* contains concrete examples of the workshop in action and valuable tips on how to implement this approach to teaching reading. In the following excerpt, Frank describes a typical day in his classroom (Serafini, 2001a, pp. 2–4):

I always begin the reading workshop with a read-aloud I have chosen specifically to go along with a study we are involved with. On this particular day, I have chosen *The Night of the Gargoyles,* written by Eve Bunting and illustrated by David Weisner. This book is part of a "focus unit," where we have been studying the various types of illustrations found in picture books and their relationship to the written text . . .

As I finish reading the book, students immediately begin to share their ideas about the story and the illustrations in particular. I turn to a large chart behind my rocking chair and begin to write down some of the ideas that are being discussed. . . .

As our discussion winds down, I check my workshop schedule to see who I am meeting with today. Every day, I schedule a short reading conference with five different students before I begin meeting with any strategy or literature study groups. . . . On this day . . . I am scheduled to meet with the *Whipping Boy* literature study group. They have just finished reading the book and today is the first day for their discussion. This should be exciting.

I say, "Okay, let's get started!" and the class disperses. A group of six children heads over to the listening center, where they are enjoying a collection of poems read aloud by various teachers in our school. . . . Another group heads over to the art supply center. They have just completed a literature study on the book *Abel's Island* by William Steig, and are creating an illustrated map of what they think the island Abel was stranded on might look like. . . . Still another nine or so children are headed for various spots in the room, books in hand, for independent or paired reading. . . .

I sit in with the literature study group reading *Whipping Boy,* written by Sid Fleischmann, for about twenty minutes. . . . After meeting with the lit group, I am scheduled to work with another group of children in what I call a "strategy group." I gather together five or six students from around the room for a short meeting. After close observation of my students, I have decided that these students need some help using context clues in their reading. It seems that they overrely on the "sound-it-out" strategy as a primary strategy during their reading. I have decided to use a "cloze" procedure, where I take a text and intentionally cover some specific words to see what strategies they will use to predict the covered words. . . .

I walk over to the tape player and put on some soft jazz music. This is the signal for students to take a few minutes and write down the names of the books they have been reading in their reading logs. . . . Within a few minutes, children begin to gather on the rug for our "sharing circle." At the end of every reading workshop, we gather together to share our ideas or concerns about our reading or the workshop itself.

You will note many aspects of our elements of "best practice" in Frank's workshop session: teacher read-alouds, direct instruction on a decoding/comprehension strategy (using context clues), lots of free-choice reading, opportunities to discuss the books that are being read, reading response activities, integrated reading and writing with the reading logs, flexible grouping, and a minimum of seatwork. Had space permitted the day to be described in more detail, the rest of the best practice elements would have shown up in Frank's workshop. This is the reason that we recommend the reading workshop so highly: it encompasses research-based principles of effective reading instruction better than any other approach to teaching reading.

In Chapter 8, we provide detailed examples of how the reading workshop can be used to teach skills and promote reading comprehension at the early primary and intermediate grade levels. In subsequent chapters, we describe two other instructional strategies that are typically used in conjunction with the reading workshop: the writing workshop (Chapters 9 and 10) and integrated, cross-disciplinary units (Chapter 11). When all three elements are combined—the reading workshop, the writing workshop, and integrated units—the result is an optimal elementary-grade language arts program.

Summary

Reading instruction has been marked by controversy and pendulumlike swings in approaches and methodology. Fortunately, in recent years, there has been a movement away from the "reading wars" toward the concept of balanced reading instruction that places emphasis both on skill instruction and opportunities for students to engage in meaningful reading activities. Children need opportunities to learn about reading by doing lots of it. In the process of extensive reading, children will learn and practice many important reading skills. At the same time, children rarely learn all the skills they need to be a proficient reader from just doing extensive reading. They also need to be taught certain skills. A balanced approach to reading instruction, such as the reading workshop, provides both types of experiences.

■ *What are the key differences between the subskill and constructivist views of the reading process? How does the inside-out/outside-in theory bridge the gap between these two opposing views of the reading process?*

A subskill view of the reading process places heavy emphasis on decoding the aspects of reading, such as letter–sound relationships, that enable readers to translate printed text into oral language. Constructivist views, on the other hand, emphasize the factors that help the reader construct meaning from text. Interactive theories, such as that proposed by Whitehurst and Lonigan (2001) maintain that both types of elements–inside-out factors that help readers decode text and outside-in factors that help them understand text— must work together to ensure successful reading.

■ *Why are research syntheses so important in the field of reading?*

Literally thousands of research studies have been conducted on the topic of reading, often with conflicting or contradictory results. Well-done, comprehensive research syntheses enable us to draw reliable conclusions across these numerous studies, pointing the way to effective practice in reading instruction.

■ *What are the key principles of "best practice" in teaching reading?*

Based on three major syntheses of reading research, we have identified the following fifteen best practice principles for reading instruction:

1. read aloud to children on a daily basis;
2. create a literate classroom environment;
3. provide direct instruction on phonemic awareness, phonics, and word recognition;
4. provide opportunities for ample independent reading of self-selected books;
5. use guided reading to develop word recognition, fluency, and comprehension;
6. activate and build prior knowledge connected with texts;
7. teach vocabulary, both directly and indirectly;
8. provide opportunities for children to discuss the books they are reading;
9. provide a variety of reading response activities;
10. directly teach comprehension strategies;
11. keep seatwork to a minimum;
12. use a range of oral reading strategies;
13. integrate reading and writing activities;
14. use flexible grouping; and
15. use authentic assessments to inform instruction.

■ *What are the main components of a reading workshop?*

We believe that the reading workshop has an ideal balance between connected reading and skill instruction. There are four main components to the workshop: focus lesson, reading time, response time, and sharing.

LINKING THEORY TO PRACTICE

1. Interview several elementary-grade teachers and ask them about their views of the reading process. Then decide how you would classify each teacher's view: subskill theory (emphasis on inside-out factors), constructivist (emphasis on outside-in factors), or interactive (emphasis on both types of factors).

2. Observe an elementary-grade teacher teaching reading. Using Table 7.1 as a guide, record how many elements of "best practice" you observe. Note if you observe any impediments to best practice, e.g., there are few books in the classroom library, resulting in limited opportunities for free-choice reading.

Embedded within Reading Workshop: Teaching Meaning and Skills

When he was in seventh grade, Jim Christie recalls spending two hours every day engaged in round robin oral reading of literary classics. He can still recall the "butterflies" that he got in his stomach as his turn to read approached. Every Friday, a lengthy multiple-choice test was given over the portion of the book that was read that week. He came to think of reading as unpleasant work, and it took years before he began reading books for pleasure again. Fortunately, fewer and fewer teachers are using this approach to literature!

Most adults remember literary experiences like Jim's. The teacher-assigned stories was followed by the teacher asking, actually reading, a set of very specific questions that typically had only one "right" answer. These "When did....?" "Who did....?" questions were designed to test the reader's comprehension of the story. Occasionally the teacher varied this routine by requiring students to complete a fill-in-the-blanks test or to write a book report. Unfortunately, this approach to reading may have taught a number of lessons unintended by the teacher, as Nancy Atwell (1987, p. 152) describes:

- Reading is difficult, serious business.
- Literature is even more difficult and serious.
- There is one interpretation of a text, the teacher's.

Instead of a single "correct" interpretation of a piece of literature, constructivist theory operates on the premise that individuals bring to the act of reading their unique prior experiences and beliefs that influence how they interpret the author's words. Likewise, a reader's interpretation may change and be influenced by ongoing life experiences (Rosenblatt, 1991). For instance, Billie remembers reading Laura Ingalls Wilder's *On the Banks of Plum Creek* (1937) when she was nine years old. In Chapter 8, Laura described Pa's reactions after she and Mary disobeyed Pa's instructions and continued to tumble down the tall straw stack that Pa had carefully raked:

PA: Did you slide down the straw-stack?

LAURA: No, Pa.

PA: Laura!

LAURA: We did not slide, Pa. But we did roll down it.

Pa got up quickly and went to the door and stood looking out. His back quivered. Laura and Mary did not know what to think (p. 60).

At nine, Billie believed Pa to be so upset with Mary and Laura that he was physically shaking with anger. However, some twenty years later, when she was rereading this story to her class, her life experiences as a parent and teacher caused her to reevaluate her original view of Pa's reaction. Billie now believes that Pa was laughing at his children's silly antics! This example illustrates the constructivist perspective of reading as being both transactive and interactive; in other words, understanding is a combination of what the reader brings to the text and what the reader takes from the text (Eeds & Wells, 1991). Thus, the act of reading is social in nature; minimally, it consists of a conversation between one reader and an author. Optimally, reading may be enhanced when several readers discuss their personal interpretations and construct shared understandings (Peterson & Eeds, 1990; Rascon-Briones & Searfoss, 1995).

Fortunately, today many teachers are engaging in the Reading Workshop as a way to help their students interact with high quality literature. Reading Workshop offers students an opportunity to:

- read independently and study texts of their own choosing;
- read independently and discuss communally;
- work in temporary small groups to learn specific skills;
- lead and participate in discussions in which each member of the group, including the teacher, has equal status;
- work in cooperative groups, governed by rules of respect. Everyone's ideas or interpretations are respected and valued;
- practice working in self-governing groups that establish their own reading assignments, set meeting times, monitor individual and group progress, and develop reading responses;
- talk, share ideas, build new understandings with peers, and consider and value others' divergent perspectives.

In this chapter, we will describe how students can learn to construct a personal understanding of text and how specific decoding and comprehension skills can be taught within a constructivist framework. We begin with the story of how Martha Linn teaches reading in her first-grade classroom. Next, we provide a description of how Anne Foley implements Reading Workshop in her fourth-grade classroom. Finally, we continue the case studies of Tiffany and Alicia, which we began in Chapter 4. We follow Tiffany's literacy development from first through sixth grades. These case studies highlight a number of instructional techniques we describe in Chapter 7 and in this chapter. Sarah Hudelson and Irene Serna describe Alicia's development as a bilingual/biliterate learner during first and second grade. They also offer a number of suggestions regarding how teachers can best assist bilingual/second-language children to learn to read and write in English.

Before You Read This Chapter, Think About . . .

- the type of reading instruction you experienced when you were in grade school. Were you in a reading group? Did you participate in "round robin" reading, where one child reads, and then another, and then another, until finally it was your turn?

- a favorite story that you read with your teacher and peers. Did you have a favorite book of poetry that you read over and over?
- how your teacher assessed your comprehension of the stories and books you read. Did you complete workbook pages? Were there weekly tests? Did you write book reports? Did you share your views with peers?

Focus Questions

- What organizational strategies do teachers use to implement Reading Workshop?
- What types of grouping strategies are used in Reading Workshop?
- How do teachers provide skill instruction in Reading Workshop?
- How do teachers help students construct meaning and expand their understanding of text?

Lessons from an Experienced First-Grade Teacher

Martha Linn views the construction of print's meaning as central to her teaching of reading. She knows that she needs to help her first-grade students bring meaning to the text in order for them to create meaning from it. She recognizes that the meaning that students create is not necessarily the meaning that the author intended; therefore, her goal is *not* to get her students to discover that one right meaning. Instead, she looks for ways to help her students bring their unique background experiences to create their individual meanings of the text. She provides numerous opportunities for her students to respond to text over the course of each day: pieces she reads to them, texts they read together, and literature they read alone.

BOX **8.1**

Definition of Terms

Literature Genres: A category of literature that has a distinctive style, form, and content. For instance, realistic fiction is unique from historical fiction. Science fiction is different from fantasy.

Literature Study Groups: Students read the same text or pieces by the same author or books in the same genre and meet to discuss the aspects of the texts they find interesting.

Read-Alouds: The teacher selects and reads a story to the whole group; the children listen and respond.

Running Record: While a student reads a story out loud, the teacher codes the student's oral reading behavior. When finished, the teacher asks the student to retell the story. This technique is used to assess students' independent, instructional, and frustration reading levels and to gain insight into the student's reading strategies.

Ms. Linn's curricular decisions are based on several factors, including:

- her students' needs and interests
- the district's curriculum guide, which reflects the state department of education's language arts objectives
- her own interests as a learner and teacher and
- her awareness of research, theory, and excellent practices in the teaching of reading

To illustrate how Ms. Linn's beliefs about reading instruction are actualized in her first-grade classroom, with her 27 students from mostly low socioeconomic-status families and many races and cultures, readers will be brought into her classroom for a portion of one day. This observation was made approximately six weeks into the school year. Some of her organizational routines are briefly described, in addition to her literacy instruction. Both the authors and Ms. Linn believe that clearly defined management routines provide a foundation for instruction and facilitate a positive learning community. Ms. Linn spent considerable time establishing the classroom's management routines at the beginning of the school year.

The Children Arrive (Until 8:35 A.M.)

As the children enter the room, they signal their presence and their lunch choices by placing a distinctively colored and labeled popsicle stick in their name pockets located on the attendance chart. If a lunch stick is not placed in a name pocket, it signals that the child is absent. The attendance helper counts the colored sticks and completes the lunch form while Ms. Linn completes the attendance slip.

As the children complete the lunch and attendance routine, they remove their coats (when worn), select both a book from the library corner and a stuffed animal (if they wish), move to the carpeted area, and read until all the children have arrived. At 8:35, the books are returned to the library corner, and the first group session begins.

Connecting Home and School (8:35–8:45)

The children's homework assignment was to bring in the printed wrappers of things they like to eat and of products used in their home. Today, the children have brought in empty boxes of Trix, Cheerios, and Tide. In addition, Snickers and Reese's candy wrappers were brought to school.

Ms. Linn begins by asking the children who brought items to read the names of their products for the other students. After the children read their environmental print, Ms. Linn selects one of the products, *Tide.* She asks, "Which alphabet letter card should *Tide,* t-t-t-, be attached to?" On the wall behind her, in alphabetical order, are large posterboard alphabet cards, one for each letter of the alphabet. Ms. Linn has modified the traditional alphabet chart by inserting several cards of consonant blends (e.g., *bl, tr, st*) and digraphs (e.g., *sh, ch, th*). (These nontraditional cards are a different color than the regular alphabet cards.) The group agrees that *Tide* should be attached to the *T t* card. A child takes the box to the

"Make It Here!" area, cuts the word from the box, and glues it to the *T t* card. While the child works on this task, the group considers the remaining wrappers.

"*Cheerios.* What card should *Cheerios* be attached to? Does *Cheerios* begin like *Couscous*? No?" Cheerios gets assigned to the *ch* card, along with *Cheer.* Later, Trix is assigned to a new card, the *tr* card. Snickers is assigned to the *sn* card and *Reese's* is assigned to the *R r* card.

Ms. Linn is aware of the research that suggests that letter symbol and sound knowledge are the best predictors of reading achievement (Adams, 1989). Hence, she wants to ensure that her students have experiences with these important predictors. Experiences with the letters, the letter names, and the names of the products that begin with each letter's sound provide opportunities daily to acquire and practice this important knowledge.

Class Calendar and Daily Schedule of Events (8:45–9:00)

Next, the teacher moves to the calendar. The children choral read the days of the week, the months of the year, and several calendar-related sentences, which have been written on large chart paper, "Today is Tuesday, October 11. There are 13 boys and 14 girls present today." Next, they consider the following sentences and decide together how to complete the sentences: "There are _____ children here today. Tomorrow will be _____. Yesterday was _____." Finally, Ms. Linn presents a schedule of the day's activities. She reviews the schedule with the children, helping them read the times and activities. The children notice that they have music class with Ms. Marks at 10:00.

Daily Read-Aloud Experiences (9:00–9:20)

Every day, Ms. Linn reads a literature selection to the class. To further the seasonal theme and to build on the children's interests, Ms. Linn has decided to use a number of Halloween poems for the daily read-aloud activity this month. For today's read-aloud activity, she has enlarged the poem "Five Little Pumpkins" on the poster machine. Ms. Linn begins by reviewing the title and discussing the illustrations with the children. During the first reading, she models directionality (top-to-bottom and left-to-right) by pointing to each of the words as she reads the entire poem (see Figure 8.1 "Five Little Pumpkins").

During the second reading of the poem, Ms. Linn uses an *echo reading strategy:* As she reads each line, she again points to the words; however, at the end of each line, she pauses and lets the children read—repeating the same line while the teacher points to the words. On the third reading, Ms. Linn uses a shared-book method—she and the children read the poem together. After three readings, Ms. Linn begins to ask questions about the poem.

MS. LINN: What is this rhyme about? Naomi?

NAOMI: It's about a bunch of silly pumpkins.

KATINA: And they're afraid of witches.

TERREL: I think it's about five talking pumpkins that roll away 'cause they're scared.

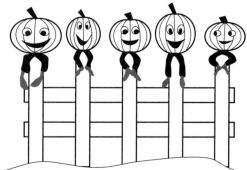

Five little pumpkins
Sitting on a gate
The first one said
"Oh, my! It's getting late."
The second one said
"There're witches in the air!"
The third one said
"But we don't care."

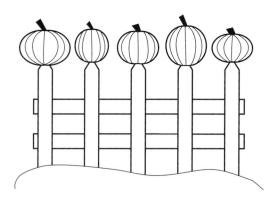

The fourth one said
"It's Halloween fun."
The fifth one said
"Let's run and run and run!"
Then whoosh went the wind
And out went the lights!
And the five little pumpkins
rolled out of sight.

FIGURE 8.1   "Five Little Pumpkins"

MS. LINN: Can pumpkins really talk? Tim?

TIM: No, but it's pretend and it's funny, 'specially when the wind goes "whoosh."

MS. LINN: This poem is make-believe and pretend and just for fun. [Pointing to the exclamation mark.] What do you think this punctuation sign means? Sasha?

SASHA: It tells you to read really loud.

MS. LINN: Does anyone know what it is called? No? It's called an **"exclamation mark."** You do read that line loudly or with lots of excitement. Let's all try reading loudly when we get to the line "Then whoosh went the wind and out went the lights!"

As the children read the poem for the fourth time, they practice using the proper expression for the exclamation mark. During the fifth reading, Ms. Linn asks if several children would like to do choral reading, reading of the poem together as she points to the words. Four children quickly volunteer. As this group reads aloud, Ms. Linn asks the other children to "whisper read" along with them. Next, she gives each child a copy of the poem, with illustrations. For the sixth reading, she asks the children to read the poem to each other, in pairs. Ms. Linn reminds the partners to make sure that each person reads with good expression and to be sure to point to the words as they read them. After partner reading, the children may color the illustration, if they wish, sometime during the day. Tonight, each child will read the poem to his or her family. This page will be added to each child's personal poem book, a collection of poems read over the year.

It is important to notice that in a 20-minute time span, Ms. Linn and the children have read the poem aloud at least six times. Each reading was slightly different, yet it called for all children to be actively involved in the oral reading process. These methods are a vast improvement over the round-robin reading technique in which one child reads in front of a whole group while all other children listen and passively wait their turn. For more information about different types of modeled reading strategies, see Figure 8.2.

Drop Everything and Read (9:20–9:50)

As discussed in Chapter 6, in a high-quality reading program, all children need to have daily opportunities for independent reading of self-selected books. The primary grades at this school use drop everything and read (DEAR), a variation of sustained silent reading (SSR; see Special Feature 7.1). Ms. Linn randomly assigned the children to four groups (circles, squares, triangles, and rectangles) for management purposes. She also provided each child with a reading folder, which contains several pages that have been divided into three columns: "Title," "Author," and "Rating." Before providing directions for movement, Ms. Linn reminds the children to rate the book(s) they have read and refers to the rating chart posted on the wall (see Figure 8.3).

Ms. Linn sends the "circle" group collect their reading journals and their storybooks. While the "square" group collects their storybooks and their journals, the children are free to choose any books they wish to read. While the first two groups are getting started, Ms. Linn asks the other children to think about the types of books they want to read today. Two or three minutes later, when the "circles" and "squares" have settled into their tasks, the teacher calls the "triangles" and "rectangles" groups to gather their storybooks and journals. For management purposes, Ms. Linn is careful not to send too many students in the same direction at one time.

In addition to choosing their own books, children are free to read in a manner with which they feel comfortable. Many children choose to read quietly to each other in pairs. Others are tucked away in corners, reading alone. Ms. Linn knows that her children are reading differently from one another in another way, as well. Some of the children are looking at the illustrations and are discussing the details. Others are using the illustrations to provide clues to their stories' content, to help them create their own stories to accompany the illustrations. Still others have selected books that are familiar to them, so they are using the pictures to prompt a fairly accurate reading or retelling of their stories. Another group of children is focusing on the print and is using both print and illustrations to read their stories.

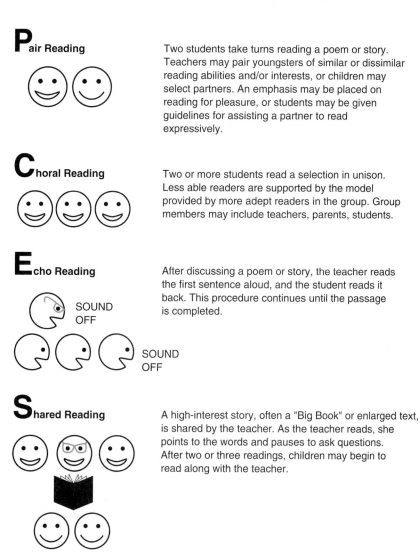

Pair Reading

Two students take turns reading a poem or story. Teachers may pair youngsters of similar or dissimilar reading abilities and/or interests, or children may select partners. An emphasis may be placed on reading for pleasure, or students may be given guidelines for assisting a partner to read expressively.

Choral Reading

Two or more students read a selection in unison. Less able readers are supported by the model provided by more adept readers in the group. Group members may include teachers, parents, students.

Echo Reading

SOUND OFF

SOUND OFF

After discussing a poem or story, the teacher reads the first sentence aloud, and the student reads it back. This procedure continues until the passage is completed.

Shared Reading

A high-interest story, often a "Big Book" or enlarged text, is shared by the teacher. As the teacher reads, she points to the words and pauses to ask questions. After two or three readings, children may begin to read along with the teacher.

FIGURE 8.2   Modeled reading strategies.

Regardless of what each child is doing, Ms. Linn believes that every child is a reader. The children read, rate, and record information about the two or three books they read during the 30-minute DEAR time. During DEAR, Ms. Linn observes the children and takes anecdotal notes about the children's interactions with print. She also circulates about the room, chatting with the children about their books and noting their responses. In addition, Ms. Linn completes a running record for one or two children during DEAR each day. Special Feature 8.1 presents a brief overview of how and why running records are conducted. It is Ms. Linn's goal to complete one running record per child each week. The information

= I liked the book a whole lot.

= I liked the book.

= I did not like the book.

FIGURE 8.3   Rate a book chart.

collected about each child's reading performance guides Ms. Linn's reading instruction for each child.

During the last five minutes of the 30-minute DEAR session, Ms. Linn asks three or four children to share one of the books they read and to explain why they rated the books as they did. As the children share their views about the books they have read, she makes notes about how these children orally described their books and how they expressed their opinions. After the rate-a-book reports, Ms. Linn dismisses the "triangles," then the "rectangles," then the "circles," and finally the "squares." Ms. Linn reminds her students to be sure to return their books to the correct book tub or shelf. Most of the books are sorted by author, content focus (e.g., science or social studies), season (e.g., Halloween), or genre (poetry, fairy tales, alphabet books). Each book in this classroom has been labeled with an identifying sticker; for example, all Halloween books and the book tub that holds them have identical witch stickers on them. This system helps the children correctly store the hundreds of literature books in the classroom library. (See Chapters 5 and 13 for more details on starting and managing a classroom library.)

Special Classes (10:00–10:30)

Special classes include music (Monday), library (Tuesday), art (Wednesday), physical education (Thursday), computers (Friday). In Ms. Linn's school, two of the special-subjects teachers (music and art) work with the primary teachers to support the children's literacy learning. Ms. Marks, the music teacher, uses stories set to music to teach singing, reading, and movement. When the children go to music instruction this day, they will learn to sing and read *The Thirteen Days of Halloween,* written by Carol Green and illustrated by Tom Dunnington (1983).

Ms. Marks begins by asking the children a number of questions designed to stimulate their interest. She asks, "Have you ever heard the song 'Twelve Days of Christmas'?" She plays a small part of the song. The children identify the main theme of the song as giving interesting presents for Christmas. Then Ms. Marks shows them the book *The Thirteen Days of Halloween,* a Halloween version of the "Twelve Days of Christmas." She asks, "What do you think a witch would give for presents?" The children excitedly

Special Feature 8.1

Running Records

The running record is a means of systematically observing and recording children's reading behavior (Clay, 1985). This procedure is very popular with classroom teachers because of its ease of use and the valuable information it provides. In a one- to-one setting, the student reads a brief passage from a book while the teacher uses a special symbol system to make a written record of what occurs: ticks (check marks) are used to record each correct response and other symbols are used to note the errors and other behaviors that occur (see Figure 7.6). No special transcript of the passage is needed. The marks are made on a blank piece of paper. After the reading is finished, comprehension can be checked by asking the student to retell the story in her or his own words.

After a running record has been taken, the written record can be analyzed to determine the accuracy of the student's reading. This is done by subtracting the number of countable errors (words supplied by the teacher and non-self-corrected substitutions, omissions, and insertions) from the number of words in the passage, then dividing this number by the number of words (see Figure 8.4). The resulting percentage indicates the

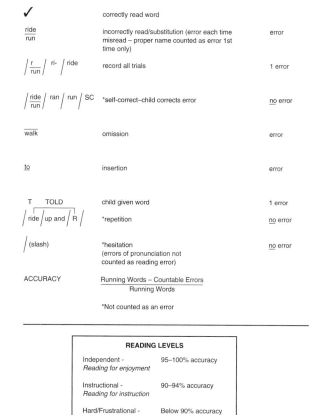

✓	correctly read word	
ride / run	incorrectly read/substitution (error each time misread – proper name counted as error 1st time only)	error
/ r / run / ri- / ride /	record all trials	1 error
/ ride / run / ran / run / SC	*self-correct–child corrects error	no error
walk	omission	error
to	insertion	error
T TOLD	child given word	1 error
/ ride / up and / R /	*repetition	no error
/ (slash)	*hesitation (errors of pronunciation not counted as reading error)	no error
ACCURACY	Running Words – Countable Errors / Running Words	

*Not counted as an error

READING LEVELS	
Independent - *Reading for enjoyment*	95–100% accuracy
Instructional - *Reading for instruction*	90–94% accuracy
Hard/Frustrational -	Below 90% accuracy

FIGURE 8.4   Conventions for recording a running record.

(continued on next page)

Special Feature 8.1 *(continued)*

proportion of words that the student recognizes accurately and is an indication of the relative difficulty of the passage for that particular student:

95–100% accuracy—*independent-level* material, suitable for pleasure reading

90–95% accuracy—*instructional-level* material, suitable for instruction

below 90% accuracy—*frustration-level* material, too difficult

This calculation gives the teacher an idea of the difficulty level of material that the student is capable of reading for different purposes. In the example running record in Figure 8.5, the student's accuracy is 90 percent, indicating that the passage is on the boundary between the frustration and the instructional level for this particular student. The only time that students should read material that is this difficult is when passage information is of particularly high interest or utility (e.g., needed for a class project).

Additional information about students' reading strategies can be obtained by using miscue analysis to analyze the errors contained on a running record (Goodman & Goodman, 1994). This involves examining errors in terms of cue systems and self-monitoring behavior. Errors are compared with their text counterparts and the surrounding context to determine whether students are attending to

- *graphophonic cues*—substituted words look like the text words;
- *syntactic cues*—substituted words are the same part of speech, and other errors maintain grammatical acceptability; and
- *semantic cues*—errors make sense in the context in which they occur.

In the example in Figure 8.5, most of the reader's substitutions look like the text words, but many do not make sense in terms of the preceding or subsequent context. Note that several are also different parts of speech than their text counterparts. This analysis indicates that the reader is relying heavily on graphophonic cues (letter–sound relationships) but is not paying adequate attention to context cues. Only one of the serious, meaning-disrupting errors was self-corrected, hinting that the reader may not be self-monitoring her reading to make sure that what is read makes sense. Detailed instructions for conducting and interpreting miscue analysis can be found in the manual by Yetta Goodman, Dorothy Watson, and Carolyn Burke (1987). Students' comprehension can be analyzed using a story-retelling checklist, such as the one illustrated in Figure 6.5.

TEXT

Jimmy was a little boy. He was walking home from school when he saw an old house on the corner. Jimmy and his dog Spot walked up to the old house. Jimmy knocked on the door, but no one answered. Jimmy was brave. He went inside.

Jimmy looked around the house, and he saw a door to his right. He opened the door and went inside. The room was very dark. Jimmy tried to find a light and he fell down. He sat on the floor and began to cry. Spot heard Jimmy crying and ran into the room, Spot found Jimmy and led him out of the dark room.

RUNNING RECORD

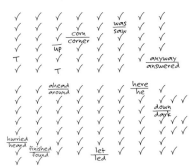

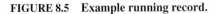

$$\text{ACCURACY} = \frac{110 \text{ (running words)} - 11 \text{ (countable errors)}}{110 \text{ (running words)}} = 90 \text{ percent}$$

FIGURE 8.5   Example running record.

offer a number of suggestions: goblins, ghosts, bats, frogs, brooms, skeletons, warts. Ms. Marks writes the suggestions.

To help children see the words and illustrations, Ms. Marks has made color transparencies of the book. As she reads the book the first time, she calls the students' attention to details in the illustrations and the descriptive language the author uses: cauldrons bubbling, fat toads, giggling ghosts, hissing cats. After hearing the whole story, the children confirm their predictions and try to guess what the last surprise present might be. As Ms. Marks begins to sing the song, the children immediately join in. This particular song is very easy to learn because it uses a cumulative pattern—the story repeats all past refrains each time a new refrain is added. During the third reading, Ms. Marks uses a pointer and underscores the words as she and the children sing the story. Because there are so many refrains to this story/song, they are only able to practice the song one more time before the music class ends. However, when the children return to Ms. Linn's class, she greets the children with the same book and an enlarged song chart. During the remainder of the week the children will practice singing and reading the song.

Later in the week, when the children go to art class, Mr. Curtis directs the children's attention to the illustrations in this same story. He and the children consider how the illustrator helps the author's words come alive. For example, how did the artist make spiders creep or goblins gobble? This activity links print and picture and provides yet another opportunity for children to use their reading skills. Next, the children are asked to draw illustrations of their favorite parts of the story and to write those parts of the story under their illustrations. Mr. Curtis circulates about the room, helping the children with their drawings and writings. At the end of art class, several students share their illustrations and read the story lines they selected.

Later in the month, Ms. Linn, the children, the art teacher, and the music teacher will work together to dramatize the students' favorite Halloween poems, stories, and songs. The children will perform these works as part of their Halloween party. These efforts provide dynamic opportunities for the children to celebrate literacy using a variety of reading-response activities.

Literature Studies (10:30–11:00)

After each day's special class, Ms. Linn conducts a whole-group literature study. This day, she has selected a popular story, *The Teeny-Tiny Woman* by Paul Galdone, a well-known author. Ms. Linn begins the study by introducing the title and the author and by focusing the students' attention on the cover illustration. "What do you think this book could be about?" She uses open-ended questions to activate the children's prior knowledge, and this, in turn, encourages them to make predictions about the story. For example,

MS. LINN: How does the teeny-tiny woman look?

SARAH: Scared, afraid, upset.

MS. LINN: I think she looks afraid too. I wonder what could be frightening her?

TONJA: Maybe she had a nightmare. Maybe she hears a robber.

MS. LINN: [Ms. Linn records the children's responses.] Look at the back cover. What do you see? [A voice is coming from the cupboard and it says, "Give me back my bone!"]

> **RAVEL:**   The cupboard has a face. Is the cupboard alive? Maybe a ghost or monster is scaring her. [Ms. Linn records the children's predictions.]
>
> **MS. LINN:**   Let's read and find out what will happen to the teeny-tiny woman and why the voice is saying, "Give me back my bone!"

Ms. Linn uses the big-book version of the *Teeny-Tiny Woman*. During the first reading, the children listen. As Ms. Linn reads (using a pointer to underline the words as she reads), she models great expression. After she reads the story the first time, she returns to the children's predictions. The children are delighted that their predictions are correct. The literature guide accompanying the series provides several suggestions to teachers regarding Paul Galdone's unique style. Using these suggestions, Ms. Linn directs the children's attention to the first illustration that shows a dialogue bubble and explains how this author uses dialogue bubbles to help tell the story.

> **MS. LINN:**   Why do you think Paul Galdone, this book's author, made the print bigger each time the ghost said, "Give me back my bone!"
>
> **STEVEN:**   The ghost is getting madder and madder.
>
> **MARIE:**   'Cuz he wants his bone back.
>
> **MS. LINN:**   Why?
>
> **JOSH:**   By this time [Josh turns pages to the last "Give me back my bone"], he's probably really mad and shouting like [Josh shouts] "Give me back my bone!"
>
> **MS. LINN:**   So the size of the print can help tell you how to read the story?
>
> **MICHELLE:**   Ah, huh [with head nods].
>
> **MS. LINN:**   What else does the author use to help you know how to read the story?
>
> **MICHELLE:**   These things [points to exclamation mark]. Expamation points.
>
> **ALL CHILDREN:**   Exclamation marks!
>
> **MS. LINN:**   Let's read this story again! This time, I'll point to the dialogue bubbles [points to one], and you read what the ghost says. Watch the size of the print. The size of the print will tell you how softly or how loudly you should read the words. [The children read beautifully, so Ms. Linn compliments them.]
>
> **MS. LINN:**   What good readers you are! You knew to read louder and louder as the print got bigger and bigger.

Now Ms. Linn turns to a story chart. The class has read and studied two other books that contain ghosts as featured characters. They now begin to compare this story to the other stories on a number of aspects, including title and author, characters, setting, time, use of magic, events in the story, and ending. Ms. Linn asks the children questions about each category on the chart. This chart provides an efficient way to summarize a story and a convenient way to compare stories (see Figure 8.6).

On Tuesday, Ms. Linn and the children reread the story, but this time as a dramatic choral reading. Some children elect to take on the part of the teeny-tiny woman, while other children elect to enact the part of the ghost. The ghosts sit to the left of Ms. Linn; the teeny-

Title and Author	Setting and Time	Characters	What Happens	Ending	Magic
Georgie's Halloween by Robert Bright	Halloween night a long time ago	Georgie Mr. & Mrs. Whittaker Miss Oliver Herman Mice	Georgie goes to a Halloween party but he is shy, gets scared and runs home	The mice give Georgie an award and Georgie blows the candle out in the Jack-O-Lantern	Yes - Georgie disappeared
The Ghost with the Halloween Hiccups by Steven Moosen Tomie De Paola	Halloween Town	Mr. Penny Bert Laura Town people	Mr. Penny has hiccups and he can't get rid of them. All the people in the town try to help him get rid of them.	The Halloween actors are all dressed up and scare the hiccups away.	No

FIGURE 8.6   **Story comparison chart.**

tiny woman characters sit to the right of her. Ms. Linn reads, stopping to let the characters read their words with much expression. The children watched the punctuation and the size of the print to guide their fluent and expressive reading.

Following the reading, Ms. Linn introduced the writing assignment. The children's task was to work together (the class was divided into three groups) to rewrite, extend, and illustrate their own versions of the *Teeny-Tiny Woman*. For the remainder of the week, during literature time, the children were to work to create their own versions of this story. The children had written versions of other stories and extended poems, songs, or chants, so they were eager to begin the task. Ms. Linn reviewed the procedures.

MS. LINN: How could you change this story? What if your group decides to create new characters? What other Halloween characters might be in your story?

CHILDREN: Pumpkins! Scarecrows! Cats! Batman! [and so forth]. [Mrs. Linn records each suggestion.]

MS. LINN: You decide. Which characters? What will your Halloween characters do? Lots of decisions to make! When your group has a draft of its story, call me over and I'll help you decide how to break it up into parts to illustrate it.

Off the groups went to different areas to begin talking, talking, and talking—and drafting.

As the groups worked, Ms. Linn circulated, offering help, as needed. She orally stretched out various words for one group of children, helping them hear the sounds (phonics instruction). She helped another group make decisions about which characters to use. When compromise was not possible, the group subdivided into two smaller groups. She helped a group consider appropriate actions for their chosen characters. One group rewrote the story, featuring a skeleton and a scarecrow. Their story began,

> Once upon a long time ago.
> A skeleton was taking a walk.
> The wind was cold and the skeleton's teeth started to chatter.
> Just then he saw some clothes on a scarecrow.
> Because he was so cold, he walked right up and took a coat right off that scarecrow.

Another group decided to extend the original story. They wrote about what they thought the teeny-tiny woman would do the next day when all of her furniture and utensils still talked to her. A third group rewrote the story's ending. In their version, Casper the Ghost saved the teeny-tiny woman and scared away the other bad ghost. All groups used dialogue bubbles, as well as text, to move the story forward; they used print size to help convey the emotional tenor of each sentence.

Over that day and the next, as groups finished their drafting, Ms. Linn heard them read their text and helped them decide on their stories' page breaks. Then, each child chose a page to illustrate, using large felt tip pens and a large piece of paper. When Ms. Larson, the classroom's foster-grandparent volunteer, came to help, she was to type the groups' texts. Later, these typed texts would be glued to the large illustrated pages.

As the children talked, wrote, and illustrated on Wednesday, Thursday, and Friday, Ms. Linn supported the children's efforts, but she also pulled individual children to read to her, one at a time. Typically, the children chose among the "Five Little Pumpkins," *The Thirteen Days of Halloween,* or *The Teeny-Tiny Woman.* All were stories, poems, or chants they had heard read to them. Ms. Linn watched how they read and how they tracked their reading with their finger. Depending on what each child did, Ms. Linn did something different. In other words, each child's needs drove the instruction. With some children, Ms. Linn focused on helping them understand the concept of a word.

MS. LINN: Derek, how many words are in this sentence? [runs finger under *once upon a time* . . .]

DEREK: Ten.

MS. LINN: See these blank spaces, these white spots? That's how writers tell us where one word ends and another begins. So, this is one word and this is another word. Then this would be a _____ [Derek fills in], and this would be a _____ [Derek fills in, and teacher continues]. I'm going to put each of these words on a card. [Ms. Linn has a pile of 1½″ × 2½″ paper prepared]. I'll put *Once* on this card, *upon* on this card, *a* on this card, and *time* on this card [and so on]. [When done, she gives the pile to Derek.] Let's make these words into the sentence. Put the first word here. [Derek puts *Once* where she points.] Put the second word here [and so forth]. Let's read this sentence together. You point to each

Children enjoy reading child-created stories.

word: Once upon a time . . . [they read, and Derek points.] I'll hand you each word and you count them for me. [She hands Derek the card with *Once* on it.]

DEREK: Once [and so forth].

MS. LINN: Would you like to keep these cards with these words to read to Mom tonight?

With other children, Ms. Linn focused on phonics. Always, the children read their chosen text first, so the pattern of the instructional time went from whole pieces to whole sentences to words within sentences to letters within words.

MS. LINN: Let's look at this word from this sentence: Five little pumpkins sitting on a gate. [In plastic letters, Ms. Linn makes the word *gate.*] Can you read this word? [The teacher returns to the sentence in the text, "Five little pumpkins sitting on a _____," helping the child use context to answer the question.]

KARMAN: Gate!

MS. LINN: Right! *Gate.* [Ms. Linn elongates the pronunciation focusing on each letter, *g-a-t.*] This *e* at the end doesn't make a sound, does it? [She covers the e with her hand.] It's not *g-a-t-e,* is it? It's a silent *e.* What would the word be if we put a *k* at the beginning instead of a *g*? Can you find the *k*? [Karman hunts among the plastic letters.]

KARMAN: A *K,* just like me!

MS. LINN: You're right! You know the letter *K*! Put it where the *g* was, at the beginning of the word. [Karman does.] Right. Now what is the word? If this was *g-a-t-e,* [makes *gate*], this must be _____.

KARMAN: Kate!

MS. LINN: Right! *Kate.* What letters stay the same?

KARMAN: [as teacher points] *a-t-e!*

> **MS. LINN:**   Let's see if we can make another word. [She puts in *h*.] *h-a-t-e*. H sounds like *h-h*, like in *house*.
>
> **KARMAN:**   [As teacher points] *H-a-t-e! Hate!*
>
> **MS. LINN:**   You can make three words from *a-t-e*, can't you? *Gate, Kate,* and *hate*. [Karman reads as the teacher changes the letters.] What a reader you are! [Karman is playing with the plastic letters.] I'll leave you to see if you can make any other words in this word family. Why don't you write the words you find here [gives her a piece of paper]. We'll read them together later. [Teacher moves on.]

Two of the children in this classroom read well. Ms. Linn's instruction is very different for them. They have each chosen a Beverly Cleary book to read. The pair joined Ms. Linn, who is also reading a Beverly Cleary book; although each of their books is by this same author, the actual selections are not the same. They talked about what had happened in their books since they last conferred together. Then they read a favorite part from their books. Ms. Linn listened for reading fluency and comprehension. She asked questions to see whether what was happening in their books ever happened to them. She shared an experience from her own youth and from an experience of her son that were just like an episode in her book. She pulled a couple of vocabulary words from each story and asked about their meaning. She pulled out a thesaurus and looked up one of the words to check for synonyms. Together these three readers carried on an authentic conversation about their books. The time with these readers ends with Ms. Linn saying, "When we conference next time, let's talk about Beverly Cleary's writing style. What are we noticing about what she does as a writer of children's stories?"

Ms. Linn does not always meet with only one child or two children. Sometimes, she pulls a group of children together who have similar instructional needs (see Special Feature 8.2). Several of these group meetings focus on instruction in the strategies for decoding print. As she did with Karman, she might focus on creating word families. Instead, she might segment words to help children hear the words' sounds and match the sounds to the symbols.

Remember, Ms. Linn uses her students' *needs* to drive her instructional decisions. Because she is presenting different information to different children, she needs to track the topics of her instruction and her children's progress.

Modeled Writing—Daily News (11:00–11:45)

Ms. Linn prompts the children to review the daily schedule posted on the board. She asks the students to quietly think about what they learned today, what they liked the most, and what they worked hardest to learn. After a few moments, she begins to call on the students to ask them to share their views.

> **KATE:**   I learned I could count by fives today.
>
> **MS. LINN:**   Kate learned to count by fives. Would you like me to write that sentence? Please, class, help me to write this sentence. What do we start with?
>
> **ALL:**   Capital *K-a-t-e*.
>
> **MS. LINN:**   Why do we start with a capital?

Special Feature 8.2

Explicit Reading Instruction in Primary Classrooms

Most children need some form of explicit instruction to help them begin the process of reading. After analyzing programs that embrace a Reading-Recovery approach (Clay, 1985), Spiegel (1995) summarized a number of guidelines for directly teaching reading skills and strategies. This special feature summarizes this research and provides an example of veteran teacher Karen Eeds conducting a small-group strategy lesson that employs these guidelines (Lubitz, 1995). Remember, once children become confident users of effective reading strategies, explicit instruction subsides.

- Children should be taught at their instructional level. Research clearly demonstrates that a child's reading development is enhanced when the child is placed in materials where the child recognizes 95 percent of the words in context (Johnston & Allington, 1991; Gambrell, Wilson, & Gantt, 1981).

- Instruction should focus on comprehension of connected text. Teaching isolated skills outside of the context of reading confuses children (Allington, 1983). When teacher and child preview the story together, it encourages the child to use all three cuing systems—context, syntax, and graphophonic—to gain meaning from text.

- Children should be taught to use and transfer strategies. Children need to be taught a variety of strategies, such as predicting, reading ahead, and looking at the pictures. Teachers may encourage the use of these strategies by using prompt questions. For example, "Does that make sense?" or "Check to see whether what you read looks and sounds right." Once strategies have been taught and reinforced through prompt questions, utilization of these strategies becomes automatic and metacognitive.

- Children are taught to use, but not depend on, letter sounds. Phonemic awareness is an outcome of literacy, not a prerequisite. Children need to learn how to effectively use their knowledge of letter sounds as one part, not the total sum, of their repertoire of strategies (Clay & Cazden, 1990).

- Teachers should monitor children's attempts to make meaning of text. Teachers' ongoing assessment of children should include both formal and informal observations throughout the day. "An alert teacher works alongside the child, observing and responding to the child's attempts to make meaning of text. The teacher seizes the teachable moments to take advantage of the child's discovery and to extend it. When a strategy has not led to success, the child is led to think about other strategies that might have been more effective" (Spiegel, 1995, p. 94).

- Explicit instruction is an essential part of learning to read for most children (Adams, 1990; Delpit, 1988). Direct instruction—such as explanation, modeling, and discussion—shows a child what a strategy is and how to use it. However, direct instruction does not imply that the teacher instructs a predetermined set of sequential skills. Instead, the teacher observes each child carefully and identifies the most appropriate manner and time to teach skills and strategies.

The following vignette provides an example of how Karen Eeds uses these guidelines to work with a small group of first-grade students.

Ms. Eeds:	This is a story called "Things Are For." I wonder what these things are for? On these pictures are all kinds of things that are for something. What do you see up there in the picture?
Matthew:	Books.

(continued on next page)

Special Feature 8.2 (continued)

Ms. Eeds:	What are books for?
David:	To read.
Ms. Eeds:	Yes. Let's look at the next page. What do you see?
Salazar:	Jump rope.
Ms. Eeds:	What are jump ropes for?
Lydia:	Jump.
Ms. Eeds:	What's next?
David:	Skates.
Ms. Eeds:	What are skates for?
Matthew:	Skating.
Ms. Eeds:	A ball is for _____.
Salazar:	Playing.
Ms. Eeds:	Crayons are for _____.
Lydia:	Coloring.
Ms. Eeds:	Let's look in this story. Put your finger on the title.
Ms. Eeds and students:	"Things Are For."
Ms. Eeds:	Now stop for just a second. When we look at the pictures, I want you to do most of the talking. Okay? What do you see here?
Salazar:	Skates.
Ms. Eeds:	What are they for?
Lydia:	For skating.
Ms. Eeds:	Can you say that? Skates are for skating.
Lydia:	Skates are for skating.
Ms. Eeds:	Tell me about the next picture.
Matthew:	Ball. Balls are for playing.
Ms. Eeds:	Keep going. Don't read. Just tell me about the pictures.
Lydia:	Jump rope.
Ms. Eeds:	For what?
Lydia:	For jumping.
Ms. Eeds:	Turn the page.
David:	Books. Books are for reading.
Ms. Eeds:	My goodness. Are we ready to read it?
Students:	Yes.
Ms. Eeds:	Sometimes in this story there might be a tricky word. You might need your cards to help you get your mouth ready for the beginning sound. Are you ready? You're going to see this word [holding up a flash card with the word "are" on it].
Ms. Eeds:	Where is that word?
Matthew:	Are. He points to the word.]
Ms. Eeds:	Good. Matthew just found it right in the title. Are. Let's do it. The teacher and the students read the title.]
Ms. Eeds and students:	Things are for.
Ms. Eeds and students:	Skates are for skating. Ms. Eeds reads the next sentence with the children but stops at the last word and waits to hear what the children say.]
Students:	Balls are for playing.
Ms. Eeds:	Hey. Wait a second.
David:	That's the letter "b" right there.
Ms. Eeds:	There is a "b." I heard you say balls are for playing. Look at that beginning letter right there [pointing to letter].
Ms. Eeds:	David, Lydia, we need to get our mouth ready for "b." Let's go back and think what else balls are good for besides playing.
Ms. Eeds and students:	Balls are for b_____.
Ms. Eeds:	Go back and get your mouth ready. Balls are for

Special Feature 8.2 (continued)

	b_____. [She motions like she is bouncing a ball with her hands.]	**Ms. Eeds:**	Jumping. See the i-n-g. The i-n-g at the end. Lets go on.
David:	Bouncing.	**Students:**	Guitars are for singing.
Ms. Eeds:	Do you think that could be? Check it. Use your finger. Balls are for bouncing. Does it look like bouncing?	**Ms. Eeds:**	Check that. Go back. What would singing start with?
		Students:	S.
Students:	Yes.	**Ms. Eeds:**	Is that right? Could that be singing? Check.
Ms. Eeds:	Yes, and look what Matthew did. He checked the picture. He could see the bouncing marks. [Ms. Eeds makes the bouncing motion again.]	**Mrs. Eeds:**	Oh, oh. I don't see an "s" there. Matthew just got his mouth ready for the "p." It says "pl." [Ms. Eeds makes he "pl" sound.] Go back and get your mouth ready for the "pl." See if a word pops in your head that guitars are good for. Guitars are for
David:	Those are basketballs.		
Ms. Eeds:	And they're bouncing.		
Ms. Eeds:	Keep going. Finger, David. Finger. Wait just a second for Lydia. [She helps Lydia find the place and points to the place in Lydia's book. While she is doing that, the children read but it is difficult to hear.]		pl_____.
		Salazar:	Playing.
		Ms. Eeds:	Is that right? Check it. Guitars are for playing. You can play a guitar. You guys are good. Matthew, you helped us get the beginning sound. Go on, Salazar.
Ms. Eeds:	Oh. Let me hear that again. I didn't get to hear that.		
Students:	Jump ropes are for jump.		
Ms. Eeds:	Jump or jumping?		
Students:	Jumping.		

CAYLA: 'Cause it's the start of the sentence.

CALEB: 'Cause it's a name. You always start a name with a capital.

MS. LINN: Both of you are correct. What's the first sound we hear in *learned*?

ALL: *L.*

MS. LINN: That's right [she spells the rest of the word]. How do I spell *to*?

Ms. Linn continues asking for the children's input throughout the writing of the sentence. She rotates between asking questions that focus the children's attention on phonetics and the mechanics of a sentence and reinforcing the correct responses. She believes that this group's writing activity and the thinking-out-loud process helps students learn more about writing. Usually, the class has an opportunity to write three to five sentences. Each week,

Ms. Linn asks the children to respond to more complex questions and to spell or sound out more of the words. The session ends with the class and her rereading of the whole daily review.

In Ms. Linn's classroom, many exciting activities are happening under the umbrella of interactions with print—choral reading, independent reading, listening to a teacher-read story, reading and singing, and writing stories, just to name a few. In addition to individual reading, children also view reading as a social activity and participate in literacy activities in pairs, small groups, and whole-class interactions. Children and teacher are actively engaged with print throughout the entire day. Since the beginning of the school year, Ms. Linn has been slowly building a foundation for small-group literature studies during group literature-studies time. The following section provides more information about literature studies and how to implement this dynamic approach to reading.

Ms. Linn's first-grade reading program gives equal emphasis to decoding and to construction of meaning. As children progress through the primary grades, this balance shifts, with less attention being given to decoding strategies and more attention given to higher-level comprehension skills and to literary appreciation.

Lessons from an Experienced Fourth-Grade Teacher

Reading Workshop does not just "happen." Teachers must thoughtfully consider the many instructional aspects discussed in Chapter 7. In this section readers will observe how Mrs. Anne Foley organizes and conducts Reading Workshop with her fourth-grade students. It is January and the students have been involved in learning how to work together in Reading Workshop since school began.

Choosing Literature

The class has been studying the Famous American Heroes and focused on Harriet Tubman and the Underground Railroad. Mrs. Foley uses the school and local city libraries to develop a comprehensive book list of high quality literature. Appendix B at the end of this chapter presents the Harriet Tubman and the Underground Railroad book list. Mrs. Foley collects and assesses the reading level of the chapter books. She is pleased that the book list offers excellent fiction and nonfiction selections and that the genres of historical fiction and biographies are well represented

Time and Scheduling

Mrs. Foley knows that her students need both sufficient and consistent time to read, discuss, write in their Literature Response Journals, and creatively respond to the stories they have read. She also know she needs time each day to read aloud to her students and time to conduct mini-lessons and to observe and assess her students' progress. Figure 8.7 presents her weekly schedule for Reading Workshop. Notice that she devotes ninety minutes a day every day to the Reading Workshop.

FIGURE 8.7   Weekly Schedule for Reading Workshop

Day & Time Frame M–F 12:00–1:30	Activity	Teacher Notes—Text and Mini-Lesson Focus
M–F 12:00–12:30	Teacher Read-Aloud Guiding Discussion Mini-Lesson &	The Story of Harriet Tubman M—Authors' description of character T—Atmosphere W—Plot development Th—Plot development F—Conflict
M & W 12:30–1:00	Silent Reading— Literature Discussion Book Literature Response Journals	Meet Addy and Sweet Clara Night John Sarny Harriet Tubman
M & W 1:00–1:30	Choice Book and Book Talks	From choice list in classroom library
T & Th 12:30–1:15	Literature Group Discussion Selected Mini-Lessons as needed	Meet Addy (meet on T) Night John (meet on T) Sarny (meet on Th) Harriet Tubman (meet on Th)
T & Th 1:15–1:30	Whole-Group Sharing	Observe Oral Expression
F 12:30–1:00	Students—Choice Book Teacher—Mini-Lessons— targeted skill groups	From choice list Skills Lesson
F 1:00–1:30	Creative Reading Responses and Sharing	Check out video for Readers Theater

Grouping

Mrs. Foley uses a number of grouping strategies during Reading Workshop. During literature study time, when the students usually read independently, she usually uses a homogeneous grouping strategy. (Students who read at about the same level read the same text.) She
rates the difficulty of the books using color stickers (see Figure 8.8, Color Coding System).
She assigns each student two colors, based on their independent and instructional reading
levels as determined by each student's performance on running records assessments. She
encourages students to choose books that are in their color range. However, because Mrs.
Foley realizes that interest and background knowledge can influence what a student can
read, she never prevents her students from trying books that she might judge to be "a little
too difficult" for them. Students do not know what level each color represents; they know
that their color reflects the book that will be at a reading level appropriate for them.

During skill-focused mini-lessons she usually uses a heterogeneous grouping strategy. Heterogeneous groups are comprised of students with different reading abilities who

FIGURE 8.8   Color Coding System

Color	Level	American Heroes Harriet Tubman
Yellow	Teacher Level Book	The Story of Harriet Tubman
Red	6th-grade reading level	Sarny
Orange	5th-grade reading level	Night John
Purple	4th-grade reading level	Harriet Tubman
Green	3rd-grade reading level	Meet Addy Sweet Clara
Blue	2nd-grade reading level	

are deliberately mixed together to learn or review concepts or skills. Mrs. Foley uses her observations of each student's performance to help her to determine what skills need to be taught to which particular students.

Teacher-Directed Activities

There are a number of teacher-directed activities that comprise Reading Workshop. The following section offers examples of how Mrs. Foley conducts the read-alouds, mini-lessons, discussions, and manages literature response journals and assesses student progress.

Read-alouds.   During the first thirty minutes of Reading Workshop, Mrs. Foley reads aloud to the students. She believes that this is an important way to help her students develop and sustain their interest in reading. She uses the read-aloud as a way to:

- develop or deepen the students' interests in the topic they are learning about;
- expand the students' vocabulary;
- model fluent and expressive oral reading;
- strengthen the students' listening comprehension skills;
- build community through discussion;
- model open-ended question strategies;
- illustrate by thinking aloud how readers think while they read; and
- model the use of post-it notes to code the text for use of beautiful language, descriptions of the main character, resolution to a problem, favorite part, unknown vocabulary word, and so forth.

Focus Lessons.   Within literature studies there are limitless possibilities for observant teachers to extend readers' understanding of literature. Focus lessons may evolve spontaneously from readers' immediate needs and concerns, or they may be based on teacher choice or district goals and objectives. There are three broad categories of mini-lessons, including procedures for managing the Reading Workshop, such as how to choose interesting books or what to write about in response journals; authors' or illustrators' craft, such as learning how authors and illustrators reveal things about their characters, and skill lessons, such as what students can do when they meet an unknown word or how to determine the main idea. In Figure 8.9 we provide an adaptation of Atwell's Categories of Mini-Lessons.

Today Mrs. Foley is teaching an author's craft lesson. She is focusing on how the author's words describe Harriet Tubman in a way that actually helps the students "see" Harriet. The students identify words and phrases that give them a picture of Harriet Tubman. She encourages the students to think about how the authors of the books they are reading in literature discussion group have used descriptive language to help them "see" the characters in their stories. She encourages them to make a note of this in their literature response journal.

Guiding Discussions. Mrs. Foley uses open-ended questions to begin the conversation about the text. In listening to the students' responses, she often redirects the questions to other students. She has found this technique to be helpful in modeling turn-taking and in guiding students to see her as a member (not leader) of the discussion. She also uses non-verbal gestures such as nods and smiles and makes encouraging comments to support her students as they elaborate their views. The following is a description of how Mrs. Foley guides discussion after the students have read *Sweet Clara and the Freedom Quilt* (D. Hopkinson, 1993). Notice how Mrs. Foley encourages the students to use the author's words to support their conclusions.

> **TEACHER:** How would you describe Clara?
>
> **NIC:** She was really brave.

FIGURE 8.9   Types of Focus Lessons: Procedures, Author's Craft, and Skills

Procedures: How To:	Authors' Craft	Skills
Find a good book	How authors reveal characters	Main idea/Supporting details
Choose a book at the right level	Types of conflict in stories	Cause-and-effect relationships
Respond to literature	Themes or authors' message	Sequence of events
• Drama	Genres	Study skills
• Art	Authors' or Illustrator's style	Understanding story elements
• Writing	Point of View	Cueing systems
Discuss literature	Use of dialog	Does it look right?
Keep a book log	Use of language	Does it sound right?
Use the classroom library	Setting	Does it make sense?
Set goals for yourself	Atmosphere	Structural analysis
Assess your progress	Book construction	Root words
Have a book conference	• Title page	Prefixes
Use the Literacy Responses Journal	• Prologue	Suffixes/endings
	• Epilogue	

Adapted from Atwell, N. (1987) *In the middle: Writing, reading, and learning with adolescents.* Portsmouth, NH: Boynton/Cook

TEACHER: Tell us how you came to that conclusion. Can you read any lines from the text that support your thinking?

NIC: [Uses his Literature Response Journal and post-it notes to find text to back-up his thinking.]

TEACHER: Marris, what do you think?

MARRIS: I agree that she was brave, because she could have been caught by the slave masters when she escaped.

TEACHER: [Nods in agreement.]

ALISHA: I think so, too, but she could have been caught when she was sewing the quilt. Don't you think the mistress might have figured out what she was doing?

BRANDON: No, I think the mistress and master didn't pay any attention to her because she was a girl, so they didn't expect it of her.

KARI: I think the masters were too busy with their own things and just didn't pay attention to any of the slaves very much. As long as Clara was quiet about what she was doing they would have ignored her.

This example illustrates some of the features of a grand conversation as the children respond to each other and raise questions themselves. No single person dominated the discussion and the speakers built on each other's comments (Eeds & Wells, 1989; Wells, 1995).

Literature Response Journals.   Another activity that Mrs. Foley initiates is that of Literature Response Journals (LRJ). At a bookkeeping level, the LRJ helps her to have a record of what the students are reading. At the management level, Mrs. Foley has found that the LRJs help her students to focus on what they are reading. But most importantly, the LRJs allow Mrs. Foley an opportunity to find out how the children are responding to the books they are reading, and they offer her a chance to respond individually to what each student is thinking and feeling. Further, as she reads several LRJs, she can see patterns across the children's journals and she uses these insights as a springboard for group discussion/sharing. Figure 8.10 provides an example of the Literature Response Journal form Mrs. Foley asks her students to complete on Monday and Wednesday after they read silently. After she reads the students LRJs, she often jots down notes about their reflections and comprehension. Her assessment of their interactions, in turn, influences her choice of mini-lessons.

Another variation of the response journal is the dialogue journal. In dialogue journals, the children continue to write their views. In addition, the teacher writes back, sharing thoughts about the text and what the child has written. The dialogue journal is a dynamic method for building a bond between student and teacher. In Trade Secret 8.1, fourth-grade teacher Lisa Wrenn describes her use of dialogue journals in her classroom.

Delaware teachers see the use of Literature Response Journals as one of several ways that they can link their instruction to the statewide reading assessment. The statewide reading assessment component of the Delaware Student Testing Program requires students to respond to numerous open-ended questions. That is, students must write responses from a couple of sentences to an extended piece of several sentences, and use details from the pas-

FIGURE 8.10 Literature Response Journal Form

Name   Date

Book title   Author   Pages read

What was the main idea or event that occurred during your reading?

How much more did you learn about the main characters?

What do you think will happen next?

Identify interesting or new vocabulary that the author used.

What language did the author use that was

Vivid?

Precise?

Colorful?

sage they have just read to support their thinking. While Delaware teachers have long used Literature Response Journals as a means to have students respond to what they have read, now they have tweaked this strategy to include asking students to justify their thinking with support from the passages they have read. Note how, in the discussion of *Sweet Clara and the Freedom Quilt,* Mrs. Foley also asked students to pull words from the book to support their thinking.

Teaching Students How to Conduct Literature Discussion Groups. Helping her students learn how to conduct Literature Study Groups is an activity that Mrs. Foley continues to refine throughout the year. Early in the year she established Rules of Respect for whole-group discussions (after the read-aloud). These rules are also expectations for student behavior during the student-directed Literature Study Groups. Mrs. Foley's Rules of Respect include the following:

- Take turns talking. Please don't interrupt.
- Give comments, but be nice.
- Help others out and be encouraging.
- Encourage each other to use the author's words to justify your thinking.

Mrs. Foley taught the students how to conduct the Literature Study Groups through mini-lessons and by modeling appropriate discussion behaviors during the Literature Study

Trade Secret 8.1

"P.S. I Love the Book!": *Using Dialogue Journals in Readers' Workshop*

Lisa C. Wrenn

Dear Mrs. Wrenn,

I like *Harriet the Spy* so far. I have read up to Book Two, 129 pages, and have loved it! My dad was right when he said it is a good book!

I think Louise Fitzhugh did a good job of leading me in, even though the beginning was slightly boring. But the rest was *fantastic*! It was hard to put down!

Harriet is a sixth grader who likes to spy on people. She has a spy route and has taken us readers on it, where we meet lots of people. Then Janie, Harriet's best friend, and Harriet are going to start dancing school. Janie wants to blow up the world! Finally, Ole Golly, Harriet's nurse, is engaged! She has just left when I stopped reading.

I think that this is going to be a great book!

Yours Sincerely,
Audrey

P.S. Next time I won't read so much!

As I closed Audrey's journal, I thought about her last comment. She was so used to teachers telling her what and how much to read that she felt it necessary to apologize for reading a lot. Instead of making me upset, however, Audrey's postscript made me smile. I knew she was on the road to being a good reader. This is the excitement I was hoping to encourage in my readers' workshop program. My students read books of their choice both during class and at home. They respond to what they read in letters written in dialogue journals. They also share ideas orally in discussion groups. I have learned a lot this year about my students. They have impressed me at every turn.

My idea for dialogue journals came from two sources: *In the Middle: Writing, Reading and Learning with Adolescents* by Nancie Atwell

(1987), and *Invitations: Changing as Teachers and Learners* by Regie Routman (1991). The purpose of the dialogue journal is to provide regular, frequent, and genuine exchange of responses about reading. "It is an excellent tool for connecting reading to writing, for extending the meaning of the text, and for giving readers' ownership of their literary experience" (Routman, 1991, p. 103).

The students write a minimum of one letter per week in their journals. This letter may be to me or to a peer, but one letter must come in to me every two weeks. When grading the letters, I agree with Routman that the focus should be on the content of the response, not the mechanics. (Routman, 1991, p. 104). I never correct mistakes in the letters, but I may comment on proper mechanics, such as underlining titles, in a minilesson. Overall, comments the teacher writes back to the students should affirm, challenge, or extend the readers' thinking. I am constantly thinking of "gossip, questions, recommendations, jokes, restatements, arguments, suggestions, anecdotes, instruction, and nudges" (Atwell, 1987, p. 275) that will benefit my students. The students rush to read my responses and those of their peers, and they love to write back right away. This is part of the magic of letters about literature.

At the beginning of the year my students receive a list of my expectations for the dialogue journal:

Dear Students,

Most of your letter should be your reaction to what you read. Some things you might tell include

- what you noticed,
- what you wondered about,
- what you thought and felt like,
- what you liked and didn't like,
- how you read and why (Where and when do you read? What are you learning about yourself as a reader?),
- what the book said and meant to you,
- what you think about the author's writing,
- connections between what you read and real life.

(continued on next page)

Trade Secret 8.1 *(continued)*

Also—ask questions, ask for help, and answer the questions that have been asked of you. Some of the letter should discuss the plot. Here are some guidelines:

- Be brief,
- mention story elements (setting, characters, problem, etc.),
- don't give away too much.
- REMEMBER—This is a letter, not a postcard. Length is a factor.

Happy writing!
Mrs. Wrenn

I want some of the letter to show their knowledge and comprehension of the book, and I need some knowledge of it to understand their response as well. (One thing you must get past if you use readers' workshop is the need to be familiar with what each student is reading. It's impossible! Allow them to introduce you to many wonderful books you knew nothing about.) The main thrust of the letters, though, is on the more critical thinking skills of analysis and evaluation. As Routman states, "Responding in writing to a question, impression, mood, or reaction generated by the reading seems to promote critical thinking" (Routman, 1991, p. 103).

The appendix in Atwell's book includes a list of "Kinds of Talk About Books," which breaks the broad statements on my expectations list into specific areas and topics. These are addressed in minilessons I teach, so that as the year goes on, the quality of students' letters increases, and students rarely are seen referring to the expectations list late in the year. They internalize the type of talk I model, and they use it when they write in their journals and share in oral discussions.

At the beginning of the year, I write a letter to the class about a book I'm reading:

Dear Students,

Last night I picked up *Midnight in the Garden of Good and Evil* by John Berendt as I got into bed. I usually like to read right before going to

sleep, even though I never read very long. Last night I caught myself reading fast. Sometimes I start almost skimming the pages, looking for the next interesting part. The only problem is I have to go back and reread those parts.

This book is a work of nonfiction, which I usually don't like. However, it's about a murder, and I love murder mysteries. As I was reading I was wondering what the truth of the murder was. There has to be more to it, otherwise Berendt wouldn't have written about it. It seems as though a lot of books I read are like that. The author is making you wait for the climax. Good authors make the buildup just as exciting or captivating.

Berendt makes his buildup exciting by surprising me. He makes me stop thinking what I was thinking and start considering the newest twist. In this case it was the return to discussing the character of Joe Odom. He really is a character! He steals people's houses in a way. If he knows someone's going to be away he just moves in! And everyone in Savannah really likes him a lot. He's very easygoing. It's amazing that he's a real person! Berendt does a very good job of description.

Anyway, I hope he gets back to the murder soon. Are you enjoying your books? Have you read any nonfiction lately?

Happy Reading!
Mrs. Wrenn

This model letter is an excellent way to specifically show the type of response I'm seeking. I put the letter on an overhead, and we discuss what I've written in terms of my expectations list. They can see that not every item from the list is included—and is never expected to be. Repeated demonstrations of appropriate responses need to be given throughout the year by thinking out loud, writing in front of the students, and—of course—by responding to the letters they write.

Earlier in the year, Alison read *Harriet the Spy* by Louis Fitzhugh. Here is the letter she wrote me:

(continued on next page)

Trade Secret 8.1 *(continued)*

Oct. 1

Dear Mrs. Wrenn,

So far *Harriet the Spy* is a very good book. Louise Fitzhugh did a good job of leading me into the book. Harriet I found out is a very good spy. So far Harriet tried to play town with Sport, but Sport wanted to play football. Harriet has gone to Miss Golly's house and met her friends. On the first day of school Harriet was ready to write about her friends and classmates in her notebook. Days passed and many little things happened. Then the day came for Ole Golly, a man asked her to be his wife and she said yes. He proposed to her at a store at night with Harriet. When they got home Harriet's mother had a fit.

A couple days passed. In school she got the part of an onion. She practiced and practiced. So thats mainly what I know so far.

Your Student,
Alison

P.S. I love the book!

Alison does a great job of retelling what she has read, but she doesn't share her reactions, thoughts, or feelings—except in her P.S.! This will develop over time, through modeling and as a focus of minilessons. Alison "caught the 'I love to read' flu" (her words). Alison's parents have also commented on the change.

May 7

Dear Mrs. Wrenn,

This week I read So Young to Die by Candice F. Ransom. It is a biography of Hannah Senesh. I thought I could read this book in one week, but I can't. It takes me a long time to read a page, but I still like the book.

It's really neat how this stuff really happened. Do you ever stop and think 'wow' about your book? What book are you reading now? Did it happen in real life? Why do you read?

In *So Young to Die* Hannah wants to work in fields with Jews at this place. She goes there. Then she thinks she is doing nothing while people are dying so now she is on this team to save Jews. I really like this book so far!

Your Student,
Alison

P.S. Hannah was living during World War II.

I can always guarantee I'll be smiling when I finish reading Alison's letters.

Nancie Atwell writes of noticing a difference between letters students write to her and those they write to each other. As for me, I haven't noticed a difference in neatness or length. They may be trying to outdo each other or may be trying to please me because they know I read the journals when I respond. The one thing I do notice is a more relaxed tone, perhaps a more genuine feeling, lacking in letters to me. However, as the year goes on and we get to know each other, the students' letters to me also take on this more relaxed tone.

Groups. Her students also came up with ideas for helping group members share ideas and ask questions during discussions.

- Look in your Literature Response Journal for ideas to share.
- Tell about your likes and dislikes.
- Compare characters.
- Compare the story to things in your life.
- Talk about reasons why the author probably wrote the story.
- Compare this author's writing to other authors' work.

Assessing Student Progress.   Mrs. Foley uses the Running Record approach to assess the students' reading level and to determine her students' ability to decode the story they are reading (see Special Feature 8.1). She tries to complete a running record for each student (particularly the students who may be struggling) every two weeks. Mrs. Foley uses the students' LRJs and her observation notes (taken when the students interact with each other during Literature Study Group) as a way to assess comprehension. Mrs. Foley stores this information in the students' working portfolios. (See Chapter 12 for more information about assessing and documenting student progress.)

Case Studies: Tiffany's Development in Literature-Based Classrooms, First–Sixth Grade

The preceding sections have described examples of how skilled teachers provide excellent practice in reading instruction at the early primary- and intermediate-grade levels. We now return to the case studies of Tiffany's and Alicia's literacy development. Chapter 3 told the story of how Tiffany, a native English speaker, and Alicia, who initially spoke only Spanish, began to read and write during the preschool and kindergarten years. The following section and Special Feature 8.2 (by Irene Serna and Sarah Hudelson) continue these stories, beginning at the point when each girl entered first grade. When reading the stories of these two girls' literacy instruction, be alert for examples of the excellent teaching practices recommended in Chapter 7.

The following is a brief example of the strategies that Ms. G, Tiffany's first-grade teacher, used with her reading group throughout a typical week of instruction. Ms. G's instructional approach was very similar to Ms. Linn's, whose teaching was described at the beginning of this chapter.

On the first day, Ms. G introduced a story by reading the story title and asking the children to predict what they thought the story might be about. After she recorded the children's ideas, she read the story to the children. As she read, Ms. G modeled fluent and dramatic reading. She also defined new vocabulary words within the context of the story. After reading a page or two, the students were asked whether they wished to revise their original story predictions. The children discarded and revised their original predictions throughout the entire story. To stimulate their interest, Ms. G occasionally asked an open-ended question, such as, "Why do you think the elves made the shoes for the shoemaker?" The next day, Ms. G asked the students as a group to complete a "Who, What, But, Then, and Finally" chart, a technique she used to help the children retell the story in a sequential manner. On this day, the children also chorally reread the story with her.

On the third day, the children worked in twos or threes and practiced rereading the story again, this time focusing on reading with fluency and dramatic expression.

By the fourth day, Ms. G listened to children individually read their favorite part of the story while she completed a running record to document their progress (see Special Feature 8.1). Tiffany's first-grade teacher also modeled the writing process at least twice each day: once in the morning as she discussed the day's activities and expectations and again as part of a closure activity at the end of the day. Ms. G also had the children keep journals, in which she encouraged them to write and illustrate their own stories.

As Tiffany entered second grade, her transformation to becoming an independent reader was almost complete. Her second-grade teacher, Ms. A, used a very similar approach to Ms. G. However, because Ms. A was particularly strong at integrating the social science curriculum, Tiffany was involved in more subject-area content. Because Ms. A used a thematic curriculum approach, Tiffany went from *learning to read* to *reading to learn,* using her reading skills to acquire knowledge about the Pilgrims' reasons for leaving Europe and about the structure of the human eye. At home, Tiffany was continuing to learn that reading is a useful, practical skill. Tiffany read cookbook recipes and package labels to make snacks, and she used *TV Guide* to determine what time her special shows were appearing on television.

Throughout her second-grade year, Tiffany continued to write and manufacture her own books by experimenting with various formats, sizes, and materials. Once, she even created a book with an inch-wide spine, which included the title of the book on the back of the spine, just like a real library book. Because one of her major interests was dance, many of her stories revolved around this theme (see Figure 8.11)

In third grade, under the gentle guidance of Mr. M, Tiffany learned that reading could have an impact on her emotions. *Nana Upstairs, Nana Downstairs* helped Tiffany deal with the death of her own great-grandmother; *The Patchwork Quilt* allowed her to understand the importance of the beautiful quilt that covered her parents' bed, and *Beezus and Ramona* helped her to understand the love and rivalry that she felt toward her sister Dawn. She discovered *Little House in the Big Woods* after watching the television series, *Little House on the Prairie.* She asked for her own set of "Little House" books so she wouldn't have to share them with her sister. However, Tiffany's third-grade favorite was the Garfield cartoon series, which she carried with her everywhere, because, as she put it, "You never know when you'll need a fast giggle."

During third grade, Tiffany was introduced to writing poetry. She found this activity to be as creative as dancing, "Only you make the words move instead of your body." Figure 8.12 is an example of one of Tiffany's poems.

Tiffany's development into a mature, independent reader and writer basically followed the developmental sequence described in Chapter 4. Though her world was print-rich and her parents were very supportive, Tiffany still required developmentally appropriate, explicit instruction by very skillful and concerned teachers to help her become a fully participating member in a literate society.

Tiffany's fourth-grade teacher, Ms. E, introduced her class to literature studies. She began by reading E. Coerr's story, *Sadako and the Thousand Paper Cranes* (1977). This story had a great impact on Tiffany, and she sobbed deeply as she retold the story to her parents that evening. Tiffany and a few of her classmates decided to celebrate this story by learning how to make origami paper cranes.

Tiffany's love of reading led her to become an official library helper. Three times a week, during her lunch hour, Tiffany helped Ms. Mimi, the school librarian, reshelve books and buddy-read to the kindergarten children. While Tiffany was studying Lynn Reid Banks's *Indian in the Cupboard* (1980) with her literature group, Ms. Banks visited Tiffany's school and signed Tiffany's copy of the book. Ms. Banks told the children that "Indian" developed from bedtime stories she told her son. A budding author herself, Tiffany found this presentation fascinating. This concept of oral storytelling inspired Tiffany to begin to create and elaborate her own stories verbally before she wrote them. On her tenth birthday, her grandmother gave her *Mrs. Piggle-Wiggle's Farm,* by Betty MacDonald (1954). This fanciful tale captured Tiffany's imagination, and by the end of the summer, Tiffany had read the entire book series.

The girl who believe in Dancing ①

One day a girl said I'm going to dance.

I'm scared but she took a deep breth and did it.

Then after class she ask her teacher a she said she did very good.

FIGURE 8.11   Tiffany's dance story (grade 2).

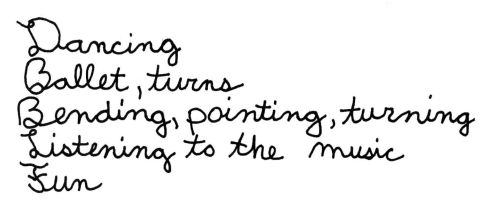

Dancing
Ballet, turns
Bending, pointing, turning
Listening to the music
Fun

FIGURE 8.12   A poem by Tiffany (grade 3).

As Tiffany entered her combination fifth–sixth grade multi-age classroom, her teachers, Mr. S and Ms. G, continued to build on the wonderful literacy foundation laid during the previous years. This teaching team hooked the students the very first day of school when they began to read *Scary Stories to Tell in the Dark,* a collection of folklore collected by Alvin Schwartz (1981). These stories were so wonderfully frightful that the students devoured them and begged for more.

That same year, Tiffany watched the video *Young Guns* (1989). The western, tall-tale genre intrigued her, and she began a quest to learn everything she could about the outlaw Billy-the-Kid and his companions. Her search took her to the city and university libraries, and she learned how to conduct a literature search on the computer. The dozens of books and articles she read about western folklore allowed Tiffany to become a classroom expert. Her passion for the subject was transmitted to her family and resulted in a family vacation traveling old roads and visiting old towns in New Mexico, following the trail of William Bonney.

The next year, as a senior sixth grader in the multi-age classroom, Tiffany helped to conduct literature studies. Her group read *The Pig Man* by Paul Zindel (1968). To facilitate group discussions, Ms. G and the students developed a list of questions that focused the students' literature journal responses and served as points of discussion during their literature group. As group organizer, Tiffany preread the story and charted the plot for each chapter (see Figure 8.13). To help document the students' involvement and interactions, Ms. G also videotaped the group as they discussed and shared their perceptions of characters and the author's intent and theme.

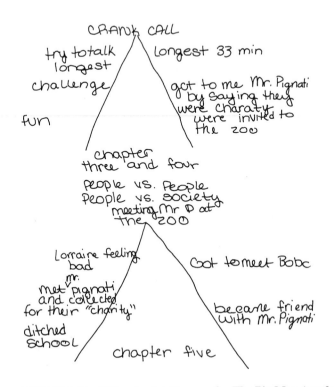

FIGURE 8.13   Tiffany's plot diagram for The Pig Man (grade 6).

Mr. S also used literature and writing to deepen his students' understanding of history. For example, while studying the Civil War, Tiffany responded to the textbook, movies, and literature by writing in diary form as Julia Elizabeth, a young slave in the midst of the Civil War (see Figure 8.14). Later, she dramatized her writings for her classmates. As the class dressed for their roles and made their presentations, the dynamic process of literature study and student learning was fully evident. For more information about using dramatic reading in literature studies, see Knipping (1993).

Tiffany's strong language development and print-rich home environment set the stage for her early love of reading, writing, and talking (Chapter 3 & 4). Her caring and observant teachers continued to extend and support Tiffany's developing literacy skills. Throughout her elementary school years, her teachers built on Tiffany's strengths and provided explicit instruction whenever the need arose. Consequently, Tiffany not only *can* read and write, but she also *does!* Tiffany loves to read and considers herself a writer in the romance-novelist tradition. For Tiffany, as for most literate adults, literacy is both useful and enjoyable. Reading and writing provide information, pleasure, and time for thoughtful reflection and introspection.

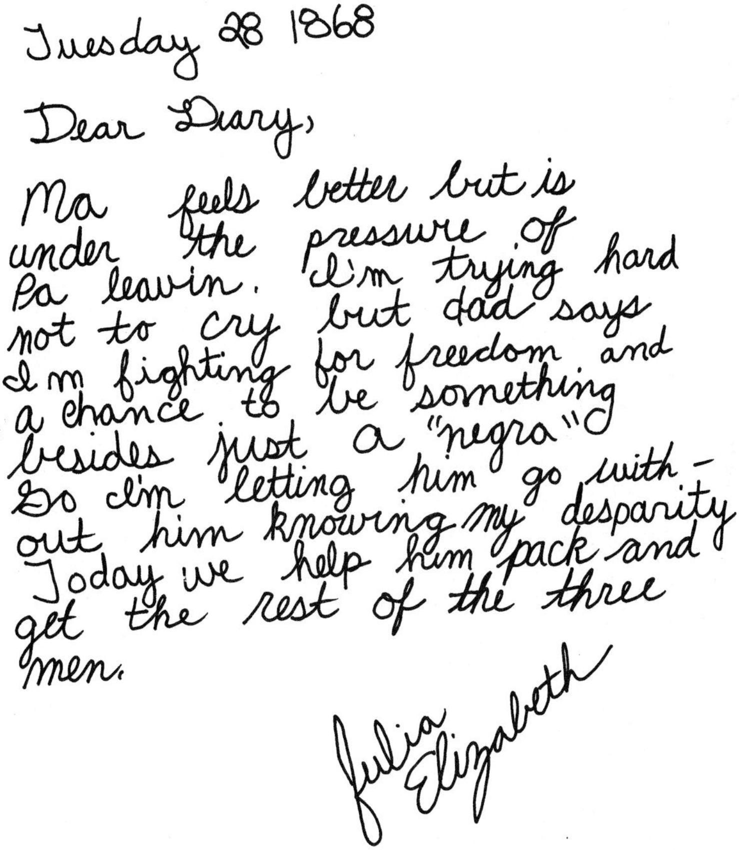

Tuesday 28 1868

Dear Diary,

Ma feels better but is under the pressure of Pa leavin. I'm trying hard not to cry but dad says I'm fighting for freedom and a chance to be something besides just a "negra." So I'm letting him go without him knowing my desparity. Today we help him pack and get the rest of the three men.

Julia Elizabeth

FIGURE 8.14   Tiffany's diary entry, written from the perspective of a book character (grade 6).

Special Feature 8.3

Alicia's Biliteracy Development in First and Second Grade

Irene Alicia Serna and Sarah Hudelson

In Chapter 4, Alicia was introduced to readers, and information was given about how she learned literacy in her native language, Spanish. In this special feature, Alicia is followed into first and second grades. Her continued literacy growth in Spanish and her addition of English literacy is described. Then Alicia's development is used as a springboard for several general comments about excellent reading practices for bilingual and second-language learners.

Becoming Biliterate in First Grade

Still more proficient in Spanish than in English at the end of kindergarten, Alicia entered a bilingual first grade composed of equal numbers of English and Spanish speakers. Her literacy instruction in Spanish continued, although English literacy events also surrounded her. Alicia wrote in Spanish in a dialogue journal, in learning and literature logs, and in several personal narratives she created in the class writing workshop. She also participated in several reading and literature-study groups conducted in Spanish. At the beginning of first grade, Alicia understood stories that were read to her in English and discussed texts in English, but she did not read or write in English. During the school year, she made significant progress in both of these aspects of English literacy.

Writing

During the first ten weeks of school Alicia wrote entries in Spanish, including the following personal recounting of a family trip to Flagstaff to play in the snow.

Alicia's Version	English Version
Nosotros vamos a Flagstaff	We are going to Flagstaff
Flagstaff esta muy lejos	It's very far
y tomamos chocolate caliente	and we drank hot chocolate
y estaba bueno	and it was good
Yo y Martincito hisiMos uN	Martin and I made a
mono de nieve	snowman
Yo y La Karina	Karina and I
nos Estabamos TiRaNDo nieve	were throwing snow
en la CARA	in each other's faces.
enTonc PARAmoS	Then we stopped at a
LA TiendDA y compRAMoS	store and bought
(rias)	(unclear)
Y YA NoS fuimoS	And then we went home
ALA cASa	

In November, on her own initiative, Alicia began to write personal narratives in English. In these narrations, she used some conventional spelling in English and some inventions influenced from Spanish. An example is provided here:

Alicia's Version	Conventional Version
i Like to go to the parke	I like to go to the park
wheth my dog.	with my dog
i thro a bal to my dog.	I throw a ball to my dog
and i run wheth my dog	and I run with my dog
and i like to take my dog	and I like to take my dog
to the parke	to the park
my dog runs to fast	my dog runs too fast
and i cant get hem	and I can't get him.
I went to the zoo	I went to the zoo
with my mom and my grama	with my mom and my grandma.

(continued on next page)

Then we war there	Then we were there.
I saw sum bears	I saw some bears
Then my mom and my grama and I went to see	Then my mom and my grandma and I went to see
the monkis	the monkeys
Then we saw a grafe eating blants	Then we saw a giraffe eating plants

During the same month, after seeing author Eric Carle at the public library, Alicia wrote, "I like Eric CARLE cuse hes Nise and He gave us THaT CarD." (I like Eric Carle because he's nice and he gave us that card.) Perhaps she wrote in English because Carle used English during his presentation. As she continued to write in English, her sentences became more complex syntactically, as in "I like my dog cuse he brings hes leesh cuse he wants me to tack hem for a walke." (I like my dog because he brings his leash because he wants me to take him for a walk.) Her spelling reflected her knowledge of phonic generalizations, phonetic features of English, her own pronunciation, and her knowledge of visual patterns in English.

In March, Alicia decided she wanted to write a report in Spanish about her Barbie dolls. Adults read her books about Barbie dolls in English and discussed the books and her dolls in Spanish. At home, Alicia began to write in Spanish, describing what each doll looked liked, how the dolls moved, the accessories she had for each doll, how she played with the dolls, and whether she thought each doll was ugly or pretty. Alicia's first drafts were all typed on the computer and returned to her for her reconsideration. As Alicia read her report, she added information and organized each chapter of her book. By May, she was satisfied with the content of her Barbie book, which totaled 20 pages. Then her English-speaking friend Lorena announced, "I would really like to read about your Barbie dolls but I can't 'cuz it's not in English." Ah, what a challenge! Would Alicia translate her book into English? Alicia was anxious for Lorena to read her

book, but she was not eager to rewrite the book herself. Her solution was this: "I know. I'll translate the book into English on the tape recorder. You [Irene] take it home and listen to it, and type what I say on your computer. Then you can bring it back to me, and I can read to see if you got it right. That way everyone can read my book." This was how Alicia's bilingual Barbie book was produced. The writing of the book entirely in Spanish facilitated Alicia's translation of the text to English. One of the chapters, "Western Fun Barbie," is presented here.

Western Fun Barbie

Spanish Version	*English Version*
Mi Western Fun Barbie se parece como	My Western Fun Barbie looks like
la muñeca en la página 97 de 1981	the doll on page 97 for 1981
por el sombrero. Western Fun	because of the hat. Western Fun
Barbie está vestida como una vaquera.	Barbie is dressed like a cowgirl.
Tiene botas y sombrero. Se puede	She has boots and a hat. You can
quitar el sombrero y ponerle un panuelo.	take off the hat and put on a scarf.
Mi Western Fun Barbie puede mover la cabeza a un lado a otro. Puede	My Western Fun Barbie can move her head from side to side. You can
doblar las manos, y el dedo gordito, y los brazos y	bend her hands, thumb, arms and
las piernas. Se puede mover la cadera	legs. You can move her hips
para atras y para adelante y splits.	forward and backward andhace make her do splits.
Su pelo es chino, rubio o moreno,	Her hair is curly, blond or light brown,

(continued on next page)

Special Feature 8.3 *(continued)*

y largo. Los ojos son azules.	and long. Her eyes are blue.
La Western Fun Barbie es bonita.	Western Fun Barbie is pretty.

After this experience, Alicia practiced writing in both languages in her dialogue journal. Sometimes, she switched languages within a single entry, particularly when influenced by a cultural topic. For example, she wrote, "I went to Cinco de Mayo. I saw India Maria and the mariachias cantando 'La Puerta Negra' and my mom bought me a snow cone." At other times, she wrote an entire entry in Spanish and then translated it into English. Thus, Alicia initiated her own writing in English, prior to receiving English language-arts instruction. She did the same with her reading, becoming fluent and independent in English as well as Spanish.

Reading

Alicia began the fall semester reading primarily predictable books written in Spanish, such as *La Oruga Hambriente* (Carte, 1994) *Harry y el Terrible Quiensabeque* (Gackenbach, 1984), *La Flautista de Jamelin* (Ladybird, 1990), *Los Tres Osos* (McKissack & McKissack, 1989), and *Jorgito* (Bright, 1991). Soon, she began reading books written in English, such as *Miss Nelson Is Missing* (Allard & Marshall, 1985) and *The Magic Nutcracker* (Hillert, 1981). Typically, she chose to read books in English with her English-speaking girlfriends and books in Spanish with her Spanish-speaking friends. When she could not read a word, Alicia typically decoded it phonetically, blended the sounds together to pronounce the word, and then reread the entire sentence to make sure that what she had read made sense. When Alicia discussed the literary elements of the stories, she attended to characters' feelings and motivations, interpretations of tension, and the problem-solution episodes. She was eager to share her personal reactions to stories. Even though she read books written in English and in Spanish, she used Spanish, as well as English, to discuss books written in English.

In March, Alicia helped an English-speaking classmate, whom she identified as the best reader in English, read *William's Doll,* by Charlotte Zolotow. When he had difficulty reading, Alicia suggested that he look at the pictures; she asked him questions focusing on semantic meaning; and she told him to read on to the end of the sentence when he could not read unfamiliar text. When some of his miscues changed the meaning of the text, Alicia asked him, "Does that make sense?" Her suggestions indicated that she was aware that (a) readers use multiple cuing systems and strategies to decode text (her teacher had worked with small groups of children on predicting unfamiliar words using syntactic, semantic, and graphophonic cues), and (b) readers read in order to construct the meaning of a text. In April, Alicia began to participate with the English-language reading and literature-study groups, while continuing to participate in the Spanish groups as well.

Biliteracy Development in Second Grade

Alicia continued in a bilingual classroom in second grade. Because she was both bilingual and biliterate, she served as a good model for literacy in Spanish and English for her peers.

Writing

During second grade, Alicia chose to write more in English. However, her ability to express her ideas more completely in Spanish and the opportunities to continue to talk through her writing in Spanish facilitated her revisions of the content of personal narratives. For example, in March, Alicia wrote a story about what she did with her dog, Cookie, and her friend, Briana. When she talked about her story, she elaborated on how she played with Cookie and stated, "Lo puedo explicar mejor en español" (I can explain it better in Spanish). Prompted by her oral description, she revised the story by adding new information in both English and Spanish. Originally, she stated that her dog played with her friend's dog. In the revised version, she explained that her dog had a ball in its mouth and that it jumped in the air and threw the

(continued on next page)

ball to Briana's dog. The other dog caught the ball and then threw it. The dogs played catch back and forth, and then the girls joined in the fun, playing keep away with the dogs.

Reading

As with her writing, Alicia's bilingual and biliteracy abilities were also evident in her participation in literature studies in both English and Spanish. Small groups of children chose a book to read independently and then gathered to discuss their interpretations (Peterson & Eeds, 1990). The children used Post-it™ notes to record (in either language) some of their ideas about passages that were meaningful to them. They referred to these notes in talking about the stories. On several occasions, these literature studies were conducted bilingually, with Alicia and Spanish-dominant Bianca often commenting in Spanish and English-speaking Susan commenting in English. Rather than translating, Alicia often mediated the group's interpretation of the story by expanding or extending comments made in either English or Spanish. An example of this occurred when the girls were discussing the character Fern in the first two chapters of E. B. White's *Charlotte's Web:*

Susan:	She [Fern] must really badly want the pig to stay. It's like she would do anything for the pig.
Alicia:	Fern quería cuidar al cerdito. Le dijeron a Fern que podría cuidar a Wilbur hasta que creciera. [Fern wanted to care for the little pig. They told Fern she could take care of Wilbur until he grew.]
Bianca:	Fern le daba botella de leche y lo paseaba en el carrito como su muñeca. [Fern would give him a bottle of milk and she would walk him in a stroller like a doll.]
Alicia:	Fern tuvo que vender el cerdito porque ya no lo podría mantener. Tuvo que vender a Wilbur a su tío que vivía en un rancho. Fern

podría visitar a Wilbur cuando se le pegará la gana. [Fern had to sell the little pig because they couldn't keep him anymore. She had to sell Wilbur to her uncle who lived on a farm. Fern could visit Wilbur when ever she wants.]

Susan:	Fern really wanted to keep the pig; she thought the pig was like her baby. Fern wanted to take care of the pig.
Alicia:	Fern's brother didn't want to take care of Wilbur.
Susan:	Fern fed him, gave him a bath. She took him for a walk every day.
Alicia:	Fern was really sad because she didn't want to lose her pet Wilbur. When she sold Wilbur, she wasn't very sad because she could go and visit Wilbur anytime she wanted.

Alicia's last statement reiterates some of the ideas she had shared previously in Spanish. Writing notes and discussing some of the text in Spanish helped Alicia express her interpretations in English. Alicia facilitated the dialogue by responding to each peer's comment, in that child's language, thus ensuring that all the children could participate in the conversation. Collectively, the children were able to construct feelings and motivations.

Conclusions About Alicia's Literacy Development

Alicia grew from a dominant Spanish speaker at the beginning of kindergarten to a bilingual–biliterate second-grader able to read chapter books in both English and Spanish. Because Alicia had opportunities to read and write in Spanish at home and at school, she quickly became literate in her native language. Her reading and writing abilities in Spanish facilitated her developing literacy abilities in English. She learned how to read first by reading her

(continued on next page)

Special Feature 8.3 *(continued)*

own Spanish-language texts (her own stories) and then literature written in Spanish. She learned to use multiple cuing systems and reading strategies. On her own, she applied her Spanish reading and writing understandings to reading familiar books in English, books she had heard read aloud or books with Spanish versions she already knew how to read. She also began to write on her own in English, using what she had learned about writing through her writing in Spanish. Also she continued to use her Spanish to mediate her learning, working through the reading of more complex English texts and the writing of more coherent English language stories by speaking in Spanish. Alicia—**not** her teachers, and **not** a structured curriculum with a predetermined scope and sequence—was in control of when she began to read and write in English. Alicia clearly demonstrated that first-language literacy supports the development of reading and writing in the second language (Edelsky, 1986; Hudelson, 1987).

Alicia also was aware of the advantages that being bilingual and biliterate afforded her as a learner and in life. In response to a question about why it's important to be bilingual, Alicia wrote, "Es muy importante aprender en inglés y español porque gente [que] no saben los dos idiomas necesitan ayuda." When asked what she meant she replied, "Personas que hablan español necesitan ayuda en inglés, y personas que hablan inglés necesitan ayuda en español. Personas bilingües no necesitan ayuda y pueden ayudar a los demás. (People who speak Spanish need help in English, and people who speak English need help in Spanish. People who are bilingual don't need help and can help others.)

Best Practice in Reading for Bilingual and Second-Language Learners

How does the example of Alicia inform the readers of this text? Alicia's story illustrates several generalizations about reading instruction, made by language educators who work in bilingual and second-language settings.

- Whenever possible, support children's literacy development in their native language, prior to helping them become literate in English. Alicia's native-language literacy gave her confidence to move into English. Further, she used what she knew about reading and writing in Spanish to navigate reading and writing in English (Hudelson, 1987). Even teachers who themselves are not bilingual can provide learners with opportunities to develop literacy in their native language.

- Allow learners to use their native language to mediate their English literacy learning (Auerbach, 1993). Some of what Alicia was able to accomplish as a reader and writer in English was influenced by the fact that she was able to work through her understandings and her ideas in her dominant language, Spanish. Even if ESL learners ultimately must read and/or write in English, they should be able to work together in their native language to produce the final product in English. Even teachers who are not bilingual should encourage children in this way. The key is trust in the learners (Freeman & Freeman, 1994b).

- Utilize natural, predictable texts for beginning reading instruction. In both the native language and English, ESL learners seem to benefit from predictable texts, which facilitate their learning to use reading strategies and multiple cuing systems by sampling the visual display (the graphophonic cuing system), predicting what will come next on the basis of syntax and semantics (what sounds right and what makes sense), pictures and real world prior knowledge, and confirming or disconfirming predictions (Heald-Taylor, 1987; Hudelson, 1994; Weaver, 1994).

- Encourage young readers to reread the same natural, predictable stories multiple times. In both the native language and English, rereading to themselves, to an

(continued on next page)

adult, or to a peer will help ESL children to become increasingly able to predict their way through stories.

- The use of predictable books in shared reading and small-group reading-strategy lessons, in both the native language and English, models for children how they can use prior knowledge, picture clues, and the language cuing systems (syntactic, semantic, and graphophonic) to predict their way through text (Nurss, Hough, & Enright, 1986). Alicia's teachers used both big books and regular-sized predictable stories for these activities (Lynch, 1988; Strickland & Morrow, 1990). They regularly covered words in stories with their fingers or with Post-it™ notes and asked children to predict a word or words that would fit in the story. They demonstrated how to use the first letter of the word to narrow the prediction. They worked with the children to generate lists of strategies to use when coming to a word that is unfamiliar. These activities also were especially important for the children who focused on one strategy for dealing with unfamiliar words: sounding out. The activities demonstrated to these children that reading is supposed to focus on the construction of meaning rather than the pronouncing of words.
- Provide in-class time for self-selected, independent reading, because bilingual and second-language-learning children need opportunities to choose some of their own reading material.
- Involve children in literature study groups so that they have experiences interpreting and responding to high-quality literature. Young children are as enthusiastic about talking about good books as are older learners (Samway & Whang, 1995).
- Encourage children to write, both in their native language and in English, and recognize the close connection between writing and reading. As Alicia exemplifies, many young

children actually begin to read (in terms of focusing on the graphophonic display) by reading their own pieces, rather than by reading stories that someone else has written. This is the text that is most meaningful and manageable to them. Children discover the process of connecting letters to sounds and sounding out (what some have called "breaking code") first through their own writing. Then they apply this understanding to other stories (Serna & Hudelson, 1993). Thus, children's phonics abilities are developed as they write daily. Writing is absolutely essential to reading development.

- Develop bilingual/ESL children's abilities to use basic skills such as phonics and spelling within the contexts of their actual writing and reading (Weaver, 1995). As noted previously, many children come to understand sound–letter correspondences through their own writing (through writing the sounds they can hear in words) rather than through isolated phonics activities and worksheets. Additionally, teachers should use such activities as reading alphabet books, written versions of rhyming poems, chants, and songs; examining children's names; and sounding out words in the creation of news of the day and dictated narrations to facilitate children's understanding and use of phonics. This contextualized approach is more understandable and meaningful to the learners, especially to learners who are working in a second language.
- Observe second-language learners' attempts to read and write carefully, and respond to what the learners are doing. Take cues from the learners rather than from a packaged program. Second-language learners work hard to construct meaning from all classroom situations, including those involving literacy. It is crucial that teachers respond to their attempts with encouragement and sensitivity.

Summary

Implementing successful literature studies requires thoughtful planning, management, and organization, and an ongoing and ever-changing understanding of student strengths, interests, and needs. For Reading Workshop to be successful, the teacher must purposefully structure a classroom environment that supports complex literacy and language communities.

■ *What organizational strategies do teacher use to implement Reading Workshop?*

Teachers thoughtfully organize large blocks of time to begin to organize Reading Workshop. Teachers need to develop weekly schedules that consistently structure time for whole-group read-alouds or shared book, small-group discussions and mini-lessons, and individual reading and written reflection. Teachers must also offer a number of procedural mini-lessons that help students learn to how to be successful contributing members of literature discussion groups.

■ *What types of grouping strategies are used in Reading Workshop?*

Teachers who use the Reading Workshop approach usually use both homogeneous (students with similar needs/abilities) and heterogeneous (students with different skills and abilities) grouping strategies. During Reading Workshop teachers may also use whole-group instruction or provide individual instruction, depending on the needs of the students and the content that needs to be taught.

■ *How do teachers provide skill instruction in the Reading Workshop?*

During Reader's Workshop, teachers usually deliver skill instruction through mini-lessons. These lessons may evolve spontaneously from readers' immediate needs and concerns, or they may be based on teacher choice or district goals and objectives. There are three broad categories of mini-lessons, including procedures for managing the Reading Workshop, such as how to choose interesting books or what to write about in response journals; authors' or illustrators' craft, such as learning how authors and illustrators reveal things about their characters; and skill lessons, such as what students can do when they meet an unknown word or how to determine the main idea.

■ *How do teachers help students construct meaning and expand their understanding of text?*

Reading Workshop provides limitless possibilities for observant teachers to extend readers' understanding of literature. This can be accomplished during the read-aloud when teachers use open-ended questions to stimulate whole-group discussions. Teachers may also use nonverbal gestures such as nods and smiles and make encouraging comments to support students as they elaborate their views. Teacher may also use authors' craft mini-lessons to give students the skills to analyze texts more carefully.

LINKING THEORY TO PRACTICE

1. With a group of colleagues, talk about classroom teachers you have observed. Did you or your colleagues observe reading instruction? Did the teachers use read-alouds or shared books? Did they conduct mini-lessons? Did you see students conducting literature study groups? How did the teachers structure time for reading instruction?

2. Conduct an oral reading activity using one or more of the modeled reading strategies (See Figure 8.2 Modeled Reading Strategies). Identify an age-appropriate poem and prepare an enlarged, chart-sized version to share with a group of primary students. Write a mini-lesson (see Figure 8.9, Types of Mini-Lessons, Procedures, Authors Craft, and Skills). How did the children respond to the different types of modeled reading strategies?

3. Interview a teacher about grouping practices for reading instruction. How does this teacher determine his or her students' reading abilities? Does this teacher use a running record or a similar reading inventory to evaluate a students' independent and instructional reading levels? How often does the teacher assess student progress? Does the teacher use homogeneous and heterogeneous group strategies?

4. Tape yourself conducting a read-aloud to a small group of elementary students. Develop a list of open-ended questions. Observe the tape. Were you successful in involving all the students? Did you redirect the student responses to other students? Did you use nonverbal actions to encourage students to share their views? What did you learn from this experience?

Appendix A

Children's Literature Listed in Text

Cleary, B. *Beezus and ramona.* Scholastic, 1955.
Coerr, E. *Sadako and the thousand paper cranes.* Dell, 1977.
de Paola, T. *Nana upstairs & nana downstairs.* Putnam's Sons, 1973.
Flournoy, V. *The patchwork quilt.* Penguin, 1985.
Galdone, P. *The teeny-tiny woman.* Clarion, 1984.
Greene, C. *The thirteen days of halloween.* Children's Press, 1983.
MacDonald, B. *Mrs. piggle-wiggle's farm.* Lippincott, 1954.
Reid-Banks, L. *Indian in the cupboard.* Doubleday, 1980.
Schwartz, A. *Scary stories to tell in the dark.* Harper & Row, 1981.
Wilder, L. I. *On the banks of plum creek.* Harper & Row, 1937.
Wilder, L. I. *Little house in the big woods.* Scholastic, 1953.
Zindel, P. *The pigman.* Bantam Starfire Book, 1968.

Appendix B

Harriet Tubman Literature and the Underground Railroad Book List

Whole Class Readings

The Story of Harriet Tubman, Conductor of the Underground Railroad, by Kate McMullan, Bantam Doubleday Dell, 1991
Breaking the Chains by William Loren Katz (pages 77, 97, 98), Aladdin, 1990.

Reading Groups–Chapter Books (level 3–6)

Meet Addy an American Girl, by Connie Porter, Pleasant Company, 1993.
Sweet Clara and the Freedom Quilt, by Deborah Hopkinson, Dragonfly, 1993.
Harriet Tubman, by George Sullivan, Scholastic, 2001.
Night John, by Gary Paulsen, Bantam Doubleday Dell, 1993.
Sarny: A Life Remembered, by Gary Paulsen, Bantam Doubleday Day, 1997.

Choice Books (level 2–6)

If You Lived at the Time of the Civil War, by Kay Moore, Scholastic, 1994.
Minty: A Story of Young Harriet Tubman, by Alan Schroeder, Dial, 1996.
Harriet and the Promised Land, by Jacob Lawrence, Simon & Schuster, 1993.
Aunt Harriet's Underground Railroad in the Sky, by Faith Ringgold, Crown, 1992.
Follow the Drinking Gourd, by Jeanette Winter, Dragonfly, 1988.
Pink and Say, by Patricia Polacco, Philomel, 1994.
Working Cotton, by Sherely Anne Williams, Scholastic, 1992
John Henry, by Julius Lester, Scholastic, 1994.
Honest Abe, by Edith Kunhardt, Mulberry, 1998.
Abe Lincoln Remembers, by Ann Turner, HarperCollins, 2001.
Grace's Letter to Lincoln, by Peter and Connie Roop, Scholastic, 1998.
The Gettysburg Address, by Abraham Lincoln, Scholastic, 1995.
The Wagon, by Tony Johnson, Tambourine, 1996.
I Have a Dream, by Martin Luther King, Jr., Scholastic, 1999.
My Dream of Martin Luther King, by Faith Ringgold, Dragonfly, 1995.
Marching to Freedom: The Story of Martin Luther King, Jr., by Joyce Milton, Bantam Doubleday Dell 1987.
The Story of Ruby Bridges, by Robert Coles, Scholastic, 1995.

9 Teaching Writing the Workshop Way

Writing and writers are important in Deirdra Aikens's classroom. Ms. Aikens invites her students to join her on the rug for a writing lesson. She begins with "I know you've been waiting for this! I'm going to reveal the next great beginning. Ta-dah!!" She uncovers the next great beginning statement on the Great Beginnings *chart and reads:*

Setting the Mood/Creating the Setting

Example: It was a deep, dark, snowy Christmas Eve and presents were under the tree.
  Referring to the example, she says, "Where do you see it happening?" The children respond. "What could come after that?" Again, the children respond. "I've pulled together some beginnings from three of our favorite books. I really like how these authors started their pieces by setting the mood and creating an image of the setting. I'll read each beginning. You tell me where you see the story happening and how it feels." With that, she reads the opening sentence of Tar Beach *by Faith Ringgold. "What did you see when you heard this sentence?" The children offer responses about the image the sentence created in their minds. Ms. Aikens accepts their answers and then shows the illustration that accompanies the sentence. "Was the picture in your head like the image created by the illustrator?" She moves on and repeats the process with the two other stories. "This is a different kind of beginning, isn't it—different from the other beginnings on our list? When you go back to your writing folders today, take a look at an old piece. Could using this kind of beginning make one of your old pieces better? If you start a new piece, think about using this kind of a beginning. Will this beginning work in all pieces?" The children respond with 'no' in unison. "Of course not! You've got to think like a writer and make decisions about which kind of beginning to use. Team leaders, please get the writing folders out. Green folder writers, let's do a quick status-of-the-class." Ms. Aikens calls on each green folder writer, gets a response ("start a new piece," "edit my piece"), and sends the writers off to write. The writing lesson is over.*
  Writers return to their desks where their writing folders have been placed. Some sit in their seat. Others move to be near a friend. One child selects the sharing chair as her writing place. In less than two minutes, all writers are writing. Children talk with each other while they write. Ms. Aikens begins a conference with a red folder writer; Monday is red folder writers' teacher–student conference day. Too quickly writing time ends and the children return their bulging folders by color group to the hanging file, all except the blue folder writers.
  Blue folder writers share today. A blue folder writer sits in the "sharing chair." His team leader stands beside him. The writer reads his piece. The team leader calls on a child to summarize. A child responds, and then several children and Ms. Aikens offer their comments. The team leader calls on another child to praise the author. The child responds, and then several children offer specific examples of what they like about the piece. The team leader calls on another child to

question the author. The child responds, and then other children and Ms. Aikens state their questions. The team leaders calls on a child to offer a suggestion. This child responds, and then another child offers his suggestion. Writing workshop is over.

This is Writing Workshop as it happens in Ms. Aikens's classroom every day for forty-five minutes. During Writing Workshop, the children are using the writing process, the same process used by young and old writers. Some children are prewriting. Some are looking off into space to discover what they know enough about to write about. Some immediately begin writing; they seem not to know what they have to say until they see the words appear on the paper. Some look at the list of topics they made for days like this, days when they need an idea about what to write about. Others are making a graphic organizer or a list. Other children are writing their "sloppy copy" or first draft. While they write, they pause to read and reread what they wrote. Still other children cross out words; they draw arrows to shift the position of sentences. These children are revising. They change the spelling of a word. These children are editing. Finally, other children are recopying their revised and edited piece; they are publishing or doing their final draft. These children are using the writing process to write their ideas.

These children know what it means to be a writer.

Before You Read This Chapter, Think About . . .

- yourself as a writer. How do you prewrite? Do you make an outline or a graphic organizer, or mull your thoughts over in your mind for several days, or just begin writing? Do you have a favorite writing tool, like a special pen or the computer? Do you make lots of revisions while you write? Do you edit while you write?
- writing instruction in your elementary school years. Did you write about topics of your choice? Did you share your writing with your peers? Did your teacher confer with you about your writing? Did you publish your writing?
- the kinds of writing you did in your elementary school years. Did you write stories? Did you write research reports? Did you write persuasive essays?
- how your writing was graded. Did your teacher write congratulatory words like "Good job!" or use a rubric to give you specific feedback about how effectively you used various writing traits, or put a grade on your paper? Did your teacher encourage you to self-assess your writing?

Focus Questions

- What are the essentials of writing workshop?
- What are the three or four components of writing workshop?
- How do teachers teach during writing workshop?
- What kinds of lessons might teachers teach during writing workshop?
- What is the structure of a writing conference?
- How might teachers assess their students' writing development?

BOX **9.1**
Definition of Terms

analytical scoring: scoring each key component of a piece of writing, trait-by-trait (organization, development or ideas, sentence variety, voice, mechanics).

conference: conversation between a teacher and a student, or between or among peers, about a piece of writing.

criteria: language used to describe how the writing traits look at various performance levels.

editing: correcting mechanical errors in writing, such as spelling, punctuation, and grammar.

focus lesson: whole-class lessons on writing that typically occur at the beginning of writing workshop.

holistic scoring: scoring by considering how all the qualities of the writing (organization, ideas or development, voice, mechanics) work together to achieve an overall effect. Scorers judge the piece based on their general impression of the piece.

primary trait scoring: scoring based on the degree of presence of the primary, or most important, traits within the piece of writing. The primary traits vary by purpose (to persuade, to express, to inform) and audience.

revising: making changes (adding, moving, deleting) in the content of a writing piece.

rubric: criteria that describe student performance at various levels of proficiency.

trait: qualities of writing (ideas, organization, voice).

writing process: the recursive behaviors all writers, regardless of age, engage in (prewriting, writing or drafting, revising, editing, final draft or publishing).

writing workshop: a time in the schedule when all children meet to study the art and craft of writing.

The Essentials of Writing Workshop

"Writing Workshop" was first described by Donald Graves (1983) in his book *Writing: Teachers and Children at Work.* During the writing workshop, all members of the shop meet to intensively study the art and craft of writing. Before the class members gather to study this craft, however, the teacher has many preparations to make.

Find Time for the Children to Write

Children need a block of time to write. More than a decade ago, Donald Graves (1983) and Lucy Calkins (1983) recommended that teachers provide at least three, though five would be better, writing workshops each week, with each workshop lasting from 45 to 60 minutes. Regular, frequent times for writing are required to help children develop as writers. As Lucy Calkins (1994) suggests, when children know to expect the writing workshop, they begin to rehearse their writing ideas between workshops. They come to school with ideas for topics and text construction. Katie Wood Ray (2001) says it like this:

> It takes lots and lots of time over the course of years for writers to get the experience they need to become good writers. Along the way, writers need time to just write and write—a lot

of it won't be very good, but all of it gives writers experience. . . . When it comes to TIME, quantity is what matters. (pp. 9–10)

Some teachers groan, "*Where* can I find time in my already overloaded daily schedule? There is no room for yet another activity!" Ralph Fletcher and JoAnn Portalupi (2001) suggest that, if the schedule is truly full then teachers need to figure out what activities writing workshop could replace. Instead of teaching punctuation, capitalization, spelling, or handwriting as separate subjects, these teachers could use the time previously devoted to these language arts skills for writing workshop. These teachers will see their students gaining competence in these mechanical skills because their students will be using the skills over and over as they construct texts for different purposes and audiences. In addition, in writing workshop teachers will see their students listening, speaking, and reading. Here all the language arts are integrated into one meaningful, purposeful activity—writing.

Arrange the Classroom Environment For Talk

Writing is a social act. Children want to share their writing with peers, to know what their peers are writing, to ask for assistance with the construction of their text. Knowing this, writing-workshop teachers cluster children at tables or at desks that have been moved together. Most writing and *conferring* (talking with peers about writing) occurs among the children in these clusters. This talk is not just any kind of talk. It's talk about the writers' texts. Writers need listeners who stop their writing, listen intently, and say, "Oh, your description of your dog is really good" or "Your characters' talk, your dialogue? Well, it sounds just like what teenagers would say" or "Hmmm . . . I don't get it. I'm confused here."

Sometimes, however, this talk interferes with a writer's writing. For these occasions, teachers designate a table or an area of the classroom where children who need privacy and quiet can go to write. Also, there are days when some children find their desk or table confining; feel like stretching out on the floor to write . . . under a table . . . with a friend.

In addition to providing places to write privately and collaboratively, writing-workshop classrooms need an area where all the writers can gather to share their drafts and their finished pieces. This area needs a special chair for the sharing author (see Trade Secret 6.2). This chair might be a rocker, perhaps outgrown by the teacher's own children or purchased at a yard sale, or it might be a stuffed chair, perhaps borrowed from the teacher's or a student's home. Regardless of its form and origin, this chair comes to hold special meaning for the children. It is *the* place the authors sit to read their pieces to their fellow writers, to receive comments and questions about the content of their pieces.

Gather the Needed Materials

Like younger children, elementary-school-aged children need materials to support their writing efforts. Return to page 162 in Chapter 6 to review the list of materials needed to support our youngest writers' writing efforts. Elementary-aged students also need many different kinds of paper (add stationery and envelopes to the list on page 162), various writing tools, writing folders, and a box or file drawer in which to store their writing fold-ers. These students will need two writing folders with pockets, one for "Works-in-Progress" and one for "Completed Works" (see Figure 9.1 for suggestions on the use of the inside covers of the "Works in Progress" folders). These students also need samples of dif-ferent writers' work on a bulletin board, posters, clipboards, and mailboxes. In addition to these items, elementary-aged students need

- tools for revising their writing (e.g., scissors, tape, staples, staplers, correction fluid, glue sticks, paper clips, gum-backed paper, sticky notes, highlighters);
- writer's notebooks for recording special language heard or read that they may want to use in their writing or ideas thought of when they are not writing);
- materials for bookmaking (e.g., construction paper or wallpaper or poster board for making book covers, colored paper in various sizes, a long-reach stapler for binding, clear plastic covers with colored plastic spines);
- reference materials (e.g., dictionaries, thesauri, spelling books and electronic spell-masters, style handbooks); and
- teacher-made charts to guide their writing efforts (see Figure 9.2 for copies of several of the charts that hang in Dierdra Aikens's classroom writing center).

Determining how to make effective use of the classroom's computers is an even greater challenge for teachers of older children than it is for teachers of younger children. Older children's writing pieces are longer and, consequently, it takes longer to compose a first draft, revise, edit, and create a final draft. Older children tend to make more changes in their writing; they need computer time to make these revisions. Some teachers assign a group of children to the computers. When this group completes its writing, another group begins using the computers. While some children write with paper and pencils, others write with the computer. Some teachers connect the writing with the word processors with a par-ticular kind of writing, such as a research report. When all the children have completed their research reports, a new kind of writing will be introduced, and all children will again have a turn with the word processor. Many teachers respond to their students' cries for more time at the word processor by permitting them access before school, during class meetings, during recess, and whenever else time permits. The effect is that writing begins to pervade the school day. Very fortunate teachers and writers have word processors for every student or every two students. Readers might consider attempting to secure simple word processors, like Dreamwriters, for their students' use (http://www2.edc.org/NCIP/library/laptops/dreamwriters.htm). They might also want to visit Nancy Carnevale's Web site (http://copland.udel.edu/~ncarnev/) to learn about how she uses computers in her class-room to support her fifth graders' writing efforts and to discover some of her and her stu-dents' favorite Web sites.

Arrange the Materials.   Return to page 164 to look again at Figure 6.1. Like their col-leagues who teach younger children, some teachers of elementary-aged children (many of whom would prefer to be called "students") also typically place the classroom's shared writing materials in a writing center (or area). One difference is that elementary-school teachers tend not to put a table and chairs in their writing centers. Instead, they ask their stu-

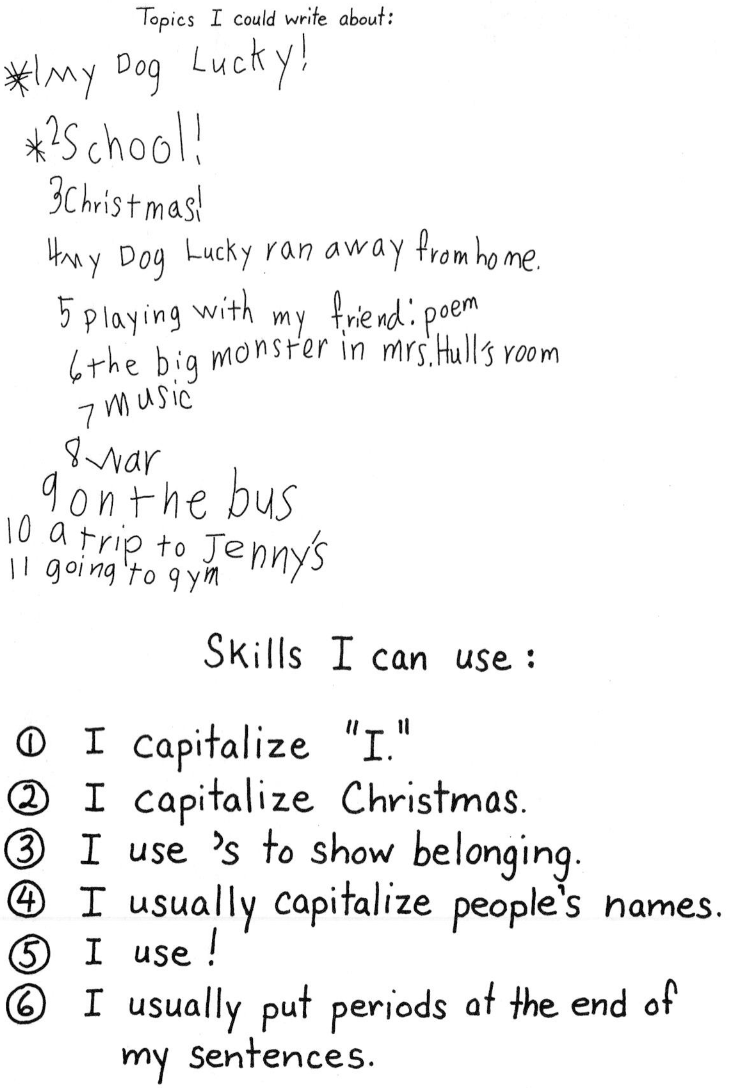

Topics I could write about:

*¹my Dog Lucky!

*²School!

3 Christmas!

4 my Dog Lucky ran away from home.

5 playing with my friend: poem

6 the big monster in mrs. Hull's room

7 music

8 war

9 on the bus

10 a trip to Jenny's

11 going to gym

Skills I can use:

① I capitalize "I."

② I capitalize Christmas.

③ I use 's to show belonging.

④ I usually capitalize people's names.

⑤ I use !

⑥ I usually put periods at the end of my sentences.

FIGURE 9.1   Use the inside covers of the "Work in Progress" folders to record valuable information.

dents to collect the materials they need from the writing center and to use them at their table or desk. Because people are known to forget to return borrowed items to their appropriate storage places, we strongly recommend that teachers create an inventory of the shared writing materials, post the inventory in the writing center, and assign a student to the task of checking the materials in the area against the inventory following each writing workshop. Other teachers of elementary-aged students make a "tool chest" (a plastic container) of

Be Different!

Give a **RARE** Response

R = **Restate the question**

A = **Answer it!**

R = **Reasons! Reasons!**

E = **Examples! Examples!**

The Best Endings

1. Surprise Ending
2. Emotional Ending
3. Circular Ending
4. Express your Feelings

and the rest are covered. Ms. Aikens hasn't taught them yet

Editing #1

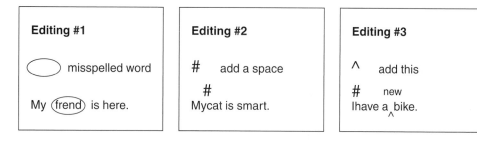

misspelled word

My (frend) is here.

Editing #2

\#   add a space

\#

Mycat is smart.

Editing #3

∧   add this

\#   new

Ihave a bike.

Editing #4

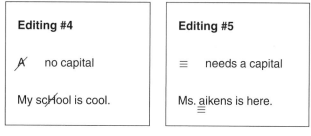

no capital

My scHool is cool.

Editing #5

≡   needs a capital

Ms. aikens is here.

Great Beginnings!

1. Question
    "Have you ever seen a cat?"
2. Arresting sentence
    "She stole my mom's present!"
3. Astonishing Fact
    The Sun is 93 million miles from earth.
4. Spoken Words
    "Daddy is coming home today, Ben."
5. Setting the Mood (setting)
    It was a deep, dark, snowy Christmas.

FIGURE 9.2   Examples of charts in Deirdra Aikens's writing center.

regularly needed writing supplies (pencils, pens, scissors, tape, stapler and staples, paper clips) for each grouping of desks or each table. Now, a student at each table or cluster of desks is responsible for ensuring that the shared supplies are returned to the "tool chest" and the tool chest is returned to the writing center at the end of writing workshop.

Teachers Who Teach Writing

> Teaching kids how to write is hard. That's because writing is not so much one skill as a *bundle* of skills that includes sequencing, spelling, rereading, and supporting big ideas with examples. But these skills are teachable.
>
> (Fletcher & Portalupi, 2001, p. 1)

Sometimes teachers say, "Oh, my kids write every day." Yes, writing every day is important. But writing every day isn't enough. Teachers need to *teach* writing every day. Teaching happens in several different ways. Teachers pull the whole class together to teach. Teachers pull groups of children who need the same information together and teach them in a small group. Teachers confer with their students and teach them one-on-one. Students confer with each other, teaching in small groups and one-on-one. The class comes together to respond to students' writings—and teach through their responses. The label given to this teaching and writing time is *writing workshop*. Teaching happens around a variety of topics. Teachers teach about where writers get ideas, about how to write great leads that make readers want to read more, about how to use telling details, about how to punctuate and capitalize correctly, about how to write different kinds of pieces for different purposes (letters to persuade, reports to inform, stories to entertain). In the following section, we detail how teachers teach writing during writing workshop.

The Components of the Writing Workshop

Nancie Atwell (1987) credits Donald Graves (1983) with helping her discover a structure that was successful with her students. Teachers across the nation (world, really) have adopted, and adapted, this structure. Each writing workshop has three or four components. While the components may be arranged differently on any given day, each writing workshop contains these components. In most classrooms, they happen in the following order:

Focus Lesson

In the early days of writing workshop, each session always began with a mini-lesson (a five- to ten-minute teacher presentation). Today, writing workshop experts are less concerned with the time factor, so they, like Katie Wood Ray (2001) and Regie Routman (1996), have shifted to calling the writing lesson a "focus lesson." Routman encourages teachers to call these lessons "focus lessons" because she believes the term *mini*-lesson trivializes the direct instruction that is so important in writing workshop. As Ralph Fletcher's and JoAnn Portalupi's (2001) new book verifies, the categories of these lessons remain the same (procedural, process, qualities of good writing, and mechanical skills), only the title has changed. The topics of these lessons are chosen based on the students' needs.

Writing Time

Students write while the teacher moves about the room conferring with the writers. Students might also confer with other students during writing time. While the teacher confers with students at the students' writing place, peer conferences might occur with those around the writer or two or more writers might move to a special section of the room.

Sharing

Each writing workshop ends with the students gathering together for a share. Here two or three children share their pieces of writing and receive feedback in the form of content-related questions and comments from their peers. Sharing might be done as a whole group, or in smaller groups, or in pairs.

Some teachers insert a **Status-of-the-Class Report** between the whole-group lesson and the children's writing time. During status-of-the-class, the teacher does a quick check of what each writer plans to do that day. Will the writer be beginning a draft of a new piece? editing a piece? making revisions to a piece based on peer feedback?

Some teachers have created other systems to check on their students' writing plans for the day. For example, some teachers ask children to report on their writing plans by attaching a clothes pin, one per student with the student's name on it, to a circular wheel depicting a combination of the writing process and the classroom writing workshop procedures (see Figure 9.3 for an example). Students move their clothes pins as they move from the whole-group focus lesson area to their table or desk to begin writing. Karen Bromley (1998) describes a different status-of-the-class procedure used by Karen Wassell. Ms. Wassel staples five library pockets to a bulletin board. Each pocket has the label of a stage in the writing process written on it (e.g., Planning, Drafting, Revising, Editing, and Publishing). Each child is given a popsicle stick with his or her name written on it. The students insert their sticks into the pocket that correctly describes their writing activity of the day.

How does the writing workshop work in a classroom? In Trade Secret 9.1 second-grade teacher Janice Medek describes how she uses this structure (focus lesson, writing time, sharing) in her classroom.

Ms. Medek's writing workshop structure and introduction is not unlike what Nancie Atwell (1987) described using with her older students. Ms. Medek's writing topic selections were chosen carefully. Because her young students have families, and many have pets they could write about, she suggested she might write about her own dog and about an experience with her daughter. She intentionally chose everyday activities, insignificant things in her life, to share as possible topics. She wants her students to realize that they, too, can write about the everyday things that happen to them. She wants the children to choose an aspect of their topics, so she described how she might write about her dog's antics while she is on the telephone or helping her daughter learn to throw and catch a ball. (Sports is another

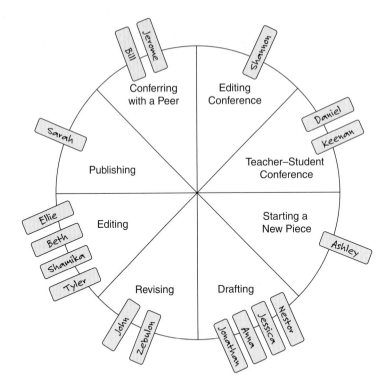

Clothes pins with Names

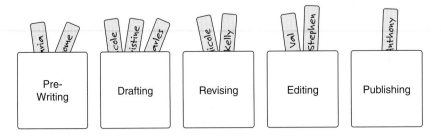

FIGURE 9.3   Status-of-the-Class Procedures

topic she knows is familiar to many of her students.) She wants them to write about things they know about—topics that they, as Donald Graves (1993) says, "have a passion for the truth" about (p. 2). For that reason, she modeled selecting and rejecting a topic that she does not know well enough to write about it. In each writing workshop, she follows this sequence: the lesson, writing, and then group sharing. In the following sections, each of the parts of the writing workshop is examined more closely.

Trade Secret 9.1

Getting Started: Writing Workshop in a Second-Grade Classroom

Janice Medek

I begin the writing workshop the second week of school. The first week, I lay the foundation for the writing workshop in several ways. First, I read several selections of high-quality literature to the children. With each reading, I give special attention to naming the author and the illustrator, to examining how the pictures relate to the print on the page, to discussing where the author may have gotten her or his idea for the book, to considering how the author began the book, and so forth. The author's literary techniques, as well as an understanding the message presented in the book, are the focus of our discussions. I tell the children they, too, can and will be authors. Second, I talk with the children about the writing workshop and the materials we will be using to write our pieces. I give them each a writing folder. We examine the materials in the writing center. We practice moving from the rug to the writing center to collect and return our folder. Third, I tell them the writing workshop rules or limits. My rules are

1. During the first five minutes of writing, there will be no talking.
2. Only writer's talk will be permitted during writing.
3. Confer with those around you.
4. Don't worry about spelling, and don't erase.
5. Put the date on everything you write.
6. Write on one side of the paper only, and skip every other line (when you use lined paper).

Now the children are ready for the writing workshop. However, because I (like Shelley Harwayne, in her book *Lasting Impressions*) see a strong relationship between hearing and reading high-quality literature and writing high-quality pieces, I continue a reading-aloud period just

before we move into the writing workshop. Then, I present a brief lesson, which is followed by the children writing and conferring, which is followed by a group share time.

On the first day of the writing workshop, I begin with a lesson showing the children how I go about selecting a writing topic. I come to school with three topics in mind. One usually has something to do with my dog, one usually has something to do with my daughter, and one has something to do with something I don't know much about. My presentation to the children goes something like this:

> Today we are all going to be authors! I've been thinking about what I might write about today. I was thinking that I might write about my dog. I really love her, but she does some things that make me angry. I thought I might write about what she does whenever I'm on the telephone. [I write "My Dog" on the board.] Or I might write about trying to teach my daughter to catch and throw a ball. We do lots of things together but I might write about just this one thing. We practiced and practiced, and then. . . . Well, I'll wait to tell you about what happened in my piece, if I decide to write about this. [I write "Catching and Throwing" on the board.] Or I've been hearing a lot about the problems in Afganistan. I think I might write about Afganistan. [I write "Afganistan" on the board.] Oh, but do I really know very much about Bosnia? I better leave that topic to someone who knows more about it than I do or until I find time to read more about what is happening there. [I cross Afganistan off my list.] What topics could you write about today? What do you know a lot about? [As the children call out topics, I list them on the board.] Wow! Look at all the topics you could write about! [I read through the list.] Which will you choose? Today, I'm going to choose to write about teaching my daughter to catch and throw. I

(continued on next page)

can't wait to get started, but I don't want to forget that I could write about my dog's antics. [I pick-up my folder. On the inside cover, I list "My Dog" under "Things I Might Write About."] You'll want to do that too. [Then, I call the children by name. They tell me their chosen topic, while I record their topics on my status-of-the-class report. They leave the rug and collect their folder to begin their writing. Of course, one or two need reminding about the procedures to be followed during the writing workshop.]

I write for the first five minutes, and then I begin conferring with the children. When children say, "I'm done, Mrs. Medek!" I say, "Fine. Reread your piece to be sure there isn't anything else you might write about your topic. If you have no more to say, start writing on another topic. This is writing time."

Soon it is time for the group share. I signal the children that I need their attention with my usual signal, a blink of the lights. Some children actually groan when it is time for them to stop writing. I invite two or three children who want to receive help from their peers to bring their piece to the rug. One child from each folder-color group collects his or her group's folders and returns them to the writing center. The remaining children come directly to the rug.

Then, I do a quick lesson on how to behave during group sharing time. I expect the children to be good listeners while a peer is reading, to raise their hand and be recognized by the author to speak, and to ask questions and make positive comments about the piece shared. With that, the first author shares, and the questions begin. I raise my hand and wait to be recognized just like the other listeners. I admit that if a child asks a particularly good question, I cannot resist saying something like, "Ohh, did everyone hear Jason's question? That was a really good question, Jason!" I tell myself that this signals the kind of questions that are helpful to writers.

Focus Lessons

Focus lessons are direct instruction lessons. (Yes, we said it; there is direct instruction in writing workshop.) Usually, these lessons are short. With the youngest students, they will rarely, if ever, be more than five to ten minutes long. Typically with older children these lessons will be about ten minutes in length, but occasionally they could be longer. When teacher Deanne McCredie plans to teach a longer lesson, she warns her students that the day's lesson will be a "mighty lesson."

The lessons are focused in three ways. First, they are focused on a specific need the teacher has determined the students' need. That is, a good focus lesson has a very clear objective. Katie Wood Ray (2001) points out that sometimes this objective is behavioral (the students should be able to do something after the lesson), and other times the objective is more cognitive (the students should have a better understanding of some aspect of writing after the lesson). Teachers' task, then, is to determine what their group of children need to help them make their writing better and to plan a lesson focused on this need. No one lesson can tell the writers everything they need to know about the topic. So, a cluster of lessons, say for a week's time, is focused on a particular need. For example, if the children need help adding rich, telling details to their pieces, the teacher would provide focused, direct, and brief instruction on this topic every day for a week. Each day's lesson would build on and extend the writers' knowledge of how to add rich, telling details. That's the second way the lessons are focused. The goal is to offer the writers pointers that they can consider as they construct their texts. Finally, a series of these lessons might be focused on the primary traits of a particular genre, like historical fiction, memoir, poetry, persuasive essay, or nonfiction. The primary traits of each of these genres is different; hence, the lessons (in addition to the students being immersed in reading quality pieces in each genre and engaging in the close study of the genre and several key authors of this genre) are aimed at helping children craft texts of their own in this genre. (An excellent resource for learning about genre study is the August 1999 issue of *Primary Voices K–6,* published by the National Council of Teachers of English. Here, readers will discover a year-long curriculum chart that details how a teacher focused on memoir, short story, revision, nonfiction, structures of texts, literary response, and more in her units of study and how other teachers tackled the teaching of various genres.)

Remember that the content of the lessons will be reinforced and reconsidered in other components of the writing workshop, particularly during the teacher–student conferences.

Regardless of grade level, topic selection is one of the first writing workshop minilessons. Using Medek's and Atwell's (1987, p. 76–83) topic-selection lessons as models will make the first day successful. What about all the days after the first day, though? Lessons for these days group themselves into four categories (procedural, craft or qualities of writing, writing process, and mechanical skills) as noted above.

Procedural lessons. The topic of many of these lessons is similar to what Ms. Medek presented to her students during their first week in school, before the writing workshop actually began. It is natural for many of the beginning-of-the-year lessons to be procedural lessons. These lessons help the children learn about the teacher's expectations for their behavior and about what they can expect from the teacher. In addition to the lessons suggested by Ms. Medek, other procedural lesson topics include discussions about conferences, editing, and publishing.

1. *Where and how to confer with peers*—Some teachers ask their students to confer with those peers seated around them. Others designate spots (e.g, in the library corner, behind the teacher's desk) in the room for conferring. The lesson might include information on (a) the volume of the voice permitted when conferring with peers; (b) the need to be kind and to remember that the piece belongs to its author, so revision decisions are the writer's; and (c) the type of questions listeners might ask of authors. Once peers begin conferring, the teacher is no longer the only teacher of writing in the classroom. Now there are 20 to 25 teacher assistants. A goal of this lesson is to alert the children to their awesome responsibility to be helpful to their fellow writers.

2. *How teacher–student content conferences will occur*—An important component of the teaching of writing is the teacher–student conferences about the content of the children's writing. These conferences will occur while the children are writing. The lesson should inform the children about two elements of teacher–student conferences. First, the lesson should describe how writers will be selected for teacher–student conferences. Teachers report that it works well for them to randomly select children for conferences and to go to the writer rather than having the writer come to them. By going to the children, teachers can control the length of the conference. Atwell (1987) describes how she carried a child-sized chair and zigzagged about the room randomly selecting children with whom to confer. By intentionally moving from one side of the classroom to the other, she was able to monitor all the children's behavior.

Second, the lesson should inform the children about the teacher's and the children's roles during the conference. The children should know that the teacher will be an attentive listener, an audience genuinely interested in learning about the topics they have chosen; that they will be asked to read their piece to the teacher; that the teacher will be asking questions to learn more about their topic and proposing suggestions for their consideration; and that the conferences will be short (two to three minutes) so that they can get back to their writing. It helps the children understand the procedures when the teacher models a teacher–student conference during the lesson.

3. *Classroom editing procedures*—Pieces that are to be published must be edited prior to publication. Writers edit by searching for the mechanical errors in their pieces and attempting to correct them. Directions on how to edit pieces and what will occur during the teacher–student editing conference should be presented in a mini-lesson. (Readers are referred to the description of one teacher's procedure on pages 321–322.) Teachers will want to wait to present this lesson until some of the children are ready to publish their first piece.

4. *How publishing will be done in the classroom*—Publishing includes preparation of the pieces for others to read. It is an important component of the writing process because most writing is meant to be read by an audience. There are many ways to publish children's writings. One teacher of young children asked each student to bring a clear, plastic 8 ½" × 11" frame to school. (Of course, she purchased frames for those children whose parents could not provide frames.) Her children published their work by mounting their selected pieces in their frames. The frames hung on the back wall of the classroom on the "Wall of Fame." A teacher of older children purchased plastic covers with colored spines from a discount store. Her students published by mounting their pieces in these covers. JoAnne Deshon's third graders publish their writing in books. Many other ideas are suggested in Sandra Brady's (1992) book, *Let's Make Books.*

Besides making books, teachers might consider making a class newspaper or magazine. Perhaps some pieces will be appropriate for submission to magazines with a broader circulation than the classroom. In Trade Secret 9.2, we provide information about the submission interests of various children's magazines. In addition, specific kinds of writing dictate publication in culturally defined ways (e.g., business letters, personal letters, invitations, thank-you notes). Each new way to publish means that the teacher must provide a lesson describing and illustrating the procedure for the children.

Craft or Qualities of Good Writing Lessons.   This second kind of lesson should make up the majority of the lessons presented during the year. These are the lessons about what Shelley Harwayne (1992) calls the "power of language." These are lessons about the content of the children's pieces and about what makes writing good.

Teachers of writing—such as William Zinsser, Donald Murray, and Ralph Fletcher—and pieces of good children's literature are the best sources for ideas for these kinds of mini-lessons. From Zinsser (1998), teachers have gathered ideas such as these. Leads must suck readers into the piece and make them want to read on; select a *corner* (a small and interest-

Trade Secret 9.2

Magazines That Accept Children's Work

Ellen Fanjoy

Bear Essential News for Kids. 2406 S. 24 Street, Phoenix, AZ 85034. (Gr. Pre K–7). Distributed without charge to children in Arizona, California, and Georgia. Publishes all types of children's creative writing.

Chickadee. P.O. Box 11314, Des Moines, IA 50340. Children's work: Great Arrow Avenue, Buffalo, NY 14207. (Gr. Pre-K–3). Publishes children's drawings on specific themes.

Creative Kids. Children's work: P.O. Box 6448, Mobile, AL 36660. (Gr. K–12). This award-winning magazine presents stories, poetry, limericks, activities, reviews, crafts, artwork, music, cartoons, puzzles, and photography by kids for kids. Its purpose is to encourage students to strive to produce work that is good enough to publish.

Highlights for Children. P.O. Box 269, Columbus, OH 43272-0002. Children's work: Hones-

dale, PA 18431. (Gr. Pre-K–6). Publishes children's letters and original drawings, poetry, and stories. Accepts jokes and riddles selected by readers.

Jack and Jill. Children's work: 1100 Waterway Boulevard, P.O. Box 567, Indianapolis, IN 46206. (Gr. 1–4). Publishes children's poetry, jokes, health questions, and artwork.

Zillions. Children's work: 256 Washington Street, Mount Vernon, NY 10553. Publishes children's questions for a child psychiatrist and letters.

Sports Illustrated for Kids. Children's work: Time and Life Building, New York, NY 10020. (Gr. 3–7). Publishes children's letters, poems, jokes, and drawings.

Stone Soup. Children's work: Children's Art Foundation, P.O. Box 83, Santa Cruz, CA 95063. (Gr. 1–8). A literary magazine of students' stories, poems, artwork, and book reviews. Contains information for contributors in each issue.

ing aspect) of the subject, and focus on it; give the last sentence a special twist, and make it a surprise; use action verbs; eliminate clutter; watch the use of adjectives. From Murray (1990), they have learned about choosing vivid, precise descriptive words; about describing the sights, sounds, and smells so that readers will be put into the scene; about using dialogue to enliven the piece; and about writing in the present tense. From Fletcher (1993), teachers have learned about the art of writing with specificity, creating a character, writing with voice, creating dramatic leads, using various kinds of endings, creating tension in pieces, designing the setting, focusing, and choosing the best language.

In addition to these teachers of writing, a growing number of authors are providing accounts of their writing process. For example, Stephen King (2000), in *On Writing*, describes his writing process. In explaining the *why* of his books, King says, "many of us [popular novelists] care about the language, in our humble way, and care passionately about the art and craft of telling stories on paper. What follows is an attempt to put down, briefly and simply, how I came to the craft, what I know about it now, and how it's done" (p. 9). From King, teachers can learn about what writers need in their "toolbox': qualities of writing like don't use long words just because you are a little ashamed of your short words, begin with the situations and then develop the characters, if you want to be a writer read a lot, and don't be afraid to imitate your favorite authors.

To present these ideas to their students, teachers typically use their own writing or children's literature to illustrate the point. For example, Maryanne Lamont, a first-grade teacher, noticed that her children were writing unfocused pieces. To help her young writers think about how to select a corner on a topic, she prepared a lesson using pieces she wrote to illustrate her point. Ms. Lamont's lesson plan is presented in Trade Secret 9.3. Ms. Lamont fussed about writing something on her students' level, in a sense an artificial piece, to illustrate the use of focus. Unfortunately, however, her lessons showing how to draw a map of a writing plan and illustrating how children's literature authors focus their writing on a corner of their topic did not help her children focus their own writing. (A point to remember is that many topics will need to be revisited and presented using various kinds of materials.) Later, she discovered what Harwayne (1992) reports having discovered: Young writers are good at discovering what is wrong with poor writing when the good and the poor are placed side-by-side. For that reason, she wrote a good and a poor piece, to use side-by-side in her lesson.

Does Ms. Lamont's lesson "show" as Katie Wood Ray (2001) says teachers should during a lesson? Ms. Ray suggests that a lesson can *show* by

- providing advice from a professional writer that explains some process of writing;
- illustrating with an example from a published text, a piece of student writing, or a piece of teacher writing that shows how some crafting technique works;
- reporting on the conversation of a teacher–student conference with one student that will help the other students;
- illustrating through having the teacher write during the lesson (on the spot); or
- using a story or metaphor to help students understand the point of the lesson (2001, p. 147).

Who does most of the talking, the students or the teacher? Typically, the teacher will do most of the talking. The teacher will draw the students into the lesson by using their names or asking them for their advice. The key, however, will be to stay focused in order to be brief so that the students have time to write. Will the students ever try something out, "have-a-go," during a lesson? Certainly, they can (and they often do in Deanne McCredie's mighty lessons), but remember that they are working on a piece of their own writing. Notice how Ms. Lamont ended her lesson. She made the connection between the topic of her lesson and their writing; she told her young writers to "have-a-go" with their writing. So, there was a try-it-out time, a practice time, later.

Do children really come to understand the qualities of good writing from such illustrations, using teacher's writing or children's literature? Harwayne (1992, p. 278) suggests that teachers reconsider the use of a sequence of lessons, such as one day teaching of "telling details, the next [of] good leads, [the following] of fresh language, [and another of] lots of showing, not telling." She suggests that children do not learn about the qualities of good writing with quick, even dynamic, teacher mini-lesson presentations. Some lessons might, as Deanne McCredie says, actually be "mighty lessons," involving the teacher and students investigating in an interactive way how various authors, including the students, craft their writing or how a trait is used in a specific genre.

Trade Secret 9.3

Selecting a Corner of the Topic: Writing Pieces with a Focus
Maryanne Lamont

"It is important for authors to choose topics that they know a lot about. It is also important for authors to write about one part of their topic. Today I need your help with a piece I've been working on. It's a piece about school. I know a lot about school! This is the first piece I wrote last night. The title of my piece is *All About School*.

> School is fun.
> We read books.
> We have three recesses.
> We make books.
> We do math.
> We eat lunch in the cafeteria.
> Our principal is Mr. Householder.
> I like school.

"When I read it over, I thought, 'Wow, I wrote about a lot of things that we do in school but I didn't really write an interesting piece because my topic was just too big. I just have one sentence about each thing I mentioned.' I decided that I needed to revise my writing. The first thing I had to do was choose one of these things to write about. Hmmm. Should I write about the cafeteria? I knew I could write about any of these things. I decided to write about recess because I had been thinking about something that happened last year on the playground."

"Listen to my revised piece. Its title is 'An Accident on the Playground':

It was Monday morning. Mrs. Jones and I had recess duty. I was watching the children on the swings. Suddenly, I heard a scream! I turned around and saw Jimmy slip and fall off the monkey bars. I raced over to see if he was alright. He was crying and couldn't move his arm. All the children came rushing over to see what had happened. Jimmy's arm really hurt. I sent John in to get the nurse. When the nurse came out and looked at Jimmy's arm, she discovered that it was broken. She took Jimmy to her office and called his mother. Jimmy's mother came to school to pick him up. She had to take him to the hospital to get a cast on his arm. When Jimmy came to school the next day, he let everyone sign his cast.

"What do you think? Does the second one tell you a lot about just one thing that happened in school—about one adventure on the playground? Do you know what happened to Jimmy? I think I'm happier with this piece. I'll keep working on it."

"When you work on your writing today, read it over and decide whether you chose a giant topic or if you focused your topic. If you chose a giant topic, think about what you might do to focus on one part of your topic. When we come together for sharing time, I'll be asking some of you to show us how you decided to focus in on one aspect of your topic. Perhaps you could read us your piece and your revised piece to help us see how your writing is different."

In writing-workshop classrooms, the serious study of authors' literary techniques begins to pervade the children's interactions with text. The qualities of good literature begin to be considered not only during the lessons before the children's writing but also when the teacher shares literature with the students and when the children engage in conversations about pieces they have read. The result is seamless reading and writing instruction—writers becoming better readers by writing, and readers becoming better writers by reading. As Harwayne says, "[While] there is no one way to run a writing workshop, . . . [high-]quality texts are nonnegotiable" (p. 337). How right she is! The teaching of writing occurs every time the teacher and the students engage in honest discussions about literature. Lessons on the qualities of good writing then serve to highlight the points garnered from these authentic interactive literary discussions.

Ralph Fletcher and JoAnn Portalupi know that teachers can sometimes use help creating their focus lessons. So few teachers had good writing instruction when they were in school; most teachers don't have a lot to draw on when they start to think about the teaching of writing. Their first book, *Craft Lessons* (1998), contains numerous lessons on the qualities of good writing, arranged by grade cluster (K–2, 3–4, and 5–8). Their goal in writing their most recent book, *Nonfiction Craft Lessons: Teaching Information Writing K–8* (2001), was to help teachers teach "the kind of writing that draws less on students' stories, memories, and histories, and more on the concrete 'out there' world" (p. 2). They know that teachers must teach their students how to write good informative pieces because this kind of writing is crucial to students as a tool to learn about the world around them.

Writing Process Lessons.   Writers engage in several behaviors as they write. When writers are asked to describe their writing process, writers speak about where they get their ideas, how they draft their pieces (e.g., how many drafts they actually write; whether they use typewriter, longhand, or computer; where they write), how they revise, and how their pieces are published. Writers make it clear that the process of writing is **not** a linear process. It is not even safe to suggest that writers begin with an idea because, as Peter Elbow (1973) suggests, some writers begin by writing and discover their idea through their writing. Similarly, it is not safe to suggest that writing ends in publication. Not all pieces written are worthy of publication; many die in the drafting stage. Hence, in lessons on the writing process, teachers want to show their writers the **behaviors** of writers, to make visible a process that is mostly invisible.

Some teachers find it helpful to children to share writers' descriptions of their writing process. Helpful resources include books such as *Worlds of Childhood: The Art and Craft of Writing for Children* by William Zinsser (1990) and *How Writers Write* by Pam Lloyd (1987). Some teachers share the videotapes produced by Houghton-Mifflin/Clarion (n.d.), showing the writing process as described by various well-known children's book authors (e.g., *A Visit with Russell Freedman*). *Booklinks*, a magazine published by the American Library Association, regularly contains author interview articles. In addition, teachers and students can access interviews, even sometimes participate in live interactions with authors, through the writers' or the writers' publishers' Web sites. For example, Scholastic (http://teachers.scholastic.com/writewith) advertises that teachers and students can meet their favorite authors and discover new ones through live interviews, classroom activities, and author profiles. Other teachers invite local authors into the classroom to write with the children. This has the advantage of making an author come alive for the children.

In addition to descriptions of writers' writing behaviors, children need to be shown the *how* of revision: how to cut and paste, how and where to insert new information, and how to use a rough draft to inform the writer of the changes needed in a second draft. Typically, children interact with other authors' final drafts, with published pieces. Hence, it is not surprising that they do not know revision procedures. Therefore, children need lessons describing how to revise, implementing the results of their reconsiderations in their texts.

Mechanical Skills Lessons. Finally, there are the lessons about punctuation, grammar, usage, handwriting, capitalization, and spelling—the conventions of language. Various sources can inform the teacher of which mechanical skill lessons need to be presented. As with all lessons, the best source is the children's writing. What conventions do children need to use, which they are not using correctly? They use dialogue, but is it incorrectly punctuated and capitalized, and there are no quotation marks? If so, the topic of at least one lesson is clear. Often, school districts have identified specific mechanical competencies that are to be covered at each grade level. Teaching these skills in lessons and then incorporating them into the editing stage of the writing process provides children with many practice opportunities. In districts where a language arts textbook is issued, teachers often examine the textbook to discover the mechanical skills they are responsible for ensuring their students encounter. These skills are then taught through the lessons and reinforced as a part of the editing process in much the same way as the district-specified competencies were taught. Even when district competencies or a textbook are used as sources for mechanical-skill topic suggestions, teachers teach the skill *when their students' writing indicates a need for that skill* rather than following the order in which the skills are presented in the textbook or on the competency list. When students have a reason to learn particular skills, and when the skills are taught in a meaningful context, children learn the skills much more quickly.

As with other kinds of lessons, the content of mechanical-skills lessons may need to be repeated in order for children's learning to occur. One mechanical-skills lesson, how to write using your best guess of how to spell each word, for example, may need to be repeated often—particularly with kindergarten and first-grade children. Teachers of older children will want to present a similar lesson to their students, though their reason will be different. These teachers want their writers to use the words in their oral vocabulary in their writings. Hence, they need to convince their students that spelling every word correctly is *not* important in their rough drafts and to show them how to spell the words the best they can so that they can read them later. After all, the students are the only persons reading their rough drafts.

Status-of-the-Class Report

When teachers use a status-of-the-class report following a lesson, they make the transition to the writing portion of the writing workshop by asking the children, "What are you planning to do today?" or "What will you be working on today?" These teacher records the children's responses on a status-of-the-class form such as the one presented in Figure 9.4.

This record provides the teacher with valuable information. First, it provides clues about which children might need a teacher–student conference. Children who seem unsure of their plans need to be seen first in order to provide support to help them proceed with the writing challenge. Children who are struggling to make their pieces say what they want them to say may need the teacher's assistance as soon as possible. Second, it informs the teacher of where the writers are in the writing process. Who is beginning a new piece? Who is publishing a piece? Who is continuing to write on a topic? Looking over several days provides a snapshot of each writer's behavior during the writing workshop.

The status-of-the-class report also provides writers with valuable information. Hearing what colleagues are doing helps to inform them about appropriate writing-workshop

STATUS-OF-THE-CLASS					
NAME	M	T	W	R	F
Alex	I	C	I		I New
Atiah	I C	I	I	S C	RV
Brandi	I	I	I C	RV C	RV
Brandy	I	C	I	S	RV
Brent	I C	I	I	I	RV
Brian	I	C	PR	P	P
Carly	2	ab	I	C	RV
Chase	I	C	I	PC	E
Christian	I	C	PR	S PR	CP
Constance	I	ab	C	I	RV C
Darren	ab	I	2	I C	I
Kara	2	I	S RV	E	P
Jessica	I C	RV	2	C	E
Kate	I C	I	2	S PR	E
Kate F.	I	I	I C	I	2
Jamie	2	C	RV	I New	I C
Julie	I	I	I C	RV	S
LaTeisha	I	2	I C	RV	RV
Lyle	2 C	I	I	2	RV
Rolandre	I C	I	I S	RV	S
Sherri	2 S	I	I	S RV	P
Stephan	I	C	RV S	RV	RV

Code: 1 - First Draft   RV - Revising
              2 - Second Draft E - Editing
              C - Conference   P - Publishing
                                  S - Sharing

FIGURE 9.4   **Status-of-the-class report.**

behaviors and gives them the vocabulary to describe their own writing activities. Hearing colleagues' writing topics often results in another child saying something such as, "Oh, I'm going to write about my birthday party!" In addition, there is the value of the status-of-the-class report as a transitional activity from the group lesson meeting on the rug to the collecting of the works-in-progress writing folder in the writing center to beginning writing at a desk or on the floor. If all children were dismissed from the rug simultaneously, chaos could ensue in the writing center.

Writing Time

As the children move from the status-of-the-class report to writing, many teachers require five minutes of silent writing before peer and teacher–student conferences begin. Like the status-of-the-class report, this five-minute period serves as a transition from the noise of children moving about the room to the seriousness of the writing task. Writers need time to reread yesterday's writing or to rehearse today's topic in their minds before writing or to get started writing in order to learn what is known about a topic. Many teachers also use this time to write themselves, thus providing themselves as a model of a writer for their children.

The teacher who looks around the classroom during this component of the writing workshop will observe writers engaged in various aspects of the writing process. Some children will be selecting new topics, so they will be thinking, talking (after the five-minute period of silence), writing, or observing. Others will be writing—with pauses to reread what they have written, to reconsider their topic, or to confer with the teacher or a colleague about the topic or the text. Others will be editing pieces in preparation for publication. Others will be publishing. In each writing workshop, young writers will be engaged in the writing behaviors of all writers. The only difference will be the physical size and the experience of these writers.

Teacher–Student Conferences. The opportunity to talk while writing is a critically important component of the writing workshop. Through interactions with others, children come to understand the needs of their audience. Because writers write about things they know about, they make decisions about what information to include from their knowledgeable perspective. In sharing a draft with an audience, writers sometimes come to understand what information is needed to make their topic clear to an audience, or they watch the glazed look in their listeners' eyes and realize that too much detail has been provided, or they recognize the need to rearrange the information.

From Carl Anderson's (2000) perspective, conferences are *conversations.* Mr. Anderson believes conferences are conversations because they share the characteristics of a conversation.

- Conferences and conversations have a point to them; the point of a conference is to help the student become a better writer.
- Conferences and conversations have a predictable structure; the structure of a conference is to talk about the work the child is doing as a writer and how the child can become a better writer.
- In conferences and conversations, listeners pursue the talkers' (or readers') line of thinking; the line of thinking in a conference is driven by the student's concerns and the text.
- In conferences and conversations, speakers engage in a pattern of exchange—one talks and then the other talks, one leads and then the other leads; in conferences the student sets the conference's agenda by describing what he or she is working on and then the teacher takes the lead in order to help the student write better.
- In conferences and in conversations, listeners show they care about each other; in conferences, teachers show students that they care by nodding, smiling, and celebrating what they did well.

The role of the teacher in a teacher–student conference is to listen, listen, listen carefully to the writer, to make considered honest responses to the writer's questions and statements, to ask genuine questions, and to offer suggestions that will help the student become a better writer. Conferences might proceed in the following way:

- *Writer's Intent.* The teacher might begin the conference with an opening like "Tell me about how your writing is going. What are you trying to do?" The goal is for the teacher to discover the student's intentions. As the student speaks, the teacher listens intently. Is it that the writer is working on telling this story in the clever way, to keep the readers' attention? Is it that the writer is working on creating a really engaging lead? Is it that the writer is working on putting spaces between his words? This is the "research" or "understand the writer" part of the conference—the teacher is searching for the way to match the teaching during the conference with the writer's goal for this piece of writing (Fletcher & Portalupi, 2001; Ray, 2001).
- *Writer's Need.* Knowing the writer's goal helps the teacher know the right questions to ask and how to focus the conversation in ways that will help the student become a better writer. In Ms. Ray's terms, the teacher is making a "what-does-this-student-need-to-know" decision (p. 163). So the second part of the conference is assessing the writer's need in order to make a decision about what to teach. Remember that the goal of a writing conference is to help the student become a better writer, not just to make this piece of writing better. The challenge is for the teacher to figure out on-the-spot what it is that will help this student as a writer now. Mr. Fletcher and Ms. Portalupi remind teachers to figure out just *one* thing that will help this writer be a better writer, one strategy, skill, or technique. All the writer's needs can not be "fixed" in a single conference.

The role of a teacher in a teacher-student writing conference is to listen carefully to the writer, to respond honestly to the writer's questions, and to offer suggestions that will help the student become a better writer.

■ *Teach the Writer.* Once the teacher has decided what would help the student be a better writer, the teacher teaches. But, beware: conferences are not mini-lectures. The teacher might grab a book to illustrate a quality of writing that this writer needs ("Hmmm. I wonder if this lead will really grab your reader's attention. What leads have you tried? Can you think of any stories we have read recently that had a really great lead? Let's take a look at these three or four books."), or the teacher might let the writer know that something is missing ("I got confused right here. As you were reading me this section, I couldn't figure out what you made out front, 'Then I made one in the front.' "), or the teacher might label what the writer is trying to do ("Ah, so you are trying to write this piece from the perspective of your cat and you're having trouble always seeing things from your cat's perspective? Let's think about a story we have read recently where the author did just what you are trying to do."), or teach a revision strategy ("Here's how you might add this information without rewriting your whole piece. Please get scissors and tape from the writing center. Now, where do you want to add more information? Right here? So, take the scissors and cut your piece apart right there. Now write the new section on this piece of paper. I'll return in a few minutes to help you insert what you write into your piece.") In Trade Secret 9.4 Jane Ragains describes her experiences teaching revision, using one of Barry Lane's revision strategies, to one of her fifth-grade writers. Exactly what the teacher says will be dependent on the writer's intent. What is it that this writer is trying to do? What can the teacher teach this writer now that will help the writer achieve his or her intent? What can the teacher teach now, what strategies or techniques, that the student can use not only in this piece but also in subsequent pieces? So, the teacher does not teach in order to make *this* draft wonderful. A perfect lead in this draft or the use of brilliant dialogue—without learning a strategy for discovering a perfect lead or making dialogue brilliant—is of little use to the writer.

■ *Writer's Plan.* What did the writer understand the teacher to say? What will the writer do now? How will the writer use the conversation to make the writing better? Katie Wood Ray (2001, p. 168) ends her conferences by asking the student to "Say back to me what I just talked to you about." Teacher Deanne McCredie ends her conferences by asking her student, "What will you do now? How will you use what we talked about?" Teacher Dierdra Aikens ends her conferences by saying, "So, what we talked about was . . . " and the student fills in the blank. Ms. Aikens then records a few key words from the student's summary on a piece of paper and staples it to the inside of the student's writing folder. Now, she and the student have a record of the content of the conference. Making a note about the content of the conferences helps to remind Ms. Aikens and the student of what she taught during the conference. Ms. Aikens departs from each conference with a comment like, "I'll check back with you in a few minutes to see how you are doing." In this way, her students know that they are to "have-a-go" at whatever strategy or technique she taught during the conference.

Like Ms. Aikens, most teachers make a record of what they taught during each conference with each student. Not every teacher staples the note to the student's writing folder. Terry Analore, for example, records her notes on 3 × 5-inch index cards. Following one conference she wrote "10/26—By reading the end of her piece, Constance saw that the

Yes, You Can Get Your Students to Revise!

Jane Ragains"

No, I don't want to write any more.""
I'm Done!"
THE END

Do these comments sound familiar? Many students respond in these ways when asked to revise their pieces of writing. Even if they are willing to revise, they don't change leads, add details, or clarify any ideas. They fix spelling, punctuation, and any other conventions that seem appropriate to them. From our frustration with the response "THE END," revision strategies need to emerge.

In order to be successful in having our students even consider revising, we need to create a classroom community of learners—students who feel comfortable enough with one another to offer constructive ideas to make writing better. This can be accomplished by showing that we value our students' work. Find something of substance that is positive about the student's work. Be sincere in the compliment. Accentuate the positives in all aspects of classroom life. Encourage all ideas as worthy of sharing. Teach students ways to listen to each other. This community needs to be established early in the year and fostered with each passing month. As this happens, students will feel comfortable sharing their work with the teacher and their peers. They will be more willing to take risks and look for ways to improve in all facets of their academic life. There is also a carryover to the unstructured moments during recess, lunch, and related art classes.

While this atmosphere of caring is being nurtured, begin teaching mini-lessons that will develop procedures to make revision easier—skip lines as you write, leave wide margins, and write only on the front of the paper. It is always wise to number the pages in any piece just in case that ten-page masterpiece is dropped to the floor and scatters in many directions. It will take several reminders to make sure students adhere to these guidelines, but they are absolutely necessary in the art of successful revision.

A favorite revision strategy comes from *After the End* by Barry Lane (1993). A "snapshot" is a description of an event using physical details. A wonderful example can be found in Laura Ingalls Wilder's *Little House in the Big Woods*:

> Ma kissed them both, and tucked the covers in around them. They lay there awhile, looking at Ma's smooth, parted hair and her hands busy with sewing in the lamplight. Her needle made little clicking sounds against her thimble, and then the thread went softly, swish! through the pretty calico that Pa had traded furs for.

After reading this to your students, you may want to ask them about the physical details Wilder considered as she was writing this paragraph. Ask them to take a series of "snapshots" of the scene. One picture might be of Ma tucking the girls into bed. Another might be of Ma's head as she bent over her sewing. The last photo might be of her hands as she pushes the needle through the calico. Have the students tell you the details they see.

Students should then be able to take a closer look at their own work. Where can they take a snapshot? How can they describe an event in more detail? A "bed-to-bed" piece, one in which the author writes an account from morning to night of an event in his or her life, can be turned into several great vignettes using the snapshot technique. Below is an example of such a piece. As you read it, look for places where Chris might give the reader a closer look.

The Trip to Nagshead
(retyped exactly as written by the student)

It was early in the morning around 6:30. When we heard a knock. I ran to the door. I opened the door.

It was my cousins! Megan brought her stuff in. Steven did not. At 7:00 o'clock we packed up the car and we were off to Nagshead.

There was a lot of food with us. There were snacks with us.

(continued on next page)

We drove onto a bridge. There were tunnels that we drove threw. They went underwater. There was a rest stop on the bridge. We got out of the car and went to the bathroom. We had lunch there. It was good. We got back in the car, and we were off again.

We met our cousin and Grandpa at a reststop. We ate some snacks. Then we went to the house. We got there too early. So my brothers, cousin and I went swimming. We went swimming because we were hot from the long ride.

Then the house was clean. We discovered the house was big. I went exploring with my cousin while the moms put away the food. First, we went to my mom and dad's room. It was big. Then we went into my aunt and uncle's room. Then we went into my girl cousin's room. Then the boy's room. It was all ready a mess.

Then we went down into the garage. We found a big raft. We ate pizza for dinner and then went to sleep.

The next day was nice. There were big waves. We got the raft out and went swimming. Everybody went down to the beach today. David and I got in the water with the raft.

Then my cousin got on the raft with us. We waited for a wave to come. My mom was video taping us when a big wave came. It hit us on my dad's head. I did a back flip off my dad's head. My brother was up in the air. He landed on the raft. My dad put my cousin down and she went in.

A big wave came right after the other one. I went under the water. I came up too early. I got caught in the raft. I got dragged up to the shore. Then David and I went back.

There was a sandbar in the water. Then right when we got out there . . . crash!! The wave knocked me back off the sandbar. My brother got me and took me back to the sandbar.

That night we went in the hot tub. It was nice. Then I watched a move and went to sleep.

Two days later we went home, unpacked and we went inside.

The End (*YES! Chris actually wrote these two words.*)

We might want to guide Chris to the part where he describes going over the Chesapeake Bay Bridge and Tunnel. He could tell us about that specific part of his trip—give us the physical details. Perhaps he would draw a picture. What more might he tell us about their rest there? Another part on which we might have him focus is his experience with the waves. How did he feel? What did it look like? Encourage him to think about how the event might have looked if someone had taken photographs of each action he described. Using pictures or words, Chris could give the reader a better idea of what really happened.

Find a particularly vivid example of physical description from the work of your students and share it with the entire class. Nothing inspires a writer more than sharing his or her work with others.

Just as dialogue is not the only way to begin a piece of writing, snapshots are not the only revision strategy. Students also need to learn how to take conference questions and insert their answers. Improving word choice is another way to enliven any piece. Once students decide where they wish to revise their piece, we can show them how to draw arrows, cut, paste, and rearrange.

It is not enough to teach revision strategies once or twice. Students need to be encouraged to routinely reread their work or share it with a friend. Teaching and reviewing ideas for revising should be an ongoing process. You will know that you have succeeded when you no longer see

THE END.

References

Lane, B. (1993). *After the end:* Teaching and learning creative revision. Portsmouth, NH: Heinemann.

last sentence didn't fit. She crossed it out and thought of a new ending." Here Ms. Analore taught the strategy of reading a piece aloud to hear how it sounds. Often this helps writers determine what needs revision. When a student's card is filled with her notes, Ms. Analore puts it in the student's working portfolio (see Chapter 12). Anabelle O'Malley records her notes on computer labels, the kind on 8 ½ × 11-inch sheets. She writes each child's name on a label. As she confers with her students, she records her notes on that student's computer label. At a glance, she can tell which students she has conferred with and which students might be in need of her support. As a student's computer label is filled with her notes, she removes it from the sheet and sticks it onto a sheet of paper in the student's working portfolio.

Conferring with student writers, with any writer really, is not easy. Students sometimes resist the teacher's suggestions, creating tensions (Nickel, 2001). Teachers need time to develop the skills needed to teach writers a new strategy or technique in a way that keeps ownership of the piece with the writer. Following each conference, it is important for teachers to step back to reflect on what they did and why they did it, and what the writer did and how the writer felt. Katie Wood Ray (2001) suggests that teachers form a study group with colleagues and read Carl Anderson's book, *How's It Going?* (2001), which is about conferring. She offers these words of advice:

Conferring is very challenging, and you will probably struggle with it for quite some time before you begin to feel at ease. But most things in teaching—as in all of life—are like that, aren't they (p. 171)?

Peer Conferences.   In addition to teacher–student conferences, peers will confer with peers, using the procedures determined by the teacher and taught in a procedural focus lesson. As children have increasing numbers of conferences with their teacher, their conferences with their peers will improve. Experience is the best teacher, and we know that social interaction with peers influences the kinds of writing strategies children internalize and use independently (Neuman & Roskos, 1991a; Rowe, 1989; Vukelich, 1993).

The ultimate purpose of teacher and peer conferences is to help the writers learn about the kinds of questions they might ask themselves in order to consider their audience's needs. As several writers (e.g., Calkins, 1986; Graves, 1983; Harwayne, 1992) have suggested, the teacher's goal is to put herself or himself out of a job. But can young writers learn to consider their audience's needs? After all, they are still quite egocentric.

Kristi, a second-grader in Margaret Hull's classroom, demonstrated how she had internalized the importance of learning about her audience's needs. One day, as she was about to begin a piece about the day she burned her hand, she said, "Well, I might as well find out what they want to know about my burning my hand before I write about it!" Having expressed that bit of wisdom, she gathered a piece of paper and a pencil and set off to interview her peers. "I'm writing a piece about the day I burned my hand. What do you want to know about it?" She learned that her peers wanted answers to such questions as, (1) How did you burn your hand? (2) What did you reach over to get? (3) Why did your dad throw you in the swimming pool? (4) What color was your hand? (5) When did it happen? (This last question seems to be the all-time favorite of young children!) When she felt she had received sufficient advice, she returned to her seat and began to write her piece. Eventually Kristi will be able to consider the questions her audience might have without having to interview her peers, but for now this seven-year-old has demonstrated that she can consider her audience's needs.

Group Share Sessions

Each writing workshop ends with a *group share session*. These sessions are a little like the teacher and peer conferences that occurred during the writing portion of the writing workshop. An important difference is that during the group share session, two or three children sit, one at a time, in the author's chair and share their pieces with the other writers in the class. Typically, the other writers are gathered at the sharing writer's feet, listening attentively while the writer reads the piece, or a portion of the piece, preparing to ask meaning-related questions. The purpose is for the author "to receive help on what is and is not working in their writing and what, if anything, they might consider doing next" (Harste, Short, & Burke, 1988, p. 221). Trade Secret 9.5 describes group sharing in Jackie Shockley's classroom.

Trade Secret 9.5

Group Sharing
Jackie Shockley

I glanced at the classroom clock—2:50.

"Boys and girls, writing time is over for today. Please put your folders away unless it is your turn to share, and meet us on the rug." Share time begins in Room 206.

The first author reads his piece in its entirety. He concludes; his audience applauds. Several hands shoot up. The author calls on a student: "I really like how you said you felt like biting him back. I liked hearing how you felt." The author smiles, replies with a thank you, and calls on another student. "I heard a lot of ands in your piece. Maybe you should go through and see if you need all of those ands." Sitting in the back of the group, I record that comment on a small piece of notepaper. The author again declines comment but calls on another student: "I liked your story a lot." I interrupt the student and ask, "What exactly did you like about it? Be specific so you can help the author." The student responds that she liked how he wrote about his gerbil because she has one, too.

I tell the audience that I really like how they are helping each other when they make comments that are specific and refer to our mini-lessons. I request another round of applause for our author and hand him the notes I wrote, asking, "Here are the suggestions that were made, but who's the boss of this piece?"

Two more authors read their pieces; each reading was followed by more comments and applause. Precious learning moments have occurred and have been reinforced during the ten-minute period. So ends a typical share time in my room.

There is concrete evidence that helpful comments during share time have a positive impact on the students' writing. During a small-group share, a writer (Kip) was reading a piece about a camping trip. In his attempts to be explicit, he included the time each activity began and ended. After one reading, a member of the audience commented, "Wow, you told the time on everything." He responded, "I know. I didn't like how it sounded. I think I'll take it out." I was thinking, "Hooray!" only to hear another member of the group saying, "I like it. I think you should leave it in." The discussion continued. Kip wavered but prior to publishing decided to include only a few of the times. His final decision is not really the issue here. What is important is that these writers were thinking critically about the piece.

There are several kinds of group share meetings that teachers might organize in their classroom. Many of these ideas originated with Lucy Calkins (1983). The typical group share session is like the sessions described in this chapter (e.g., see Trade Secret 9.5). In this kind of share session, called a *share meeting,* as many writers as possible share their drafts and receive their peers' and teacher's questions in the 10- to 15-minute session. Some teachers select children who volunteer to be the presenters. Other teachers select children they have identified as having made a significant discovery to be the presenters. For example, Margaret Hull asked Charlie to share his piece about his fishing trip because he discovered how to use parentheses to explain words possibly unknown to his readers. Still other teachers ask writers who tried the strategy or technique taught in the focus lesson to share their revised draft and to talk about how they used the strategy or technique. Many use a combination of these means of selecting writers for group share presentations.

A second kind of group share session is *writers' circle.* In this kind of share session, the teacher divides the class into several small groups of five or so children. Writers then simultaneously share pieces with their peers. Obviously, many experiences with share meetings are needed before young children can be expected to independently and effectively run writers' circles. Harste, Short, and Burke (1988) insist that each participant in this kind of share session bring a piece of writing to the writers' circle.

A third kind of share session is a *quiet share.* This kind of share session requires the listeners to have access to paper; a writing tool; and a desk, table, or clipboard. When each of the two or three writers has finished reading their pieces, the listeners write their questions or comments. They may or may not sign their comments. These are then given to the writers for their consideration.

Focused shares occur when the teacher asks the writers to read a specific aspect of their pieces. For example, the teacher might ask the children to gather to read their leads, or their titles, or their sentence or sentences that describe the setting of their piece, or to show how they focused their topic, or . . . whatever. Sometimes, teachers link focused shares with the day's mini-lesson topics (as Maryanne Lamont did). On the day when the topic of her mini-lesson was the writing of focused pieces, Ms. Lamont decided that the group share session would be a focused share, where some of her young writers would read their old pieces and their revised pieces, to illustrate how they had revised to focus on one aspect of their topic.

Occasionally, teachers will use the group share session for a *process share.* During these kinds of group share sessions, the children may be asked to bring illustrations of revisions they made in their texts and to be prepared to tell about why they made the changes. The student may also be asked to share their notes (like brainstorming webs), created to help them discover what they know about a topic, or their handling of problems they have solved in their pieces (such as Charlie's use of parentheses).

Giving or celebration shares are unlike all other group share sessions. During these share sessions, writers share the pieces they have published. Because the writers have completed their writing of these pieces, only comments are offered by the listeners. These authors' works then join those by other published authors (writers such as Maurice Sendak, Chris Van Allsberg, Tomie de Paolo, and Eric Carle) in the classroom library corner. Like all other books in the library corner, these works are available to be checked out and read by an appreciative audience. Like the other books in the library corner, these books need to have a library checkout card and a pocket in which to keep the card.

Assessment: Discovering What Students Know and Can Do

The observant reader realized the important role of the teacher in the implementation of a writing program pages ago. Central to teachers' implementation of a high-quality writing program is their ability to answer the following kinds of questions: What do these writers need? Do they need information on how to pull their readers into their pieces, on good leads? Do they, perhaps, need information on how to make their writing come alive, using dialogue? When children use dialogue, do they know how to punctuate their texts? By examining the pieces in the students' writing folders and by rereading the anecdotal notes made during teacher–student conferences and the vignettes of significant breakthroughs demonstrated by their writers, and by reading and evaluating their students' writing pieces, teachers can acquire the information needed to inform their instructional decisions. This information will also serve as the basis for making judgments about their writers' development and accomplishments.

Using Writing Rubrics

Rubrics are an important tool teachers use to make judgments about their students' writing. They use them to help them answer the questions: How good is this piece of writing? What qualities of good writing did this writer use effectively in crafting this piece? (The answer to this question helps teachers know what to celebrate in their students' writing, and celebrating what is good is as important as uncovering each writer's instructional needs.) What qualities of good writing did this writer not use as effectively in crafting this piece? (The answer to this question helps teachers know what lessons to teach this student.) Rubrics, then, help teachers understand their students' development. They provide the "criteria that describe student performance at various levels of proficiency" (O'Neill, 1994, p. 4). Rubrics enable teachers (and students) to assign a score or rating (beginning, developing, proficient) to a piece of writing. Classic writing rubrics typically describe student writing in several areas (writing traits), for example, organization, development or ideas, sentence variety, word choice, voice, and conventions. Descriptors outline the expectations or criteria for each of the possible point values or performance levels, usually on a three- to six-point scale, for each area. The clearer the criteria, the more likely the student writers will know what is expected of them in each writing trait. Vicki Spandel (2001, p. 21), for example, describes the level of detail needed to describe the *organization* writing trait. She suggests that the criteria describing proficient organization might be: "(1) inviting, purposeful lead; (2) effective sequencing; (3) smooth, helpful transitions; (4) good pacing; and (5) effective conclusion that makes the reader think." The criteria describing developing performance might be: "(1) introduction and conclusion present, (2) sequencing sometimes works, (3) transitions attempted, and (4) pacing sometimes too rapid or too slow." Finally, the criteria for beginning organization might be: "(1) no real lead or conclusion yet, (2) sequencing creates confusion, and (3) pacing slows reader down—or pushes the reader too hard." Notice how these criteria are clearly written, identify significant aspects of an important writing trait, give clear distinctions among the three performance levels, and describe what the writer should do. The students could use these criteria to guide their development of their writing, and they and their teachers could use this rubric to judge the quality of this writing trait (organization) in the students' writing pieces.

There are three kinds of scoring rubrics for teachers and students in use today: primary trait, holistic, and analytical.

- Primary trait scoring rubrics vary with the writing's purpose and audience. If the writers are to write to persuade a person in authority, for example, then the traits that are central to putting forth an argument might be to articulate a position and to prepare a well-written discussion on the reasons for the position, taking into account the knowledge of the audience about the topic. Because the audience is a person in authority, an additional trait might be to offer a counterargument for at least one of the audience's possible positions on the topic. We provide an example of a primary trait scoring rubric in Figure 9.5. Using this rubric, how would you score the persuasive letter in Figure 9.6?

- Holistic scoring rubrics require raters to consider how the writer used all the writing traits (organization, ideas or development, voice, word choice, sentence variety, mechanics) in harmony in a piece to achieve an overall effect. In essence, the scorer reads the piece and gets a general impression of how well the writer has used the writing traits in the crafting of the piece. To help scorers, exemplars (or anchor papers) are selected to illustrate typical performance at each score point. The scorers, then, can compare the piece they are reading against the anchor papers to help them arrive at a single score for this piece. Unlike primary trait scoring rubrics, the same holistic scor-

FIGURE 9.5   Primary Trait Scoring Rubric for Persuasive Writing

6   **Extensively elaborated.** In these pieces, students articulate a position for or against the topic, or they suggest a compromise, and they present an extended, well-written discussion on the reasons for their position. These responses may be similar to "5" responses, but they provide an extended discussion of the reasons for their position.

5   **Elaborated.** In these responses, students articulate a position for or against the topic, or they suggest a compromise, and they provide an extended discussion of the reasons for their position.

4   **Developed.** In these responses, students take a position for or against the topic, or they suggest a compromise, and they discuss the reasons for their position. Although the reasons may be more clearly stated than in papers that receive lower scores, the discussions may be unevenly developed.

3   **Minimally developed.** In these responses, students state or imply a position for or against the topic. Rather than support their position with reasons, however, these papers tend to offer specific suggestions or to elaborate on the students' opinions.

2   **Undeveloped.** In these responses, students state or imply a position for or against the topic, but they offer no reasons to support their point of view.

1   **Off-topic or no response.** In these responses, students do not take a position or write nothing.

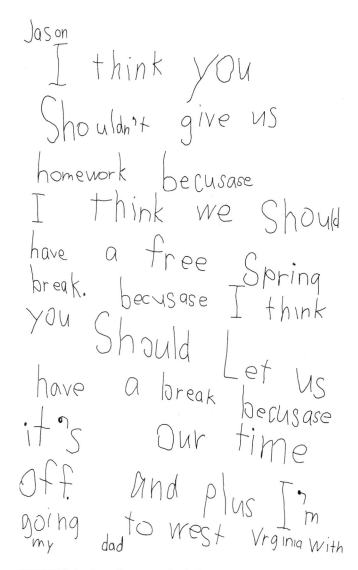

FIGURE 9.6   Jason's persuasive letter.

ing rubric can be used to score writing in all discourse categories (persuasive, expressive, information, narrative). We provide an example of a holistic scoring rubric developed by a group of teachers in Figure 9.7. Consistent with suggestions regarding how
a rubric should be created, these teachers researched the characteristics of expressive
texts and read published pieces in order to make a list of the important characteristics
exhibited by these kinds of texts. They incorporated these characteristics into the highest category, a category they labeled "advanced," on their rubric. Using this rubric,
how would you score the writing in Figure 9.8?

Three Rubrics: Basic, Proficient, Advanced

Pieces rated as basic *should exhibit the following characteristics:*

- The piece has a good topic sentence.
- Piece focuses on one topic.
- The sequence of the events is appropriate.
- The description of the setting (where the event occurred) might be stated or implied.
- The piece has a beginning, a middle, and an end. The beginning and middle probably are more developed than the end.
- The transition between sentences and paragraphs is typically clear.
- The piece has a title that is consistent with its main idea.

Pieces rated as proficient *should exhibit the preceding characteristics, with some elaboration, and the following characteristics:*

- The setting is stated and developed, probably through the use of an adjective or two.
- The piece has a beginning, a middle, and an end that exhibits more development (particularly of the middle) than pieces rated as basic. One event may be detailed, or there may be brief details for multiple events.
- The vocabulary is selected to create a picture of the event or events, the character, the setting, and so on. Fresh adverbs and adjectives are often used.

Pieces rated as advanced *should exhibit the following characteristics:*

- The lead is catchy; grabbing the reader's attention and making him or her want to read on.
- The setting is explicitly described, using imagery.
- The beginning catches the reader's attention, arousing his or her interest and helping him or her to anticipate the middle. It provides the information necessary to understand the rest of the narrative. The middle sustains interest by depicting events with details. The piece ends with an effective "bang" that reveals the outcome.
- The dialogue provides insights into the character's (or characters') thoughts and feelings, in addition to advancing the plot/storyline.
- The writer uses appropriate words to signal transitions.
- There is cohesion within the paragraphs (each idea is developed in a paragraph) and coherence across paragraphs. One event moves smoothly to another.
- Multiple events are described. Events, details, and dialogue are carefully chosen with the purpose of telling the story.
- The writer selects and sustains
  - a language natural to the narrative,
  - a point of view appropriate to the narrative, and
  - a tense (or tenses) consistent with the flow of the narrative.

FIGURE 9.7   Teacher-designed expressive rubric.

■ Analytical scoring "acknowledges the underlying premise that, in writing, the whole is more than the sum of its parts, but it adds that, if we are to teach students to write, we must take writing apart—temporarily—in order to focus on one skill at a time" (Spandel, 2001, p. 26). An analytical scoring rubric, then, takes each significant writing trait and describes, using specific language and criteria, what each trait looks like at various levels of proficiency. It is the analytical scoring rubric that is most useful to

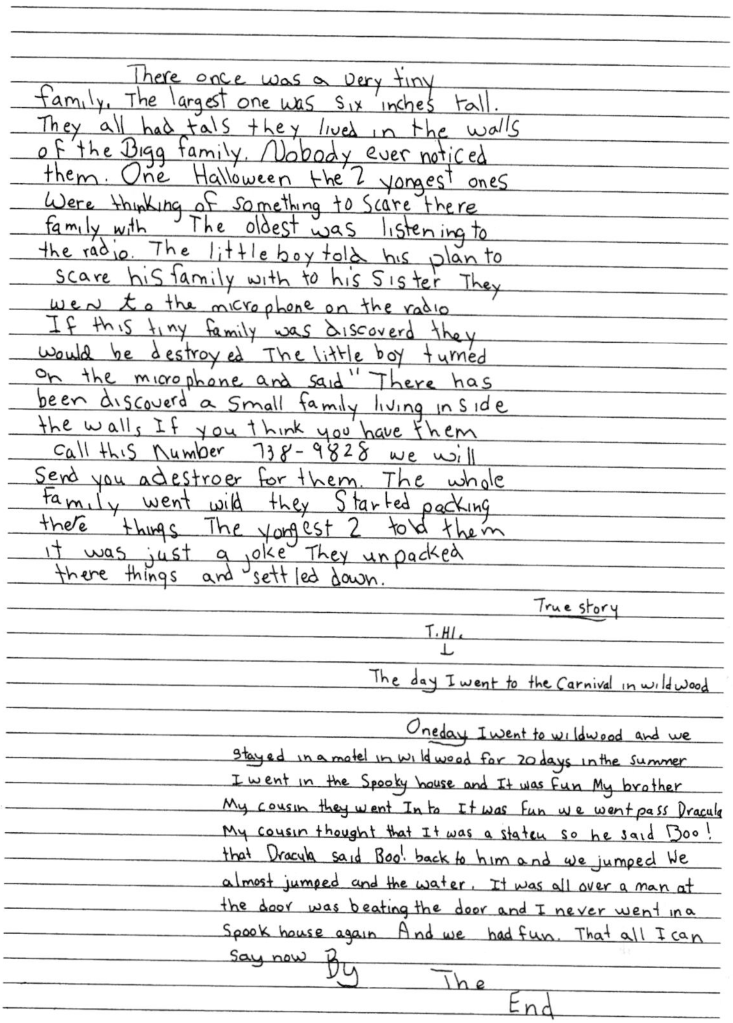

There once was a very tiny
family. The largest one was six inches tall.
They all had tals they lived in the walls
of the Bigg family. Nobody ever noticed
them. One Halloween the 2 yongest ones
were thinking of something to scare there
family with   The oldest was listening to
the radio. The little boy told his plan to
scare his family with to his Sister They
wen to the microphone on the radio
If this tiny family was discoverd they
would be destroyed The little boy turned
on the microphone and said" There has
been discoverd a small family living inside
the walls, If you think you have them
call this number 738-9828 we will
Send you a destroer for them. The whole
family went wild they Started packing
there things The yongest 2 told them
it was just a joke They unpacked
there things and settled down.

True story

T.Hl.

The day I went to the Carnival in wildwood

One day I went to wildwood and we
stayed in a motel in wildwood for 20 days in the summer
I went in the Spooky house and It was Fun My brother
My cousin they went Into It was Fun we went pass Dracula
My cousin thought that It was a staten so he said Boo!
that Dracula said Boo! back to him and we jumped We
almost jumped and the water. It was all over a man at
the door was beating the door and I never went in a
Spook house again And we had fun. That all I can
say now   By   The
                        End

FIGURE 9.8   Two third graders' stories.

teachers. By scoring students' writing along each significant writing trait, teachers
can determine each student's writing needs and the class's writing needs. Now, the
teacher knows what to teach and what the topics of the classroom's focus lessons
should be. In Trade Secret 9.6 Peggy Dillner describes this critical link between
assessment and instruction. We provide an example of an analytical scoring rubric in
Figure 9.9. Using this rubric, how would you score the writing in Figure 9.10?

Rubrics not only help teachers, but they also help students if teachers teach their students how to use the rubric for self-assessment purposes. (In fact, George Hillocks, Jr.

FIGURE 9.9   Analytical Scoring Rubric

The following characteristics determine the success of the response in meeting the needs of the audience and fulfilling the writing purpose.

		Score of 5	Score of 4	Score of 3	Score of 2	Score of 1
Organization		*Score point 5 meets all the criteria listed in score point 4. In addition, a paper receiving this score shows an exceptional awareness of readers' concerns and needs.*	Unified with smooth transitions, a clear and logical progression of ideas, and an effective introduction and closing.	Generally unified with some transitions, a clear progression of ideas, and an introduction and closing.	Minimally unified and may lack transitions or an introduction or closing.	Lacks unity.
Development			Sufficient, specific, and relevant details that are fully elaborated.	Specific details but may be insufficient, irrelevant, or not fully elaborated.	Some specific details but may be insufficient, irrelevant, and/or not elaborated.	No or few specific details that are minimally elaborated.
Sentence Formation		*The student may have shown an exceptional use of:*	Consistently complete sentences with appropriate variety in length and structure.	Generally complete sentences with sufficient variety in length and structure.	Some sentence formation errors and a lack of sentence variety.	Frequent and severe sentence formation errors and/or a lack of sentence variety.
Style/Word Choice		*Development strategies specific to the purpose for writing*	A consistent style with precise and vivid word choice.	Some style and generally precise word choice.	Sometimes general and repetitive word choice.	Often general, repetitive, and/or confusing word choice.
Lang. Conventions		*Distinctive style, voice, tone* *Literary devices* *Compositional risks*	Few, if any, errors in standard written English that do not interfere with understanding.	Some errors in standard written English that rarely interfere with understanding.	Several kinds of errors in standard written English that interfere with understanding.	Frequent and severe errors in standard written English that interfere with understanding.

Source: Delaware Department of Education

(1986) suggests that of all the methods used to teach writing over the past decades, well-defined criteria is one of the two research-supported instructional techniques. The other instructional technique he suggests the data support is providing good models.) To make the state's scoring rubric useful for their students, the teachers at Jennie Smith Elementary School rewrote the language of the criteria of the state's rubric into "kid-friendly language" (see Figure 9.11). The principal, then, contracted with the district's vocational students to make poster-size rubric charts to hang in each classroom's writing center. In addition, the teachers placed a copy of the kid-friendly rubric in each student's writing folder. Through

Do you know how to play soccer? Well, Matt and I do. This is how you start. First, you sign up. Then you get your coach. After that, the coach gets the whole team together and you have your first practice. Then you practice all the kicks and moves. Now we are going to tell you how to do them.

(1)

First we will tell you the way you should use your feet. You use the inside of your feet to dribble, pass and score. Also, you use the inside of your feet to block the ball.

Now we will tell you about kicks. One kick is the dribble and kick. It is when you dribble and then you kick the ball.

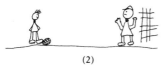

(2)

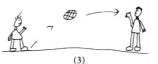

(3)

Since we have been talking about dribbling, we will tell you how to dribble. You use the inside of your feet. Then you kick it with the inside of your feet. If you kick it with your toes, sometimes it will hurt. Also if you kick it with the outside of your foot, the person can steal the ball. Also you might twist your ankle. But if you want to kick the ball like that you should be a professional or if you had a lot of experience. If you want to, you can try it; but we're just telling you that you shouldn't try it.

Now we will tell you more kicks. This play is called the "give and go." First, you dribble the ball. Then you pass it to your teammate. Then their teammate kicks the ball and makes a score.

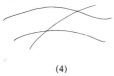

(4)

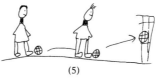

(5)

Now we will tell you about the banana kick. The banana kick is when the defender is charging. You should strike the ball with the outside of your foot. It will curve around him to your teammate. The banana kick is a very famous kick because it is made by famous Peli.

(6)

Now we will tell you how to act on the field. First, you be kind to your teammates. If you yell at the ref, you will get a yellow card. If you yell at the ref again, you will get another yellow card. That means you got a red card and you will get kicked out of the other next game.

(7)

FIGURE 9.10   How to play soccer by Matt and Scott.

(continued)

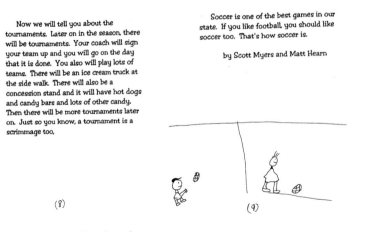

Now we will tell you about the tournaments. Later on in the season, there will be tournaments. Your coach will sign your team up and you will go on the day that it is done. You also will play lots of teams. There will be an ice cream truck at the side walk. There will also be a concession stand and it will have hot dogs and candy bars and lots of other candy. Then there will be more tournaments later on. Just so you know, a tournament is a scrimmage too,

Soccer is one of the best games in our state. If you like football, you should like soccer too. That's how soccer is.

by Scott Myers and Matt Hearn

(8)

(9)

FIGURE 9.10   Continued

teacher–student conferences and the group sharing session at the end of writing workshop, the teachers teach the students to use the language of the rubrics to describe their writing.

Katie Wood Ray (2001) suggests that teachers form a study group around Carl Anderson's book on conferring. We suggest that, once the study group has read and discussed Anderson's book, they read and discuss Vicki Spandel's (2001) book on writing assessment and instruction. An excellent Web site provides numerous support materials for teachers attempting to integrate six-trait assessment into their classrooms (http://www.nwrel.org/assessment/department).

Large-Scale Assessments

In the previous section, we described how teachers might use rubrics to make judgments about their students' writing performance. In addition to teachers assessing their students' writing performance, a growing number of states assess students' writing performance. Typically, these assessments occur at particular grades, like grades 3, 5, 8, and 10. On a specific day, typically in the spring, all students at those grade levels are required to produce a piece of writing. The procedures for gathering this sample of students' performance are standardized. Typically, teachers across the state, at each of the grade levels, present their students with the same prompt. For example, the students might be directed to write to the following prompt: The editor of your newspaper is putting together a student section of the newspaper. Students have been asked to write about their favorite holiday or tradition for this section. Write an article about your favorite holiday or tradition to send to the newspaper (Source: Delaware Department of Education). All students have the same number of minutes to prepare their response. Once the allotted time has passed, the teachers box the students' writing samples and deliver them to the school's office. The office staff, then, forwards the test to the district office or the state for scoring by trained scorers. (For additional prompt suggestions, see Vicki Spandel ([2001], pp. 32–33].)

Trade Secret 9.6

From Assessment to Instruction
Peggy Dillner

Assessment with a rubric is only the beginning of the cycle. If the assessment is to be truly meaningful, it must drive instruction (Hansen, 1994). Looking at an individual student's writing, and the class's writing as a whole, the teacher must make instructional decisions. Such lessons may be quick individual lessons given during a conference, lessons involving several children who exhibit the same weakness, or instruction to the entire class for a need they all share. "The long term benefit of effective instructional assessment is the implementation of a process for moving schools from a remedial toward a developmental approach" (Fradd & McGee 1994). The subtlety is between telling students what is wrong with their writing versus telling them how to improve their writing.

In assessment one of the biases to which teachers are prone is to note the errors in conventions and stop the assessment at that point (Spandel & Stiggins, 1997). Faulty grammar, missing punctuation, and poor spelling jump out at teachers, jangle their nerves, and undoubtedly point to instructional needs. However, weaknesses in development, organization, word choice and style, and sentence structure also point to instructional needs.

Teachers must assess and instruct in all areas, focusing on areas of greatest need. John Collins (1987) writes about "focus correction areas," reminding educators that many students will be overwhelmed if expected to fix everything. Teachers need to force themselves to examine closely the needs exhibited by their students' writing according to a reliable rubric. Then instruction can focus on one or two weaknesses at a time. Following instruction there should be immediate application as students return to their writing.

The following ideas are for mini-lessons appropriate for weaknesses in organization,

development, word choice/style, and sentence structure. *Conventions* is not listed since most teachers have an excellent repertoire of lessons on spelling, punctuation, and grammar.

Organization

Problem: Lacks unity and smooth transitions

Possible lesson: Find a well-written published piece that illustrates unity with good use of transition words or phrases. Such an example is from page 10 of *The Midwife's Apprentice* by Karen Cushman (1995). Retype it in discrete sentences and cut the text apart. Have students work in groups to put the text back together. Discuss how they knew the sequence into which to arrange the piece. Then have students return to their pieces and read them looking for unity and transition for possible revision.

Development

Problem: Many irrelevant details

Possible lesson: Have student(s) list everything they know about a particular subject (the Titanic, basketball, MTV, the local mall). Then have that list divided into two: one for critical information, the other for trivial information. Discuss what would be included in a good paper on this topic. Remind them of the quotation by Elmore Leonard (as quoted in Lane, p. 120): "I try to leave out the parts that people skip." Have the student(s) return to their writing. If necessary, have them list on another piece of paper all the details about the subject in their pieces. Then have them determine if all these details belong in a critical information column or in the trivial information column.

Word Choice/Style

Problem: Lacking in distinctive tone or character

Possible lesson: Pick one of the biographies written by Russell Freedman (Abraham Lincoln, Eleanor Roosevelt, Franklin Delano Roosevelt, Crazy House, The Wright Brothers, Louis Braille,

(continued on next page)

Trade Secret 9.6 *(continued)*

Martha Graham). Read a section from the Freedman biography and then part of an encyclopedia article about the same individual. Discuss the difference. Have students return to their pieces to see if they believe their distinctive voice shines through.

The best practice is for teachers to use pieces of student work (with the student's permission, of course) and/or quality literature from their classroom in the development of minilessons. So much good literature is available today to enrich students' literary world; this literature can be easily woven into lessons on writing strategies.

Instruction based on the needs of students is where constructivist research says to begin (Herman, Aschbacher, and Winters, 1992). One then builds on the learner's prior knowledge to enable movement forward. Assessing a student's writing to determine instructional needs and making decisions on how to best meet those needs is what good teachers of writing are all about.

References

Collins, J. J. (1987). *The effective writing teacher: 18 strategies.* Andover, MA: NETWORK.

Cushman, K. (1995). *Midwife's apprentice.* New York: Clarion Books.

Fradd, S. H., & McGee, P. L. (1994). *Instructional assessment: An integrative approach to evaluating student performance.* New York: Addison Wesley.

Hansen, J. (1996). Evaluation: The center of writing instruction. *Reading Teacher, 50,* 188–195.

Herman, J. L., Aschbacher, P. R., & Winters, L. (1992). Linking assessment and instruction: A practical guide to alternative assessment. Alexandria, VA: Association for Supervision and Curriculum Development.

Lane, B. (1993). *After the end: Teaching and learning creative revision.* Portsmouth, NH: Heinemann.

Spandel, V., & Stiggins, R. J. (1997). *Creating writers: Linking writing assessment and instruction* (2nd ed.). New York: Longman.

This kind of writing is different from what typically occurs in writing workshop classrooms. In writing workshop classrooms, students write about topics in which they have vested interests. Real audiences read their writing. Students have time to prewrite, write, revise, edit, and write a final copy. Students use the resources (e.g., dictionary, thesaurus, spell checkers) they need. Perhaps it is not surprising that, given such differences, all teachers are not enthusiastically supportive of such large-scale assessments. Some teachers find them threatening and intimidating, especially when their students' performance is used to judge their or their school's or education's performance.

How do teachers survive, and flourish, in this accountability climate? Volunteer to serve as a scorer, a prompt writer, or an anchor selector. Typically, the state will bring teachers from across the state together to engage in each of these activities. Teachers who participate in such activities repeatedly declare their participation to have provided them with excellent information, knowledge they can use in their classroom with their instruction and assessment practices. Remember that the large-scale assessment is just one assessment of students' writing. The students' writing folders will house multiple other indicators of their day-to-day efforts. Most states have developed a process whereby teachers can provide classroom evidence to support their claim that a student's writing score is atypical to that student's day-to-day writing performance. And yes, periodically, ask the students to

FIGURE 9.11 **Kid-friendly Writing Rubric**

Organize	Develop	Sentences	Words
4	4	4	4
My writing is in an order that makes sense.	My details are all about my topic.	I use complete sentences.	I use many exciting, sparkling words.
I use words to connect the beginning, middle, and end.	My details are important to my topic.	I use different words to start my sentences.	I use many powerful action words.
I always stay on topic.	I use many details to tell about my topic.	I use long and short sentences.	I use many different words.
My piece's beginning tells about the topic in an exciting way.			
My writing has an effective ending.			
3	3	3	3
My writing is mostly in an order that makes sense.	My details are mostly about my topic.	I usually use complete sentences.	I use some exciting, sparkling words.
My writing has a beginning, middle, and end.	I use some details to tell about my topic.	I usually use different words to start my sentences.	I use some powerful action words.
I usually use words to connect the beginning, middle, and end.	My details are good.	I use long and short sentences.	I use a lot of different words.
My writing has a good ending.			
2	2	2	2
My writing might be in an order that is confusing.	I use just a few details to tell about my topic.	I sometimes use complete sentences.	I use a few exciting, sparkling words.
My writing might be missing a beginning, middle, or end.	Some of my details might not tell about my topic.	I start most of my sentences the same.	I use few powerful action words.
My writing might include sentences that are not about the topic. My ending is just "The End."		My sentences are short.	Many of my words are the same.
1	1	1	1
My writing is in an order that is confusing.	I have few or no details.	My sentences might not be complete.	I do not use exciting sparkling words.
I might have written about more than one topic.	My piece is very short.	I might use the same words to begin my sentences.	I do not use powerful action words.
My writing may be missing a beginning, middle, or ending.		My sentences are short.	I often use the same words.
			I leave out words.

Source: Jennie Smith Elementary School.

respond to a prompt like that they will need to address on the state test. (In fact, Katie Wood Ray (2001) suggests teaching writing to a prompt as a "genre" study before the large-scale assessment test.) Score their responses using the state's writing rubric. Ask the students to score their writing using the state's writing rubric. Talk about what the students could have done to make their writing better.

Large-scale assessment has served to remind everyone—students, teachers, administrators, the public—of the importance of writing. It has provided a strong reason for teachers to find time in their already packed daily schedules to teach, not just assign, writing. It has provided a reason for students to attend to how they might make their writing better. Sadly, it is the *how* of doing the assessment that does not always match good writing instruction.

Summary

To become a competent teacher of writing in a writing workshop context will require considerable effort. Not only is this approach to the teaching of writing likely different from what most readers experienced as elementary students themselves, most elementary-school teachers do not feel they know much about good writing. We encourage our readers to begin collecting models of good writing in all genres and to add copies of the many new books on the teaching of writing to their personal professional library. There are whole books written on conferring, on mini-lessons, on evaluating, and new books every year on teaching writing the writing workshop way.

■ *What are the essentials of writing workshop?*

Before writing workshop begins, teachers need to make preparations. They need to consider their daily schedule. Where will forty-five to sixty minutes of writing workshop each day fit into the schedule? They need to arrange the classroom environment for talk among peers and for quiet writing. They need to create an area where all the writers can gather to share their drafts and finished pieces. They need to gather the needed materials and determine how to arrange these materials for the writers' easy access. They need to make plans to teach their students how to write.

■ *What are the components of writing workshop?*

In most classrooms, the three or four components of writing workshop happen in the following order each day: a focus lesson in which the teacher teaches the students something about writing or writing workshop procedures; writing time during which the students write, confer with the teacher, and confer with each other; and group sharing time during which two or three students share their writing with the group and receive responses. Some teachers insert a status-of-the-class report between the focus lesson and writing time. Here the teacher does a quick check on what each writer plans to do that day during writing workshop.

■ *How do teachers teach and what kinds of lessons might they teach during writing workshop?*

Teachers teach through the focus lessons. Focus lessons might be procedural lessons in which students learn the teachers' expectations for their behavior during writing workshop; the craft or qualities of good writing lessons in which students learn about what makes writing good; writing process lessons in which students learn about the recursive nature of the writing process (prewriting, drafting, revising, editing, publishing) and how to use this process themselves; or mechanical-skills lessons in which students learn the rules of capitalization, punctuation, grammar, or usage. Teachers can teach these same lessons, one-on-one, during teacher–student conferences. They can reinforce these lessons through the group share at the end of writing workshop.

■ *What is the structure of a writing conference?*

Conferences have a predictable structure. The teacher begins by attempting to discover the student's intentions. Here, the teacher is searching for the way to match the teaching during the conference with the writer's goal for this piece of writing. Knowing the writer's goal helps the teacher decide what the writer needs to achieve the goal. So the second part of the conference is assessing the writer's need in order to decide what to teach. The third step is to teach the writer a needed strategy or skill. The teacher teaches something the student needs now but also something that will be useful in subsequent pieces of writing. The fourth step is to create a plan with the writer. What did the writer understand the teacher to say and what will the writer do now? The teacher makes a record of the student's plan

■ *How might teachers assess their students' writing development?*

In their classrooms, teachers gather evidence about students' writing development every time they confer with them. Most teachers make judgments about their students' writing performance through the use of analytical, holistic, or primary trait rubrics. Rubrics not only help teachers, but also students, if teachers teach their students how to use rubrics for self-assessment purposes. In addition to classroom-based assessments, many states require that students at particular grade levels participate in the state's large-scale assessment. Here students respond to prompts, someone other than the teacher scores the students' writing, and the teacher and student (and the student's parents) receive a score or rating of the student's performance.

LINKING KNOWLEDGE TO PRACTICE

1. Visit a classroom to observe a writing workshop. Make field notes of your observations of the classroom environment (the materials, the furniture arrangement, the writing area), the procedures used to implement writing workshop, the topic and content of the focus lesson, the models provided for the writers, how the teacher confers with the students, how peer conferring occurs, the availability of rubrics for the students' use, and how group sharing happened. Compare your observation data with that of your colleagues.

2. Use the rubrics to rate the writing pieces in this chapter. In addition to the rating, make a written record of your reasons for your rating. Share your ratings and rationales with your colleagues. Did you agree? Why or why not?

3. Teaching writing through writing workshop likely will be different from what most students' parents experienced as elementary-school students. Using the information in this chapter, work with a colleague to write a brochure or handout for parents describing this approach to teaching writing.

4. Begin a writing support group with a group of colleagues. Challenge each other to write pieces in various genres. Gather models in each genre to "teach" you about the genre. Aim to publish your pieces.

CHAPTER 10

Embedded within Writing Workshop: Teaching Skills and Meeting Special Needs

Zebulon is ready to publish his story on his piece about his trip to Virginia Beach. He knows the classroom editing procedures. He collects the classroom's editing checklist from the writing center. With a blue pen, he circles any words he thinks might be misspelled. Then he searches his story to be certain he has put a punctuation mark at the end of each sentence, capitalized the first word in each sentence, indented the first word of each paragraph, capitalized the important words in the title, and capitalized the names of people and places. When he finishes with his search, he staples the editing checklist to his story and places both in "The Editing Box" in the writing center. He knows that before the next writing workshop his teacher will examine his edited piece and maybe will write him some notes, notes like "I see two more words that are misspelled. Can you find them?" or "I see three sentences in your second paragraph. Can you find them?" His teacher will also add the mechanical skills he used correctly to the list of skills he knows how to use on the inside cover of his writing folder (see Figure 10.1). The next day during writing workshop, Zebulon will take a green pen and search the piece again to see if he can make the corrections the teacher's notes suggested. He can ask a friend to help him if he wishes. Following this search, he will sign up for an editing conference with his teacher. When he confers with his teacher, his teacher will celebrate the mechanical skills that he used correctly and teach him one or two additional skills. Then, he will publish his story by rewriting it on special theme paper using a felt-tip pen. He'll make a cover page with the title and his name. Then, he'll insert the final draft and cover into a plastic sleeve and select a colored spine to hold it in place. His story will be placed in the library center, alongside the work of other published authors.

Recall Ralph Fletcher's and JoAnn Portalupi's (2001) suggestion that to "fit" writing workshop into the daily schedule teachers might need to determine what activities writing workshop could replace? Instead of teaching punctuation, capitalization, spelling, or handwriting as separate subjects, teachers can teach most of these important mechanical skills of writing within the context of the classroom's writing workshop. As explained in Chapter 9, some focus lessons will be on topics in these areas. But focus lessons alone are insufficient; students will not learn these skills by hearing their teachers talking about or seeing their teachers demonstrating their use. These skills come to the forefront during editing conferences, after the children have made the content of their pieces as good as they can. Thus, the teaching of mechanical skills is embedded in the writing workshop and in the writing process itself.

In the sections that follow, the mechanical skills of writing—capitalization, punctuation, handwriting, spelling, and grammar—are temporarily removed from their supporting context (the writing workshop) and examined in isolation. This chapter highlights one additional significant feature embedded within the writing workshop: meeting the special needs of children, particularly bilingual and second-language learners who come to school exhibiting varying degrees of competence in writing in English. Today in the United States, native speakers of Spanish compose the largest group of these learners. Special Feature 10.1 (by Sarah Hudelson and Irene Serna; presented later in this chapter) provides suggestions on how to support these students' writing development within the writing workshop.

Before You Read This Chapter, Think About . . .

- how you learned to spell words. Did you learn to spell words by studying lists of words—the same list your peers studied—for Friday spelling tests?
- how you learned the rules of capitalization, punctuation and grammar. Did you complete practice exercises?
- how you learned to form the letters of the alphabet. Did you practice by writing a page of "a's" just like a model and than a page of "b's" just like a model?
- how you might support bilingual and second-language learners' writing development.

Focus Questions

- When will children learn about the mechanics of writing—spelling, grammar, capitalization, punctuation, and handwriting—in writing workshop?
- Given a choice, which handwriting style and form should teachers use?
- How should teachers teach children to form the alphabet letters correctly?
- Is writing workshop and teaching the mechanical skills of writing within writing workshop appropriate for non-native speakers of English?

BOX 10.1

Definition of Terms

cursive style writing: flowing form of writing in which the strokes of the letters in each word are joined

early phonemic spelling: children represent one or two phonemes in words with letters

editing conference: time when the teacher discusses the mechanical rules he or she used correctly and teaches one or two rules he or she did not learn correctly

letter-name spelling: children break words into phonemes and choose letters to represent the phonemes based on similarity between the sound of the letter names and the respective phoneme

manuscript style writing: vertical form of writing with letters made with circles and straight lines

prephonemic spelling: children form letters correctly, but they have not yet discovered that letters represent the sounds or phonemes in words

transitional spelling: children write words that look like English words, though the words are not all spelled correctly

The Mechanical Skills of Writing

If you answered "yes" to the questions in the *Before you read this chapter, think about . . .* section, you were taught the mechanical skills of writing through a "drill and practice" approach. By drilling you on the skills, your elementary-school teachers hoped you would be able to apply your knowledge to your writing. In all likelihood, you did not.

Today, students are taught to form letters correctly when it matters (e.g., when they are ready to publish a piece). Students do not practice forming the letters by copying models or tracing letters. Instruction occurs when the teacher teaches the child how to form a letter correctly. Today, teachers help students learn to spell by helping them understand how words work—the conventions that govern the structure of words and how these structures signal sound and meaning. Rather than studying lists of words, students pull words out of the immediate contexts of reading and writing in order to examine and explore them for common patterns. Today, teachers teach students the capitalization, punctuation, and grammar rules in focus lessons and by helping them correct errors in the pieces they plan to publish. The rules taught are those that the students need, as demonstrated by errors in the pieces they are ready to publish.

As you read the following sections, you will find that we often suggest that correcting a writing piece's mechanical problems will occur in an editing conference. These are conferences that teachers hold with their students who have selected a piece to publish. Many teachers ask their students to examine their pieces, using an editing checklist to support their searching, before an editing conference. Typically the editing checklist includes punctuation, capitalization, and grammar rules that the teacher has taught during focus lessons. When students hunt through their writing pieces to discover whether or not they have used each rule correctly, the act of hunting is a way to reinforce the skills the teacher has taught. As the teacher teaches new skills, the editing checklist changes and the number of items on the checklist grows. Readers will find an example of an editing checklist in Figure 10.1.

Spelling

Learning to spell words correctly is important. However, until children demonstrate sufficient understandings of how the English language works, teachers must permit their writers to use their best guesses to construct their texts. Encouraging children to use invented (or temporary) spellings means that every word in the children's oral vocabulary can be used in their written texts. To insist that children use correct spellings, look up the words they cannot spell in a dictionary, or seek help in spelling unknown words, will result in their abandoning their use of sophisticated words they do not know how to spell in favor of simple words they do know how to spell. The early school years are a time for experimentation, a time to risk making a mistake, a time for children to use the linguistic principles they know to construct their texts. So, the time for fixing the spelling in texts—like the time for fixing handwriting, punctuation, and capitalization—is after the writing, as a part of the editing process.

After the children are confident that the content of their texts is as they wish it to be, their attention can turn to spelling. They can, as Zebulon did, circle the words that they think are misspelled when they edit their pieces. When teachers hold editing conferences with their writers,

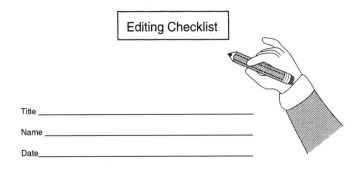

Title _____

Name _____

Date_____

Are you ready to publish?

Check ✓ your piece for the following:

____   1. Have you circled all the words you think might be misspelled?

____   2. Have you punctuated the end of each sentence? (? ! .)

____   3. Does each sentence begin with a capital letter?

____   4. Have you capitalized the names of people and places?

____   5. Did you indent the first word of each paragraph?

____   6. Is your title capitalized?

____   7. Have you read your piece aloud to check for errors?

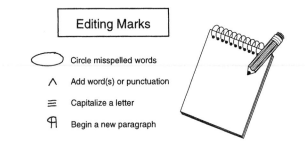

FIGURE 10.1   Editing checklist.

they can *teach* them spelling strategies (e.g., write the word several different ways until you discover the one that looks correct) and patterns or rules (e.g., [long vowel]–[consonant]–*e,* as in *take* or *bite*). In addition, teachers can pull words from the children's writing to explore the patterns that can be detected in sound, structure, and meaning features.

How Children Learn to Spell.   Encouraging children to use invented spellings in their writings is a concern to some parents. Teachers who know how children learn to spell can better explain the role of children's use of invented spellings to these concerned parents.

As explained in Chapters 4 and 6, children's emergent writing starts as pictures or scribbles and gradually becomes similar to conventional writing. Elizabeth Sulzby (1990) has identified seven broad categories of emergent writing: drawing as writing, scribble writing, letterlike units, nonphonetic letter strings, copying from environmental print, invented spelling, and conventional spelling (see Figure 6.4). For primary-grade teachers, invented spelling is the category of greatest interest because most children go through the multistage transition between invented and conventional spelling between ages six and eight years (described later in this chapter).

A number of studies have focused solely on invented spelling, providing very detailed information about this stage of spelling development. These studies have provided important information to assist teachers in explaining invented spelling and in determining how to help children develop their ability to spell words conventionally. The following three points briefly summarize this research:

1. Children who have had many experiences with print learn about how written language works through a process of discovery and experimentation. As explained in Chapters 1 and 3, children construct their own knowledge of written language as they interact with print and with people in everyday situations. Among the factors that contribute to children's discoveries about writing are being read to regularly, seeing adults who are important to them writing, and having access to writing tools. According to J. Richard Gentry and Jean Gillet (1993, pp. 22–24), three of children's first discoveries are that "print . . . stays the same," that "writing . . . is arranged horizontally" and moves from left to right across a page, and that "print . . . is made up of . . . certain kinds of marks."

2. At an early age, most children are able to detect the phonetic characteristics of words. They break words into their individual sounds and find a letter to represent each phoneme. These "finds," as Charles Read (1971, 1975) discovered, are not random. English-speaking children spell words by

   - using letter names (e.g., *C* for see, *LADE* for *lady*),
   - using only consonant sounds (e.g., *GRL* for *girl*),
   - omitting nasals within words (e.g., *ED* for *end*),
   - using phonetically based spelling patterns to represent artifacts (e.g., *chr* for *tr* as in *CHRIBLES* for *troubles*),
   - substituting *d* for *t* (e.g., *prede* for *pretty*).

   Children also employ several different strategies to spell words with short vowels, based on the place of articulation in the mouth. Short *i*, for example, is represented with an *e* (e.g., *FES* for *fish*), and short *o* is represented with an *i* (e.g., *CLIK* for *clock*).

3. Children's invented spelling changes as they become aware of the many rules and patterns that govern the English language. Most children pass through the different stages of spelling in the same order. The five stages (using Temple, Nathan, Temple, & Burris's, 1993, categories and labels) are as follows:

   a. *Prephonemic stage*—Children can form letters correctly, but they have not yet discovered that letters represent the sounds or phonemes in words. Letters are strung together randomly. This stage is typical of three- to five-year-olds (for example, "RAVRDJRV" may be used for "ocean road").

b. *Early phonemic stage*—Children attempt to represent phonemes in words with letters, but they usually only represent one or two letters in words. Typically, the initial and the final sound are represented. This stage is typical of five- and six-year-olds (for example, "MNMDF" may be used for "me and my dad fishing").

c. *Letter-name stage*—Children break words into phonemes and choose letters to represent the phonemes based on the similarity between the sound of the letter names and the respective phonemes. This stage is typical of six-year-olds (for example, "I WAT TO MAI FRNDZ BRATHDAY WE MAD AOI ON SUNDAY" for "I went to my friend's birthday. We made our own sundae.")

d. *Transitional stage*—Children write words that look like English words, though the words are not all spelled correctly. Typically, each syllable has a vowel. Unlike children in the earlier stages, transitional spellers no longer rely mostly on sounds to present written words; transitional spellers use a morphological and visual strategy also (e.g., *eightee* instead of *ate* for *eighty*). The child has a visual memory of spelling patterns. This stage is typical of seven- and eight-year-olds. (for example, "Out back thar is a pass. it is hils. and thar is a huj hil. and I krassd on my bike." may be used for, "Out back, there is a pass. It is [between] hills. And there is a huge hill. And I crashed on my bike.)

e. *Correct spelling stage*—Children spell nearly all words correctly, though like all of us, assistance may be needed with occasional troublesome words. Children typically reach this stage by age 8 or 9 years. (for example, "I am nice, talented and aspeily smart BECAUSE. . . . I moved up to second grade. The week was very easy in first grade and just right in second grade. I really like second grade. In lunch a fly landed on Allen's nose today and it went buzzzzzzz!")

So, learning to spell begins in the early years of children's literacy development. Children's early years, when they play with the forms and functions of print, are important because they lay the groundwork for children's later exploration of the alphabetic layer of spelling. By the early phonemic stage, children have some knowledge of the names of the alphabet letters and some awareness of sounds within spoken words. Now they can invent their spellings as they write. Notice how children are using consonants almost exclusively in the early phonemic stage. In English, according to Shane Templeton and Darrell Morris (1999) consonants emerge first in children's invented spellings because they are more salient acoustically and the children can feel their articulation. Vowels emerge later, in the letter-name stage.

By the time children move into the transitional stage of spelling, they have begun to understand how groups or patterns of letters work together to represent sound. A key indicator that children have progressed to this point is their use of silent letters in their invented spellings to represent long-vowel sounds. For example, for *tied* they might write *tide*. From letter patterns within single syllables, children will progress to understanding syllable patterns. Now, they grasp the understanding of "consonant-doubling/e-drop principles as it applies to simple base words and suffixes" (Templeton & Morris, 1999, p. 106). Understanding how syllables and suffixes work in spellings leads students to attending to the role of meaning in spelling. Now they correct words by relating words to the base. For example, they might write *oppisition,* look at it, see the word *oppose,* and understand how to correct their error.

By closely examining children's writings, teachers can understand the strategies children are using to construct written words. Each word can be categorized into one of the five spelling stages, and the percentage of words spelled using prephonemic, early phonemic, letter-name, transitional, and correct spelling strategies can be calculated. For example, if the word looks a lot like conventional English spelling, with a vowel in each syllable (e.g., "EGLE" for "eagle"), then the teacher knows the child used the sounds in the word and a visual pattern (*gle*) in constructing the word—strategies characteristic of a transitional speller. By engaging in this kind of analysis and calculating the percentage of words written at each stage, the teacher can identify the child as *primarily* exhibiting the strategies of a particular stage of spelling. (Children typically do not use strategies of one stage only.) Comparing two or more of a child's writing samples, written at different times during the year, helps the teacher understand the child's growth in spelling knowledge. With this information, the teacher can answer the question, Is the child becoming a better speller?

Helping Children Become Better Spellers. Will children learn to spell words correctly by discovery on their own? Today's spelling experts (e.g., Gentry & Gillet, 1993; Temple, Nathan, Temple, & Burris, 1993; Templeton & Morris, 1999) suggest that independent discovery is not enough; children need instruction to become expert spellers.

Unfortunately, while the theoretical and descriptive research has been "quite rich in describing what is happening cognitively as children learn to spell," the literature on what adults should *do* to assist children's development is not as clear (Sipe, 2001, p. 266). In fact, there is considerable disagreement about how spelling skills are best acquired. Can these skills be acquired by immersing children in a literacy-rich environment, where they have numerous opportunities to read and write for real purposes and audiences? Or do children need instruction in order to acquire these mechanical skills? The natural learning approach advocates argue with the direct instruction advocates. We have chosen a middle-of-the-road approach, an approach that recognizes the importance of children's immersion in a literacy-rich environment *and* of teachers providing their students with direct instruction in important mechanical skills. In essence, we have chosen a "balanced" approach. There is some evidence that this "caught" and "taught" approach yields greater gains in spelling performance than either one alone (Clarke, 1988; Gettinger, 1993). Below we detail some strategies that the literature currently recommends. The instruction we suggest will probably differ from the spelling instruction received by most readers. We believe instruction should vary, depending on the students' needs.

Prephonemic and **early phonemic spellers** need help learning more about how alphabet writing works. Appropriate goals for these young spellers include learning letter names and sounds, developing a stable concept of what constitutes a word, and discovering both how to break words into their constituent parts—to phonemically segment words—and how to represent the parts with letters. Bernadette Watson's mini-lesson on invented spelling is an example of an appropriate activity (see Trade Secret 8.8). As Bernadette wrote her piece on traveling to New York, she helped her young students break words into sound segments and select the best letter to represent these parts. She left spaces between the words and told the children why (e.g., "I need to leave a space here between these two words. The space tells me where this word ends and where this word begins"). As her children worked at writing their own pieces, Bernadette provided one-on-one instruction in these important skills as she conferred with each child.

These same kinds of activities are appropriate for **letter-name spellers.** As children move into this stage and have had many experiences with segmenting words and selecting the best letter to represent the spoken parts of each word, their accuracy will increase. More sounds are heard, including vowels. Occasionally, teachers might do as Elizabeth Sulzby has recommended. When a child says *went* is spelled *YNT,* the teacher might suggest that *YNT* is the way many children spell *went,* but soon they will learn that adults spell it a little differently—WENT.

Lawrence Sipe (2001) suggests another strategy, using an organizer such as Elkonin boxes to help students stretch out the phonemes or individual sounds in the words. As they stretch out the sounds and identify the corresponding letters, they fill in the individual sound boxes to complete the word. For example, to write the word *trap,* the teacher might present the child with three boxes.

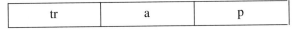

| tr | a | p |

The use of such a strategy gives students a visual representation of how phonemes are combined to make words. It also emphasizes the number of letters that are used to make each word.

Teachers might also wish to help each child at the **letter-name** stage to construct a personal dictionary of those words frequently misspelled in the child's writing. In some classrooms, these dictionaries are small spiral-bound notebooks, with one page per letter. In other classrooms, the dictionaries are 3- × 5-inch note cards. In still other classrooms, some teachers create a word wall where they list words frequently used and misspelled by members of the class. Typically, these teachers have each letter of the alphabet posted on the wall, and words troublesome to many children in the class are written on cards under the letter. Copying the correct spelling of frequently misspelled words from a personal dictionary when the words are needed in a piece of writing helps to establish the children's memory bank of how the words look and are spelled.

As letter-name spellers begin to move into the **transitional stage,** it is appropriate to begin asking the students to study a short list of not more than ten words per week (Temple et al., 1993). Recall that, for the typical speller, this will occur sometime during the second half of first grade. Other children do not reach the transitional stage until later in the primary grades.

So, which words exactly? Shane Templeton and Darrell Morris (1999) suggest several principles that teachers might use in the selection and organization of spelling words. First, the words selected should reflect the spelling features that students use but confuse when they write. For example, if the children are using but confusing short-vowel spellings, then they should work with words with this pattern. Attempting to teach these children long-vowel patterns would not be productive. Students who are using but confusing one-syllable long-vowel patterns should be studying these words; it would be inappropriate to ask them to study polysyllabic words.

Secondly, the words should be organized according to spelling patterns. Younger children might explore vowel patterns; older children might explore syllable patterns or spelling–meaning relationships (like *oppisition* and *oppose*). For younger children, the words should be organized around common features or patterns, for example the CVC short-vowel pattern.

Thirdly, at the primary level (grades 1–3) the children should be able to read the words automatically as sight words. At the upper grade levels, the students should be familiar with most words, but some new words might be included.

Direct Instruction. According to J. Richard Gentry and Jean Gillet (1993), formal instruction in spelling should possess six characteristics: self-selection, student ownership, self-monitoring, collaboration, feedback, and needs-based direct instruction.

In the past, the words to be studied were selected by textbook writers. Today, the recommendation is for teachers and students to select the words to be learned. Which words should be chosen? Two teams of researchers (i.e., Gentry & Gillet, 1993, and Temple, Nathan, Temple, & Burris, 1993) provide comparable advice: Some words should come from each child's reading and writing. As indicated above, words should be selected that the child will use frequently, which show a particular spelling pattern (e.g., [long vowel]-[consonant]-*e: name, hide, cute*), or which follow a consistent spelling generalization with no more than two different spelling patterns being evident in a child's weekly list. Good sources for these words include the books the child is reading, the child's personal dictionary, and the child's personal writings. Using these personalized words as the base, the teacher should add two or three words that share the same spelling pattern (e.g., *cat* and *fat* with *sat*), meaning pattern (e.g., synonyms and antonyms), or visual pattern (e.g., *ough* in *rough, cough,* and *enough*). Because the teacher and the child selected the initial words to be studied from the child's reading and writing, **self-selection** and **student ownership** is inherent in the word-selection process. According to Steve Graham (1999), each of these means for selecting words is equally as appropriate for students with learning disabilities as with those who do not.

Collaboration describes how students might study their selected words. Working with others helps students discover patterns in the spelling of words. Peers might study their words in pairs or they might administer tests of their words to each other. Working with other students reduces the tedium of studying for all students, learning disabled and non-learning disabled. J. Richard Gentry and Jean Gillet (1993) and Charles Temple and his colleagues (1993) recommend using the following five-day schedule:

- *Monday*—Each student's words should be called out, and each student should attempt to write the correct spellings. Obviously, because each student's list of words is different, the teacher cannot possibly call out each child's list. Students can work in pairs, taking turns calling out each other's list. Then, each list should be returned to its owner so that the owner can compare the correct spellings against his or her spellings. Words spelled incorrectly should be crossed out, and the correct spelling should be written beside each incorrectly spelled word. The processes of **collaboration, feedback,** and **self-monitoring** are evident.
- *Tuesday, Wednesday, and Thursday*—The students can work to learn those words they misspelled on the Monday pretest. Lynnette Bradley and Peter Bryant (1985) suggest that children be taught to study their words using a multisensory study technique such

as the one outlined in the following eight steps (a technique that provides image feedback and a lot of self-monitoring):

1. **Look** at the word, and **say** it aloud.
2. **Read** each letter in the word.
3. **Close** your eyes, try to **picture** the word, and **spell** it to yourself.
4. **Look** at the word. Did you spell it correctly?
5. **Say** each letter of the word as you **copy** it.
6. **Cover** the word, and **write** it again.
7. **Look** at the word. Did you write it correctly?
8. If you made any mistakes, **repeat** these steps.

On these days, the teacher might also bring the children together who are working on words with a common pattern for some group work. Games and exercises that play on the spelling patterns of the group's words can be profitable and fun. Thursday might also be a practice-test day. This instruction is clearly **direct** and **based on needs.** It is also fun.

■ *Friday*—Students are tested on the words they selected (with the teacher's assistance) for studying that week. Tests are administered and corrected, as they were on Monday. The new words each child has learned to spell are celebrated. The students can record the words they learned to spell correctly in a personal record-keeping book. Words that the child misspelled might be returned to the list for additional study next week or retired to be reviewed at a later appropriate time. **Self-monitoring, immediate positive feedback,** and **student ownership** are evident.

This test–study–test method works equally as successfully with good and poor spellers, although the efficacy of this procedure has not been specifically examined with learning-disabled students. Of course, the presumption is that the children can spell some of the words on the pretest. Otherwise, imagine the resentment against taking such tests. Further, the procedures suggested for studying the spelling words are equally as effective with learning-disabled students as with non–learning-disabled students. However, some data suggest that testing the students daily is an effective means of supporting daily practice (Graham, 1999).

This kind of spelling program—one that focuses on each child's word needs, that provides direct instruction based on the child's spelling stage and demonstrated knowledge, that celebrates each child's growth without comparing a child's growth against that of other class members, that supports invented spellings as developmentally appropriate for writers and not as errors—provides support for growing writers and spellers, helping them to tackle the challenges of writing and learning to spell with confidence and enthusiasm.

Remember that each of the strategies described here is equally as appropriate for learning-disabled children as it is for nonlearning-disabled students. As Steve Graham (1999, p. 96) notes: "teachers of learning disabled students need to explicitly teach [spelling] skills while simultaneously capitalizing on incidental and less formal methods of instruction. It is important to realize that an overemphasis on meaning, process, or form in writing instruction is not in the best interest of the child."

Grammar

Children come to school knowing a lot about how language works. By the age of six years, they know the basic grammar of the language used in their home. They have internalized the rules for creating language. Their grammatical knowledge is *implicit*—that is, children cannot tell their teachers the rules they are using, but they can intuitively use the rules to construct their oral texts. As Neil Daniel and Christina Murphy (1995, p. 226) point out, "All normal humans have full control of the grammar they use every day."

For some children, the grammar that works well at home is different from the grammar they meet at school. School's grammar is "a set of conventions, collectively known as usage, that govern written [and oral] discourse" (Daniel & Murphy, 1995, p. 226). School's grammar is an arbitrary system of rules, rules to be learned and demonstrated by students.

In the past, teachers tried to teach their students the rules of grammar or usage through drill. Readers may recall filling in tedious workbook exercises such as, **"The children _____ (was or were) playing."** Years of researching the effectiveness of this approach to teaching grammar led diverse scholars to the same conclusion: Students make almost no connection between this traditional grammar instruction and the production of their own texts (Hillocks, 1986). Even those children who successfully completed the exercises and scored well on the Friday tests rarely used what they had learned in their own writing and speaking. The main predictable outcome was that most students developed an aversion to studying grammar. A new method of teaching grammar was clearly needed. Note that the question was not: To teach grammar or not to teach grammar. As Constance Weaver, Carol McNally, and Sharon Moerman (2001) suggest, "That is *not* the question."

The constructivist perspective suggests that grammar should be taught as children engage in meaningful uses of language. More than anything else, humans need to be engaged with significant tasks (Csikszentmihalyi, 1990). Within these meaningful tasks, grammar instruction can help children understand that there are many ways of saying the same thing. As George Hillocks, Jr. (1986) suggests, teachers should show writers how to use a variety of syntactic structures (word orderings) and how to select the most effective structure for the current situation. For example, the grammatical structures used in writing a letter for publication in a newspaper are different from those used to write a letter to a grandmother.

The teaching of grammar, then, does not mean requiring children to memorize a collection of do's and don'ts! It does mean helping children learn how to manipulate language. For example, students can be assisted in selecting words to modify nouns, or they can learn to combine sentences by discovering the processes of embedding, deletion, substitution, and rearrangement of elements (Brosnahan & Neuleib, 1995). Yes, teachers should expose their students to grammar's vocabulary: *noun, verb, adjective, adverb,* and *clause,* yet students need very little of this to learn the conventions of written English. The difference today is that grammar's vocabulary and the structure of the language is studied within the context of a meaningful task.

The writing workshop provides a meaningful context within which to facilitate children's study of grammar. A significant component of the writing workshop is helping children use the writing process used by all writers. Within the writing workshop, writers produce products that are published in various forms for others to read. As Wendy Bishop (1995, p. 187) points out, "There is nothing like [publishing] to make us try to make ourselves and our writing presentable!" The opportunity to publish supplies considerable motivation for children to follow the conventional rules of grammar.

The components of the writing workshop—focus lesson, writing and conferring (content and editing conferences), and group sharing—provide grammar teaching and learning opportunities. For example, during a focus lesson, Deanne McCredie shared with her students a piece that she had written about her dogs. She finished by saying, "You remember I was working on this last week? Well, I thought it got kind of boring. It was funny when it happened, but my story didn't sound funny. I remembered the story of the wolf's view of his adventures with the three little pigs, and I thought, 'Why don't I try this piece from my dogs' perspective!' Here's what it sounds like now." Her students agreed that the story from the dogs' perspective made it "funnier"—though they professed to liking the story from her perspective also. The lesson continued with a brief comparison of the two perspectives. Ms. McCredie ended by saying, "When you work on your pieces today, you might think about writing about your topic from one of the character's perspective." So, as Weaver and her colleagues suggest and Deanne McCredie demonstrates, the important question to ask is, "What aspects of grammar can we teach to enhance and improve students' writing, and when and how can we best teach them (p. 19)?" Dawn Downes (see Trade Secret 10.1) would respond, "in the context of writing in writing workshop." The goal is to see students incorporating the grammatical constructions teachers teach into their writing, to see them using the grammatical constructions in their writing.

Focus lessons on grammatical constructions can take many forms. For example, teachers might model and ask students to generate sentences with particular kinds of grammatical constructions like those found in literature, or they might show students how to use the five senses in their writing to sharpen the details in their descriptions of objects and experiences in their writing. Carol McNally (Weaver, McNally, & Moerman, 2001) used Lois Lowry's *The Giver* (1993) in one of her focus lessons, a "mighty" focus lessons. She selected a paragraph from Chapter 9 and, "through a regression process," turned it into a piece of writing that sounded just like what her students wrote (p. 24). When her students read the passage, they thought it was "too choppy." So they combined sentences, rewrote the altered passage, and revised the paragraph to make it sound like what they thought Lowry would have written. Then they compared what they had written with what Lois Lowry wrote. Ms. McNally encouraged her students to think about how they might incorporate what they had learned about how to combine sentences in their own writings. What she discovered was a great use of participial phrases, appositives, and subordinate clauses in her students' writing—all without telling them they were studying grammar. So, grammatical constructions can be topics of focus lessons.

During teacher–student conferences, teachers can discuss the decisions their students made about their sentences or the perspective they decided to take on their topic, or many of the other grammatical and stylistic decisions writers must make to construct text. During editing conferences, teachers can help their writers consider the conventions of grammar needed to meet the demands of this text's situation. Is it going to the writer's grandmother or to the newspaper? As different grammatical constructions are taught in focus lessons, they can—as Judy Patton did—be added to the editing checklist. Joan Berger (2001) also did this. As well as providing instruction during focus lessons, Ms. Berger's peer editor's checklist gave specific directions on what peers should look for as they edited each other's

Trade Secret 10.1

Building Language: A Constructivist Approach To Grammar

Dawn Downes

The first year that I initiated a writing workshop in my classroom my students drafted writing, conferred with each other, and published their writing in a class anthology. I gave mini-lessons on topics, leads, revision, poetry, organization, and other parts of the writing process. I felt good about what was happening in my classroom. The kids were writing, and I felt like I was making a difference in the literate lives of my students. Several weeks into the workshop, however, one of my students came up to me and very innocently asked, "When are we going to do English?"

After I recovered from the surprise of her question, I stammered that we were doing English. To write is to accomplish what all of those grammar skills add up to. Satisfied with my less than polished answer, Sarah walked away to join her writing circle, but she left me with a nagging question in the back of my head that wouldn't go away: What was I doing about grammar?

I knew that many teachers teach formalized grammar lessons because they believe that it improves the quality of their students' writing. They also think that learning grammar makes language empirical, promotes "mental discipline," improves standardized test scores, facilitates the learning of a foreign language, improves social status, and makes our students better users of language (Weaver, 1996).

In reality, *more than fifty years of research suggest that teaching the grammar book in a traditional manner does not improve the quality of students' writing*. In fact, "if schools insist upon teaching . . . concepts of traditional school grammar (as many still do), they cannot defend it as a means of improving the quality of writing" (Hillocks, 1986, p. 138). Moreover, "the conclu-

sion can be stated in strong and unqualified terms: the teaching of formal grammar has a negligible or, because it usually displaces some of instruction and practice in actual composition, even a harmful effect on the improvement of writing" (Braddock, Lloyd-Jones, & Schoer, as quoted in Calkins, 1986, p. 195). Such strong words confirm what I had known instinctively all along: teaching the grammar book is a waste of instructional time.

To teach grammar in the context of student writing means that we follow a constructivist approach to teaching. In traditional grammar curricula, the language (or whole) is broken down into a system of rules (parts) that describe and prescribe how we use language. English teachers hope that their students will manage somehow to apply these "rules" and transfer their writing (and speech). However, students enter school with a knowledge of some version of English (a grammar), and learn best when their teachers help them to apply what they already know about the language in their writing, and then instruct them on those aspects they don't know. This contrasts sharply with a traditional grammar classroom where students are overwhelmed with rules and structures that are not directly applied to their writing and cannot be internalized. The rules and patterns may be momentarily memorized for a test or quiz, but in the end they are lost. Instead, in a constructivist classroom, students build their knowledge by learning in the context of authentic tasks. Students have the opportunity to write, and, as the teacher sees a need for grammatical coaching, a lesson is taught. However, since the grammatical rule and its authentic application are taught simultaneously, the new knowledge will be valued and attached to the existing knowledge about composition. Instead of learning the grammatical skills in isolation, they will be attached to meaningful texts in a powerful way (Brooks & Brooks, 1993).

There are four different kinds of grammar lessons that can be embedded in writing

(continued on next page)

Trade Secret 10.1 *(continued)*

workshop. All of these lessons start with student work; the teacher assesses the work, determines the grammatical needs of the writing, and plans lessons (coaching sessions) around those needs.

Incidental Lessons are lessons that are not taught through direct instruction. They take place during a student conference or casually as the teacher moves about the room, coaching students on their writing. The emphasis is on exposing students to the rules of grammar at the moment of greatest impact: right when they find that they don't know how to do or say something. The application is immediate and meaningful (Weaver, 1996).

Inductive Lessons are some of the most powerful lessons that students can learn. This is when students are presented with a collection of data (like student work) and they draw conclusions and formulate a rule based on the work (Weaver, 1996). As suggested by Brooks & Brooks, inductive lessons require students to construct knowledge and come to their own conclusions based on their own observations. Because the lesson came out of students' needs, the application of the rule derived inductively is immediate.

Mini-Lessons are described by Lucy Calkins (1986) as short, five- to ten-minute lessons that are direct with limited student interaction. The teacher is simply presenting an idea to the class. Several lessons in a sequence may be used to teach larger concepts. In general, the students are not required to practice the skill immediately, outside of the context of their writing, and the skills that are presented are not tested in isolation from the student writing.

Extended Lessons should take place when a concept is complex and the students would benefit from some practice of the idea. The teacher teaches a regular focus lesson and then the students are asked to apply it in a short activity. The focus of the practice is to clarify the concept, not necessarily to master it. Again,

the students will not be tested in isolation on this topic. Instead, the teacher should assess whether or not the students grasp the ideas based on their writing.

Altogether, grammar lessons that are taught in this manner fit into a curriculum in which the application of grammatical patterns is contextualized in response to student work and taught in an active learning curriculum. I was misguided in my original application of writing workshop. I thought that writing was the cumulative activity that grows from the application of other discrete skills. I was approaching the workshop from a parts to whole pedagogy. The students were "doing English" by using their grammar in writing.

Now I approach English and grammar from a different perspective. Students must use their prior knowledge of grammar to create a new piece of writing. Then, as a coach, I study their writing and create a grammar game plan that teaches them the grammar that they need to know in the context of when they need to know it. Grammatical knowledge makes writing effective and purposeful. I am not afraid to teach grammar. My students will learn grammar as they craft their writing around meaningful experiences, playing with language inside and outside the rules of grammar, searching for a clear voice to express their thoughts and ideas.

Bibliography

Calkins, L. (1986). *The art of teaching writing.* Portsmouth, NH: Heinemann.

Hillocks, G., Jr. (1986). *Research on written composition: New directions for teaching.* Urbana, IL: ERIC Clearinghouse on Reading and Composition Skills and the National Conference on Research in English.

Noguchi, R. R. (1991). *Grammar and the teaching of writing: Limits and possibilities.* Urbana, IL: National Council of Teachers of English.

Weaver, C. (1996). *Teaching grammar in context.* Portsmouth, NH: Boynton/Cook.

papers. For example, items on this checklist included: "Commas are used correctly after adverb phrases or with compound sentences. Place a check mark in the margin where commas are not used or used incorrectly." Through focus lessons, her students had the "verbal equipment" to recognize "adverb phrases" and "compound sentences" (p. 47).

This kind of grammar teaching provides support for growing writers and users of the language. It helps them to tackle the challenges of writing and to begin "to share in what every writer knows is grammar's 'infinite power' " (Hunter & Wallace, 1995, p. 246).

Now, it is possible that some readers are feeling moderately unsure that the grammar instruction *they* received helped *them* recognize adverbial phrases and compound sentences. For assistance with personal grammar questions, readers might wish to visit the Guide to Grammar and Writing site maintained by Charles Darling (http://webster.commnet. edu/grammar/index.htm). Readers who find themselves overwhelmed with all the information on this site might turn to the Big Dog's Grammar site, a bare bones guide to English (http://gabiscot.com/bigdog/). For numerous other sites to support teachers' teaching of grammar in the context of meaningful language activities, we recommend Nancy Patterson's article in *Voices from the Middle,* March 2001.

Capitalization and Punctuation

Children who learned capitalization and punctuation rules, as needed, in the context of their own writing perform equally as well on a standardized test as children who are taught using the more traditional skill-and-drill method (e.g., Calkins, 1980; Cordeiro, Giacobbe, & Cazden, 1983). Lucy Calkins (1980) also discovered that the students who learned the rules as needed within the context of their writing used more kinds of punctuation correctly within their pieces and explained the reasons why punctuation is used more clearly than did students taught using the traditional approach. Further, Pat Cordeiro, Mary Ellen Giacobbe, and Courtney Cazden (1983) discovered that teaching the rules in the context of the children's writing actually seems to provide children with **more** opportunities to practice using the rules than does the language-arts book and workbook they might have used.

Once a rule is introduced in Judy Patton's classroom, it becomes an item on the classroom's editing checklist. As with all items on this checklist, writers search the pieces they have selected for publication for words that should be capitalized that are not or words that are capitalized that should not be, as well as for punctuation that is missing or is used incorrectly. The practice of searching for errors and correcting them in one's own work provides instruction. Additional instruction occurs during the editing conference. The teacher can reinforce the rule supporting each self-correction made by the child and can call the child's attention to one or two words incorrectly capitalized or one or two punctuation marks used incorrectly. As in handwriting instruction, during the editing conference, the teacher has the opportunity to provide direct instruction on those rules of capitalization and punctuation the child needs.

Unfortunately, however, a child's piece typically has many capitalization and punctuation errors. The teacher cannot teach all rules simultaneously! Which rule should the teacher focus upon first? Teacher Judy Patton used her school district's language-arts textbook to guide her decision making. Ms. Patton decided to teach those punctuation and capitalization rules that her students' writings indicated they needed and that her district (by its selection of the language-arts textbook) identified as important. Teachers who have no textbook to guide their decisions have the advantage of focusing solely on their students' needs, selecting those most in need of attention, as determined by frequency of use in the children's pieces. Teachers may wish to use *The Elements of Style* (Strunk & White, 1979) and *Writers Express* or *The Write Track* (Kemper, Nathan, & Sebranek, 1995) as resources to guide their recall of capitalization and punctuation rules.

Handwriting

Before considering how to help children learn to make legible alphabet forms, teachers need to decide which handwriting style and form to use: manuscript or cursive style, vertical or slanted manuscript form.

Manuscript or Cursive Style?   Prior to the 1920s, U.S. children of all ages were taught only the cursive style (Hackney, n.d.b). Marjorie Wise's 1921 arrival in the United States from England marked the commencement of U.S. children being taught the manuscript style. Wise's introduction of the manuscript style, a vertical form with letters made with circles and straight lines, was quickly embraced by teachers as the writing style most appropriate for young children. Several reasons have been put forth to support the teaching of the manuscript style to young children (Barbe & Milone, 1980; Duvall, 1985; Farris, 1982; Graham, 1993/94, 1999; Hackney, n.d.b). These include the following:

- Manuscript letters are very similar to the print forms used in books. Only two lowercase letters, "a" and "g," are different in type than in handwriting.
- The print in children's world outside the classroom (e.g., "STOP," "SCHOOL BUS") is mostly in manuscript style.
- The manuscript style is easier to produce than is the cursive style.
- The basic strokes (mostly circles and lines) used in the manuscript style parallel young children's perceptual and motor development; the basic shapes are in their drawings.

The typical pattern has been to introduce children to the manuscript style first and then to the teach them cursive style in second or third grade.

Vertical or Slanted Form?   Which manuscript form: vertical or slanted? The title of Steve Graham's (1993/1994) article, "Are Slanted Manuscript Alphabets Superior to the Traditional Manuscript Alphabet?" summarizes the debate. Beginning in the 1960s, some educators began to question children's introduction to the vertical manuscript alphabet—a form like that used by the Zaner-Bloser Company in their handwriting program, *Handwriting: A Way to Self-Expression* (1993) (see http://www.zaner.Bloser.com). (Directions for how to form Zaner-Bloser's manuscript and cursive letters can be found in Figure 10.2.) Two concerns have been raised most frequently: (1) Young children often reverse some of the very similar lowercase letters (e.g., "b" and "d"), and (2) young children are being required to learn two distinctly different handwriting forms in the span of only two or three years. Concerns such as these resulted in the introduction of slanted manuscript alphabets, a

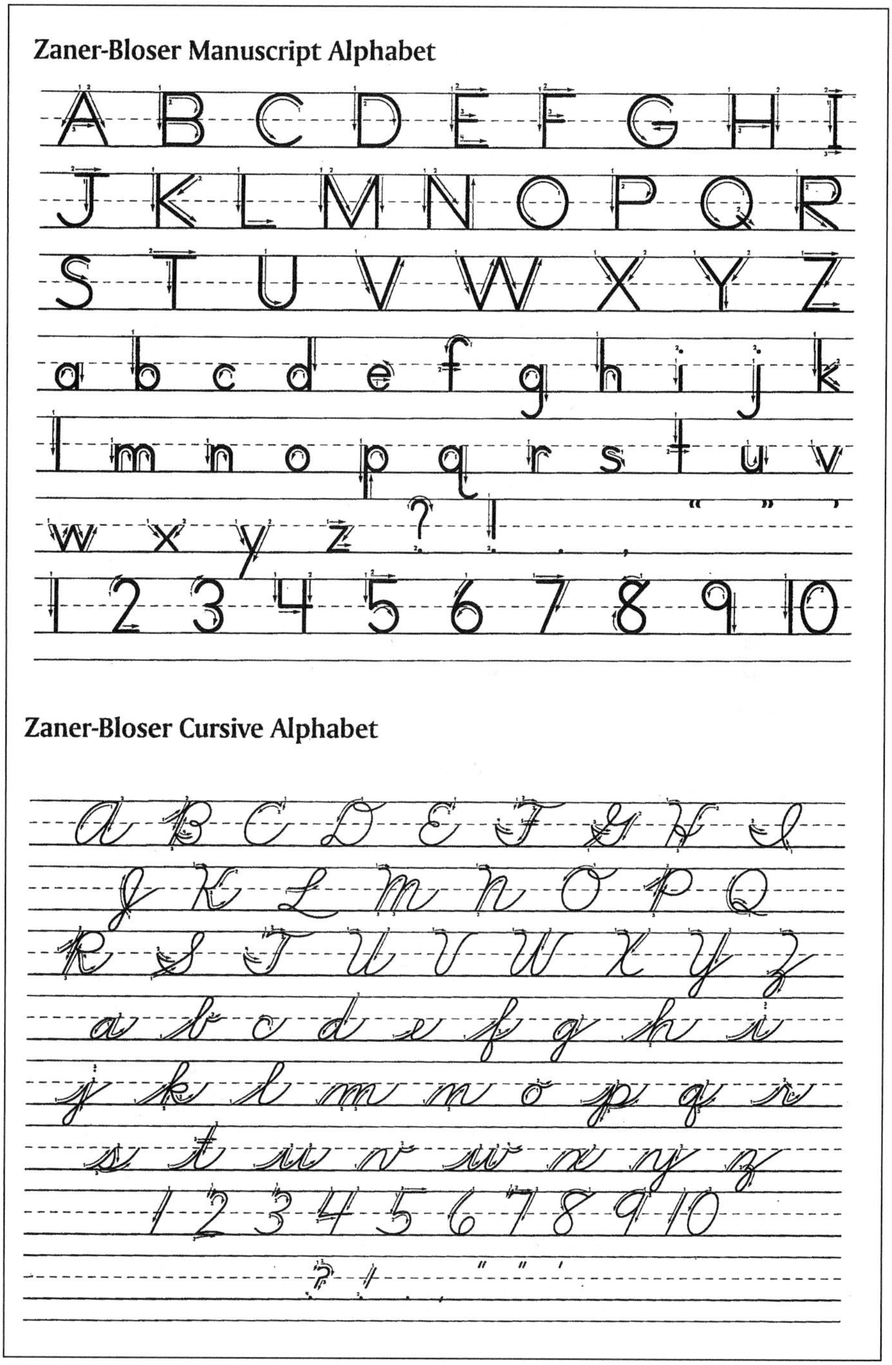

Zaner-Bloser Manuscript Alphabet

Zaner-Bloser Cursive Alphabet

FIGURE 10.2   Zaner-Bloser's manuscript and cursive handwriting forms.

Used with permission from Zaner Bloser, Inc.

manuscript form purportedly more similar than the vertical form to cursive writing. Today, for example, Donald Thurber's D'Nealian slanted manuscript alphabet is used in Scott, Foresman (1993) handwriting program, *D'Nealian Handwriting* (see www.scottforesman.com/language/dnealian.html). Another handwriting program, *Handwriting Connections* (1993), using a slanted alphabet is published by the McDougal, Littell Company.

Do the slanted alphabets really ease children's transition from the manuscript to the cursive style? Does the use of a slanted alphabet truly help children become better cursive writers? Several researchers (e.g., Duvall, 1985; Farris, 1982; Graham, 1992, 1993/1994, 1999; Ourada, 1993) contend that there is insufficient evidence to support the claims made by the supporters of slanted alphabets of the benefits of this form to writers. Instead, their findings indicate the following:

- The use of slanted alphabets does not help children to learn cursive more easily or quickly.
- The slanted alphabets' manuscript and cursive letter forms are, like the vertical manuscript and cursive forms, dissimilar.
- There is no evidence that using the slanted alphabets' continuous strokes to form manuscript letters resulted in children having a better writing rhythm, a faster writing speed, or a smaller number of reversed letters than when using single strokes.
- Slanted alphabets require young children to engage in fine-motor motions that are beyond their physical developmental level.

Hence, the present evidence seems to suggest that, if given a choice, teachers should choose to introduce their students to the vertical manuscript style like that from the children's environment outside the school. Learning the vertical manuscript style is also recommended for students with learning disabilities, even though there is no research examining the effectiveness of different scripts with these special needs students (Graham, 1999). Steve Graham adds a word of caution, however. Regardless of which script teachers teach their students, children will develop their own style. Teachers ought not to insist on a strict adherence to any particular model.

Teaching Children How to Form Letters.   Attention to how letters have been and should be formed is part of the editing stage of writing. The procedures used by first-grade teacher Donna Hutchins provide an illustration of how handwriting instruction can be woven into this stage of the writing process. When her first-graders are ready to publish their pieces, they compare their letters against models and circle the letters that they think are formed incorrectly. When Ms. Hutchins meets with each child during an editing conference, she selects a letter or two from among those circled by the child. Sometimes the letters selected are those that are most illegible; often they are those in the child's name; sometimes they are the two letters that appear most frequently in the child's piece.

Once the letters are identified, Ms. Hutchins provides *direct instruction* in how to form these few selected letters. She uses a procedure recommended by researchers such as Beatrice Furner (1985) and Karl Koenke (1986). She gives verbal directions for how each of the two letters should be formed; models how to construct the letters; observes as the child repeats the steps in making the letters while saying the directions softly; and provides the child with corrective feedback and reinforcement. Ms. Hutchins observes as the child forms the selected letters three or four times each. Then she asks the child to select the best formed letter.

The exception is with her learning-disabled students; she does not ask them to verbalize the steps for forming a letter while learning it. What seems to work best with learning-disabled students is to have them examine a model of the letter marked with numbered arrows and then to reproduce the letter from memory (Berninger et al., 1997). All children seem to benefit from the brief kind of supervised practice Ms. Hutchins provides for her students.

This procedure provides direct instruction in correct letter formation. Rather than introducing all students to each letter, instruction is individualized, focusing only on those letters each student needs assistance in learning to form. This teaching approach demands that the teacher maintain careful records of which letters have been introduced to which child and which letters each child writes correctly. Usually, a checklist is used to help the teacher track the students' handwriting progress and to recall which letters have been introduced to which children. When the teacher notices that some children have been introduced to the correct way to form a letter more than once, but they persist in forming that letter incorrectly, these children can be brought together for a brief session of direct instruction and practice in the formation of the problematic letter.

Left-Handed Writers.   Given that 10 to 15 percent (a percentage that is growing) of the population is left-handed, most teachers will have at least some left-handed students in their classrooms. Instruction for left-handed students is only slightly different from the instruction provided for right-handed students. First, it is important for the teacher to determine each student's hand preference. Most children develop a preference for their left or right hand sometime during the first four years of life (Bloodsworth, 1993). When unsure of the child's choice, the teacher can ask the child to throw a ball, to cut with scissors, to paint, to string beads, or to hold a pencil or crayon. These will provide **clues** regarding the child's hand preference. Sometimes, these observations will provide conflicting information. Carol Vukelich, one of the authors of this book, writes with her left hand, holds a tennis racket in her right hand, paints walls with her right hand, throws a ball with her right hand, manipulates puzzle pieces with her right hand, pours water with her left hand, and pours sand with her right hand. Fortunately, her first-grade teacher, Ms. Peggar, permitted her to choose which hand she preferred to use to write.

Three instructional adjustments are recommended for left-handed writers (Hackney, n.d.a; Howell, 1978):

- Left-handed writers might wish to hold their writing tools an inch or more farther back from the tip than right-handed writers. This change permits them more easily to see what they have just written.
- Left-handed writers should tilt the paper to slope downward slightly to the right about 30 to 40 percent, with the lower right corner pointed toward their midsection. (Right-handed writers tilt the paper slightly upward and to the left.) Too severe a tilt results in a backward slant to the letters.
- Teachers should permit left-handed writers to slant their handwriting slightly backward.

Of the three suggestions, the paper tilting is the most critical (see Figure 10.3). If the left-handed child fails to position the paper correctly, the child may end up writing with a

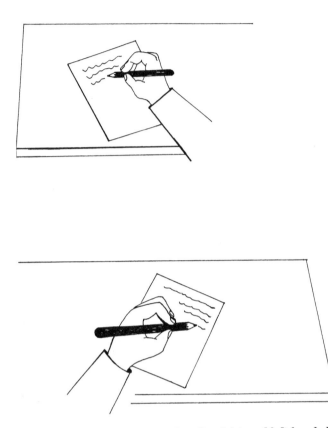

FIGURE 10.3 **Correct paper slant for right- and left-handed writers.**

hooked wrist, a problem that affects legibility and fluency and can cause erasure or smudging of what has been written. Carol Vukelich knows about these problems from personal experience. She has received many smudged notes from her left-handed father, whose teacher, Ms. Peggar, would not let him tilt his paper to the right. Fortunately, a generation later, when Ms. Peggar was Carol's first-grade teacher, she had changed her approach to teaching handwriting and allowed Carol to tilt her paper in the proper direction.

The kind of support needed by developing writers comes from handwriting instruction that focuses on each child's letter-formation needs, provides direct instruction in how to form the selected letters, and adapts to children's hand preferences.

Special Populations

Recall that one of the underlying themes of this book is respecting the tremendous diversity of children who are enrolled in today's early childhood programs. It is not surprising, therefore, that the general strategies we have recommended will sometimes need to be modified to meet the needs of specific children.

As explained throughout this book, ongoing assessment is a key requirement for providing this type of individualized instruction. Another important requirement is for teachers to be aware of the needs of special populations—groups of children who face common problems and challenges.

This section contains information on adapting instruction to meet the needs of two groups of children—bilingual second-language learners and children with various types of disabilities. Teachers will undoubtedly encounter many members of both groups of children during their teaching careers. Tailoring instruction to meet the needs of linguistically and developmentally diverse children is one of the hallmarks of excellent teaching. The special features that follow give practical tips to assist teachers in this challenging task.

Bilingual and Second-Language Learners

Currently, more than one in seven students in U.S. schools speak English as a second language (Barone, 1998), and the proportion is much higher in some areas such as California and other parts of the Southwest. In addition, the percentage of second-language learners tends to be higher in the earliest grades, forecasting even greater linguistic diversity in future classrooms. For example, one survey of Head Start programs reported that 22 percent of the students spoke Spanish at home and that 4 percent came from families who spoke one of 139 other languages (Tabors, 1998)! It is vitally important for early childhood educators to be prepared to help these children learn to speak, read, and write English. These children also need to be helped to learn content knowledge in subjects such as math, science, and social studies. Whenever possible, second-language learners should also be helped to continue to master their native languages.

In Special Feature 10.1, Sarah Hudelson and Irene Serna describe how the writing workshop can be adapted for use with second-language learners. As you will see, the writing workshop is ideally suited to the needs of children learning English as a second language. The main adaptation is to allow opportunities for children to become competent writers in their native language and then provide authentic opportunities and purposes for writing in English. The children's writing in their native language will mediate and facilitate their acquisition of written English.

Children with Special Needs

Recent legislation has mandated that children with disabilities be placed in the least restrictive environment. The goal is inclusion, allowing each child with special needs to have the maximum amount of integration into general education classrooms that is possible. The resulting mainstreaming of children with special needs into regular classrooms has radically changed the role of classroom teachers at all grade levels. Teachers are now expected to work as part of a multidisciplinary team (along with special education teachers, psychologists, and other specialists) to develop an individualized education program (IEP) for each child with identified special needs.

Meeting Special Needs of Bilingual and Second-Language Learners

Sarah Hudelson and Irene Serna

Question: How applicable is the writing workshop approach to non-native speakers of English? Answer: Totally! Bilingual programs (especially Spanish-to-English programs) have used this approach to teaching writing and have found that bilingual children can and do engage in writing for multiple purposes and audiences. These children need the same kinds of opportunities as nonbilingual speakers do. Through this kind of instruction, non-English-speaking children discover both the forms and the functions of their native written language (Edelsky, 1986; Flores, Garcia, Gonzalez, Hidalgo, Kaczmarek, & Romero, 1985, Freeman & Freeman, 1992a, 1994; Serna & Hudelson, 1993). Alicia, the Spanish-speaking kindergarten child introduced in Special Feature 3.3, demonstrates well the kinds of understandings that can emerge when children are given opportunities to write in a writing workshop. In her bilingual classroom, Alicia learned to write by engaging in writing. Through writing and through having others respond to her written works, Alicia learned about how written Spanish works, and she also learned that she could use written language to express herself, to communicate her intentions.

Developments in the field of English as a second language (ESL) teaching also support the workshop approach to the teaching of writing. At one time, ESL pedagogy advocated the sequential introduction of listening, speaking, reading, and *finally* writing and suggested devoting substantial amounts of time to children's oral language development before worrying about their reading and writing development. This traditional ESL writing instruction prescribed the writing of words,

then phrases, then sentences, and finally paragraphs from models. The assumption was that second-language learners needed extended, structured practice with the language before they could be asked to create text. When this method was used, these learners were never given the opportunity to write their own pieces. Fortunately, brave teachers began to test the use of the writing workshop with ESL students. Virginia Allen (1991) and Sarah Hudelson (1989) summarize these teachers discoveries:

- Young ESL learners can write from early on in their second-language learning experiences, while they are developing oral proficiency in the language.
- Young ESL writers' texts display features similar to those seen in native speakers' texts, providing evidence of ESL learners' experimentation with the new language, English.
- The texts produced reflect the learners' abilities in English at a particular time. As the learners' competence grows, the learner's texts change, offering evidence of how the learners are constructing and reconstructing the written language.
- Young ESL learners learn to write in English (a) by engaging in writing with varied audiences, for varied purposes; and (b) by having others respond to what they are writing—just as native speakers do.
- Like native speakers of the language, young ESL speakers are able to respond to the writing of others and to make changes in their writing.
- Writing ability in the native language facilitates writing in the second language.
- The teacher's role is crucial. ESL children are extremely sensitive to the teacher's beliefs about writing.

Given this new knowledge, what are the best practices in the teaching of writing to

(continued on next page)

Special Feature 10.1 *(continued)*

bilingual and second-language learners? How can teachers use the writing workshop to meet the special needs of ESL and bilingual students?

Facilitating First-Language Competence.
Encourage and support children to become competent writers in their *first* language. There is substantial evidence that time spent in becoming a writer of one's native language is time well-spent (Freeman & Freeman, 1994; Hudelson, 1987, 1989). The reasons for this benefit are many. Writing is the creation of meaning from one's intellectual and linguistic resources and activity. Construction of meaning will be enhanced if writers are able to use well-developed linguistic resources (the native language) rather than resources that are not as well developed (the second language). When ESL children write in their native language, their knowledge of how written language functions can be more easily constructed from a strong foundation in the spoken language (the native language) rather than from the weaker language (the second language). Native language writing provides children with opportunities to experience what writing is and does, how it functions for writers, and the uses or purposes it serves. Native language writing also gives children confidence in themselves in writers. Once ESL children know what writing is, how it functions, and how it can be used, they begin to experiment with writing in their second language, English. The specific time for this experimentation will be different for each young writer. Teachers should be guided by each child's timetable, not the calendar.

Teachers who speak and read the same language as the children can encourage and respond to their children's native language writing, even if they are not nearly as proficient in that language as they are in English. If the teachers do not know the children's native languages, then they might enlist the help of parents or community volunteers or other older children in the school. Response is important.

Encouragement of First-Language Use
When ESL learners begin to write in English, allow and encourage them to continue to use their native language to mediate their learning. There is considerable evidence that it may take second-language learners from four to six years to achieve full proficiency in English (Ramirez, Yuen, & Ramel, 1991). To deny access to the first language is to deny children the broadest, most complete access to learning. Additionally, if children are able to use both their native language and English, they may be able to articulate more completely what they know.

Benjamin, a Spanish-speaking second-grader, illustrates the importance of allowing ESL learners to use their native language freely. In the spring of second grade, Benjamin's bilingual second-grade class was studying China. Each child was to choose a topic of interest related to China, collect information about that topic, and prepare a report. Benjamin chose kung fu as his topic. School and public library resources were limited to English language materials, so Benjamin read about his topic in English. Then he switched into Spanish to write what he had learned. He needed to articulate what he had understood about his topic from his reading in English into his native language:

Benjamin's text in Spanish:	The English translation of Benjamin's text (Hudelson & Serna, 1994, p. 292)
Como pelean ConFoo	How do they fight kung fu?
ai muchos typos de CongFu.	There are many types of kung fu.
TiHe I CongFu	Tai chi and kung fu
En Ti He tocas con quien estas peleando	In tai chi you touch the person you're fighting with.

(continued on next page)

Special Feature 10.1 (continued)

Kungfu si pegas a
las personas

Y wingchum le pesieron
ese nombre porque
asi se llama el ombre
que inbento kungfu.

In kung fu you hit
the people.

after the man who
invented kung fu.

Third-grader Juan provides a second illustration. Juan chose to prepare a report on polar bears. His learning-log notes—notes taken from his readings, his interview of a zookeeper, and his viewing of a documentary—were written in both Spanish and English. After conferring in English with his teacher, Juan added information to his notes, which he then orally reviewed in Spanish with a group of peers. Juan was able to explain more coherently in Spanish than in English how the polar bear adapted to the Arctic. Juan then wrote the first draft of his report in Spanish. After peer and teacher response, he wrote a final draft in English. (The children chose whether to produce their final drafts in English or in Spanish.) Juan's Spanish writing facilitated construction of an informative text, which he wanted to write in English.

Juan's first draft written in Spanish:	Juan's second draft written in English:
Los osos polares viven in en artico donde hace mucho fio. Hay mucho hielo y nieve. Ellos tienen pel muy greso para que o tengan frio. El piel is negro y cuando el sol le pega se pone caliente para que no tengan frio.	Polar bears live in the Arctic in the north where it is very cold. day jave thick fur so day won't be cold. Polar Bears jave blak skin when the sun hits the fur ut terns warm so the polar Bear esn't cold.
Las garras y el pelo entre los dedos les ayundan andar en el hielo y nieve sin rebalarse. Osos polares tiene piel entre los dedos. El piel les ayuda a nadar porque pueden mover mas agua.	polar bears jave big claws and fur between their toes so they won't slip of the ice when they're walking. Polar Bers hae skin bituin their toes

which helps them
muve more water
and that's whi they're
good suimrs.

Pueden nadar abajo agua
por dos minutos. Cuando
estan nandando no tiene
frip porque el pelo es
muy greso.

Los senores los estan
matando porque quieren
su piel para chamaras. Han
matado muchos y por eso
estan en peligro.

Multiplicity of Opportunities for Authentic Uses of Second Language Recognize that children need multiple, authentic opportunities and purposes for writing in English. Children should not be asked to write in English simply for the sake of writing in English. Real reasons occur naturally within classroom life, particularly within the writing workshop; reasons do not need to be invented (Hudelson & Serna, 1994). For example, in Benjamin's second-grade classroom, there were both Spanish speakers and English speakers. When one of Benjamin's English-speaking friends moved to another school, Benjamin missed him a lot. He decided to write to him. Because he knew that Jimmy did not know Spanish, Benjamin wrote in English:

Benjamin's letter Jimmy:	Conventional to spelling (Hudelson & Serna, 1994, p. 283):
Dear jimmy, I mist jou sow moch ver du eu Lib uiarnt yu coming bac we d misiu Tichur ddyt tu Hector Tu I lov iu	Dear Jimmy, I miss you so much. Where do you live? Why aren't you coming back? We all miss you. Teacher did too. Hector too. I love you, Jimmy. Sincerely.
jemmy sensirali	

(continued on next page)

Special Feature 10.1 *(continued)*

Benjamin used a considerable amount of Spanish orthography in his letter, but he wrote in English because he wanted to communicate with Jimmy, and he knew that to do so, he needed to write in English (Hudelson & Serna, 1994). Later in the year, Benjamin's teacher established a pen-pal program, pairing Spanish-speaking children from her class with English-speaking children from another school and English-speaking children in her classroom with Spanish-speaking children from the other school. This provided all the children another opportunity to engage in communicating through writing, and it offered the Spanish-speaking children another opportunity to communicate in English.

Other examples of pen-pal programs are described in the ESL literature. For example, teachers have paired intermediate-grade native English speakers with primary-grade ESL learners in dialogue journal-writing programs (Bromley, 1995). In a third-grade class, children made biweekly visits to nursing-home residents. At Christmas-time, the children wanted to make cards for their senior "buddies." One child who had been reluctant to write in English produced the following card, her first English writing. She knew the card had to be written in English because her buddy could not read Spanish.

Child's card:	Conventional spelling:
Dar Arty,	Dear Arty,
I lav u dices u ar nas tu mi.	I love you because you are nice to me.
I lav yu tu.	I love you too.
Ga old ar u?	How old are you?
I em 8. I lac u tu mah	I am 8. I like you too much.
fam _____	From _____ .

These examples demonstrate that young ESL learners are very much aware of the contextual demands on their spoken and written language and illustrate how they respond to these demands.

Interdependence of Language Processes
Acknowledge that the language processes of listening, speaking, reading, and writing in a second language develop simultaneously and interdependently. That is, writing should not be isolated from the other language arts. Rather, writing is, and should be, connected to talking, to reading literature, and to study of content (such as thematic units or theme cycles).

Acceptance of All Attempts at Writing Communication
During children's early ESL writing experiences, be especially encouraging and accepting of all their efforts, encouraging the learners simply to write, to become comfortable and fluent as second language writers. If second-language writers are to become better at the craft of writing, they need to be willing to take risks, to experiment, to ask questions, and to make mistakes. They will be more willing to adopt this stance of experimentation if they receive encouragement, and if their efforts are acknowledged and celebrated (Peyton & Reed, 1990).

First-grader Catalina, for example, came to school knowing no English. She began writing in her journal after a month in school. She started by drawing pictures and labeling them with words that she copied from around the room. She asked her teacher for help with her writing. Her teacher accepted Catalina's efforts, assisted her, and always responded to her entries, but she also kept encouraging her to try writing independently. For several months, Catalina insisted on writing only words that she could spell accurately by copying or by asking an adult or a peer. The consequence was that her writing took on the form of patterns, such as "I drink milk for dinner. I drink milk for breakfast." It was not until the end of March of her first-grade year that she took a

(continued on next page)

Special Feature 10.1 *(continued)*

risk and wrote independently, using inventing spelling.

Catalina's writing:	Conventional spelling (Peyton & Reed, 1990, p. 86):
Friday I psie a psow the psow is read and Today I pie a crayons to.	Friday I buy a pencil. The pencil is red. And today I buy a crayons too.

Catalina's teacher celebrated the fact that Catalina finally had taken a risk in her writing and wrote back to her, "I didn't see your new red pencil. I did see your new crayons. Now you can do good work." This was a turning point for Catalina. Now, freed from the constraints of standard spelling, she could write about whatever she wanted. Her teacher continued to encourage her and to support her efforts. By the end of the school year, Catalina had added imaginative stories, science journal entries, and letters to her friends to her repertoire of writing. When interviewed before starting second grade, Catalina indicated that when she first started school she was afraid to write and always asked for help. Now, however, she judged herself to be a good writer who could figure out the answers to her own questions. Catalina had gradually developed confidence as a writer, and her teacher's attitude played a crucial role in that evolution.

Providing Special Assistance   **Adapt practices (such as writing workshop, dialogue and literature response journals, and learning logs) to meet the specific needs of second language learners.** While it has been demonstrated, for example, that young ESL learners are able to participate meaningfully in writing workshop (Samway, 1992; Peyton, Jones, Vincent, & Greenblat, 1994), they may need more assistance with their writing than native speakers. They may

benefit from extended talking about their chosen topics before and during drafting. They may need assistance with vocabulary and contextual cues such as how to use pictures or planning webs. They may be more successful with writing that is connected to a topic the class is studying rather than a personal experience since class activities may have provided more schema within which to write. Initially they may be less comfortable revising than native speakers or make more revisions that are word-based. A teacher's goal is to meet the needs of all her students within writing workshop, to provide the support each child needs to become a better writer.

Keeping Corrections to a Minimum   **Recognize that young ESL learners are individuals with individual personalities, interests, varying degrees of interest in and commitment to writing, and varying rates of learning the second language.** Remember the words of warning from Chapter 8? All learners do not learn at the same rate or in the same way. All ESL learners will not begin writing in English at the same time or under the same circumstances. Be patient. Be encouraging. Be supportive. Be reasonable about correcting the child's text—making the corrections fit the writing purpose and learner's language abilities. As with any writer, overcorrection will probably result in a decrease in the writer's interest in writing. How much correction should be done? What would be helpful to and manageable for this child? As was suggested earlier this chapter, choose one or two variations from conventional English, and focus on helping the learner correct those one or two errors. Think of this writing as learning in progress; over time, the child's writing will change and will move toward becoming more conventional. Also, over time, as ESL children develop more proficiency in English through many experiences writing, talking about their writing, hearing other students' writing, and talking about other students' writing, they will become competent writers of English texts.

While this movement toward full inclusion has generated new challenges and responsibilities for teachers, it has also created wonderful new opportunities for children with disabilities. Koppenhaver, Spadorcia, and Erickson (1998, p. 95) explain:

> The importance of inclusive instruction for children with disabilities is that they receive instruction from the school personnel who have the greatest knowledge of literacy theory and practice, the most training, and the greatest print-specific resources. They are surrounded by models of varied print use, purposeful reading and writing, frequent peer interaction and support, and the expectation that children can, should, and will learn to read and write.

These types of positive literacy experiences are especially important for children with disabilities. Marvin and Mirenda (1993) investigated the home literacy experiences of children enrolled in Head Start and special education programs. They found that the parents of children with special needs placed a much higher priority on oral communication than on learning to read and write. Parents of preschoolers with disabilities reported less adult-initiated literacy activity in the home, less exposure to nursery rhymes, and fewer trips to the library.

In Special Feature 10.2, Karen Burstein and Tanis Bryan describe how teachers can make accommodations to promote language and literacy learning for children with a variety of special needs. These adaptations, when combined with the activities described in this book, should enable teachers to get all students off to a good start in learning language and literacy.

Special Feature 10.2

On Your Mark, Get Set, Go: Strategies for Supporting Children with Special Needs in General Education Classrooms

Karen Burstein and Tanis Bryan

Previous chapters in this book have described how to set up and implement a balanced language and literacy program for young children. In this special feature, two early childhood special needs experts describe strategies for supporting children with special needs in such programs.

On Your Mark

Teachers in preschools, kindergartens, and the primary grades are increasingly likely to have children with special needs in their classrooms. Typically, the majority of these children have speech and/or language impairments, developmental delays, and learning disabilities. A smaller number of these children have mental and or emotional disturbances, sensory disabilities (hearing or visual impairments), and physical and health impairments. The latter reflects increases in the number of children surviving serious chronic conditions (e.g., spina bifida, cystic fibrosis) and attending school as well as increases in the number of children with less life-threatening but nonetheless serious health (e.g., asthma) and cognitive (e.g., autism) problems.

Public policy and law, including the 1997 Individuals with Disabilities Education Act (IDEA), along with humane and ethical considerations dictate that children with disabilities receive optimal educational programs, given our knowledge bases and resources. Further, *IDEA* stipulates that children with special needs be provided their education in classes with their age-same peers to the greatest extent possible.

One of the primary goals of early education is to prepare all young children for general education classrooms. Making this a reality for children

(continued on next page)

with special needs requires that teachers make accommodations and adaptations that take into account the individual child's special needs. Teachers' willingness to *include* children with disabilities and their skillfulness in making adaptations are critical determinants of effective instruction. This special feature outlines strategies and suggestions for teachers who have young children with special needs in their classrooms. Our purpose is to provide suggestions for making adaptations so that teachers feel comfortable, confident, and successful including these children in their classrooms.

Get Set

Cognitive, physical, sensory, developmental, physical, emotional—there are so many variations in development! It is not reasonable to expect general education teachers or special education teachers to be experts on every childhood malady. The primary lesson to remember is that children are far more alike than they are different from one another. Whatever their differences, children desire and need the company of other children. They are more likely to develop adaptive behaviors in the presence of peers. Children with special needs can succeed academically and socially in mainstreamed settings (Stainback, & Stainback, 1992; Thousand & Villa, 1990).

Setting the stage for an inclusive classroom takes somewhat more planning. Effective planning includes input and support from the school administration, other teachers, parents of children with special needs, and possibly the school nurse. Early and frequent collaboration with your special education colleagues is particularly helpful. There are significant differences between general and special education teachers' perspectives on curriculum and methods of instruction. Sometimes they differ in expectations for children.

Collaboration works when teachers constructively build on these different points of view. Collaboration produces multiple strategies that can be tested for effectiveness (as in the proverbial "two heads are better than one"). For collaboration to work, teachers have to respect different points of view, have good listening skills, and be

willing to try something new. It also requires systematic observation and evaluation of strategies that are tested. Teachers have to ask, "How well did the strategy/adaptation work? What effect did it have on the children in the class?" Here are some strategies for collaboration:

- Attend the student's multidisciplinary team meeting.
- Keep a copy of the individual family service plan (IFSP) or individualized education plan (IEP) and consult it periodically to ensure that short- and long-term goals are being achieved.
- Arrange to have some shared planning time each week with others who work with children with special needs.
- Brainstorm modifications/adaptations to regular instructional activities.
- Identify who will collect work samples of specific tasks.
- Assess the student's language, reading, and writing strengths, and give brief probes each week to check on progress and maintenance.
- Share copies of student work with your collaborators and add these artifacts to the child's portfolio.
- Collaborate with families. Parents are children's first and best teachers. Additionally, they possess personal knowledge of their children that far surpasses any assessment data we may collect.

Go

As previously mentioned, the majority of children with special needs have difficulties in language, reading, and written expression. Research indicates that these problems stem from deficits in short-term memory, lack of self-awareness and self-monitoring strategies, lack of mediational strategies, and inability to transfer and generalize learned material to new or novel situations. Hence, many children with special needs may have difficulty in classroom setting that utilize a high degree of implicit teaching of literacy. These children typically can benefit from explicit instruction. Here are some general teaching strategies

(continued on next page)

that teachers can use to support children with special needs:

- Establish a daily routine on which the child with special needs can depend.
- Allocate more time for tasks to be completed by children with special needs.
- Structure transitions between activities, and provide supervision and guidance for quick changes in activities.
- Adapt the physical arrangement of the room to provide a quiet space free of visual and auditory distractions.
- Plan time for one-on-one instruction at some point in the day.
- Use task analysis to break learning tasks into components.
- Recognize the different learning styles of all students, and prepare materials in different ways—for example, as manipulatives, audio recordings, visual displays, and the like.
- Try cross-ability or reciprocal peer tutoring for practice of learned material.
- Begin teaching organization skills such as the use of a simple daily planner.
- Teach positive social behaviors to all children.
- Consistently implement behavior change programs.
- Recognize and help children with special needs deal with their feelings.
- Encourage all children to respect and include children with special needs in their academic and play activities.
- Establish a routine means of communication with parents.
- Locate strategies that help parents that select materials that are developmentally and educationally appropriate for their children.

Speech Development

When children come to school, they are expected to be able to communicate. Language is the ability to communicate using symbols; it includes comprehension of both oral and written expression. Speech is one component of oral expression.

Many young children come to school with delays in speech and language (comprehension and expression). Speech problems such as misarticulations and dysfluencies are frequently seen in young children with and without special needs. Less obvious are problems understanding others' speech. Fortunately, the majority of children with language problems are able to successfully participate in all aspects of general education with a few modifications to the environment or curriculum.

Frequently, children with language problems receive special education services provided by a speech and language pathologist. However, the classroom teacher also has important roles to fulfill: (1) monitoring children's comprehension of instructions and classroom activities, and (2) providing opportunities for oral language practice and interaction with peers and adults.

The following are strategies that classroom teachers can use to help promote speech development in children with oral language delays:

- Collaborate with the speech and language pathologist in selecting activities, materials, and games that promote language development.
- Model appropriate grammar, rhythm, tone, and syntax.
- Keep directions simple, brief, and to the point.
- For students who have difficulty expressing themselves, do not rely solely on open-ended questions. Use yes or no questions that are easier to answer.
- When students with speech problems speak, give them your full attention and ensure that other students do the same.
- Errors should not be criticized. Pay attention to the content of the child's message. Do not call attention to misarticulations, especially dysfluencies, as the problem may become more serious if attention is called to it (Lewis & Doorlag, 1999).
- Children who stutter may have improved speech quality if alternate styles of communication are used, such as whispering, singing in a higher or lower pitch, or choral reading.

(*continued on next page*)

Special Feature 10.2 (*continued*)

- Give children with special needs multiple opportunities across the day to converse with you.
- Encourage parents to routinely engage in conversations using children's new words, experiences, and relationships.

Special strategies are also needed to help language-delayed children learn the meanings of new words (receptive vocabulary) and be able to use these new words in their speech (expressive vocabulary):

- Teach vocabulary in all subjects: math, science, social studies, health, and so on.
- Assess the child's prior knowledge before introducing a new topic.
- Have the student develop a word book of new words for practice. Pair these words with pictures.
- Encourage children to ask about words they do not understand. Pair these new words with concepts already known.
- Have the students paraphrase new words they are acquiring.
- Use physical demonstrations of words, such as verbs and prepositions, that are difficult to explain. Show children the meanings of these words.
- Have the students physically demonstrate the meanings of words.
- Use manipulatives that children can handle to teach new words.
- Give multiple examples of word meanings.
- Teach students to use picture dictionaries to locate unfamiliar words.
- Keep parents informed of these special strategies and urge them to continue their use outside of school.

For children with more severe special needs, secure the services of a specialist in augmentative communication. These individuals have specific skills in communication boards, electronic communication devices, and computer voice synthe-

sis. For more information about this special area, contact the Assistive Technology On-Line Web site at www.asel.udel.edu?at-online, sponsored by the DuPont Hospital for Children and the University of Delaware.

Reading Assessment and Instruction

For many young children with or at-risk for special needs, reading is a very difficult task. Many of these children benefit greatly from explicit instruction in the basic tools of reading (Chall, 1989, 1989; Slavin, 1989; Stahl & Miller, 1989) using a direct instruction model. Assessments of children's phonemic awareness (Torgesen, 1994) provide valuable information about the student's skills and deficits in basic manipulation of phonemes. Additionally, it is essential for teachers to match reading materials to the skills of students with special needs.

Once a student's instructional reading level has been identified and appropriate reading materials have been obtained, teachers can use the following strategies to help promote the reading development of the child with special needs:

- Use books without words to provide early readers with an overview of the sequence of story content.
- Teach students to use the context clues available in the text such as the title and pictures.
- Use cross-age tutors, pairing older children such as second-graders with kindergarteners, for drill and practice of sight words and newly learned words.
- Increase fluency by having students repeat readings often.
- Have students use a straightedge under a line of text to eliminate visual distractions and keep place and pace.
- Have students use their finger to point and keep place and pace.
- Tape text read by the teacher or other children. Have the student follow along and

(continued on next page)

Special Feature 10.2 (*continued*)

read aloud while listening to correct pronunciation, expression, phrasing, and punctuation.

- Echo read with the students. Sit behind and to the side of the child out of his or her line of sight. Read the text with the child softly into his or her ear, providing a model of pacing, pronunciation, and corrective feedback.

Writing Instruction

Most young children with special needs do not have physical impairments. However, many may experience delays in both fine and gross motor development. These delays may affect a child's ability to effectively grasp a pencil or shape letters and numbers. Large or ball-shaped crayons are often effective writing tools for children who have not developed a pencil grip. Many commercial built-up pencils or pencil grips are also available. When using these grips, be sure to instruct the child in the proper finger and hand placement on the pencil. For very young children with special needs, tracing letters in sand is a good place to start. Practicing letter structure in fingerpaints or liquid soap is also effective. Paper used by young children can be brightly colored in order to produce a contrast between the writing and the background. Initially, plain paper without lines is preferable to that with lines, as printing is similar to drawing. Using successive approximation of the appropriate size and shape of letters can be accomplished with wide-lined paper with different colored lines. These lines serve as cues for the child to stop or go. Young children with more severe special needs may require the support and services of occupational therapists. These therapists can provide you with expertise and specialized equipment to promote fine motor development.

Written expression by young children with special needs may present several problems for the teacher and the child, as writing is both a process and a product that requires physical and cognitive skills. The written product should be assessed using observable and measurable goals that correspond with the strengths and weaknesses of the child. Teachers need patience and repeated observations of children's written work in order to effectively evaluate and plan for writing instruction. The following are strategies for promoting written expression by young children with special needs:

- Allocate time for writing each day.
- Have children create simple stories from tangible objects that they can touch and manipulate, rather than asking for a memory or a concept. For example, give a ball to the child and ask the child to tell you about this ball. Have an adult serve as a scribe for the child and take dictation, writing down the story as it is composed. When the child is able, ask the child to copy the dictated copy and draw a picture of the ball.
- Compliment children on the content of their stories. Ask for more information about the topic and help them expand their stories.
- Develop a template for writing—for example, putting name and date on a specific area of the paper.
- Celebrate the child's successes!
- Exhibit examples of all children's work.

Including young children with special needs in the general education setting can be a rewarding experience for the children and their teachers. Assisting children to meet their potential is a teacher's responsibility. These strategies have proven to be effective for teachers supporting children with special needs in special and general education classrooms. However, the most effective tool for teachers is shared planning and collaboration. We urge teachers in all settings to share their skills, experience, and techniques with one another and celebrate the diversity of learners in the schools of this new century.

Summary

As we mentioned in the introduction to this chapter, the way in which skills are taught in the writing workshop is quite different from the way these skills were taught in the past. This change often makes parents uncomfortable and leads them to question whether handwriting, spelling, and grammatical conventions are being given adequate attention. Assure parents that skills are addressed in a writing workshop program. In fact, skills are being taught more effectively now than they were when the parents were students. Years of researching the drill-and-test approach to teaching skills have shown that students rarely used what they were believed to have learned in drill exercises in the texts they wrote! The writing workshop method is a definite improvement over the old method.

■ *When Will Children Learn about the Mechanics of Writing—Spelling, Grammar, Capitalization, Punctuation, and Handwriting—in Writing Workshop?*
Instruction in the mechanics of writing is embedded in the writing workshop. First, children are provided instruction on the mechanics of writing during the focus lessons that begin each writing workshop. The students' needs determine which mechanical skills are taught. For example, the observant teacher notices when many of the children are not capitalizing the names of the months in their pieces and teaches a lesson on the importance of capitalizing the name of each month. Or the teacher might notice that the students write in short, choppy sentences and decide to teach a lesson on sentence combining. Second, when the writers have decided that the content of their pieces is just right, and they wish to publish their pieces, they then turn their attention toward the mechanical details. They search their piece, attempting to discover their errors. They circle the words they think are misspelled. They look for words that should be capitalized that are not or words that are capitalized that should not be. They look carefully at how their letters are formed, circling those they think look odd. They search for places that need punctuation marks. They look carefully at the grammatical structures they have used. They might search with a friend after they have searched alone for their errors. Then, the students and the teacher edit the pieces to be published, and the teacher provides one-on-one direct instruction on one or two rules the students need in order to correct mistakes in their pieces because the pieces will be read by a particular audience.

■ *One mechanics of writing skill requires not only teaching within the context of writing workshop but also more direct teaching. That writing skill is spelling.*
When children begin to write, it is important that children are encouraged to use what they know about words and their sounds to write their pieces. Becoming a competent speller is a developmental journey, with all children progressing through five stages at their own rate. At each stage, children need to be provided with spelling instruction; formal spelling instruction—being assigned particular words to study each week—will begin when the child reaches the fourth stage. The words the children will study will be constructed from their writing and reading. The teacher will also add some words that share the same spelling pattern (e.g., if a particular child needs to learn to spell *cough,* then *rough* and *tough* might also be added to the week's spelling list). There will be spelling tests on Friday for students who receive formal spelling instruction. There is some evidence that spelling

instruction embedded in writing workshop and taught directly yields greater gains in spelling performance than either one alone. This is true for students who are learning-disabled and those who are not. This is also true for non-native English-language speakers.

■ *Given a choice, which handwriting style and form should teachers use? Manuscript or cursive style? Vertical or slant form?*

The answers are: manuscript and vertical for children who are learning-disabled and those who are not.

■ *How should teachers teach children to form the alphabet letters correctly?*

Children *do* need instruction in how to form letters. We recommend that this instruction take place during the editing stage of the writing process. Select one or two letters that the student seems to be having difficult forming correctly. Give verbal directions for how to form each of the two letters. Model how to construct the letters. Observe the student as the student repeats the steps in making the letters while saying the directions softly. Provide the student with corrective feedback. Observe while the student correctly forms the letters three or four times. Ask the child to select the best-formed letter. With learning-disabled students, do not ask them to verbalize the steps for forming a letter while learning it. Instead, have them examine a model of the letter marked with numbered arrows and then reproduce the letter from memory.

■ *Is writing workshop and teaching the mechanical skills of writing within writing workshop appropriate for non-native speakers of English?*

Absolutely! Non-native speakers of English have the same needs as native speakers of English. The focus of the writing workshop is to address the needs of each child. Hence, within the writing workshop, teachers can meet the needs of many different kinds of learners. Through writing workshop, second-language learners can and do engage in writing for multiple purposes and audiences, at first in their native language and then later in English. In the process, they learn about written language and about how to use it effectively.

LINKING KNOWLEDGE TO PRACTICE

1. Work with a colleague to develop a focus lesson plan on capitalization, punctuation, or grammar for a group of students.

2. Write the letters of the alphabet in manuscript vertical form. Check your letter formations against the letters in Figure 10.2. Repeat the task with cursive letters.

11 Using Literacy to Learn: Integrating the Curriculum

Pam Morse's third-grade students showed a growing interest in the outdoor environment, so Ms. Morse initiated a pond life project. She began the project by asking the children to tell her what they already knew about ponds (a typical KWL strategy) and by taking the children on a field trip to the Outdoor Learning Center. During the weeks that followed, the children returned to the Outdoor Learning Center often and engaged in such activities as checking the water temperature around the shore of the pond and comparing it with the temperature of water taken from a central location of the pond, estimating the pond's depth, comparing water samples from the shore with samples from the middle of the pond, studying the life that thrives in the pond, and comparing living and nonliving objects around the pond. Finally they were ready to begin their research studies. They decided on the topics they wanted to study and began gathering information from library books, the Internet, and magazines. They decided how to represent their knowledge (i.e., dioramas, a large poster, clay sculptures, reports). At the project's end, the children focused on what they had learned. Ms. Morse again used the KWL strategy. She asked the children to share what they learned during their study of the pond and she recorded their thoughts on chart paper. (Warner & Morse, 2001)

For many years, teachers have connected, or integrated, the curriculum. This approach to curriculum planning and implementation has had a variety of labels. Some teachers use the term *interdisciplinary curriculum* (Jacobs, 1989), while others speak about immersing their children in the study of a theme (Manning, Manning, & Long, 1994). More recently, many teachers suggest they are using the project approach (Katz & Chard, 1993).

Whatever the label, these teachers are heeding the advice of the National Council of Teachers of English (NCTE, 1993):

> Rather than working on subjects in isolation from one another, studying reading apart from writing, and apart from math, science, social studies, and other curricular areas, children learn best when they are engaged in inquiries that involve using language to learn, and that naturally incorporate content from a variety of subject areas.

When the language arts are woven into the very fabric of all subject matter areas, it is a classic win-win situation. Subject matter content and the language arts are both learned more effectively. As teacher Tarry Lindquist (1995, p. 1) points out:

> It is through the language arts that my students most often reveal their knowledge and apply their skills. Reading, writing, listening, and speaking are integral to all learning. Without language arts, the construction of meaning in specific topics is impossible.

An integrated approach to curriculum has three basic requirements: (1) a classroom environment rich with materials to support children's investigations, (2) a daily schedule that permits interweaving the various subject matter areas and focusing on a topic for sustained periods of time, and (3) teachers who view their role as a facilitator of learning rather than as a transmitter of knowledge. According to Goodlad and Oakes (1988, p. 19), these teachers "function more like orchestra conductors than like lecturers: getting things started and keeping them moving along, providing information and pointing to resources, coordinating a diverse but harmonious buzz of activity."

In this chapter we describe how many teachers are connecting the language arts, helping children use literacy to learn, planning integrated curricula designed to meet their children's interests and needs, designing classroom environments that support their children's investigations, and arranging for the time that is needed for their children's study.

Before Reading This Chapter, Think About . . .

■ The types of projects and units that you participated in when you were in school. What topics do you remember studying? Were these topics selected by the teacher, by the students, or both? What sorts of activities were included in the projects or units? How did you share the findings or products?

Focus Questions

■ What are the major differences between the subject-by-subject, correlated, and integrated approaches to curricula?
■ How can teachers plan and implement an integrated curriculum unit or project?
■ How can teachers arrange the classroom's physical environment and daily schedule to support the integrated curriculum?

Approaches to Curriculum Design

Before examining just how teachers are connecting the language arts and implementing an integrated curriculum, we briefly consider the range of curriculum choices available to teachers.

Subject-by-Subject

Some teachers use a subject-based approach in which each subject (language arts, mathematics, science, social studies, art, music, and physical education) has a separate time block during the day. These teachers make no deliberate effort to show the relationship between or among the subjects. When reading is over, the children put their reading books away and take out their spelling books. In these classrooms, the textbook determines the curriculum. These teachers seem to believe that children are vessels into which knowledge can be

BOX **11.1**

Definition of Terms

content standards: statements that specify the essential knowledge (the important and enduring ideas, issues, dilemmas, principals, and concepts from the disciplines) and processes (ways of thinking, working, communicating, and investigating) that should be taught and learned. Local, state, and national groups of teachers, administrators, parents, and representatives from businesses typically set these standards.

correlated curriculum: activities in different subjects are selected that are related to to a given theme or topic.

integrated curriculum: activities in different subject areas are selected in order to help children find answers to questions about a topic that is of interest to them.

KWL chart: a strategy for facilitating comprehension. Prior to studying a topic, the teacher makes a chart listing what children already know about the topic and what they want to learn about the topic. After the topic has been studied, the teacher makes a list of new things that the students learned about the topic.

learning log: a notebook in which children record their thinking about the topic being studied in a project or unit.

subject-by-subject curriculum: a curriculum in which each subject area has a separate time block during the day. For example, math is scheduled from 9:00 to 9:30, and the language arts are taught from 9:30 to 10:30.

webbing: a visual organizer that shows how various facets of a topic are related to each other. Teacher use webs to help children to generate ideas linked to a topic and to organize the investigation of the topic.

---

poured. Fortunately, this compartmentalized option is used less often in preschool and kindergarten classrooms than in the primary and intermediate grades. The authors of this book encourage teachers not to use this approach in any grade.

Correlated

Many teachers use a correlated approach to curriculum planning (also commonly referred to as the multidisciplinary approach). These teachers choose a topic for study, such as the circus, weather, monsters, or pigs. Sometimes the topic is selected because its study is required by the state or district social studies or science curriculum. For example, the district may require that all children in a specific grade study sinking and floating. Other times, the topic is selected because teachers know it is of interest to their children.

Typically, these teachers begin their planning by examining their district's suggested learning goals, objectives or standards in each subject area for their grade level. Then, they design activities or learning experiences that correlate with the selected topic and that permit their students to achieve these learning goals. Often, activities exhibit the planner's creativity, and usually these activities are fun for the children. Typically, these teachers plan lots of activities, and they gather all the children's books they can find on the topic.

One group of teachers chose rabbits as a topic of study for their students in April. These teachers made a deliberate decision to bring together the various discipline areas. Together, they planned a range of activities that would be placed in the various centers (e.g., the mathematics center, the writing center) in their classrooms. Figure 11.1 provides an illustration of the activities offered to the children on one day.

There are several shortcomings with this approach to designing curriculum. First, what did the children learn about the rabbits during this day? What major concepts or understandings about this animal were addressed? Often when teachers seek to have each of the subject matter areas represented in a theme, the topic serves as the conduit to teach or reinforce skills. Learning about the topic is subjugated to a minor position.

One Day of a Multidisciplinary Rabbit Study

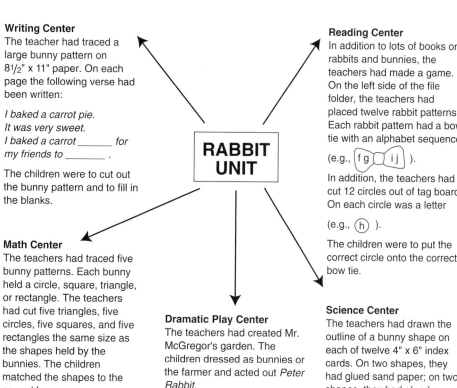

Writing Center
The teacher had traced a large bunny pattern on 8½" x 11" paper. On each page the following verse had been written:

I baked a carrot pie.
It was very sweet.
I baked a carrot _____ for
my friends to _____ .

The children were to cut out the bunny pattern and to fill in the blanks.

Math Center
The teachers had traced five bunny patterns. Each bunny held a circle, square, triangle, or rectangle. The teachers had cut five triangles, five circles, five squares, and five rectangles the same size as the shapes held by the bunnies. The children matched the shapes to the correct bunny.

Dramatic Play Center
The teachers had created Mr. McGregor's garden. The children dressed as bunnies or the farmer and acted out *Peter Rabbit.*

Reading Center
In addition to lots of books on rabbits and bunnies, the teachers had made a game. On the left side of the file folder, the teachers had placed twelve rabbit patterns. Each rabbit pattern had a bow tie with an alphabet sequence (e.g., f g   i j).

In addition, the teachers had cut 12 circles out of tag board. On each circle was a letter (e.g., h).

The children were to put the correct circle onto the correct bow tie.

Science Center
The teachers had drawn the outline of a bunny shape on each of twelve 4" x 6" index cards. On two shapes, they had glued sand paper; on two shapes, they had glued a cotton ball; on two shapes, they had glued corduroy; and so on. The children took turns matching the bunnies by the textures of their tails.

FIGURE 11.1   One day of a multidisciplinary rabbit study

A second problem relates to the activities themselves. Was matching the shapes in the math center or matching the textures in the science center right for all children in the three classrooms? In all likelihood, some children could already sort and even label the shapes. Was this activity an appropriate use of their valuable school time?

Were these activities worth the tremendous investment of the teachers' time? A comparison of the teachers' preparation time with the children's doing time would reveal that the teachers spent far more time constructing the activities than the children spent doing them.

Finally, is the activity in the writing center a writing activity? To provide activities in each of the centers sometimes results in a deviation from the principles of quality instruction we have described in this book. Clearly, the links or connections across the various curricular areas are artificial.

Integrated

The topic of dinosaurs was chosen by a group of teachers in Colorado and was developed into an integrated unit. Judith Gilbert (1989) described these teachers' unit. First, the teachers decided on the concepts they wanted to address and queried their students about the questions they wanted answered during their study of dinosaurs. For example, one concept centered on one of the children's question about the size of dinosaurs: How big were dinosaurs? The teachers designed an activity to help their young children understand dinosaurs' size and to answer their question. One of the teachers drew a full-sized outline of a dinosaur on the school's parking lot. The number of children who could fit inside a dinosaur was estimated and calculated. Many children could fit inside the dinosaur outline! Then the teachers had the children lie flat, with one child's feet touching the top of another child's head, on the parking-lot outline, extending from the bottom of the dinosaur drawing's feet to the tip of the dinosaur's nose. In this way, the children were able to determine that a dinosaur was about ten children tall. Did that mean a dinosaur could see over the school building? To help the children answer this question, ten children's silhouettes were traced vertically on a roll of butcher paper. The school's custodian kindly climbed to the roof of the building and hung the butcher paper from the top of the school building. The children discovered that the paper was longer than the school building was high! This helped the children understand that dinosaurs could see over their school building. Numerous other activities were implemented to help the children answer their questions and understand the major concepts about dinosaurs.

In the preceding example, concepts about dinosaurs and children's questions drove the teachers' creation of the educational activities. Subject-matter areas appropriate to the activities or projects were woven naturally into the children's investigations. The seams among the subject-matter areas were erased. Notice that school time was structured around the children's needs. Thus, the schedule had to be flexible. The teachers had to be alert to the knowledge and skills the children were acquiring through the activities. In addition, the teachers had to consider new ways to legitimately weave subject areas and skill development into the activities.

This integrated curriculum approach (also called the interdisciplinary approach) "trusts the teacher to be a good problem solver and wise decider" (Lindquist, 1995, p. 2).

This kind of instruction, which is an integral element of the constructivist philosophy, requires a teacher who

- Shows innate curiosity, sharing children's interests and enthusiasm about the world
- Supports children's intellectual curiosity by organizing the environment and the schedule in ways that encourage children to pursue their ideas
- Willingly collaborates with children in the designing of the curriculum. (Klein, 1991)

How do teachers make the right decisions and design quality curricula? What might their classroom schedules look like? How do they design their classroom environments? These questions are the foci of this chapter.

Erasing the Seams: Designing Integrated Curricula

Phase 1: Selecting a Topic

Some experts believe topic selection should be negotiated between the teacher and the students, with the teacher attempting to be responsive to as many children's interests as possible. Topics would emerge from collective planning with the children. Teachers might begin by holding a brainstorming session during which the children identify topics they want to study. As the group discusses each of the topics listed, some topics might be combined. Then the class might narrow the options by identifying what they would like to learn about first.

Which topics might these children study? Several writers provide teachers with words of advice, for example, select topics that are

- not too broad and not too narrow and that lend themselves to children's study (Jacobs, 1989);
- broad, such as endangered species, homelessness, and human rights (Manning, Manning, & Long, 1994);
- relevant to children's daily lives, for example, topics like the children's homes, families, and food; the local community's people and businesses; important local events and current affairs; nearby landmarks, rivers, hills, or woods; and natural phenomena like the weather, water, wind, and air (Katz & Chard, 1993).

However, in a growing number of public schools, teachers are not completely free to work with their students to select the topics of study. In many areas of the country, committees of teachers, administrators, parents, businesspeople, and community leaders in states and districts have agreed on the knowledge and processes children must learn in each discipline area. These statements are called "content standards." In these states and districts, teachers must use these content standards in their instructional units and learning–teaching activities planning.

Douglas Harris and Judy Carr (1996) suggest there are several ways teachers might use their state and district standards to help them identify relevant topics. Topics could be based on student questions or interests (e.g., Pam Morse's children's study of the pond); on community resources (e.g., Pam Morse's use of the Outdoor Learning Center); on curriculum expectations (e.g., all fourth-grade children study the history of the state); or on a topic or essential questions suggested by the standards themselves (e.g., all children need to learn to write persuasively). Once the topic is tentatively identified, the teacher then must consider which content standards can be addressed through the study of this topic. Those interesting topics that are unrelated to the standards must be ignored if children are to learn the content the state and the district have stated they must know.

Teachers' use of standards in their curriculum planning is relatively new. The public believes that high and rigorous academic standards are a way to establish what all students need to know and be able to do and to ensure that all children have access to high quality education. Further, the public believes that students, teachers, and parents need a clear idea of what students should learn each year. In this way, the public can hold schools accountable for ensuring that all students meet or exceed that stated standard. Judy Carr and Douglas Harris (2001, p. 7) elaborate: "Should all teachers teach 'Y'?.... Ultimately these conversations lead to meaningful and sustained reform in curriculum, instruction, and assessment." Ultimately these conversations also lead to groups of teachers at the district or the school level having a strong voice in which topics children need to study at each grade level. States and districts are struggling to determine how they can ensure that all their students are exposed to the same content, and that their teachers have sufficient time to supplement the required content with topics of specific interest to their students and to take advantage of serendipitous learning opportunities.

Phase 2: Determining What the Children Already Know and What They Need and Want to Learn about the Topic

Once the topic has been selected, it is important for the teacher to know what the children already know and what misconceptions the children possess about the topic before activity planning begins. Often teachers begin by constructing a KWL chart with their children—a chart with three columns, the first two of which show the answers to the questions: What do you already know? What do you want to learn? After the study of the topic is completed, the third column of the chart shows the answer to: What did you learn? (Ogle, 1986). The teacher serves as the recorder of the children's collective knowledge.

At this stage of information-gathering, it is important to accept and record all comments made and questions generated by the children. Not only is knowing what children know important for their teachers, but knowing children's misconceptions also provides their teachers with insights into needed learning experiences. As Sandra Wilensky (1995, p. 43) suggests, teachers "have an obligation . . . [to] dissolve stereotypes and generalizations such as 'All Africans live in huts.' and 'All Eskimos live in igloos.' "

Certainly, during the group discussion, because teachers are members of the classroom learning community, the teacher might raise questions to extend the children's thinking about what they might learn. For example, as the children consider the topic of dinosaurs, a popular topic with many groups of children, if no child raises the question about how big they really were, the teacher might suggest that this is something she or he would like to learn. "Do we know how big dinosaurs really were? I've seen them on television, but I've always wondered: If a dinosaur stood beside me, how much taller than me would it be? I've also wondered: Could a dinosaur fit in this room? I don't think so, but how tall and long were they? I'm interested in answers to these questions." With that, the teacher's question (How big were dinosaurs?) could be added to the What do you want to learn? column on the KWL chart.

Observant teachers often see links between the topics the children want to study and what their districts or states say the children must study. When such links are possible, they alert their children to the questions the district or state wants them to be able to answer. All teachers are not free to do anything they choose! As suggested earlier, many teachers must also be alert to what the children *need* to know about this topic. For example, before Pam Morse's children studied the pond, Ms. Morse likely considered the Texas science content standards. Perhaps she added questions like "What happens when objects made of different materials are left out for a long time? Do they change?" Because her children would be reading, writing, and speaking during their pond study, she probably also considered the Texas English language arts standards. Perhaps she added a question like "How can I persuade people not to pollute the pond?" Because her children might be drawing posters or making clay sculptures, she might have also considered her state's visual and performing arts standards. Perhaps she added a question like "What color best expresses my concern for what people are doing to the pond?" As a member of the classroom learning community, Ms. Morse is free to add specific questions to the *What do you want to learn?* column on the KWL chart.

Carol Avery (1993) described another reason teachers need to understand what their children know about a topic before they plan activities. In a 45-minute discussion, her young students demonstrated their knowledge of all of the concepts about urban, suburban, and rural communities outlined in the Lancaster County, Pennsylvania, district curriculum guide. Her students had lived in the area for all their young lives and had attended to their environment. Life had provided her children with this knowledge. Had Carol not begun with a What do you already know? discussion, she would have wasted time presenting information and offering her children activities on concepts they already understood.

In Figure 11.2, we present the KWL charts generated by two of Denise Cusanelli's third graders before and after their investigation of rocks. These charts are good illustrations of what two students knew, wanted to know, and learned about the topic of rocks. (Note that Ms. Cusanelli had some work to do to correct one student's belief that rocks "are glued to stay together.")

What subtopics are represented by the children's questions? By looking over all the questions, it is possible to develop a list of subtopics. For example, following a group discussion on the environment, a teacher identified the following subtopics embedded within the children's questions: recycling/disposing, pollution, litter, and garbage.

After the list of subtopics has been generated, the teacher can construct a web. "A web is a kind of visual brainstorm that helps to generate ideas and link them to a theme or central focus" (Huck, Hepler, Hickman, & Kiefer 1997, p. 652). It is also "a mapping of the key ideas and concepts that a topic comprises and some of the major subthemes related to it" (Katz & Chard, 1993, p. 88). By preparing a web, teachers can see whether the topic has sufficient depth and breadth to warrant the children's investigation. Figure 11.3 is a sample web on trash prepared by a second-grade teacher.

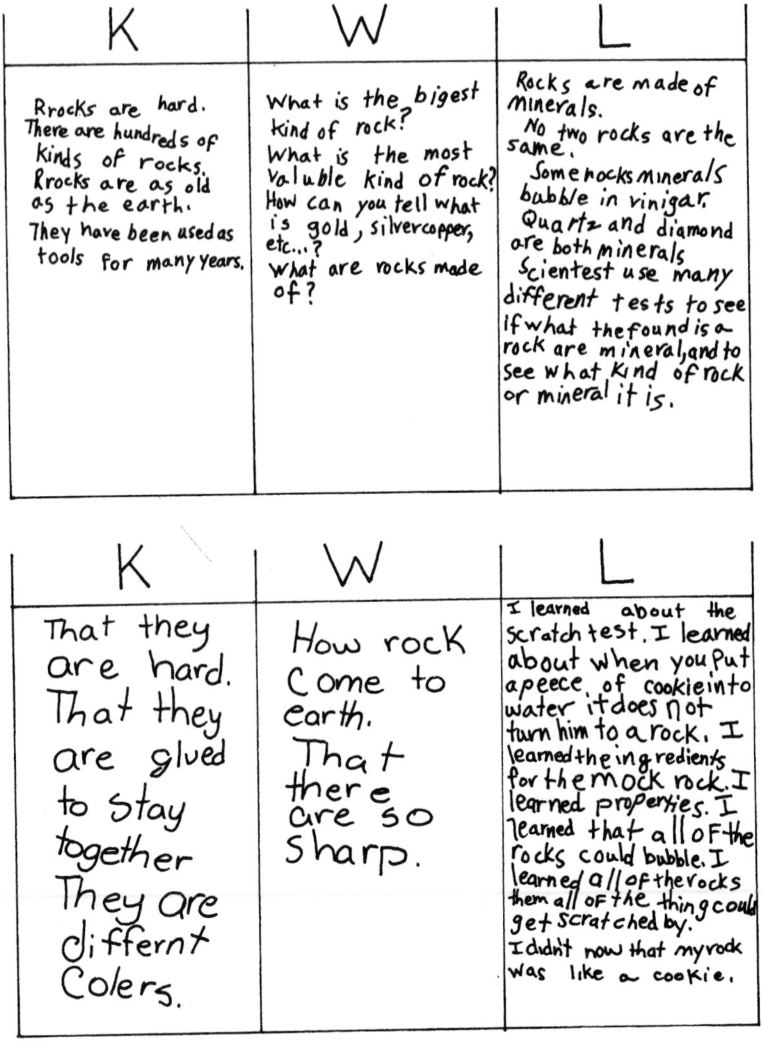

K	W	L
Rrocks are hard. There are hundreds of kinds of rocks. Rrocks are as old as the earth. They have been used as tools for many years.	What is the bigest kind of rock? What is the most valuble kind of rock? How can you tell what is gold, silvercopper, etc..? what are rocks made of?	Rocks are made of minerals. No two rocks are the same. Some rocks minerals bubble in vinigar. Quartz and diamond are both minerals Scientest use many different tests to see If what the found is a rock are mineral, and to see what kind of rock or mineral it is.

K	W	L
That they are hard. That they are glued to stay together They are differnt colers.	How rock come to earth. That there are so sharp.	I learned about the scratch test. I learned about when you put a peece of cookie into water it does not turn him to a rock. I learned the ingredients for the mock rock. I learned properties. I learned that all of the rocks could bubble. I learned all of the rocks them all of the thing could get scratched by. I didn't now that my rock was like a cookie.

FIGURE 11.2   Two third-graders' KWL charts.

Phase 3: Determining Ways to Answer Children's Questions: The Activities or Projects

The concepts and standards to be addressed, the questions generated, and the children's misconceptions drive the decisions about which activities these children will do during their study of the topic of interest. Since major concepts relative to each topic are embedded in children's and teachers' questions, teachers know their children will come away from their study with important understandings. In addition, teachers know that the vari-

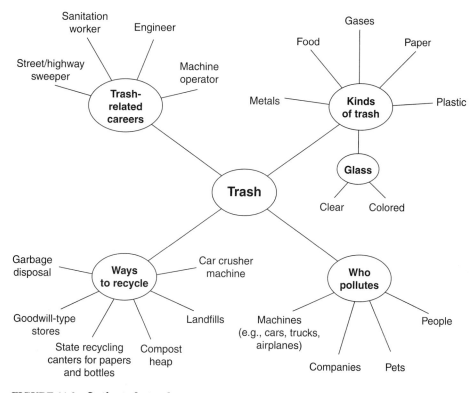

FIGURE 11.3   Let's study trash

ous subject matter areas are embedded in the questions. In contrast to when the multidisciplinary approach is used in curriculum planning, integrated curriculum teachers are not concerned that every subject matter area or every classroom learning center is blended into the study of each topic. Teachers using the integrated approach do not set out at the beginning of their planning with the intention of ensuring that all subject matter areas are covered. They know that most, if not all, subject areas will be embedded in each topic's study using this approach. If activities are planned thoughtfully, the activities will draw heavily on a variety of disciplines for facts, skills, concepts, and understanding. In fact, it will be nearly impossible not to weave the language arts into nearly all of the activities. The children will be doing lots of listening, reading, writing, enacting, speaking, and observing.

Judy Helm (1999) describes how a group of children approached their study of photography. The children interviewed and worked with experts. That is, their teacher made arrangements for them to interact with adults who knew a lot about photography. Helm reminds teachers to talk with the experts before their visit to the classroom about the children's developmental level and to encourage the experts to consider leaving something with the children, perhaps something like "a small light table so that the children can view slides they've taken together" (p. 28). The class also went on various field trips. Helm reminds teachers to make the following preparations before each field trip:

- Make a pre-trip visit to explain that the children will have specific tasks they are hoping to do while they are at the site.
- Prepare the children by reviewing what they want to learn from their visit to the site.
- Decide how the children will make a record of their trip.
- Make a list of the questions they want to have answered.

Children might bring clipboards, paper, and pencils with them to make sketches of what they see, or they might bring cameras.

Some teachers believe that, because the content standards are written in each discipline area, they cannot use the integrated curriculum approach. That is what Adrian DeTullio thought until she worked with Susan Drake and learned that it is possible to do both—use an integrated curriculum and address the standards (Drake, 2001). These two educators began their planning by

- studying the mandated curriculum for possible connections among required units of study. They selected Medieval Times (social studies) and Pulleys and Gears (science and technology). They quickly realized that the language arts and art standards would be woven into the study also.
- reading all the relevant standards in those discipline areas to discover the broad-based and cross-disciplinary standards. They discovered, for example, research and inquiry standards in social studies, science, language arts, and the arts.
- refreshing their knowledge of medieval times by gathering information from other teachers, reading children's literature, viewing a CD-ROM, and using the Internet.
- using the *know, do, be* framework to help them put the project together (Drake, 1998). The *know* component identifies the facts and knowledge—the big ideas—that they wanted the students to understand (e.g., heritage, citizenship, and systems). The *do* component identifies what the students needed to demonstrate (design and construction, research and inquiry, presentation). The *be* component addresses how they wanted the students to act during the project (collaboration, responsibility, respect).

King DeTullio introduced his fourth graders to Medieval Times by holding court. As the children worked through the project's or unit's activities of creating a portcullis or drawbridge, designing and constructing a castle, writing research reports and stories, dancing, drawing portraits, role-playing, giving oral reports, and reading literature, Mr. DeTullio simultaneously covered the mandated standards. In fact, more standards were addressed than Mr. DeTullio and Dr. Drake originally thought would be. In addition, they realized that they could have incorporated math and physical education standards into this integrated project. Now, teacher DeTullio sees the connections across subject areas and across the standards.

In Adrian DeTullio's classroom, collaboration was important. Collaboration is also important in Bobbi Fisher's (1995) classroom. Bobbi puts her children into study groups, called "committees," to answer their questions. As stated in a letter to parents requesting the parents' assistance with the study of Africa (a topic required by the school district's social studies curriculum), each committee's task was to "research its topic, arrange activities, and plan ways to present information to the rest of the class." (p. 25). Committees were formed in this classroom, as follows: Ms. Fisher made a graph with the six subtopic choices (animals, clothing, the arts, food, houses, and languages), and she wrote each child's name on a Post-it™ so that the names could be moved easily (see Figure 11.4). The children put their

Topics	Children's Choices			
Animals	Anne	Chris	Linda	Jeff
Clothing	Carol	Rob	Marie	Steven
The Arts	Amy	Tom	Emily	Joe
Foods	Mary	Jack	Susan	Jim
Houses	Dianne	Bill	Brenda	Ron
Languages	Tony	Lois	Brad	Pam

FIGURE 11.4   Making committee assignments.

names on the column of their first choice. As a class and as committees, the children were now ready to investigate the Africa topic and its subtopics. After about two weeks of reading, writing, talking, and reflecting, each committee meets with Ms. Fisher to determine the projects they will develop to teach others about their subtopic.

Sharing Learning with Others.   As teachers plan for and consider various ways for students to express their learning, they want to be cognizant that knowledge can be expressed in many different ways. In most instances, several different kinds of products will be possibilities. Typically, the children will choose the product that seems most appropriate for them.

Maryann Manning, Gary Manning, and Roberta Long (1994) describe several different ways that children can express their knowledge. They suggest that "*replicating,* copying something someone else has created, has its place" in the study of a topic (p. 47). For example, when Bobbi Fisher's (1995) first-graders studied Africa, they made masks, adinkra cloth, and traditional African foods. While studying local Native Americans, Denise Cusanelli's students wove baskets, made a small replica of the type of shelter used by the Native Americans studied, dyed cloth using berries and roots, wove cloth, and made food eaten by these early Americans.

Of course, learning can be demonstrated by "many forms of *original expression*" (Manning et al., 1994, p. 48). Children might create a time line, build a model, design a diorama, or prepare a reader's theatre. (In *readers theatre,* the players read their lines, and there are no elaborate sets or costumes.) They might prepare an oral presentation or a debate.

Often, children will use writing as a form of original expression to demonstrate their learning. Of course, what is written need not always be a report. Perhaps the written product will be a petition, such as the one Carol Avery's children's produced. Teachers should be alert to the diversity of writing products that their children might create. Maryann Manning, Gary Manning, and Roberta Long (1994) provide two and one-half pages of different forms of written expressions of knowledge that children might prepare! Their list includes such ideas as advertisements, ballads, billboards, cartoons, demonstrations, editorials or letters to the editor, fashion shows, game boards, manuals, newspapers, obituaries, pamphlets, posters, and puppet shows. Nancie Atwell (1990a, p. 163–166) suggests 29 options. While Atwell's list was constructed with older children in mind, several of the suggestions (e.g., how-to book, math-concepts book, friendly letter, coloring book) are appropriate for young children.

These numerous suggestions include examples from the three major discourse categories: expressive (e.g., construction of the script for puppet shows), persuasive (e.g., letters to the editor, editorials, advertisements), and informative (e.g., newspaper articles, pamphlets, reports). It is important to provide children with numerous experiences and options for presenting their findings.

Informative Reporting.   Many teachers teach their students about writing informative reports during their study of a topic. For example, in Laurel Bok Swindle's first-grade classroom, while studying animals, each student completed a research project on one animal. In Trade Secret 11.1, Ms. Swindle describes her first graders' first adventure with the writing of an informative piece.

Trade Secret 11.1

Teaching Report Writing to First-Grade Children
Laurel Bok Swindle

For five months, my first graders had been writing personal narratives in our "Authors' Workshop," a writing class held twice a week. When I decided to teach them a new form of writing, I chose research reports. I knew it would be my task to surround the children with the information and experience they would need in order to have something on which to report. In addition, the children would need to learn how to take notes so that they could organize and retrieve information for inclusion in their reports. Because I wanted the children to write interesting reports, which involved the reader and expressed the children's sizeable personalities, I would need to find good informational books to serve as models. With these concerns in mind, I introduced the project to the children.

Topic Selection

I had three requisites to fulfill when selecting the area for study. If I wanted the children to be committed to their work, the topic would have to be of interest to them. If I wanted them to gather information, there had to be a wealth of resource material available to them. If I wanted to be able to justify the project academically, the topic had to be extracted from the curriculum. I chose the category Animals, taken from our science curriculum.

At the outset of the project, I explained that each child would choose an animal on which to become an expert. As we progressed through the science unit, I introduced them to a variety of animals they might wish to consider. Some of the children decided on a topic immediately. Keith wanted to write about snakes—cobras especially. He told us about the cobra conversations he and his brother held, snugly tucked into their beds, lights out. Keith truly owned his topic from the beginning. Other children made their choices as they read books, watched films, or listened to their friends and classroom visitors.

Research

Once every child had selected a topic, I sent the list to the school librarian. Although she was able to locate a book for every child, many of these books were inappropriate for beginning readers. The children could not read or understand them without adult guidance. Few could serve as models for the kind of writing I wanted the children to do.

Therefore, I was dependent on the children's families to help the children to digest the material. Unfortunately, some families did not cooperate. For those children, I squeezed in time to read and discuss their books with them.

As Lucy Calkins (1986) suggested, I instructed the children to "fill up their heads" with information about their topics. They were not yet to write a single word. During this prewriting period, we spent much time talking, viewing films and filmstrips, reading, and even singing about animals. Our bulletin boards and windows were crammed with animal pictures. We were getting into the mood to write.

Note Taking

Each child had a writing log in which to keep notes and drafts. The first page contained the child's name, topic, and bibliographic information. The second page was for note taking.

Before I allowed the children to write, I asked them to tell a friend what they had learned. I hoped that these conversations would help fix ownership of the topic in their minds. Perhaps talking first would facilitate writing—not pedantic, stilted writing, but writing with a personal voice and commitment.

After their conversations, the children listed all of the facts that they felt they might need. Later, during the writing of their drafts, I encouraged them to check this fact sheet for ideas and for accuracy of information.

Copying

The note-taking lesson seemed like a good time to talk about plagiarism. Being authors themselves,

(continued on next page)

Trade Secret 11.1 *(continued)*

the children understood the concept of literary ownership. They did not want others to steal their work, so they were comfortable with avoiding this offense themselves.

Writing

Selecting a Literary Model

With the data gathered, we were ready to begin our first drafts. I experienced my first uneasy moment when it became apparent that some of the children thought note taking was the report. It was then that I appreciated my search for appropriate literary models. I found an excellent model in *What's Wrong with Being a Skunk?* by Miriam Schlein.

Reader Involvement

Because Schlein's book involves the reader from the first sentence, maybe from the title, reader involvement seemed like a good first writing lesson. I explained that when a writer speaks to his or her audience as though they were holding a conversation, the writer makes the readers want to read more. I read the first page:

> Sometimes, when someone has done something very nasty to you, something mean and rotten and unfair, you might say "YOU'RE A REAL SKUNK." Why do you say that? What's so bad about skunks?

The children agreed that Miriam Schlein had pulled us into her piece. As it appeared that they understood this writing element, I left them to begin their first drafts. When we reconvened 30 minutes later, I was astonished by their attempts to master reader involvement. Following are three successful examples:

> Did you ever go to the zoo? Did you see a monkey? Did you know that monkeys are like humans because they got hands and belly buttons like humans?
>
> Larry

> When you hear a bounce, guess what? What you hear is a kangaroo.
>
> Ann

> Do you know that the mother rabbit cannot go to the baby rabbit in the morning? Do you know why?
>
> Alexis

It was clear that using Miriam Schlein's book had made an impact on my children's writing.

Focus

One aspect of writing that we had learned about was the difference between real writing and listing. When an author lacks commitment to a given topic, she or he often lists facts without developing the supporting information. Ironically, the work then becomes listless, without vigor. Many of the children understood this difference, but because of their limited knowledge and experience, many of them resorted to listing.

Once again we returned to the skunk book for guidance. We talked about how Miriam Schlein devoted eight pages to discussing the skunk's ultimate weapon, the stink, before continuing to another aspect of the skunk's life.

Many of the children began with good intentions regarding focus. Few were able to sustain their intentions throughout the reports. Lists of unrelated facts tended to trail at the end of their work.

Revising

The revision process during this unit was continuous. The children had learned to confer both with their peers and with me to help improve their writing. I found that they were more serious about their revisions of informative text than they had been when writing personal narratives. Perhaps they respected the material because it had come from books rather than from their own lives. Perhaps my attitude about the project being grown-up influenced them. Maybe they were just

(continued on next page)

Trade Secret 11.1 (continued)

becoming accustomed to revision as a natural process of writing.

Publishing

Using the charming pen-and-ink drawings done by Ray Cruz in the skunk book as a model, the children illustrated their reports. I typed and made copies of each child's work. We collated the pages into one book, which the children entitled *Animals in Action*. We made a table of contents with four subheadings.

Extension Activities

We kept the books in the classroom for several days so that we could use them for extension activities. Using a guide sheet I had prepared, the children worked with the Table of Contents page and individual reports to find information and answer questions. The children drew posters to advertise their work, and we invited their families to join us in the celebration of the completion of our book at our "Authors' Reception." Their first research reports were a great success!

Second-grade teacher Marianne Bors's students also wrote informational reports. Ms. Bors had not intended to have her students prepare polar-animal reports. However, as the unit on polar regions came to a close, the children complained that they had not had enough time to study the animals of the region. They decided that if they each prepared a report, they could learn about the animals from each other. Ms. Bors questioned, "Well, which polar animals would you like to know something about and what information would you like to know about these polar animals?" Together, they decided they wanted to know about penguins, polar bears, seals, walruses, Arctic foxes, and snowy owls. They also decided that each person's report should include information on the animal's home, color, food, and some interesting facts selected at the writer's discretion.

Ms. Bors suggested that each student select one of the animals and that they write their report alone or with a co-author. Sarah Marsh chose to investigate the walrus alone. She read about walruses on her CD-ROM encyclopedia on her home computer. She handwrote her notes on a form provided by Ms. Bors, with a column for each of the four items the children had decided were important for them to know about each animal. During the writing workshop, Sarah prepared the draft of her written report and shared it with her peers and teacher in conferences. She typed her final draft on her home computer.

A comparison of Ms. Swindle's and Ms. Bors's approaches to teaching informational writing reveals many similarities.

- Both teachers permitted their young writers to *select topics of interest* to them within the broader topic under study (i.e., polar regions, animals).
- Both teachers helped their young writers consider what information should be gathered. They helped their students *identify the questions* they wanted to answer through their research. As one young writer of an informational report is quoted as saying about the data-gathering process: "We wanted to write things we wanted to learn about or teach to people" (Winship, 1993, p. 8).
- Both teachers found a way to solve the problem in which much of the written information was too difficult for most of their children to read independently: Both issued a *call for help*—and parents, grandparents, the principal, and other adults responded.

- *Plagiarism* was discussed in both classrooms. These first- and second-graders learned that you summarize the information you want to record in your own words.
- As drafting began, the children used the *familiar components of the writing workshop* (teacher and peer conferring and group share time) to receive feedback and response to their work. These teachers used the mini-lesson time during the writing workshop to inform their students about the process of being writers of informational texts and about what makes informational pieces good. After the students edited their drafts, they *published* their pieces in books. Ms. Swindle's students published one edited class book, which was photocopied so that each child could have copy of this important first informational writing effort. Both classes of children used *writing and reading to learn.*

The product of such information gathering need not always be a written report. In Ms. Bors's state, the English language arts content standards (Delaware Department of Public Instruction, 1995) suggests that children of all ages should have opportunities to present what they know, not only in writing but also orally. Given the children's enthusiasm for their written reports about polar-region animals, Ms. Bors decided to have the children present their reports orally. First, the children and Ms. Bors decided on the criteria that would make an oral report good. They decided that the presenters should

- show that they knew the information about their animal,
- wait to begin until they had everyone's attention,
- speak slowly,
- speak loudly enough so that everyone could hear,
- look at the audience, and
- look at their reports only when they needed to and not very often.

Before making their oral presentations to the class, the children practiced presenting their reports in school with a peer and at home as homework. After each child finished making his or her report, the class discussed how well the child had exhibited the six criteria of a good oral presentation.

Note Taking.   One skill that Ms. Swindle's and Ms. Bors's students needed to acquire in order to prepare their informative reports was how to make notes on what they read, heard, or viewed. Regie Routman (1991) describes how she and third-grade teacher Julie Beers taught note taking to Ms. Beers's students. First, Ms. Routman and Ms. Beers demonstrated note taking. They reproduced a page of an article on the left-hand side of a transparency, leaving the right-hand side blank for their notes. They projected the page for the children to read along with them as they read the words aloud. As they read, they underlined the key phrases and important points. As they read and highlighted the key points, they verbalized their thinking for the students. Why was this phrase or point important? Then they showed the students how to prepare notes from each of the key phrases and important points.

Next, they divided the students into small groups. Each group was given a copy of a portion of a different article, written on a transparency. Each group was directed to underline the key phrases and important points. Then each group wrote its notes for each important point on the right-hand side of the transparency. When this task was completed, the groups shared their work and received their peers' feedback.

When the students had seen the teachers' demonstration, had collaborated with a group of colleagues to do what Ms. Routman and Ms. Beers had done, and had received their peers' feedback to their work, they were ready to make notes on the materials they read for their research projects. Notice that the teachers had provided direct instruction in the mini-lesson and that the lesson had an immediately applied reason for being taught.

Integrating Literature into the Study.   As children engage in investigation activities, they will be reading many different materials (books, encyclopedias, pamphlets), or having information read to them. The teacher's role is to gather trade books (fiction and nonfiction) that are correlated with the topic under study. For example, when Nancy Edwards' kindergartner's studied the pond, Nancy's library corner was filled with books about water and the animals who live in it. When Tarry Lindquist's (1995) students studied pre-Revolutionary War America, they read historical fiction novels.

Readers should become familiar with the American Library Association bimonthly magazine *Book Links: Connecting Books, Libraries and Classrooms.* This magazine lists books, suggests activities, and recommends literature useful across the curriculum. Each month it contains annotated bibliographies of books connected to a theme, possible discussion questions, author interviews, activities, and lists of related books.

Learning Logs.   Many teachers request their children to keep learning logs while they engage in the learning activities or projects. Learning logs are notebooks in which children record their thinking and their discoveries. Unlike diaries, they are meant to be shared with others and to be reflected upon. In their logs, children

- systematically record the data they obtain through observations, reading, talking, and interviewing (e.g., the number of pets each classmate has, their classmates' favorite colors or sports);
- make predictions and speculations;
- describe experiences;
- record descriptions of activities;
- identify problems; and
- write summaries.

Carol Avery (1993) summarizes: Learning logs "are vehicles that can be used for speculating, predicting, recording, documenting, webbing, charting, listing, sketching, brainstorming, questioning, imagining, hypothesizing, synthesizing, analyzing, and reflecting" (p. 444). They are, says Nancie Atwell (1990b, p. xviii), "tools [for children] to generate their own knowledge."

While students write in their learning logs, their teachers can have informal conferences with them. As her children wrote in their learning logs, Carol Avery (1993, p. 444) moved among them, asking "How do you know this?" "Why is this important?" "What do you think?" She reports that the children began posing similar questions to each other. Children really can keep learning logs. They will write using personalized, emergent forms of writing to record their information.

Phase 4: Assessment and Evaluation

Recall what you read in Chapter 1: Assessment and evaluation are intricately woven into the learning process; teachers gather data about their children's study of topics (assessment), and they make judgments about what their children have learned and need to learn (evaluation) while their children are engaged in learning.

While children work, teachers gather evidence to document their children's learning, skill development, and dispositions toward learning. Using these data, teachers and the children themselves make judgments about the children's learning. Note that, unlike in past years, it is not just the teacher making judgments about the children's learning. Child self-evaluation is a critical component of the new assessment and evaluation procedures.

Two teachers, Lisa Burley Maras and Bill Brummett (1995, p. 100), summarize their new view of assessment:

> We no longer viewed assessment and evaluation as something that comes at the end of a learning experience. For us, they occurred at all stages of the study—from our first wonderings and formulations of questions, through our active engagement, to our final products, and beyond to new topics. Assessment constantly functioned to support learners by enabling them to move beyond their current understandings.

Carli Carra (1995) described the assessment-and-evaluation process she uses in her classroom, relative to her third-graders' study of the rain forest. Ms. Carra searches for evidence of her students' learning in the content of their reports, poems, and stories. To learn about the processes her students use to uncover what they know and need, she observes, listens in on their conversations with their peers, and monitors their dialogue with her. To recall the details of these data sources, she keeps anecdotal notes. She uses the rain-forest display to inform her of the students' level of understanding and knowledge. She considers the product of their collaborative writing—a play—for more information on what they know about the rain forest. She takes photographs to preserve her own and the children's memories. She has each child fill out a self-evaluation sheet. Through these data sources, she comes to know and to form a judgment about what her students have learned about the rain forest.

Evidence, then, of the children's learning is demonstrated by the products created during the children's investigations, constructions, dramatic play, writing, and speaking while they study topics. Not only is the teacher gathering information about what the children are learning about the topic of study, but the teacher is also gathering information about each child's reading, writing, speaking, and listening learning. Every activity is an opportunity to gather data about the children. Much more information about assessment and evaluation will be found in Chapter 12.

Phase 5: Involving Parents

While "Involving Parents" is listed as the fifth phase of designing and implementing an integrated unit, parents can and should be involved throughout the study of a topic. If teachers want parents to be involved in what is going on in the classroom, then parents must be brought into each topic's study.

Lilian Katz and Sylvia Chard (1993) suggest that teachers can help parents become involved in their children's study by:

1. Helping children share information about their study with their parents while the study is progressing. For example, newsletters, written by or with the children, detailing the classroom activities can provide information for conversations. Similarly, occasionally photocopying a page form the children's learning logs provides a record of what the children learned on a particular day. Some teachers bring parents together regularly as a group to speak to them about their curricular intentions. Knowing that some parents will be unable to attend such a meeting, a follow-up summary can be sent to those parents who were unable to attend. Perhaps a parent with secretarial skills would be willing to prepare minutes of the meeting. Many parents want to be involved and need teachers assistance in the how of their involvement.

2. Encouraging parents to ask questions of their children about their study and to become involved in their children's study. Some children are excellent at responding to the age-old parent question, "What did you learn in school today?" Many children, however, answer "Nothing." Effective teachers look for ways to help parents structure their questions so that they generate a genuine parent–child conversation about children's learning. These teachers might include illustrations of possible kinds of questions (sometimes constructed with the children) at the end of a classroom newsletter. Other teachers hold a meeting for helping parents ask the kinds of questions that generate more than a "yes," "no," or "nothing" answer.

3. Involving parents "in providing information, pictures, books, and objects for the whole class in its pursuit of knowledge on the topic" (Katz & Chard, 1993, p. 106). Are there parents who hold jobs who are willing to speak to the children about their occupations? Could the children interview their parents to discover what they do?

4. Involving parents in the study's culminating activity, to come see the products of their children's work. Sandra Wilensky (1995) described how her children held conferences with their parents to share their works-in-progress and their completed efforts. Ms. Wilensky described how her role in the process was to assist the children in "preparing and organizing for the conference" (p. 49). Her children wrote a letter to their parents as part of their preparation for the conferences. The children outlined the things they wanted to discuss with their parents. They wrote about their feelings about their conferences afterward.

Laurel Bok Swindle's first-grade students held a publishing party to share their *Animals in Action* book with their parents. They wrote invitations to their parents and siblings, baked cookies, and made placemats. When their families gathered, they proudly read their pieces to their audience. They also autographed their report in each other's books!

It is these kinds of involvement activities that help parents feel that they take an active part of their children's education. Parents are important partners in their children's education. For additional suggestions on ways to involve parents in their children's education, see Chapter 13.

Designing the Classroom's Physical Environment to Support the Integrated Curriculum

The classroom is the stage on which the drama will be played. The props it contains and how it is set up are critically important to the successful implementation of an integrated curriculum. Both the materials provided and the physical arrangement of these materials in the available space affects children's behaviors (Gump, 1989; Morrow & Weinstein, 1982, 1986). The classroom floor plan used by one teacher, Sandra Lawing, is shown in Figure 11.5 as an illustration of several points teachers need to consider in arranging their classrooms.

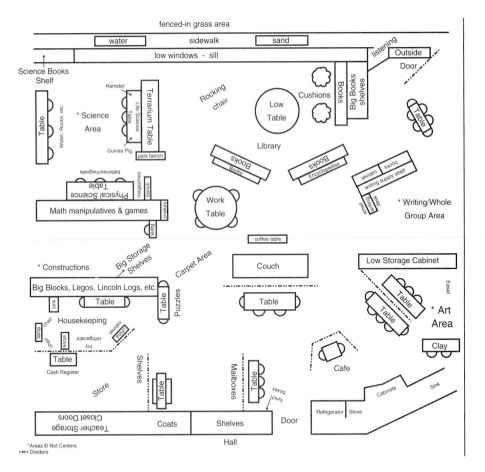

FIGURE 11.5   Sandra Lawing's classroom floor plan

Reprinted from "Building Generative Curriculum" by Lester L. Laminick and Sandra Lawing, *Primary Voices K–6*, August 1994. Copyright 1994 by the National Council of Teachers of English.

Carve the Large Classroom Space into Small Areas

Notice how Sandra Lawing's classroom is divided into small, well-defined activity areas. Small, clearly defined areas encourage more interaction and sustained activity than do large areas. In addition, smaller areas accommodate fewer children, which leads to a quieter classroom and fewer behavior problems. Each area (or center, as it is often called) needs to be clearly evident to its users. Areas can be clearly defined by using available classroom movable furniture (such as book shelves, cupboards, tables, boxes), screens, and large plants (real, if possible, but if not, artificial will do).

Typically, these centers are designed around each content area. Hence, classrooms have a science center, a mathematics center, a library center, a writing center, a dramatic play center, and so forth. To assist children's understanding of the purposes of the areas, each area should be clearly labeled with a sign mounted near the children's eye level. With young children, an appropriate picture or symbol should accompany the written label.

Gather Appropriate Resources to Support the Children's Learning

Typically, the materials needed to support children's engagement in activities are housed in the various centers. For example, we include a list of the materials found in Sandra Lawing's classroom's centers in Figure 11.6. In addition, suggestions for materials for the writing center can be found in Chapter 9 and for the reading/library area in Chapter 5.

Each item should have a designated storage place. This designation helps children to find the materials with ease and to replace the materials for the next child's use. This means that each center needs shelves, tables, or boxes for the materials, with the designated spot for each material clearly labeled.

Within each center, the method of exhibiting the materials should be considered. For example, blocks of like sizes, like shapes, or like materials should be grouped together in the block center (sometimes called the construction site). The labels might read: long, rectangular, wooden blocks; or small square wooden blocks; or red Lego blocks. Pictures of each kind of block by the words will support the youngest children's reading. Similarly, paper in the writing center can be grouped by color, kind, and size. Labels might include those for publishing paper, rough-draft paper, stationery, and cards.

Functional signs (e.g., "Make construction plans here!") can also be used to guide children's behavior in each center. Experiences with such signs encourage even the youngest children to attend to the functional purposes of print and to begin to make use of signs to achieve their purposes.

In addition, many teachers prepare an inventory of the items available in each center in enlarged print. Remember that with young children, the use of print with pictures on the inventory list is important. Posting the inventory in a location visible from various spots in the classroom assists the children in independently gathering the resources they need to support their work. Because the children will be engaged in interdisciplinary projects, they may need materials from several different centers.

In addition to the regularly used resources, centers often will contain special displays and materials related to the topic under study. Like the regularly used center resources, these also need to be grouped into meaningful collections, labeled, and displayed attractively.

Items found in the various areas of Sandra Lawing's classroom:

Reading Area
- low table and chairs
- rocking chair
- pillows for comfortable reading
- large variety of books in plastic tubs, organized by first letter of author's name
- books in tubs by genre (such as poetry or fairy tales) or by topics we are studying

Science Area
- physical science table with magnets; batteries; hand lenses; Capselas (plastic bubbles with batteries and wheels to make cars that are motorized); books about magnetism, electricity, and science experiments
- life science table with a terrarium; guinea pig; hamster; snake; seeds; soils; and cups (for planting); balance scales; tripod; magnifying glass; and books, charts, and posters on plants and animals
- earth science table with dinosaur models, rocks, a fish net with starfish and shells, plastic models of crabs, rock books, dinosaur books, and a tub of books with information on water
- tape recorder and tapes

Construction Area
- big blocks
- Legos
- manipulatives for building
- books (about everything from castles to architecture to building)

Math Area
- bank
- manipulatives including unifix cubes, teddy bears, counting items
- hundreds boards
- measurement items, rulers
- math games
- books that deal with math concepts

Housekeeping
- grocery store
- kitchen
- household items

Class Cafe
- a table and two chairs behind a puppet screen
- menus that the students have made
- placemats (also student designed and made)
- order blanks
- books about food, recipe books

Art Area
- table
- easel
- clay
- watercolors
- sequins, dyed macaroni, glitter, old lace— anything to glue and decorate

Writing Area
- paper
- pencils
- publishing items: editing cards (with directions such as, "Read for periods at end of each sentence"), spelling cards (e.g., "Circle words you think the author needs help with"), and revising cards
- needles and thread for book binding and sewing

Listening Center
- tapes of songs or books
- books to accompany tapes
- tape player (three in the classroom)
- blank tapes for students to record their reading or singing
- earphones

FIGURE 11.6   Resource materials to support children's learning.

Place Similar or Related Centers Near Each Other

Sandra Lawing placed the library center and the writing center close to each other. These two centers belong together because they both encourage children's development and use of literacy. In fact, some educators combine these centers together into a literacy center because their focus is children's literacy development. The two centers occupy a major portion of the classroom space: the library center with its posters, many books of many different genres displayed in different kinds of ways (e.g., as in a public or school library with spines visible, with the covers visible), puppets, literature on tapes, flannel boards with story characters, magazines, stuffed animals wanting to hear stories read to them, a rocking chair, pillows, and more; and the writing center with its many writing tools, different kinds of paper, cards, resources to assist with the writing process, and more.

Many educators divide the centers into potentially noisy centers and potentially more quiet centers. Based on their predictions, they place the potentially noisy centers near each other (e.g., the block center is placed near the dramatic play center, and both centers are near the art center) and the potentially quiet centers are near each other (e.g., the literacy center is placed near the science and mathematics centers, as they are in Ms. Lawing's classroom).

Involve the Children in Designing the Classroom

After years of teaching in the same classroom, kindergarten teacher Dee Dougherty was required to move to a new classroom. In August, as she surveyed the boxes and boxes of materials and reflected on what she had learned in a summer design technology workshop she had attended, she decided to try meeting the children on the first day of school in a different manner than previously. The classroom would be undecorated, and they would design it together. They talked about what they needed and considered where the various centers might be located. They drew blueprints, drawings done on beige construction paper in blue pen or blue crayon. They considered safety rules, traffic patterns, electrical outlet placement, and much more. Eventually, they voted upon the best design. With the help of the custodian, materials were moved to the designated areas, materials were arranged, and their placements were labeled. (A note to new teachers: Make friends immediately with the custodian!)

Some teachers find that this level of involvement by their children in the classroom's construction makes them feel uncomfortable. However, these teachers look for other ways for their children to feel ownership of the classroom. Instead of decorating the walls with displays of commercial items, these teachers look for ways to celebrate their children's products. They mount exhibitions of their children's work. They look for ways to provide opportunities for the children to share messages with each other. Recall the mailboxes recommended as equipment in the writing center in the Chapter 9. How about a suggestion box for sharing ideas, recommendations, and complaints? How about a message board where children exchange personal notes? How about a picture gallery where children can hang their favorite photographs of themselves or their favorite drawings or paintings?

A special effort should be made to include items that reflect the children's cultures. Recall that in selecting topics for study, teachers look for topics that have meaning to the children. Similarly, as the environment is considered, teachers might ponder what to include that is representative of what is important to the children. Posters, photographs, objects, and so forth representative of their cultures should be embedded into each center. The intention is to celebrate the class's diversity in visible ways.

Make Literacy Materials a Part of the Fabric of Each Center

Sandra Lawing's classroom's science center has many science books in it. So does her block area. By including books, writing tools, posters with print, magazines, and other relevant materials in each center, each center's potential for developing children's literacy is enhanced.

Jim Christie (1995) described how, in his early teaching days, he believed that literacy should not be woven into each center; only the library and writing centers had literacy materials. He recalled wondering whether he would confuse his students by putting books in the dramatic play center when the center was a housekeeping center. He now knows that putting literacy materials in the various centers supports children's literacy development and is an important way for teachers to enhance children's literacy learning. By enriching all centers, children read, write, speak, listen, and observe to learn.

Create an Aesthetically Pleasing, Inviting Environment

Attention to detail and careful organization of each center will be rewarded by children's increased attention to the activities and materials offered in each center and by children's increased care in maintaining the center and using the materials.

Cleotis Stevens' classroom immediately communicates a positive message to the observer. The color scheme of blues and grays projects a feeling of calmness. Extra table and floor lights in various areas lessen the harshness of the overhead fluorescent lighting. On occasion, Ms. Stevens can turn off the overhead lights, turn on the large table lamp in the library center, and create a new atmosphere for sharing a story with her children. Large soft pillows and beanbag chairs make the library center an inviting atmosphere for reading books, listening to tapes of stories, using the flannel board and story characters, and so forth. The rugs in most centers in the classroom (not the art center) absorb the sound of many little feet traveling about the room to collect needed resources. Ms. Stevens' classroom is in an older building; the classroom floors are tiled, not carpeted. When a friend of a friend replaced her family-room carpeting, Ms. Stevens was able to secure the used carpet. Teachers need to be scroungers!

Lots of natural objects from the world outside the classroom are available for the children's manipulation. For example, different kinds of seashells are available in the math center for the children's sorting, counting, and examination. Ms. Stevens borrowed an idea from another teacher, Roxanne Nelson: When the children went to a pond that had been overrun with *phagmites* (a weed that grows in ponds), they returned to the classroom with a pile of these destructive weeds. (This is one of the few items environmentalists eagerly support having removed from a pond area.) Together, the children wove an area divider from the weeds. Ms. Stevens looks for ways to bring natural items from the children's outside world into the classroom.

Creating this kind of environment required thought, work, and scrounging on Ms. Stevens' part. Ms. Stevens is expert at knowing which yard sales in which neighborhoods to shop. She's even learned that if she arrives the night before and pleads her case as a teacher in need of resources for her classroom, often the owner will permit her early access to the goods at a reduced rate. The outcome for her classroom is worth the work, evoking a sense of pride in Cleotis and enhancing her children's learning.

Organizing the Classroom's Daily Schedule: Creating a Rhythm to the Day

Recall that children need chunks of time to investigate topics alone, with small groups of other children, and with the whole group. On the one hand, there needs to be flexibility in the schedule to permit students to focus on flowers or insects for a block of time when their needs and interests dictate. On the other hand, there needs to be some predictability to life in the classroom. In this section, we consider how to create a schedule that supports children's engagement in meaningful learning.

Sample classroom schedules are provided in Figure 11.7. In each of these schedules, the teachers followed several common principles. They have

- balanced quiet times with noisier times, and sitting and listening time with movement time;
- provided large chunks of time for individual and small-group investigations and shorter amounts of time for whole-group activities;
- recognized their children's need for time to work together as a whole group, to work with peers in small groups, and to work independently;
- shown that they value having children choose and make decisions about how to structure their personal time.

Through the use of these principles, these teachers demonstrate their recognition of children's need for diversity and variety in their daily activities. They also recognize children's need for predictability and a not-so-hidden structure to each day—a rhythm.

How firmly should teachers hold to a time schedule? Carol Wien and Susan Kirby-Smith (1998) suggest that teachers consider having an order of events, but allowing the children to dictate the timing of the changes in activities. They contend that the " 'Schedule,' determined by the 'clock,' often interrupts productive play and intrudes upon young children's natural, creative activities. This creates unnecessary transitions and stress" (p. 9).

What Happens during Whole-Group Time?

Some teachers call whole-group sessions group time or circle time. Of course, it is during these times that the children and their teacher come together, typically in a carpeted area of

A Third-Grade Classroom's Daily Schedule

8:15 – 8:40	Opening exercises: Flag salute, calendar, current events, and overview of the day
8:40 – 10:00	Teacher read-aloud followed by reading workshop
10:00 – 10:15	Recess
10:15 – 11:15	Writing workshop
11:15 – 11:45	Lunch
11:45 – 12:00	Drop everything and read
12:00 – 1:30	Interdisciplinary theme study
1:30 – 2:00	Specials (art, music, P.E., library)
2:00 – 3:00	Mathematics
3:00 – 3:15	Learning logs (student reflection on what they learned that day)

A Half-Day Kindergarten Classroom's Schedule

9:00 – 9:20	Opening exercises
9:20 – 10:20	Activity time
10:20 – 10:30	Clean-up
10:30 – 10:45	Snack and quiet reading
10:45 – 11:10	Group time
11:10 – 11:30	Outside play
11:30 – 11:45	Literature
11:45	Dismissal

A Second-Grade Classroom's Schedule

8:15	Children begin to arrive; gather books to read
8:30 – 9:00	Opening exercises: Flag salute, calendar, news, songs and chants
9:00 – 10:15	Mathematics
10:15 – 10:45	Specials (music, library, art, P.E., computer lab)
10:45 – 11:15	Read-aloud
11:15 – 12:15	Writing workshop
12:15 – 12:45	Lunch
12:45 – 2:00	Reading workshop
2:00 – 2:15	Recess
2:15 – 3:00	Interdisciplinary theme study (science or social studies)
3:00 – 3:15	Group time
3:15	Dismissal

FIGURE 11.7   Three daily schedules.

the classroom. During the first group time of the day, teachers usually take attendance; make announcements; with kindergarten and older children, recite the pledge of allegiance to the flag; check the date on the calendar; report on the news of the day; and discuss plans for the day. Other whole-group sessions are used to introduce and to discuss the integrated unit being studied, for the teacher to read literature aloud, for teacher presentation of a lesson on a writing or reading strategy, for singing songs, for the choral reading of poems, and for bringing closure to the day.

These group sessions typically last 10 to 30 minutes, depending on the children's developmental needs and the teacher's intentions. Many of these whole-group times have been discussed in detail in other chapters. As Susan Neuman and Kathy Roskos (1993, p. 147) suggest, teachers' intent during whole-group sessions often is "to actively engage [all the children] in thinking and talking, reading and writing about ideas related to [the] topic of interest."

What Happens During Small-Group Activity Time?

Typically, the children's curiosity will be aroused or their focus will be directed during the whole-group meetings. During the small-group activity times (a bit of a misnomer, since the children will also be engaged in independent activities during these times), the children can act on their interests. During these times, the children might move freely about the classroom, selecting the area or center of interest to them. They might write in the writing center, read books in the cozy corner library, build structures in the block or construction center, or investigate and record their observations in the science center. It is important for teachers to provide children with time to engage in activities of their choice and to plan the use of their time.

It is also important for teachers to actively engage in learning with their children during these free-choice times. This is not the time for teachers to work at completing administrative tasks. It is the time to read a book with a child or two, take a child's dictation, happen upon a child at just that moment when she or he needs instruction, or play with the children in dramatic play area.

During these free-choice times, the children might work with a small group of peers to answer questions of shared interest. In other instances, groups might form spontaneously; those five children who are interested in playing in the dramatic play area come together for play and stay until they are tired of playing in the center.

An Integrated Unit Alive in a Classroom

How do the parts of the day come together in the interdisciplinary study of a topic of interest to the children? How is it that children engage in purposeful activities that support the development of their abilities to speak, listen, read, and write? In Special Feature 11.1, Deanne McCredie describes aspects of her students' study of immigration, highlighting how she used this social studies topic to support her students' literacy development. Ms. McCredie illustrates how this topic was woven into many, though not all, aspects of the classroom's schedule. In Ms. McCredie's classroom, the schedule and the environment provided the foundation on which the children's investigations were based.

The Immigrant Experience: An Integrated Unit

Deanne McCredie

Over the year, my children had selected many topics for study. However, in this instance, topic selection was driven by my state's and district's standard curriculum-content mandates and by my interest in providing my students with meaningful multicultural experiences and learning events. Specifically, I wanted my students to consider America's ethnic diversity. This diversity is possibly America's greatest national challenge, as people of all backgrounds learn to live together and to appreciate one another's contributions to American life. One reason that America is so diverse is that it was settled by immigrants; everyone who lives in the United States is an immigrant or a descendent of an immigrant. I wanted my students to understand that their own family history is part of the story of America's immigration.

During the period of 1820–1920, the United States experienced the largest wave of immigrants in its history. I wanted my students to understand these immigrants' experiences, why they chose to leave their homelands, and to realize that immigrants continue to come to America in search of a new life for many of the same reasons immigrants came to America nearly a century ago.

What did my students already know about immigration? I began the unit with an introductory discussion to assess their existing knowledge about the topic. I learned quickly that my children knew very little about immigration. Therefore, defining what they wanted to learn was difficult. I decided to begin the unit by having the students engage in the behaviors of social scientists—historians—by examining primary sources of historical information and by recording and interpreting their findings. As the students acquired some knowledge about immigration, I asked them what **else** they wanted to learn, and I used their questions and discoveries to guide the direction of our investigations.

I wanted the students to understand that primary sources give us a first-hand look at the past and that studying primary sources helps us to experience history. These were eight- and nine-year-olds, though. How might we begin? I decided to begin by examining primary sources that were significant to these children. I sent a letter to the children's parents requesting that they consider sending an item from their families' history to school for their child to share with the class. I suggested that the primary sources might include artifacts such as letters, journals, documents, photographs, art, and so forth.

The next day the children arrived with many different pieces of their families' histories for sharing. A great deal of talk ensued. The artifact of greatest interest was an old glass bottle, probably dating from the Civil War. The students excitedly guessed who the bottle might have belonged to and how it came to be buried in the ground. I closed this sharing session by asking, "Has anyone read *Homeplace* by Crescent Dragonwagon (1993)? It's a story about a family who discovers several artifacts buried in the ground and imagines to whom the items might have belonged. You'll find a copy of it in the library corner."

In addition to *Homeplace,* the children found many other books dealing with the topic of immigration in the library corner. During the class's reading workshop, the children read books they chose from among the books in the library corner. As always, I conferred with the children; discussing their selections, learning what they had learned, and listening to them read selections they chose. The children also gathered in literature circles to discuss their books with other students. In addition, they raised questions, copied quotes they particularly liked, wrote drafts of letters to authors, wrote drafts of letters to peers recommending their book—regular reading-response activities—in their reading-response journals.

In addition to their independent reading, my read-aloud sessions played a significant role in building the children's knowledge. I believed that the inclusion of children's literature would be

(continued on next page)

crucial to the students' understanding of the immigrants' experiences. I selected books for specific purposes, all about children who had immigrated to this country. Each time we read a story, we wrote the child's name on his or her homeland's flag, attached it to the child's homeland on a large map, marked the map indicating where the child landed in the United States, and connected the two locations with a string.

For example, I read and we discussed *Gooseberries to Oranges* (Cohen, 1982). First, however, we brainstormed a list of reasons why immigrants might choose to leave their homeland. What I thought would take 5 minutes took 20 minutes! The children had many thoughtful ideas on why people might leave their homeland. On another day, I read *Klara's New World* (Winter, 1992). The children commented on the similarities and differences between these two stories. To visualize the commonalities and differences, we created interconnecting circles, much like a Venn diagram.

I planned to have the children use learning logs to record their findings during our study. To illustrate how historians record their findings, I showed a slide of immigrants arriving on Ellis Island (photos, still and video, being important primary sources) and modeled how historians record their findings. I looked carefully at the slide. "What did this picture tell me about these immigrants?" I voiced some of my findings. I provided justification for each finding. I asked for the children's help. Together, we constructed a list of findings from this one slide; I recorded our findings on the board. Then it was their turn. Over the remainder of our study, as we carefully considered the information in slides, in print, and in oral forms, we recorded our findings in our logs. Always, as the children wrote in their logs, I circulated about the classroom, speaking with them about their findings and learning much about their developing understandings of immigration.

By chance, there was a piece on the evening news about people immigrating from Mexico into the United States. Our focus to this point had been immigrants of the past; this news clip connected our study to today. As homework, the children were directed to skim newspapers and to watch the evening news broadcasts for information on immigration. (I brought copies of newspapers for those children who did not have access to them at home; none of my students lacked access to television.) Copies of the newspaper articles and notes taken while observing the news broadcasts were mounted on a classroom bulletin board. These became the topic of our morning current-events discussions. These articles and broadcasts verified that the items on our brainstormed list of reasons why people immigrated to the United States in the past were equally relevant today. We decided that this discovery was important to record in our learning logs.

One child observed that it seemed as though when people immigrate, they do not bring much with them. "What would you choose to bring with you?" I brought a trunk to school the size of the trunks used by turn-of-the century immigrants. "If you could only bring what would fit in a trunk this size, what would you bring and why?" In groups, the children considered the possibilities. All groups concluded that money was important—even if it was not the currency of the new country—because any currency could be exchanged for appropriate currency. Perhaps stimulated by some of the family artifacts they had seen, the groups thought it would be important to bring things to remind them of their homeland and family (e.g., photographs, special gifts, favorite toys—small ones, of course). Also, they thought they would need food. One group thought carrots would be a good idea; since no one likes them very much, they would not have to worry about their being stolen!

As the number of pieces of strings on our classroom map grew, the children's conversations around the map naturally turned to "My Pop-Pop immigrated [They liked to use that word, *immigrated.*] from Sweden, just like Klara." Children made mental and written notes to check

(continued on next page)

Special Feature 11.1 (continued)

on their families' heritages. The children suggested making flags with their names on them and attaching the flags to the map to denote their own families' original homelands. Soon, conversations around the map indicated that the children were noting the many different original homelands represented by the children in the class: Puerto Rico, someplace in Africa, Poland, Croatia, Ireland, England, and many more.

I had wanted to introduce the children to the conditions that early African immigrants (i.e., unwilling immigrants) faced when they were brutally forced to come to this country. The children's interest in their families' countries of origin provided a reason for this discussion. I read excerpts from *Days of Slavery* (Kallen, 1990); *The Story of the Henrietta Marie* (Sullivan, 1994), showing the photographs of the actual shackles from the sunken slave ship; and Alex Haley's *Roots* (1974), the section describing the conditions of the slave ship that brought Kunta to America. Many of the students' recordings in their learning logs indicated their genuine concern regarding the conditions on the slave ships.

A colleague's middle-school students had been studying the slave experience. The day following our examination of the evidence of the conditions of the slave ships, three of her students came to our class to make brief speeches summarizing their research on life in America for the African-Americans who were sold into slavery and how people such as Harriet Beecher Stowe helped them escape to freedom. We ended this session with the reading of *Nettie's Trip South* (Turner, 1987), an excellent story told from the point of view of a ten-year-old girl, and the singing of "Follow the Drinking Gourd" (Winter, 1988), an African-American freedom-trail song. (The drinking gourd is the Big Dipper, which points the direction northward at night.) Again, the children's learning logs indicated their concern with the plight of the early African immigrants to this country. Throughout the unit, I continually reinforced the connection between the immigrant experience and the slave experi-

ence so the children would understand that both groups contributed to the hopes and dreams that have built America.

One of the reasons that people have immigrated to this country has been to worship their god or gods as they pleased. (We had noted this reason on our early brainstorming list, an indication that the children recalled our Thanksgiving-time discussion of why the Pilgrims came to America.) I decided to reread *Molly's Pilgrim* (1983), a book the children had enjoyed in November. Before reading the story, I wrote the Yiddish words used in the story on the board: *malkeleh, shaynkeit, paskudnyaks.* As I pronounced them, Zoe proudly told the class what they meant. As I read the book, we stopped often to discuss such points as why Molly's English was not perfect, why the other children teased Molly and how that must have made Molly feel, who the Cossacks were, why Molly's family left Russia, what her class learned from Molly's doll, and Molly's definition of *Pilgrim.* I ended the presentation by indicating that we were going to make our own immigrant dolls to symbolize all the different people who came to live in America. Each student would select a different country and a specific person to research to understand how people in that country dressed when this immigrant came to America. They would use this information to dress their immigrant dolls. They would complete an immigration identification card for their dolls, with details such as the name of the immigrant, how old the immigrant was, the country of origin, the year of arrival, the reason(s) for immigrating, the conditions during the journey to the United States, and the challenges faced when living in America. Finally, the students would use their research to write a piece that would inform their peers about their immigrant's coming to America. I closed the session with "Think about the country of your choice overnight."

The next day, I posted a sign-up sheet for the children to note their selected countries. I provided sheets of poster board with the outline of a child traced on each board; various kinds of mate-

(continued on next page)

rials gathered from every neighbor of mine who sewed or knitted, to use for clothing and hair; informational books; an encyclopedia on CD-ROM; passes for trips to the library—and the children were off. Of course, I conferred, guided, formed discussion groups to resolve common problems or to consider clothing-customs discov-

eries made by children working on immigrants from similar parts of the world, negotiated material selections, conferred with writers, listened in on peer writing conferences, did minilessons addressing the needs I observed in the children's writing and researching, and so forth. The draft of one child's piece is presented in Figure 11.8.

X "Pack up!" "Where going to America
X Julia your only aloud to bring one
X doll. "Oh no!" said Julia "Which one
X do I bring?" "Bring Stacey," said nana
X Nana why are we going to America?
X "Because we are in the middle of a
X war sweety and we don't want to get
X hurt." "Oh. It was 1930 in
X the middle of world war 2. Very
X dangerous "Paul" A bullet just broke
X the window. Julia started crying.

X It's ok. sweety. It's just the war. Julia
X is only 4. "O h!n"let's go!" Run!
X oh!oh!oh!oh! oh! oh! Then we're
X on the boat. It was very crowded on
X the boat, but I held my moms hand
X as tight as possible. I got sick on
X the 3rd day but I got better before
X anyone noticed. It wasn't very fun
X on the boat, but I had my doll on
X the boat. Stacey my doll was very
X scared also. My mom was with

X me. We only ate a little. The food
X that the people gave us was stale.
X I threw-up because of it. After we
X ate we went to see the water on the
X top of the boat. The water was on
X rough it looked like a snake shaking
X like crazy. I thought it was real
X neat. Finally they got to Ellis
X Island safe and sound. We were
X in a big line for something. When
X It was my turn and my moms

X said "Go ahead. Then we went
to an inntelligent test they
X said we were brillent so we went on
suddenly we heard someone say Julia
X that was my dad!! He told us everything
X that happend to him on his
X way to America too
X When we got home. I was very
X shocked! It was a beautiful
X wooden house much better than
X our house. It was 12:00 A.M.
X My dad said to get to sleep

X because I had school tomorrow.
X I loved my house in America!
X Home Sweet Home I said.

The End

FIGURE 11.8   The story of Julia's coming to America.

(continued on next page)

Our culminating experience for the unit was to take a bus trip to Ellis Island. While everything we had studied and learned was in preparation for this trip, I wanted to review the use of photographs as primary historical sources. I marked three photographs in each of several different books (e.g., *Ellis Island: New Hope in a New Land* by W. J. Jacobs [1990], *Ellis Island: Echoes from a Nation's Past* edited by S. Jonas, [1989], *Ellis Island: A Pictorial History* by B. Benton [1985], *Keepers of the Gate: A History of Ellis Island* by T. M. Pitkin [1925]), divided the children into eight groups, and gave each group three overhead transparencies. The children were to work cooperatively as historians, examining the photographs and recording their findings about the immigrants pictured on the overhead transparencies. The transparencies would be used to present their discoveries to the class the next day. As groups finished their observations and writing, they practiced their presentation. Well, the children worked one day longer than I thought they would to carefully consider the information they gathered from the photographs, to write their sentences, and to practice their presentations.

One day late, the groups made their presentations. Photographs were shown. Observations were read and justified. After each group's presentation, the class participated in an oral evaluation of their presentation. "What did this group do well? What might they do better next time?" Generally, the presentations were marvelous! (See Figure 11.9 for the information one group presented on its overhead transparencies.)

Because we would be seeing the Statue of Liberty, we needed to learn something about it before we boarded the buses. I began by asking the children what they already knew about the Statue of Liberty. I listed the few known points on the board. I read *The Story of the Statue of Liberty* by Betsey and Guilio Maestro (1986). "Would the Statue of Liberty fit in this classroom?" Showing the students a meter stick, I asked the students to estimate the height of the Statue of Liberty in meters. I recorded their estimates on the board.

Then I told them that the statue is 100 meters tall. "How tall is that?" Though guesses were offered, the children seemed very unsure. We would measure the Statue of Liberty to exact scale on the grass outside the school building. I divided the class into four groups and made each group responsible for laying out a section of the statue (e.g., one group would mark the distance from the statue's chin to the top of the flame, another mark the distance from the statue's waist to its chin). I gave each group a container of popsicle

1st picture. ELLIS ILAND

1. The first thing we noticed was that you can not fit another person on the ship
2. Next we saw that most women are wearing scarfs on their heads.
3. Most of the men are wearing top hats or some sort of hat on his head, because of his religion.
4. We also noticed that the ship was huge! (As you can see.)
5. You know, if I were on that ship I would be so confused!! (Just think how they feel.)

2nd picture.

1. The thing we really noticed most about this picture was that there is a huge American Flag on top of the front wall.
2. The Immigrants are waiting on benches or standing in long lines inside the railings
3. We also noticed that the ceiling is large and round, like a dome.
4. These are lots of huge windows.

FIGURE 11.9 Using photographs to gather information about the past.

(continued on next page)

sticks. They were to place their meter stick on a beginning line and insert the popsicle stick into the ground at the end of the meter stick. Then they would butt the meter stick to the popsicle stick and place a second popsicle stick at the end of the meter stick. The process would be repeated until they had reached the top of their section. Then the group cut a piece of twine exactly as long as from their beginning line to their last popsicle stick. When all groups had completed their tasks, we carefully laid the four pieces of twine end-to-end. "Wow! That's how big the Statue of Liberty is!" "It looks as big as two 18-wheelers!!"

Fortunately, I had enlisted the assistance of several middle-school students to help with our measuring. This hands-on measurement activity was meaningful to the children, but they definitely needed helpers. The next day, I used the middle-school students' participation to teach the students about the social convention of writing a thank-you note when someone does something that pleases you. We talked about what might be included in a thank-you note. Interested students wrote thank-you notes.

Before leaving the unit, I wanted to pull the discussion back to our classroom and the 24 people who lived in it. During a read-aloud session, I read *Make a Wish, Molly* (Cohen, 1995). We live in a pluralistic culture in our society and in our classroom. We talked about what that meant.

We also talked about several metaphors that describe our pluralistic culture: salad bowl, melting pot, and patchwork quilt. We decided our classroom was a patchwork quilt. Our class was composed of different students with different backgrounds. We decided to make a patchwork quilt to symbolize our cohesiveness. Alone, each square would be lovely; together, all the squares would be a wonderful illustration of how we work together—just like how all the immigrants had to work together to make our country. The children decorated their squares with symbols telling about them and their heritage. Once the squares were sewn together, we proudly displayed the quilt in our classroom.

On May 30th, we boarded the buses for the long bus ride to Ellis Island and the Statue of Liberty. Throughout this unit of study, my students read, wrote, listened, talked, and observed. The materials in the classroom and in the school's library supported their investigations. While the classroom schedule suggested readers' workshop, writing workshop, social studies, and so forth, from the children's perspective, the day was seamless. Our investigation of immigration flowed across and was embedded within the various curriculum content areas. Although I had outlined goals and objectives for this interdisciplinary unit, the students' questions and observations guided our study as we learned together about the dreams and hopes that have built America.

Summary

Children learn best when they are engaged in inquiries that involve using their language to learn. For this to happen, the various content areas need to be naturally integrated. Through immersion in the study of a broad topic that is relevant to the lives of the students and their community, children read, write, speak, listen, and observe. How does this approach to integrated curriculum match with your memories of projects and units when you were in school?

To summarize the key points about facilitating oral language learning, we return to the guiding questions at the beginning of this chapter:

■ *What are the major differences between the subject-by-subject, correlated, and integrated approaches to curricula?*

A subject-by-subject curriculum has a separate time block for each subject area. In this type of compartmentalized curriculum, each subject is taught in isolation. In a correlated curriculum, activities in different subjects are selected that are related to a given theme or topic. The goal is to master subject-area content and skills, not to learn about the topic. There is some degree of subject-area integration in this approach, but the links or connections across the various curricular areas tend to be artificial. In an integrated curriculum, activities in different subject areas are selected in order to help children find answers to questions about a topic that is of interest to them. In this approach, subject-matter areas appropriate to the topic are woven naturally into the children's investigations, and there is true curricular integration.

■ *How can teachers plan and implement an integrated curriculum unit or project?*

The teacher begins by selecting a topic for study and by determining what the children already know; need to learn, as defined by the content standards; and want to learn about the topic. Next, the teacher helps the children plan learning activities or projects. As children work on their investigations, the teacher engages in ongoing assessment and evaluation of children's learning. The teacher also involves parents in all phases of the unit.

■ *How can teachers arrange the classroom's physical environment and daily schedule to support the integrated curriculum?*

Teachers can create a classroom environment that supports an integrated curriculum by (1) carving classroom space into small, well-defined areas; (2) gathering appropriate resources to support the children's learning; (3) placing similar or related centers near each other, (4) involving children in designing the classroom; (5) making literacy materials part of the fabric of each center; and (6) creating an aesthetically pleasing environment.

The daily schedule should also support the integrated curriculum. A wonderful environment without blocks of time to use it is worthless. There need to be large chunks of time for individual and small-group investigations and shorter amounts of time for whole-group activities. Quiet times during which children sit and listen should be balanced with active times. The schedule should also feature flexibility, so that children have the freedom to pursue their interests, and predictability, so that there is a rhythm to the day.

L I N K I N G   K N O W L E D G E   T O   P R A C T I C E

1. Kathy Roskos (1995) worked with a group of teachers to design a set of criteria and a scale that can be used to assess the quality of integrated units. An adaptation of these teachers' and Kathy's ideas is presented in Table 11.1. Visit a classroom and use this scale to evaluate an ongoing unit or project.

TABLE 11.1   **Evaluating the Quality of Interdisciplinary Units**

	Yes	Somewhat	No

The topic is . . .
- child-centered
- broad in scope
- relevant to these children
- relevant to real-life in these children's community

During the study of the topic . . .
- the teacher begins by discovering what these children know (their prior knowledge) and what they want to learn
- children are given choices about which aspect of the topic they wish to investigate
- reading, writing, speaking, and listening are naturally woven into the activities
- activities are planned to help develop concepts and to answer the children's questions
- children share what they have learned with others
- the teacher provides information (e.g., how to take notes, how to write an informative report, how to make an oral presentation) the children need to successfully complete their projects and activities
- quality literature is woven into the study

Assessing students' learning . . .
- is ongoing, while the children complete the activities
- includes student self-evaluation

Teaching this unit, the teacher . . .
- involves the students' parents
- functions like an orchestra conductor, getting things started and moving them along, providing information and resources, and coordinating the buzz of activities
- conferences with the students

2. While visiting the classroom, observe the physical environment. How does the classroom match up with the six criteria for a supportive physical environment presented in this chapter?

3. What is the daily schedule in this classroom? Does this schedule support or hinder integrated curriculum?

CHAPTER

12

Assessment: Determining What Children Know and Can Do

In the preceding chapters we have presented strategies for implicit and explicit instruction in literacy. While these instructional activities form the core of an effective reading, writing, and speaking program, they cannot stand alone. To ensure that the instructional strategies meet the needs of every child in the class, teachers need to assess whether these activities achieve their intended aims.

We begin this chapter by discussing the goals literacy professionals have identified as those that teachers should help their students to meet. Then, we consider the two general assessment approaches that teachers might use to gather information about their students' literacy development: ongoing, or portfolio, assessment and on-demand assessment. We focus mostly on ongoing assessment because this is the approach that best fits the constructivist orientation of this book. Portfolio assessment is the approach that is consistent with the literacy assessment principles we presented in Chapter 1 and the various assessment strategies we have described in the previous chapters.

Before You Read This Chapter, Think About . . .

- how your teachers assessed your literacy progress. Did you take a spelling test on Fridays? Did you read stories and answer comprehension questions? Did you ever evaluate your own progress? Did you keep a portfolio?
- how information about your literacy progress was shared with your parents. Did your parents learn about your progress by reading your report card? Did your parents attend conferences? Were you involved in sharing information about your progress with your peers or your parents?
- the on-demand tests you have taken. Did you take reading and writing tests throughout elementary school? Were you required to take a test, like the Scholastic Aptitude Test or the Graduate Record Examination, and score above a minimum level to gain admission to your undergraduate or graduate program?

Focus Questions

- What is important for teachers to know about children's literacy development?
- What are the two general approaches teachers might use to assess their students' literacy learning?
- What are the differences between working and showcase portfolios?
- How do teachers use the information they collect?

BOX **12.1**

Definition of Terms

achievement test: a standardized test designed to measure how much a student has learned and to compare this student's learning with a standard or norm

analytic scoring: a type of rubric scoring that separates the whole into categories of criteria that are examined one at a time. For example, a rater might judge a piece of writing in the categories of organization, development, sentence sense, word choice/style, and mechanics, one score per category.

assessment: the process of observing; describing, collecting, recording, scoring, interpreting, and sharing with appropriate others (like parents) information about a student's learning

benchmark: examples of actual student performance that illustrate each point on a scale and then are used as exemplars against which other student's performance can be measured

criterion-referenced test: a test used to compare a student's progress toward mastery of specified content, typically content the student had been taught. The performance criterion is referenced to some criterion level such as a cutoff score (e.g., a score of 60 is required for mastery).

evaluation: use of information from assessments to make a decision about continued instruction for a student

holistic scoring: assigning a single score based on the overall assessment of the student's performance

on-demand assessment: a type of assessment that occurs during a special time set aside for testing. In most cases, teaching and learning come to a complete stop while the teacher conducts the assessment. *See also* standardized test.

ongoing assessment: a form of assessment that relies on the regular collection of student work to illustrate students' knowledge and learning. The students' products are created as they engage in daily classroom activities, thus students are learning while they are being assessed.

performance task: an activity that allows students to demonstrate what they know and can do

rubric: a scoring guide that describes the characteristics of performance at each point on a scale

showcase portfolio: samples of student work that illustrate the student's efforts, progress, and achievements. The showcase portfolio is shared with others, usually the student's parents.

standardized test: The teacher reads verbatim the scripted procedures to the students. The conditions and directions are the same whenever the test is administered. Standardized tests are one form of on-demand testing.

working portfolio: where the student and teacher place work that is reflective of the student's achievement. Both the student and the teacher may place work in the working portfolio.

What Is Important for Teachers to Know About Children's Literacy Development?

Sheila Valencia (1990) and Grant Wiggins (1993) agree on a primary component in assessment: Teachers must begin assessment by determining what they value. "Only after goals have been established and clarified can attention turn to the appropriate tasks and contexts for gathering information" (Valencia, Hiebert, Afflerbach, 1994, p. 10). Teachers must answer the question, What is important for us to know about our children's development as readers, writers, speakers, and listeners?

The ideas in every chapter in this book help readers to answer this question. In addition, readers can use one or more of the sets of English language-arts *content standards* (or *outcomes, goals* or *accomplishments*, the terms are used interchangeably) that are available. School districts from Bellevue, Washington to Dover, Delaware, have prepared goals for their students. Most states have defined *content standards*—what their young citizens (grades K–12) should know and be able to do. (See Figure 12.1 for an illustration of the English language-arts standards developed by teachers for one state's young citizens.) Representatives of the two major literacy organizations, the International Reading Association (IRA) and the National Council of Teachers of English (NCTE), have worked collaboratively to construct a set of content standards for the whole nation.

In addition, the Committee on the Prevention of Reading Difficulties in Young Children, a committee appointed by the National Research Council, has provided educators interested in children's literacy learning with a list of accomplishments that successful learners are likely to exhibit each year (Snow, Burns, & Griffin, 1998). Similarly, the International Reading Association and the National Association for the Education of Young Children (NAEYC) have jointly issued a position statement on developmentally appropriate reading and writing practices for children that includes a list of what children of various ages and grade levels likely can do (IRA/NAEYC, 1998). The authors of this book strongly encourage readers to obtain copies of these important national publications.[1]

Such assessment tasks **do** have an impact on classroom instruction. For example, teachers not previously teaching children how to write persuasively might begin to do so. Also, teachers will probably introduce their students to the criteria that will be used to judge the quality of the students' work. The impact of the assessment, then, is on the children as a group.

Ongoing Assessment

Ongoing assessment relies on the regular collection of artifacts to illustrate students' knowledge and learning. The artifacts are gathered while the children engage in their daily

---

[1]For a complete copy of the position statement, *Learning to Read and Write: Developmentally Appropriate Practices for Young Children,* and the IRA/NCTE content standards, readers are encouraged to write to the International Reading Association, 800 Barksdale Road, Newark, Delaware, 19714. For a copy of *Preventing Reading Difficulties in Young Children,* write to the National Academy Press, 2102 Constitution Avenue, NW, Lockbox 285, Washington, DC 20053. Readers can also download this book off the Internet at the National Academy Press Web site (http://www.nap.edu/readingroom/books/prdyc).

English Language Arts Content Standards

Standard One: Students will use written and oral English appropriate for various purposes and audiences.
Standard Two: Students will construct, examine, and extend the meaning of literary, informative, and technical texts through listening, reading, and viewing.
Standard Three: Students will access, organize, and evaluate information gained through listening, reading, and viewing.
Standard Four: Students will use literary knowledge gained through print and visual media to connect self to society and culture.

(Indicators of required performance for each standard at four grade clusters—K-3, 4-5, 6-8, and 9-10—are provided. One such set of indicators for K-5 students for one standard, Standard One, is detailed below.)

Performance Indicator for the End of K–Grade 5

Writers will produce texts that exhibit the following textual features, all of which are consistent with the genre and purpose of the writing:

Development: The topic, theme, stand/perspective, argument, or character is fully developed.
Organization: The text exhibits a discernible progression of ideas.
Style: The writer demonstrates a quality of imagination, individuality, and a distinctive voice.
Word Choice: The words are precise, vivid, and economical.
Sentence Formation: Sentences are completed and varied in length and structure.
Conventions: Appropriate grammar, mechanics, spelling, and usage enhance the meaning and readability of the text.

Writers will produce examples that illustrate the following discourse classifications:

1. **Expressive** (author-oriented) texts, both personal and literary, that
   a. reveal self-discovery and reflection;
   b. demonstrate experimentation with techniques, which could include dialogue;
   c. demonstrate experimentation with appropriate modes, which include narration and description;
   d. demonstrate experimentation with rhetorical form.
2. **Informative** (subject-oriented) texts that
   a. begin to address audience;
   b. exhibit appropriate modes, which could include description, narration, classification, simple process analysis, simple definitions;
   c. conform to the appropriate formats, which include letters, summaries, messages, and reports;
   d. contain information from primary and secondary sources, avoiding plagiarism.
3. **Argumentative and persuasive** (audience-oriented) texts that
   a. address the needs of the audience;
   b. communicate a clear-cut position on an issue;
   c. support the position with relevant information, which could include personal and expert opinions and examples;
   d. exhibit evidence of reasoning.

Speakers demonstrate oral-language proficiency in formal and informal speech situations, such as conversations, interviews, collaborative group work, oral presentations, public speaking, and debate. Speakers are able to

1. **Formulate** a message, including all essential information.
2. Organize a message appropriately for the speech situation.
3. **Deliver** a message,
   a. beginning to control volume, tone, speed, and enunciation appropriately for the situational context;
   b. using facial expression to reinforce the message;
   c. maintaining focus;
   d. creating the impression of being secure and comfortable, and in command of the situation;
   e. incorporating audiovisual aids when appropriate.
4. **Respond** to feedback, adjusting volume and speed, and answering questions.

FIGURE 12.1   Delaware's English language-arts content standards and the performance indicators for the end of K–5.

classroom activities, such as those described in every chapter in this book. The products of these activities, then, serve the dual purposes of instruction **and** assessment. Because the children's artifacts are stored in portfolios, ongoing assessment often is called "portfolio assessment."

Ongoing assessment exhibits the following features:

- Children work on their products for varying amounts of time, and the procedures or directions probably vary across all children in a classroom or across classes in the building.
- What each child, with the teacher's assistance, selects as evidence of literacy learning may be different, not only across the children in the school but also across children in a teacher's class.
- The classroom teacher analyzes each child's performance on each of the tasks and makes judgments about each child's learning.
- The children know the criteria against which their products will be judged, and examples of students' work are often displayed to help them understand the criteria.
- The students engage in making judgments about how their work compares with the criteria. The students' self-evaluation is seen as an integral component of the process.
- The teacher's and child's judgments are used immediately to define the child's next learning goal. The assessment, then, has an immediate impact on instruction for **each** child.
- The assessment of the work produced over time in many different contexts permits the teacher and the child to gather more than a quick snapshot of what the child knows and is able to do at a given moment.

Ongoing assessment, then, permits both the teacher and the student to examine the child's knowledge and learning. First-grader Phyllis shares what this means as she uses her journal to describe her growth as a reader and writer.

> I comed to this school a little bit nervous, you know. Nothin'. [She shakes her head for added emphasis.] I couldn't read or write nothin'. Look at this. [She turns to the first few pages of her writing journal.] Not a word! Not a word! [She taps the page and adds an aside.] And the drawin's not too good. Now, look at this. [She turns to the end of the journal.] One, two, three, four. Four pages! And I can read 'em. Listen. [She reads.] Words! [Nodding her head.] Yup! Now I can read and write alotta words!

Information-Gathering Tools

Phyllis's journal is one of several tools her teacher uses to gather information about Phyllis's literacy learning. Like Phyllis, her teacher can compare the writing at the beginning and at the end of the journal to learn about Phyllis's literacy development over time. Each tool used permits teachers to gather information about their children's literacy learning **while** the children perform the kinds of activities described in this book. Readers were introduced to several of these tools in previous chapters.

Anecodotal records. These are a teacher's notes describing a child's behavior. Peter Winograd and Harriette Johns Arrington (1999) suggest that teachers make their anecdotal notes as they "kidwatch," a term coined by Yetta Goodman (1978). They suggest that teachers often find it helpful to focus on a series of questions like the following: "What can this child do? What does this child know? What kinds of questions does the child have about his/her work? What does the child's attitude reveal about his/her growth and progress?" (p. 231). Fairfax County Public Schools (1998) offers additional suggestions for ways to avoid making the writing of anecdotal notes overwhelming. This school system suggests that teachers decide on a focus for their note taking. For example, in reading, teachers might focus on how fluently the children are reading, or how well the children are comprehending the text, or the children's interest in reading as reflected in their free-choice book selections. In writing, teachers might focus on how the children are organizing their pieces, or how the children are incorporating voice into their pieces. The school system also suggests that teachers begin their note taking by focusing on those children whose progress most concerns them.

Teachers use many different kinds of paper (e.g., computer address labels, notepads, paper in a loose-leaf binder, index cards, Post-it Notes) to make their anecdotal records of children's behavior. Figure 12.2 shows an inexpensive flip chart a teacher developed to aid her anecdotal note record-keeping. The teacher used a clipboard and 3 × 5″ index cards. She wrote each child's name on the bottom of a card, arranged the cards in alphabetical order, then, starting at the bottom of the clipboard, taped the child's card whose name began with the last letter of the alphabet onto the clipboard, so that the bottom of the card was even with the bottom right-hand corner of the clipboard. Then she placed the card of the child whose name began with the next-to-last letter of the alphabet on the clipboard slightly above the first card. She mounted it so that the name of the other child was still visible. She continued this process with the remaining cards. When she finished, she had constructed an inexpensive flip chart.

Patty Kopay writes anecdotal notes on computer address labels. In addition to the child's name and date, she describes the specific event or product exactly as she saw or heard it. Lynn Cohen (1999, p. 27) suggests that a teachers' goal when writing an anecdotal note is to "get the basic story and most significant details, keeping the information as factual as possible" with no judgment or interpretation applied. The following is an example of one of Patty's anecdotal notes:

> Ronnie 10/12
> Read self-selected book (*The Biggest, Best Snowman*). Skipped unknown words, read to the end of the sentence, and reread sentence with filling in the skipped word. When done, he said, "I know just how Little Nell felt. Everyone in my house thinks I'm too little to do everything, too!" Read s-l-o-w-l-y, haltingly!

Teachers use anecdotal notes to describe the strategies children use to decode words, the processes children use while they write, the functions of writing children use while they play, and characteristics of children's talk during a presentation to the class. "Taken regularly, anecdotal notes become not only a vehicle for planning instruction and documenting progress, but also a story about an individual" (Rhodes & Nathenson-Mejia, 1992, p. 503).

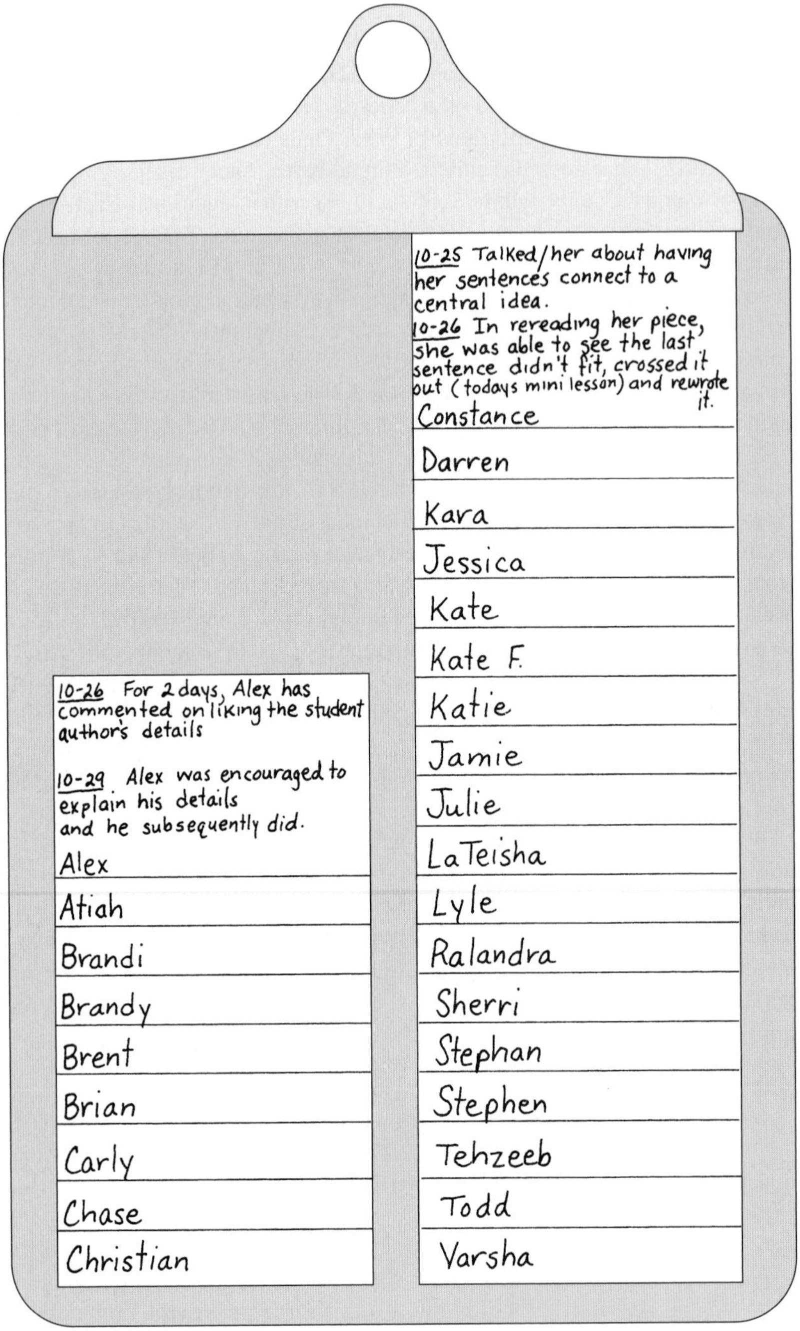

10-25 Talked/her about having her sentences connect to a central idea.
10-26 In rereading her piece, she was able to see the last sentence didn't fit, crossed it out (todays mini lesson) and rewrote it.

Constance

Darren

Kara

Jessica

Kate

Kate F.

Katie

Jamie

Julie

LaTeisha

Lyle

Ralandra

Sherri

Stephan

Stephen

Tehzeeb

Todd

Varsha

10-26 For 2 days, Alex has commented on liking the student author's details

10-29 Alex was encouraged to explain his details and he subsequently did.

Alex

Atiah

Brandi

Brandy

Brent

Brian

Carly

Chase

Christian

FIGURE 12.2   One record-keeping system: An inexpensive flip chart.

Vignettes or Teacher Reflections.   These are recordings of recollections of significant events made after the fact, when the teacher is free of distractions. Because vignettes are like anecdotal notes except that they are prepared sometime after a behavior has occurred and are based on a teacher's memory of the event, vignettes are used for purposes such as those identified for anecdotal notes. These after-the-fact descriptions or vignettes can be more detailed than anecdotal notes and are particularly useful when recording literacy behavior that is significant or unique for a specific child.

For example, Karen Valentine observed one of her students attempting to control his peers' behavior by writing a sign and posting it in an appropriate place. Because she was involved with a small group of children, she did not have time to record a description of the student's behavior immediately. However, as soon as the children left for the day, she recorded her recollection of the event:

> Jamali 3/7
> For days, Jamali had been complaining about the "mess" left by the children getting drinks at the classroom water fountain after recess. "Look at that mess! Water all over the floor!" At his insistence, the class discussed solutions to the problem. While the problem wasn't solved, I thought there was less water on the floor. Evidently, Jamali did not. Today he used the "power of the pen" to attempt to solve the problem. He wrote a sign:
> > BEWR!! WTR SHUS UP
> > ONLE TRN A LITL
> > (Beware! Water shoots up. Only turn a little.)
> He posted his sign over the water fountain. This was the first time I had observed him using writing in an attempt to control other children's behavior.

Vignettes, then, are recollections of significant events. As such, they look much like an anecdotal note, except they are written in the past tense. Also, because teachers can write vignettes when they are free of distractions, they can be more descriptive about the child's concern that drove the literacy-oriented behavior, and they can connect this event to what is known about the child's previous literacy-oriented behaviors.

Checklists.   These are observational aids that specify which behaviors to look for and provide a convenient system for keeping records. They can make observations more systematic and easier to conduct, and can be used in a variety of instructional contexts.

Checklists are useful because they provide lists of items that teachers can see at a glance, showing what children can do. Teachers have learned that (1) children sometimes engage in a behavior on one day that does not reappear for several weeks, and (2) many different variables can affect the literate behaviors children show (e.g., the storybook being read and the other children in the group). Hence, teachers are careful to record the date of each observation and to use the checklists many times over the year in an attempt to create an accurate picture of students' literacy development.

The number of checklists available to describe children's literacy development seems almost endless. The writers of this textbook have provided several examples in previous chapters (see, for example, Figures 6.3 and 6.4). Teachers interested in looking for additional ideas might investigate such resources as Bill Harp (1996), Regie Routman (1991), Lauren Leslie and Mary Jett-Simpson (1997), Fairfax County Public Schools (1998), David Cooper and Nancy Kiger (2001), or The Wright Group (1999).

Conferencing.   A conference is a conversation between a teacher and an individual student. Teachers confer to obtain information they cannot uncover any other way. Sometimes it is difficult to determine the significance of a literacy behavior. For example, a teacher observed several young children playing airport. They were cutting dollar-sized pieces of paper and writing on each piece with scribbles.

> TEACHER: I wonder what you guys are making. Is it money? Are you making a lot of money?
>
> BUDDY: These aren't money. They're tickets for the airplane!

Note how this brief, informal interview cleared up the teacher's initial misconception about the make-believe identity of the pieces of paper.

Conferences can be quick and informal, like the one above, or more structured and systematic. Regardless of length, conferences must be conducted in a "secure and comfortable manner so that students feel encouraged to take risks and share their ideas" (Winograd & Arrington, 1999, p. 234) otherwise the data gathered will be highly suspect. Scott Paris (1995) suggests that comfort occurs if the teacher does not ask too many questions; if the student does most of the talking; if the teacher appears interested and enthusiastic; and if the teacher celebrates the student's strengths.

Whether long or short (and conferences typically are short, about five to ten minutes), teachers begin the conference with a clear purpose in mind. Purposes might include asking questions to understand: (1) what the student is learning or has learned and would like to learn next, (2) the student's interests and attitudes, (3) the strategies the student is using to decode or comprehend text, and (4) what the student sees as difficult. The teacher should make a written record of each conference, noting the purpose of the conference, the child's thinking, and any conclusions reached.

Teachers must take great care in how they structure conference questions. Peter Johnston (1992) suggests that there are three kinds of questions teachers might ask: (1) descriptive questions (e.g., "What happens during the writing workshop in your classroom?" "What do you usually do during the readers' workshop?"), (2) structural questions (e.g., "Do you read during the writing workshop? Can you tell me about when and how?"), and (3) contrast questions (e.g., "Who are your two favorite authors? How are their stories the same? How are their stories different?") To Johnston's list, we could add Graves's (1983) process questions (e.g., "I see you made a change here in your writing; you added some new information. I wonder why it was important to add this information? How did you know to add this information?")

Johnston noted that teachers might want to consider adding a pretend audience for the question. For example, teachers might say, "Suppose a new student was added to our classroom. What things would you tell him or her about reading to help him or her know what to do and how to be good at reading?"

Surveys.   Many teachers use reading or writing surveys to gather information about children's attitudes, interests, and their home literacy environments, and often design their own surveys to help them acquire the information they wish to know. For example, Marianne Kellner wanted to learn about her children's home literacy experiences, so she designed the survey in Figure 12.3. Other teachers ask children to mark a picture (perhaps from a series of happy to sad faces) or circle the appropriate words (*very, kind of, not at all*) to indicate how they feel about reading and writing. These attitude surveys include statements like (1) I like to write, (2) I like to read, (3) I am a good writer, (4) I am a good reader.

Video and Audio Recordings. Teachers often use audiotaping to document children's progress. To assess their children's reading ability, for example, teachers record their students'

Parent Literacy Survey

Child's Name:_____Parent Signature:_____
Date: _____

Please circle the most appropriate of the six responses under each item.

1. My child and I discuss family happenings, school, and current events.
   Every Day   Every Other Day   Twice a Week   Once a Week   Twice a Month   Never

2. I read to my child.
   Every Day   Every Other Day   Twice a Week   Once a Week   Twice a Month   Never

3. My child reads to me.
   Every Day   Every Other Day   Twice a Week   Once a Week   Twice a Month   Never

4. How often does your child see you reading at home?
   Every Day   Every Other Day   Twice a Week   Once a Week   Twice a Month   Never

5. How often does your child see you writing at home?
   Every Day   Every Other Day   Twice a Week   Once a Week   Twice a Month   Never

6. How often does your child visit the public library?
   Every Day   Every Other Day   Twice a Week   Once a Week   Twice a Month   Never

7. How many books does your child have?
   30+ Books   20-30 Books   10-20 Books   5-10 Books   A Few Books   None

8. About how many hours of TV does your child watch each day?
   4+ Hours   3 Hours   2 Hours   1 Hour   Less Than 1 Hour   None

9. My child reads for his or her own enjoyment.
   Every Day   Every Other Day   Twice a Week   Once a Week   Twice a Month   Never

10. I would describe my child as a capable and confident reader.

← ——————————————————————————————————— →

Strongly Agree   Somewhat   Strongly Disagree

FIGURE 12.3   **Example of parent literacy survey.**

oral reading. In this way, teachers learn about their students' fluency in reading a text. Teachers also record children's retellings of stories that were read previously and literature-group discussions to study their students' comprehension of texts.

Teachers use videotaping to capture children's literacy behaviors in a variety of contexts. Some teachers focus the camera lens on an area of the classroom, such as the dramatic-play area or the writing center, to gather information about the children's literacy-related social interactions during their play and work. Viewing of the tapes provides valuable information, not only about the children's knowledge of context-appropriate oral language and their ability to engage in conversations with others, but also about the children's knowledge of the functions of writing.

Running Records.   Running records are used to document students' reading behaviors. In Chapter 8, readers are introduced to how to make a running record on a child's reading of a piece of text (Special Feature 8.1). As Peter Johnston suggests, "learning to record oral reading errors and figure out what they [mean]" takes practice (1992, p. 69). The recording and interpretation of oral reading errors are very important skills for teachers to develop. Once teachers have learned the procedures, they can record their students' oral reading behaviors at any time, from any book, without any preparation such as photocopying of the story's pages or having extra copies of the book available.

Products or Work Samples.   Some products, such as samples of children's writing, can be gathered together in a folder. If the children's original works cannot be saved (e.g., a letter that is sent to its recipient), a photocopy can be made of the product. Other products, such as structures the children have created, might not be conveniently saved. In these cases, a photograph—still or video—can be made. Because memories are short, the teacher or the child should record a brief description of the product or the activity that resulted in the product.

Many teachers find that folders with pockets and with center clasps for three-hole-punched paper serve as better storage containers than file folders. Interview forms, running-record sheets, and other similar papers can be three-hole-punched, thus permitting their easy insertion into each student's folder. When anecdotal notes and vignettes are written on computer mailing labels, the labels can be attached to the inside covers of each child's folder. When these notes are written on index cards, the cards can be stored in one of the folder's pockets. Also, a Ziploc® sandwich bag might be stapled inside each child's folder to hold an audiotape. The self-sealing feature of the bag means that the tape can be securely held inside the folder. The class's folders might be housed in a plastic container or in hanging files in a file cabinet.

Typically, products or work samples demonstrate children's literacy knowledge and skill in performing an authentic, real-world literacy task. The children might write a report on their favorite animal, design a poster encouraging other children not to pollute the environment, create a commercial for a new cafeteria offering, or write a persuasive letter to the principal for more recess time, and so forth. Each of these products is different; each requires a different set of criteria to judge the product's "goodness." David Cooper and Nancy Kiger (2001) suggest that teachers use general criteria similar to the following to guide their assessment of such products. Teachers need to *first,* think through the strategies, skills, and knowledge the product will require the children to use. Which strategies and skills have the children already been taught? Which strategies and skills will the children need to be taught? The answer to this question will impact the immediate instructional plans.

second, describe the task. This might be done alone or with the children. What is it that the children need to produce?

third, develop a rubric, or scoring guide, of the specific criteria, to evaluate the product. The teacher alone or with the children should clearly identify and define the criteria to be used to judge whether or not each objective on the rubric has been met. Varying degrees of meeting the objective might also be described. Children should know what is expected before they begin creating their product. Samples of products produced by other children that illustrate varying "degrees to which an individual has attained something," in other words "anchor products," give children points of reference for their work. (See Special Feature 12.1 on constructing rubrics.)

fourth, share the rubric with the children. Do the children understand what they are being asked to do?

fifth, once the products have been created, invite the children to self-evaluate their product.

sixth, compare your assessment with each child's assessment and meet with each child to discuss this comparison. Consider which criteria were not met because additional teaching was needed, and which criteria were not met because the child needed to work harder. Plan for future teaching and learning.

The development of rubrics for assessing quality is a difficult and time-consuming —but worthwhile—task. Finding the correct language to describe the different performance levels for each facet is a challenge. In Special Feature 12.1, we describe a set of procedures for constructing a rubric.

Often, rubrics are developed by teachers for use by and with their students. Two teacher-developed rubrics used to judge the quality of children's writing were presented in Chapter 8 (see Figure 8.15 and 8.16). Rubrics might also be developed by teachers **with** their students. The NSP (1994) suggests that this is the way to begin. The teachers involved in the NSP say that constructing a rubric with students helps the students to understand the expectations for their behavior and helps them know what needs improvement to meet the required performance level.

Tarry Lindquist (1995) has agreed. At the beginning of a unit of study, she helps her students consider what they might produce. She saves copies of her students' work from the previous years and shares these models with her students. "What is effective about this particular model? What could have been done to make it more effective?" (p. 150). Ms. Lindquist has commented,

> Student-created criteria predict what the children hope to accomplish and with what degree of mastery, creativity, and/or cooperation. By setting up the criteria prior to the practice, students have a guide to success in terms they comprehend because they fashioned the measurement. (p. 150–151)

Special Feature 12.1

Developing Item-Specific Rubrics

Considerations

- Scoring Levels (degrees of performance)
- Outcome(s)
- Descriptors (qualities for each outcome at each scoring level)

Scoring Levels

Decide on the number of scoring levels. An even number of levels (4 works well) requires the

Adapt/Adaptation	Demonstrate/Demonstration
Analyze/Analysis	Describe/Description
Apply/Application	Determine/Determination
Appraise/Appraisal	Differentiate/Differentiation
Clarify/Clarification	Evaluate/Evaluation
Compare/Comparison	Examine/Examination
Consider/Consideration	Explain/Explanation
Contrast/Contrast	Explore/Exploration
Define/Definition	

Descriptors

The descriptors are words that indicate the various degrees of performance across the scoring

scorer to discriminate above or below a mid-point or average score.

Outcomes

The outcome(s) indicate the product that the student is expected to generate. Some items may require students to produce more than one outcome. When possible, the outcome should be a noun or a noun form of the verb used in the wording of the item. For example, if the item says " Explain the reasons for the author's decision," the outcome would be stated as an "explanation." Here's a verb/noun list to consider when writing items and rubrics:

Express/Expression	Predict/Prediction
Identify/Identification	Propose/Proposition
Integrate/Integration	Reflect/Reflection
Interpret/Interpretation	Represent/Representation
Investigate/Investigation	Select/Selection
Justify/Justification	Support/Support
List/Listing	Synthesize/Synthesis
Modify/Modification	Utilize/Utilization
Organize/Organization	

levels. They describe depth, breadth, quality, scope, extent, complexity, degree, and/or accuracy of the response. Here are some examples:

	Four-Point Rubric	Two-Point Rubric:
Score Point 4	complete and thorough, sufficient and relevant, specific	
Score Point 3	adequate, accurate, some	
Score Point 2	limited/sketchy, few	accurate and complete, appropriate and thorough, logical
Score Point 1	attempted, irrelevant, insufficient	incomplete, illogical

Steps

1. Determine the number of **scoring levels** to be used when evaluating responses.
2. Determine the learner **outcome(s),** and prioritize them if multiple outcomes are expected.
3. Write the **descriptors** for each outcome at the highest level of performance. Focus on

terms of qualification rather than quantification, and avoid stating descriptors in the negative.

4. Write the **descriptors** for each outcome at each of the lower levels of performance. Focus on words or phrases that clearly capture the actual differences among the levels

(continued on next page)

Special Feature 12.1 *(continued)*

of performance, and avoid the overuse of adjectives and adverbs.

5. Don't fall in love with the rubric. Chances are, once you actually use it to score student work, you'll discover ways to **revise and improve** the rubric, the item, or both.

Rubric Development Template and Example

Item: Although they are friends, Sheila and Michael are very different. Using information from the story, explain how they are different.

Template

Score Point	Outcome 1	Descriptors 1	Outcome 2	Descriptors 2	Outcome 3	Descriptors 4
4	Explanation	Thorough	Support	With sufficient, relevant details from the text		
3	Explanation	Adequate	Support	Wits some relevant details from the text		
2	Explanation	Limited	Support	With few, if any, relevant details from the text		
1	Explanation	Mostly inaccurate	Support	With irrelevant details, if any, from the text		
0	Explanation	Inappropriate or incorrect	Support	Totally irrelevant or incorrect		

Final Rubric:

Score Point:	Description
4	Response is a thorough explanation of how the characters are different, supported by sufficient, relevant details from the text.
3	Response is an adequate explanation of how the characters are different, supported by some relevant details from the text.
2	Response is limited explanation of how the characters are different, supported by few, if any, relevant details from the text.
1	Response is a mostly inaccurate explanation of how the characters are different, supported by irrelevant details, if any, from the text.
0	Response is totally inappropriate or inaccurate.

Adapted by materials provided by Michael C. Kelly at http://www.doe.state.de.us

Rubrics, then, provide criteria against which students can compare their work to determine how good it is and to select their best work for their portfolios.

Rubrics also provide the means by which teachers use portfolios to inform their instruction, to establish future learning goals for each child, and to report to parents or to school and district administrators. Comparing each child's performance against the appropriate rubrics permits the teacher to make ongoing determinations about the student's literacy development. For example, consider the teacher who uses an appropriate rubric for assessing a child's letter to the principal, attempting to convince her that he and his classmates need more than 20 minutes for lunch. By comparing the child's writing against an appropriate writing rubric, the teacher can identify the strengths and weaknesses in the child's writing of a persuasive letter. The resulting analysis informs the teacher of the instruction this child needs, and it defines learning goals for child.

It is not **just** the teacher who uses rubrics to make informed judgments. Teachers report that students learn to "understand and internalize the criteria in a rubric, . . . using the criteria to assist their peers in revising work and [in assessing] their own work" (O'Neil, 1994, p. 5). Knowing the criteria especially helps children to acquire the language they need in order to offer specific feedback to their peers. Many teachers ask their students to rate their work before the teachers assess the product. Even teachers of young children have discovered that children can be accurate in their assessment of their performance.

Creating Portfolios: Working and Showcase

What exactly is a portfolio? F. Leon Paulson, Pearl Paulson, and Carol Meyer (1991, p. 60) define a portfolio as "a purpose collection of [a sample of] student work that exhibits the student's efforts, progress, and achievements." The purposes of portfolios, as defined by Frank Serafini (2001b, p. 388), are "to uncover the possibilities for students, to understand each child as a whole, and to attempt to provide a window into a student's conceptual framework and ways of seeing the world."

There are at least two kinds of portfolios, the working portfolio and the showcase portfolio. The working portfolio should provide "accurate documentation about how a child is growing and developing" (Gronlund, 1998, p. 5). The work samples, anecdotal notes, and so forth described above will be housed in the students' working portfolios. The items housed in working portfolios are not representative of the student's best work. Rather, the items housed in working portfolios evidence a student's typical, everyday performance. From the working portfolios, children and their teachers select specific pieces for inclusion in each child's showcase portfolio. The items in the showcase portfolio exhibit the best work the student has produced.

What each portfolio will look like will vary from teacher to teacher and school to school. Some teachers maintain a folder on each student. For example, the majority of teachers in a Delaware portfolio project used expandable file folders for their children's portfolios. Manila folders were placed inside each expandable file folder. Each class's portfolios were placed inside a large plastic container with a lid. These teachers liked having a lid on their portfolio boxes because it helped to reduce the amount of classroom dust on the children's portfolios.

Other teachers have created different kinds of portfolios. For example, a Colorado teacher used gallon-size Ziploc® bags, bound together with large metal rings. The teacher's students decorated poster board covers, which the teacher then laminated (Wilcox, 1993). Some teachers use pizza boxes decorated by the children. One teacher used a handmade fabric wall-hanging with a pocket for each child. Still other teachers ask their students to decide what they want their portfolios to look like.

Deciding what to use is the practical starting point with portfolio assessment. As Gaye Gronlund (1998) notes, "Decisions in this area must be made, experiments tried, and a comfortable style selected." There is no one right storage scheme for children's portfolios. Teachers might use one kind of system for their children's working portfolios and another for their children's showcase portfolios.

Selecting Artifacts for Inclusion. Maintaining a classroom portfolio system does not mean saving everything the child does and sending nothing home. Saving everything creates what Gaye Gronlund calls "a storage nightmare!" The pieces placed in a working portfolio are selected because they show students' everyday performance related to the literacy accomplishments or standards the teacher or school district or state has determined the children should know and be able to do. The pieces placed in the showcase portfolio are selected from the working portfolio because they show the student's best accomplishment relative to the literacy accomplishments.

Having a specific reason for selecting each artifact is critically important. What are the specific reasons? Recall that content standards (or goals, outcomes, or accomplishments) drive teachers' decisions about which data to gather (see Figure 12.1). These same content standards drive the teachers' and the children's decisions about what should be selected for inclusion in the children's portfolios. For example, to demonstrate each child's accomplishments relative to the state English language arts standards in Figure 12.1, teachers and children might include artifacts like those described in Figure 12.4 in children's working portfolios. The teacher and the students will select the artifacts that best illustrate the students' behavior relative to each literacy accomplishment for inclusion in the showcase portfolios.

Sharing Information on Artifact Selection for Showcase Portfolios. To encourage the thoughtful selection of items, portfolio advocates suggest that an entry slip should be attached to each artifact included in the children's showcase portfolios. "Writing the entry slips is a way for students to reflect on their work, as well as to give the background for the work to others" (New Standards Project [NSP], 1994, p. 12). Entry slips require students to engage in a "dialogue with their inner, critical selves" (Wilcox, 1993, p. 20). The NSP teachers and Carol Wilcox agree: An entry slip helps readers of children's portfolios know the importance of the work selected for inclusion. "Why do I want this artifact in my (or this child's) portfolio? What does it show about me (or this child) as a reader, a writer, a learner, a literate individual?"

Just what does an entry slip look like? See Figure 12.5 for an example of an entry slip used by the five-, six-, and seven-year-olds in a multi-age classroom. Notice that entry slips are dated. Many teachers have discovered that it is helpful to have a date stamp, like those used by librarians, readily available in the classroom in the area where the portfolios are stored. Dating each item selected for inclusion in portfolios permits the teacher and the child to arrange the items in chronological order to show changes or learning over time.

FIGURE 12.4   Possible artifacts for inclusion in students' working portfolios linked to a state's content standards

Content standard	Students will	Possible artifacts
Standard One	use written and oral English appropriate for various purposes and audiences.	Writings illustrating different stages of the writing process (e.g., drafts, edited pieces, published pieces) Examples of writing in three discourse categories (e.g., expressive, informative, and persuasive) Best writing in September and in May All drafts from one piece to show changes within a piece of writing Notes from teacher/student conferences Videotape of a presentation Drafts of a speech from initial planning to final draft Teacher's anecdotal notes of student's speaking behavior Peer and teacher evaluations of oral presentations Checklist of oral discussion skills
Standard Two	construct, examine, and extend the meaning of literary, informative, and technical texts.	Reading response log entries Text-based writing responses Teacher anecdotal notes of reading or discussion observations Running records Retellings Attitude surveys Literature discussion checklist List of books read Reading strategy checklist
Standard Three	access, organize, and evaluate information gained through listening, reading, and viewing.	Research reports with graphs and figures Teacher anecdotal notes on computer skills; narrowing research topics; reading of graphs, tables, charts Copies of graphic organizers of information gained Samples of notes taken while reading
Standard Four	use literary knowledge gained through print and visual media to connect self to society and culture.	Teacher anecdotal notes of self-to-text and text-to-text connections Reading response log entries

Frequency of Artifact Selection for Showcase Portfolios.   The NSP recommends that the selection of items for inclusion in children's portfolios should occur at least three times a year. The NSP teachers have discovered that too much accumulated work overwhelms children, making it difficult for them to be selective, so it seems wise to follow this rule: The

Portfolio Entry Slip

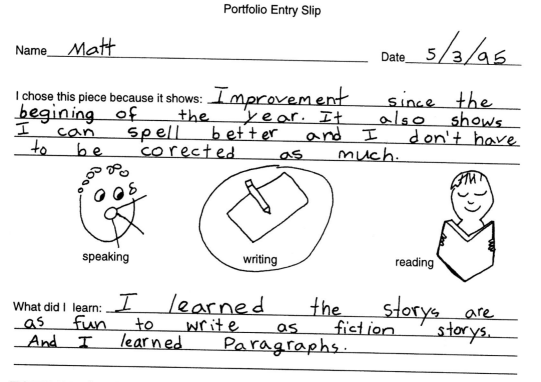

Name ___Matt_____   Date ___5/3/95___

I chose this piece because it shows: _Improvement   since   the_
begining   of   the   year.   It   also   shows
I   can   spell   better   and   I   don't   have
to   be   corected   as   much.

speaking   writing   reading

What did I learn: ___I   learned   the   storys   are_
as   fun   to   write   as   fiction   storys.
And   I   learned   Paragraphs.

FIGURE 12.5   Sample portfolio entry slip.

younger the child, the more frequently the artifacts should be selected. Perhaps once every four weeks would be a prudent guide. However, a key to the decision regarding frequency of selection will be the number of artifacts the children and their teacher have created and stored in their various storage bins. Too few items also limits the children's and teacher's ability to select.

Another variable in determining when to select items will be the school's identified times for reporting to parents through report cards and parent–teacher, parent–teacher–child, or parent–child conferences. The portfolio items will serve as the information base for these reporting systems.

Sharing Portfolios with Others.   Carol Wilcox (1993, p. 33) reports teacher Karen Boettcher as saying, "The heart of portfolios is sharing." Following are some ways in which the information in portfolios can be shared with others.

Sharing with Peers.   One important audience for portfolios is the children's classmates. "Sharing portfolios is a powerful tool for building community within the classroom" (Wilcox, 1993, p. 33). Wilcox has elaborated this statement by noting that by sharing, children learn unique things about their classmates. They learn about the learning strategies their colleagues have used successfully. They learn what peers are struggling to learn, and they learn to offer assistance in their peers' struggles. They learn about peers' special talents. They learn about books they might read, new ways of writing their own pieces, and new goals they might set for themselves.

Teachers can structure different kinds of ways for peers to share. Here are some options:

- Children are asked to share something that teaches others about them as a reader, that shows a new skill they have learned to use in writing, or that shows how they have changed as a reader, writer, or speaker.
- Children form a circle with an artifact of their choice from their portfolio in hand, each sharing the artifact and receiving the audience's response.
- Children take selected artifacts or their portfolios to another class at the same or a different grade to share with members of this other class. The children might meet in pairs, for example, to consider what development as a reader looks like in first and second grade. What better way to introduce first-graders to what to expect in second grade?

In addition to teaching children how and what to share, teachers need to teach children how to respond to their peers' portfolios. Carol Wilcox (1993) has described how second-grade teacher Kathy Busick had her students generate a list of statements they could use to help them respond to each other's portfolios. The list included statements such as,

I learned . . . about you.
I like how you showed. . . .
I never knew that. . . .

Sharing with Parents.   Parents (interpret this term broadly to mean the significant adults in each child's life) are another important audience for portfolios. Of course, teachers will use the children's portfolios during parent–teacher conferences. Sometimes, children will join in these conferences to provide their own perspective on their own development as readers, writers, and speakers. At other times, children will independently use their portfolios to explain their literacy development to their parents. Even Bernadette Watson's kindergartners ran their own portfolio conferences for their parents! (Ms. Watson and other teachers have discovered that it is important to have children practice how they plan to share their portfolios with their parents before they actually do so.) See Chapter 13 for details of a conference where a portfolio is used to share a description of the child's literacy development.

Teachers not only need to teach children how to respond to their peers, but also to inform parents how to respond to their children's portfolios. Carol Wilcox (1993) has detailed the story of Michael, a six-year-old, who had a devastating experience when sharing his portfolio with his parents. Their response focused on his poor spelling and handwriting performance, rather than on his accomplishments and his literacy development. He was not, after all, spelling words conventionally!

Children may not always be present during the sharing of their portfolios. When the child is not to be present when her or his portfolio is examined by the parents, the child might write a letter explaining the portfolio to the reader. We present an example of a letter written by a third-grader to his portfolio's readers in Figure 12.6. This student's awareness of his learning is clearly evident in his letter to his readers.

Dear Reviewer,

I think my story about the tiny family is my best piece. I organized the story real good. I tried to help my readers know how worried the tiny family would be when it heard the news that the police were coming for them. I thought I gave it a good ending. I wrote it around April Fool's Day. That's how I came up with the idea of the ending. I had two other ideas for endings, but this was the one I liked best. I liked when my friends said, "That's good!" when they heard my ending. I like to get good responses to my pieces from my friends.

I think my writing has really improved this year. In September, I wrote short pieces. I wrote a lot about playing with my friends. Now I write about lots of different topics. I like writing stories. I'm good at paragraphing now. I used to just start writing. Now, I think about what I'm going to write about before I fall asleep. I come to school ready to write. I really like writing time. But I don't think I'll be a writer when I grow-up. I want to be a soccer player.

Do you like my writing?

Sincerely,

FIGURE 12.6   A letter written to introduce a child's portfolio to readers.

Many school districts continue the policy of having four reporting periods per year, with two of these reports being oral and two being written. Teachers who use portfolios in their classroom as the means of tracking their students' literacy development can be frustrated if their district requires them to use a letter-grading system in their written report to parents. To translate the children's rich portfolio data into a single letter grade seems a formidable task. These teachers prefer to report progress to parents using a conference (see details of how in Chapter 13), and, when a written report is required, they prefer to use a narrative report. Peter Afflerbach (1993) has provided a hint about why teachers using portfolios prefer narrative reports over letter-grade reporting systems. He suggests that "within a narrative report, teachers can provide detail about [a] student's development. . . . The narrative can include relatively detailed information about a student's strengths and needs, personal challenges and accomplishments, and describe the variety of a student's . . . experiences" (p. 461).

While teachers may **prefer** to report progress to parents through a conference or a written narrative, teachers in districts that have not abandoned reporting progress to parents through letter grades on report cards, typically **must** translate their students' rich portfolio data into letter grades to meet their districts' requirements. Some years ago, the teachers at Townsend Elementary School faced this challenge by working together to prepare rubrics to define what their students needed in order to earn an "A," a "B," and so forth in the immediate grades and "Excellent," "Satisfactory," or "Needs Improvement" in the primary grades. Because effort, growth, and performance were important to these teachers, these elements were central to their grading scale. Using the data in each student's portfolios, the teacher and the student graded the student's performance over the marking period. (Of course, the teachers and children had developed and used rubrics for various classroom activities, so the rating of performance was not a new task.) Differences were resolved through teacher–student conferences. In addition, the teachers enclosed a written narrative in each student's report card. The parents discovered how much more they learned about their children's development from the narratives than from the letter grades. The following year, the teachers **and the parents** petitioned the school board for permission to report progress to parents using narratives and conferences only. The school board granted their request.

Sharing with School Administrators.   Center directors, principals, and central-office administrators (e.g., the superintendent, the center's advisory board, the school board, the language-arts supervisor) want to know about the progress that all the children in each classroom or school are making toward the defined standards, outcomes, or goals. A data-collection form often is created, on which classroom teachers can summarize their students' portfolio information and arrive at a conclusion about how their students are progressing as a group. An example of such a form is presented in Figure 12.7. Using the information on this form, it is possible to aggregate the data across all children in a classroom or the school. Comparing the data from the fall to the spring permits school administrators to see changes in the percentages of children in each category within each teacher's classroom, within each grade level, and within the school who have met the standard or achieved the goal. Central-office administrators can calculate this information across all schools in the district. In this way, the portfolio data can become an integral component of the school's and the school district's accountability system.

Teacher's Name _____ Grade _____

School _____ Date _____

Key:

✔ Meets or exceeds standard

★ Approaching standard

● Significantly below standard

Teachers within the school or district will have defined what students at each grade level need to know and be able to do to earn each rating.

Standards	Students				
	Adam	Ainya	Collin	Shane	and other students in the class
I. Writer produces texts that exhibit the following textual features:					
• Development: The topic, theme, stand/perspective, argument, or character is fully developed.					
• Organization: The text exhibits a discernible progression of ideas.					
• Style: The writer demonstrates a quality of imagination, individuality, and a distinctive voice.					
• Word Choice: The words are precise, vivid, and economical.					
• Sentence Formation: Sentences are complete and varied in length and structure.					
• Conventions: Appropriate grammar, mechanics, spelling, and usage enhance the meaning and readability of the text.					

Additional standards and indicators as defined by the district or state would be added to the form.

FIGURE 12.7   Sample portfolio data summary form.

On-Demand Assessment

There is another kind of assessment that teachers use, or are required to use, to understand their students' literacy learning: **on-demand assessment.** Each of the following examples illustrates a kind of on-demand assessment.

A teacher pulls each of her students aside, one at a time, to have them read the same book, a book unknown to all of them. While each child reads, the teacher records the child's reading errors. When the child finishes reading, the teacher asks the child to retell the story. Later, the teacher might use a miscue analysis system to analyze the children's reading errors and a story structure form to analyze the children's retellings. The teacher analyzes every child's reading and retelling exactly the same way.

A group of children finish reading *Charlotte's Web* by E. B. White (Harper Collins, 1952). The teacher has participated occasionally in the group's book discussions so the teacher has a sense of the group's understanding of the story. However, the teacher wants to know more about each child's understanding of the text. The teacher develops a set of four open-ended questions to which all children will respond in writing and identifies the criteria to be used to score the children's work. All children in the group take the test on the same day, writing for as much time as they need, and are given the same directions: to use details from the story to support their answers. To score the test, the teacher compares what the children wrote and the degree to which they supported their ideas (rarely to thoroughly and sufficiently) against the previously defined criteria.

On two days in March, all third, fifth, eighth, and tenth graders in the state read several passages and demonstrate their understanding of the passages by bubbling-in answers to multiple-choice questions and writing answers to open-ended questions. The multiple-choice questions are scored by machine; the open-ended questions are scored by trained raters using a rubric written by and anchor papers selected by teachers. (Because the items on the test have been linked to the state's content standards, this on-demand assessment would be called a "standards-based state-mandated" assessment because it is linked to the state's standards and mandated by the state's legislators.)

Notice the shared features of these on-demand assessments. A central feature is that during on-demand assessments the teacher stops instruction and the children stop their learning to demonstrate what they know and are able to do. The children are, as the name implies, required to show what they know "on-demand." (Recall that, in ongoing assessment, assessment and instruction were interwoven.)

Standardized Tests

Many on-demand assessments, such as those in the third example above, are administered, scored, and interpreted in the same way for all test takers. Each student taking the test reads the same passages, answers the same questions, and hears the same directions or writes to the same prompt in the same amount of time. When all variables are held constant, the assessment would be known as a "standardized" on-demand test.

There are two types of standardized tests:

1. **Criterion-referenced tests** are developed using a specific set of objectives that reflect district and state learning standards. For instance, the district or state has a standard that fourth-grade students should be able to identify the main idea of a passage. Mrs. Bette, a fourth-grade teacher, has taught a specific unit on comprehending the main idea. Two weeks later Mrs. Bette administers the district criterion-based test that focuses on several reading comprehension skills, including identifying the main idea. The test has fifty items; ten items deal directly with identifying the main idea. The students read a short passage and choose the correct multiple-choice answer that identifies the main idea from each passage. To demonstrate their mastery of this skill,

students must correctly identify the main idea for eight out of ten passages. The goal in criterion-referenced tests is for all students to demonstrate mastery of the information and skills they have been taught.

2. **Norm-referenced tests** are designed to measure the relative accomplishment of one student to the whole class, or to compare one classroom of fourth-grade students to another classroom within the same school, or to compare all fourth-grade classrooms in a district, or to compare all fourth graders across the country. Norm-referenced standardized tests can be used to determine whether a school's curriculum reflects national expectations of what children should know at a specific grade level.

Unfortunately, many people use norm-referenced tests to compare students to one another. Another concern is that norm-referenced tests reflect a transmission (behaviorist) theory of learning. As discussed in Chapter 1, transmission learning assumed that knowledge could be broken into separate bits and that children learned when teachers organized these pieces into a sequence. Constructivist theory helps us to understand that knowledge is not separable bits and that children learn by connecting what they already know with what they are trying to learn.

Today it is common practice for states to mandate that children take a standards-based standardized test, typically in the spring of the academic year. The state's aim is to gather information on how a school and the school district are achieving with respect to the standards. Lucy Calkins, Kate Montgomery, and Donna Santman (1998) suggest that teachers hired to teach in a new district ask questions like the following to help them understand the district's testing policies:

- Is the district's test norm-referenced or criterion-referenced and standards-based?
- How are the children's scores reported to the public? Raw scores? Percentile scores? Cut-score percentages (below standard, meets the standard, above the standard)?
- Is the school's score compared with that of other schools used to rank the school? Are all children's (special education, bilingual) scores counted in the school's ranking?

Reconsidering Teaching Practices

The authors of this book acknowledge that no single test score should be used alone to judge a student's progress in reading and writing. However, *if* most of the children in the classroom do not perform as expected on a standardized test, then teachers must be prepared to reconsider their methods of teaching reading and writing. Teachers need to ask themselves, "What could I have done better or differently?" Others certainly will raise this question. "Is it the reading curriculum?" A district administrator might recommend that a new basal anthology be purchased. Someone, maybe even a state legislator, might mandate that phonics be taught to all kindergarten through third-grade children for thirty minutes a day. Teachers must be able to respond by defending their teaching practices and by learning what legitimately needs revising to support children's development as readers and writers. Teachers at each grade level and within each school need to study the reported testing data to understand what their students could do well and what was challenging for their students. These data can guide teachers' examination of their teaching practices.

Summary

In the earlier chapters in this book, we presented the instructional strategies that create the framework for an effective language and literacy program. However, these strategies by themselves are not sufficient to construct a program that ensures optimal language and literacy learning for all children. In this chapter, we present information on a key ingredient—assessment.

■ *What is important for teachers to know about children's literacy development?*
    Teachers need a thorough knowledge of the language and literacy accomplishments or goals or objectives that have been judged by the professional community and the public as important. This information may be obtained from several sources, including state and local school district guidelines. In addition to information provided throughout this text, the authors also recommend reports prepared by the Committee on the Prevention of Reading Difficulties in Young Children, the joint position paper issued by the International Reading Association and the National Association for the Education of Young Children (IRA/NAEYC), and the joint standards issued by the International Reading Association and the National Council of Teachers of English (IRA/NCTE).

■ *What are the two general approaches teachers might use to assess their students' literacy learning?*
    Changes in what we know about literacy learning have necessitated major changes in our ways of measuring children's literacy learning. There are two general approaches teachers might use to gather information about their students' literacy development: ongoing assessment and on-demand assessment. Ongoing assessment makes use of such information-gathering tools as anecdotal notes, vignettes or teacher reflections, checklists, conferences, surveys, video and audio recordings, running records, and the collection of children's work samples. These artifacts of children's literacy learning are produced while the children engage in their daily classroom activities and the teacher is teaching. The artifacts, then, serve the dual purpose of instruction and assessment. These artifacts are stored in portfolios. Hence, ongoing assessment is often called "portfolio assessment." On-demand assessment occurs when the teacher stops teaching to assess the students' performance and asks them to demonstrate what they know and can do. The children are required to show what they know "on-demand." Typically, on-demand assessments are administered, scored, and interpreted in the same way for all test takers. In reality, the two approaches work hand-in-hand in the classroom. Teachers gather ongoing data while instructing about children's daily performances and on-demand data periodically in order to form a comprehensive picture of each student's literacy learning.

■ *What are the differences between working and showcase portfolios?*
    The goal of the working portfolio is to provide documentation of how the child is growing and developing. The items housed in the working portfolio are evidence of a student's typical, everyday performance. From the working portfolio, the teacher and student will select specific pieces for inclusion in the student's showcase portfolio. The items housed in the showcase portfolio will exhibit the best work the student has produced.

■ *How do teachers use the information they collect?*

Teachers (and children) collect information and store it in the working portfolios. Teachers (and students) analyze the products and information contained in the working portfolio to assess each student's progress over time. These types of authentic assessment provide just the type of information that teachers need to know to provide effective literacy learning experiences for children.

Teachers also use the information they collect in portfolios to share with parents. Parents need to know how their children are progressing, and most parents need concrete examples with explicit information provided by the teacher, so teachers share the working and the showcase portfolios with children's parents.

Teachers also share information with parents that has been gathered through on-demand assessment. Teacher-made and district-mandated on-demand assessment data is housed in the children's showcase portfolios. The teacher uses these data to show what the child can do independently, unsupported by the teacher and peers.

LINKING KNOWLEDGE TO PRACTICE

1. One way teachers determine what they want and need to know about children's literacy development is by reviewing national, state, and local standards. Search the state's Web site or contact the state or a school district to obtain a copy of the state or local standards of language arts. Given what you have learned about children's literacy development in this textbook, do these standards appear reasonable goals for language arts instruction at the grade level of your choice? Why or why not?

2. Interview a teacher about the information-gathering tools that he or she typically uses to collect information about children's literacy development. How does the teacher organize this information to share with parents?

3. Interview a principal, teacher, or someone from the state's Department of Education. What are the district-mandated on-demand assessments? What are the state-mandated on-demand assessments? How are these tests constructed? Ask the questions Lucy Calkins and her colleagues (see page 399) suggested that teachers new to a district ask.

4. Examine one of the Web sites in Special Feature 12.1 and find a strategy for ongoing assessment. Report your findings to the class.

Special Feature 12.2

Web Sites with Assessment Information

Elaine Coxon's Web page (http://www. odyssey.on.ca/~elaine.coxon/rubrics. htm): Need a rubric? Check out teacher Elaine Coxon's Web site for sample rubrics that will help readers create their own.

Reading Online (http://www.readingonline. org/electronic): This is the site of the International Reading Association's on-line journal; the section is the electronic classroom. Readers will find both practical and research articles related to literacy education in this journal, including many dealing with assessment. Each article contains links to numerous appropriate Web sites.

Kathy Schrock's Guide for Educators (http:// school.discovery.com/schrockguide/ assess.html): Kathy Schrock has prepared a collection of assessment rubrics for teachers to use as guides to design their own. This Web site contains numerous student rubrics, subject-specific and general rubrics, and educator skills rubrics. Ms. Schrock provides links to numerous articles on rubrics and assessment in general. She also provides links to report cards and progress reports.

National Center for Research on Evaluation, Standards, and Student Testing (http:// www.cse.ucla.edu): The site includes full text of the CRESSTLINE Newsletter, a description of CRESST print, video, and audio products, and full text presentations delivered at some CRESST conferences and several articles. The "Parents' Page" provides a range of helpful information about assessment written in a straightforward way for parents.

Scholastic-Assessment (http://teacher. scholastic.com/professional/classplan. htm#Assessment): This site is sponsored by Scholastic and advertises itself as having the "latest on rubrics, performance, and other strategies for assessing student performance."

13 Parents as Partners in Language Education

Nestling close on Grandma's big, soft, feather bed, Grandma reads Billie her favorite book, The Little Engine That Could. *Grandma barely finishes the last word in the book when Billie asks her to read it again. As Grandma rereads, Billie echoes the refrain, "I think I can, I think I can, I think I can!" After the story, Grandma always says, "If you think you can, you can do anything." To this day, whenever Billie is challenged to learn new concepts or deal with difficult situations, she remembers Grandma saying, "Just think you can, just think you can!"*

If you share memories like Billie's, you are indeed fortunate. Research demonstrates that a family's role in a child's language and literacy development is directly related to the child's communicative competence (Hart & Risley, 1995), positive attitudes toward reading and writing, and literacy achievement (e.g., Christian, Morrison, & Bryant, 1998; Epstein, 1986; Sulzby, Teale, & Kamberelis, 1989).

When parents and teachers share information, the child benefits.

Before Reading This Chapter, Think About . . .

- Your early literacy experiences. Do you remember precious moments snuggling with a special person and sharing a book? Do you remember talking with an adult who provided you with many experiences and the words to describe these experiences? Do you remember an adult helping you read words in your environment?
- Your memories of a parent's report of a parent–teacher conference about your classroom behavior and learning. Do you remember if your parents always heard positive reports about your learning? Do you remember what happened if the teacher made suggestions for home learning activities?
- News flashes, newsletters, and other written communication you carried home from school. Do you remember these being posted in your home, perhaps on the refrigerator door? Do you remember them helping you answer the question: What did you do in school today?

Focus Questions

- What is known about the relationship between what parents do and children's language and literacy development?
- In what ways might early childhood teachers communicate personally with parents?
- How might teachers run a parent–teacher conference?
- In what ways might teachers communicate with parents in writing?
- What resources might an early childhood teacher provide to parents and parents provide to teachers to support young children's early literacy learning?

What Roles Do Families Play?

Collin (1992, p. 2) refers to the parents' nurturing role in their child's literacy development as "planting the seeds of literacy." Almost all parents want to plant these seeds, but many are unsure of the best way to begin. Similarly, most parents and other primary caregivers vastly underestimate the importance of their role in helping children become competent language users. In this chapter, we discuss strategies teachers can use to inform parents of all cultures and other primary caregivers about the critical role they play in their child's language and lit-

---

B O X   13.1

Definition of Terms

developmental spelling: another name for invented spelling, where children use two or three letters to phonetically represent a word (e.g., *happy* might be spelled as *hape*).

---

eracy development, and how parents and teachers can work together to enhance language and reading and writing opportunities in the home. Special Feature 13.4, Parental Involvement in Bilingual/Second-Language Settings, provides a multicultural perspective on this issue.

Language Development

In Chapters 2 and 3, we discussed how families provide the rich social context necessary for children's language development. The thousands of hours of parent–child interactions from the moment of birth through the preschool years provide the foundation for language. As children acquire language, they are able to share with others what they feel, think, believe, and want. While most children begin to use their expressive vocabulary in the second year of life, research has long documented that children differ in their ability to learn and use new words (Smith & Dickinson, 1994). In an effort to understand what accounts for these differences, researchers Betty Hart and Todd Risley (1995) documented parent and child interactions during the first three years of children's lives. The research team observed 42 families from different socioeconomic and ethnic backgrounds one hour each month for two-and-a-half years. Their data revealed vast differences in the amount of language spoken to children. Children from welfare homes heard an average of 616 words an hour; children from working-class families heard 1251 words an hour; while children from professional homes heard 2153 words per hour! If one thinks of words as dollars, the children from these different socioeconomic homes would have significantly disparate bank accounts. Further, this long-term study revealed that early language differences had a lasting effect on childrens' subsequent language accomplishments both at age three and at age nine. In other words, talk between adults and children early in life makes a significant difference. It is equally important for older children to have consistent opportunities in their homes to express their views on current events, offer their opinions about movies and television programming, and recount the daily details of their school lives.

Reading and Writing Acquisition

Parents also play a critical role in helping children learn about print. Many children learn about literacy very early. This task is accomplished quite naturally as children sit on the laps of parents, other family members, or caregivers sharing a storybook. Surrounded by love, these children easily learn about the functions of print and the joys of reading. Being read to at home facilitates the onset of reading, reading fluency, and reading enjoyment. Unfortunately, a growing number of studies have documented a lack of parent–child reading opportunities, especially in low-income homes (Christian, Morrison, & Bryant, 1998; Griffin & Morrison, 1997). Lesley Morrow (1988) surveyed parents of children in three preschools serving poor families (incomes of less than $10,000, 40 percent minority, 75 percent single-parent headed). Ninety percent of these parents indicated that they read to their children only once a month or less! This lack of parental involvement may have a significant effect on the children's learning throughout their schooling. For example, Billie Enz's (1992) study of 400 high school sophomores revealed that 70 percent of the remedial readers could not recall being read to by their parents as children, while 96 percent of the students in advanced placement courses reported that their parents had read to them regularly. In essence, it appears that a child's future literacy and subsequent success in school depend on parents' ability and will-ingness to provide the child with thousands of planned and spontaneous encounters with print (Enz & Searfoss, 1995).

Parental involvement also has an important effect on children's writing development. In the following example, notice how four-year-old Timeka's early attempts at writing are subtly supported by her mother:

> Sitting at a table with crayon in hand, Timeka is engrossed in making squiggly lines across a large paper. Timeka's mother, sitting across from her, is busy writing checks. After Timeka finishes her writing, she folds her paper and asks her mother for an envelope so she can "pay the bank, too." As mother smiles and gives Timeka the envelope, she remarks, "Good, our bank needs your money."

This brief example illustrates how Timeka is taking her first steps to becoming literate. While most children need formal instruction to learn to read and write conventionally, children who have parents who guide and support their beginning literacy efforts learn to read and write more quickly. As Timeka observes her parents and other adults writing, she discovers that these marks have purpose and meaning. Timeka then imitates, to the best of her ability, this process. Since the adults in Timeka's life also regard her efforts as meaningful, Timeka is encouraged to refine both her understanding of the functions of print and her writing skills. In that regard, Timeka's scribbles are to writing as her babbling was to talking. Because her parents approve and support her attempts instead of criticizing or correcting them, Timeka practices both talking and writing. This dual effort also simultaneously develops her under-standing that words and thoughts can be expressed both orally and in print (Fields, Spangler, & Lee, 1991; Sulzby, Teale, & Kamberelis, 1989). Parents who value their children's grow-ing literacy abilities also encourage their development. The following example demonstrates how ten-year-old Jeffery and his dad use Jeffery's literacy ability to accomplish an exciting task of putting together a mini-car using parts from the lawn mower engine.

> **DAD:**   Jeff, reread that last part of the directions again.
>
> **JEFFERY:**   It says to bolt the gas-o-line engine to the metal crossbars at right angles Dad. But Dad, what we have doesn't look like the drawing. (Both Jeffery and Dad study the diagram and go back to read the previous steps.)
>
> **DAD:**   Good going, Son!

Jeffery and his dad are using their ability to read to accomplish a task that is of great inter-est to both of them. Dad's reliance and genuine appreciation of his son's literacy reinforces reading as a great tool to achieve a big goal.

Dilemmas Facing Modern Families

The "family in America—Black, White, Hispanic, and Asian—is actually in the throes of basic upheaval" (Carlson, 1990, p. xv). As evidence, Carlson cites the three factors most likely to affect school performance: the employment of both parents in more than 70 percent of nuclear families, the high divorce rate, and the increase in single-parent families. Recent research studies report that 40 percent of today's school children will have lived with a single parent by the time they reach the age of 18 (Flaxman & Inger, 1991). The financial and psychological stresses many single-parent families face may not allow parents either the time or emotional energy to sustain conversation or read to their children on a regular basis.

Another significant factor is the cycle of poverty and undereducation. Research consistently reveals that a child whose parent has poor literacy skills is at great risk of repeating the illiteracy cycle (Christian, Morrison, & Bryant, 1998; Lonigan & Whitehurst, 1998). Likewise, Betty Hart and Todd Risley's (1995) study clearly demonstrates that welfare parents often transmit their limited vocabulary and lower oral communicative competence to their children.

Two factors span socioeconomic and cultural differences. First, as educators we must help parents understand the crucial role they play in helping their children become successful communicators, readers, and writers (Epstein, 1995). Secondly, we must build parents' knowledge of how to support their child's language and literacy development. How else will parents be able to fulfill their role as their child's first and most important teacher?

Helping Parents and Primary Caregivers Become Effective First Teachers

Helping parents become successful language and literacy models is one of a teacher's most important tasks. To fulfill this responsibility, teachers at all grade levels must interact with parents constantly! However, this role may be more challenging than many teachers initially anticipate. In this chapter, we describe two categories of communication efforts—personal interactions and classroom instructional publications.

Personal Interactions

Personal interactions are opportunities for parents, other family members, and early childhood teachers or caregivers to share information about a child's individual needs in two-way conversations. Personal interactions also offer unique opportunities for modeling communication and literacy strategies. These personal interactions include home visits, parent workshops, parent–teacher conferences, and telephone calls.

Today's teachers need to be aware that English may not be their children's parents' dominant language; therefore, a teacher may need to have a translator help with communication during personal interactions. Regardless of how teachers choose to communicate, observation shows that whatever the content, medium, or language, any message is enhanced if it is delivered warmly, respectfully, and with genuine concern.

Home Visits.   Perhaps the best way to reach parents prior to children's formal entry into preschool or kindergarten is through home visits.

> "We are going to be heroes today," Dana Donor said as she sat down on the couch in the living room of the Youtie family. She was met by four-year-old Tate and three-year-old Darrin. They watched as Dana opened the children's storybook, *One Duck Stuck.*

"Are you ready to help?" Dana asked as she sat between Tate and Darrin. For the next 15 minutes, Dana and Marie, the children's mother, take turns reading to the children and encouraging them to interact with the pictures in the book. "How many frogs are trying to help this silly duck? Let's count them," Marie suggests, and Tate and Darrin use their fingers to count the fearless frogs. Dana asks, "What animal do you think will try to help next? How many animals do you think will be on the next page? How would you have helped the duck?" After they had read the story, two very happy children asked to have it read again!

After the second reading, Dana passes out crayons and paper and asks the children to draw their favorite animal. "I'm gonna write my name," says Tate. "See T-A-T-E." Tate has recently begun using conventional print to write her name. Darrin announces loudly, "Me too!" Darrin uses scribble writing for his name. As the children work on their pictures, Dana and Marie step back to engage in a brief conversation about the children's stage of development in the writing process. After the children complete their pictures, they tape them to the refrigerator.

Dana Donor is a teacher-demonstrator in a well-documented parent–child home program that has a long track record of helping at-risk families. Her job is to help bring stories to life for children as young as two. The demonstrator also helps parents learn how to make reading fun. During the twice-a-week visits, Marie is able to observe Dana model story reading strategies, encourage language interactions, and support beginning writing opportunities. Marie and Dana also discuss age appropriate language and literacy behavior (see Table 13.1). After several weeks of participating in the program, Marie is more confident and has begun to try some of these techniques using the storybooks Dana leaves in the home for between-visits use. Marie is pleased that she is learning how to keep her children actively engaged during storytime.

Teachers of school-aged children also need to continue their efforts to help parents support their child's rapidly growing reading and writing skills. Table 13.2 offers age-appropriate activities that parents can use at home.

Since the 1970s, these types of home-visit programs have increased in number, especially as states and communities refocus attention and resources on young children. The programs can have long-term benefits, by offering maternal and child health care, parenting education, school readiness skills, guidance on how to create a literate home environment, and a direct link to other social services (Jacobson, 1998).

Parent Workshops.   Another strategy for involving and directly informing parents of preschool and kindergarten students about how to support their children's language and literacy learning is through parent workshops. The purpose of the workshops is to share explicit information about the children's development and the class curriculum, and to provide practical suggestions that parents may use at home to support their child's learning (Brown, 1994).

To begin, the teacher should design a needs assessment survey to determine parents' special interests and needs. In Figure 13.1, we provide an example of a survey that covers possible workshop topics, meeting times, and child care needs.

After the survey has been returned and the results tallied, the early childhood teacher should publish and advertise the schedule of workshops. We recommend selecting the top two or three topics and identifying the time(s) and day(s) listed as convenient for most of the parents. Generally the most convenient meeting place is the classroom or the school's or center's multipurpose room. Scout troops, parent volunteers, or older students may provide child

TABLE 13.1   Age-Appropriate Language and Literacy Activities: Birth to Age 5

Months		Language Speaking/Listening	Print Recognition Receptive/Reading	Expressive/Writing
0–6	CD	Babbling, extensive sound play.		
	PS	Talk to baby. Sing to baby. Make direct eye contact with baby when speaking. Use parentese.		
6–12	CD	Echolia, vocables, first words.	Is able to listen to short stories. Wants to handle books.	
	PS	Label objects. Scaffold child's language efforts.	Provide cloth and cardboard book. Read to your child.	
12–24	CD	Begins to use words and gestures. Responds to simple requests.	Begins to recognize environmental print/logos.	Begins to use writing implements to make marks.
	PS	Listen and actively respond. Read stories. Engage in frequent conversations.	Confirm print recognition, "Yes, that is Coke." Read to your child.	Offer chalk/chalkboard, paper, and crayons.
24–36	CD	Uses simple sentences, adds new words rapidly, and experiments with inflection.	Attends to pictures—describes pictures, then begins to form oral studies reflecting pictures.	Knows print has meaning and serves practical uses. Uses scribble marking.
	PS	Engage child in complex conversations frequently. Listen to child.	Read, read, read to your child. Ask child to label characters and objects.	Provide access to many types of writing implements/paper.
36–48	CD	Proficient language user. Engages in dramatic play. Likes to learn songs.	Attends to pictures. Repeats familiar story phrases.	Print recognition—may write letter-like units, and nonphonetic letter-like string.
	PS	Serve as co-player in dramas. Teach new songs. Ask child questions to encourage two-way dialogue.	Reread familiar stories. Ask open-ended questions. Begin home library.	Model writing process. Demonstrate your interest in your child's writing efforts.
48–60	CD	Uses language to obtain and share information.	May begin to recognize individual words.	Conventional writing emerges as letter–sound relationship develops.
	PS	Offer logical explanations. Listen and respond thoughtfully and thoroughly.	Shared reading. Frequent visits to library and expand home library. Demonstrate your enjoyment of reading.	Begin writing notes to child. Read your child's writing.

CD: Child's development

PS: Parental support

TABLE 13.2   Age-Appropriate Literacy Activities: Age 6–12

Age	Literacy Activities
6–7	Develop a shopping list with child's input
	During the shopping trip, ask child to find specific items on the aisle you are currently shopping.
	Write/draw a card to send to relatives.
	Find specific items in a pantry.
	Read storybooks to child; ask child to read to you.
8–10	Ask child to sort coupons for shopping trip.
	Ask child to review the *TV Guide.*
	Ask child to find a phone number in the phone book.
	Ask child to look up a word for you in the dictionary.
	Ask child to look up a word for you in the dictionary.
	Ask child to read to younger sibling(s).
	Ask child to read directions for a recipe.
11–12	Ask child to write shopping list will you dictate.
	Ask child to find specific sites on the Internet.
	Ask child to read movie reviews.
	Ask child to read a short article from the newspaper.
	Read a brief magazine to child.

care. Teachers should be sure to have parents confirm their participation in the workshop (see Figure 13.2). This will allow the teacher to prepare sufficient materials and secure appropriate child care arrangements. Send reminders the day before the workshop. Don't be surprised if only a few parents attend initially. Parent workshops may be a new concept, and it might take a little time for parents to become comfortable with this approach to parent–teacher interactions.

Teachers must prepare for a parent workshop. They need adequate supplies. They may need to organize the room. They need to set up refreshments. (Parent Teacher Organizations or center budgets can often reimburse teachers for refreshments.) Teachers need to prepare name tags, double-check child care arrangements, develop an evaluation form for the workshop, and create a detailed lesson plan!

There are several points for teachers to remember when running a parent workshop. First, the workshop should begin promptly. Second, start with a get-acquainted activity to put people at ease and begin the workshop on a relaxed, positive note. Third, remember that parents should not be lectured to; instead, they should experience hands-on, highly engaging activities. After the parents have engaged in the activity, provide brief, specific information about the theory underlying the process. Most importantly, remember to smile. When the teacher has a good time, the parents will also! Finally, have parents complete the workshop evaluation form; this will help to continually refine the quality of the workshops (see Figure 13.3).

Dear Parents,

   Did you know you are your child's first and most important teacher? One of my responsibilities as a teacher is to work and share all my teaching colleagues for the benefit of the special student we share—your child. I would like to conduct several workshops this year, and I need to know what topics you are most interested in learning about. Please complete the survey and have your child return it by _____. Place "X" by topics you would like to attend.

____Storytelling techniques   ____Linking Play and Literacy

____Writers Workshop   ____Kitchen Math and Science

____Rainy Day Fun   ____Learning Motivation

____Other_____

_____

What is the most convenient day? What time is the most convenient for you to attend a workshop?

____Monday   ____Tuesday   ____9:00am ____4:00pm ____7:00pm____

____Wednesday   ____Thursday

____Friday   ____Saturday

Would I use a child-care service if one was provided?

____Yes—list number of children needing care ____.

____No.

FIGURE 13.1   Needs assessment survey

Phone Calls.   Another powerful tool for communicating with parents is the telephone. Unfortunately, phone calls have traditionally been reserved for bad news. However, successful teachers have found that brief, positive, frequent telephone conversations help establish a strong partnership with parents (Fredericks & Rasinski, 1990). When parents receive a phone call about something exciting at school, they immediately sense the teacher's enthusiasm for

Dear Parents:

The topics that most most of you wanted to learn more about were

Writing Workshop, Kitchen Math and Science, and Rainy Day Fun!

The times that were convenient for most of you were:

    Wednesdays at 7:00 p.m. and Saturdays at 9:00 a.m.

I have used this information to create a schedule of workshops for the Fall semester. Please fill out the personal information and put an X by the workshops you plan to attend. All workshops will be in my classroom. Refreshments will be served. Dress comfortably as we might be getting messy. Children will be cared for in the cafeteria by the Girl Scouts and their leaders.

Name_____ Phone_____

Number of children needing child care_____.

____Writers Workshop—Wednesday, October 2, 7:00–8:30 p.m.

____Kitchen Math and Science—Saturday, November 4, 9:00–10:30 a.m.

____Rainy Day Fun—Wednesday, November 9, 7:00–8:30 p.m.

FIGURE 13.2   Workshop confirmation form

teaching their child and are more likely to become involved in classroom activities. Thus, whenever possible, the phone should be used as an instrument of good news. Whenever a call is made and for whatever reason, it is important to have the parents' correct surname; there are many stepfamilies in today's schools. All calls to parents should be documented. A phone log can be effective method to manage and maintain a record of phone conversations (see Fig-

Workshop Name_____ Date_____

List two activities you enjoyed or learned the most about.

1.

2.

List any information that was not useful to you.

The workshop was (mark all that apply):

____clear   ____confusing   ____enjoyable   ____boring

____too short   ____too long ____informative

Any other comments?

Thanks for attending!

FIGURE 13.3   Workshop evaluation

ure 13.4). This log should contain a separate page or section for each child in the class, making it easy to trace the contacts with specific parents (Enz & Cook, 1993).

Parent–Teacher Conferences.   Children are complex, social individuals who must function appropriately in two very different cultures—school and home. Parents need to

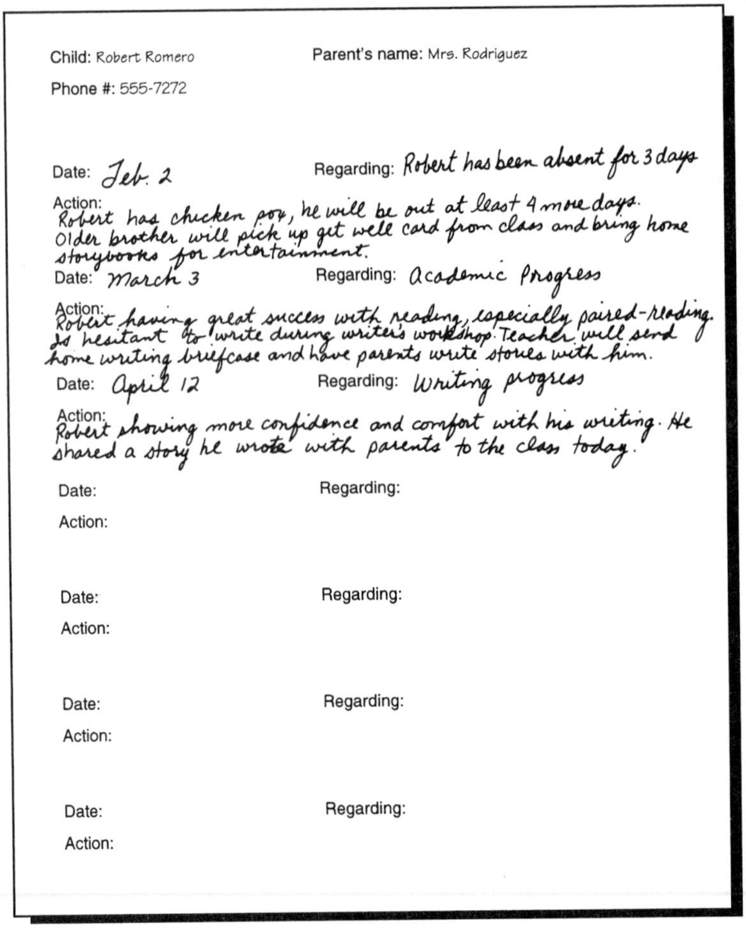

Child: Robert Romero   Parent's name: Mrs. Rodriguez

Phone #: 555-7272

Date: *Feb. 2*   Regarding: *Robert has been absent for 3 days*

Action: *Robert has chicken pox, he will be out at least 4 more days. Older brother will pick up get well card from class and bring home storybooks for entertainment.*

Date: *March 3*   Regarding: *Academic Progress*

Action: *Robert having great success with reading, especially paired-reading. Is hesitant to write during writer's workshop. Teacher will send home writing briefcase and have parents write stories with him.*

Date: *April 12*   Regarding: *Writing progress*

Action: *Robert showing more confidence and comfort with his writing. He shared a story he wrote with parents to the class today.*

Date: Regarding:

Action:

Date: Regarding:

Action:

Date: Regarding:

Action:

Date: Regarding:

Action:

FIGURE 13.4   Phone call log

understand how a child uses his or her social skills to become a productive member of the school community. Likewise, experienced teachers appreciate the child's home life and recognize its significant influence on a child's behavior and ability to learn. Partnerships reach their full potential when parents and teachers share information about the child from their unique perspectives, value the child's individual needs and strengths, and work together for the benefit of the child.

The best opportunity teachers have for engaging parents in this type of discussion is during parent–teacher conferences. Conferences should feature a two-way exchange of information. There are generally two types of parent–teacher conferences—pre-established conferences that review the child's classroom progress, and spontaneous conferences that deal with a range of specific concerns that occur throughout the year.

Progress Review Conference. The progress review conference is an opportunity for parents and teachers to share information about children's social interactions, emotional maturity, and cognitive development. One way to help a parent and teacher prepare to share information during the conference is a preconference questionnaire. The teacher sends the questionnaire home to the parent to complete and return prior to the conference. In Figure 13.5, we present the notes made by Manuel's mother as she prepared for her conference with Ms. Jones, her son's kindergarten teacher. The information Mrs. Rodriguez provides also tells Ms. Jones what concerns she has; therefore, Ms. Jones has a better idea about how to focus the conference. Remember, it may be necessary to have this letter and questionnaire translated into the language spoken in the home.

During the progress review conference, the teacher, of course, will share information about the child's academic progress. In Chapter 12, we discussed how to develop and

---

Dear Parent,

To help us make the most of our time, I am sending this questionnaire to help facilitate our progress review conference. Please read and complete the questions. If you have any other concerns, simply write them down on the questionnaire and we will discuss any of your inquiries during our time together. I look forward to getting to know both you and your child better.

1. How is your child's overall health?
   Good, but Manuel gets colds alot.
2. Are there specific health concerns that the teacher should know about? (include allergies)
   Colds and sometimes ear infections.
3. How many hours of sleep does your child typically get?
   About 9
4. Does your child take any medication on a regular basis? If so, what type?
   He takes penicillin when he has ear infections.
5. What are the names and ages of other children who live in your home?
   Maria, 9; Rosalina, 7; Carlos, 3.
6. How would you describe your child's attitude toward school?
   He likes school.
7. What school activity does your child enjoy most?
   P.E. and art
8. What school activity does your child enjoy least?
   Math
9. What are your child's favorite TV shows?
   Power Rangers, Ninja Turtles
   How many hours of TV will your child generally watch each night?
   Three
10. What is the title of your child's favorite storybook?
    Where the Wild Things Are.
11. How often do you read to your child?
    His sisters read to him most nights.
12. What other activities does your child enjoy?
    Playing soccer.
Other concerns:
    I can't read his writing. His sisters' was good in Kindergarten.

FIGURE 13.5 Preconference questionnaire

maintain assessment portfolios and document observational data for each child. The portfolio allows the teacher an opportunity to document the child's development over time. In addition to academic progress, most parents want to know about their children's social interactions and classroom behavior. The observational data that the teacher has recorded helps provide a more complete picture of the child in the classroom context.

When working with parents, teachers are encouraged to use a structured format during the progress review conference. The structure keeps the conference focused and increases the chance of both teachers' and parents' concerns being adequately discussed. Billie Enz and Susie Cook (1993) recommend that progress review conferences be structured as follows:

- *Positive statement and review conference format*—The teacher's first sentence helps establish a foundation for a proactive conference. Positive statements are sincere and usually personal—for example, "Your child is so eager to learn." Next, the teacher should briefly review the three steps of the conference: (1) parent input, (2) teacher input, and (3) closure. Reviewing the conference process relieves stress and actually helps keep the conference moving in a positive direction.
- *Ask for parental input*—"First, I am going to ask you to share with me what you have observed about your child this year that makes you feel good about his learning and then what concerns you have about his progress." It is important for parents to focus on their child's academic and social strengths when they meet with you. It is also important for you to know the parents' view of their child's major academic and social concerns.
- *Offer teacher input*—"Then I will share some of your child's work with you and my observations about his progress. We'll discuss ideas that will continue to encourage his learning."
- *Closure*—"So, let's review the home and school (or center) activities that we think will best help your child continue to progress."

The success of the parent–teacher relationship depends on the teacher's ability to highlight the child's academic and social strengths and progress. When areas of concern are discussed, it is important to provide examples of the child's work or review the observational data to illustrate the point. Often, the issues the parents reveal are directly related to the concerns the teacher has. Whenever possible, connect these concerns, as this reinforces the feeling that the teacher and the parents have the same goals for helping the child learn. It is essential to solicit the parents' views and suggestions for helping the child and also to provide concrete examples about how they might help the child learn.

To make sure both teacher and parents reach a common understanding, briefly review the main ideas and suggestions for improvement that were discussed during the conference. Allow parents to orally discuss their views of the main ideas of the conference. Check the parents' perceptions. Finally, briefly record the parents' oral summary on the conference form. Figure 13.6 is a progress review conference form from Manuel's conference.

Child–Parent–Teacher Conferences.   A rather new innovation in progress review conferences is the inclusion of the student. The child participates equally—sharing work,

---

Student's name: *Manuel Romero*   Parent's name: *Mary Romero*

Conference date: *Nov. 1*   Time: *4:30 p.m.*

Positive Statement: *manuel is so eager to learn*

Review Conference steps:
Our conference today will consist of three parts. First, I will ask you to review your child's progress, sharing with me both academic/social strengths and areas of concern. Next, I'll review Manuel's work with you and discuss his academic/social strengths and areas in which we will want to help him grow. Finally, we will discuss the main points we discussed today, and review the strategies we decided would help Manuel continue to make progress.

1. Ask for Parent Input: What have you observed about Manuel this year that makes you feel good about his learning? (Take notes as parent is sharing)

Manuel likes school, drawing, friends, stories.

What are your main concerns?

His writing looks like scribbles. He's not reading yet but he likes stories read to him.

2. Teacher Input: I would like to share some observations about Manuel's work and review both areas of strengths and skills that need to be refined. *Manuel interest in reading is wonderful. He is eager to write in class journal. Though his printing is still developing, he is beginning to use "invented" spelling. Look at this example in his portfolio.*

MT M ρN PR RG2

Mighty Morphin Power Rangers

Notice how he is separating the words. Ask him to read his work for you if you are having difficulty decoding or deciphering it. His printing skills will improve naturally with time and encouragement. He is really progressing well. Sometimes young girls develop finger muscles sooner. We need to support his efforts. Manuel enjoys sharing his writing in class with his friends and his art work is full of detail. Manuel has many friends and gets along easily with others.

3. Closure: Let's review those things we talked about that will facilitate continued success. (Teacher needs to write down this information as the parent talks)

a. *Manuel's printing is "Okay" for him.*

b. *Manuel is writing. I am surprised to see that he really is writing. I just need to have him read for me. Then it's easier for me to figure out what his*

c. *letters say.*

FIGURE 13.6   Progress review conference form

discussing areas in which he or she has noticed improvement, and establishing academic and/or social goals. This type of conference requires that the children are active participants in selecting what work will be featured in their portfolios. In addition, the teacher must begin to help children develop the skill to evaluate their own performance. For example, an editing checklist, such as the one described in Chapter 8, may be created with the children, for use in the writing workshop. The checklist also serves as an instructional guide. Children consult the checklist to make sure they have used correct punctuation, have begun sentences with capital letters, or have asked another student to proofread their work. Child–parent–teacher conferences are a natural outgrowth of frequent child–teacher conferences.

Because a three-way conference may be a new experience for parents, it is important for the teacher to establish guidelines for parents and students. A letter sent home explaining the format of the conference and discussing each person's role is essential. Parents are encouraged to ask open-ended questions, such as:

"What did you learn the most about?"
"What did you work the hardest to learn?"
"What do you want to learn more about?"

Questions such as these encourage students to analyze their own learning and also help them to set new goals. Parents should not criticize the child's work or focus on any negative aspect of any material that is presented during the conference. Negative comments, particularly from parents, will only inhibit learning and dampen excitement about school.

The following is a brief excerpt of a three-way conference at the last conference of the year. Notice that six-year-old Manuel does most of the talking:

MOTHER: Manuel, what have you worked hardest to learn?

MANUEL: My writing. I can do it faster and all of my friends can read my stories now. I draw really good ill-stra-suns—everybody likes them.

TEACHER: Manuel, can you read your parents a favorite story you wrote? [Manuel begins to read his five-page, illustrated story with great confidence. He underlines the words with his fingers and reads with great fluency. His parents smile and are impressed with their son's comical pictures.]

TEACHER: Manuel, what else have you been working on?

MANUEL: My counting and adding. I can add really good and I helped Shelly and Robbie put together the 100 number board. [Manuel proudly takes his parents over to the 1–100 number board.]

FATHER: Manuel, what do you want to learn next year?

MANUEL: I want to read more big books [referring to the multichapter books]. I want to get my own library card. I want to learn the number tables, you know, like María [his fourth-grade sister] can do. I want to write more books about the rangers and stuff.

Student-Led Conference.   The older child may actually run the conference with the teacher serving as conference recorder (see Figure 13.7). Once again it is important to prepare the parents for their role in the student-led conference.

Student name _____   Date: _____

Parent Name _____   Teacher's Name _____

Grade Level _____   School _____   District _____

_____, discussed the following topics during the conference:
(student's name)

1.

2.

3.

_____ was pleased with his/her progress in the following area(s):

Area _____   Reason _____

Area _____   Reason _____

Area _____   Reason _____

_____ is working to improve his/her progress in the following area(s):

Area _____   Plan _____

Area _____   Plan _____

Area _____   Plan _____

FIGURE 13.7   Student-Led Conference Summary Form

The following is a brief excerpt of a student-led conference being conducted by fourth through fifth multi-age student Jasmine Jackson.

JASMINE: Mom, Dad, this term we studied fantasy as a genre. We studied the features of popular stories like the J. K. Rowling's Harry Potter series and *The Lion, The Witch and the Wardrobe* by C. S. Lewis. After we analyzed the features we began to write our own fantasy stories. I co-wrote and illustrated with Amee this story, "The Witch's Wand."

TEACHER: Jasmine, what part of this project pleased you most about your progress? Why?

JASMINE: It made it easier to write a good fantasy story after we studied the parts of a good fantasy and talked about the story elements.

MR. JACKSON: You really wrote a good story. The illustrations are also really good, honey.

Specific Problem Conference.   Occasionally, concerns will emerge that require the teacher to work with the family immediately. The following case studies illustrate how teacher and parents worked together to help identify and resolve a specific problem in the home that was creating tension in the child's school life.

Sibby

Four-year-old Sibby started preschool as a happy, confident child. She loved story-time and had memorized several stories that she had heard her family read to her over and over again. Sibby had learned to print her name and was excited about writing her own letters and stories (scribble writing and some letter-like streams). Sibby was interested in environmental print and often brought empty product boxes and wrappers to preschool because she was proud that she recognized words and specific letters. She loved playing in the dramatic play center and frequently demonstrated her understanding of the many practical functions of print. After winter break, Sibby's behavior changed abruptly. She said she didn't know how to read when she went to the library center, and she refused to write during journal time. Her teacher, Mrs. Role, quickly called Sibby's parents.

Mr. and Mrs. Jacobs came to preschool the following day. Mrs. Role described the dramatic change in Sibby's behavior and asked the Jacobs' if they had any ideas about what may have caused the change. The Jacobs had also noticed a change in Sibby's confidence. After discussing her behavior, they mentioned that Sibby's grandmother, a retired high school English teacher, visited their home over winter break. They were surprised that Sibby's grandmother had been critical of their display of Sibby's stories on the refrigerator. Grandmother stated "That youngster needs to know the correct way to write!" She felt that "Praising Sibby's scribbles kept her from wanting to learn the right way to form letters," but they were sure Sibby had not overheard any of these comments. However, they remembered that Grandmother baby-sat Sibby one afternoon just before her visit was over. Mrs. Jacobs promised she would talk to Grandmother about the baby-sitting episode.

The following week, Mrs. Jacobs reported that Grandmother had decided "It was time someone taught Sibby how to print her letters properly." During the afternoon Grandmother and Sibby were together, Sibby had spent most of the time practicing making letters correctly. In addition, Grandmother required Sibby to say the letter sounds as she repeatedly wrote each letter. Grandmother told Sibby that she "would not be able to read and write until she knew all her letters and their sounds."

The Jacobs and Mrs. Role attributed Sibby's reluctance to read and write to her Grandmother's inappropriate instructional efforts. Sibby was going to need a great deal of encouragement and support from her parents and her teacher to regain her confidence.

Steven

Mrs. Garcia, Steven's mother, called Mr. R., Steven's third-grade teacher. Mrs. Garcia was concerned that, for the past few mornings, Steven, a new student, had complained of a stomachache. On this morning, Steven had begun to cry and stated that he did not want to go to school. Mr. R. suggested that Mrs. Garcia come to school that afternoon for a conference. During the day Mr. R. observed Steven carefully. As Mr. R. watched Steven, he noticed that Steven could easily read and comprehend the materials during a running record, yet, during paired reading, he seemed less confident in his oral reading and hesitant to participate in the story discussion. Mr. R. was puzzled. During recess, he watched to see who Steven was playing with. Mr. R. soon realized that Steven was not playing with the children; instead, he just walked around the perimeter of the playground or watched the others play. During center time in class, Steven again worked by himself.

That afternoon, when Mrs. Garcia came to the conference, Mr. R. thanked her for calling. Mr. R. asked Mrs. Garcia who Steven played with at home. Mrs. Garcia named one boy, who was in the fourth grade. Mr. R. then told Mrs. Garcia about his observation. He told Mrs. Garcia that he suspected that, because Steven was new to the neighborhood and school, he had not had a chance to make new friends. Steven might be feeling self-conscious and lonely. Mr. R. felt that Steven would eventually make friends in class and would regain his confidence. Mr. R. was planning to move Steven's desk closer to two very friendly children in the class. However, he wondered if Mrs. Garcia could help by encouraging Steven to invite one or two of the children in the class home to play. Mrs. Garcia agreed that Steven was sometimes shy and had difficulty making new friends. She also felt that she could talk to Steven about his feelings about being the new kid at school. Both Mr. R. and Mrs. Garcia agreed that Mrs. Garcia would call Mr. R. the next week to again share information about Steven's adjustment.

Classroom Instructional Publications

Classroom instructional publications are designed to describe the children's learning activities or directly inform parents about specific literacy concepts. They may include informal news flashes, weekly notes, and a more formal monthly newsletter that features regular columns, such as Dear Teacher, Family Focus, and Center Highlights. With the growing number of homes with computers and Internet access, some teachers may be able to publish their classroom instructional publications on a classroom Web site or listserve. Of course, teachers must check with their children's parents to learn which homes have access to these services. Sadly, those teachers who work with young children from low socioeconomic families likely will find few families with Internet access. The digital divide is widening, rather than narrowing, in the United States. Communities are struggling to learn how to increase Internet access to families of modest financial means.

Informal Weekly Notes. Because consistent communication helps create a sense of community, the authors strongly recommend weekly, or at minimum, bimonthly notes. Frequent communications allow teachers the opportunity to

- provide a bond between school and home experiences,
- extend parents' understanding of developmentally appropriate curricula,

- involve parents in assessing the child's growth and development,
- encourage parents to reinforce and enrich children's learning, and
- strengthen the working partnership between parents and teacher.

Weekly notes are typically one page in length and generally include (1) information about upcoming events; (2) items about children's achievements; (3) explanations about the curriculum that help parents understand how children learn to read and write; (4) practical and developmentally appropriate suggestions for working with children; and (5) recognition of parents who have helped support classroom learning—for example, parents who accompanied the class on a field trip (Gelfer, 1991).

It is important for informal weekly notes to be reader-friendly and brief and to suggest successful activities for parents and children to do together. These suggestions typically are well received if they are stated in a positive, proactive manner—for example, "Reading to your child just ten minutes a day helps your child become a better reader," not, "Your child will not learn to read unless you read to her or him."

Figure 13.8 is a sample of an informal weekly note. Observe how Ms. Jones reviews the previous week's activities, taking the opportunity to thank parents who have provided supplies or support. Next, she describes the focus of this week's curriculum and provides suggestions that will help parents reinforce this information at home. Notice how Ms. Jones uses friendly, everyday language to introduce and explain new concepts, and suggests realistic, content-appropriate literacy activities that encourage parents to become involved in classroom learning. Trade Secret 13.1 presents another way that children can participate in sharing their views of the week—a child-authored "Student Note" that summarizes their perceptions of what they have learned.

News Flashes.   There are times when events occur that require immediate publication or an upcoming activity warrants attention, such as reminding parents that their children will attend school for only a half day because of parent–teacher conferences or alerting parents that their children will be on the TV news tonight. Teachers may use news flashes to inform parents about TV programming that is relevant to curriculum the class is currently studying. News flashes might also be used to tell a parent about a noteworthy event in the child's life that day (e.g., Zack wrote his first letter today!)

Monthly Newsletters.   Like weekly notes, monthly newsletters create a sense of community. The goal of monthly newsletters should be to provide parents with specific information about children's literacy development. In addition, monthly newsletters offer parents an opportunity to preview the curriculum and classroom projects for the upcoming month. As most parents have extremely busy schedules, monthly newsletters help them plan ahead and thus increase the likelihood that they will be able to participate in school activities. Monthly newsletters are generally two or three pages in length and typically use a two- or three-column format. Regular features, such as Dear Teacher, Family Focus, Curriculum Overview, Center Highlights, and Monthly Calendar inform parents in a direct,3 but fun and interesting manner. In Figure 13.10, we provide a sample kindergarten newsletter written for the month of October. Notice the regularly featured columns.

Dear Parents:

Last week our field trip to the hospital was exciting and we learned even more about how doctors and nurses serve our community. Have your child read you the story he or she wrote and illustrated about what we learned on our hospital journey. One of the most exciting stops in the hospital was the nursery. All of the children were interested in their own first stay at the hospital. Perhaps you will be able to share your memories about that event. A great big thank you to Mrs. Delgato and Cecille Ortiz for helping to chaperon. They also helped our students write their stories.

This week we will discuss fire safety at home and school. Our first lesson is called "Stop, Drop, and Roll," which teaches us what to do if our clothes catch on fire. Next, we will discuss the proper use and storage of matches and lighters. We will also map a safe exit from our room in case of fire and review appropriate behavior during an emergency (no talking, listen to teacher's directions, leave all possessions, walk the planned escape route). We will actually have a schoolwide fire drill to practice these skills. Because you and your child's safety is so important, I am asking that you work with your child to draw and label a map of your house and design the best fire escape route. Drawing the map and labeling the rooms of your house teach your child vocabulary words and reinforce the fire safety concepts I am teaching in school. On Friday we will go to our local fire station. Attached to this note is a permission slip. Since this is a walking field trip, I will need at least four parent volunteers. I hope you can join us. To help all of us learn more about fire safety, the Fire Marshall will provide the children and their families with a booklet called "Learn Not To Burn." The book is available in Spanish also. If you would like additional copies, let me know. Please review this informative and entertaining booklet with your child.

To learn even more about fire safety and fire fighters, you might wish to read the following books to your child. These books are available in the classroom, school, and local public library.

EL Fuego, by Maria Ruis and Josep McParramon, Harron's.
Pumpers, Boilers, Hooks and Ladders: A Book of Fire Engines, by Leonard Everett Fisher, Dail Press.
Fire Fighters, by Ray Brockel, Children's Press.
Curious George at the Fire Station, by Margret and H.A. Rey, Houghton Mifflin.
Puedo Ser Bombero, by Rebecca Hankin, Children's Press.
The Whole Works: Careers in a Fire Department, by Margaret Reuter, Children's Press.

If you have any personal experiences in the area of fire safety, please let me know and you can be an Expert Speaker for our classroom.

Sincerely, Mrs. Jones

FIGURE 13.8 Informal weekly note

Dear Teacher Letters. As the sample newsletter demonstrates, parents frequently have questions about reading to their children. An effective way to address these inquires is through Dear Abby type letters. The teacher frames the questions based on common concerns she hears from the parents. The following are examples of typical parent questions, answered by advice based on Jim Trelease's (1989) work.

DEAR TEACHER: My three-year-old often becomes restless when I read stories to him. What can I do to keep his interest? *Signed, Wiggle-Worm's Mom*

DEAR WIGGLE-WORM'S MOM: While most children enjoy having stories read to them, most young children also have a short attention span. Hence, younger children

Student Notes

Dawn Foley

As a third-grade teacher, I have found another way that children can communicate about what they are learning in school with their parents: a personal weekly summary letter called a "note." For example, in Figure 13.9, Abby describes her view of things that she has learned during the week, ranging from the concept of probability in math to the literature she is reading. The letter is written in a form that leaves space for the teacher to make comments also. In this case, I commented on the fact that Abby won first place in our Academic Fair Project.

FIGURE 13.9   Abby's "note" to her parents

need to be actively involved in the reading. Asking your son to predict what he thinks will happen next or asking him to point to a character or discuss some aspect of the illustration is an excellent way to keep his attention.

DEAR TEACHER: I have three children, and our evenings are hectic to say the least! I also work, so the time I have is limited. When is the best time and for how long should I read to my kids? *Signed, Watching the Clock*

DEAR WATCHING: Excellent question! Many parents have multiple responsibilities, and time is always an issue. The best time is whenever you can consistently schedule about 15 to 20 minutes alone. For most parents, that time appears to be just before bed. However, some parents report that they find time right after the evening meal. Whenever you feel rested and can give your children 15 to 20 minutes of undivided time is the best time to read to them.

DEAR TEACHER: My four-year-old son wants to hear the same story over, and over, and over. Is this normal? Shouldn't I read a new book each night? *Signed, Repeating Myself*

DEAR REPEATING: As adults we tend to like variety, but most young children between the ages of two and seven have a favorite story, and this storybook may be as comforting to them as their best-loved stuffed toy. So the question becomes how to have both variety and comfort. At this age, favorite books tend to be short, so one suggestion is to read two or three books at storytime. Try reading the new books first and the favorite book last. When your child begins to read along with you, this is the perfect time to have him read this favorite book to you or to another child in your household. Frequently a child's favorite book becomes the first one he will read independently.

DEAR TEACHER: When I read my five-year-old daughter a book at storytime, I worry about her comprehension skills. Should I ask questions? *Signed, Just the Facts*

DEAR FACTS: I'm so glad you asked that question. The stories you read will frequently inspire your child to share many of her thoughts, hopes, and fears. These discussions are obviously more important than reciting any particular detail. In fact, quizzing children about story details will only make storytime an unpleasant activity for both of you. Instead, ask open-ended, opinion questions, such as "Which was your favorite part?" or "Why do you think Max stared at the Wild Things?" Storytime will also motivate your children to ask you questions! Take your time, share your views, and allow your child to hear your thought process. This activity will do more to teach them about story interpretation than 1000 fact questions! P.S. Did you know that Sendak's relatives served as the model for the Wild Things?

Family Focus. Because many parents have a number of questions about how their child will learn to write, it becomes essential for teachers to proactively communicate information about the normal developmental process of writing. To help parents learn about emergent writing, teachers may wish to use a more formal, direct instruction approach, such as a Your Child Learns to Write column in the monthly newsletter, like the

Ms. Jones' October Newsletter

Kindergarten Curriculum

 It's October and the Kinder- gartners in Ms. Jones' class are learning about our 5 senses— Halloween style! During this month we will learn about sight: how our eyes work, and eye health and safety. We will also have our vision tested. We will study the super sense of smell: How the nose and olfactory nerves work, and how smell and memory are related. We will learn how the ear hears and discover how hearing aids work. We will test our tongues to determine how the sense of taste works to detect sweet, salty, sour, and bitter. Finally, we will learn about the largest organ on our bodies—our skin! The sense of touch can teach us many things about our world.

Dear Teacher: Questions about Reading.

Dear Teacher,
Hola! Both my husband and I speak and read Spanish. Though our son speaks both languages, would it confuse him if we read him story books in Spanish?
Signed, Bilingual/Biliterate

Dear Bi-double L,
How wonderful it is that your son is already speaking two languages! It is perfectly fine to read books written in Spanish to him in Spanish—just as you would read books written in English to him in English. While he is learning to read in both languages, he will also begin to write in English and Spanish.

Parent Partnership: Your Child Learns to Write.

DR TUTH FRE ILS MI TUTH
PLS HEL ME FD et

Can you read this? This is a note to the tooth fairy. It was written by a child who lost her first baby tooth. Let's decode this note together.

DR TUTH FRE ILS MI TUTH

Dear Tooth Fairy, I lost my tooth.

PLS HEL ME FD et

Please help me find it.

As adults, we have been conditioned to read only conventional spelling. On first glance, this note may resemble only a string of letters. On closer inspection, we detect that its writer is trying to convey an important message. When young children begin to use print, their parents and teachers should encourage all attempts. Treating a child's scribbles or letter streams as important and meaningful encourages the child to continue her efforts. As she experiments with reading and writing, her understanding of the rules of our language increases. Eventually, develop- mental or invented spelling matures into more conventional spelling. To read more about this process you might want to read *Spell. . . is a four letter word* by J. Richard Gentry, (1987) from Heinemann Publishing Company in Portsmouth, New Hampshire.

(cont.)

FIGURE 13.10   Monthly newsletter

example in Figure 13.10. We recommend that before any children's writing is sent home, the teacher educate parents about the developmental writing stages. The following is an example of the most common questions parents ask about their child's writing develop- ment. The answers provide a sample of the tone and depth of information the column should contain.

Preparing for Parent/Student/Teacher Conferences

Conferences are wonderful opportunities for parents, student, and teacher to sit beside one another to share the students' work and review their progress. In our class each student will share the contents of his/her portfolio with both parents and teacher.

In the first half of the 20-minute conference, students will display and discuss their writing and perhaps read some of their stories. They will explain why certain products were included in the portfolio and why they believe these particular pieces best demonstrate their learning efforts. The students will also show the parents and teacher some of the work they completed at the beginning of the school year and compare it to how they are performing today. During this part of the conference, it is important for parents to listen to the student's self-evaluation. Parents are encouraged to ask open-ended questions, such as:

• What did you learn the most about?
• What did you work the hardest to learn?
• What do you want to learn more about?

These questions encourage students to analyze their own learning and also help them set new learning goals for themselves. Parents should not criticize the child's work or focus on any negative aspect of any material that is presented from the portfolio. Negative comments will only inhibit learning and dampen excitement about school. During the last ten minutes of the conference, the student will be excused so that parents and teacher have an opportunity to talk about any concerns the parents may have. Be sure to complete the Preconference Questionnaire and return it prior to the conference so that the teacher may be better prepared to discuss your concerns.

October Calendar

3rd	– Visit with the eye doctor: vision testing
7th	– Visit the audiologist: hearing tests
15th	– My Favorite Smells Day: bring in your favorite smell
18th	– Taste-testing day
19th	– School pictures day – dress bright
23rd	– Touch and tell day
28th–29th	– Parent/Student/Teacher Conference
31st	– Halloween/5 senses party

Remember: Weekly notes will provide details for each event.

Story Books for October

Georgie's Halloween, by Robert Bright (Doubleday)
The Teeny-Tiny Woman, by Paul Galdone (Clarion)
The Berenstain Bears: Trick or Treat, by Stan and Jan Berenstain (Random House)
Clifford's Halloween, by Norman Bridwill (Scholastic)
ABC Halloween Witch, by Ida Dedage (Garrard)
Who Goes Out on Halloween, by Sue Alexander (Bank Street)
It's Halloween, by Jack Prelutsky (Greeenwillow)

FIGURE 13.10 *(continued)*

When does my child really start to write? We live in a culture where print is used to communicate. Therefore, children begin to read and write informally long before they enter school. By the time children are able to pick up a pencil or crayon and draw or scribble, they are demonstrating their knowledge that these marks mean something, and the first step toward written communication has begun.

When my child draws or scribbles, does that mean that I should begin to teach him or her how to hold the pencil and form letters correctly? When your child first began to sing songs, did you start teaching him to play the piano? No, of course not! But you did enjoy the songs he or she sang, and you sang along. This is exactly the approach parents should take when their child first begins to draw or scribble write. Say, "Tell me about what you wrote about." Listen to the answer and compliment the effort.

How can I encourage my child's writing? When children watch adults write a grocery list or a letter or pay bills, they are often motivated to imitate this writing. Usually, all children need are the writing materials—paper, markers, crayons, pencils—and they will take the ideas from there. Occasionally, you could suggest that they might wish to write a letter to Grandmother or leave a note for the tooth fairy. Another perfect opportunity to encourage writing is during their dramatic play. When children play house, they can write grocery lists or leave phone messages—all you need to do is provide the writing materials and praise. A particularly exciting activity is to have your child choose a favorite stuffed animal. The stuffed animal takes a field trip to Grandmother's house or to preschool with the child. That night, parents and child may write about and illustrate a story about "The Adventures of _____ at _____." Children will write frequently if they feel their attempts to communicate are accepted and valued as meaningful.

Isn't handwriting practice important for learning to read and write? Learning the correct written form of a letter is called *handwriting.* It is an opportunity for children to gain control of the small muscles in their fingers and hands. However, handwriting drills do not teach children how to read and write. A child who exhibits excellent penmanship will not necessarily learn to read or communicate in written form any faster than the child whose writing still resembles scribbles. Critical comments about a child's handwriting efforts can stifle the joy of communicating. When a new scribe begins to learn the "how" of writing, it is far better to praise the efforts. This will encourage the child to write more.

How do I read my child's written work? Start by asking your child to tell you what was written. The information provided will give you context. These clues should enable you to figure out what the scribble, shapes, or letters represent. Children tend to progress through predictable developmental stages on the way to conventional spelling. This progression may proceed from scribbles, to letter strings, to single letters representing whole words or thoughts, to invented spelling, to conventional spelling. Invented spelling is using two or three letters to phonetically represent a word—this is sometimes called developmental spelling.

| H | → | hpe | → | hapy | → | happy |
| (happy) | | (happy) | | | | (happy) |

Should I correct my child's invented/developmental spelling? Have you ever changed what you wanted to write simply because you were unsure of the spelling of a word? Research reveals that children write less and use only a limited vocabulary of known words if their spelling is criticized. However, young children of six or seven who are encouraged to use their invented spelling will often write extensive stories with complex vocabularies. Parents may help children sound out phonetic words or spell more difficult words if the child asks for assistance.

Student-Authored Newsletters.   Teachers of older students may wish to involve their classes in writing their own monthly newsletter. This provides students with an authentic purpose for writing and allows them to share their perceptions of important events at school. In Trade Secret 13.2, middle-school teacher Michelle Gerry describes how she helps her students produce a monthly newsletter.

Thus far, this chapter has provided a number of communication strategies and highlighted the importance of ongoing communications to parents. One-shot publicity campaigns (e.g., read to and write with your child) do not provide parents with sufficient information or the long-term motivation they need to become involved in a meaningful literacy program. Instead, consistent, frequent, positive information that includes highly practical suggestions will help parents support their child's education. Beyond communicating, however, teachers may also need to provide other types of support to help parents fulfill their role as their child's first teachers. In the remainder of this chapter, we discuss the teacher's role as educational resource and community connection.

Teachers and Schools as Professional Resources

"In some schools there are still educators who say, 'If the family would just do its job, we could do our job.' And there are still families who say, 'I raised this child; now it is your turn to educate her' " (Epstein, 1995, p. 702). Most often, children who need the most help come from families that need the most support. Schools and centers that wish to make a significant difference in the lives of these children must find ways to offer support and forge successful school–family partnerships (Gardner, 1993–1994). Fortunately, most early childhood educators find that educating a child requires at least two teachers—the one at school or the center and the one at home. Following are concrete suggestions that teachers may use to help parents fulfill their role as first teacher.

Sharing Instructional Materials and Offering Guidance

Preschool teachers frequently recommend that parents read to their young children (Becker & Epstein, 1982). Unfortunately, many parents face great financial hardships and cannot provide a large number of quality reading materials in their homes. Further, parents may not know how to encourage and engage their children's interest in reading (Richgels & Wold, 1998). To help parents to fulfill their role as partners in literacy programs, it is vital for teachers to work with these families to offer easy access to both books and writing materials (Brock & Dodd, 1994) and guidance in how to use them (McGee & Richgels, 1996).

Classroom Lending Library.   Susan Neuman's 1999 study examined the effect of flooding more than 330 child care centers with storybooks. The results of her study confirm that children who have access to high-quality storybooks and teachers who are trained to support children's storybook interactions score significantly higher on several early reading

Trade Secret 13.2

Student-Authored Monthly Newsletter

Michelle Gary

Most intermediate-grade-level teachers assume that, because their students are older and more verbal, they will share pertinent information about their classes with their parents. This is simply not the case. Likewise, many intermediate-grade-level teachers believe that most parents are not as interested in what their children do in school as the parents of younger children are. This, too, is a false assumption. I have found that most parents of intermediate students feel out of touch with the activities and requirements of the classrooms and greatly appreciate newsletters that inform them of school activities.

I have found that monthly newsletters create a sense of community and offer parents an opportunity to preview the curriculum and classroom projects for the coming month. The monthly sixth-grade language arts class newsletters are generally one to two pages in length. The students include features such as "What I Learned" and "From a Student's Eye View." I supply the calendar for the coming month and curriculum overview.

At the middle-school level, I involve students in the following ways:

1. The last fifteen to twenty minutes on Friday, my students review the week's learning and suggest their views of the most important and interesting events.
2. I list their responses on the board.
3. Each of my students then chooses a topic from the list and writes a short descriptive paragraph.
4. I collect the paragraphs and select several to use in the newsletter.

The student-authored monthly newsletter has several positive features:

- It serves as a closure and summarization activity each Friday.
- My students have an opportunity to practice journalistic writing.
- Each of my students can author at least one article during the year.
- Parents receive frequent communications about classroom activities from the students' perspective.
- My students have an opportunity to publish their works for others to read and appreciate.

achievement measures than children who have not experienced high-quality storybooks and trained teachers. In other words, it is critically important for young children to have easy access to high-quality storybooks. Further, it is essential that parents and child care providers know how to support a child's early interactions with print. Though most public schools possess libraries, children generally are restricted to borrowing only one or two books a week. Some child care centers use public libraries with similar restrictions. While this may be appropriate for older children who can read chapter books, this quantity is insufficient for young children who are learning how to read. Young children should have the opportunity to have at least one new book an evening. One way to ensure early literacy development at home and foster the home–school connection is through a classroom lending library. A classroom lending library allows children to check out a new book each day, thus ensuring that all parents have an opportunity to read to their child frequently.

The acquisition of quality books for daily checkout is the first step in establishing a classroom lending library. Since the children will exchange their book each day, all a teacher needs to begin a library is one book per child.

Managing the classroom lending library requires that all books contain a library pocket and identification card. The teacher needs to create a classroom library checkout chart. When a child borrows a book, she simply removes the book's identification card and replaces it in her or his name pocket on the classroom checkout chart. The teacher can easily see what book each child has checked out at a glance.

The rules that accompany the classroom lending library are simple. A child may borrow one book each day. When the book is returned, the child may check out another. Teaching the children to manage the checkout routine is easy. When the children enter the classroom in the morning, they return their books to the library by removing the book's identification card from their name pocket. They place the identification card back in the book's library pocket, and they place the book back on the shelf. The children may select new books anytime throughout the day.

Writing Briefcase.   Another popular option that may be included as part of the classroom lending library is the writing briefcase. The briefcase can be an inexpensive plastic carrying

FIGURE 13.11   Sample book bag themes

Counting Theme

Hillanbrand, W. (1997). *Counting Crocodiles.* Orlando: FL: Harcourt Brace.

Kirk, D. (1994). *Miss Spider's Tea Party.* New York: Scholastic Editions Inc.

Barbieri-McGrath, B. (1998). *Hershey's Counting Board Book.* Wellesley, MA: Corporate Board Book.

Alphabet Theme

Wilbur, R. (1997). *The Disappearing Alphabet.* New York: Scholastic.

Alexander, M. (1994). *A You're Adorable.* New York: Scholastic.

Martin, B., & Archambault, J. (1989). *Chicka, Chicka, Boom Boom.* New York: Simon & Schuster Children's Publishing.

Rhyming Books

Goldston, B. (1998). *The Beastly Feast.* New York: Scholastic.

Slate, J. (1996). *Miss Bindergarten Gets Ready for Kindergarten.* New York: Scholastic.

Wood, A. (1992). *Silly Sally.* Orlando: FL: Harcourt Brace.

Getting Dressed

Degen, B. (1996). *Jesse Bear, What Will You Wear?* New York: Simon & Schuster Children's Publishing.

London, J. (1997). *Froggy Gets Dressed.* New York: Viking Children's Press.

Regan, D. (1998). *What Will I Do if I Can't Tie My Shoe?* New York: Scholastic.

case or a canvas portfolio. Inside the briefcase, the teacher may provide writing paper, colored construction paper, markers, pens and pencils, glue, tape—anything that might stimulate a child to write a story, make a greeting card, design a book cover, or create whatever they can imagine. Depending on the size of the class, teachers may have seven or eight writing briefcases—enough so that four or five children may check out the materials each day, and two or three extras so that the teacher has time to replenish the briefcase supplies frequently and conveniently. The briefcases are numbered, and each has a library pocket and identification card. The checkout procedures follow the same routine as for library books.

The writing briefcase may also contain explicit suggestions that encourage parents to use writing to communicate with their children. In Special Feature 13.1, we describe how one father used notes to spark his child's interest in learning to read and write.

Book Bags. Yet another way to encourage family participation and successfully engage and guide parents' literacy interactions with their children is through book bags (Barbour, 1998–1999). Like writing briefcases, book bags may be checked out of the classroom lending library for a week at a time. Book bags contain a collection of high-quality books and offer informal, interactive activities for extending children's language and literacy acquisition. When designing the bags, teachers need to consider their children's developmental stages, interests and experiences, and literacy levels. The book bags (nylon gym bags) typically contain three or four books and activities inspired by a specific theme (see Figure 13.11 for sample book bag themes). In addition, each bag contains two response journals (one for the child and one for the parent). Some bags contain tape recorders and the tapes that accompany the books. The tapes and tape recorders are particularly important for parents who may not be able to read English. Each bag also contains an inventory that helps parents and children keep track of and return materials assigned to each bag.

Special Feature 13.1

Love, Letters, and Literacy Learning
Mikeal Killeen

My plan was simple. I would write a short love note to my five-year-old daughter and leave it by her bed after she had fallen asleep. When she awoke she would see the note and come running to find me. My first message was "Come hug me. Love, Daddy." To my dismay there was no enthusiastic visitor the next morning. At the breakfast table, my daughter informed me that "It was fun to get a note, but it was too hard to read." I learned a valuable lesson that morning, for in my excitement I used cursive! My daughter emphati-

cally made me promise to "Print the letters neatly, Daddy, cause I can't read that scribble stuff."

True to my promise, the next few notes were neatly printed and contained several symbols to help my daughter decode my messages. Soon our communication developed into a treasure hunt; one note would give clues about where to find the next note and, occasionally, a treat. As you might guess, my modeling was quickly imitated, and it was not long before notes began to appear under my pillow or on the mirror. As you can imagine, the paper, tape, and pencil consumption in our house went way up, but those things are just the tools of the trade of communicating your ideas to the world.

Teachers typically initiate the program by sending home a letter describing the program. In addition to the introductory letter, each family also receives a contract. The terms of the contract are simple: Parents promise to spend time regularly reading to their children; children promise to spend time with the books and activities and treat each bag with care; and teachers promise to instill a love of reading in children and to manage the program. All three participants sign the contract.

The book bag project has been highly successful in many teachers' classrooms. The book bags supply parents the appropriate materials and explicit guidance, which in turn

- empower and motivate them to become teachers of their own children,
- encourage them to provide supportive home learning environments, and
- expand their knowledge of how to interact with their children.

Videotape.   As more schools have access to video cameras, another option to consider is creating a videotape lending section for the classroom library. Videotape has the potential to become an exceptional tool for teaching parents about storybook reading skills. The teacher may wish to videotape himself or herself reading an exciting storybook. While reading a book to the children, the teacher has the opportunity to demonstrate oral fluency, enthusiasm, and the use of different voices to make the story characters come alive. In addition, the teacher can illustrate how open-ended, predictive questioning strategies can facilitate children's active involvement during storytime. Likewise, using retelling prompts, the teacher can demonstrate how children discuss story events with each other and share their unique and meaningful perspectives. These informal instructive videos may significantly help parents improve and expand their own story-reading skills. Children may check out both the videotape and the storybook. The video and accompanying storybook may be stored in a large self-sealing plastic bag. The same checkout procedures as for the library books or writing briefcases may be used.

Schools as Community Resources

Because literacy is a critical component for success in all aspects of community life, schools are beginning to extend opportunities for all community members to become involved in producing literate citizens. In extending our view of literacy beyond the classroom, we also expand our views of the traditional roles of schools. In the past decade, an increasing number of schools have chosen to provide for the social, medical, and educational needs of the families in their community (Liu, 1996; Patton, Silva, & Myers, 1999). In Special Feature 13.2, readers will find a discussion of the major components of family resource schools.

Teacher as Community Contact

Teachers also need to think beyond the classroom and consider the many ways reading, writing, talking, and listening enhance all facets of a person's life in the home, school, church, and workplace. Teachers then must consider how they can provide opportunities for students to learn about community literacy activities.

Special Feature 13.2

Family Resource Schools

The way schools care about children is reflected in the way schools care about the children's families. If educators view children simply as students, they are likely to see the family as separate from the school. That is, the family is expected to do its job and leave the education of children to the schools. If educators view students as children, they are likely to see both the family and the community as partners with the school in children's education and development (Epstein, 1995, p. 701).

The major goal of family resource schools (also called *learning community schools*) is to strengthen the social and economic foundations of the neighborhood community. This goal is accomplished by providing extensive support to families, both before and after school. Family resource schools offer a broad range of services, including:

Student achievement and activity programs, such as

- community study hall with volunteer tutors,
- family read-alongs and family math classes,
- physical activity classes (gymnastics, dance, etc.),

- fine arts classes (arts and crafts, chorus, guitar, etc),
- community garden.

Adult education and skill building, such as

- adult basic education,
- general equivalency diploma,
- English as a second language,
- Spanish as a second language,
- conflict management seminars,
- employment workshops.

Parent education courses, such as

- parenting education programs,
- positive discipline workshops,
- sex education workshops,
- gang prevention workshops.

Family support services, such as

- on-site case management,
- alcohol and drug prevention programs,
- before- and after-school child care,
- baby-sitting co-ops,
- food and clothing banks,
- primary health care,
- mental health services.

VIP Program.   The VIP, or very important person, program is an effective strategy for involving community members in classroom activities. Community members of all types—secretaries, politicians, lawyers, construction workers, computer programmers, maids, chefs, fire fighters, flight attendants, store clerks, doctors, farmers, and professors—are invited to visit the classroom. When they arrive, they may read their favorite childhood story or perhaps an appropriate story that provides information about their career. After the VIP reads the story, she or he may wish to tell how reading and writing are used in the job. Children are sometimes surprised to hear how all types of jobs require literacy.

Another version of VIP is "Very Important Parents." As the name implies, this program features the children's parents. Parents may read their favorite childhood story to the class, share a favorite oral story, engage in a cooking activity using a favorite recipe, or perform another interesting activity.

Business Adoption Programs.   In this type of community involvement program, the school or classroom is adopted by a business in the community. Businesses often provide some financial support for the purchase of books or writing briefcases. In addition, employees of the businesses may be encouraged to be VIPs or help arrange a field trip to see business literacy in action (Rasinski & Fredericks, 1991). Children viewing the work of adults may be inspired to imitate and practice many of the reading and writing activities they see performed. Teachers may capitalize on this interest by creating dramatic play centers where the adopted business is a play theme, including all the literacy props and activities the children observed.

Community Tutors.   Perhaps the most inclusive and dynamic method for involving adult community members in your classroom is as volunteer reading tutors. Retirees in particular enjoy the role of classroom grandparents. Classroom tutors regularly volunteer each week to cuddle with and read to a child. This consistent involvement is pleasurable for the volunteer and benefits the young children. The value of spending individual time with another caring adult is beyond calculation.

Buddy Reading Programs.   To make a significant improvement in family literacy practices, it is essential that educators begin to develop the skills of tomorrow's parents. Older students may benefit greatly by participating in a parent apprenticeship program called Buddy Reading. Unfortunately, many older children do not have strong reading skills themselves. One major strength of the Buddy Reading program is that it has the potential to simultaneously improve older students' skills while supporting young students as they learn to read.

Primary, middle, or high school teachers may arrange to have their students work with preschool children during the school day, during lunch or recess, or in an after-school program. Whatever the time arrangement, the older reading buddies need to

- learn appropriate read-aloud behaviors, such as using an expressive voice, sharing and discussing pictures and print, and facilitating comprehension;
- identify characteristics of appropriate trade books, such as predictable books with repetitive, cumulative, rhythm and rhyme, and/or chronological patterns; and
- determine the younger reading buddy's interests and how to select appropriate books of interest to the child.

Sharing your literacy program within the school and throughout the local community is a win-win proposition. Older children learn how and why it is important to read to young children, while community members learn to appreciate the work of children and teachers in the schools. The following is a list of agencies that teachers may contact for more information and specific brochures about family involvement in the literacy process:

- Association for Childhood Education International
  The Olney Professional Building
  17904 Georgia Avenue, Suite 215
  Olney, MD 20832

■ National Association for the Education of Young Children
15009 16th Street, NW
Washington, DC 20036-1426

■ American Library Association
50 E. Huron Street
Chicago, IL 60611

■ International Reading Association
800 Barksdale Road
Newark, DE 19714

■ Reading Is Fundamental
P.O. Box 23444
Washington, DC 20026

Summary

Families play a critical role in nurturing young children's literacy learning. Early childhood teachers must be prepared to reach out to parents to form two-way partnerships aimed at building parents' awareness of the important role they play in their children's literacy learning and providing them with strategies for nurturing their children's early reading, writing, and speaking development. Here, we return to the questions posed at the beginning of the chapter and briefly summarize the information presented.

■ *What is known about the relationship between what parents do and children's language and literacy development?*
Research demonstrates that when parents converse a great deal with their young children, the children's vocabulary and language fluency increase. Likewise, if parents consistently engage their children in storytime and storytelling, there is a greater likelihood that their children will enjoy reading and become interested in and knowledgeable about the reading process. Parents who support young children's early reading and writing attempts encourage their children to begin to read and write. In short, what parents do makes a great deal of difference in their children's literacy learning and success. The data suggest that many parents need their children's teachers' assistance in understanding the crucial role they play in helping their children become successful readers, writers, and speakers and that all parents need teachers to share strategies for nurturing their young children's early literacy learning.

■ *In what ways might early childhood teachers communicate personally with parents?*
Communication is the key to successful parent–teacher partnerships. True two-way communication must take place between parents and teachers. Teachers can communicate personally with parents through regular phone calls and conferences. Phone calls should be used to communicate good news, not just troubling news. Regularly scheduled progress review conferences offer opportunities for parents and teachers to share information about factors influencing children's reading and writing development. Specific

Parental Involvement in Bilingual and Second-Language Settings

Sarah Hudelson and Irene Serna

This chapter discusses the importance of involving parents in their children's education. In the home setting, parents are their children's first teachers. There is no reason for this role to cease when children begin their formal schooling. In this special feature, the perspective already developed in this chapter is extended by exploring several issues that are particularly important to keep in mind when planning for the involvement of parents who are native speakers of a language other than English.

The Problem of Stereotyping

Even in the 1990s, when educators worked to be more sensitive to diversity (Brandt, 1992), comments about parents, especially parents of color, parents who do not speak English, and parents who are not middle class were heard.

- "Those parents are poor and uneducated; they don't have any idea of how to help their children."
- "The parents at my school don't value education; they don't even come to parent-teacher conferences."
- "Some parents can't even speak English and read and write themselves. How are they supposed to help their kids?"
- "These poor babies come from homes with no books; no wonder they are so behind. They have no understanding of literacy before they come to school."

Comments such as these reflect stereotyping and negative attitudes toward some parents. Some non-English-speaking parents have not been fortunate enough to complete even elementary school; some have had limited opportunities to develop literacy. Some are

uncomfortable in the school setting because they do not speak English; some have difficulty attending school functions because they are holding down two or three poorly paying jobs in order to support their families. The presence of these challenging obstacles does not mean that parents are unable and unwilling to participate in their children's education. In fact, non-English-speaking parents are especially concerned about education because they view education as the key to a better life for their children.

Recent studies (Allexsaht-Snider, 1991; Delgado-Gaitan & Trueba, 1991; Schieffelin & Cochran-Smith, 1984; Vasquez, 1991) (e.g., of home literacy practices in working-class, non-English-speaking, immigrant families) have found that these families do engage in a variety of literacy practices. However, these practices tend to be focused on literacy for daily life, survival, and communication with relatives in their native countries, rather than on more middle-class purposes for reading (for example, literacy for pleasure or to pass leisure time). Reading for pleasure or leisure is difficult when a parent is working multiple jobs.

Therefore, educators must avoid making assumptions about non-English-speaking parents. Instead teachers are encouraged to (1) acknowledge and understand parental and family realities; (2) work to establish relationships with parents that will allow them to feel valued for who they are; and (3) help parents recognize the important contributions they make to their children's continued education.

Understanding Different Cultural Norms regarding Schooling

For individuals raised in mainstream, middle-class settings, parental involvement in education may be considered a given. Parents assume that they are welcome at school and that they ought to have a say in their children's educational experiences. However, such assumptions are not necessarily the case in all communities, and they are

(continued on next page)

particularly unlikely in culturally and linguistically diverse settings.

In the Miami community of Little Haiti, for example, Creole-speaking parents from Haiti historically had been excluded from the French-language schools their children attended. Parents viewed the schools as places where they sent their children to do as the schools instructed, with no input from parents. The schools, in turn, emphasized learning via memorization rather than through active construction of knowledge (Hudelson, 1990).

Similarly, in many communities populated by Mexican and other Latin American immigrants, parents believe that when they send their children to school, they turn over the responsibility for the child's education to that institution. Traditionally, there has been a separation of functions. The parents' role is to instruct their children to behave and to listen carefully to their teachers. The parents' job is also to discipline children who misbehave in school. The teachers' function is to teach (Delgado-Gaitan & Trueba, 1991). Additionally, Mexican and Mexican-American parents have not been schooled in the constructivist perspective advocated by so many educators today. These parents may hold views of literacy learning that may be much more traditional than those of the teacher. Also like most parents, they may be reticent to participate in pedagogies that they have not experienced (Enz & Searfoss, 1995; 1996).

Authoritarian views of schooling and the separation of parents from schools and teachers, then, have been experiences that parents from many cultural backgrounds may have shared. Given such socialization, it is understandable that parents may initially be uncomfortable seeing themselves in formal teaching roles and working in more interactional ways. They may also believe that they should come to school only for disciplinary reasons. It is important, therefore, to appreciate that parents may have been socialized to view schools and teacher-parent roles in ways that significantly differ from the views that the teacher expects. Teachers need to learn from

community members what parents' views about schools and about experiences with schools have been so that they may more effectively invite parents to work with them.

Encouraging Native Language Use

One of Irene Serna's most vivid memories of her own elementary schooling is having a teacher tell her parents that they should not use Spanish with her in their home. If her parents continued to speak Spanish to her, they were told, Irene would be retarded in her academic development. The way to help Irene was to use English. More than 30 years later, this advice continues to be given to parents who are not proficient users of English. Simply stated, this advice is wrong.

In Special Feature 2.3 accompanying Chapter 2, you read about immigrant parents' problems in communicating effectively with their young children who no longer acknowledged their native languages. How were these adults who spoke little or no English to raise their children to be decent human beings if they could not use the language they spoke fluently (Fillmore, 1991)? In addition, think about what language means to humans, what humans use language for. People use both spoken and written language for a broad spectrum of purposes: to provide information, to persuade others to a point of view, to argue, to tell jokes, to share stories, to scold, to ask questions, to share opinions, to make interpersonal connections, to express emotions, and so on. Language is a powerful force in our lives.

In order to understand language's potential, children need to be exposed to a wide range of language uses (Heath, 1986). Such exposure is much more likely to happen when adults interact in a language they control (i.e., their native language), rather than in a language they are still struggling to learn. Unless second-language learners have achieved high levels of proficiency in the second language, they will not use this newer tongue for the full range of uses in which

(continued on next page)

they will use the native language. To deny children access to this full range of language functions is to impoverish children's language and to put them at risk for lower achievement in school. David Dolson (1985) has demonstrated that children who come from monolingual homes where a language other than English is spoken perform better in school than children from homes where parents try to use their second language, English, with their children.

Therefore, parents who are more proficient in their native language than in English must be encouraged to use the native language with their children, thus providing the young learners with demonstrations of a broad range of possibilities of language use. Learners then take these understandings into the second-language setting.

Expanding Our Views of the Roots of Literacy

As this book has demonstrated, one place where children learn about reading and writing is the home, where the children see their parents engage in reading and writing and where they themselves engage in a variety of literacy events. One such event is storybook reading. Because storybook reading has been found to be a predictor of later success in reading (Wells, 1986), suggestions to parents for assisting their children to become literate generally include reading out loud.

For many non-English-speaking parents, economic circumstances and limited availability of materials in their native languages often mean that storybook reading is limited. However, in many cultures, a tradition of oral storytelling exists. Research has demonstrated that the elements of story, as well as the strategies or ways of thinking about or responding to text that schools expect (for example, sequencing, evaluating, elaborating, clarifying) are developed during these storytelling events (Guerra, 1991; Pease-Alvarez, 1991; Vasquez, 1991).

Juan's family is an example. Juan came from a home in which oral storytelling was a family rit-

ual that took place as Juan's mother prepared the family dinner. Juan's mother would tell a story, and then the children were expected to tell stories. This home literacy practice provided Juan with a sophisticated understanding of story development. His stories demonstrated a complexity and creativity that many of his classmates (who did not engage in such storytelling) did not have. For example, during kindergarten, Juan created "Los Osos Malos" (The Bad Bears). In Juan's story, some bad bears chased him, even turning themselves into ghosts in an effort to capture him. However, through a series of moves and countermoves, Juan finally escaped. Juan's story was by far the most complex of any produced by the kindergarten children, and this, at least in part, can be attributed to his background in hearing and then telling stories.

Non-English-speaking parents who come from cultures with strong oral traditions should be encouraged to tell stories at home. Parents could be invited to tell stories at school. By broadening our base of understanding of what contributes to children's school literacy success, another avenue is provided for meaningful participation by non-English-speaking parents.

Family Literacy Demonstrations

The present chapter makes a series of excellent suggestions for providing workshops for parents on aspects of curriculum. The workshop format allows parents to participate in and try out some classroom instructional strategies that promote literacy. Educators involved with parents in bilingual and second-language settings also have worked in this hands-on way, but they have found particular success in organizing the workshops somewhat differently. They have involved parents and young children together in carrying out the kinds of activities and strategies that are a part of the children's ongoing literacy development; thus, the focus is on family and intergenerational literacy (Weinstein-Shr & Quintero, 1995).

In an elementary school in central Phoenix, Arizona, primary-grade bilingual teachers have

(continued on next page)

invited parents and children to participate in literature study groups with high-quality picture books. The teacher begins by reading the story aloud, followed by opportunities for adults and children to share their responses to the book. Often, parents and children then choose other books to take home. While this activity is usually carried out in Spanish, a variation of it could involve parents and children in listening, one time or several times, to a carefully selected predictable book in English. Parents who are ESL learners have reported that they themselves learn more English when they listen to predictable stories.

In a family literacy project involving Spanish-speaking mothers and their four-year-old preschoolers, experienced early childhood educators engaged parents and children in hands-on activities, followed by language-experience-type dictation. These parent- and child-generated stories became comprehensible reading material for the workshop participants. Teachers also urged the mothers to encourage their young children's experimentations with written language, even though the writing was not conventional (Macías-Huerta & Quintero, 1990).

In a project in Atlanta, Georgia, ESL parents with some ability in English came together with their children so that the parents could share stories of their lives in their various homelands. Teachers involved in the program helped put these stories into written English narratives, which then became a source of reading material for children and their parents. This project also utilized computers, motivating adults and children to learn to use the computer so that they could produce final versions of their stories.

Consider bringing parents and children together in workshop sessions that will both facilitate better understanding of your philosophy and pedagogy and contribute to children's and adult literacy.

Use Parental Knowledge

There is substantial evidence indicating that working-class immigrant families engage in a variety of home literacy practices. However, because these events often do not match the schools' views of literacy, family literacy practices may go unacknowledged or may even be viewed as standing in the way of children's academic development. For several years, educator Luis Moll and some of his colleagues have been working with teachers both to investigate literacy practices in U.S. and Mexican households and to develop innovations in literacy teaching in the schools based on these practices, related to what Moll calls, "funds of knowledge" (Moll, Amanti, Neff, & González, 1992). Moll has used the term *funds of knowledge* to describe bodies of skills and knowledge that accumulate in all communities and households. He and his colleagues contend that family and local community knowledge and skills can be tapped strategically by teachers and used to promote academic achievement (González, 1995).

Early childhood education teacher Marla Hensley (1995) wrote about how she applied the concept of funds of knowledge to her kindergarten classroom. Hensley chose the family of one of her students for a series of extended home visits in which, with the assistance of a questionnaire, she learned about this family in depth. As she got to know the child's father, she discovered that he was an expert gardener, and she recruited him to help her class prepare and plant both a vegetable and a flower garden. As she continued to visit in the home, Hensley found that the father had excellent communication skills and that he was a skilled musician, playing both keyboard and guitar and composing original songs. This parent agreed to write some children's songs and to help create a musical based on the folktale "The Little Red Hen." Then Hensley and this parent worked together to help the children learn the songs and later to rehearse and perform the musical.

Learning in detail about the talents and abilities of one parent gave this teacher an appreciation for parental funds of knowledge in general. This teacher developed a sensitivity to the possi-

(continued on next page)

bilities of making use of parental experts across her school curriculum.

It may not be feasible for you to spend extensive amounts of time visiting families and conducting in-depth interviews with parents. Nonetheless, it is still possible to learn something about the kinds of knowledge and skills possessed by the parents of your learners. Parent-teacher conferences might be one venue for asking parents about their talents and interests.

You may want to send a letter home asking parents to jot down hobbies, areas of expertise, and so on that they would be willing to share with the children. Listen to your children as they talk about the activities they engage in at home. Bring parental expertise into the classroom. Make parents' real-life knowledge an integral part of your curriculum, thus providing children with the opportunity to use spoken and written language to accomplish real-world learning.

problems conferences are needed when difficulties arise between regularly scheduled conferences. Sharing information about the child's literacy development might occur during a home visit, another forum for personal communication. Home visits also can be used to share information with parents on how to support their children's literacy learning. While teachers can share information one on one with parents during home visits, groups of parents can learn and interact together during parent workshops.

■ *How might teachers run a parent–teacher conference?*

Structuring the parent–teacher conference keeps the conference focused and increases the chance of both the teacher's and the parents' concerns being addressed. The teacher might begin with a positive statement and review the conference format, then ask for the parents' input, then offer input, and finally summarize points agreed on in the conference.

■ *In what ways might teachers communicate with parents in writing?*

Teachers can send home a variety of written publications including informal weekly notes, news flashes, and monthly newsletters. News flashes might be about classroom-related events, or they might be about something special the child has done that day. Some teachers might be able to use electronic mail to communicate with parents.

■ *What resources might an early childhood teacher provide to parents and parents provide to teachers to support young children's early literacy learning?*

Teachers of young children are an important resource for parents. Through the use of classroom lending libraries, book bags, and writing briefcases, teachers can provide parents with the materials needed for home literacy activities. In addition, teacher-made videos can be sent home to show parents what they might do during an activity, like storybook reading, to help their child get the most from the activity.

Parents can be an important resource for teachers also. Teachers can recruit parents and other community adults to assist them in their efforts to offer young children the best literacy education possible. Parents and members of the community might come to the classroom to read favorite stories to the class; local businesses might adopt the school or center and offer material and people resources; senior citizens might serve as classroom volunteers, offering a lap and cuddle for one-to-one sharing of a story; and older students might be reading buddies. Bringing parental and community expertise into the classroom does much to help build powerful partnership links between home and classroom and between classroom and community. These links are critical for all children. They offer young children the opportunity to use spoken and written language to accomplish real-world learning.

LINKING KNOWLEDGE TO PRACTICE

1. With a group of colleagues, plan a workshop for parents on some aspect of children's language and literacy learning. Write a letter to invite parents to the workshop. List the supplies you will need. List the refreshments. Develop an evaluation form. Create a detailed lesson plan. Offer your workshop to a group of parents.

2. Based on a classroom experience, write a one-page weekly note for parents.

3. Work with a group of colleagues to write a monthly newsletter for your class (the one for which you are reading this book).

4. Write a Dear Teacher question-and-answer for inclusion in a preschool classroom's newsletter. Make a photocopy for everyone in your college class.

5. Visit a school or public library. Question a librarian about the check-out policy for children. If this library allows children to check out only one book per week, write a letter to convince the librarian that this is inappropriate for children.

6. With a colleague, develop a bookbag around a theme for use by parents of children.

REFERENCES

Adams, M. (1990). *Beginning to read: Thinking and learning about print.* Cambridge, MA: MIT Press.

Adams, M. (1991). A talk with Marilyn Adams. *Language Arts, 68,* 206–212.

Adams, M., Foorman, B., Lundberg, I., & Beeler, T. (1998). The elusive phoneme: Why phonemic awareness is so important and how to help children develop it. *American Educator, 21*(1&2), 18–29.

Afflerbach, P. (1993). Report cards and reading. *Reading Teacher, 46,* 458–465.

Allen, R. (1976). *Language experiences in communication.* Boston: Houghton Mifflin.

Allen, V. (1991). Teaching bilingual and second-language learners. In J. Flood, J. Jensen, D. Lapp, & R. Squires (Eds.), *Research in the teaching of the English language arts* (pp. 356–365). New York: Macmillan.

Allexsaht-Snider, M. (1991). Family literacy in a Spanish-speaking context: Joint construction of meaning. *Quarterly Newsletter of the Laboratory of Comparative Human Cognition, 13,* 15–21.

Allington, R. (1983). The reading instruction provided readers of differing reading abilities. *Elementary School Journal, 87,* 548–559.

Allington, R., & Woodside-Jiron, H. (1999). The politics of literacy teaching: How "research" shaped educational policy. *Educational Researcher, 28,* 4–13.

Altwerger, B., Diehl-Faxon, J., & Dockstader-Anderson, K. (1985). Read-aloud events as meaning construction. *Language Arts, 62,* 476–484.

Anderson, C. (2000). *How's it going?* Portsmouth, NH: Heinemann.

Anderson, G., & Markle, A. (1985). Cheerios, McDonald's and Snickers: Bringing EP into the classroom. *Reading Education in Texas, 1,* 30–35.

Anderson, R., Heibert, E., Scott, J., & Wilkinson, I. (1985). *Becoming a nation of readers: The report of the Commission on Reading.* Washington, DC: National Institute of Education.

Anderson, R., & Pearson, P. D. (1984). A schema-theoretic view of basic processes in reading comprehension. In P. D. Pearson (Ed.), *Handbook of reading research* (pp. 255–291). New York: Longman.

Anderson, R., Wilson, P., & Fielding, L. (1988). Growth in reading and how children spend their time outside of school. *Reading Research Quarterly, 23,* 285–303.

Archbald, D., & Newman, F. (1988). *Beyond standardized testing: Assessing authentic academic achievement in secondary schools.* Washington, DC: National Association of Secondary School Principals.

Ashton-Warner, S. (1963). *Teacher.* New York: Simon & Schuster.

Atwell, N. (1987). *In the middle.* Portsmouth, NH: Heinemann.

Atwell, N. (1990a). *Coming to know.* Portsmouth, NH: Heinemann.

Atwell, N. (1990b). *Workshop 1: By and for teachers* (Vol. 1). Portsmouth, NH: Heinemann.

Au, K. (1993). *Literacy instruction in multicultural settings.* Fort Worth, TX: Harcourt Brace Jovanovich.

Au, K., Carroll, J., & Scheu, J. (1997). *Balanced literacy instruction: A teacher's resource book.* Norwood, MA: Christopher–Gordon.

Au, K., & Jordan, C. (1981). Teaching reading to Hawaiian children: Finding a culturally appropriate solution. In H. Tureba, B. Guthire, & K. Au (Eds.), *Culture and the bilingual classroom* (pp. 139–152). Rowley, MA: Newbury House.

Au, K., & Kawakami, J. (1991). Culture and ownership: Schooling of minority students. *Childhood Education, 67,* 280–284.

Auerbach, E. (1993). Reexamining English only in the ESL classroom. *TESOL Quarterly, 27,* 9–32.

Aukerman, R. (1984) *Approaches to beginning reading.* New York: Wiley.

Avery, C. (1993). *And with a light touch: Learning about reading, writing, and teaching with first graders.* Portsmouth, NH: Heinemann.

Baghban, M. (1984). *Our daughter learns to read and write.* Newark, DE: International Reading Association.

Baker, L., Serpell, R., & Sonnenschein, S. (1995). Opportunities for literacy learning in the homes of urban preschoolers. In L. Morrow (Ed.), *Family literacy: Connections in schools and communities* (pp. 236–252). Newark, DE: International Reading Association.

Barbe, W., & Milone, M., Jr. (1980). *Why manuscript writing should come before cursive writing* (Zaner-Bloser Professional Pamphlet No. 11). Columbus, OH: Zaner-Bloser.

Barbour, A. (1998/99). Home literacy bags: Promote family involvement. *Childhood Education, 75*(2), 71–75.

Barone, D. (1998). How do we teach literacy to children who are learning English as a Second Language? In S. Neuman & K. Roskos (Eds.), *Children achieving: Best practices in early literacy* (pp. 56–76). Newark, DE: International Reading Association.

Barrentine, S. (1996). Engaging with reading through interactive read-alouds. *Reading Teacher, 50,* 36–43.

Barrera, R., Ligouri, O., & Salas, L. (1992). Ideas a literature can grow on: Key insights for enriching and expanding children's literature about the Mexican American experience. In V. Harris (Ed.), *Teaching multicultural literature in grades K–8* (pp. 203–243). Norwood, MA: Christopher-Gordon.

Bateson, G. (1979). *Mind and nature.* London: Wildwood House.

Bear, D., Invernizzi, M., Templeton, S., & Johnston, F. (2000). *Words their way: Word study for phonics, vocabulary, and spelling instruction.* Upper Saddle River, NJ: Merrill.

Beck, I., McCaslin, E., & McKeown, M. (1981). Basal readers' purpose for story reading: Smoothly paving the road or setting up a detour? *Elementary School Journal, 81,* 156–161.

Becker, H., & Epstein, J. (1982). Parent involvement: A study of teacher practices. *Elementary School Journal, 83,* 85–102.

Benton, B. (1985). *Ellis Island: A pictorial history.* New York: Facts on File.

Berger, J. (2001). A systematic approach to grammar instruction. *Voice from the Middle, 8,* 43–49.

Berninger, V., Abbott, S., Reed, E., Greep, K., Hooven, C., Sylvester, L., Taylor, J., Clinton, A., & Abbott, R. (1997). Directed reading and writing activities: Aiming intervention to working brain systems. In S. Dollinger & L. DiLalla (Eds.), *Prevention and intervention issues across the life span* (pp. 123–158). Hillsdale, NJ: Erlbaum.

Bhavnagri, N., & Gonzalez-Mena, J. (1997). The cultural context of infant caregiving. *Childhood Education, 74,* 2–8.

Bishop, R. (Ed.). (1994). *Kaleidoscope: A multicultural booklist for grades K–8.* Urbana, IL: National Council of Teachers of English.

Bishop, W. (1995). Teaching grammar for writers in a process workshop classroom. In S. Hunter & R. Wallace (Eds.), *The place of grammar in writing instruction: Past, present, future* (pp. 176–187). Portsmouth, NH: Boynton/Cook.

Bissex, G. (1980). *GNYS AT WRK: A child learns to read and write.* Cambridge, MA: Harvard University Press.

Black, J., Puckett, M., & Bell, M. (1992). *The young child: Development from prebirth through age eight.* New York: Merrill.

Blanchowicz, C., & Fisher, P. (2000). Vocabulary instruction. In M. Kamil, P. Mosenthal, P. D. Pearson, & R. Barr (Eds.), *Handbook of reading research* (vol. 3, pp. 503–523). Mahwah, NJ: Erlbaum.

Bloodsworth, J. (1993). *The left-handed writer.* Arlington, VA: ERIC Document Reproduction Service, ED356494.

Bosma, B. (1992). *Fairy tales, fables, legends and myths* (2nd. ed.). New York: Teachers College Press.

Bradley, P., & Bryant, L. (1985). *Children's reading problems.* New York: Oxford University Press.

Brady, S. (1992). *Let's make books.* Dubuque, IA: Kendall/Hunt.

Brandt, R. (1992). Overview: A caring community. *Educational Leadership, 49,* 3.

Bravo-Villasante, C. (1980). *Historia y antologia de la literatura infantil iberoamericana* (Vols. 1 and 2; 2nd ed.). Madrid: Edita Doncel.

Bredekamp, S. (1989). *Develop mentally appropriate practice.* Washington, DC: National Association for the Education.

Brice-Heath, S. (1993). Inner city life through drama: Imagining the language classroom. *TESOL Quarterly, 27,* 177–192.

Brock, D., & Dodd, E. (1994). A family lending library: Promoting early literacy development. *Young Children, 49*(3), 16–21.

Bromley, K. (1988). *Language arts: Exploring connections.* Boston: Allyn & Bacon.

Bromley, K. (1995). Buddy journals for ESL and native-English-speaking students. *TESOL Journal, 4*(3), 7–11.

Bromley, K. (1998). *Language arts: Exploring connections.* Needham Heights, MA: Allyn.

Brooks, J., & Brooks, M. (1993). *In search of understanding: The case for constructivist classrooms.* Alexandria, VA: Association for Supervision and Curriculum Development.

Brosnahan, I., & Neuleib, J. (1995). Teaching grammar affectively: Learning to like grammar. In S. Hunter & R. Wallace (Eds.), *The place of grammar in writing instruction: Past, present, future* (pp. 204–212). Portsmouth, NH: Boynton/Cook.

Brown, J. (1994). Parent workshops: Closing the gap between parents and teachers. *Focus on Early Childhood Newsletter, 7*(1).

Brown, M. (1947). *Goodnight moon.* New York: Scholastic

Bruner, J. (1980). *Under five in Britain.* Ypsilanti, MI: High/Scope.

Bruner, J. (1983). Play, thought, and language. *Peabody Journal of Education, 60*(3), 60–69.

Bus, A., van Izendoorn, M., & Pellegrini, A. (1995). Joint book reading makes for success in learning to read: A meta-analysis on intergenerational transmission of literacy. *Review of Educational Research, 65,* 1–21.

Butler, A., & Turbill, J. (1984). *Towards a reading–writing classroom.* Portsmouth, NH: Heinemann.

Calkins, L. (1980, February). Punctuate! Punctuate! Punctuate! *Learning Magazine,* 86–89.

Calkins, L. (1983). *Lessons from a child: On the teaching and learning of writing.* Portsmouth, NH: Heinemann.

Calkins, L. (1991). *Living between the lines.* Portsmouth, NH: Heinemann.

Calkins, L. (1994). *The art of teaching writing.* Portsmouth, NH: Heinemann.

Calkins, L. (2001). *The art of teaching reading.* Portsmouth, NH: Heinemann.

Calkins, L., & Harwayne, S. (1987). *The writing workshop: A world of difference.* Portsmouth, NH: Heinemann.

Calkins, L., Montgomery, K., Santman, D., with Falk, B. (1998). *A teacher's guide to standardized reading tests.* Portsmouth, NH: Heinemann.

Cambourne, B. (1988). *The whole story: Natural learning and the acquisition of literacy in the classroom.* Auckland, New Zealand: Ashton Scholastic.

Canizares, S. (1997). Sharing stories. *Scholastic Early Childhood Today, 12*(3), 49–52.

Carey, S. (1979). The child as word learner. In M. Halle, J. Bresnan, & G. Miller (Eds.), *Linguistic theory and psychological reality* (pp. 264–293). Cambridge, MA: MIT Press.

Carlile, E. *Little Cloud.* New York: Scholastic.

Carlson, A. (1990). *Family questions.* New Brunswick, NJ: Transaction.

Carr, J., & Harris, D. (2001). *Succeeding with standards: Linking curriculum, assessment, and action planning.* Alexandria, VA: Association for Supervision and Curriculum Development.

Carra, C. (1995). Reflecting on the rain forest in the third grade. In P. Cordeiro (Ed.), *Endless possibilities: Generating curriculum in social studies and literacy.* Portsmouth, NH: Heinemann.

Cazden, C. (1976). Play with language and meta-linguistic awareness: One dimension of language experience. In J. Bruner, A. Jolly, & K. Sylva (Eds.), *Play: Its role in development and evolution* (pp. 603–608). New York: Basic Books.

Cazden, C. (1988). *Classroom discourse.* Portsmouth, NH: Heinemann.

Chall, J. (1967). *Learning to read: The great debate.* New York: McGraw-Hill.

Chall, J. (1989). *Learning to read: The great debate 20 years later—A response to* "Debunking the great phonics myth." *Phi Delta Kappan, 70,* 521–538.

Chomsky, C. (1969). *The acquisition of syntax in children from 5 to 10.* Cambridge, MA: MIT Press.

Chomsky, N. (1965). *Aspects of the theory of syntax.* Cambridge, MA: MIT Press.

Christian, K., Morrison, F., & Bryant, F. (1998). Predicting kindergarten academic skills: Interaction among child-care, maternal education, and family literacy environments. *Early Childhood Research Quarterly, 13,* 501–521.

Christie, J. (1987). Play and story comprehension: A critique of recent training research. *Journal of Research and Development in Education, 21,* 36–43.

Christie, J. (1991). *Play and early literacy development.* Albany, NY: State University of New York Press.

Christie, J. (1995). *Linking literacy and play.* Newark, DE: International Reading Association.

Christie, J., & Enz, B. (1992). The effects of literacy play interventions on preschoolers' play patterns and literacy development. *Early Education and Development, 3,* 205–220.

Christie, J., Johnsen, E. P., & Peckover, R. (1988). The effects of play period duration on children's play patterns. *Journal of Research in Childhood Education, 3,* 123–131.

Christie, J., & Stone, S. (1999). Collaborative literacy activity in print—enriched play centers: Exploring the "zone" in same-age and multi-age groupings. *Journal of Literacy Research, 31,* 109–131.

Chukovsky, K. (1976). The sense of nonsense verse. In J. Bruner, A. Jolly, & K. Sylva (Eds.), *Play: Its role in development and evolution* (pp. 596–608). New York: Basic Books.

Clark, E. (1983). Meanings and concepts. In J. Flavell & E. Markman (Eds.), *Handbook of child psychology: Vol. 3: Cognitive development* (4th ed., pp. 787–840). New York: Wiley.

Clark, M. (1976). *Young fluent readers.* London: Heinemann.

Clarke, A., & Kurtz-Costes, B. (1997). Television viewing, educational quality of the home environment, and school readiness. *Journal of Educational Research, 90,* 279–285.

Clarke, L. (1988). Invented spelling versus traditional spelling in first graders' writing: Effects on learning to spell and read. *Research in the Teaching of English, 22,* 281–309.

Clay, M. (1972). *Reading: The patterning of complex behaviour.* London: Heinemann.

Clay, M. (1975). *What did I write?* Auckland, New Zealand: Heinemann.

Clay, M. (1985). *The early detection of reading difficulties* (3rd. ed.). Portsmouth, NH.: Heinemann.

Clay, M. (1989). Telling stories. *Reading Today, 6*(5), 24.

Clay, M. (1991). *Becoming literate.* Portsmouth, NH: Heinemann.

Clay, M. (2000). *Concepts about print: What children have learned about the way we print language?* Portsmouth, NH: Heinemann.

Clay, M., & Cazden, C. (1990). A Vygotskian interpretation of Reading Recovery. In L. Moll (Ed.), *Vygotsky and education: Instructional implication and application of socio-historical psychology* (pp. 206–222). New York: Cambridge University Press.

Cochran-Smith, M. (1984). *The making of a reader.* Norwood, NJ: Ablex.

Cochran-Smith, M., Kahn, J., & Paris, C. (1986, March). *Play with it; I'll help you with it; Figure it out; Here's what it can do for you.* Paper presented at the Literacy Research Center Speaker Series, Graduate School of Education, University of Pennsylvania.

Cohen, L. (1999). The power of portfolios. *Early Childhood Today, 13*(5), 23–29.

Collin, B. (1992). *Read to me: Raising kids who love to read.* New York: Scholastic.

Collins, M. (1997). Sounds like fun. In B. Farber (Ed.), *The parents' and teachers' guide to helping young children learn* (pp. 213–218). Cutchoque, NY: Preschool Publications.

Cooper, J., & Kiger, N. (2001). *Literacy assessment: Helping teachers plan instruction.* New York: Houghton Mifflin.

Copeland, J., & Gleason, J. (1993). *Causes of speech disorders and language delays.* Tucson, AZ: University of Arizona, Speech and Language Clinic.

Corballis, M. C. (1991). *The lopsided ape: Evolution of the generative mind.* New York: Oxford University Press.

Cowley, F. (1997, Spring/Summer). The language explosion. *Newsweek: Your Child* (special edition).

Cordeiro, P., Giacobbe, M. E., & Cazden, C. (1983). Apostrophes, quotation marks, and periods: Learning punctuation in the first grade. *Language Arts, 60,* 323–332.

Crystal, D. (1995). *Cambridge encyclopedia of the English language.* New York: Cambridge.

Csikszentmihalyi, M. (1990). *Flow, the psychology of optimal experience.* New York: Harper.

Cunningham, A., & Stanovich, K. (1998). What reading does for the mind. *American Educator, 21*(1 & 2), 8–15.

Cunningham, P. (1995). *Words they use: Words for reading and writing* (2nd ed.). New York: Harper Collins.

Dailey, K. (1991). Writing in Kindergarten: Helping parents understand the process. *Childhood Education, 3,* 170–175.

Daniel, N., & Murphy, C. (1995). Correctness or clarity? Finding answers in the classroom and the professional world. In S. Hunter & Ray Wallace (Eds.), *The place of grammar in writing instruction: Past, present, future* (pp. 225–240). Portsmouth, NH: Boynton/ Cook.

Daniels, H. (1994). *Literature circles: Voice and choice in the student-centered classroom.* York, ME: Stenhouse.

Danst, C., Lowe, L., & Bartholomew, P. (1990). Contingent social responsiveness, family ecology, and infant communicative competence. *National Student Speech-Language-Hearing Association Journal, 17*(1), 39–49.

Degroff, L., & Galda, L. (1992). Responding to literature: Activities for exploring books. In B. Cullinan (Ed.), *Invitation to read: More children's literature in the reading program* (pp. 122–137). Newark, DE: International Reading Association.

Delacre, L. (1989). *Arroz con leche: Popular songs from Latin America.* New York: Scholastic.

Delaware Department of Public Instruction. (1995). *New directions: English language arts curriculum framework.* Dover, DE: Author.

Delgado-Gaitan, C., & Trueba, H. (1991). *Crossing cultural borders: Education for immigrant families in America.* Philadelphia, PA: Falmer Press.

Delpit, L. (1988). The silenced dialogue: Power and pedagogy in educating other people's children. *Harvard Educational Review 58,* 280–298.

Delpit, L. (1997). Ebonics and cultural responsive instruction. *Rethinking School Journal 12*(1), 6–7.

Demo, D. (2000). *Dialects in education* (ERIC/CLL Resources Guide online). Washington, DC: ERIC Clearinghouse on Language and Linguistics.

Dewey, J. (1938). *Experience and education.* New York: Collier.

Dickinson, D., & Tabors, P. (2000). *Beginning literacy with language: Young children learning at home and school.* Baltimore: Paul H. Brookes.

Dodge, D., & Colker, L. (1992). *The creative curriculum for early childhood education.* Washington, DC: Teaching Strategies.

Doiron, R. (1994). Using nonfiction in a read-aloud program: Letting the facts speak for themselves. *Reading Teacher, 47,* 616–624.

Dolson, D. (1985). The effects of Spanish home language use on the scholastic performance of Hispanic pupils. *Journal of Multilingual Multicultural Development, 6,* 135–155.

Downing, J., & Oliver, P. (1973–74). The child's concept of a word. *Reading Research Quarterly, 9,* 568–582.

Dragonwagon, C. (1993). *Homeplace.* New York: Alladin Books.

Drake, S. (1998). *Integrated curriculum: A chapter in the Curriculum Handbook.* Alexandria, VA: ASCD.

Drake, S. (2001). Castles, kings . . . and Standards. *Educational Leadership, 59,* 38–42.

Durkin, D. (1966). *Children who read early.* New York: Teachers College Press.

Durkin, D. (1984). Is there a match between what elementary teachers do and what basal manuals recommend? *Reading Teacher, 37,* 734–744.

Durkin, D. (1987). *Teaching young children to read* (4th ed.). Boston: Allyn & Bacon.

Durkin, D. (1993). *Teaching them to read* (6th ed.). Boston: Allyn & Bacon.

Duvall, B. (1985). Evaluating the difficulty of four handwriting styles used for instruction. *ERS Spectrum, 3,* 13–20.

Dyson, A., & Genishi, C. (1983). Children's language for learning. *Language Arts, 60,* 751–757.

Edelsky, C. (1986). *Writing in a bilingual program: Habia una vez.* Norwood, NJ: Ablex.

Edelman, G. (1995, June) Neuroscience Institute, La Jolla, California cited in J. Swerdlow, Quiet Miracles of the Brain, *National Geographic, 187*(6).

Eeds, M., & Wells, D. (1989). Grand conversations: An exploration of meaning construction in literature study groups. *Research in the Teaching of English, 23,* 4–29.

Eeds, M., & Wells, D. (1991). Talking and thinking and cooperative learning: Lessons learned from listening to children talk about books. *Social Education, 55*(2), 134–137.

Ehri, L. (1991). Development of the ability to read words. In P. D. Pearson (Ed.), *Handbook of Reading Research* (Vol. II, pp. 383–417). New York: Longman.

Ehri, L. (1997). Phonemic awareness and learning to read. *Literacy Development in Young Children, 4*(2), 2–3.

Ehri, L., Nunes, S., Willows, D., Schuster, B., Yaghoub-Zadeh, Z., & Shanahan, T. (2001). Phonemic awareness instruction helps children learn to read: Evidence from the National Reading Panel's meta-analysis. *Reading Research Quarterly, 36,* 250–287.

Elbow, P. (1973). *Writing without teachers.* Oxford, England: Oxford University Press.

Elkind, D. (1990). Academic pressures—Too much, too soon: The demise of play. In E. Klugman & S. Smilansky (Eds.), *Children's play and learning: Perspectives and policy implications* (pp. 3–17). New York: Teachers College Press.

Ellis, R. (1985). *Understanding second language acquisition.* New York: Oxford University Press.

Elster, C. (1998). Influences of text and pictures on shared and emergent readings. *Research in the Teaching of English, 32,* 43–63.

Enright, D. (1986). Use everything you have to teach English: Providing useful input to young second language learners. In P. Rigg & D. Enright (Eds.), *Children and ESL: Integrating Perspectives* (pp. 113–162). Washington, DC: Teachers of English to Speakers of Other Languages.

Enright, D., & McCloskey, M. (1988). *Integrating English: Developing English language and literacy in the multilingual classroom.* Reading, MA: Addison-Wesley.

Enz, B. (1992). *Love, laps, and learning to read.* Paper presented at International Reading Association Southwest Regional Conference, Tucson, AZ.

Enz, B., & Christie, J. (1997). Teacher play interaction styles: Effects on play behavior and relationships with teacher training and experience. *International Journal of Early Childhood Education, 2,* 55–69.

Enz, B., & Cook, S. (1993). *Gateway to teaching: From pre-service to in-service.* Dubuque, IA: Kendall-Hunt.

Enz, B., & Searfoss, L. (1995). Let the circle be unbroken: Teens as literacy teachers and learners. In L. Morrow (Ed.), *Family literacy: Multiple perspectives* (pp. 115–128). Reston, VA: International Reading Association.

Enz, B., & Searfoss, L. (1996). Expanding our views of family literacy. *Reading Teacher, 49,* 576–579.

Epstein, J. (1986). Parent's reactions to teacher practices of parent involvement. *Elementary School Journal, 86,* 277–294.

Epstein, J. (1995). School/family/community partnerships: Caring for the children we share. *Phi Delta Kappa, 76,* 701–712.

Ericson, L., & Juliebö, M. (1998). *The phonological awareness handbook for kindergarten and primary teachers.* Newark, DE: International Reading Association.

Ernst, G. (1994). "Talking circle": Conversation and negotiation in the ESL classroom. *TESOL Quarterly, 28,* 293–322.

Espinosa, C., & Fournier, J. (1995). Making meaning of our lives through literature: Past, present, and future. *Primary Voices, 3*(2), 15–21.

Fairfax County Public Schools. (1998). *Expanding expectations: Assessing.* Annaudale, VA: Author.

Faltis, C. (2001). *Joinfostering* (3rd ed.). Upper Saddle, NJ: Prentice-Hall.

Farris, P. (1982). *A comparison of handwriting strategies for primary grade students.* Arlington, VA: ERIC Document Reproduction Service.

Fein, G., Ardila-Rey, A., & Groth, L. (2000). The narrative connection: Stories and literacy. In K. Roskos & J. Christie (Eds.), *Play and literacy in early childhood: Research from multiple perspectives* (pp. 27–43). Mahwah, NJ: Erlbaum.

Feitelson, D., & Goldstein, Z. (1986). Patterns of book ownership and reading to young children in Israeli school-oriented and nonschool-oriented families. *Reading Teacher, 39,* 924–930.

Fernandez-Fein, S., & Baker, L. (1997). Rhyme and alliteration sensitivity and relevant experiences among preschoolers from diverse backgrounds. *Journal of Literacy Research, 29,* 433–459.

Ferreiro, E., & Teberosky, A. (1982). *Literacy before schooling.* Exeter, NH: Heinemann.

Fessler, R. (1998). Room for talk: Peer support for getting into English in an ESL kindergarten. *Early Childhood Research Quarterly, 13,* 379–410.

Field, T., Woodson, R., Greenberg, R., & Cohen, D. (1982). Discrimination and imitation of facial expressions by neonates. *Science, 218,* 179–181.

Fields, M., Spangler, K., & Lee, D. (1991). *Let's begin reading right: Developmentally appropriate beginning literacy.* New York: Merrill-Macmillan.

Fillmore, L. (1976). *The second time around: Cognitive and social strategies in second language acquisition.* Unpublished doctoral dissertation, Stanford University.

Fillmore, L. (1982). Instructional language as linguistic input: Second language learning in classrooms. In L. Wilkinson (Ed.), *Communicating in the classroom.* New York: Academic Press.

Fillmore, L. (1983). The language learner as an individual: Implications of research on individual differences for the ESL teacher. In J. Handscombe & M. Clarke (Eds.), *On TESOL '82: Pacific perspectives on language learning and teaching* (pp. 53–67). Washington, DC: Teachers of English to Speakers of Other Languages.

Fillmore, L. (1991). When learning a second language means losing the first. *Early Childhood Research Quarterly, 6*(3), 323–346.

Fisher, B. (1995). Things take off: Note taking in the first grade. In P. Cordeiro (Ed.), *Endless possibilities: Generating curriculum in social studies and literacy.* Portsmouth, NH: Heinemann.

Flanigan, B. (1988). Second language acquisition in the elementary schools: The negotiation of meaning by native-speaking and nonnative-speaking peers. *Bilingual Review/ La Revista Bilingue, 14*(3), 25–40.

Flaxman, E., & Inger, M. (1991). Parents and schooling in the 1990s. *ERIC Review, 1*(3), 2–5.

Fletcher, R. (1993). *What a writer needs.* Portsmouth, NH: Heinemann.

Fletcher, R., & Portalupi, J. (1998). *Craft lessons: Teaching Writing K–8.* York, ME: Stenhouse.

Fletcher, R., & Portalupi, J. (2001). *Writing workshop: The essential guide.* Portsmouth, NH: Heinemann.

Flood, J., Lapp, D., Flood, S., & Nagel, G. (1992). Am I allowed to group? Using flexible patterns for effective instruction. *Reading Teacher, 45,* 608–616.

Flores, B., Garcia, E., Gonzalez, S., Hidalgo, G., Kaczmarek, K., & Romero, T. (1985). *Holistic bilingual instruction strategies.* Chandler, AZ: Exito.

Fountas, I., & Pinnell, G. (1996). Guided reading: Good first teaching for all children. Portsmouth, NH: Heinemann.

Fournier, J., Lansdowne, E., Pastenes, Z., Steen, P., & Hudelson, S. (1992). Learning with, about and from children: Life in a bilingual second grade. In C. Genishi (Ed.), *Ways of assessing children and curriculum: Voices from the classroom* (pp. 126–168). New York: Teachers College Press.

Fractor, J., Woodruff, M., Martinez, M., & Teale, W. (1993). Let's not miss opportunities to promote voluntary reading: Classroom libraries in the elementary school. *Reading Teacher, 46,* 476–484.

Fredericks, A., & Rasinski, T. (1990). Involving the uninvolved: How to. *Reading Teacher, 43,* 424–425.

Freeman, D., & Freeman, Y. (1992). *Whole language for second language learners.* Portsmouth, NH: Heinemann.

Freeman, D., & Freeman, Y. (1994a). *Between worlds: Access to second language acquisition.* Portsmouth, NH: Heinemann.

Freeman, Y., & Freeman, D. (1994b). Whole language learning and teaching for second language learners. In C. Weaver, *Reading process and practice: From sociopsycholinguistics to whole language.* Portsmouth, NH: Heinemann.

Furner, B. (1985). *Handwriting instruction for a high-tech society: Will handwriting be necessary?* Paper presented at the annual spring conference of the National Council of Teachers of English, Houston, TX.

Galda, L., Cullinan, B., & Strickland, D. (1993). *Language, literacy, and the child.* Fort Worth: Harcourt Brace Jovanovich.

Gallas, K. (1992). When the children take the chair: A study of sharing in a primary classroom. *Language Arts, 69,* 172–182.

Gambrell, L., & Mazzoni, S. (1999). Principles of best practice: Finding the common ground. In L. Gambrell, L. Morrow, S. Neuman, & M. Pressley (Eds.), *Best practices in literacy instruction* (pp. 11–21). New York: Guilford.

Gambrell, L., Wilson, R., & Gantt, W. (1981). Classroom observations of task-attending behaviors of good and poor readers. *Journal of Educational Research, 74,* 400–404.

Gardner, S. (1993–94). Training for the future: Family support and school-linked services. *Family Resource Coalition, 3*(4), 18–19.

Garvey, C. (1977). *Play.* Cambridge, MA: Harvard University Press.

Garvey, C. (1984). *Children's talk.* Cambridge, MA: Harvard University Press.

Gavelek, J., Raphael, T., Biondo, S., & Wang, D. (2000). Integrated literacy instruction. In M. Kamil, P. Mosenthal, P. D. Pearson, & R. Barr (Eds.), *Handbook of reading research* (Vol. 3, pp. 587–607). Mahwah, NJ: Erlbaum.

Gelfer, J. (1991). Teacher–parent partnerships: Enhancing communications. *Childhood Education, 67,* 164–167.

Geller, L. (1982). Linguistic consciousness-raising: Child's play. *Language Arts, 59,* 120–125.

Genishi, C. (1987). Acquiring oral language and communicative competence. In C. Seefeldt (Ed.), *The early childhood curriculum: A review of current research* (pp. 75–106). New York: Teachers College Press.

Genishi, C., & Dyson, A. (1984). *Language assessment in the early years.* Norwood, NJ: Ablex.

Gentry, J., & Gillet, J. (1993). *Teaching kids to spell.* Portsmouth, NH: Heinemann.

Gesell, A. (1928). *Infancy and human growth.* New York: Macmillan.

Gettinger, M. (1993). Effects of invented spelling and direct instruction on spelling performance of second-grade boys. *Journal of Applied Behavior Analysis, 26,* 281–291.

Gilbert, J. (1989). A two-week K–6 interdisciplinary unit. In H. Jacobs (Ed.), *Interdisciplinary curriculum: Design and implementation* (pp. 46–51). Arlington, VA: Association for Supervision and Curriculum Development.

Glass, G., McGaw, B., & Smith, M. L. (1981). *Meta-analysis in social research.* Beverly Hills, CA: Sage.

Gleason, J. (1967). Do children imitate? In C. Cazden (Ed.), *Language in early childhood education.* Washington, DC: National Association for the Education of Young Children.

Golinkoff, R. (1983). The preverbal negotiation of failed messages: Insights into the transition period. In R. Golinkoff (Ed.), *The transition from prelinguistic to linguistic communication* (pp. 57–78). Hillsdale, NJ: Erlbaum.

González, N. (1995). The funds of knowledge for teaching project. *Practicing Anthropology, 17*(3), 3–7.

Gonzalez-Mena, J. (1997). *Multicultural issues in childcare* (2nd ed.). Mountain View, CA: Mayfield.

Goodlad, J., & Oakes, J. (1988). We must offer equal access to knowledge. *Educational Leadership, 45,* 16–22.

Goodman, K. (1970). Reading: A psycholinguistic guessing game. In H. Singer & R. Ruddell (Eds.), *Theoretical models and processes of reading* (pp. 259–271). Newark, DE: International Reading Association.

Goodman, Y. (1981). Test review: Concepts about Print Test. *Reading Teacher, 34,* 445–448.

Goodman, Y. (1986). Children coming to know literacy. In W. Teale & E. Sulzby (Eds.), *Emergent literacy: Writing and reading* (pp. 1–14). Norwood, NJ: Ablex.

Goodman, Y., & Goodman, K. (1994). To err is hman: Learning about language processes by analyzing miscues. In R. Ruddell, M. Ruddell, H. Singer (Eds.), *Theoretical Models and processes of reading* (4th ed.), Newark, DE: International Reading Association.

Graham, S. (1992). Issues in handwriting instruction. *Focus on Exceptional Children, 25,* 1–4.

Graham, S. (1993/94). Are slanted manuscript alphabets superior to the traditional manuscript alphabet? *Childhood Education, 70,* 91–95.

Graham, S. (1999). Handwriting and spelling instruction for students with learning disabilities: A review. *Learning Disability Quarterly, 22,* 78–98.

Graves, D. (1983). *Writing: Teachers and children at work.* Portsmouth, NH: Heinemann.

Graves, D. (1993). Children can write authentically if we help them. *Primary Voices K–6, 1,* 2–6.

Graves, D., & Hansen, J. (1983). The author's chair. *Language Arts, 60,* 176–183.

Greenewald, M. J., & Kulig, R. (1995). Effects of repeated readings of alphabet books on kindergartners' letter recognition. In K. Hinchman, D. Leu, & Kinzer, C. (Eds.), *Perspectives on literacy research and practice: Forty-fourth yearbook of the National Reading Conference* (pp. 231–234). Chicago: National Reading Conference.

Griffin, E., & Morrison, F. (1997). The unique contribution of home literacy environment to differences in early literacy skills. *Early Child Development and Care, 127/128,* 233–243.

Gronlund, G. (1998). Portfolios as an assessment tool: Is collecting of work enough? *Young Children, 53,* 4–10.

Guerra, J. (1991). The role of ethnography in the reconceptualization of literacy. *Quarterly Newsletter of the Laboratory of Comparative Human Cognition, 13,* 3–8.

Gump, P. (1989). Ecological psychology and issues of play. In M. Bloch & A. Pellegrini (Eds.), *The ecological context of children's play* (pp. 35–36). Norwood, NJ: Ablex.

Guthrie, J., & Wigfield, A. (2000). Engagement and motivation in reading. In M. Kamil, P. Mosenthal, P. D. Pearson, & R. Barr (Eds.), *Handbook of reading research* (Vol. 3, pp. 403–422). Mahwah, NJ: Erlbaum.

Hackney, C. (n.d.) *Standard manuscript or modified italic?* Columbus, OH: Zaner-Bloser.

Hakuta, K. (1986). *Mirror of language: The debate on bilingualism.* New York: Basic Books.

Haley, A. (1974). *Roots: The saga of an American family.* New York: Doubleday.

Hall, N. (1987). *The emergence of literacy.* Portsmouth, NH: Heinemann.

Hall, N. (1991). Play and the emergence of literacy. In J. Christie (Ed.), *Play and early literacy development* (pp. 3–25). Albany, NY: State University of New York Press.

Hall, N. (1999). Real literacy in a school setting: Five-year-olds take on the world. *Reading Teacher, 52,* 8–17.

Hall, N., & Duffy, R. (1987). Every child has a story to tell. *Language Arts, 64,* 523–529.

Hall, N., & Robinson, A. (1995). *Exploring writing and play in the early years.* London: David Fulton.

Halliday, M. (1975). *Learning how to mean: Explorations in the development of language.* London: Edward Arnold.

Han, M., Chen, Y., Christie, J., & Enz, B. (2000). *Environmental Print Assessment Kit.* Tempe, AZ: Arizona State University.

Hansen, C. (1998). *Getting the picture: Talk about story in a kindergarten classroom.* Unpublished doctoral dissertation, Arizona State University.

Hansen, J. (1994). Literacy profiles: Windows on potential. In S. Valencia, E. Hiebert, P. Afflerbach (Eds.), *Authentic reading assessment.* Newark, DE: International Reading Association.

Harp, B. (1996). *The handbook of literacy assessment and evaluation.* Norwood, MA: Christopher-Gordon.

Harris, D., & Carr, J. (1996). *How to use standards in the classroom.* Alexandria, VA: Association for Supervision and Curriculum Development.

Harris, V. (Ed.). (1992). *Teaching multicultural literature in grades K–8.* Norwood, MA: Christopher-Gordon.

Harste, J., Short, K., & Burke, C. (1988). *Creating classrooms for authors: The reading–writing connection.* Portsmouth, NH: Heinemann.

Harste, J., Woodward, V., & Burke, C. (1984). *Language stories and literacy lessons.* Portsmouth, NH: Heinemann.

Harwayne, S. (1992). *Lasting impressions.* Portsmouth, NH: Heinemann.

Hart, B., & Risley, T. (1995). *Meaningful differences in the everyday experience of young American children.* Baltimore, MD: Paul H. Brookes.

Hazen, K. (October, 2001). *Teaching about dialects.* Educational Resources Information Center, ERIC Clearinghouse on Language and Linguistics. EDO-FL-01-01.

Heald-Taylor, G. (1987). Predictable literature selections and activities for language arts instruction. *Reading Teacher, 40,* 6–12.

Healy, J. (1994). *Your child's growing mind: A practical guide to brain development and learning from birth to adolescence.* New York: Doubleday.

Healy, J. (1997, August-September). Current brain research. *Scholastic Early Childhood Today, 12*(1), 42–44.

Heath, S. (1982). What no bedtime story means: Narrative skills at home and school. *Language in Society, 11,* 49–76.

Heath, S. (1983). *Ways with words.* Cambridge, England: Cambridge University Press.

Heath, S. (1986). Sociocultural contexts of language development. In Bilingual Education Office, California State Department of Education (Ed.), *Beyond language: Social and cultural factors in schooling language minority students* (pp. 143–186). Los Angeles: Evaluation, Dissemination and Assessment Center, California State University.

Hedrick, W., & Pearish, A. (1999, April). Good reading instruction is more important than who provides the instruction or where it takes place. *Reading Teacher, 52,* 716–725.

Helm, J. (1999). Projects! Exploring children's interests. *Scholastic Early Childhood Today,* 24–31.

Hidi, S. (1990). Interest and its contribution as a mental resource for learning. *Review of Educational Research, 60,* 549–571.

Hiebert, E. (1981). Developmental patterns and interrelationships of preschool children's print awareness. *Reading Research Quarterly, 16,* 236–260.

Hillocks, G., Jr. (1986). *Research on written composition: New directions for teaching.* Urbana, IL: NCRE/ERIC.

Holdaway, D. (1979). *The foundations of literacy.* Sydney: Ashton Scholastic.

Hong, L. (1981). Modifying SSR for beginning readers. *Reading Teacher, 34,* 888–891.

Howard, S., Shaughnessy, A., Sanger, D., & Hux, K. (1998). Lets talk! Facilitating language in early elementary classrooms. *Young Children, 53*(3), 34–39.

Howell, H. (1978). Write on, you sinistrals! *Language Arts, 55,* 852–856.

Huck, C., Hepler, S., Hickman, J., & Kiefer, B. (2000). *Children's literature in the elementary school.* New York: Holt, Rinehart & Winston.

Hudelson, S. (1987). The role of native language literacy in the education of language minority children. *Language Arts, 64,* 827–841.

Hudelson, S. (1989). *Write on: Children writing in ESL.* Englewood Cliffs, NJ: Prentice-Hall.

Hudelson, S. (1990). Bilingual/ESL learners talking in the English classroom. In S. Hynds & D. Rubin (Eds.), *Perspectives on talk and learning* (pp. 267–284). Urbana, IL: National Council of Teachers of English.

Hudelson, S. (1994). Literacy development of second language children. In F. Genesee (Ed.), *Educating second language children: The whole child, the whole curriculum, the whole community.* New York: Cambridge University Press.

Hudelson, S., Fournier, J., Espinosa, C., & Bachman, R. (1994). Chasing windmills: Confronting the obstacles for literature based reading programs. *Language Arts, 71,* 164–171.

Hudelson, S., & Serna, I. (1994). Beginning literacy in English in a whole language bilingual program. In A. Flurkey & R. Meyer (Eds.), *Under the whole language umbrella: Many cultures, many voices.* Urbana, IL: National Council of Teachers of English.

Huey, E. (1908). *The psychology and epdagogy of reading.* New York: Macmillan.

Hunt, L. (1971). Six steps to the individualized reading program (IRP). *Elementary English, 48,* 27–32.

Hunter, S., & Wallace R. (1995). Afterword. In S. Hunter & R. Wallace (Eds.), *The place of grammar in writing instruction: Past, present, future* (pp. 243–246). Portsmouth, NH: Boynton/Cook.

Huttenlocher, J. (1991). Early vocabulary growth: Relations to language input and gender. *Developmental Psychology, 27,* 236–248.

International Reading Association. (1999). *Using multiple methods of beginning reading instruction: A position statement of the International Reading Association.* Newark, DE: Author.

International Reading Association. (2000). Teachers' choices for 2000. *Reading Teacher, 54,* 269–276.

International Reading Association/National Council of Teachers of English. (1994). *Standards for the assessment of reading and writing.* Newark, DE & Urbana, IL: International Reading Association & National Council of Teachers of English.

International Reading Association/NAEYC. (1998). Learning to read and write: Developmentally appropriate practices for young children. *Young Children, 53*(4), 30–46.

Jackman, H. (1997). Early education curriculum: A child's connection to the world. Albany, NY: Delmar.

Jacobs, H. (1989). *Interdisciplinary curriculum: Design and implementation.* Alexandria, VA: Association for Supervision and Curriculum Development.

Jacobs, W. (1990). *Ellis Island: New hope in a new land.* New York: Scribner.

Jacobson, L. (1998, February 11). House calls. *Education Week,* 27–19.

Jacobson, R., & Faltis, C. (Eds.). (1990). *Language distribution issues in bilingual schooling.* Clevedon, UK: Multilingual Matters.

Jalongo, M. (1995). Promoting active listening in the classroom. *Childhood Education, 72*(1), 13–18.

Jaramillo, N. (1994). *Grandmothers' nursery rhymes/Las nanas de abuelita.* New York: Henry Holt.

Johnson, D. (2001). Vocabulary in the elementary and middle school. Boston, MA: Allyn & Bacon.

Johnson, J., Christie, J., & Yawkey, T. (1999) *Play and early childhood development* (2nd ed.). New York: Allyn & Bacon/Longman.

Johnston, P. (1992). *Constructive evaluation of literate activity.* White Plains, NY: Longman.

Johnston, P., & Allington, R. (1991). Remediation. In R. Barr, M. Kamil, P. Mosenthal, & P. D. Pearson (Eds.), *Handbook of reading research* (Vol. 2, pp. 984–1012). New York: Longman.

Jonas, S. (Ed.). (1989). *Ellis Island: Echoes from a nation's past.* Montclair, NJ: Aperture.

Jones, E., & Reynolds, G. (1992). *The play's the thing: Teachers' roles in children's play.* New York: Teachers College Press.

Joyce, B. (1999). Reading about reading: Notes from a consumer to the scholars of literacy. *Reading Teacher, 52,* 662–671.

Kalb, C., & Namuth, T. (1997, Spring/Summer). When a child's silence isn't golden. *Newsweek: Your Child* (special edition).

Kallen, S. (1990). *Days of slavery: A history of black peple in America.* Edina, MN: Abdo & Daughters.

Karmiloff-Smith, A. (1979). Language development after five. In P. Fletcher & M. Garman (Eds.), *Language acquisition* (pp. 455–474). Cambridge, England: Cambridge University Press.

Katz, L., & Chard, S. (1993). *Engaging children's minds: The project approach.* Norwood, NJ: Ablex.

Kember, D., Nathan, R., & Sebranek, P. (1995). *Writers express.* Burlington, WI: The Write Source.

King, S. (2000). *On writing.* New York: Scribner.

Klein, A. (1991). All about ants: Discovery learning in the primary grades. *Young Children, 46,* 23–27.

Knipping, N. (1993). Using dramatic talk to explore writing. In K. Pierce & C. Oates (Eds.), *Cycles of meaning.* Portsmouth, NH: Heinemann.

Koenke, K. (1986). Handwriting instruction: What do we know? *Reading Teacher, 40,* 214–216.

Koppenhaver, D., Spadorcia, S., & Erickson, K. (1998). How do we provide inclusive early literacy instruction for children with disabilities? In S. Neuman & K. Roskos (Eds.), *Children achieving: Best practices in early literacy* (pp. 77–97). Newark, DE: International Reading Association.

Kotulak, R. (1997). Inside the brain: Revolutionary discoveries of how the mind works. Kansas City, MO: Andrews McMeel.

Krashen, S. (1982). *Principles and practices in second language acquisition.* Oxford, England: Pergamon.

Krashen, S. (1987). Encouraging free reading. In M. Douglass (Ed.), *51st Claremont Reading Conference Yearbook.* Claremont, CA: Center for Developmental Studies.

Kuhl, P. (1993). *Life language.* Seattle, WA: University of Washington.

Laminack, L., & Lawing, S. (1994). Building a generative curriculum. *Primary Voices K–6, 2,* 8–18.

Lass, B. (1982). Portrait of my son as an early reader. *Reading Teacher, 36,* 20–28.

Leslie, L., & Jett-Simpson, M. (1997). *Authentic literacy assessment: An ecological approach.* New York: Addison Wesley Longman.

Lessow-Hurley, J. (1990). *Foundations of dual language instruction.* New York: Longman.

Levin, D., & Carlsson-Paige, N. (1994). Developmentally appropriate television: Putting children first. *Young Children, 49,* 38–44.

Lewis, R., & Doorlag, D. (1999). *Teaching special students in general education classrooms.* Columbus, Ohio: Prentice-Hall.

Lindfors, J. (1987). *Children's language and learning* (2nd ed.). Englewood Cliffs, NJ: Prentice-Hall.

Lindquist, T. (1995). *Seeing the whole through social studies.* Portsmouth, NH: Heinemann.

Liu, P. (1996). Limited English proficient children's literacy acquisition and parental involvement: A tutoring/family literacy model. *Reading Horizons, 37*(1), 60–74.

Lloyd, P. (1987). *How writers write.* Portsmouth, NH: Heinemann.

Lomax, R., & McGee, L. (1987). Young children's concepts about print and reading: Toward a model of word reading acquisition. *Reading Research Quarterly, 22,* 237–256.

Lonigan, C., & Whitehurst, G. (1998). Relative efficiency of parent and teacher involvement in a shared-reading intervention for preschool children from low-income backgrounds. *Early Childhood Research Quarterly, 23,* 263–290.

Lubitz, D. (1995). Unpublished field notes. Tempe, AZ: College of Education, Arizona State University.

Luke, A., & Kale, J. (1997). Learning through difference: Cultural practices in early childhood language socialization. In E. Gregory (Ed.), *One child, many worlds: Early learning in multicultural communities* (pp. 11–29). New York: Teachers College Press.

Lynch, P. (1988). *Using predictable books and big books.* New York: Scholastic.

Macias-Huerta, A., and Quintero, E. (1990). *All in the family: Bilingualism and biliteracy. Reading Teacher, 44,* 306–314.

MacLean, P. (1978). A mind of three minds: Educating the triune brain. In J. Chall & A. Mirsky (Eds.), *Education and the brain, 77th Yearbook of the National Society for the Study of Education.* Chicago: University of Chicago Press.

Maestro, B., & Maestro, G. (1986). *The story of the Statue of Liberty.* New York: Lothrop, Lee & Shepard.

Manning, J. (2001). *Who stole the cookies from the cookie jar?* New York: Harper Festival.

Manning, M., Manning, G., & Long, R. (1994). *Theme immersion: Inquiry-based curriculum in elementary and middle schools.* Portsmouth, NH: Heinemann.

Manning-Kratcoski, A., & Bobkoff-Katz, K. (1998). Conversing with young language learners in the classroom. *Young Children, 53*(3), 30–33.

Maras, L., & Brummett, B. (1995). Time for a change: Presidential elections in a grade 3–4 multi-age classroom. In P. Cordeiro (Ed.), *Endless possibilities: Generating curriculum in social studies and literacy.* Portsmouth, NH: Heinemann.

Martinez, M., & Roser, N. (1985). Read it again: The value of repeated readings during storytime. *Reading Teacher, 38,* 782–786.

Martinez, M., & Teale, W. (1987). The ins and outs of a kindergarten writing program. *Reading Teacher, 40,* 444–451.

Martinez, M., & Teale, W. (1988). Reading in a kindergarten classroom library. *Reading Teacher, 41,* 568–572.

Marvin, C., & Mirenda, P. (1993). Home literacy experiences of preschoolers in Head Start and special education programs. *Journal of Early Intervention, 17*(4), 351–366.

Mason, J. (1980). When do children begin to read?: An exploration of four-year-old children's letter and word reading competencies. *Reading Research Quarterly, 15,* 203–227.

Masonheimer, P., Drum, P., & Ehri, L. (1984). Does environmental print identification lead children into word reading? *Journal of Reading Behavior, 16,* 257–271.

Mathews, M. (1966). *Teaching to read: Historically considered.* Chicago: University of Chicago Press.

McCaslin, N. (1987). *Creative drama in the primary grades.* New York: Longman.

McCracken, R., & McCracken, M. (1978). Modeling is the key to sustained silent reading. *Reading Teacher, 31,* 406–408.

McGee, L., & Richgels, D. (1989). "K is Kristen's": Learning the alphabet from a child's perspective. *Reading Teacher, 43,* 216–225.

McGee, L., & Richgels. D. (1996). *Literacy's beginnings: Supporting young readers and writers* (2nd ed.). Boston, MA: Allyn & Bacon.

Menyuk, P. (1988). *Language development: Knowledge and use.* Glenview, IL: Scott-Foresman.

Miller, S. (1997). Family television viewing: How to gain control. *Childhood Education, 74*(1), 38–40.

Miller-Lachman, R. (Ed.). (1995). *Global voices, global visions: A core collection of multicultural books.* New Providence, NJ: R. R. Bowker.

Moffett, J., & Wagner, B. (1983). *Student-centered language arts and reading, K–13: A handbook for teachers* (3rd ed.). Boston: Houghton Mifflin.

Moir, A., & Jessel, D. (1991). *Brain sex: The real differences between men and women.* New York: Carol.

Moll, L., Amanti, C., Neff, D., & González, N. (1992). Funds of knowledge for teaching: Using a qualitative approach to connect homes and classrooms. *Theory into Practice, 31*(2), 132–141.

Morgan, A. (1987). The development of written language awareness in black preschool children. *Journal of Reading Behavior, 19,* 49–67.

Morisset, C. (1995). Language development: Sex differences within social risk. *Developmental Psychology, 31,* 851–865.

Morrow, L. (1983). Home and school correlates of early interest in literature. *Journal of Educational Research, 76,* 221–230.

Morrow, L. (1985). Reading and retelling stories: Strategies for emergent readers. *Reading Teacher, 38,* 870–875.

Morrow, L. (1988). Young children's responses to one-to-one story readings in school settings. *Reading Research Quarterly, 23,* 89–107.

Morrow, L. (2001). *Literacy development in the early years: Helping children read and write* (4th ed.). Boston: Allyn & Bacon.

Morrow, L., & Rand, M. (1991). Preparing the classroom environment to promote literacy during play. In J. Christie (Ed.), *Play and early literacy development* (pp. 141–165). Albany, NY: State University of New York Press.

Morrow, L., & Tracey, D. (1997). Strategies used for phonics instruction in early childhood classrooms. *Reading Teacher, 50,* 644–651.

Morrow, L., Tracey, D., Gee-Woo, D., & Pressley, M. (1999). Characteristics of exemplary first-grade literacy instruction. *Reading Instructor, 52,* 462–476.

Morrow, L., & Weinstein, C. (1982). Increasing children's use of literature through program and physical changes. *Elementary School Journal, 83,* 131–137.

Morrow, L., & Weinstein, C. (1986). Encouraging voluntary reading: The importance of a literature program on children's use of library centers. *Reading Research Quarterly, 21,* 330–346.

Murray, D. (1990). *Write to learn.* New York: Holt, Rinehart and Winston.

Murray, B., Stahl, S., & Ivey, M. (1996). Developing phoneme awareness through alphabet books. *Reading and Writing: An Interdisciplinary Journal, 8,* 307–322.

Nagy, W. (1988). Teaching vocabulary to improve reading comprehension. Newark, DE: International Reading Association.

National Council of Teachers of English. (1993). *Elementary school practices: Current research on language learning.* Urbana, IL: Author.

National Education Goals Panel. (1997). *Special early childhood report.* Washington, DC: Author.

National Reading Panel. (2000). *Teaching children to read: An evidence-based assessment of the scientific research literature on reading and its implications for reading instruction.* Washington, DC: U.S. Government Printing Office.

Neuman, S. (1995). *Linking literacy and play.* Newark, DE: International Reading Association.

Neuman, S. (1998). How can we enable all children to achieve? In S. Neuman & K. Roskos (Eds.), *Children achieving: Best practices in early literacy* (pp. 5–19). Newark, DE: International Reading Association.

Neuman, S. (1999). Books make a difference: A study of access to literacy. *Reading Research Quarterly, 34*(3), 286–311.

Neuman, S., & Celano, D. (2001). Access to print in low-income and middle-income communities: An ecological study of four neighborhoods. *Reading Research Quarterly, 30,* 8–26.

Neuman, S., & Roskos, K. (1991a). Peers as literacy informants: A description of young children's literacy conversations in play. *Early Childhood Research Quarterly, 6,* 233–248.

Neuman, S., & Roskos, K. (1991b). The influence of literacy-enriched play centers on preschoolers' conceptions of the functions of print. In J. Christie (Ed.), *Play and early literacy development* (pp. 167–187). Albany, NY: State University of New York Press.

Neuman, S., & Roskos, K. (1992). Literacy objects as cultural tools: Effects on children's literacy behaviors during play. *Reading Research Quarterly, 27,* 203–223.

Neuman, S., & Roskos, K. (1993). *Language and literacy learning in the early years: An integrated approach.* Fort Worth, TX: Harcourt Brace Jovanovich.

Neuman, S., & Roskos, K. (1997). Literacy knowledge in practice: Contexts of participation for young writers and readers. *Reading Research Quarterly, 32,* 10–32.

Neuman, S., & Roskos, K. (Eds.). (1998). *Children achieving: Best practices in early literacy.* Newark, DE: International Reading Association.

New Standards Project. (1994). *Elementary English Language Arts Teacher Portfolio Handbook: Field Trial Version, 1994–1995.* Urbana, IL: Author.

Nickel, J. (2001). When writing conferences don't work: Students' retreat from teacher agenda. *Language Arts, 79,* 136–147.

Norris, A., & Hoffman, P. (1990). Language intervention with naturalistic environments. *Language, Speech, and Hearing Services in the Schools, 21,* 72–84

Noyce, R., & Christie, J. (1989). *Integrating reading and writing instruction in grades K–8.* Boston, MA: Allyn & Bacon.

Nurss, J., Hough, R. & Enright, D. S. (1986). Story reading with limited English children in the regular classroom. *Reading Teacher, 39,* 510–515.

Nurss, J., & McGauvran, M. (1976). *Metropolitan readiness tests.* New York: Harcourt Brace Jovanovich.

Ogle, D. (1986). KWL: A teaching model that develops active reading of expository text. *Reading Teacher, 39,* 564–570.

Oken-Wright, P. (1998) Transition to writing: Drawing as a scaffold for emergent writers. *Young Children, 53*(2), 76–81.

O'Neill, J. (1994). Making assessment meaningful: "Rubrics" clarify expectation, yield better feedback. *Association for Supervision and Curriculum Development Update, 36*(1), 4–5.

Opitz, M. (1998). Children's books develop phonemic awareness—for you and parents, too! *Reading Teacher, 51,* 526–528.

Opitz, M., & Ford, M. (2001). *Reaching readers: Flexible & innovative strategies for guided reading.* Portsmouth, NH: Heinemann.

Orellana, M., & Hernández, A. (1999). Taking the walk: Children reading urban environmental print. *Reading Teacher, 52,* 612–619.

Ourada, E. (1993). Legibility of third-grade handwriting: D'Nealian versus traditional Zaner-Bloser, In G. Coon & G. Palmer (Eds.), *Handwriting research and information: An administrators handbook* (pp. 72–87). Glenview, IL: ScottForesman.

Ovando, C., & Collier, V. (1998). *Bilingual and ESL classrooms: Teaching in multicultural context.* New York: McGraw-Hill.

Paley, V. (1981). *Wally's stories.* Cambridge, MA: Harvard University Press.

Paley, V. (1984). *Boys and girls: Superheroes in the doll corner.* Chicago: University of Chicago Press.

Paley, V. (1990). *The boy who would be a helicopter.* Cambridge, MA: Harvard University Press.

Pappas, C. (1993). Is narrative "primary"? Some insights from kindergartners' pretend readings of stories and information books. *Journal of Reading Behavior, 25,* 97–129.

Pappas, C., & Brown, E. (1987). Learning how to read by reading: Learning how to extend the functional potential of language. *Research in the Teaching of English, 21,* 160–177.

Paris, S. (1995). *Coming to grips with authentic instruction and assessment.* Presentation sponsored by the Education Center, Torrance, CA.

Paris, S., Wasik, B., & Turner, J. (1991). The development of strategic learners. In R. Barr, M. Kamil, P. Mosenthal, & P. D. Pearson (Eds.), *Handbook of reading research* (Vol. 2 pp. 609–640). New York: Longman.

Patterson, N. (2001). Just the facts: Research and theory about grammar instruction. *Voices from the Middle, 8,* 50–55.

Patton, M., Silva, C., & Myers, S. (1999). Teachers and family literacy: Bridging theory to practice. *Journal of Teacher Education, 50,* 140–146.

Paulson, F., Paulson, P., & Meyer, C. (1991). What makes a portfolio a portfolio? *Educational Leadership, 48,* 60–63.

Pearson, P. D., & Raphael, T. (1999). Toward an ecologically balanced literacy curriculum. In L. Gambrell, L. Morrow, S. Neuman, & M. Pressley (Eds.), *Best practices in literacy instruction* (pp. 22–33). New York: Guilford.

Pease-Alvarez, L. (1991). Oral contexts for literacy development in a Mexican community. *Quarterly Newsletter of the Laboratory of Comparative Human Cognition, 13,* 9–13.

Peck, S. (1978). Child–child discourse in second language acquisition. In E. Hatch (Ed.), *Second language acquisition: A book of readings* (pp. 383–400). Rowley, MA: Newbury House.

Peterson, R., & Eeds, M. (1990). *Grand conversations: Literature groups in action.* New York: Scholastic.

Peyton, J., & Reed, J. (1990). *Dialogue journal writing with non-native English speakers: A handbook for teachers.* Alexandria, VA: Teachers of English to Speakers of Other Languages.

Peyton, J., Jones, C., Vincent, A., & Greenblatt, L. (1994). Implementing Writer's Workshop with ESL students: Visions and realities. *TESOL Quarterly, 28,* 469–488.

Piper, T. (1993). *Language for all our children.* New York: Macmillan.

Pitkin, T. (1975). *Keepers of the gate: A history of Ellis Island.* New York: New York University Press.

Power, B. (1998). Author! Author! *Early Childhood Today, 12,* 30–34.

Pressley, M. (2000). What should comprehension instruction be instruction of? In M. Kamil, P. Mosenthal, P. D. Pearson, & R. Barr (Eds.), *Handbook of reading research* (Vol. 3, pp. 545–561). Mahwah, NJ: Erlbaum.

Purcell-Gates, V. (1989). What oral/written language differences tell us about beginning reading instruction. *Reading Teacher, 43,* 290–294.

Purcell-Gates, V. (1996). Stories, coupons, and the *TV Guide*: Relationships between home literacy experiences and emergent literacy knowledge. *Reading Research Quarterly, 31,* 406–428.

Raines, S., & Isbell, R. (1994). *Stories: Children's literature in early education.* Albany, NY: Delmar.

Ramirez, D., Yuen, S., & Ramel, D. (1991). *Executive summary: Longitudinal study of structured English immersion, early-exit, and late-exit transitional bilingual education programs for language minority children.* San Mateo, CA: Aguirre International.

Rascon-Briones, M., & Searfoss L. (1995, December). *Literature study groups in a preservice teacher education class.* Paper presented at the meeting of the National Reading Conference, New Orleans.

Rasinski, T., & Fredericks, A. (1991). Beyond parents and into the community. *Reading Teacher, 44,* 698–699.

Ray, K. (2001). *The writing workshop: Working through the hard parts (and they're all hard parts).* Urbana, IL: National Council of Teachers of English.

Read, C. (1971). Pre-school children's knowledge of English phonology. *Harvard Educational Review, 41,* 1–34.

Read, C. (1975). *Children's categorization of speech sounds in English.* Urbana, IL: National Council of Teachers of English.

Reutzel, D. R. (1999). Organizing literacy instruction: Effective grouping and organizational plans. In L. Gambrell, L. Morrow, S. Neuman, & M. Pressley (Eds.), *Best practices in literacy instruction* (pp. 271–291). New York: Guilford.

Reyes, M., & Franquiz, M. (1998). Creating inclusive learning communities through English language arts: From chanclas to canicas. *Language Arts, 75,* 211–220.

Reyes, M., Laliberty, E., & Orbansky, J. (1993). Emerging biliteracy and cross-cultural sensitivity in a language arts classroom. *Language Arts, 70,* 659–668.

Rhodes, L., & Nathenson-Mejia, S. (1992). Anecdotal records: A powerful tool for ongoing literacy assessment. *Reading Teacher, 45,* 502–509.

Rice, M., Huston, A., Truglio, R., & Wright, J. (1990) Words from *Sesame Street:* Learning vocabulary while viewing. *Development Psychology, 26,* 421–428.

Richgels, D., Poremba, K., & McGee, L. (1996). Kindergarteners talk about print: Phonemic awareness in meaningful contexts. *Reading Teacher, 49,* 632–642.

Richgels, D., & Wold, L. (1998). Literacy on the road: Backpacking partnerships between school and home. *Reading Teacher, 52,* 18–29.

Rosenblatt, L. (1985). The transactional theory of literary work: Implications for research. In C. Cooper (Ed.), *Researching response to literature and the teaching of literature* (pp. 33–53). Norwood, NJ: Ablex.

Rosenblatt, L. (1991). Literacy theory. In J. Flood, M. Jensen, D. Lapp, & J. Squire (Eds.), *Handbook of research on teaching the English language arts* (pp. 57–62). New York: Macmillan.

Roser, N. (1998, February). Young children as competent communicators. *Scholastic Early Childhood Today, 9*(6), 45–47.

Roser, N., & Martinez, M. (1985). Roles adults play in preschoolers' response to literature. *Language Arts, 62,* 485–490.

Roskos, K. (1995, October). *Integrated curriculum: Criteria for assessment.* Personal conversation.

Roskos, K., & Christie, J. (Eds.). (2000). *Play and literacy in early childhood: Research from multiple perspectives.* Mahwah, NJ: Erlbaum.

Roskos, K., & Neuman, S. (1993). Descriptive observations of adults' facilitation of literacy in play. *Early Childhood Research Quarterly 8,* 77–97.

Routman, R. (1991). *Invitations: Changing as teachers and learners K–12.* Portsmouth, NH: Heinemann.

Routman, R. (1996). Literacy at the crossroads: Crucial talk about reading, writing, and other teaching dilemmas.

Rowe, D. (1989). Author/audience interaction in the preschool: The role of social interaction in literacy learning. *Journal of Reading Behavior, 21,* 311–348.

Rowe, D. (1994). *Preschoolers as authors: Literacy learning in the social world.* Cresskill, NJ: Hampton Press.

Rudnick, B. (1995, October). Bridging the chasm between your English and ESL students. *Teaching Prek–8, 28,* 48–49.

Rumelhart, D. (1977). Toward an interactive model of reading. In S. Dornic (Ed.), *Attention and performance, VI* (pp. 573–603). Hillsdale, NJ: Erlbaum.

Samway, K. (1992). *Writer's Workshop and children acquiring English as a second language.* Washington, DC: National Clearinghouse for Bilingual Education.

Samway, K., & Whang, G. (1995). *Literature study circles in a multicultural classroom.* York, ME: Stenhouse.

Saville-Troike, M. (1988). Private speech: Evidence for second language learning strategies in the 'silent period'. *Journal of Child Language, 15,* 567–90.

Schickedanz, J. (1986). *Literacy development in the preschool* (sound filmstrip). Portsmouth, NH: Heinemann.

Schieffelin, B., & Cochran-Smith, M. (1984). Learning to read culturally: Literacy before schooling. In H. Goelman, A. Oberg, & F. Smith (Eds.), *Awakening to literacy* (pp. 3–23). Exeter, NH: Heinemann.

Schon, D. (1983). *The reflective practitioner: How professionals think in action.* New York: Basic Books.

Schon, I. (1994). *Tito, tito: rimas, adivinanzas, y juegos infantiles.* Leon: Editorial Everest.

Schwartz, J. (1983). Language play. In B. Busching & J. Schwartz (Eds.), *Integrating the language arts in the elementary school* (pp. 81–89). Newark, DE: International Reading Association.

Scieszka, J. (1989). *True Story of the three little pigs.* New York: Puffin Books.

Searfoss, L., & Readence, J. (1994). *Helping children learn to read* (3rd ed.). Boston: Allyn & Bacon.

Segal, M., & Adcock, D. (1986). *Your child at play: Three to five years.* New York: Newmarket Press.

Serafini, F. (2001a). *The reading workshop: Creating space for readers.* Portsmouth, NH: Heinemann.

Serafini, F. (2001b). Three paradigms of assessment: Measurement, Procedure and inquiry. *Reading Teacher, 54,* 384–393.

Serna, I., & Hudelson, S. (1993). Emergent literacy in a whole language bilingual program. In R. Donmoyer and R. Kos (Eds.), *At-risk students: Portraits, policies and programs.* Albany, NY: SUNY Albany Press.

Shanahan, T. (1988). The reading–writing relationship: Seven instructional principles. *Reading Teacher, 41,* 636–647.

Shanahan, T. (2000). Research synthesis: Making sense of the accumulation of knowledge in reading. In M. Kamil, P. Mosenthal, P. D. Pearson, & R. Barr (Eds.), *Handbook of reading research* (Vol. 3, pp. 209–226). Mahwah, NJ: Erlbaum.

Shore, R. (1997). *Rethinking the brain: New insights into early development.* New York: Families and Work Institute.

Sipe, L. (2001). Invention, convention, and intervention: Invented spelling and the teacher's role. *Reading Teacher, 55,* 264–273.

Slavin, R. (1989). Students at risk of school failure: The problem and its dimensions. In R. Slavin, N. Karweit, & N. Madden (Eds.), *Effective programs for students at risk.* Boston: Allyn & Bacon.

Skinner, B. (1957). *Verbal behavior.* East Norwalk, CT: Appleton-Century-Crofts.

Smilansky, S. (1968). *The effects of sociodramatic play on disadvantaged preschool children.* New York: Wiley.

Smith, F. (1988). *Understanding reading* (4th ed.). Hillsdale, NJ: Erlbaum.

Smith, M., & Dickinson, D. (1994). Describing oral language opportunities and environments in Head Start and other preschool classrooms. *Early Childhood Research Quarterly, 9,* 345–366.

Snow, C., Burns, M., & Griffin, P. (1998). *Preventing reading difficulties in young children.* Washington, DC: National Academy Press.

Snow, C., Chandler, J., Lowry, H., Barnes, W., & Goodman, I. (1991). *Unfulfilled expectations: Home and school influences on literacy.* Cambridge, MA: Harvard University Press.

Snow, C., & Ninio, A. (1986). The contracts of literacy: What children learn from learning to read books. In W. Teale & E. Sulzby (Eds.), *Emergent literacy: Writing and reading* (pp. 116–137). Norwood, NJ: Ablex.

Sochurek, H. (1987, January). Medicine's new vision. *National Geographic, 171*(1), 2–41.

Spandel, V. (2001). *Creating writers through 6-trait writing assessment and instruction.* New York: Addison Wesley Longman.

Spiegel, D. (1992). Blending whole language and systematic direct instruction. *Reading Teacher, 46,* 38–44.

Spiegel, D. (1995). A comparison of traditional remedial programs and Reading Recovery: Guidelines for success for all programs. *Reading Teacher, 49,* 86–97.

Sprenger, M. (1999). *Learning and memory: The brain in action.* Alexandria, VA: Association for Supervision and Curriculum Development.

Stahl, S. (1992). Saying the "p" word: Nine guidelines for exemplary phonics instruction. *Reading Teacher, 45,* 618–625.

Stahl, S. (1999). Why innovations come and go (and mostly go): The case of whole language. *Educational Reseacher, 28*(8), 15–22.

Stahl, S., Duffy-Hester, A., & Stahl, K. (1998). Everything you wanted to know about phonics (but were afraid to ask). *Reading Research Quarterly, 33,* 338–355.

Stahl, S., & Miller, P. (1989). Whole language and language experience approaches for beginning reading: A quantitative research synthesis. *Review of Educational Research, 59,* 87–116.

Stainback, S., & Stainback, W. (1992). *Curriculum considerations in inclusive classrooms.* Baltimore, MD: Brookes.

Stallman, A., & Pearson, P. D. (1990). Formal measures of early literacy. In L. Morrow & J. Smith (Eds.), *Assessment for instruction in early literacy* (pp. 7–44). Englewood Cliffs, NJ: Prentice-Hall.

Stanovich, K. (1986). Matthew effects in reading: Some consequences of individual differences in the acquisition of literacy. *Reading Research Quarterly, 21,* 360–407.

Strickland, D., & Morrow, L. (1990). Family literacy: Sharing good books. *Reading Teacher, 43,* 518–519.

Strong, M. (1983). Social styles and the second language acquisition of Spanish-speaking kindergarteners. *TESOL Quarterly, 17,* 241–258.

Strunk, W., & White, E. B. (1979). The elements of style. New York: MacMillan.

Sullivan, G. (1994). *Slave ship: The story of the Henrietta Marie.* New York: Dutton.

Sulzby, E. (1985a). Children's emergent reading of favorite storybooks: A developmental study. *Reading Research Quarterly, 20,* 458–481.

Sulzby, E. (1985b). Kindergartners as writers and readers. In M. Farr (Ed.), *Advances in writing research, Vol. 1: Children's early writing development* (pp. 127–200). Norwood, NJ: Ablex.

Sulzby, E. (1990). Assessment of emergent writing and children's language while writing. In L. Morrow & J. Smith (Eds.), *Assessment for instruction in early literacy.* (pp. 127–200). Englewood Cliffs, NJ: Prentice-Hall.

Sulzby, E., & Barnhart, J. (1990). The developing kindergartner: All of our children emerge as writers and readers. In J. McKee (Ed.), *The developing kindergarten: Programs, children, and teachers.* Ann Arbor, MI: Michigan Association for the Education of Young Children.

Sulzby, E., Barnhart, J., Hieshima, J. (1989). Forms of writing and rereading from writing: A preliminary report. In J. Mason (Ed.), *Reading and writing connections* (pp. 31–63). Boston: Allyn & Bacon.

Sulzby, E., & Teale, W. (1991). Emergent literacy. In R. Barr, M. Kamil, P. Mosenthal, & P. D. Pearson (Eds.), *Handbook of reading research* (Vol. 2 pp. 727–757). New York: Longman.

Sulzby, E., Teale, W., & Kamberelis, G. (1989). Emergent writing in the classroom: Home and school connection. In D. Strickland & L. Morrow (Eds.), *Emerging literacy: Young children learn to read and write* (pp. 63–79). Newark, DE: International Reading Association.

Swain, M. (1972). *Bilingualism as a native language.* Unpublished doctoral dissertation, University of California at Irvine.

Swanborn, M., & de Glopper, K. (1999). Incidental word learning while reading: A meta-analysis. *Review of Educational Research, 69,* 261–285.

Sweet, A. (1993). *State of the art: Transforming ideas for teaching and learning to read.* Washington, DC: Office of Research, U.S. Department of Education.

Sylwester, R. (1995). *A celebration of neurons: An educator's guide to the human brain.* Alexandria, Virginia: Association for Supervision and Curriculum Development.

Tabors, P. (1998). What early childhood educators need to know: Developing Effective programs for linguistically and culturally diverse children and families. *Young Children, 53*(6), 20–26.

Tabors, P., & Snow, C. (1994). English as a second language in preschool programs. In F. Genesee (Ed.), *Educating second language children: The whole child, the whole curriculum, the whole community* (pp. 103–126). New York: Cambridge University Press.

Taylor, D. (1983). *Family literacy.* Portsmouth, NH: Heinemann.

Taylor, D. (1986). Creating family story: "Matthew! We're going to have a ride". In W. Teale & E. Sulzby (Eds.), *Emergent literacy: Writing and reading* (pp. 139–165). Norwood, NJ: Ablex.

Taylor, D., & Dorsey-Gaines, C. (1988). *Growing up literate: Learning from inner-cities families.* Portsmouth, NH: Heinemann.

Taylor, D., & Strickland, D. (1986). *Family storybook reading.* Portsmouth, NH: Heinemann.

Taylor, N., Blum, I., & Logsdon, D. (1986). The development of written language awareness: Environmental aspects and program characteristics. *Reading Research Quarterly, 21,* 132–149.

Teale, W. (1986a). The beginnings of reading and writing: Written language development during the preschool and kindergarten years. In M. Sampson (Ed.), *The pursuit of literacy: Early reading and writing* (pp. 173–205). Dubuque, IA: Kendall Hunt.

Teale, W. (1986b). Home background and young children's literacy development. In W. Teale & E. Sulzby (Eds.), *Emergent literacy: Writing and reading* (pp. 173–205). Norwood, NJ: Ablex.

Teale, W. (1987). Emergent literacy: Reading and writing development in Early Childhood. In J. Readence and R. Baldwin, (Eds.), *Research in literacy: Merging perspectives* (pp. 45–74). Thirty-sixth yearbook of the National Reading Conference. Rochester, NY: National Reading Conference.

Teale, W. (1989, February/March). Assessing young children's reading and writing. *Reading Today, 6*(4), 24.

Teale, W. (1990). The promise and challenge of informal assessment in early literacy. In L. Morrow & J. Smith (Eds.), *Assessment for instruction in early literacy* (pp. 45–61). Englewood Cliffs, NJ: Prentice-Hall.

Teale, W., & Martinez, M. (1988). Getting on the right road: Bringing books and children together in the classroom. *Young Children, 44*(1), 10–15.

Teale, W., & Sulzby, E. (1986). Emergent literacy as a perspective for examining how young children become writers and readers. In W. Teale & E. Sulzby (Eds.), *Emergent literacy: Writing and reading* (pp. vii–xxv). Norwood, NJ: Ablex.

Teale, W., & Sulzby, E. (1989). Emergent literacy: New perspectives. In D. S. Strickland & L. M. Morrow (Eds.), *Emerging literacy: Young children learn to read and write* (pp. 1–15). Newark, DE: International Reading Association.

Temple, C., Nathan, R., Temple, F., & Burris, N. A. (1993). *The beginnings of writing.* Boston, MA: Allyn & Bacon.

Templeton, S., & Morris, D. (1999). Questions teachers ask about spelling. *Reading Research Quarterly, 34,* 102–112.

TESOL. (1997). ESL standards for prek–12 students. Alexandria, VA: Author.

Tharp, R., & Gallimore, R. (1988). *Rousing minds to life: Teaching, learning and school in a social context.* Cambridge: Cambridge University Press.

Thousand, J., & Villa, R. (1990). Sharing expertise and responsibilities through teacher teams. In W. Stainback & S. Stainback (Eds.), *Support networks for inclusive schooling: Interdependent integrated education* (pp. 151–166). Baltimore: Brookes.

Thurber, D. (1993). *D'Nealian handwriting.* Glenview, IL: ScottForesman.

Tierney, R., & Pearson, P. D. (1983). Toward a composing model of reading. *Language Arts, 60,* 568–580.

Tierney, R., Readence, J., & Dishner, E. (1995). *Reading strategies and practices: A compendium* (3rd ed.). Boston, MA: Allyn & Bacon.

Tompkins, G. (2001). *Literacy for the 21st Century* (2nd ed.). Columbus, OH: Merrill.

Tough, J. (1977). *The development of meaning: Talking to some purpose with young children.* London: Allen and Unwin.

Torgesen, J. (1994). *Torgesen test of phonemic awareness.* Shoal Creek, TX: Pro-Ed.

Trelease, J. (1989). *The new read-aloud handbook.* New York: Penguin.

Turner, A. (1987). *Nettie's trip south.* New York: Macmillan.

Turner, E. (1994). *Emerging bilingualism and biliteracy in a primary, multi-age bilingual classroom.* Unpublished Honors Thesis, Arizona State University, Tempe.

Valencia, S. (1990). A portfolio approach to classroom reading assessment: The whys, whats, and hows. *Reading Teacher, 43,* 338–340.

Valencia, S., Hiebert, E., & Afflerbach, P. (1994). *Authentic reading assessment: Practices and possibilities.* Newark, DE: International Reading Association.

van Manen, M. (1995). On the epistemology of reflective practice: Teachers and teaching. *Theory and Practice, 1,* 33–50.

Vasquez, O. (1991). Reading the world in a multicultural setting: A Mexicano perspective. *Quarterly Newsletter of the Laboratory of Comparative Human Cognition, 13,* 13–15.

Veatch, J. (1986). *Whole language in the kindergarten.* Tempe, AZ: Jan V Productions.

Veatch, J., Sawicki, F., Elliot, G., Flake, E., & Blakey, J. (1979). *Key words to reading: The language experience approach begins.* Columbus, OH: Merrill.

Ventriglia, L. (1982). *Conversations of Miguel and Maria.* Reading, MA: Addison-Wesley.

Vernon-Feagans, L., (1996). *Children's talk in communities and classrooms.* Cambridge, MA: Blackwell.

Vernon-Feagans, L., Hammer, C., Miccio, A., & Manlove, E. (2001). Early language and literacy skills in low-income African American and Hispanic children. In S. Neuman & D. Dickinson (Eds.), *Handbook of early literacy research* (pp. 192–210). New York: Guilford.

Volk, D. (1997). Continuities and discontinuities: Teaching and learning in the home and school of a Puerto Rican five-year-old. In E. Gregory (Ed.), *One child, many worlds: Early learning in multicultural communities* (pp. 47–61). New York: Teachers College Press.

Vukelich, C. (1992). Play and assessment: Young children's knowledge of the functions of writing. *Childhood Education, 68,* 202–207.

Vukelich, C. (1993). Play: A context for exploring the functions, features, and meaning of writing with peers. *Language Arts, 70,* 386–392.

Vukelich, C. (1994). Effects of play interventions on young children's reading of environmental print. *Early Childhood Research Quarterly, 9,* 153–170.

Vygotsky, L. (1962). *Thought and language.* Cambridge, MA: MIT Press.

Vygotsky, L. (1978). *Mind in society: The development of psychological processes.* Cambridge, MA: Harvard University Press.

Waggoner, D. (1992, October/November). The increasing multiethnic and multilingual diversity of the U.S.: Evidence from the 1990 census. *TESOL Matters, 1,* 1, 5.

Wagstaff, J. (1997/1998). Building practical knowledge of letter–sound correspondences: A beginner's word wall and beyond. *Reading Teacher, 51,* 298–304.

Walker, D., Greenwood, C., Hart, B., & Carta, J. (1994). Prediction of school outcomes based on early language production and socio-economic factors. *Child Development, 65,* 606–621.

Warner, L., & Morse, P. (2001). Studying pond life with primary-age children. *Childhood Education, 77,* 139–143.

Watson, D. (1983). Bringing together reading and writing. In U. H. Hardt (Ed.), *Teaching reading with the other language arts* (pp. 63–82). Newark, DE: International Reading Association.

Weaver, C. (1994). *Reading process and practice: From sociopsycholinguistics to whole language.* Portsmouth, NH: Heinemann.

Weaver, C. (1995). *Facts on teaching skills in context.* Prepared for the Michican Language Arts Framework project. Distributed by the Michigan Department of Education Curriculum Development Project.

Weaver, C., McNally, C., & Moerman, S. (2001). To grammar or not to grammar: That is *not* the question. *Voices from the Middle, 8,* 17–33.

Weinstein-Shr, G., & Quintero, E. (1995). *Immigrant learners and their families.* McHenry, IL: Delta Systems.

Weir, R. (1962). *Language in the crib.* The Hague: Mouton.

Weiss, C., Lillywhite, H., & Gordon, M. (1980). *Clinical management of articulation disorders.* St. Louis: Mosby.

Wells, D. (1995). Leading grand conversations. In N. L. Roser & M. Martinez (Eds.), *Book talk and beyond: Children and teachers respond to literature* (pp. 132–139). Newark, DE: International Reading Association.

Wells, G. (1986). *The meaning makers: Children learning language and using language to learn.* Portsmouth, NH: Heinemann.

White, B. (1985). *The first three years of life.* Englewood Cliffs, NJ: Prentice-Hall.

Whitehurst, G., & Lonigan, C. (2001). Emergent literacy: Development from prereaders to readers. In S. Neuman & D. Dickinson (Eds.), *Handbook of early literacy research* (pp. 11–29). New York: Guilford.

Wien, C., & Kirby-Smith, S. (1998). Untiming the curriculum: A case study of removing clocks from the program. *Young Children, 53*(5), 8–13.

Wiggins, G. (1993). *Assessing student performance.* San Francisco, CA: Jossey-Bass.

Wilcox, C. (1993). *Portfolios: Finding a focus.* Papers in Literacy Series. Durham, NH: The Writing Lab.

Wilensky, S. (1995). Social studies and literacy in the second grade. In P. Cordeiro (Ed.), *Endless possibilities* (pp. 33–53). Portsmouth, NH: Heinemann.

Willett, J. (1995). Becoming first graders in an L2: An ethnographic study of L2 socialization. *TESOL Quarterly, 29,* 473–503.

Winograd, P. (1989). Introduction: Understanding reading instruction. In P. Winograd, K. Wixson, & M. Lipson (Eds.), *Improving basal reading instruction* (pp. 1–17). New York: Teachers College Press.

Winograd, P., & Arrington, H. (1998). Best practices in literacy assessment. In L. Gambrell, L. Morrow, S. Neuman, & M Pressley (Eds.), *Best practices in literacy instruction* (pp. 210–241). New York: Guilford.

Winship, W. (1993). Writing information books in a first-grade classroom. *Primary Voices K–6, 1,* 7–12.

Wixson, K. (1992, May). *Anchoring assessment to curriculum goals.* Paper presented at the International Reading Association Conference, Los Angeles.

Wong-Fillmore, L., & Snow, C. (April, 2000). *What teachers need to know about language.* Educational Resources Information Center, ERIC Clearinghouse on Language and Linguistics. ED-99-CO-0008.

Woodard, C. (1984). Guidelines for facilitating sociodramatic play. *Childhood Education, 60,* 172–177.

The Wright Group. (1998). *Phonemic awareness handbook.* Bothell, WA: Author.

The Wright Group. (1999). *The story box: Reading program assessment guide.* Bothell, WA: Author.

Yaden, D., Rowe, D., & MacGillivray, L. (2000). Emergent literacy: A matter (Polyphony) of Perspectives. In M. Kamil, P. Mosenthal, P. D. Pearson, & R. Barr (Eds.), *Handbook of reading research* (Vol. III, pp. 425-454). Mahwah, NJ: Erlbaum.

Yaden, D., Smolkin, L., & Conlon, A. (1989). Preschoolers' questions about pictures, print conventions, and story text during reading aloud at home. *Reading Research Quarterly, 24,* 188–214.

Yaden, D., Smolkin, L., & MacGillivray, L. (1993). A psychogenetic perspective on children's understanding about letter associations during alphabet book readings. *Journal of Reading Behavior, 25,* 43–68.

Yopp, H. (1992). Developing phonemic awareness in young children. *Reading Teacher, 45,* 696–703.

Yopp, H., & Yopp, R. (2000). Supporting phonemic awareness in the classroom. *Reading Teacher, 54,* 130–143.

Zaner-Bloser. (1993). *Handwriting: A way to self-expression.* Columbus, OH: Author.

Zinsser, W. (1998). *Worlds of childhood: The art and craft of writing for children.* Boston, MA: Houghton Mifflin.

AUTHOR INDEX

SUBJECT INDEX